ABOUT THE AUTHORS

Author **James Marti** is Executive Director of the Holistic Medical Research Foundation in San Francisco, and the Clinica Holistica in Puerto Vallarta, Mexico. He was former Executive Director of the San Francisco Medical Research Foundation, and has held several academic and administrative positions at Syracuse University and the College of Notre Dame. He served as coordinator of Syracuse's Nonviolence Studies Program, the first program of its kind in the U.S. to offer yoga, meditation, and stress reduction for academic credit. He subsequently founded the National Academy of Peace Committee which successfully lobbied Congress to create the U.S. Peace Institute in 1976. His other books include *The World Model*, *New Book of World Rankings*, *The Ultimate Consumer's Guide to Diets and Nutrition*, and *Holistic Pregnancy and Childbirth*.

Andrea Hine earned her bachelor's degree in cultural anthropology from Stanford University, graduating Phi Beta Kappa and magna cum laude, and holds a master's degree from the University of London's School of Oriental and African Studies. She is the editor of *New Book of World Rankings* and *Small Business Success*. Her other credentials include executive speech writing, producing an award-winning employee newsletter, and copywriting.

MEDICAL ADVISORY BOARD

ALTERNATIVE HEALTH & MEDICINE

Encyclopedia

Highlights

Persons interested in a comprehensive reference providing information and documented research on all aspects of alternative medicine and whole body preventive care can turn to one accurate source: *The Alternative Health & Medicine Encyclopedia.* The book is composed of 19 chapters covering both traditional and alternative therapies on a broad range of topics, including:

- Aging
- Botanical Medicines
- Cancer
- Coping with Stress
- Dental Care
- Drug Abuse and Addiction
- Exercise
- Eye, Ear, Nose, and Throat Disorders
- Heart Disorders
- Male and Female Health Problems
- Mental Health Disorders
- Minerals and Trace Elements
- Nutrition and Diet
- Pregnancy and Childbirth
- Strengthening the Immune System
- Stress-Related Disorders
- Vitamins

Arrangement Allows for Quick Information Access

The Alternative Health & Medicine Encyclopedia provides an abundance of information, and its topical format makes it easy to use. The chapters contain subject-specific bibliographies and are enlivened by over 100 sidebars and tables of invaluable guidelines, statistics, and recommendations for the various topics discussed in each chapter. Other value-added features include:

- Contents section detailing each chapter's coverage
- List of references, organizations, and sources for further reading at the end of each chapter
- Glossary of terms
- General bibliography
- Comprehensive subject index

ALTERNATIVE HEALTH & MEDICINE Encyclopedia

James Marti
with Andrea Hine

Foreword by
Dr. Michael T. Murray

VISIBLE
INK
PRESS

DETROIT • SAN FRANCISCO • LONDON • BOSTON • WOODBRIDGE, CT

CONTENTS

Chapter 1:
WHAT IS ALTERNATIVE MEDICINE? 1

Acupuncture and Acupressure • Ayurvedic Medicine •
Biofeedback • Botanical Medicine • Chiropractic Medicine •
Exercise • Homeopathy • Hypnosis • Meditation • Transcendental
Meditation • Naturopathic Medicine • Nutrition • Osteopathic
Medicine • Visualization Therapies • Yoga • Aromatherapy •
Bach Flowers and Flower Essences • Hydrotherapy •
Hyperthermia • Massage • Music Therapy • Ozone Therapy •
Alexander Technique • Aston Patterning • Feldenkrais Method •
Hellerwork • Kinesiology • Rolfing • Rosen Method

Chapter 2:
DIET AND NUTRITION. 33

Required Nutrients • Proteins • Carbohydrates • Fiber • Lipids
(Fats) • Cholesterol • Calories • Recommended Dietary
Allowance • Nutrition for the Elderly • Nutrition for Children •
The "Good Diet" • Food Diary • Overweight Americans • Weight-
Loss Programs • Obesity • Anorexia Nervosa • Bulimia

FOREWORD
ALTERNATIVE MEDICINE'S ROLE IN THE EMERGING MEDICAL PARADIGM

A paradigm is defined as a model used to explain events. As our understanding of the environment and the human body evolves, new paradigms emerge, including a new one for medicine. While the old medical paradigm viewed the body basically as a machine, the new paradigm focuses on the interconnectedness of body, mind, emotions, social factors, and the environment in determining health status. Rather than relying on drugs and surgery, the new model utilizes natural, noninvasive techniques to promote health and healing. Many of these healing techniques are now labeled as "alternative."

The Alternative Health & Medicine Encyclopedia provides information on some of the major components of this new medical paradigm. As this book details, alternative medicine emphasizes achieving health, not just eliminating disease; treatments that address underlying causes rather than just symptoms; and an integrated approach that treats the whole patient as opposed to specialization. The alternative therapies covered in this volume stress the role of diet, lifestyle, and preventive measures, a distinct contrast to conventional medicine's use of high technology. An additional difference of the new model is the importance of empathy and caring on the part of the physician. The alternative medicine practitioner is looked upon as a partner in the healing process—someone who informs, counsels, and assists the patient in making health-care choices.

An interesting aspect of the emerging medical paradigm is that it draws from the healing wisdom of many lands and cultures, including India (Ayurvedic), China (Taoist), and Greece (Hippocratic). Based on these traditions, four time-tested medical principles are being incorporated into modern medicine. I believe these four principles define the philosophy and foundation of natural medicine whether they are utilized by a naturopath (N.D.), medical doctor (M.D.), osteopath (D.O.), chiropractor (D.C.), or other health practitioner. These principles will assuredly continue to stand the tests of time.

Principle 1. The Healing Power of Nature. The human body has considerable power to heal itself. The role of the physician is to facilitate and enhance this process. Increasing evidence supports the contention that the healing process is best enhanced with the aid of natural, nontoxic therapies. The tremendous healing power of the mind is of particular interest.

Principle 2. First Do No Harm. As Hippocrates said, "Above all else, do no harm." In our current medical system, potential harm lies not only in drugs and surgical operations, but also in the inappropriate application of medications and procedures.

Principle 3. Identify and Treat the Cause. Of vital importance is the treatment of the underlying causes of a disease rather than simply suppressing the symptoms. Evidence is accumulating that many drug treatments are effective only in suppressing the symptoms, while many natural treatments actually address the cause.

Principle 4. The Physician as Teacher. The primary meaning of the word "doctor" is teacher. The physician's role is to teach the patient about achieving health and avoiding disease. As Thomas Edison once said, "The doctor of the future will give no medicine, but will interest his patient in the care of the human frame, in diet, and in the cause and prevention of disease."

The conventional medical doctor simply does not have time to teach. The typical first office visit lasts less than seven minutes, which usually provides only enough time for a doctor to make a quick diagnosis and write a prescription. In contrast, a typical first office visit with an alternative health-care practitioner is much more in-depth and may last an hour or longer. But making a careful assessment of a patient's health status and diagnosing disease is only one part of the healing process. Since alternative health-care providers consider teaching to be one of their primary goals, the time devoted to discussing and explaining principles of health is one of the aspects that sets them apart from conventional medical doctors.

Alternative medicine is a term I believe will be short-lived because what is now considered "alternative" will soon become part of the conventional medical approach. The nineteenth-century German philosopher Arthur Schopenhauer stated that all truth goes through three steps: First, it is ridiculed. Second, it is violently opposed. Finally, it is accepted as self-evident. At one time, alternative therapies were violently opposed by conventional medical groups, although numerous medical organizations that in the past had spoken out strongly against alternative medicine now endorse many aspects of it. For example, since the early 1900s, naturopathic physicians have extolled the value of eating more high-fiber foods; reducing the intake of refined sugars, fats, and cholesterol; and increasing the intake of dietary antioxidants. These same recommendations are now endorsed by the U.S. National Academy of Sciences, American Cancer Society, American Heart Association, and the American Diabetic Association. Another example is that at one time acupuncture was viewed as total quackery by the medical establishment. Now it is becoming much more widely accepted and is even taught at several medical schools across the United States.

The growing adoption of the principle and healing techniques of alternative medical practitioners by conventional medicine illustrates the paradigm shift occurring in medicine. Treatments once scoffed at are now becoming generally accepted as effective. In fact, in many instances clinical research is demonstrating that natural alternatives offer significant benefits over conventional medical treatments. In the future many of the concepts, philosophies, and techniques now considered alternative will be incorporated into conventional medical practice. How soon this shift occurs will depend upon how effectively the alternative medical community can get the information to consumers. *The Alternative Health & Medicine Encyclopedia* is a powerful step in the right direction.

—Michael T. Murray, N.D.

Michael T. Murray is widely regarded as one of the world's leading authorities on natural medicine. In addition to maintaining a private medical practice, he serves on the faculty and the board of trustees at Bastyr University in Seattle, Washington. He is the coauthor of A Textbook of Natural Medicine, *the definitive textbook on naturopathic medicine for physicians,* The Encyclopedia of Natural Medicine, *and* Botanical Influences on Illness. *He has also written* The Healing Powers of Herbs, The Getting Well Naturally Series, The Healing Power of Foods, *and* Natural Alternatives to Over-the-Counter and Prescription Drugs.

PREFACE

In 1988, my mother developed breast cancer at the age of 76. She was a full-time tennis instructor and was told that she would have to discontinue her physical activity and undergo radiation therapy. At the time, I was the executive director of the San Francisco Medical Research Foundation, one of the first American holistic medical foundations researching orthomolecular, nutritional, and psychoimmunological treatments for chronic degenerative diseases. I was familiar with Dr. Bernie Siegel's pioneering work with cancer patients and advised my mother to visualize her radiation treatments as white healing light which would kill her cancer cells. I also sent her daily supplies of vitamin C crystals, chlorophyll, Green Magma (a green barley leaf from Sweden), and aloe vera juice to maintain the strength of her immune system. My mother took the botanical supplements each morning, underwent radiation treatments in her tennis togs, and afterwards went out and played competitive senior tennis matches. Her cancer went into remission within three months.

My mother had been a competitive athlete for most of her life, and, given her physical fitness, her recovery did not seem unusual to me. Recently, however, quite a number of remarkable cases of "spontaneous remission" or "self-healing" cases involving ordinary people of different ages and fitness levels have been documented. We now know from the studies of Dr. Siegel, Dr. David Spiegel, Dr. Dean Ornish, Dr. Deepak Chopra, and other leading alternative medical specialists that exceptional healing is a power that all of us have.

Alternative medicine is composed of many specialized therapies, each of which might be said to constitute a spoke on a wheel. Taken as a whole, they provide a comprehensive program for maintaining robust health and extending our life spans. Each of us inherits a set of biogenetic cards from our parents, which to some extent determines our ability to resist disease. Yet whatever advantages or limitations we inherit, we are ultimately responsible for our own personal health. Consciously or unconsciously, we daily make choices in the areas of nutrition, exercise, vitamins and minerals, botanical supplements, stress reduction, avoiding toxins, and living harmoniously with our environment.

This book presents the latest international medical research drawn from the disciplines of orthomolecular medicine, homeopathy, naturopathy, biochemistry, nutrition, psychoimmunology, genetics, chiropractic, bodywork, and Ayurvedic and Chinese medicines. Primary research for this book was conducted at the University of California Berkeley Medical Library and the Lane Medical Library at Stanford. For international and foreign language journals, we used computerized Medline searches at Marin General Hospital Library. Once again, Head Librarian Kathy Resnick helped us comb through hundreds of foreign journal articles which had been translated and summarized in English. In some cases, the month, volume number, or page numbers were not provided, especially for Chinese, Japanese, and Russian journals. Nevertheless, readers can still find the articles cited in this *Encyclopedia* by author, title, and year in most medical libraries, or by Medline.

My hope in writing this book was to clearly present the different specialized therapies which fall under the umbrella of alternative medicine. Which program or therapy will be right for you is a highly individual matter. It will depend partly on the cards you have been dealt, and also, importantly, what feels right for you. The diversity of alternative medicine is its strength. There are many different paths to total whole body health, although the goal is always the same: to help empower the individual to achieve his or her personal best–the highest level of health possible. In one sense, holistic medicine is ultimately about attaining higher levels of self-knowledge. I sincerely hope the information provided in this book empowers you to live a long, meaningful, and healthy life.

—James Marti

Suggestions Are Welcome

The editor and publisher of *The Alternative Health & Medicine Encyclopedia* will appreciate any suggestions for additions or changes that will make future editions more accurate and useful. Please send comments to:

Editor
The Alternative Health & Medicine
   Encyclopedia
Gale Research
835 Penobscot Bldg.
Detroit, MI 48226
Phone: (313)961-2242
Fax: (313)961-6741
Toll-free: 1-800-347-GALE

ACKNOWLEDGMENTS

The Alternative Health & Medicine Encyclopedia is dedicated to the competent and compassionate physicians and researchers who served on its Medical Advisory Board. They are all prominent in their areas of specialty, and I personally owe each of them an immense debt of gratitude.

I have benefitted from a number of personal and professional acquaintances, without whose support this book would not have been possible. Foremost among these is Andrea Hine, my Stanford University colleague, with whom I have collaborated since 1989. This book is very much a product of her remarkable mind, careful research, and meticulous editing and writing–and she rightfully deserves to be credited as its co-author.

Personally, I am especially grateful to Jane Hoehner, Larry Baker, Diane Dupuis, Ellen Pare, and Dedria Bryfonski at Gale Research, who believed in the importance of providing readers with holistic medical alternatives. Kyung Lim Kalasky, editor in the Science Department, expertly guided the revised edition from start to finish. Laurie Harper, my literary agent, is the best at what she does, combining integrity, intelligence, competence, and a wry sense of humor. I am also deeply indebted to Dr. Raphael Ornstein, founder of the San Francisco Medical Research Foundation, who has been my friend and colleague since 1980. Many of the discussions in this book are derived from our conversations over the years.

I also wish to thank Dr. Carlos Rodriguez, Dr. Abel Jimenez, Dr. Edward Treitler, Margit Bauer, Dr. Jean Fryer, Jesse Molesworth, Karen McChrystal, Mr and Mrs. Phil Little, Matt Wagner, and Linda Ellen. I also wish to thank Alan Davis for his enduring friendship and kindness.

Most of all, I remain very grateful to the pioneers of alternative medicine. In the 1970s it was difficult for holistic practitioners to find a forum to present their life-enhancing views. In the last 25 years, the works of Dr. Herbert Benson, Dr. Joan Borysenko, Dr. Bernie Siegel, Dr. Andrew T. Weil, Dr. Dean Ornish, Dr. Raphael Ornstein, Dr. Kenneth Pelletier, and Dr. Deepak Chopra have achieved international prominence. The popularity of their work is due, I believe, to their vision and compassion. These practitioners, like holistic practitioners everywhere, believe passionately in the remarkable powers of the body to heal itself, in the higher powers of the mind, and in the idea that life is for all of us a journey towards higher consciousness. This book serves as a testament to their work.

INTRODUCTION TO THE SECOND EDITION

The first edition of *The Alternative Health & Medicine Encyclopedia,* published in 1995, presented new breakthroughs in holistic medicine, which offer the promise that each of us may live longer, healthier lives free of medical complications. More than 30 million Americans have used alternative or holistic medical therapies and spend more than 14 billion dollars annually on alternative treatments. As a medical system, alternative medicine is holistic–it views the mind and body as a living integrated system, and is based on the premise that the mind and body continually interact. For example, negative thoughts and emotions can adversely affect the body and lead to physiological disorders. In turn, physiological imbalances can directly impact the mind and lead to psychological or emotional disorders.

The first edition of the *Encyclopedia* presented more than 200 alternative therapies for more than 50 common medical disorders and was designed to acquaint readers of different ages, backgrounds, and interests with the major components of alternative medicine. This expanded and revised second edition adds more than 100 new therapies for 20 additional disorders. The following chapter outline provides more detailed information about what's new in the second edition.

How to Use This Book

Chapter 1 presents an overview of each specialty in alternative medicine, from complete systems such as Ayurvedic medicine to very specialized bodywork therapies such as Aston Patterning. After reading Chapter 1, readers can turn directly to chapters that may be of particular interest to them. Beginning with Chapter 2, the specific components of alternative medicine are described in detail. As with the first edition, the progression of the 19 chapters in this edition provides a comprehensive manual to maintaining vibrant health through nutrition, orthomolecular medicine, botanical medicine, detoxification, stress reduction, and psychoimmunological therapies such as positive thinking. Chapter 9 begins the discussion of alternative treatments for specific disorders. The index at the back of the book provides a quick reference to pages that discuss specific topics. There is a listing of resources included at the end of each chapter that cites references and additional books and articles on the topics discussed, as well as related organizations that can provide more information.

Chapter 1: What Is Alternative Medicine?

The major components of modern alternative medicine detailed in Chapter 1, which now includes new therapies such as aromatherapy and ozone therapy, are based on holistic concepts of health that have been an integral aspect of the belief systems and healing practices of many cultures throughout history. Respect for and understanding of the unity of mind and body, for example, have been basic precepts of the healing systems of Ayurvedic medicine, Chinese medicine, homeopathy, naturopathy, and chiropractic. In alternative medicine, health is defined as more than the absence of disease–it is the result of all our bodily systems being harmoniously in balance with each other and with the environment. In this state of equilibrium, our defense mechanisms and our immune system can efficiently respond to most of the hazards that life presents, whether these are pathogenic (disease-causing) organisms, toxic substances, or environmental or emotional stress factors.

Chapter 2: Diet and Nutrition

Nutrition has always been one of the key components of alternative medicine. Chapter 2 summarizes studies which identify foods, such as fats, oils, meats, and processed products, that contribute to the risk of chronic diseases. It also discusses foods and supplements–namely, fresh organically grown fruits and vegetables, whole grains, seeds, nuts, and fish–that have proven effective in clinical trials in preventing and reversing chronic disorders. The revised chapter also includes helpful nutritional tips and guidelines, as well as a Food Diary to help readers monitor their daily nutritional intake.

Chapter 3: Vitamins

Chapter 3 summarizes more than 200 studies linking vitamin deficiencies to certain diseases and describes how vitamin supplements have proven helpful in preventing them. All of the major vitamins are discussed, including revised Recommended Dietary Allowances (RDAs). Readers will find the revised chapter an ideal way to acquaint themselves with the growing field of orthomolecular medicine. Important disease-preventing information is offered, including the role of vitamin C in reducing the risk of some cancers; the role of vitamin E in preventing cardiovascular ailments and blood clots; and the role of the B vitamins in treating depression and alcoholism.

Chapter 4: Minerals and Trace Elements

Minerals and trace elements are essential parts of enzymes which play an important role in many physiological processes. Most minerals and trace elements are available in foods, especially fresh fruits and vegetables. This revised chapter discusses all of the important minerals and trace elements, the foods which contain them, daily recommended dosages, and how specific mineral deficiencies or excesses have been linked to chronic diseases.

Chapter 5: Botanical Medicines

Botanical (plant) medicines have been the basis of all medical traditions since the dawn of civilization, and their importance was reemphasized recently by President Clinton who declared the 21st century to be the "century of biological medicine." More than 5,000 botanical plants have been extensively tested for medicinal uses. The first edition summarized 30 of the most important botanical plants, herbs, and supplements used to prevent or reverse disease. The revised chapter now adds 30 new botanicals, including black walnut husks, cat's claw, kombucha mushroom, nettles, St. John's wort, suma, and astralagus, among others.

Chapter 6: Exercise

The first edition detailed 11 important medical benefits of exercise, and provided physical activity guidelines for children, the elderly, the handicapped, and people who work in offices. The revised edition adds a comprehensive survey of specific forms of exercise that are most effective in preventing, treating, or reversing specific diseases.

Chapter 7: Strengthening the Immune System

Every day people risk being exposed to more than 10,000 environmental toxins, many of which are poisonous. Many people suffer from chronic health problems simply because their bodies do not effectively eliminate toxins which can weaken the immune system. This new chapter details 10 new therapies for strengthening the immune system, including hydrotherapy, new vitamin, mineral, and botanical therapies, chelation therapy, colonic therapy, fasting, lymphatic massage, osteopathy, and chiropractic lymphatic draining.

Chapter 8: Coping with Stress

The modern Western lifestyle is physically and emotionally stressful, and an estimated 70-80% of Americans who visit a physician suffer from a stress-related disorder. This chapter highlights new alternative therapies for reducing stress, including aromatherapy, hypnotherapy, visualization, imagery, nutritional, vitamin, and mineral therapies, mindful exercise, music, yoga, meditation, biofeedback, massage, and qi gong.

Chapter 9: Stress-Related Disorders

The direct relationship between stress and disease is now well-known and widely accepted. Chapter 9 presents a variety of alternative therapies for preventing, treating, or reversing such stress-related disorders as headaches, hypertension, irritable bowel syndrome, ulcers, and atherosclerosis. The revised chapter discusses the effectiveness of acupuncture, Bach flowers, and biofeedback in relieving headaches; the use of botanical medicines in lowering high blood pressure; and the use of bayberry, chamomile, goldenseal, and licorice power to relieve ulcers.

Chapter 10: Drug Abuse and Addiction

Addiction is the most expensive medical problem in the U.S., consuming billions of dollars and causing immeasurable human suffering. An estimated 520,000 Americans die each year as a result of drug abuse. Chapter 10 describes alternative treatments for drug dependencies and addiction that combine nutrition, exercise, vitamin and botanical supplements, and lifestyle changes. Updated information is provided on vitamin, mineral, and botanical therapies for alcoholism, as well as new acupuncture and acupressure treatments for cocaine, opium, heroin, marijuana, caffeine, and nicotine addictions. New sections have been added that deal with new treatments for childhood addiction, and codependency.

Chapter 11: Mental Health Disorders

This chapter discusses alternative or holistic therapies for such mental disorders as anxiety, depression, panic disorders, phobias, and schizophrenia. When used in combination with psychotherapy, behavioral therapy, or psychoanalysis, nutrition, vitamins, minerals, amino acids, hormones, botanical medicines, exercise, and massage can help treat many mental health disorders. New sections discuss vitamin and mineral therapies which double the recovery rate of acute schizophrenics and prevent relapses of schizophrenia; new treatments for childhood emotional disorders; biofeedback, yoga, meditation, tai chi, and visualization treatments for phobias and anxiety; and new alternative treatments for depression and compulsive disorders.

Chapter 12: Common Male Health Problems

The most common health problems among men involve disorders of the genitourinary system, which includes the bladder, urethra, prostate gland, penis, and testicles. Chapter 12 discusses alternative treatments as well as the latest findings on low sexual energy and impotence, enlarged prostate (benign prostatic hypertrophy), and prostatitis.

Chapter 13: Common Female Health Problems

This chapter presents the latest alternative medical therapies for common health problems of women. Women readers will find effective therapies for relieving PMS, dysmenorrhea, vaginitis, and fibrocystic breast disease.

Chapter 14: Holistic Pregnancy and Childbirth

This completely revised chapter outlines a comprehensive, holistic program that takes prospective parents from preconception through pregnancy, birthing, and early infant care. It answers important questions about diet, vitamin, mineral, and botanical supplements, and the best forms of exercise for each trimester. New sections detail 15 therapies for relieving pregnancy and labor symptoms.

Chapter 15: Dental Care

Dentists are often the first practitioners to diagnose cancers of the mouth, bulimia, diabetes, and other medical disorders. This chapter includes new sections on state-of-the-art dental therapies, including the effectiveness of natural toothpastes, new therapies for children, guided tissue regeneration, holistic first-aid for toothaches and knocked-out teeth, as well as treatments for common abscesses and mouth infections.

Chapter 16: Eye, Ear, Nose, and Throat Disorders

Along with the mouth and skin and mucous membranes, the eyes, ears, nose, and throat serve as the body's first line of defense against external toxins and infectious organisms. Chapter 16 details new alternative approaches to keeping these organs healthy, and treating a wide variety of disorders that can affect them.

Chapter 17: Cancer

Currently, one out of every five Americans is likely to develop cancer during his or her lifetime, and among those with cancer, one person in five is likely to die from it. Chapter 17 reviews the latest alternative therapies developed in the U.S., Europe, and Japan for treating cancer, including antineoplaston therapy, hydrazine sulfate therapy, hydrogen peroxide therapy, and the use of shark cartilage and maitake mushrooms.

Chapter 18: Heart Disorders

Although heart disease causes nearly half of all deaths in the U.S., it is one of the most preventable chronic diseases. Chapter 18 outlines therapies that help reverse coronary artery diseases, including exercise, yoga, meditation, weight loss, stress reduction programs, and diet modifications. These alternative programs have proven so effective that they are now reimbursed by some insurance companies.

Chapter 19: Aging

Too often, people assume that once elderly persons reach a certain chronological age, they become biologically infirm and mentally deficient. That view is fast changing, especially among the elderly. Chapter 19 outlines therapies that people can use to improve their strength, flexibility, and energy levels. It also presents new hope for patients suffering from Alzheimer's disease, senile dementia, and osteoporosis and discusses newly documented therapies such as estrogen replacement therapy, calcitonin therapy, and chelation treatments.

Epilogue: The Future of Alternative Medicine

The rising costs of health care around the world and the public's demand for safer, less expensive medical therapies will produce in the next 50 years new medical treatments that more fully integrate the mind and body. The epilogue forecasts what alternative medicine will be like in the year 2050 and what new treatments might be available, including Super Foods, Utopian hospitals and hospital supermarkets, and holistic telemedicine.

One criticism shared by many people who find themselves dissatisfied with conventional medicine is that it tends to overlook the emotional and psychological aspects of healing. One reason alternative or "holistic" medicine has become increasingly popular is that it puts the human touch back into medical treatment. This approach is aptly summarized by Dr. Ed Weiss, who states: "I think it's being a human being, acting like a human being, being perceptive like a human being, and expressing love for your patient that leads to health. That's the most important thing holistic medicine should offer."

Chapter 1

WHAT IS ALTERNATIVE MEDICINE?

In the winter of 1988, San Francisco cardiologist Dean Ornish shocked the medical community when he proved that 40 advanced heart patients could actually shrink the fatty plaque deposits that were progressively blocking their coronary arteries. As the deposits disappeared, their arteries began to open and fresh oxygen was able to reach their hearts. As a result, most of the patients no longer suffered from chest pains or were at risk of having another heart attack.

There were two astonishing things about Ornish's findings. First, he was the first Western doctor to prove that a chronic disease could be reversed once it has started. Millions of people throughout the world who suffered from heart disease now realized that they were not helpless victims. What was even more amazing about Ornish's clinical experiment was the therapy he used to make the plaques disappear. Ordinarily, Western heart specialists use surgery to reopen the clogged artery or bypass the artery altogether. Instead, Ornish used the innate healing power of the body itself; his patients "reversed" their disease with yoga, meditation, a low-cholesterol diet, and group therapy. After approximately one year of lifestyle changes, their clogged heart arteries had repaired themselves. The process is described in his 1990 book, *Dr. Dean Ornish's Program for Reversing Heart Disease.*

The medical therapies Ornish incorporated into his treatment represent the nucleus of an emerging body of world medicine called "holistic medicine"—or whole body medicine. Holistic medicine attempts to treat the whole body by combining many different Eastern and Western medical specialties: Ayurvedic medicine, Chinese medicine, acupuncture and acupressure, nutri-

tion, exercise, naturopathic medicine, homeo-pathic medicine, botanical medicine, chiro-practics and massage. However, just as there is no universal language, no single medical specialty—Eastern or Western, ancient or modern, scientific or unscientific—can pro-vide the magic lantern that reveals all of the mysteries of the human body. Each specialty has its strengths and weakness, its insights and limitations. Yet taken together, the many specialties of holistic medicine offer great promise in helping people maintain optimal health.

The fact that a vast number of people are seeking new ways to stay healthy outside of surgery and drugs was confirmed in a study reported in the *New England Journal of Medicine* which concluded that 60 million Americans used some type of alternative medical therapy in 1992, spending more than $14 billion. Holistic options are increasing for those who wish to explore whole body therapies to maintain health and prevent or treat chronic illness and disease.

An old Chinese prayer says: "When you have a disease, do not try to cure it. Find your chi and you will be healed." Chinese medi-cine is based on the belief that humanity is part of a larger creation, the universe, and subject to the same laws that govern nature. All life and the entire material universe origi-nate from a single unified source, called Tao, which is an integrated whole present in every-thing. Tao created two opposing forces, yin and yang—archetypical opposites that are incomplete without the other and combine to create all phenomena.

According to Dr. Yuan-Chi Lin, an Associate Professor of Anesthesia and Pediatrics at the Stanford University Medical Center, "Yin is present in the qualities of cold, rest, passivity, darkness, inwardness and decrease. Yang is associated with heat, activ-ity, stimulation, light, outwardness and increase." In his book, *Pain in Infants,*

Children, and Adolescents, written with John D. Yee and Paul A. Aubuchon, Lin says, "Health requires a balance of yin and yang within a given person, while disease is char-acterized by a disharmony or lack of balance between these two dynamic forces."

Within the body, the balance of yin and yang is manifest in the flow of an energy called chi (or the life force), which flows through the body in precise and orderly pat-terns called meridians. There are 14 meridi-ans, 12 of which are associated with organs in the body, while two are responsible for unify-ing various systems. Each meridian, which runs vertically from the head to the feet, mov-ing chi to specific parts of the body, is classi-fied as being either yin or yang. Every part of the body is nourished with chi energy unless a meridian becomes blocked or stagnant, which causes an imbalance in the flow of life force. Certain organs, for example, can become excessive or hyperactive (yang), while others can become deficient and hypoactive (yin). There can also be excessive swelling or expansion (yang), or too much contraction (yin). Without adequate life force, tissues and organs become stagnant and can no longer eliminate waste from cells. As waste prod-ucts accumulate, the blood-cleansing organs become stressed, and eventually their capacity to clean the blood is exceeded. This accumu-lation of toxins (such as fat, cholesterol, ammonia, uric acid, triglycerides, and carbon dioxide) weakens the immune system suffi-ciently to allow a virus to take hold in the body. More specifically, the accumulation diminishes the life force which is the founda-tion of health.

In Chinese medicine, all treatment is meant to bring about harmony between effi-ciency and excess, or between yin and yang. Foods, herbs, and other therapeutic techniques are used to restore this balance. Thus, a Chinese doctor might use acupuncture, acu-pressure, herbs, Tai Chi Chuan, moxibustion (heat applied to acupuncture points), or massage to increase or decrease the chi flow as needed.

Acupuncture and Acupressure

In his "Healing and The Mind" television series on PBS, Bill Moyers visits a hospital in China where a 35-year-old woman was undergoing a brain operation to remove a large tumor in her pituitary gland. Amazingly, the woman was conscious and able to talk to her doctor during the surgery. She felt no pain despite being given only half the drugs that would be administered in the West because her physician used acupuncture needles to help anesthetize her.

In China, acupuncture is most commonly applied for anesthesia. But it can also be used to rebalance a chi disturbance in a patient—whether caused by an external influence such as coldness, an emotional influence such as excess anger, poor diet, or an organ imbalance. Acupuncture, like all Chinese medical therapies, seeks to diagnose a chi imbalance before a detectable, physiological impairment occurs. Acupuncturists focus on helping patients balance the chi energy within and between the five major organ systems: the heart, lungs, liver, spleen, and kidneys.

To restore health, an acupuncturist uses tiny needles as antennae to direct chi to organs or functions of the body. The needles can also be used to drain chi where it is excessive; to warm parts of the body that are cool or stagnant; to decrease or increase moisture; and to reduce excessive heat. The acupuncturist does this by pinpointing specific points along the body's 14 meridians, which affect the functioning of specific organs, and using needles to slightly puncture and stimulate tissue at these specific points to bring about the desired results. The needles penetrate just below the epidermis and do not draw blood or cause discomfort. The application of heat is also sometimes used, along with massage or electrical pulses.

According to the World Health Organization (WHO), 104 different conditions have been treated by acupuncture, including migraines, sinusitis, the common cold, tonsillitis, asthma, inflammation of the eyes, addictions, myopia, duodenal ulcer and other gastrointestinal disorders, neuralgia, and osteoarthritis. Acupuncture is now widely used in American hospitals, for example, to reduce pain in patients with sore throats, sickle-cell anemia, dysmenorrhea, dental pain, hysterectomies, chronic back disorders and migraine headaches. It has also been used to help people stop smoking, and to treat alcoholism and opiate addiction.

The December 1, 1992 issue of *National Acupuncture Detoxification Association Newsletter* cites a significant number of clinical studies which suggest that acupuncture may be the most effective alternative medicine therapy for treating a variety of addictions. It reports two controlled studies on treatment of alcoholic recidivism, for example—one with 80 patients and the other with 54 patients—which found that acupuncture treatment at fixed points was more effective than sham points in reducing expressed need for alcohol, drinking episodes, and hospital admissions for detoxification.

Dr. Jeffrey Holder, founder and director of Exodus, a residential treatment for addictions based in Miami, Florida, states in *New Auricular Therapy* that every addiction corresponds to a different set of ear acupoints. Every drug of choice thus has a receptor site mechanism located in the ear. What acupuncturists do is satisfy the needs of that receptor site by supplying and directing the endorphins or enkephalins. Using auriculotherapy, Holder reports success rates of over 80% for curing addiction to nicotine, alcohol, cocaine, heroin, and other mood-altering substances.

The National Institute of Drug Abuse is currently conducting several clinical trials using acupuncture on heroin addicts in New York City outpatient drug detoxification programs. Detoxification from chronic use of prescribed opiates (morphine, Demeral, etc.) usually takes from three to six months. Even "brief" detoxification programs take more than a month. One uncontrolled trial found that after electrical stimulation at ear acupuncture points, 12 out of 14 pain patients (86%) were able to completely withdraw from narcotics in 2-7 days. They also experienced fewer or no side effects.

Several studies, reported in *Alternative Medicine: The Definitive Guide*, found that acupuncture was equal to or better than methadone in helping people withdraw from heroin. Methadone treatment programs only substitute a less expensive, longer-acting, government-sanctioned drug. Researchers now think that acupuncture, in combination with a relapse prevention program, can eliminate the heroin addict's need for both methadone and heroin. Acupuncture also claims good success rates with nicotine addiction, where a newly discovered acupoint called "Tien Mi" is used in conjunction with other traditional acupoints, particularly those located in the ear.

In a study conducted at the Lincoln Substance Abuse/Acupuncture Clinic in New York City, reported in the *National Acupuncture Detoxification Association Newsletter*, 68 pregnant women addicted to crack or cocaine participated in a program in which they received acupuncture treatments in conjunction with a detoxification regimen, counseling, and daily urinalysis tests. The women who attended the program for 10 visits or more showed significantly higher infant birth weights than those who attended less than 10 times.

Currently, there are more than 300 acupuncture clinics worldwide which use acupuncture to treat a variety of mental disorders. In Portland, Oregon, for example, four new acupuncture programs address chronic mental illness. Professor Pierre Huard of the Medical Faculty of Paris, author of Chinese Medicine, and Dr. Ming Wong of the Medical Faculty of Rennes have found that acupuncture is equivalent to the effect of tranquilizers in cases of depression, worry, insomnia, and nervous disorders.

The *National Acupuncture Detoxification Association Newsletter* also documents a six-month study conducted by Tom Atwood which found that acupuncture may be beneficial in the treatment of schizophrenia and paranoia. In the study, 16 patients in a residential care home received auriculotherapy for a variety of conditions, including paranoid schizophrenia and borderline personality disorders. Hospital stays dropped from 27 to eight days following the initiation of acupuncture, compared to records of the previous year. Hypertensive patients experienced reduced blood pressure, and patients generally reported sleeping better. In addition, they became more productive. Atwood notes that "these patients who are normally the most resistant, and the most likely to be readmitted for hospitalization, were also more willing to have acupuncture as opposed to other treatments offered at our center."

Acupuncture is also used with Chinese herbs to improve AIDS patients' immune function, and reduce uncomfortable or dangerous symptoms, including night sweats, fatigue, and digestive disturbances. Chinese acupuncturist Dr. Wu Bo Ping has used acupuncture with Chinese herbs to treat 160 AIDS patients in Tanzania, according to the *National Acupuncture Detoxification Association Newsletter*. Holder also states that he has used acupuncture to significantly extend the life span and improve the quality of life in AIDS patients. In addition, the patient's lesions disappeared. Preliminary results of a pilot study conducted at the Kuan Yin Clinic in San Francisco with HIV patients show acupuncture to be beneficial in increasing immune function, white blood cell production, and T-cell production, as well as alleviating many of the symptoms relating to HIV infection and AIDS. Clinic physicians working with AIDS patients have been able to increase T-cell counts from 210 to 270 with just three acupuncture treatments.

Acupressure is a form of acupuncture in which fingers and thumbs rather than needles are used to press chi points on the surface of the body. Acupressure relieves muscular tension, which enables more blood—and therefore more oxygen and nutrients—to be carried to tissue throughout the body. This helps promote both physical calmness and mental alertness, and aids in healing by removing waste products. Like acupuncture, acupressure is now believed to trigger the release of endorphins, the neurochemicals that relieve pain.

Acupressure has been used successfully to release mental tension and stress, provide relief from tired and strained eyes, headaches, premenstrual cramps, and arthritis. It is also used for promoting general health care, relieving stiff shoulders, preventing and combating colds, improving muscle tone, and boosting energy levels.

More than 15 million Americans have visited acupuncturists or acupressurists. Today, there are approximately 9,000 acupuncturists practicing in the U.S. In most states, acupuncturists must be medical doctors and must have certification from the National Commission for the Certification of Acupuncturists. However, as some states do not regulate the practice at all, it is advisable to check a practitioner's credentials.

Consulting an Acupuncturist

According to Dr. Yuan-Chi Lin, Associate Professor of Anesthesia and Pediatrics at Stanford University Medical Center, these factors may be involved in a visit to an acupuncturist:

- The acupuncturist uses patient history and physical examination in making a diagnosis.

- The acupuncturist will focus on the character of the pulse and the appearance of the tongue.

- Unlike Western medicine, sophisticated biological testing is not employed.

- The goal of therapy is to assess the balance of yin and yang in the patient and to restore deficiencies or correct excesses of chi, thus restoring health.

- Several treatments may be required over the course of weeks or months.

Ayurvedic Medicine

In Boston, a 39-year-old woman with extensive cancer in her lymph nodes and 12 different sites in her bones consulted a well-known Ayurvedic doctor because her chemotherapy sessions left her without energy, her blood count was consistently low, and her chances of survival was only 1%. The physician prescribed a long-term Ayurvedic regime that included meditation, revised diet and sleep patterns, massage, herb preparations, yoga routines, and even exposure to certain sounds and aromas. After several years of treatment, her cancer went into complete remission, her general health was good, and her blood chemistry returned to the normal range, according to Craig Lambert in his article, "The Chopra Prescriptions," published in the September-October 1989 issue of *Harvard Magazine*.

This woman's case is far from an isolated one. While Westerners might consider her treatment to be "alternative," Ayurvedic medicine has been practiced in India for more than 6,000 years. In Sanskrit, "Ayurveda" means the "science of life and longevity." The Aruyvedic approach treats the person, not just the disease, so each treatment is highly individualized. It is based on the premise that health is a state of "balance" among the body's systems—physical, emotional, and spiritual. Illness is seen as a state of imbalance.

Ayurvedic medicine has been popularized in the West by Dr. Deepak Chopra, whose best-selling books, *Perfect Health* and *Ageless Body/Timeless Mind*, describe how it works. According to Chopra, "the guiding principle of Ayurveda is that the mind exerts the deepest influence on the body, and freedom from sickness depends upon contacting our own awareness, bringing it into balance, and then extending that balance to the body. This state of balanced awareness…creates a higher state of health."

Ayurvedic medicine stresses a holistic approach to health. It defines disease as the result of climatic extremes, bacterial attack, nutritional deviance, and stress as well as other forms of emotional imbalance. Optimal health is achieved by cultivating mental and physical habits that are conducive to physical and spiritual well-being, and treatment often includes hatha yoga, diet, and developing positive attitudes.

Biofeedback

For thousands of years, Eastern mystics have demonstrated their ability to control their heart rate, skin temperature, blood pressure, and other "involuntary" functions through concentration and will power. Western physicians have begun experimenting with biofeedback machines to accomplish the same result. People suffering from migraine headaches, for example, can be connected to biofeedback machines which monitor their bodily functions such as skin temperature, blood pressure, sweat, and electrical responses. Once they are hooked up to a machine, patients learn to consciously will a desired result, such as lowering their blood pressure. Electrodes attached to the body provide readings, giving patients the feedback necessary to determine whether their mental powers are causing the desired physiological change.

Biofeedback training has a range of applications in medicine, particularly in cases where psychological factors play a role. Sleep disorders, hyperactivity in children, and other behavioral disorders respond well to biofeedback training, as do dysfunctions stemming from inadequate control over muscles or muscle groups. Incontinence, postural problems, back pain, temporamandibular joint syndrome (TMJ), and loss of control due to brain or nerve damage have been relieved when patients undergo biofeedback training, according to *Alternative Medicine: The Definitive Guide.*

Biofeedback has also been effective in treating heart dysfunctions, gastrointestinal disorders (acidity, ulcers, irritable bowel syndrome), difficulty in swallowing, esophageal dysfunctions, ringing in the ears, twitching of the eyelids, fatigue, and cerebral palsy. Severe structural problems such as broken bones and slipped discs, on the other hand, do not appear to respond to biofeedback therapy.

Biofeedback offers promise as one method of partially treating depression. R. Kaiser, for example, reports in the July 1992 issue of *Headaches* that biofeedback relieved depression in 85% of 28 patients between the ages of 13 and 18 who complained of chronic daily headaches caused by depression.

Along with pelvic muscle exercises, biofeedback has been used to effectively treat urinary or sphincter incontinence. Several studies found symptom reduction rates of 78-90%. *Alternative Medicine: What Works*, for example, reports one single-blind clinical trial conducted by Dr. P. Burns of the School of Nursing at the State University of New York at Buffalo which showed that biofeedback and pelvic muscle exercises maintained and improved urinary functioning in 135 women. Burns concluded that "the number of incontinent episodes decreased significantly in the biofeedback and pelvic muscle exercise subjects but not in the control subjects for all severity of incontinence frequency subgroups." Biofeedback has also been used as an adjunct therapy in physical training of people with spinal cord injuries, although exercise therapy has proven much more important.

M. A. Bennings, in the January 1993 *Archives of Disease in Childhood*, and N. R. Binnie, in the September-October *World Journal of Surgery*, report how clinicians have used biofeedback to treat rectal ulcer syndrome, pediatric sickle-cell anemia, and cerebral palsy in children. R. E. Thomas, in the April 1993 issue of *Ergonomics*, writes that it may prove helpful in treating carpal tunnel syndrome (CTS) as well.

Biofeedback has also been incorporated as a noninvasive technique for controlling parasympathetic cardiac arryhmia. One Australian study suggests that biofeedback therapy can help patients recover from strokes. Biofeedback has also proven very effective in treating alcoholism, and preventing relapses. E. Saxb in the September 1995 issue of *Journal of Clinical Psychology* reports a very promising clinical trial in which 14 alcoholic outpatients used biofeedback brainwave treatment for alcohol abuse. After temperature biofeedback pretraining, subjects completed two 40-minute session of alpha-theta brainwave neurofeedback training (BWNT). Twenty-one month follow-up data indicated sustained prevention of relapse in 12 alcoholics who completed treatment.

Biofeedback has also been used to relieve posttraumatic stress disorder (PTSD) in Vietnam War veterans, according to an article by Dr. S. Vilerin the April 1995 issue of the *Journal of Traumatic Stress*. The program resulted in significant improvement in anxiety, anger, depression, isolation, intrusive thoughts (of combat experiences), flashbacks, nightmares (of combat experiences), and relationship problems.

Limited trials have shown the ability of biofeedback to control hyperactivity in children. Finally, it may offer a direct symptomatic treatment for reflex sympathetic dystrophy (RSD), an unusual debilitating chronic pain syndrome thought to be associated with continuous excessive discharge of regional sympathetic nerves. For a complete list of clinical trials using biofeedback and more information and referrals, contact the Association of Applied Psychophysiology and Biofeedback.

Botanical Medicine

In China, when patients go to a clinic to pick up their medicine, they do not normally receive pills. Instead, they are likely to be given either a packet or pot containing a mixture of botanical plants and herbs which a physician has prescribed as the appropriate medicine for the patient's specific disorder. Some prescriptions are 600 years old. Each has a written formula and may contain a combination of herbs, plants, plant roots and, in some cases, a variety of animal parts such as antlers' horns, or even parts of a scorpion.

Western scientists assume that the botanical plants work because they contain chemicals which help a diseased part of the body to heal itself. Interestingly, Chinese doctors do not prescribe botanical medicines because of their active chemical ingredients. Instead, they give their patients botanical medicines to either increase or decrease their vital life energy (or chi).

The World Health Organization (WHO) estimates that 80% of the world's population relies primarily on traditional medicine for health care. A major part of these traditional therapies involves the use of plant medicines. In the U.S., botanical plants were used as primary agents in medicine until the development of new pharmaceutical drugs in laboratories during the 1940s and 1950s. Even today, 25% of pharmaceutical drugs are derived directly from plants, according to Dr. Andrew Weil, author of *Health and Healing* and *Natural Health, Natural Medicine*. Among the most important are: the birth-control pill, derived from the Mexican yam; the heart medication digitalis, which comes from the foxglove plant; and the bark of the Pacific yew tree, which has yielded a new drug that is one of the most promising for treating ovarian and breast cancers. Betacarotene, found in abundance in certain fruits and vegetables, also shows promise as a powerful preventative agent. Herbal preparations from leaves, seeds, stems, flowers, roots, and bark have also proven very useful for chronic and mild conditions by aiding natural healing and stimulating the body's return to balanced health.

Natural botanical medicines taken wholly and directly from plants are widely available in the U.S., and sales of herbal medicines have grown as much as 20% a year for the last several years, according to an August 1993 article in *The Boomer Report*. However, the vast majority of Americans take pharmaceutical medicines. Natural botanical medicines, including herbs, are not the same as the pharmaceutical drugs that are synthesized from them. For example, natural herbs are

much milder in effect. Natural botanical drugs also release more slowly into the bloodstream when they are bound up with other inert components contained in the plant. As a result, Aruyvedic physicians only prescribe herbs extracted from whole plants because the herb's active ingredient is packaged along with other natural chemicals that offset any possible undesirable effects.

Chiropractic Medicine

Therapeutic manipulation of the skeleton, particularly of the spine, has ancient roots. Hippocrates (fifth century B.C.), Aesklepiades (100 B.C.) and Galen (second century A.D.) all used some form of it, and it was common practice among physicians as early as the fourth century A.D. The most common form of therapeutic skeletal manipulation practiced today—chiropractic and osteopathy—are two of the most important holistic therapies originally developed in the U.S. The word "chiropractic" is taken from the Greek "done by hand."

Chiropractic was invented by Daniel David Palmer who performed his first spinal adjustment in 1895 and claimed that he'd cured an African-American janitor of deafness. From this miraculous event, Palmer deduced that the nervous system was the ultimate control mechanism of the body and that even minor misalignment of the spine, which he termed "subluxations," could significantly impact a person's health. And thus, the term chiropractic, a method of restoring wellness through adjustments of the spine, was coined. Palmer, however, credited the ancient Greeks with inventing the technique as early as 1250 B.C.

Palmer opened his own school of chiropractics in 1895. According to Thomas Weisman, the basis of Palmer's teaching was that "as many as 31 different pairs of spinal nerves travel through openings in the vertebrae to and from the brain." If one of the vertebrae is partly displaced from its correct position, it can cause an impingement and put pressure or irritation on the surrounding nerves. As a result, essential nerve messages are distorted, which may cause damage to the surrounding muscles or tissues. Since the nervous system regulates all systems of the body, including the digestive, respiratory, circulatory, immune, muscular, and elimination systems, subluxations can have far-reaching effects.

Today, there are an estimated 39,000 chiropractors practicing in the U.S. The largest group (approximately 32,000) consists of "broad scope" chiropractors who manipulate the spine to restore nerve flow and function, but their goal is to diagnose, treat, and eliminate specific symptoms and conditions. They sometimes incorporate other methods of treatment such as physical therapy, nutrition, and acupuncture.

The remaining 7,000 American "straight" or "network" chiropractors practice in Palmer's tradition. Rather than diagnosing or treating specific conditions or symptoms, they treat subluxations (or partial dislocations of the spine) in an effort to restore normal nerve flow. Also, whereas "broad scope" chiropractic focuses entirely on physical stress and trauma to the spine, the scope of "network" chiropractic includes emotional, mental, and chemical factors which can create tension in the spinal system and soft tissues.

Weisman states that "everybody is born with their own internal organizing power or innate intelligence." The chiropractor's sole function is to adjust the spine to eliminate any subluxations he is able to detect which are obstructing the expression of this innate intelligence through the nervous system. "There are no diseases, only dis-ease," Weismann continues. "Diseases, symptoms or conditions which are distressing our physical or emotional make-up are reflections of the mind-body being out of sync with its natural rhythm."

Fugh-Berman cites more than 20 studies reviewed by the Office of Alternative Medicine documenting the benefits of chiropractic therapy in relieving pain. A 1990 study, for example, found that chronic low-back pain patients who were treated at chiropractic clinics ended up with less pain and more mobility than those treated at conventional hospitals. Another study published in 1991 concluded that people with acute low-back pain not caused by neurological complications could significantly boost their odds of recovering within three weeks by undergoing spinal manipulation.

Weisman related a 1986 study conducted at the University of Lund in Lund, Sweden, suggesting that chiropractic treatment may significantly reduce the risk of immune breakdown and disease The study involved three different control groups of people who had been exposed to hazardous environmental chemicals linked to cancer: Group 1 consisted of healthy individuals who received long-term chiropractic care; Group 2 included healthy individuals who did not receive chiropractic care; and Group 3 consisted of people with cancer or other serious diseases. Those individuals who received chiropractic care had 200% greater immune competence than Group 2, and 400% greater immune competence than Group 3. All chiropractic patients were "genetically normal"—that is, they had no obvious genetic reasons for increased resistance or susceptibility to disease. Ronald Pero, one of the investigators, concluded that "chiropractic may optimize whatever genetic abilities you have. I'm very excited to see that without chemical intervention…this particular group of patients under chiropractic care did show a very improved response."

In the U.S., chiropractors constitute the third largest medical profession after physicians or dentists, and are licensed to practice without supervision or referral from medical doctors in every state. They cannot, however, prescribe drugs or perform surgery. Those with a D.C. degree (Doctor of Chiropractic) have completed at least four years of training at an accredited chiropractic college.

Hospitals are increasingly adding chiropractors to their medical staffs, and their services are widely reimbursed by Medicare, Medicaid, workers' compensation, and private insurance. Surveys indicate that 15-20 million Americans visited a chiropractor in 1992, the majority of them for treatment of low-back pain.

Exercise

In the Orient, there is an old expression: The body is like a hinge on a door. If it is not swung open, it will rust.

Indeed, virtually all cultures recognize the importance of regularly moving all parts of the body. In India, yogic exercise has played an important role in Aruyvedic medicine for over 6,000 years. Similarly, in China, exercise has been practiced for 2,500 years using martial arts such as tai chi.

Given the critical importance of regular exercise, it is surprising that as many as an estimated 75% of all Americans, including children, do not exercise enough.

Many studies, as cited in Chapters 6 and 7, have shown that people who exercise regularly have fewer illnesses than sedentary persons. Vigorous exercise benefits the body both directly and indirectly by stimulating the immune system and enabling people to cope with a variety of stressors and toxins. The psychological benefits are equally as important, and exercise has been successfully used to treat several disorders such as depression.

Regular exercise is almost always a key component of any holistic medical program because next to diet it most effectively produces total body health. In fact, the American Cancer Society now recommends regular exercise as part of its 10-step program to prevent cancer. The many functions exercise plays in maintaining health and preventing disease are documented in Chapter 6.

Homeopathy

In his book, *Health and Healing*, Weil describes how he once developed sudden attacks of pain starting in the center of his chest that eventually radiated to the center of his back, left shoulder, throat, and jaw. The pain was accompanied by difficulty in swallowing, as if something were lodged in the bottom of his esophagus. After consulting with several orthodox physicians who were not able to relieve the pain, Weil visited a friend who was a homeopath. The friend asked him a number of questions not directly related to the specific pain, including questions pertaining to lifestyle and sleeping patterns.

The homeopath then diagnosed Weil as having symptoms provoked by elemental sulfur and gave him a vial of tiny white pellets which were lactose (milk sugar) covered with a drop of a dilute suspension of sulfur. After Weil took the pellets, the pains completely disappeared, and never returned again.

Homeopathy was founded in the late 18th century by the German physician Samuel Hahnemann, who became discouraged by prevailing medical techniques such as bloodletting and blistering to treat illness, and the use of toxic substances such as mercury. He began experimenting with cinchona bark which contains quinine, then a well-known medicine for fever and malaria. He found that while cinchona produced fever in healthy individuals, it relieved fever in people with malaria. Based on these experiments, Hahnemann stated, "A substance that produces a certain set of symptoms in a healthy person has the power to cure a sick person manifesting those same symptoms." He coined the name homeopathy, joining the Greek words "homoios," which means like, and "pathos," for suffering or sickness. Hahnemann maintained that the presence of an illness stimulates the body's defense system to combat the illness. That defensive reaction produces symptoms, which are part of the body's effort to rid itself of the underlying disease. The symptoms are not the illness, Hahnemann claimed, but part of the curative process. This contrasts with traditional views that symptoms are the manifestation of the disease itself.

Once a homeopath has diagnosed a disorder in a patient, a diluted solution to treat the problem is prescribed. This is done by matching ("proving") symptoms with the one substance that most closely reproduces these symptoms in a normal person.

Since Hahnemann's pioneering work, homeopaths have kept detailed clinical records of the results of giving small amounts of many different substances to volunteer subjects in good health. As Weil relates, these substances contain chemicals, minerals, plant extracts, dilute preparations of animal and insect venoms, disease-causing germs, and some standard drugs. Matching the patient's symptoms with the one substance that most closely reproduces them is crucial because a single dose of that substance, highly diluted and properly prepared, has the capacity to cure the ailing patient.

To date, there have been an extensive number of controlled clinical studies evaluating the effectiveness of homeopathic treatment. The April 1991 issue of *Health Facts* reports an exhaustive review of 107 controlled experiments in which homeopathic remedies or placebos (dummy pills) were prescribed. The researchers concluded that the homeopathic remedies were more effective than the placebos in treating a variety of common problems, including migraine headaches, dry cough, and ankle sprains.

Since Hahnemann first published his findings in 1810, millions of people have relied exclusively on homeopathy for the treatment of all types of illnesses. According to the National Center for Homeopathy, sales of homeopathic medicine grew 50% between 1988 and 1990, reaching $150 million. Despite homeopathy's documented effectiveness, however, the American Medical Association (AMA) does not recognize homeopathic medicine because it believes it is not based on scientific principles. Currently, only three states (Arizona, Connecticut, and Nevada) license homeopaths, and in these states, a homeopathic practitioner is licensed under one of the other accepted forms of medicine, such as a medical doctor, acupuncturist, osteopath, or chiropractor.

Hypnosis

In *Beyond Biofeedback*, Elmer Green and Alyce Green of the Menninger Clinic describe the case of a patient with a large and painful pelvic cancer the size of a grapefruit. The patient was hypnotized and asked to find the room in his brain that had the valves controlling the blood supply to his body and to turn off the valve that controlled the blood flow to his tumor. He did so, and during the two month-session, the tumor shrank to one-fourth its former size.

Hypnotherapy has proven effective in treating both psychological and physical disorders. In perhaps the most interesting study, conducted by the University of Colorado Health Sciences Center, hemophiliacs under hypnosis were able reduce their need for blood transfusions, significantly reducing

A Typical Hypnotherapy Session

- A hypnotherapy session usually lasts from one hour to 90 minutes. The number of sessions required to produce results varies according to each individual and his condition. Six to 12 sessions, once a week, is the average length of treatment.

- Although hypnosis is a safe practice in the hands of a qualified practitioner, it should be used with discretion. WHO cautions that hypnosis should not be performed on patients with psychosis, organic psychiatric conditions, or antisocial personality disorders.

their exposure to the AIDS virus and lowering their risk of liver and kidney damage. Self-hypnosis apparently provided the hemophiliacs with increased feelings of control and confidence and improved the quality of their lives.

Maurice Tinterow, an anesthesiologist at the Center for the Improvement of Human Functioning in Wichita, Kansas, has successfully employed hypnotherapy to control pain for conditions that include headaches, facial neuralgia, sciatica, osteoarthritis, rheumatoid arthritis, whiplash, menstrual pain, and tennis elbow. He has also used hypnotherapy in place of anesthesia in a variety of surgical operations, including hernias, hysterectomies, breast biopsies, hemorrhoidectomies, cesarean sections, and for the treatment of second- and third-degree burns.

Office of Alternative Medicine (OAM) studies, according to Fugh-Berman, show that hypnosis has also proven effective in relieving chronic back pain, ulcers, and morning sickness. In one study, 32 patients with high hypnotizability recovered faster from cardiac surgery after being treated with formal hypnosis. Psychiatrists have also used hypnosis to treat diseases that manifest as behavioral compulsions, such as phobias and eating disorders, and to help patients remember and deal with traumatic events. In most cases, patients learn self-hypnosis, which they can then apply themselves if the problem resurfaces.

Hypnosis has also been used to help patients with eating disorders, and several studies have shown that it is an effective therapy for weight loss. In a controlled study reported in *Alternative Medicine: What Works*, obese patients received either hypnosis, hypnosis plus an audiotape, or certain amount of attention. Both hypnosis groups lost an average of 17 pounds in six months, while the control group gained a half pound. In another study, 45 obese subjects who received hypnosis with specific food aversion suggestions lost an average of 14 lbs (6.4 kg). Those who received hypnosis but not the food aversion suggestions lost 7.5 lbs (3.4 kg), while those who received no hypnosis lost only 2.8 lbs (1.3 kg).

Alternative Medicine: What Works cites another trial in which 12 asthmatic subjects who were highly susceptible to hypnosis had improved symptoms, decreased use of medications, and dramatically decreased response to methacholine (a substance that usually worsens asthma), as compared both to the 17 controls and to 10 other subjects who also were hypnotized but whose susceptibility to it were low.

Another larger, controlled trial of 252 asthmatics found that progressive relaxation therapy and hypnosis both reduced symptoms, but hypnosis was more effective. Independent assessment found 59% of the hypnosis group "much better" compared to 43% of the relaxation group (a statistically significant difference). Another controlled trial of 62 asthmatics found that hypnosis reduced both the use of drugs and the number of days on which wheezing occurred.

Hypnotherapists are not regulated or licensed by the federal government or by state agencies. It is therefore important to find someone who is licensed by the American Society of Clinical Hypnosis, whose members include medical doctors, dentists, psychiatrists, psychologists, nurses, and social workers.

Meditation

In his book, *Love, Medicine & Miracles*, Dr. Bernie Siegel defines meditation as "an active process of focusing the mind into a state of relaxed awareness. There are many ways of doing this. Some teachers recommend focusing attention on a symbolic sound or word (a mantra) or on a single image, such as a candle flame or a mandala. Others teach people to focus on the sound and flowing of the breath. The result of all meditation methods is ultimately the same: to induce a restful trance which strengthens the mind by freeing it from its accustomed turmoil."

In the last 25 years, a considerable body of research by Chopra, Siegel, Dr. Jon Kabat-Zinn, Dr. Herbert Benson, and others has demonstrated how meditation benefits health. For example, blood chemistry reports have shown a lessening of lactate in the blood (lactate is related to high levels of anxiety). Also, electroencephalograms have shown an increase in alpha brain wave activity (alpha waves are present during states of deep relaxation and creativity). Meditation tends to lower or normalize blood pressure, pulse rate, and the levels of stress hormones in the blood. It also lowers abnormally high cholesterol levels and reduces mild hypertension. There is also evidence that with regular practice over a substantial period of time, meditation may increase concentration, memory, intelligence, and creativity.

In the October 1995 issue of *Journal of Physiology and Pharmacology*, Dr. S. Telles relates that one group of seven meditators who mentally chanted "OM" showed a statistically significant reduction in heart rate during meditation compared to a control group. *Alternative Medicine: What Works* reports a small clinical trial in which meditation helped decrease anxiety in 45 college students. Laughing meditation, according to an article by D. Sutorisu in the September issue of 1995 *Patient Education and Counseling,* has also been used as an effective adjutant in stress reduction therapy. J. Miller reports in the May 1995 issue of *General Hospital Psychiatry* that 22 medical patients with anxiety disorders and panic phobias significantly improved with 8-week outpatient physician-referred stress reduction intervention based on meditation.

Because meditation helps patients with a variety of disorders control their involuntary nervous system, it has been used successfully to reduce epileptic seizures. Dr. U. Panjwani conducted a study of 11 adults suffering from epilepsy who were taught meditation and yoga, while another nine adults acted as controls. All patients were on antiepileptic drugs and their serum drug levels were monitored regularly. Panjwani reports in the April 1995 issue of *Indian Journal of Physiology and Pharmacology* that the meditation group showed a "significant reduction in seizure frequency and duration, an increase in dominant background EEG frequency."

Other studies have confirmed that meditation can increase personal happiness and decrease negative thinking and anger. W. Smith reports a clinical trial in the March 1995 issue of the *Journal of Clinical Psychology* in which meditators scored signif-

Medical Benefits of Meditation

- Lessens lactate in the blood, which is related to high levels of anxiety.
- Increases alpha brain wave activity (alpha waves are present during states of deep relaxation and creativity).
- Lowers or normalizes blood pressure, pulse rate, and the levels of stress hormones in the blood.
- May increase concentration, memory, intelligence, and creativity.
- Lowers abnormally high cholesterol levels.
- Reduces mild hypertension.
- Lowers immune system resistance.
- Induces the "relaxation response."

icantly higher on Personal Happiness Enhancement Program (PHEP) inventory than a control group who did not meditate. In the 1992 *Scandinavian Journal of Psychology*, Dr. J. Dua reviews a clinical trial in which patients who were taught meditation significantly reduced negative thinking and anger scores across a wide variety of situations.

Transcendental Meditation (TM)

Transcendental Meditation (TM) was introduced to the West in the 1960s by Maharishi Mahesh Yogi, and currently boasts more than 3 million practitioners in 110 countries. The aim of TM is to transcend normal thought processes to a heightened level of awareness called cosmic consciousness, producing in the body and mind a sense of profound rest and relaxation. The technique involves the mental repetition of a mantra, or Sanskrit sound, that is given to new practitioners by a TM instructor. TM's technique involves sitting comfortably in a chair with the spine erect, the body relaxed and the eyes closed while the mantra is repeated silently for 20 minutes.

In 1975, Dr. Herbert Benson's *The Relaxation Response* documented that TM evoked an innate mechanism in the body that is the opposite of the "fight-or-flight response," the involuntary reaction to perceived danger which speeds up the body's processes (affecting heart beat, blood pressure, and metabolic rate) while lowering immune system resistance. Dr. Benson called this opposite mechanism which causes the beneficial physiological effects the "relaxation response." The relaxation response can be evoked by sitting quietly and willing the body to relax and assume its natural state of internal harmony. Two vital factors are required: the repetition of a word or phrase (as in meditation) and relaxation of the entire muscle system. According to Benson, the key to relaxation in all of these exercises is the passive disregard for intruding thoughts.

TM is a form of physical and mental relaxation which produces changes in the secretion and release of several stress hormones. The hormonal changes induced by TM mimic the effects of endorphins in runners who reportedly experience a "runner's high," according to an article by Dr. C. Maclean in the November 1994 *Annals of the New York Academy of Sciences*. Maclean has also found that TM reduces cortisol and testosterone levels associated with stress and anger.

Chopra observes in the August 1992 issue of the *Journal of Behavioral Medicine* that TM also increases serum DHEA (dehydroepiandrosterone sulfate [DHEA-S])

A Naturopathic View of Disease

Dr. Ross Trattler, naturopath and author of *Better Health Through Natural Healing,* summarizes the basic disease process and its causes as follows:

- Accumulation of toxic material within the body due to poor circulation, poor elimination, and lack of exercise.

- Unhealthy diet that is rich in harmful ingredients (fat, cholesterol, sugar, artificial ingredients, and excess protein) and low in essential vitamins, minerals, and fiber.

- Improper posture and body structure, including spinal misalignment, poor muscle tone, and blood and lymph stagnation.

- Destructive emotions, including fear, stress, resentment, hatred, and self pity, all of which have a debilitating effect on internal organs and the immune system.

- Suppressive drugs, such as antibiotics and vaccinations, which some studies have found depress the immune system.

- Excessive alcohol, coffee, and tobacco.

- Environmental agents in the soil, air, water, and work place.

- Parasites, virus, and infection.

- Genetic factors that create specific weaknesses, which allow accumulated toxins and other factors to manifest as disease.

levels, which may increase the practitioner's lifespan. Chopra suggests his findings indicate TM may help practitioners reverse age-related diseases.

TM also effectively lowers high blood pressure (hypertension). Dr. T. Nder reviews a study in the August 1996 issue of *Hypertension* documenting that TM helped 127 African American men and women, aged 55-88 years, lower their diastolic and systolic blood pressure.

T. McClanahan reports in the October 1995 issue of *Psychological Report* that TM and operand learning proved effective in helping a 32-year-old Caucasian woman overcome her compulsion for biting her nails. Dr. J. Lamarra relates in the April 1996 issue of *American Journal of Cardiology* that TM is useful for treating patients with coronary artery disease (CAD).

Naturopathic Medicine

The term "naturopathic" was first coined in 1895 by Dr. John Scheel to describe a combination of natural therapies which included nutritional therapy, herbal medicine, homeopathy, spinal manipulation, exercise therapy, hydrotherapy, electrotherapy, stress reduction, and natural cures. Naturopathy was subsequently popularized by a German-born healer named Benedict Lust, who in 1902 founded the American School of Naturopathy. Lust defined naturopathy as the use of nontoxic healing methods derived from Greek, Asian, and European medical traditions.

Consulting a Naturopath

Naturopath Michael Murray, coauthor of the *Encyclopedia of Natural Medicine,* and a member of the faculty of Bastyr College in Seattle, Washington, describes how naturopaths counsel patients:

- During the first visit, which normally lasts an hour, a naturopath uses history taking, physical examination, laboratory tests, and other standard diagnostic procedures to learn as much as possible about the patient.

- Diet, environment, exercise, stress, and other aspects of lifestyle are also evaluated.

- Once a good understanding of the patient's health and disease are established (making a diagnosis of a disease is only one part of this process), the doctor and patient work together to establish a treatment and health-promoting program.

Naturopathy shares with these systems a belief in an underlying life force and views disease as the result of a healing effort of nature.

Naturopathic medicine begins by assuming that the body is always striving for health. If an illness develops, the symptoms accompanying it are the result of the organism's intrinsic attempt to defend and heal itself. A naturopathic physician thus focuses on aiding the body in its effort to regain its natural health, rather than initiating a treatment that might interfere with this process.

Naturopathic doctors prefer nontoxic and noninvasive treatments which minimize the risks of harmful side effects. They are trained to distinguish which patients they can treat safely and which need referral to other health care practitioners. Naturopaths are currently licensed to practice in all but seven states in the U.S. Naturopathic physicians who have attended an accredited four-year program are trained in most of the same scientific disciplines taught in conventional medical schools. Consequently, most naturopaths use medical tests, such as blood and urine analysis, for diagnosis. Many naturopaths may use modern medicine, including drugs and surgery in certain extreme crisis situations, although they remain committed to using nontoxic and noninvasive methods. Currently, licensing for naturopathic physicians is available in seven states: Alaska, Arizona, Connecticut, Hawaii, Montana, Oregon, and Washington. There are two accredited colleges in the United States that offer degrees in naturopathic medicine: Bastyr College in Seattle, Washington, and Southwest College in Scottsdale, Arizona.

Nutrition

It is impossible to maintain optimal health without eating natural, nutritious foods. Many holistic physicians consider nutrition the most important aspect of holistic medicine. Why is what we eat so important? Because, like automobile engines, the human body cannot run without fuel. While certain people may be genetically strong, physically fit, and free of disease, if they ate strictly sugar, saturated fats, cholesterol, salt, and additives, the likelihood is that they would eventually become sick. On the other hand, if they ate strictly natural, unprocessed foods, particularly fruits, vegetables, grains, beans, seeds and nuts, they would probably live healthier lives.

Traditional medicine in China, Japan, and India has always stressed the key role that nutrition plays in health and healing. George Ohsawa, founder of the macrobiotic diet in the early 20th century, believed that a return to the more traditional Japanese diet of 50% grains, 25% vegetables, and 10% beans could prevent the major diseases directly related to diet.

The importance of nutrition for maintaining health was contested for many years by conventional doctors in the U.S. who argued that nutritional factors could not reverse (or cure) chronic diseases. However, a growing body of clinical evidence suggests that certain whole foods and nutritional supplements help maintain positive health and assist in the prevention or cure of a variety of diseases. In the last 20 years, a number of studies have repeatedly shown that dietary factors play a role in at least five of the 10 leading causes of death for Americans: heart disease, cancers, strokes, diabetes, and arteriosclerosis (hardening of the arteries).

The documented results of Ornish's "Reversal Program," described at the beginning of this chapter, also provide dramatic proof that ordinary people can reverse chronic illness with a combined program of nutrition, exercise, yoga, and group therapy. As a result, one major U.S. insurance company, Mutual of Omaha, now reimburses policy holders who enroll in Ornish's program.

Chapter 2 highlights a number of studies which detail specific food groups and foods that have been scientifically proven to enhance healthful living. Vitamins and minerals also play a critical role in maintaining optimal physical and mental health, and chapters 3 and 4 analyze the major vitamins and minerals and how they may be used in disease prevention and treatment.

Osteopathic Medicine

Osteopathy, or "bone treatment," was developed by a Civil War physician named Andrew Taylor Still, who became frustrated with the unpredictability and ignorance involved in prescribing the toxic medications commonly used in the late 1800s. He subsequently founded the American School of Osteopathy in Kirksville, Missouri, in 1892 after three of his children died of spinal meningitis, and he dedicated himself to find a way to enhance nature's own ability to heal.

As described by Weil in his book, *Health and Healing*, "Still gave up the use of drugs completely and, instead, tried to promote healing by manipulating bones to allow free circulation of blood and balanced functioning of nerves. The technique he developed was the same used by generations of children to crack their knuckles: placing tension on a joint until an audible click or pop results." Still was able to find positions and motions to crack most of the larger joints of the body. He reportedly used his manipulations to treat cases including pneumonia, bacterial infections of the skin, typhoid fever, and diarrhea.

Osteopaths assume that the structure of organs, skeleton, and tissues directly affect the body's various functions. Thus the shape and position of the skeletal structure are central to maintaining optimal health. Osteopaths believe that the correction of posture problems, mobilization of joints, and alignment of the spine can improve health and aid in the healing of diseases.

Osteopathic medicine is very similar to chiropractic medicine with two important exceptions. First, chiropractors normally only adjust the spine, whereas osteopaths manipulate all joints, even the difficult immobile joints of the cranium. Osteopathic medicine also focuses more on the health of the arteries because osteopaths believe that when blood and lymphathics flow freely, the tissues are able to perform their physiological functions without restriction. When an individual suffers emotional or physical trauma, the tissues often contract and the fluid flow becomes obstructed. Osteopathic manipulation restores the fluid flow throughout the impaired tissues and regenerates the body's inherent healing powers.

Osteopathic manipulation has been used successfully to treat young children with impaired inherent physiologic motion disorders. It has also been used to treat patients suffering from low-back pain, particularly women experiencing menstrual cramping, as well as dysmenorrhea. Recently, osteopathic manipulation has been introduced in clinical trials to help patients recover from coronary bypass graft surgery. In an October 1989 article in *INED*, J. L. Dickey reports that patients undergoing osteopathic manipulative treatment often perceive a sense of deep relaxation, tingling, energy flows, and relief of pain.

According to *Alternative Medicine: The Definitive Guide,* metastudies have shown that osteopathy has provided aid for patients with spinal and joint conditions, arthritis, allergies, cardiac disease, breathing dysfunctions, chronic fatigue syndrome, hiatal hernias, high blood pressure, headaches, sciatica, and various neuritis (inflammation of nerves disorders).

Most osteopaths are primary care physicians, and practice holistic medicine, including diet and exercise. Like MDs, osteopaths (Doctors of Osteopathy or "DOs") provide comprehensive medical care, including preventative medicine, diagnosis, surgery, prescription medications, and hospital referrals. DOs are licensed in all 50 states in the U.S.

Visualization Therapies

In *Love, Medicine & Miracles*, Siegel reported a clinical trial in which a young boy who suffered from an inoperable brain tumor was taken by his parents to the Biofeedback and Psychophysiology Center at the Menninger Clinic in Topeka, Kansas. The staff then taught him self-regulation techniques to help him to "control his body with his mind." He learned, for example, to imagine rockets ships, as in a video game, flying around in his head and shooting at the tumor. Several months later, he told his father, "I can't find my tumor anymore." A subsequent CAT scan showed that the tumor had entirely disappeared.

The boy, in effect, was using visualization to eradicate his tumor. Visualization is a generic term which describes a variety of visual techniques used to treat disease. It is based on inducing relaxation in patients, having them visualize their medical problems, and literally willing them away.

Visualization has been used to treat cancer patients. In one clinical trial documented in Siegel's book, a man with advanced throat cancer was given radiation treatment and told to visualize his white blood cells regenerating. His cancer dramatically disappeared within four months, and the patient subsequently cured his arthritis and a 21-year-old case of impotence using visualization techniques. In experiments conducted at the Stanford University Medical School, cancer patients who used guided imagery and other counseling techniques survived twice as long as patients who did not, according to an article by Spiegel and others in the 1989 issue of *The Lancet*.

Therapists have used visualization or guided imagery to help heal patients suffering loss due to disease, altered body image, or the threat of death. Positive results have been documented even when a total cure may be out of the question. Writing in the December

1992 issue of *Perceptual and Motion Skills*, S. Hu states that many patients with phobias, for example, have also been treated with visualization and positive thinking.

Yoga

As far back as the third century B.C., Patanjali, the father of classical yoga philosophy, defined yoga "as the cessation of the modification of the mind." Yoga, which in Sanskrit which means "union," focuses on altering the state of a person's mind, and using the powers of the mind to generate healing within the body. Through assuming a series of asanas (positions), and concentrating on breathing, people who practice yoga keep their spine supple and systematically exercise all of the body's major muscle groups. This in turn strengthens the organs by increasing respiration and blood flow.

The importance of breathing is central to all yogic teachings because the breath is considered to be the vehicle of "prana," or the vital life force. Prana enters the body when we inhale. How we breathe—whether shallow or deep, hurried or slow—controls how prana influences the body and mind. Indian yogis have long taught that to control the breath means to control universal energy within, or to control the physical health and state of mind. According to Swami Rama, one of the most influential figures to demonstrate the authenticity of yoga to western medicine, and reported by Tom Monte in *World Medicine: The EastWest Guide to Healing Your Body*, "All breathing exercises—advanced or basic—enable the student to control his mind through understanding prana."

A study in the April 1992 *Indian Journal of Physiology and Pharmacology* summarized by Dr. M. Satyanarayana suggests that Santhi kriya yoga, combining yogic breathing and relaxation, effectively helps reduce body weight, increase alpha activity of the brain, lower respiration rates, and increase a sense of "calmness" in eight healthy male volunteers aged 25-39. Another variant of yoga, Sahaja yoga, effectively reduces stress and blood lactate levels, according to Panjwani's article in the *Journal of Physiology and Pharmacology*. In his study, 32 Indian patients with epilepsy reduced periodic seizures by decreasing stress and blood lactate levels using yoga breathing.

A small study of five patients with obsessive compulsive disorder (OCD), reported by L. Beckett in the March 1996 *Journal of Neuroscience,* found that yogic breathing reduced their symptoms by 83%, 79%, 65%, 61%, and 18%. Three patients stopped medication after seven months or less, and two significantly reduced it, one by 25% and the other by 50%.

An article by Dr. P. Raju in the August 1994 *Indian Journal of Medical Research* showed that yogic breathing decreases blood lactate levels, often associated with stress-related disorders, and helps patients breathe more efficiently. Subjects in Raju's study who practiced pranayama achieved "higher work rates with reduced oxygen consumption per unit work and without increases in blood lactate levels."

S. Telles' article in the April 1994 *Indian Journal of Physiology and Pharmacology* suggests that yogic breathing, using alternate nostrils "can have a marked activating effect or relaxing effect on the sympathetic nervous system." Forty-eight male subjects ranging in age from 25-48 were randomly assigned to three groups: the first group practiced right nostril pranayama breathing, the second group practiced left nostril breath, and the third alternate nostril breathing. The alternate pranayama group showed an 18% increase in oxygen consumption, the right nostril group 37%, and the left nostril group 24%.

An increasing number of traditional medical doctors, chiropractors, back specialists, and physical therapists recommend yoga physical exercises such as stretching to their patients both as a preventive and remedial measure for the spine and as a stress-reduction technique. Many athletes have found that yoga is an excellent adjunct to their training because it tones, stretches, and relaxes muscles and ligaments, which in turn improves their range of motion and helps prevent injury.

Yoga relaxation exercises have been useful in Czechoslovakia in psychiatric treatment, especially for low self-esteem, social skills training, impulse control, and group and family therapy, according to an article by K. Nespor in the June 1994 *Cezheslovania Psychiatry*. Nespor adds that yoga has been used effectively to treat alcoholism, psychosomatic disorders and some neuroses. In the May 1994 *Journal of Biometerology*, S. Rawal suggests that yoga can be used to treat thyroid disorders. His study found that 10 male subjects with thyroid disorders used hatha yoga exercise effectively to increase thyroidal activity.

Like TM, yoga directly lowers heart rates, blood pressure levels, cortisol and prolactin levels, and increases growth hormone levels. Several studies reviewed by the OAM, and Fugh-Berman, suggest that on personality inventories, people who regularly practice yoga showed markedly higher scores in life satisfaction and lower scores in excitability, aggression, openness, emotionality, and somatic complaints.

Several studies also demonstrate that yogic exercises significantly improve young children's ability to focus and perform on mental and motor skill tests. S. Telles reports one study in the April 1994 *Indian Journal of Physiology and Pharmacology* of 20 subjects ranging from 17-22 years of age who practiced asanas'(physical postures), pranayama (voluntary regulation of breathing), medita-tion, devotional exercises, and tratakas (visual focusing exercises). These subjects showed fewer errors on mental tests.

Other Alternative Medical Therapies

Many other therapies are included in holistic medicine which are not complete medical systems, but nevertheless have proven successful in treating or preventing specific ailments or diseases. Descriptions of several of the more popular therapies appear below.

Aromatherapy

Essential oils and aromas extracted from plants have long been used in medicine. The Egyptians buried their cats and kings in antiseptic oils of natural essences such as myrrh and cedarwood to arrest putrefaction. Treating patients with incense was practiced throughout the Middle Ages, and the Arab physician Avicenna is known to have first developed the technique of distilling, or extracting, the essential oils of plant.

Aromatherapy uses essential oils derived from the leaves, barks, roots, flowers, resins, or seeds of plants to treat physical and psychological health problems. Typically the oils are inhaled for respiratory and nervous problems or applied topically or added to a bath for skin and muscle problems. The sense of smell, according to Marcel Lavarbre's *Aromatherapy Workbook*, acts mostly on a subconscious level; the olfactory nerves are directly connected to the most primitive part of the brain. "In a sense," says Lavarbre, "the olfactory nerves are an extension of the brain itself, which can then be reached directly through the nose."

The pathways by which aromatherapy heal are not fully understood. Some plants contain compounds which act as pesticides, bactericides, and fungicides, and their aromas perform these functions on humans with observable effects. Other plants are stimulants or aphrodisiacs, and their aromas, presumably, have the same effect. Lavarbre's thesis is intriguing: that the olfactory nerves are connected to the brain's limbic system, which also regulates sensory motor activities and affects sexual urges and behavioral mechanisms.

Olfactory nerves affect memory and aromatherapy has been particularly useful for treating psychological disorders. French psychoanalyst Andre Virel, for example, has used fragrances effectively to bring out patients' hidden memories. Like smelling salts, different odors wake up the brain, evoking images and feelings associated with each smell. *Alternative Medicine: The Definitive Guide* reports on one study conducted at Warrick University in England which found that inhaling beach aromas, for example, induced the relaxation response. Aromatherapy is primarily useful, according to *Alternative Medicine: The Definitive Guide,* for combating wrinkles, acne, and other skin problems as well as for treating poor circulation, obesity, broken capillaries, rheumatism, sinusitis, depression, anxiety, and stress. It may also be effective for bacterial infections of the respiratory system, immune deficiencies such as Epstein-Barr virus (the form of herpes believed to be the causative agent in infectious mononucleosis), and numerous skin disorders.

Dr. Kurt Schnaubelt, director of the Pacific Institute of Aromatherapy, states in *Alternative Medicine: The Definitive Guide,* "the chemical makeup of essential oils gives them a host of desirable pharmacological properties ranging from antibacterial, antiviral, and antispasmodic, to uses as diuretics (promoting urine production and excretion),

vasodilators (widening blood vessels), and vasoconstrictors (narrowing blood vessels). Essential oils act on the adrenals, ovaries, and thyroid gland, and can energize or pacify, detoxify, and facilitate the digestive process."

Bach Flowers and Flower Essences

Olsten's *The Encyclopedia of Alternative Health Care* states that flower essences, homeopathic dilute liquid remedies made from wildflower blossoms, can relieve symptoms of stress-related disorders. Flower essences were first developed into a healing system by British homeopath Edward Bach, a physician and pathologist, who experimented with "the healing secrets of wildflower" to cure himself of depression. He found that certain wildflowers had subtle life energies which could heal specific emotional disorders, and by the time of his death, he had invented 38 wildflower remedies, including honeysuckle, holly, and wild rose. Bach postulated that emotions such as guilt, fear, or doubt create personality fixations, which eventually lead to physical consequences—stress, pain, and illness. He developed a remedy system using flower essences that was based on identifying personality types with chronic patterns of mental or emotional imbalance that created tendencies for certain chronic disease.

Chiropractors, homeopaths, and other natural health practitioners use flower essences as remedies to heal the body *indirectly.* The essences address not specific physical illness but moods, attitudes, and emotions, such as fear, anxiety, and restlessness. As in homeopathy, flower essence therapy is a form of subtle energy medicine. The remedies work on a vibrational rather than biochemical level, the flowers serving as gentle catalysts promoting health from within.

Scientific evidence for the effectiveness of Bach flower or aromatherapies is still lacking. The FDA considers Bach Remedies and other flower essences as over-the-counter homeopathic drugs, and they are widely available at most health food stores. Some flower essences are also included in first-aid creams. As with all homeopathic remedies, flower essences are largely nontoxic.

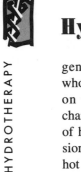

Hydrotherapy

Hydrotherapy, the use of heated water, is generally attributed to Vinzenz Priessnitz who, in the 1820s, collected data in Austria on the powers of water and temperature change to heal the body. Different methods of hydrotherapy use water and water immersion, including sitz baths, douches, spas and hot tubs, whirlpools, saunas, showers, immersion baths, poultices, and foot baths.

The healing properties of water include its buoyancy (which makes movement easier); its temperature (which promotes relaxation and decreases pain); its viscosity (which provides resistance so injured patients can maintain muscle tone and aerobic capacity); and its hydrostatic or circumferential pressure (which enhances blood circulation). One of hydrotherapy's most important benefits is that it allows therapists to treat a wide variety of patients sooner. After an injury or surgery, patients are able to begin an active program of stretching and conditioning right away instead of having their muscles atrophy. Recovery time can be reduced by as much as 50% in some cases, according to Wade Boyle and Andre Saine in *Lectures in Naturopathic Hydrotherapy*.

Hydrotherapy has proved particularly effective with many discomforts associated with spinal stress. Clinical success has also been demonstrated on patients with steroid-dependent asthma, coughs, head colds, hoarseness, and burn injuries. People with learning disabilities have benefited from spa therapy. Repeated water immersion has also been used as an alternative to medicine for patients with liver cirrhosis, arterial hypertension, rheumatoid arthritis, lumbar pain syndrome, pneumoconiosis and dust-induced bronchitis, and hypertension, reports A. Ader in the September 1993 issue of *Contributions to Nephrology*.

Hyperthermia

Hyperthermia, or heat therapy, raises the body temperature, which has several important physiological effects. First, elevated body temperatures increase immune resistance by increasing antibody production, and the growth of some microorganisms is inhibited by raising body heat above their normal temperature. Second, a slight increase of body temperature to 102°F (38°C) also stimulates the activity of certain enzymes which are heat sensitive. Increased sweating, for example, increases the elimination of salt and water through the skin.

Maria Abdin reports in the June 1995 *Townsend Letter for Doctors* that heat helps eliminate toxins from the body, including metals (such as nickel, copper, zinc, and lead), toxic volatile hydrocarbons (benzene, styrenes, toluene, and trichloroethylene), drugs (cocaine, methadone, barbiturates, and benzodiazepine), fluorine, nitrogen-containing chemicals (urea, creatinine, and ammonia), and immunoglobulins.

Heat therapy may become an important component of treating AIDS, and HIV-related diseases. Abdin reports that an initial clinical trial has shown that heat therapy has effectively induced remission of Kaposi's sarcoma and hairy leukoplakia in seven of 10 patients, with no activation of HIV.

Hyperthermia can result in skin burns,

Medical Uses of Hyperthermia

- Localized infections. Localized infections/abscesses are often helped by heat application.

- Psoriasis. Regular sauna bathing reduces symptoms, provided a vitamin E skin cream is used after the sauna.

- Muscle spasm. Hot packs have been used to alleviate muscle spasms, including those of poliomyelitis.

- Arthritic and rheumatic disorders. Exposure to hot, moist air has been shown to alleviate symptoms of arthritic conditions. Saunas have helped reduce pain and improve joint mobility in rheumatic patients. In some cases, how-

ever, symptoms have been reported to worsen the following day unless the sauna was followed by cooling with cold water.

- Malignancies. Hyperthermia has been used in conjunction with chemotherapy and radiation to treat malignancies. The methods of inducing hyperthermia include localized heating by means of ultrasound or microwaves with careful temperature regulation.

- Respiratory conditions. Symptoms of the common cold and allergic rhinitis have been improved by the use of local hyperthermia.

prolonged rectal temperature, brain damage, and can cause heat stroke and death. Thus, heat therapy is contraindicated for patients with heart disorders, hemorrhage (such as active pulmonary tuberculosis or gastric ulcer), active alcoholism, diabetes, and high blood pressure.

Massage

In China, every medical student must study massage for two years before graduating from medical school. All doctors must complete at least one year of residency in massage and then pass an examination. While people in the West tend to think of massage as a therapy for relaxation, the Chinese use massage to treat chronic illness.

Massage has proved very effective in treating back pain, and shows promise for depression. The Touch Research Institute (TRI) at the University of Miami Medical

School studied the effect of massage on adolescent mothers and their infants, abused and neglected children in shelter care centers, adolescent psychiatric patients, anorexic and bulimic girls, and survivors of Hurricane Andrew. They found that after a 30-minute massage, people had consistently lower levels of stress-related hormones—cortisol and norepinephrine—and were more alert, less restless, and better able to sleep, according to a November/December 1993 report in *Natural Health* by Meredith Gould Ruch.

Music Therapy

In the ancient cultures of China, Greece, and India, music was understood to have transformational power. In ancient China, sages were custodians of the fundamental tone called the "kung," which was considered to be a bridge between the celestial and earthly scales. Master musicians of the Vedic civi-

Uses of Ozone Therapy

Ozone is now routinely utilized in the following medical fields:

- Opthamalogy. To treat retinitis pig-mentosa, glaucoma, optic nerve dysfunction, thrombosis, and corneal ulcers.

- Dermatology. To treat allergies, acne, mycosis, fistulae, and furunculosis.

- Internal medicine. To treat hepatitis, metabolism dysfunctions, blood alteration, hypercholesterolemia, cerebral sclerosis, constipation, and cirrhosis of the liver.

- Gynecology. To treat vulvovaginitis

- Oncology. As an adjunct to combined cancer therapies—healing radiation scars, for example.

- Blood treatments for transfusions to prevent hepatitis.

- Angiology. To treat venous and arterial circulatory disturbances, gangrene, thrombophlebitis, and chronic ulcerations.

- Gerontology. To treat senile dementia, Alzheimer's disease, and vascular dementia.

- Urology. To treat cystitis and prostatitis.

- Gastroenterology. To treat mucous colitis, diarrhea, giardia, and amoebas.

- Ear disorders. To treat chronic otitis and sinusitis.

- Orthopedics. To treat arthritis, polyarthritis, spondylitis, and osteomyelitis.

- Rheumatology. To treat rheumatoid arthritis.

- Neurology. To treat Parkinson's disease and Friedreich's ataxia.

- Stomatology. To treat stomatitis and clean and disinfect the buccal membrane.

- Aesthetics. To treat cellulitis.

lization were seers or rishis who were believed to understand the musical structure of the cosmos, and lived and breathed music that resonated with all the laws of nature. In Greece, Greek philosopher and mathematician Pythagoras taught his students to cleanse themselves of worry, sorrow, fear, and anger through daily singing and music making. In the ancient temples of India, China, and Tibet, Buddhist and Hindu monks used prolonged chants, ecstatic rhythms, and ancient melodic patterns to awaken their chakras, believed to be powerful center of energy in the body.

Music may be an effective therapeutic tool because it stimulates peptides and endorphins, natural opiates secreted by the hypothalamus that produce a pleasurable feeling. Because it is nonverbal, music moves quickly through the auditory cortex directly to the center of the limbic system, the midbrain network that governs most emotional experiences as well as basic metabolic responses such as body temperature, blood pressure, and heart rate. Music may also be able to activate the flow of stored memory material across the corpus callosum, the network of fibers connecting the left and right sides of the brain. British osteopaths have claimed they can transmit the "correct" frequency of health to a diseased organ. While this treatment is not yet fully accepted in the United States, it has been successfully used to treat certain neuromuscular problems such as arthritis and degenerative bone condition.

American physicians now use music to treat patients recovering from grief and stress. In one clinical trial, the University of Massachusetts Medical Center in Worcester treated outpatients with Buddhist meditation and harp music. The program also taught patients how to pay attention to their bodies, their breathing patterns, and their thoughts, according to Pamela Bloom's article in *New Age Journal*'s March/April 1987 issue.

Ozone Therapy

In *Oxygen Healing Therapies*, Nathaniel Altman reports that the Cuban Department of Ozone has treated more than 25,000 patients with ozone therapy for more than 20 major diseases, including cancer and HIV-related disorders. Altman details five primary methods of ozone therapy.

1. *Major autohemotherapy.* Autohemotherapy involves removing between 50-100 milliliters of a patient's blood, bubbling ozone and oxygen into it for several minutes, and then reintroducing the ozonated blood back into the patient through a vein. These methods have been used successfully to treat a wide variety of health problems, including herpes, arthritis, cancer, heart disease, and HIV-infection. This is the most commonly use type of ozone therapy used worldwide today.

2. *Rectal insufflation.* This method is considered one of the safest ways to apply ozone, and is used primarily for children and elderly patients whose veins are too delicate for autohemotherapy. Rectal insufflation involves introducing a mixture of oxygen and ozone through the rectum where it is absorbed through the intestine.

3. *Ozone Bagging.* This non-invasive method uses specially made plastic bags that are placed around the area to be treated. An ozone oxygen mixture is pumped into the bag and is absorbed into the body through the skin. Ozone bags are ideal for treating leg ulcers, burns, gangrene, fungal infections, and slow-healing wounds.

4. *Injections.* Used primarily to treat arterial circulatory disturbances, a small amount of ozone and oxygen are injected through intra-arterial application. Ozone can also be injected directly into joints to treat arthritis and other joint diseases.

5. *Ozonated oil.* Used primarily to treat skin problems, ozone gas is added to olive oil and applied as a balm or salve for long-term, low-dose exposure. In Cuba, ozone is usually combined with sunflower oil, and applied externally to treat fungal infections such as athlete's foot, fistulae, leg ulcers, bed sores, gingivitis, herpes simplex, hemorrhoids, vulvovaginitis, bee stings, insect bites, and acne. The Cubans also use capsules filled with ozonated oil to treat gastroduodenal ulcers, gastritis, giardia, and peptic ulcers.

Other Body Therapies

Body therapies, or bodywork, refers to a range of therapies that attempt to improve the structure and functioning of the human body. The goal of bodywork is for a person to become more aware of his or her body and movement patterns.

Alexander Technique. The Alexander Technique was developed by an actor who created the method after concluding that bad posture was responsible for his own chronic voice loss. Practitioners teach simple, efficient physical movements designed to improve balance, posture and coordination, and to relieve pain. Instructors offer gentle hands-on guidance and verbal instruction to retrain students in the optimal use of their bodies. A session may focus on movements as basic as getting up from a chair properly.

Aston Patterning. Founded by former dancer Judith Aston, this method is an integrated system of movement education, bodywork, and environmental evaluation. In specifically designed sessions, teacher and client work together to reveal and define the body's individual posture and movement patterns while training the body to move more efficiently and effortlessly.

Sessions can include any one or a combination of the following: movement education which teaches alternatives to stressful habits; massage-like body work which can relieve chronic physical and mental stress; and environmental consultation which modifies the individual's surroundings to reduce unnecessary stress and promote ease of movement.

The Feldenkrais Method. As part of his recovery after suffering a sports-related injury, nuclear physicist Moshe Feldenkrais developed a way to help people create more efficient movement by combining movement training, gentle touch, and verbal dialogue. Feldenkrais takes two forms. The first involves individual, hands-on sessions ("Functional Integration") where the practitioner's touch is used to improve the subject's breathing and body alignment. The second form involves a series of classes of slow, non-aerobic motions ("Awareness Through Movement"), in which the subjects "relearn" the proper ways their bodies should move. The method is frequently used to help reduce stress and tension, to alleviate chronic pain, and to help athletes and others improve their balance and coordination.

Hellerwork. Developed by former aerospace engineer Joseph Heller, this technique combines deep-tissue muscle therapy and movement reeducation with counseling about the emotional issues that may underlie a physical posture. For example, feelings of insecurity may manifest themselves in stooped shoulders. Participants go through eleven 60-90-minute sessions. Hellerwork is used to treat chronic pain or to help "well" people learn to live more comfortably inside their bodies.

Choosing a Holistic Physician

The American Holistic Medical Association (AHMA) recommends that new patients ask the following questions when making a final decision about a holistic physician:

- Do you feel comfortable and cared for when you visit the office?

- Is your appointment time honored, or do you have to wait?

- How do you feel when you are in this environment? Is the practitioner accessible?

- Is the practitioner sensitive enough to place him/herself in your position regarding your fears and anxieties about an illness or proposed treatment?

- Does the practitioner appear to represent a healthy lifestyle, or does he or she show signs of overweight, overwork, smoking, or drinking?

- Did the physician diagnose your condition fully?

- Did the physician order expensive tests?

- Did the practitioner prescribe prescriptions that have known side effects or cause adverse reactions?

- Do you trust both the physician's tone and the therapy outlined for you?

- Were you given a reasonable amount of time to evaluate the recommendations before beginning treatment, or do you feel you were rushed unnecessarily?

Kinesiology. Kinesiology is a diagnostic system based on the premise that individual muscle functions can be used to provide information about a patient's overall health. Practitioners test the strength and mobility of certain muscles, analyze a patient's posture and gait, and inquire about lifestyle factors that may be contributing to an illness. Nutrition, muscle and joint manipulation, diet, and exercise are then used as part of a treatment plan. Kinesiology is used by professionals licensed to diagnose, including chiropractors, dentists, medical doctors, and osteopaths.

Rolfing. Rolfing is a deep massage technique developed by biochemist Ida Rolf which uses deep manipulation of the fascia (connective tissue) to restore the body's natural alignment, which may have become rigid through injury, emotional trauma, or inefficient movement ha-bits. The process typically involves 10 sessions, each focusing on a different part of the body. Rolf practitioners are certified through the Rolf Institute in Boulder, Colorado.

Rosen Method. Developed by former physical therapist Marion Rosen, the Rosen Method combines gentle touch and verbal communication to evoke relaxation and self-awareness. The work can bring up buried feelings and emotions and is sometimes used in conjunction with counseling.

Summary

Alternative medicine emphasizes that health is a state of optimal well-being and not simply the absence of disease. The philosophy of holistic health emphasizes the unity of the mind, spirit, and body. Alternative medicine focuses on the whole person, and emphasizes self-healing, the maintenance of health, and the prevention of illness, rather than the treatment of symptoms and disease.

Determining appropriate medical advice and treatment must be a combination of many factors. Each individual's needs will be different. All holistic physicians share the belief that the body has an inherent healing mechanism that can be stimulated through natural means such as diet, nutrition, exercise and botanical medicines, and by triggering the relaxation response through yoga, meditation, visualizations, biofeedback, or hypnosis. As with conventional MDs, there is wide variation in the background and training of holistic physicians and medical practitioners. Licensing regulations governing specific fields often vary from state to state. Therefore, it is important for patients to research a practitioner's background. As further elaborated throughout this book, the goal of alternative medicine is to empower patients to participate in their own healing process.

Resources

References

Abdin, Maria. "Heat, Sauna and Healing: A Review." *Townsend Letter for Doctors* (June 1995): 46-50.

Ader, A.J. "Water Immersion: Lessons from Antiquity to Modern Times." *Contributions to Nephrology* (1993): 171-86.

Beckett, J. "Clinical Case Report: Efficacy of Yogic Techniques in the Treatment of Obsessive Compulsive Disorders." *Journal of Neuroscience* (March 1996): 1-17.

Benninga, M.A. "Biofeedback Training in Chronic Constipation." *Archives of Disease in Childhood* (January 1993): 126-29.

Berger. B. "Mood Alternation with Yoga and Swimming." *Perceptual and Motor Skills* (December 1992):1331-43.

Binnie, N.R. "Solitary Rectal Ulcer: The Place of Biofeedback and Surgery in the Treatment of the Syndrome." *World Journal of Surgery* (September/October 1992): 836-40.

Bloom, Pamela. "Soul Music." *New Age Journal* (March/April 1987): 58-63.

"Boomers Are Biggest Users of Alternative Medicine." *The Boomer Report* (August 15, 1993): 6.

Boulter, P. "Learning Disabilities. Using Hydrotherapy: Maximizing Benefits." *Nursing Standard* (October 14-20, 1992): 5-7.

Boyle, Wade, and Andre Saine. *Lectures in Naturopathic Hydrotherapy.* East Palestine, OH: Buckeye Naturopathic Press, 1988.

Bullock, M. "Controlled Trial of Acupuncture for Severe Recidivist Alcoholism." *The Lancet* , No 8652 (June 1989):1435-39.

The Burton Goldberg Group. *Alternative Medicine: The Definitive Guide.* Puyallup, WA: Future Medicine Publishing, Inc., 1993.

Chopra, Deepak. *Perfect Health: The Complete Mind/Body Guide.* New York: Harmony Books, 1991, p. 6.

———. "Elevated Rum Dehydroapiandorsterone Sulfate Levels In Practitioners of the Transcendental Meditation (TM) and TM-Sidhi Programs." *Journal of Behavioral Medicine* (August 1992): 327-41.

Dickey, J.L. "Postoperative Osteopathic Manipulative Management of Median

RESOURCES

Sternotomy Patients." *INED* (October 1989): 1319-22.

Dua, J. "Effectiveness of Negative Thought Reduction, Meditation and Placebo Training Treatment In Reducing Anger." *Scandinavian Journal of Psychology* (1992): 135-46.

Eisenberg, D. *Encounters with Qi: Exploring Chinese Medicine.* New York: Penguin Books, 1987.

Eisenberg, D., et al. "Unconventional Medicine in the United States: Prevalence, Costs, and Patterns of Use." *New England Journal of Medicine* 328 (March 1993): 246-52.

Fugh-Berman, Adriane. *Alternative Medicine: What Works.* Tucson, AZ: Odonian Press, 1996.

Gerber, R. *Vibrational Medicine.* Sante Fe, NM: Bear & Company, 1988.

Gould Ruch, Meredith. "Feeling Down? Study Shows Massage Can Lift Your Spirits." *Natural Health* (November/December 1993): 48-50.

Hau, D. "Effects of Eclctroacupuncture on Leukocytes and Plasma Protein." *American Journal of Chinese Medicine* (1980): 354-66.

"Homeopathic Remedies: Safe, Inexpensive...And They Seem to Work." *HealthFacts* (April 1991): 1-2.

Hu, S. "Positive Thinking Reduces Heart Rate and Fear Responses to Speech-Phobic Imagery." *Perceptual & Motion Skills* (December 1992): 1067-73.

Jayasuraiya, A. *Textbook on Acupuncture.* Colombo, Sri Lanka: Open University, 1987.

Kaiser, R. "Depression in Adolescent Headache Patients." *Headache* (July 1992): 340-44.

Kranhold, C. "Hypnotizability in Bulimic Patients and Controls: A Pilot Study." *European Archives of Psychiatry & Clinical Neuroscience* (1992): 72-76.

Krieger, Dolores. *Accepting Your Power to Heal.* Sante Fe, NM: Bear and Co. Publishing, 1993.

Laidlaw, T.M. "Hypnosis and Attention Deficits after Closed Head Injury." *International Journal of Clinical & Experimental Hypnosis* (April 1993): 97-111.

Lamarra, J. "Usefulness of the Transcendental Meditation Program in the Treatment of Patients with Coronary Artery Disease." *American Journal of Cardiology* (April 1996): 867-70.

Lambert, Craig. "The Chopra Prescriptions." *Harvard Magazine* (September-October, 1989): 23-28.

Lavarbre, Marcel. *Aromatherapy Workbook.* Healing Arts Press.

LeBaw, W. "The Use of Hypnosis with Hemophilia." *Psychiatric Medicine* (1992): 89 98.

Maclean, C. "Altered Responses of Cortisol, Testosterone to Acute Stress after Four Month's Practice of Transcendental Meditation." *Annals of the New York Academy of Sciences* (November 1994).

McClanahan, T. "Operand Learning (R-S) Principles Applied to Nail-Biting." *Psychological Reports* (October 1995): 507-14.

Miller, J. "Three-Year Follow-Up and Clinical Implications of a Mindfulness Medication." *General Hospital Psychiatry* (May 1995):192-200.

Mitchell, Ellinor. *Plain Talk about Acupuncture.* New York: Whalehall, Inc., 1987.

Monte, Tom. *World Medicine: The EastWest Guide to Healing Your Body.* New York: Putnam Berkley Group, Inc., 1993.

NADA Newsletter Committee. *National Acupuncture Detoxification Association Newsletter (*December 1, 1992): 1-6.

Nder, T. "Trial of Stress Reduction for Hypertension in Older African Americans." *Hypertension* (August 1996): 228-37.

Nespor, K. "Use of Yoga in Psychiatry." *Czech Psychotherapy* (May 1994): 295-97.

Ornish, Dean. *Dr. Dean Ornish's Program for Reversing Heart Disease.* New York: Ballantine Books, 1990.

Panjwani, U. "Effect of Sahaja Yoga Practice on Stress Management in Patients of Epilepsy." *Indian Journal of Physiology and Pharmacology* (April 1995): 111-16.

Raju, P. "Comparison of Effects of Yoga & Physical Exercise in Athletes." *Indian Journal of Medical Research* (August 1994): 81-86.

Rawal, S. "Effect of Yogic Exercises on Thyroid Function." *Journal of Biometerology* (May 1994): 44-47.

Satyanarayana, M. "Effect of Santhi Kriya on Certain Psychophysiological Parameters." *Indian Journal of Physiology and Pharmacology* (April 1992): 88-92.

Saxb, E. "Alpha-Theta Brainwave Neurofeedback Training: An Effective Treatment for Male and Female Alcoholics with Depressive Symptoms." *Journal of Clinical Psychology* (September 1995): 685-93.

Siegel, Bernie. *Love, Medicine & Miracles.* New York: Harper & Row, 1986.

Silver, S. "Treatment of Vietnam War Veterans With PTSD." *Journal of Traumatic Stress* (April 1995): 337-42.

Smith, W. "Meditation as an Adjunct to a Happiness Enhancement Program." *Journal of Clinical Psychology* (March 1995): 269-73.

Spiegel, David, et al. "Effect of Psychosocial Treatment on Survival of Patients with Metastatic Breast Cancer." *The Lancet* (1989): 888-91.

Spiegel, David. "Predictors of Smoking Abstinence Following a Single-Session Restructuring Intervention with Self-Hypnosis." *American Journal of Psychiatry* (July 1993): 1090-97.

Sutorisu, D. "The Transforming Force of Laughter." *Patient Education and Counseling* (September 1995): 367-71.

Tanizaki, Y. "Clinical Effects of Complex Spa Therapy on Patients with Steroid-Dependent Intractable Asthma." *Japanese Journal of Allergology* (March 1993): 423.

Telles, S. "Breathing through a Particular Nostril Can Alter Metabolism and Autonomic Activities." *Indian Journal of Physiology and Pharmacology* (April 1994):133-37.

———. "Plasticity of Motor Control Systems Demonstrated by Yoga Training." *Indian Journal of Physiology and Pharmacology* (April 1994):143-44.

———. "Autonomic Changes during 'OM' Meditation." *Journal of Physiology and Pharmacology* (October 1995): 418-20.

Thomas, R.E. "The Effects of Biofeedback on Carpal Tunnel Syndrome." *Ergonomics* (April 1993): 353-61.

Tisserand, Robert. *The Art of Aromatherapy.* Destiny Books.

Torem, M.S. "The Use of Hypnosis with Eating Disorders." *Psychiatric Medicine* (1992): 105-18.

Tredget, E.E. "Epidemiology of Infections with Pseudomonas Aeruginosa in Burn Patients: The Role of Hydrotherapy." *Clinical Infectious Diseases* (December 1992): 941-49.

RESOURCES

Weil, Andrew. *Health and Healing.* Boston: Houghton Mifflin Company, 1983.

Weiss, Rick. "Bones of Contention." *Health* (July/August, 1993): 44.

Worsley, J.R. *Acupuncture: Is It for You?* New York: Harper & Row, 1973.

Yee, John, Yuan-Chi Lin, and Paul A. Aubuchon. "Acupuncture." *Pain in Infants, Children, and Adolescents.* Baltimore, MD: Williams & Wilkens, 1992.

Organizations

American Chiropractic Association.
1701 Clarendon Boulevard, Arlington, VA 22209

American Institute of Homeopathic Education and Research.
5910 Chabot Crest, Oakland, CA 44018.

American Institute of Homeopathy.
1500 Massachusetts Avenue N.W., Washington, D.C. 20005.

American Society of Clinical Hypnosis.
2200 East Devon Avenue, Suite 291, Des Plaines, IL 60018.

Council on Chiropractic Education.
44011 Westown Parkway, Suite 120, West Des Moines, IA 50265.

Homeopathic Education Services.
2124 Kittredge Street, Berkeley, CA 94904.

International Chiropractors Association.
1901 L Street. N.W., Suite 800, Washington D.C. 20036.

Additional Reading

Altman, Nathaniel. *Everybody's Guide to Chiropractic Health Care.* Los Angeles: Jeremy P. Tarcher, Inc., 1989.

Brassard, C. "Biofeedback and Relaxation for Patients with Hypertension." *Canadian Nurse* (January 1993): 49-52.

Bricklin, Mark. *The Practical Encyclopedia of Natural Healing.* New York: Penguin Books, 1990.

Cerney, J.V. *Acupuncture without Needles.* Parker Publishing Co., Inc. 1983.

Chopra, Deepak. *Creating Health: How to Make Up the Body's Intelligence.* Boston: Houghton Mifflin, 1987.

———. *Ageless Body, Timeless Mind.* New York: Harmony Books, 1993.

Cott, A. "Long-Term Efficacy of Combined Relaxation: Biofeedback Treatments for Chronic Headache." *Pain* (October 1992): 49-56.

Cummings, Stephen, and Dana Ullman. *Everybody's Guide to Homeopathic Medicine.* New York: St. Martin's Press, 1991.

Enomiya-Lassalle, Hugo. *The Practice of Zen Meditation.* San Francisco: HarperCollins, 1992.

Frymann, V.M., and R.E. Carney. "Effect of Osteopathic Medical Management on Neurologic Development in Children." *Mimeo* (June 1992).

Goodhart R., and V. Young. *Modern Nutrition in Health and Disease.* Philadelphia: Lea & Febiger, 1988.

Greenleaf, M. "Hypnotizability and Recovery from Cardiac Surgery." *American Journal of Clinical Hypnosis* (October 1992): 119-28.

Grundy, Scott, and Mary Winston, eds. *Low-Fat, Low-Cholesterol Cookbook.* Dallas: American Heart Association, 1989.

Holmes, P. "Cranial Osteopathy." *INED* (May 29-June 4, 1991): 36-38.

Jin, P. "Efficacy of Tai Chi, Brisk Walking, Meditation and Reading in Reducing

Mental and Emotional Stress." *Journal of Psychosomatic Research* (May 1992): 361-70.

Jordan, Sandra. *Yoga for Pregnancy.* New York: St. Martin's Press, 1987.

Laffan, G. "Alternative Therapies: A New Holistic Science." *Nursing Standard* (January 13-19, 1993): 44-45.

Mills, Simon. *Out of the Earth: The Essential Book of Herbal Medicine.* New York: Penguin Books, 1991.

Murray, Michael, and Joseph Pizzorno. *Encyclopedia of Natural Medicine.* Rocklin, CA: Prima Publishing, 1991.

National Research Council. *Diet, Nutrition and Cancer.* Washington, D.C.: National Academy Press, 1982.

Ng, R.K. "Cardiopulmonary Exercise: A Recently Discovered Secret of Tai Chi." *Hawaii Medical Journal* (August 1992): 216-17.

Ody, Penelope. *The Complete Medicinal Herbal.* London, UK: Dorling Kindersley, 1993.

Porkett, Manfred. *Chinese Medicine.* New York: Henry Holt & Co., 1992.

Reid, Daniel. *Chinese Herbal Medicine.* Boston: Shambhala Publications Inc., 1993.

Sabatino, F. "Mind & Body Medicine: A New Paradigm?" *Hospitals* (February 1993): 66, 68, 70-72.

Saltman, Paul, Jeol Gurin, and Ira Mothner. *The University of California San Diego Nutrition Book.* Boston: Little Brown & Company, 1993.

Santillo, Humbart. *Natural Healing with Herbs.* Prescott, AZ: Hohm Press, 1991.

Stein, Diane. *The Natural Remedy Book for Women.* Freedom, CA: The Crossing Press, 1992.

Vishnu-devanda, Swami. *The Complete Illustrated Book of Yoga.* New York: Harmony Books, 1988.

Weil, Andrew. *Natural Health, Natural Medicine.* Boston: Houghton Mifflin, 1990.

RESOURCES

Chapter 2

DIET AND NUTRITION

"There is only one good, knowledge," Socrates once said, "and one evil, ignorance." His observation is certainly true about nutrition because the nutrients we consume—or do not consume—each day help determine our health, our risk of developing chronic diseases, and even our life span.

While these claims may seem extreme, they are, in fact, the conclusions of the largest research effort ever conducted on the ways nutrition directly affects health. For four years, U.S. nutrition experts in the federal government, aided by hundreds of colleagues in universities, professional schools, industries, communities, and state and local government agencies, examined the results of more than 2,500 scientific studies in order to determine the links between diet and disease. Their conclusions were released in 1988 in the first *Surgeon General's Report on Nutrition and Health*

What we eat may affect our risk for several of the leading causes of death for Americans, notably coronary heart disease, stroke, atherosclerosis, diabetes, and some types of cancer. These disorders together now account for more than two-thirds of all deaths in the United States.

"The *Report's* main conclusion is that overconsumption of certain dietary components is now a major concern for Americans. While many food factors are involved, chief among them is the disproportionate consumption of foods high in fats, often at the expense of foods high in complex carbohydrates and fiber that may be more conducive to health."

This chapter details the key recommendations contained in the *Surgeon General's Report* and summarizes dietary guidelines

Recommendations of the *Surgeon General's Report*

Issues for Most People:

- **Fats and cholesterol:** Reduce consumption of fat (especially saturated fat) and cholesterol. Choose foods relatively low in these substances, such as vegetables, fruits, whole-grain foods, fish, poultry, lean meats, and low-fat dairy products. Use food preparation methods that add little or no fat.

- **Energy and weight control:** Achieve and maintain a desirable body weight. To do so, choose a dietary pattern in which energy (caloric) intake is consistent with energy expenditure. To reduce energy intake, limit consumption of foods relatively high in calories, fats and sugars, and minimize alcohol consumption. Increase energy expenditure through regular and sustained physical activity.

- **Complex carbohydrates and fiber:** Increase consumption of whole-grain foods and cereal products, vegetables (including dried beans and peas), and fruits.

- **Sodium:** Reduce intake of sodium by choosing foods relatively low in sodium and limiting the amount of salt added in food preparation and at the table.

- **Alcohol:** To reduce the risk for chronic disease, take alcohol only in moderation (no more than two drinks a day), if at all. Avoid drinking any alcohol before or while driving, operating machinery, taking medications, or engaging in any other activity requiring judgment. Avoid drinking alcohol while pregnant.

Other Issues for Some People:

- **Fluoride:** Community water systems should contain fluoride at optimal levels for prevention of tooth decay. If such water is not available, use other appropriate sources of fluoride.

- **Sugars:** Those who are particularly vulnerable to dental caries (cavities), especially children, should limit their consumption and frequency of use of food high in sugars.

- **Calcium:** Adolescent girls and adult women should increase consumption of foods high in calcium, including low-fat dairy products.

- **Iron:** Children, adolescents, and women of childbearing age should be sure to consume foods that are good sources of iron, such as lean meats, fish, certain beans, and iron-enriched cereals and whole-grain products.

subsequently issued by four respected U.S. agencies. It also explains how to administer a personal nutritional assessment in order to monitor intelligently a healthy diet as well as daily food and nutrient intake. The central component of this assessment is a food diary that encourages taking an active role in achieving dietary goals.

Everyone knows that the human body is a complex organism that needs certain essential chemical constituents to stay alive. The body cannot produce most of these chemicals itself, however, and must get them from the environment. For example, 60% of the human body is composed of water. Thus it needs a continual supply of fresh water to continue functioning. Otherwise it becomes dehydrated and eventually dies.

Water, however, cannot supply all the chemicals the body needs to grow and rejuvenate itself. The other essential chemicals must be provided by nutrients contained in foods. It is this combination and amounts of foods eaten that constitutes nutrition.

Nutrition is the most important factor in human life and health. In less developed parts of the world too many people do not get enough food or water, and become ill or die as a result. Shortages of water due to droughts cause many deaths annually as do scarcities of food due to famines, poverty, and other adverse circumstances.

The absence of food or water deprives the body of one or several essential nutrients. The absence of a particular essential nutrient in the body is called a nutritional deficiency, while diseases that are caused by a specific nutrient deficiency are called nutritional deficiency diseases. If the body contains too little iron, for example, it is said to have an iron deficiency, and one result is that the body will not produce enough red blood cells. Without adequate red blood cells, a person becomes weak and lacks energy, resulting in an iron deficiency disease called anemia.

Nutritional deficiencies are common in less developed parts of the world, where finding enough essential foods is a daily struggle. In developed countries such as the United States, on the other hand, most people can easily supply themselves with all of the essential foods they need to live long, healthy lives. In the United States, this is accomplished at a grocery or health food store. The challenge lies in deciding which foods to eat and in what amounts.

Because of the complexities of the human body as a biochemical organism, scientists still do not know all of the nutritional chemical factors that contribute to optimal health. For one thing, every person's body is different—it is composed of a chemical structure of atoms and molecules. Even identical twins do not have the same exact proportion of atoms and molecules in their bodies. In addition, every person's body continually changes as chemical constituents are utilized and replaced.

Nevertheless, scientists have learned that although each body does vary to some degree, everyone needs five basic types of chemical substances in addition to water: proteins, carbohydrates, lipids (fats), vitamins, and minerals. How much of these substances people require depends on their age, sex, heredity (their unique genetic structure), amount of exercise, and the amount of toxins (poisons) that exist in the body. Proteins, most carbohydrates, and fats contained in foods are too large to be absorbed directly into the body. They must first be metabolized (broken down) into smaller chemical constituents before they can be utilized. Vitamins and minerals (see Chapters 3 and 4) do not need to be broken down and can be directly absorbed.

When a person eats a piece of meat, for example, it must first be ground down by the teeth and mixed with saliva into smaller particles which can then enter the gastrointestinal tract. These particles eventually reach the stomach and intestines where they are further broken down into proteins and fat and absorbed directly into the blood. The elements of the meat which are not absorbed into the blood are later eliminated through the colon.

Each person's digestive system breaks down proteins, carbohydrates, and fats at slightly different rates. Some people eat faster than others and also eat differing amounts of these substances. Also, everyone's body metabolizes foods at a different rate (their metabolic rate). What people consume and the speed and efficiency by which their bodies convert the food they eat into needed chemicals (proteins, carbohydrates, fats, vitamins, and minerals) largely determines their energy levels and the overall state of their health.

Proteins

All humans require proteins to survive because they regulate virtually every bodily function. Approximately 20% of the human body consists of proteins, including the skeleton, muscle fiber, hair, skin, and nails.

Once a protein-containing food such as meat is eaten, the protein is broken down in the stomach into different amino acids. The human body needs 20 different amino acids to function, although it can only actually manufacture 12 of these itself. The eight most important amino acids that cannot be manufactured internally must be obtained from animal and plant protein foods. These eight essential amino acids–called so because the body requires them for optimal cell functioning–are phenylalanine, tryptophan, valine, threonine, lysine, isoleucine, leucine, and methionone. If they are not present, some normal body processes will be impaired. Consuming the right amount of food each day is extremely important in order to supply the proper amount of the eight essential amino acids.

The difficulty for many people lies in knowing exactly how much protein their bodies need each day and which foods contain the right amounts of the required amino acids. Nutritionists agree that adults need approximately 50-60 grams daily, which is fulfilled easily by a normal American's diet of meat, fish, eggs, and dairy products. Although both meat and plant foods contain proteins, meat is a better source because it contains all eight essential amino acids. Most vegetables are lacking in at least one essential amino acid and consequently vegetarians usually need to consume both grains and legumes to obtain their amino acid requirements.

If people consume too little protein, they will develop symptoms of a protein deficiency. Children who do not eat enough protein, for example, will have retarded skeletal and muscle growth. Pregnant women who do not eat enough protein will suffer from poor weight gain and fatigue. Adults who lack protein often have weak immune systems, which make them susceptible to infections and diseases. This is because proteins form a critical part of the antibodies which protect the body from viruses and bacteria.

Obtaining adequate amounts of high-quality protein is not a problem for most people in developed countries. In fact, most Americans consume twice the amount of protein they actually need, two-thirds of which comes from meat. Overconsuming protein is potentially dangerous because an excess of protein eaten at any one time cannot be fully absorbed by the body. This excess protein then enters the blood stream as partially digested protein (peptides), which are now thought to cause inflammation of some organs, tissues, and joints.

Scientists have begun to link the consumption of too much meat protein to other health problems such as cancer and heart attacks. Americans who eat large amounts of meat tend to have higher rates of cancer of the colon, for example, although scientists are not yet sure precisely why. Most meat sold commercially, according to Gordon Edlin and Eric Golanty, also contains nonfood chemicals such as pesticide residues and hormone growth promoters, all of which may be co-contributors to cancer. Overconsumption of animal fat, especially the fat in red meat, also appears to increase men's risk of developing prostate cancer. Scientists at Harvard University and the Mayo Clinic compared the health records and eating habits of more than 47,000 American men by dividing them into two groups: those who ate large amounts of red meat and those who did not. The men whose diets included large quantities of red meat were more than 2 1/2 times as likely to develop cancer as those who ate little red meat. And according to an article in the *Journal of the American Medical Association*

(JAMA), reviewed in the October 6, 1993 issue of the *San Francisco Chronicle,* eating excessive amounts of protein-rich meat (which is also high in fats and cholesterol) can lead to heart disease.

Carbohydrates

Carbohydrates are the principal source of the body's energy and are also used in the synthesis of some cell components such as DNA. The two principal types of carbohydrates are simple sugars (found predominantly in fruit) and complex carbohydrates (found in grains, fruits, and vegetables). Of the simplest sugars, glucose is the most common. Glucose is a carbohydrate freely soluble in blood and cell fluids, and supplies energy to all the body's tissues. Although only small amounts of glucose are ingested, most foodstuffs (with the exception of fatty acids) must be converted to glucose before being utilized for energy in the body. Other simple sugars include fructose (one of the sweetest sugars) found in fruits and honey, sucrose (or common table sugar) harvested from sugar cane and sugar beets, and lactose, which is found almost exclusively in dairy products.

So long as it is consumed in the proper amounts, sugar is not harmful. Unfortunately, since many food manufacturers use sugars to flavor their products, Americans tend to consume an excess of sugar. It is estimated that the average American now consumes almost a third of a pound of refined sugar each day in synthetic foods. Some scientists, according to Peter Jarret, think that overconsumption of sugar may be related to several degenerative diseases and may cause a person's body to age more rapidly.

Complex carbohydrates are present in such foods as grains (wheat, rice, corn, oats, and barley), legumes (peas and beans), plant roots, leaves and stems (most vegetables), and some animal tissues. They consist of two

---

Benefits of Fiber

- Helps prevent constipation.

- Prevents diverticulosis by relieving stress on the colon wall.

- Increases enzyme secretion and activity.

- Lowers serum lipid levels (i.e., cholesterol and tryglycerides) by preventing their manufacture in the liver.

- Maintains healthy bacterial flora in the colon.

- Decreases incidence of most degenerative diseases, including diabetes, irritable bowel syndrome, ulcerative colitis, appendicitis, and cancer.

---

major classes: starch, which is digestible and utilized to supply molecules for energy production and cellular structure; and fiber, which is not digestible but nevertheless important for removing wastes from the body. Starch is present in granules within seeds, pods, or roots of plants. The animal form of starch, glycogen, is found in muscle and liver. Most of the starch in an average person's diet comes from foods made from flour, such as bread, noodles, and pastries.

Fiber

Fiber foods provide the other major form of complex carbohydrates in the human diet–cellulose–the primary constituent of all plant material. Cellulose is composed of glucose molecules which humans cannot digest. However, though cellulose cannot be digested, its importance–along with bran and other fibers–lies in aiding digestion and preventing several disorders of the gastrointesti-

FIBER

nal tract. Fiber also adds bulk to the feces, thereby preventing constipation and related disorders such as hemorrhoids. It is now thought that fiber lowers the risk of appendicitis, and cancer of the colon and rectum, by decreasing the time it takes for waste material and bacteria to pass through the gastrointestinal tract. Nutritionists recommend that people consume 20-30 grams of fiber daily. The best sources of fiber include vegetables, whole grains, fruit, legumes, bread, uncooked oats, pumpkin seeds, and psyllium seeds.

Lipids (Fats)

Lipids are chemical substances that are relatively insoluble in water. The most familiar is triglyceride (body fat). Other lipids, including cholesterol and lecithin, are essential components of cell membranes. Vitamins A, D, E, and K are also lipids, as are substances in the liver bile (bile acids) which help digest fats.

The lipids that most people eat in ordinary foods come in three principal forms: cholesterol, saturated fats (found primarily in animal products), and unsaturated fats—either polyunsaturated fats (as in sunflower and safflower oil) or monounsaturated fats (as in olive and canola oil). Cholesterol levels depend largely on the type of fats an individual consumes. In general, saturated fats raise cholesterol levels in the blood, while unsaturated fats appear to reduce cholesterol, including "bad" (LDL) cholesterol, without adverse side effects.

Most Americans are now familiar with the danger of consuming too much fat, especially saturated fats, which are believed to contribute to heart disease. Saturated fats are found in animal foods such as beef, pork, lamb, veal, egg yolks, whole milk, cream, cheese, ice cream, butter and lard, chocolate, coconuts, and oils often used in processed foods, like coconut, palm, and palm-kernel. Many studies have shown a relationship between dietary fat consumption and cancer of the breast, colon, and prostate gland—one reason experts recommend eating no more than 10% of calories in the diet as saturated fat.

Cholesterol

Though many physicians warn their patients about consuming too much cholesterol, everyone needs a certain amount of the right forms. Cholesterol helps produce hormones, contributes to development of the brain, and aids the functioning of the nervous system. It is not necessary to consume high levels of cholesterol in foods because the liver manufactures all that the body needs.

Because cholesterol is insoluble in water and because it cannot mix with the blood, it is carried through the bloodstream in protein "packets" called lipoproteins. The two most common kinds of lipoproteins are low-density lipoproteins (LDL) and high-density lipoproteins (HDL). Blood cholesterol consists largely of LDL and HDL, although there are several other types of blood fats, including very low-density lipoproteins (VLDL), intermediate-density lipoproteins (IDL), and triglycerides.

Most of the cholesterol typically circulating in the bloodstream is carried by LDL. LDL is often called "bad" cholesterol because extra LDL cholesterol that is not used by the body tends to collect on the lining of the blood vessels and can cause arteriosclerosis (build up of fatty deposits, or plaque, in the arteries). Arteriosclerosis can reduce the supply of blood carrying oxygen and other vital nutrients to the heart and other organs and cause several heart disorders. Blood clots (thrombosis) that form around cholesterol deposits can also clog the arteries supplying the brain with oxygen and cause brain damage as well as strokes.

HDL cholesterol usually is called "good" cholesterol because it can be eliminated by the body more easily. HDL cholesterol also appears to help prevent the formation of fatty plaques in the arteries, and thus may help protect against heart disease.

Cholesterol is highly concentrated in egg yolks and organ meats such as liver, and is also found in milk, dairy products, poultry, and seafood. Only animal products contain cholesterol, although prepared foods, including crackers or bakery goods, also contain high-cholesterol ingredients such as lard, eggs, or butter.

Many people find it difficult to determine whether they eat foods which contain too much cholesterol, especially "bad" cholesterol. Part of the problem is that many foods which are high in cholesterol are also high in saturated fat—meat, butter, cheese, whole milk, cream, and ice cream, for example. It is not clear whether cholesterol alone, especially "bad" cholesterol, is harmful, but it is clear that a diet high in LDL and saturated fats should be avoided.

Blood tests are the only means of determining whether a person's cholesterol is too high. If cholesterol numbers are borderline, a cholesterol-lowering diet along with a yearly check-up is likely to be prescribed. The doctor may also recommend other lifestyle changes like exercising, quitting smoking, and limiting alcohol and coffee consumption. If the LDL ratio is unusually high, some physicians may prescribe cholesterol-lowering drugs to bring blood lipids down to normal levels.

A Few Health Facts

- Frequency of heart attacks in the U.S.: every 25 seconds.
- Frequency of fatal heart attacks in the U.S.: every 45 seconds.
- Average American male's risk of death from heart attack: 50%.
- Average vegetarian American male's risk of death from heart attack: 4%.
- Reduction of heart attack risk by eliminating consumption of meat, dairy products, and eggs: 90%.
- Rise in blood cholesterol from consuming one egg per day: 12%.
- Rise in heart attack risk from a 12% rise in blood cholesterol: 24%.

Calories

In addition to supplying the basic chemical materials for the body, foods also supply a continuous source of energy needed for human life. The amount of energy provided by food is measured in calories. As already discussed, the human body derives its energy from the breakdown of carbohydrates and fats. Carbohydrates and proteins supply approximately four calories per gram, while fats supply approximately nine calories per gram.

Recommended Dietary Allowances (RDA)

In order to help people determine the proper amounts of these nutrients for optimum health, the Food and Nutrition Board (which operates under the National Academy of Sciences) has established the daily

Guidelines for Nutrition

1. **General Recommendations:** Eat a diet rich in whole "natural" and unprocessed foods such as fruits, vegetables, grains, beans, seeds, and nuts, as these foods contain not only valuable nutrients but also dietary fiber.

2. **Proteins:** Eat moderate quantities of protein, especially animal protein. Fish and many shellfish are excellent sources of low-fat protein.

3. **Fats:** Maintain total fat intake at or below 30% of total caloric intake and saturated fats at less than 10%. Eat leaner cuts of meat, trim off excess fat, remove skin from poultry, and consume smaller portions.

4. **Carbohydrates:** Carbohydrates should comprise between 60 and 70% of the total intake of calories. Only 10% of carbohydrates should be refined or concentrated sugars such as honey, fruit juices, dried fruit, sugar, or white flour. Eat foods high in calories from whole-grain cereals and bread rather than foods or drinks containing sugar.

5. **Dairy Products:** Eat dairy products for calcium, but avoid excessive amounts of whole milk, whole-milk cheeses, yogurt, ice cream, and other milk products which are high in saturated fats.

Recommended Dietary Allowances (RDA) for protein, 11 vitamins, and seven minerals. The World Health Organization (WHO) also recommends a set of dietary standards which are very similar to the RDAs.

RDAs are generally set about 30% higher than the average amount the body requires, which, on a statistical basis, usually accommodates most healthy individuals. The RDA is designed for people who are in good health, are not suffering from clinical disease, and are not under an unusual amount of stress. The RDA also lists nutrient requirements for children and for pregnant and lactating women. By eating a balanced diet of natural foods each day, most people are able to acquire the essential nutrients in amounts suggested by the RDA.

Several other U.S. agencies have also suggested general dietary guidelines which people can follow and modify, if necessary. For example, the U.S. Department of Agriculture and U.S. Department of Health and Human Services published dietary guidelines in 1990 which urged Americans to adopt diets which are lower in fat, especially saturated fat, and higher in complex carbohydrates and fiber. They also recommended that Americans consume only moderate amounts of sugar, salt, and alcoholic beverages.

The American Council on Science and Health has also issued a publication entitled *Food and Life: A Nutrition Primer* which defines "a good diet" for all Americans to follow. The Council, for example, strongly recommends that all Americans consume enough calories to maintain their optimal body weight, adequate carbohydrates and fats to fulfill energy requirements, enough fat to absorb fat-soluble vitamins, essential fatty acids, and sufficient vitamins and minerals to facilitate enzyme processes.

Previously, the National Academy of Sciences (NAS) had issued a report which recommended virtually the same diet. The NAS also recommends that people maintain total fat intake at or below 30% of total caloric intake and saturated fatty acid at less than 10%. In addition, the NAS urges Americans to consume only moderate amounts of meat protein, and obtain more calories from carbohydrates, especially whole-grain cereals and breads.

Nutritional Needs of the Elderly

Illness and multiple medications, along with the aging process itself, necessitate that the elderly be particularly conscientious about daily nutrition, especially caloric intake. In some cases, elderly people may need to increase the calories in their diet in order to maintain their body cell mass. Also, according to an article by M.F. Martin in the April 1992 issue of the *American Journal of Clinical Nutrition*, if elderly people inadvertently decrease their caloric intake, it takes longer for them to subsequently restore body cell mass.

Elderly people should also monitor their energy expenditure regularly. One U.S. study reviewed by S. B. Roberts in the December 1992 issue of the *International Journal of Obesity* compared the energy requirements (listed in the RDAs) for healthy elderly men and the total energy they used in their daily activities. The study concluded that the RDAs for the elderly significantly underestimate their particular energy requirements. The study also found that the low levels of nutrients suggested by the RDAs may favor the build-up of unnecessarily high levels of body fat mass. Therefore, elderly people may find they need to consume more than the RDAs recommended for their age group, and should be sure to monitor both their body cell mass and body fat mass.

Nutritional Needs of Children

Small children, particularly infants, require more of certain specific nutrients, including vitamins and minerals, than adults. The RDAs for vitamins and minerals for children are listed in Chapters 3 and 4. All children need more protein for energy, as well as some carbohydrates and fats, to ensure satisfactory growth and development. It is well known that many American children, however, consume too much sugar, and along with American adults, too much red meat.

Many parents attempt to follow sound nutritional guidelines for their children at home, but worry—with good reason—about the lunches and snacks their children eat at school. A 15-year study of the American school lunch program showed that school lunches contribute less than one-third of total daily nutrient requirements, and that intakes of dietary components related to cardiovascular disease risk were excessive. Sixty to 80% of children exceed RDA amounts of daily total fat, saturated fat, cholesterol, and sodium. The study reported by R. P. Farris in the May 1992 issue of the *Journal of School Health* concluded that schools could reduce the risk of cardiovascular disease by providing students with healthier foods and educational programs which promote healthier lifestyles.

The "Good Diet"

Following publication of the *Surgeon General's Report on Nutrition and Health,* several U.S. agencies–the American Council on Science and Health, the National Academy of Sciences (NAS), the U.S. Department of Agriculture, and the U.S. Department of Health and Human Services–issued their own dietary guidelines, as summarized below.

Professionally Administered Nutritional Assessments. There are several ways people can monitor their nutritonal intake to ensure that their diets meet national guidelines. Physicians, nutritionists, and dietitians use several techniques, including physical examinations, to assess a person's nutritional status. Compiling a medical and diet history helps detect nutritional imbalances, deficiencies, usual eating habits

and food preferences, and intake of medications, nutritional supplements, and alcohol. Biochemical or clinical laboratory tests (including blood and urine samples) can also directly measure nutrients and detect deficiencies, while other laboratory tests, such as the Schilling test of vitamin B_{12}, detect how well a person absorbs certain essential nutrients. Immune function tests measure the type and amount of white blood cells present, which provides an indicator of both the body's nutritional status and resistance to disease.

Self-Administered Nutritional Assessments. In addition to consulting with a physician, people can also conduct a self-administered nutritional assessment to monitor their current diet and their daily food and nutrient intake intelligently. One of the most effective is a food diary, which helps determine factors associated with food consumption such as time of day, place eaten, level of hunger, and mood. Among other advantages, this alternative (along with a food frequency checklist) encourages the diary keeper to assume an active role in achieving dietary goals, and helps people be more conscious of the lifestyle and home factors that affect their food choices and consumption patterns.

How to Keep a Food Diary

A food diary records everything eaten for at least three days–the minimum period in which to gather reliable information about nutritional intake and food consumption patterns. Completing the diary for seven days is better, while a 30-day period is even more helpful. Nutritionists recommend that the diary be kept throughout the day so that the required information can be recorded immediately after eating.

A sample one-day food diary appears below. It can be xeroxed and the additional pages stapled or bound together to make a diary for longer periods of time.

To make entries: 1) Record the date and type and amount of each food you consume in a 24-hour period. 2) Using a calorie-counting guide, nutritional handbook, or computer diet software program, calculate the number of calories and nutrient composition for each food eaten. 3) Record the time and place of consumption, and whether the food was a meal or a snack. 4) Note how hungry you were, and what, if any, mood accompanied the food.

Foods and Amounts. In the "Food Consumed" column, record the type of *every* food and beverage you consume during the course of a day and its product name. For example, if you ate cereal, toast, and coffee for breakfast, record in column 1:

> *Food*
> Grapenuts cereal
> Whole wheat toast
> Coffee with cream

In the "Amount" column, enter the amount of each food or beverage you consumed. Thus, in the second column you would enter:

Food	*Amount*
Grapenuts cereal	1 serving
Whole wheat toast	2 slices
Coffee with cream	1 cup w/ 2 tablespoons cream

Calories. While not all of the diets "count" calories, it's a good idea–particularly at the beginning of any diet–to know how many calories you consume each day. By way of comparison, carbohydrates and proteins supply approximately four calories per gram, while fats supply approximately nine calories per gram.

In May 1994, the Food and Drug Administration (FDA) began requiring companies that produce packaged foods to provide substantial information about fat content, calories, and other nutritional values in large type on a "Nutrition Facts" panel on their labels, and to show how items fit into a daily diet of 2,000 calories. The new laws, which took 10 years to develop, have now forced companies to substantiate claims for their products such as "low fat" or "high fiber." This newly required information will help dieters filling out a food diary calculate the amounts of various nutrients–listed as grams or milligrams, as well as a percentage of recommended daily intake–they are consuming.

Protein. Identifying the protein content of foods is important in order to determine whether you are receiving adequate daily amounts of essential amino acids. As noted, national dietary guidelines now recommend that people consume moderate quantities of protein, especially animal protein, and suggest that fish is an excellent source of protein and is low in saturated fat.

Fats and Saturated Fats. Recording total daily fat and saturated fat intake is especially important for people on weight-loss diets. Normally, when people consume excessive amounts of fat (more than 30% of daily calories), they experience weight gain. However, there are exceptions, and by paying close attention to this column in the food diary, you can determine how well your body metabolizes fat. Some dieters may find that even if they restrict fats to 20% of calories, they still gain weight.

Cholesterol. According to the *Surgeon General's Report*, a 1% reduction in total blood cholesterol is accompanied by a 1.5% reduction in heart disease risk. National dietary guidelines currently recommend that Americans consume no more than 300 milligrams of cholesterol per day. People who suspect that they may be at risk of heart disease should further restrict their cholesterol intake to less than 200 milligrams daily.

Carbohydrates. In this column, enter your daily intake of the two principal types of carbohydrates: complex carbohydrates and simple sugars (found predominantly in fruit). National dietary guidelines currently recommend that 60-70% of total daily caloric intake should consist of complex carbohydrates.

Fiber. Monitoring intake of fiber foods is important because they provide cellulose which helps in digesting food and preventing several disorders of the gastrointestinal tract. As a result, nutritionists recommend that people consume 20-30 grams of fiber daily.

Sugar. Sugar is not considered to be harmful when consumed in the proper amounts. However, sugar flavors many manufactured food products, and Americans tend to consume it to excess. The average American, for example, is estimated to take in almost a third of a pound of refined sugar each day in synthetic foods. Refined sugar–which are rich in calories and do not provide essential nutrients–also deplete other essential nutrients in the bloodstream and prevent nonsugar foods from being easily metabolized.

Alcohol. It's very important to monitor daily intake of alcohol because heavy drinkers tend to overconsume other sugar-rich foods, and underconsume nutrient-dense, nonsugar foods. Since alcohol contains the energy equivalent of seven calories per gram, a few beers or mixed drinks several evenings a week can also substantially increase weight and body fat. In addition, alcohol irritates and damages the digestive tract, interferes with the body's use of many nutrients, and depletes tissue stores of protein, B vitamins, and essential minerals.

Meal or Snack. Recording the number of meals and snacks consumed each day will help identify food patterns that may be counterproductive. For example, eating one large meal a day, which supplies the majority of caloric intake, increases the difficulty of losing weight. Instead nutritionists recommend eating smaller amounts of food more frequently. Many of the diets reviewed in this book stress the importance of eating three balanced meals–and consuming small, nutritious snacks throughout the day. This pattern tends to stabilize blood sugar and blood fat levels. Eating a balanced breakfast, in particular, is key to weight loss, as studies show that dieters who eat breakfast, compared to those who do not, have more healthful dietary patterns overall.

Hunger Level. Everyone becomes hungry during the day when the body signals that it needs nutrients to provide energy for its many physiological processes. Keep in mind that hunger is different than appetite. Appetite is defined as the brain's psychological perception that it needs food (often as a response to external cues), while hunger is the body's physiological demand for sustenance. Healthy people respond only to hunger.

To record your hunger level in the food diary, use a scale of 0 to10–0 being empty, 5 being comfortable, and 10 being completely full. Note at what level of hunger you were when you ate a particular food. You may find that your brain sometimes tricks your appetite to convince you that you need food when, in fact, you may already be satiated.

Many overweight individuals find that their eating behavior is triggered by external stimuli that are unrelated to feelings of hunger or satiety. For example, some people eat at predetermined times each day, regardless of whether or not they are hungry. Mealtimes are often an important form of socializing, and family gatherings or taking a break from work can trigger appetite.

In addition, some people are "recreational" eaters, meaning that their principal forms of recreation–playing cards, for exam-ple–include eating food. Again, these people do not necessarily eat because they are hungry, but because it is part of the social ritual surrounding that form of recreation.

Time of Day. Because foods are metabolized differently depending on when they are ingested, it is also essential to record the time of day you consume each food and beverage. Foods consumed at breakfast, for example, are more quickly metabolized–i.e., the calories are burned–because most people perform some physical activity (even if it is just going to work) immediately following breakfast. A large meal eaten just before going to bed, on the other hand, is not metabolized as quickly because sleeping involves very little physical exertion.

Place. Locale can also influence when and how much people eat. Studies have shown, for example, that certain rooms in a house are often subconsciously linked with eating. People who spend a lot of time in the kitchen tend to eat more–and often overeat. Many people eat more when they are close to a refrigerator, while others are more susceptible to overeating when they shop for food. Dining at the home of friends, family gatherings, parties, and at restaurants also encourages overeating–especially foods rich in fats and sugars, including alcohol.

Finally, watching television tends to encourage people to eat, even after they have consumed a large meal and presumably are no longer hungry. Michael Murray and Joseph Pizzorno state in the *Encyclopedia of Natural Medicine* that next to prior obesity, television watching is the strongest predictor of subsequent obesity. In fact, the more TV watched, the greater the degree of obesity.

Mood. Many people with weight problems are unaware of the emotional cues that can trigger overeating. Psychologists have observed, for example, that stress, anxiety, and feeling lonely, bored, or angry can prompt food cravings. Unfortunately, giving in to these cravings ultimately tends to make a person feel worse, because it can lead to weight gain and guilt, and may even contribute to wavering self-esteem.

Some people derive a kind of emotional comfort from ingesting food. This may be because as early as when they were nursing infants, most people learned to associate eating with receiving love, affection, and comfort. This strong association may persist throughout life, reinforced by various cultural events revolving around food, such as socializing and celebrations. As a result, overindulgence can become a generalized behavioral pattern for dealing with psychological distress.

In the "Mood" column, write down the mood that best summarizes your emotional status each time you consumed food or beverages.

Overweight Americans

Holistically healthy people attempt to eat all the essential foods they need in the proper proportions. Unfortunately, 60% of Americans now consume excessive amounts of the wrong foods. According to a series of eight annual surveys conducted by Louis Harris and Associates in 1993 for *Prevention Magazine*, 64 million Americans are now overweight. Life insurance company tables taking into account age, sex, and body build were used to determine whether or not a person was overweight. Interestingly enough, almost a third of those who were overweight did not know it, or at least did not admit it. Instead, they told interviewers that they were "at about the right weight." Overweight men were nearly twice as likely as women to feel that their weight was acceptable. The survey also found that fewer Americans are trying to avoid eating too much sugar and sweets than in 1983. And fewer are making an attempt to

Elements to Include in a 24-Hour Food Diary

1. Food consumed
2. Amount (serving)
3. Protein
4. Total fat
5. Saturated fat
6. Cholesterol
7. Carbohydrate
8. Fiber
9. Sugar
10. Alcohol
11. Meal or snack
12. Hunger
13. Time
14. Place
15. Mood
16. Self-esteem

consume enough vitamins and minerals or eat fish twice a week.

Weight-Loss Programs. What should overweight people do to regain holistic health? Basically, they need to adopt a weight-loss program consistent with the major tenets of holistic medicine–proper diet, adequate exercise, and a positive mental attitude. The basic equation for losing weight is the same whatever diet program is followed. In order for an individual to lose weight, energy intake must be less than energy expenditure. This can be accomplished by decreasing caloric intake (dieting), increasing the rate at which calories are burned (exercising), or a combination of the two.

As Murray and Pizzorno explain in the *Encyclopedia of Natural Medicine*, people must take in 3,500 fewer calories than they expend in order to lose one pound of body weight. Therefore, to lose one pound each week, a negative caloric balance of 500 calories a day is required. This could be accomplished through exercise alone by jogging for 45 minutes, playing tennis for an hour, or taking a brisk walk for one hour and 15 minutes, assuming that caloric intake remained the same.

The most sensible approach to weight loss is to decrease calorie intake and increase energy expenditure. Most individuals will begin to lose weight if they keep their caloric intake below 3,000 calories per day and do aerobic exercise for 15-20 minutes 3-4 times per week. Starvation and crash diets usually result in rapid weight loss (largely muscle and water), but cause rebound weight gain. The most successful approach to weight loss, according to Murray and Pizzorno, is gradual weight reduction (0.5-1 pound per week) through adopting dietary and lifestyle modifications.

Obesity

An estimated one to two million Americans are morbidly obese, or so overweight that their bodies cannot function normally, and because of many complications, may be putting themselves at a high risk for death. An additional 1.24 million people fall into the category of medically significant obesity. Obesity is a potentially fatal condition because it can lead to diabetes, heart disease, and cancer. In men, for example, obesity has been directly linked to cancer of the colon, prostate, and rectum. Alan Reesand Charlene Willey (*Personal Health Reporter*) report that obesity in women is directly associated with cancer of the breast, gall bladder, ovaries, and

uterus. Obese people also have higher incidences of arthritis, gallstones, and gout.

There is no single reason why obese people obsessively overeat. Genetic, psychological, and dietary factors all contribute to obesity. Data suggests that if an obese person has one parent with a weight problem, the chance of developing morbid obesity is 60%. If both parents have a weight problem, the probability rises to 90%, according to Armour Forse, Peter N. Benotti, and George Blackburn in an article in the September-October 1989 *Nutrition Today*.

In addition, obesity is influenced by a person's metabolism and the interactions between appetite, metabolic rate, adipose tissue, and brain neurochemicals. Diet, of course, always contributes to obesity–even someone with a poor metabolism would not become obese without overeating. Frequenty, the problem is complicated by a lack of cardiopulmonary exercise.

Treatments for Obesity

How do health practitioners attempt to treat obesity? There are several basic approaches for helping obese people lose weight without regaining it. One approach is to psychologically condition an obese patient to avoid overeating. Another approach is to use gastric bypass surgery to shrink the stomach, thereby reducing its storage capacity. This typically involves applying stainless steel staples across the top of the stomach which shortens the stomach and results in early satiety. Although somewhat extreme, gastric bypass surgery generally works, and obese patients normally achieve a 20 pound weight loss, according to Forse, Benotti, and Blackburn.

Conventional physicians also use toxic drugs such as dexfenfluramine (dF) to decrease hunger in obese patients. Further experiments with dF are needed, however, to test for toxicity, drug tolerance morbidity, and mortality from obesity. Very Low Calorie Diets (VLCD) in conjunction with prolonged use of dF have also been shown to be effective, according to Michelle Homes in the January 1990 *American Family Physician*.

Alternative Treatments for Obesity

It is extremely difficult to help obese patients lose a large amount of excess weight. Rather than using staples to shrink the stomach, or dF-like drugs which may be toxic, a holistic weight-loss program may be the answer. Some holistic diet programs have been successful in a limited number of clinical trials. But they must be total mind/body programs incorporating nutritional counseling, VLCDs, exercise, and group therapy.

VLCDs clearly produce rapid weight loss in the first several weeks of a treatment program. However, obese patients tend to regain the same amount of weight–or even more–once the VLCD is discontinued unless their lifestyle is altered through behavior modification. Holistic physicians emphasize educating patients to monitor their own health and eating habits, and help them dramatically alter the amount and pattern of what they eat. The patients must also exercise to increase their energy expenditure and demonstrate self-awareness and assertiveness. In one clinical trial, only 10% of obese patients who were given two weeks of behavior modification (BMOD) prior to a VLCD regained weight, whereas 33% who were not given the BMOD prior to the VLCD regained weight, reports R. O. Kramath in the *American Journal of Clinical Nutrition*'s July 1992 issue.

Anorexia Nervosa

Individuals with anorexia nervosa are usually people of normal or slightly above normal weight who start on an "innocent" diet and eventually begin suppressing hunger sensations to the point of self-starvation, according to the California Medical Association's July/August 1989 *Health Tips*. They may subsist on as few as 250 calories a day. The causes of anorexia nervosa are primarily psychological, although some people with the disorder may have a genetic predisposition which can be triggered by psychological factors. Psychological factors are suspected because the vast majority of anorexics are Caucasian, North American women between the ages of 13 and 22. Many of these women are starting to menstruate or have just graduated from high school. The widespread pressure on these women to diet and stay thin just as they enter society may contribute to anorexia.

Treatments for Anorexia Nervosa

Treatment for anorexia typically involves reducing patients' fears of a normal body weight by encouraging them to gradually regain their natural body weight. Group support and medication play an important role in subsequently reducing their anxiety about eating. Some nutrient supplements and nasogastric or intravenous feeding also have proven successful. Nutritional supplements alone are usually insufficient, however, because the underlying psychological causes must be treated as well.

The diet for an anorexic prescribed by a physician should reflect nutrient needs and identify energy allowances that take into account the degree of starvation. For these patients, relatively small, gradual increases are usually made in caloric level of the diet during treatment. It is very important, however, that meal plans always consider individual needs.

Bulimia

An increasing number of young Americans, particularly females, overconsume enormous amounts of food in one sitting, and then purge the food by inducing vomiting, or using laxatives or diuretics. This is a chronic eating disorder called bulimia with both short- and long-term complications. Bulimia usually begins in conjunction with a diet and, once the binge-purge cycle begins, victims cannot stop themselves from either eating excessive amounts, vomiting, or abusing laxatives or diuretics. The average meal for a normal nonbulimic person contains approximately 1,000 calories. People with bulimia may eat from 5,000 to as many as 50,000 calories in one extended meal and then purge once the binge is over. Some bulimics may be underweight and a few may be obese,

but most tend to maintain a fairly normal weight. In some bulimic women, the menstrual cycle becomes irregular and sexual desire usually declines.

There are two potentially fatal aspects of bulimia. If people dramatically increase their body weight in a short amount of time, they may develop heart problems and high blood pressure. In addition, vomiting for extended periods of time can cause chloride and potassium deficiencies which often lead to heart arrhythmias and heart damage. Bulimics commonly have very low self-esteem and are often depressed, according to an article by Dixie Farley in the May 1986 *FDA Consumer Reports*.

Treatments for Bulimia

Some bulimic patients have been treated successfully with behavioral modification programs. Patients with severe cases, however, sometimes require intensive treatment, either in a hospital or an inpatient unit. Medication, including antidepressants, may also be useful in certain circumstances, although there is to date no antibulimia drug per se, as reported by D. B. Woodside and P. Garfinkel in *Nutrition Today* (June 1989).

The nontraditional approach to bulimia recognizes that while genetic and physiological factors may contribute to the disorder, any successful elimination of the problem must involve rebuilding the patient's self-esteem. Holistic physicians normally avoid prescribing antidepressant drugs because they have side effects, including dependency, and do not eliminate the underlying psychological causes of bulimia. A controlled pharmacological approach, however, can prove useful, particularly in the early stages. For example, a study conducted at the University of Pittsburgh School of Medicine found that bulimic women eat more when supplies of the brain chemical serotonin are depleted. Small doses of natural or synthetic serotonin might help prevent binge eating, and hopefully further study will lead to a more successful treatment, according to an article by A. James Giannini in the April 1990 *American Family Physician*.

Psychological approaches may also prove effective. For example, bulimic patients often mistakenly think that vomiting helps them lose weight quickly. In fact, however, vomiting does not immediately cause weight loss because calories are retained in the gastrointestinal tract even after vomiting. Bulimic patients in several studies have been shown to eat slower than control groups, and they also take significantly longer to start eating. If bulimic patients are placed in support groups that stress exercise and intervention begins before the bulimic person initiates binge eating, eventually it may be possible to cure their disorder.

According to Maurice Shils in *Modern Nutrition in Health and Disease*, underweight patients with anorexia and bulimia usually do not need to consume above-average quantities of food. The initial use of small quantities meets the psychological needs of the patient, who is fearful of gaining weight rapidly. Eating large quantities and high-caloric snacks can actually be counter-therapeutic. Treatment includes the following phases: obtaining a detailed diet history, determining the calorie content of the initial diet, designing an appropriate diet plan, planning gradual progression in the diet, considering weight gain expectations, and designing a diet plan for weight maintenance.

In general, both anorexics and bulimics must avoid fasting, skipping meals, and eating inadequate amounts at meals, since they often contribute to a recurrence of destructive eating habits. Keeping food records is also extremely helpful and should include a nota-

Weight Gain Diet for Bulimics

1. Determine actual caloric expenditure by measuring oxygen consumption.
2. Have a physician counsel the patient about a diet that provides an appropriate nutrient composition and caloric content.
3. Design a diet to include foods from each of the basic food groups, with portions being increased as caloric increase is made. Foods should provide all vitamins and mineral needs, and supplements should not be necessary.
4. Emphasize a varied diet which reflects the patient's likes and dislikes.
5. Weigh foods to ensure that adequate portions are consumed and to give bulimics greater confidence that overeating will not occur.
6. Create individualized meal plans ensuring that a wide variety of foods are included in three meals and snacks.
7. Make sure the bulk content of meals is not excessive in the initial stages in order to minimize discomfort.
8. Gradually increase weekly intake by 200 calories during the early stages of the diet, following with greater increases when the patient becomes more comfortable eating.

tion of the times of the binges, the kinds of foods eaten, and the occurrence of vomiting and laxative and/or diuretic abuse.

Summary

Eating wholesome natural foods is the most important factor in maintaining optimum holistic health. Everyone needs to consume the proper amounts of the essential nutrients of water, proteins, carbohydrates, fats, vitamins, and minerals in order for the body to function smoothly and maintain its natural balance. Eating less than the minimum daily recommended amounts of foods can cause severe physiological disorders, while over-consuming unnecessary foods can also cause serious medical complications. By applying the nutritional guidelines outlined in this chapter, and keeping a food diary, most people will be able optimize their diet.

Resources

References

American Council on Science and Health. *Food and Life Primer* (July 1990): 34-35.

California Medical Association. *Health Tips* (July/August 1989): L1.

Edlin, Gordon, and Eric Golanty. *Health and Wellness.* Boston, MA: Jones and Barlett Publishers, 1992, p. 69.

Farley, Dixie. "Eating Disorders: When Thinness Becomes an Obsession." *FDA Consumer Reports* (May 1986): 20-21.

Farris, R. P. "Nutrient Contribution for the School Lunch Program." *Journal of School Health* (May 1992): 180-84.

Forse, A. "Morbid Obesity: Weighing the Treatment Options." *Nutrition Today* (September-October 1989): 14-15.

Giannini, A. James. "Anorexia and Bulimia." *American Family Physican* 41, no. 4 (April 1990): 175.

Holmes, Michelle. "Current Therapies for Obesity." *American Family Physician* (January 1990): 317.

Jarret, Peter. "Are We Slowly Dying from Pollution Overload?" *Longevity* (June 1990): 64.

Kamrath,R. O. "Repeated Use of VLCD in a Structured Multidisciplinary Weight Management Program." *American Journal of Clinical Nutrition* (July 1992): 288S-289S.

Martin, M. F. "The Effect of Age on the Caloric Requirement of Malnourished Individuals." *American Journal of Clinical Nutrition* (April 1992): 783-89.

Murray, Michael, and Joseph Pizzorno. *Encyclopedia of Natural Medicine* Rocklin, CA: Prima Publishing, 1991, pp. 45-48.

National Institute of Mental Health, Public Inquiries Branch. *Facts About Anorexia Nervosa.* November 1990.

Public Health Service. *The Surgeon General's Report on Nutrition and Health.* 1988.

"Red Meat Linked to Fatal Prostate Cancer." *San Francisco Chronicle* (October 6, 1993): 5

Rees, Alan, and Charlene Willey. *Personal Health Reporter.* Detroit, MI: Gale Research, 1993, p. 427.

Roberts, S. B. "What Are the Dietary Energy Needs of Elderly Adults?" *International Journal of Obesity* (December 1992): 969-76.

"Serotonin Depletion Affects Bulimic Women." *Associated Press* (June 13, 1993).

Shils, Maurice, James A. Olson, and Moshe Shike. *Modern Nutrition in Health and Disease.* Philadelphia, PA: Lea & Febiger, 1994.

SUMMARY

"2 Out of 3 Americans Are Overweight, Survey Finds." *San Francisco Chronicle* (May 3, 1993): A4.

U.S. Department of Agriculture and U.S. Department of Health and Human Services. "Nutrition and Your Health: Dietary Guidelines for Americans." *Home and Garden Bulletin* (November 1990): 3-4.

Woodside, D. B., and P. Garfinkel. "An Overview of the Eating Disorders Anorexia Nervosa and Bulimia Nervosa." *Nutrition Today* (June 1989): 27-29.

Organizations

American Anorexia/Bulimia Association, Inc.
133 Cedar Lane, Teaneck, NJ 07666.

American Dietetic Association.
208 South LaSalle Street, Suite 1100, Chicago, IL 60604.

American Nutritionists Association.
P.O. Box 34030, Bethesda, MD 20817.

American Society for Clinical Nutrition.
9650 Rockville Pike, Bethesda, MD 20814.

American Society of Bariatric Physicians.
5600 South Quebec, Suite 310B, Englewood, CO 80111.

Center for the Study of Anorexia and Bulimia.
1 West 91 Street, New York, NY 10024.

Food and Nutrition Information Center.
National Agricultural Library, Beltsville, MD 20705.

National Anorexic Aid Society, Inc.
P.O. Box 29461, Columbus, OH 43229.

National Association of Anorexia Nervosa and Associated Disorders.
P.O. Box 7, Highland Park, IL 60035.

Pamphlets

National Research Council, National Academy of Sciences. *Diet and Health: Implications for Reducing Chronic Disease Risk.* 1989.

Recommended Dietary Allowances. 10th edition. 1989.

Additional Reading

Blundell, J.E. "Dietary Fat and the Control of Energy Intake: Evaluating the Effects of Fat on Meal Size and Postmeal Satiety." *American Journal of Clinical Nutrition* (May 1993): 55-57.

Brody, Jane. *The Good Food Book.* New York: Bantam Books, 1990.

Buery, V.J. "Across-the-Day Monitoring of Mood and Energy Intake Before, During and After a Very-Low-Calorie Diet." *American Journal of Clinical Nutrition* (July 1992): 277S-278S

Carper, Jean. *Food–Your Miracle Medicine.* San Francisco: Harper Collins, 1993.

Hamilton, M. *The Duke University Medical Center Book of Diet and Fitness.* New York: Ballantine, 1990.

Hirschman, Jane. *Overcoming Overeating.* Reading, MA: Addison-Wesley, 1988.

Ikeda, Y. "Comparison of Clinical Usefulness of VLCD and Supplemental LCD." *American Journal of Clinical Nutrition* (July 1992): 275S-276S

Leibel, R.L. "Energy Intake Required to Maintain Body Weight Is Not Affected by Wide Variation in Diet Composition." *American Journal of Clinical Nutrition* (February 1992): 350-55.

McDougall, John. *The New McDougall Cookbook.* Boston: Dutton, 1992

Ornish, Dean. *Eat More, Weigh Less.* San Francisco: HarperCollins, 1993.

Pauling, Linus. *How to Live Longer and Feel Better*. New York: W.H. Freeman, 1986.

Phinny, S.D. "Exercise During and After VLDC." *American Journal of Clinical Nutrition* (July 1992): 190S-194S.

Pope, H. *New Hope for Binge Eaters*. New York: Harper/Coliphon, 1985.

Sadur, C.N. "Body Composition and Weight Maintenance with a Very Low Calorie Diet for the Treament of Moderate Obesity."

American Journal of Clinical Nutrition (July 1992): 286S-287S.

Siegel, M. *Surviving an Eating Disorder*. New York: Harper, 1988.

Spalter, A.R. "Thyroid Function in Bulimia Nervosa." *Biological Psychiatry* (March 1993): 408-14.

Urbain, W. *Food Irradiation*. New York: Academic Press, 1986.

RESOURCES

Chapter 3

VITAMINS

In 1976, Linus Pauling, the Nobel Prize-winning chemist, announced that vitamins (especially vitamin C) could help prevent strokes, mental illness, heart disease, cancer, and infection. With "optimal intake," he claimed, people could extend their lives an extra 12-18 years. (Pauling defined "optimal intake" as falling somewhere between 3,200 and 12,000 milligrams a day, or what a person could obtain from consuming 45 to 170 oranges.) Pauling's dramatic claim, although subsequently challenged by many scientists, set off international studies of possible links between vitamins and disease prevention. By the late 1980s, one of every three Americans was taking vitamin C supplements, and today Americans spend $2 billion a year on vitamins, according to David Zimmerman, author of *Zimmerman's Complete Guide to Nonprescription Drugs.* A growing body of evidence gathered from both underdeveloped and fully industrialized countries now strongly reinforces the late Pauling's once-maverick contention that vitamins play a significant role in maintaining good health and in helping to treat infection and disease.

The Role of Vitamins

Vitamins are chemical compounds that must be included in the human diet to ensure growth and health. They are needed only in small amounts to build, maintain, and repair tissues and usually are available in a balanced diet that features a variety of fresh fruits and vegetables.

To obtain sufficient vitamins, most nutritionists recommend that a daily diet include multiple servings of cereal or bread;

Recommended Daily Allowance (RDA) for Vitamin A

	Mcg (micrograms)
Infants (0-1 year)	375
Children (1-10 years)	600
Males (11-24 years)	1,000
Males (25-51+ years)	1,000
Females (11-24 years)	800
Females (25-51+ years)	800
Pregnant Females	800
Breastfeeding Mothers	1,300

dairy products (milk, cheese, ice cream, cottage cheese); meat, fish, or eggs; and vegetables and fruits. Several vitamins are recommended as supplements, either because they are deficient in the diet or because the body does not produce them.

However, vitamins alone will not take the place of a good diet, nor will they provide energy. The human body needs substances found in food such as protein, minerals, carbohydrates, and fats, and vitamins themselves often cannot work without the presence of various foods.

There is substantial controversy as to whether people should take vitamin supplements and whether such supplements can prevent chronic diseases. Individuals should be fully informed of the supplements' potential levels of toxicity because they are medicines and can cause either desirable or undesirable changes in the body's physiology or internal anatomy. Some vitamins, when taken in excessive doses, can cause side effects, adverse interactions with other drugs, and other problems.

This chapter analyzes each of the essential vitamins and describes its chemical composition, its physiological functions, its occurrence in natural foods or supplements, and the current Recommended Daily Allowance (RDA). The RDA for each vitamin represents the best current assessment of safe and adequate intakes and serves as the basis for information that appears on product labels. Each section discusses concerns about deficiency and toxicity and concludes with results of clinical trials of vitamin therapies.

Vitamin A

Vitamin A is a fat-soluble, solid terpene alcohol essential for skeletal growth, testicular and ovarian function, embryonic development, and differentiation of tissues. It is crucial for the normal functioning of the eye. In addition, vitamin A is required for adequate immune system response, builds the body's resistance to respiratory infections, and helps form and maintain healthy skin, hair, and mucous membranes.

Vitamin A is available in several forms. Retinols are a derivative of vitamin A found in foods that come from animals (meat, milk, and eggs), as well as fish liver oils, cheese, and butter. Betacarotene, a pre-vitamin found in leafy green vegetables and yellow fruits, is converted by the body into vitamin A.

Symptoms of vitamin A deficiency include lack of tear secretion, dry or rough skin, weight loss, poor bone growth, weak tooth enamel, night blindness, changes in mucous membranes, susceptibility to respiratory infections, and diarrhea. Many months of a vitamin A deficient diet are required before any adverse symptoms develop, however, and most healthy individuals have a two-year supply of vitamin A stored in the liver.

Vitamin A deficiency can cause several major eye diseases and is a major health problem in many developing countries. One of these diseases, xerophthalmia, characterized by conjunctival dryness with hardening of the tissue, is contracted by approximately 500,000 people each year in India. Half of these reported cases lead to blindness, and only 30% of children with severe xerophthalmia are likely to survive, according to a report by K. Vijayaraghavan in the December 1, 1990, issue of *Lancet.*

Overdoses of vitamin A can lead to hypervitaminosis A, resulting in fatigue, abdominal upset, brittle nails, and other adverse side effects.

Vitamin A and Cancer. Vitamin A and its derivatives (betacarotene, retinol) represent one class of anticarcinogenic phytochemicals. Vitamin A has been demonstrated to reduce cancerous tumors in animals and may reduce the risk of lung cancer in humans. In a study published in March 1992 by the *New England Journal of Medicine,* researchers reported that high doses of a derivative of vitamin A, marketed as the acne drug Accutane, prevent lung, throat, and mouth cancers in people who are at high risk of developing them.

Researchers at the M.D. Anderson Cancer Center of the University of Texas in Houston also successfully treated patients with head and neck cancer using Accutane. Because these patients' tissues already were primed to become cancerous, they were very likely to grow new, separate cancers that were more life-threatening than the first. Accutane prevented new cancers from forming in most patients in the study for nearly three years. However, the drug did not prevent the recurrence of the original tumors, as reported by Frank Murray in *Today's Living,* October 1992.

Accutane has serious side effects when administered in high doses, but researchers reported that if lower doses also work, the stage will be set for giving Accutane to people who smoke or drink heavily and are there-

Benefits of Vitamin A

- Builds resistance to infections, especially of the respiratory tract and mucous membranes.

- Counteracts night blindness and weak eyesight.

- Promotes healthy skin.

- Helps prevent lung, throat, and mouth cancers in people who are high risk of developing them.

- Helps prevent head and neck cancer.

- Strengthens pregnancy (when taken in conjunction with iron) by combatting a deficiency of red blood cells in anemic women.

fore at relatively high risk for head or neck cancers. The findings strongly indicated that other cancers might also be preventable.

Vitamin A also appears to lower the risk of breast cancer, according to *Alternative Medicine: What Works.* In a study of the diets of 89,494 nurses, those who ingested the most vitamin A had 16% less risk of breast cancer. When vitamin A supplements were given to those with the least of it in their diets, their risk also went down. In another analysis of the same data, the nurses with the most vitamin A in their diets had 39% fewer cataracts than those who had the least.

Vitamin A and Cervical Dysplasia. Fugh-Berman also reports a controlled study of 301 women with cervical dysplasia in which derivatives of vitamin A called retinoids were applied to the cervix, or neck of the uterus. This treatment completely reversed the dysplasia in 43% of women, compared to 27% of those who used placebo cream.

B Vitamins

The B family consists of thiamine (B$_1$), riboflavin (B$_2$), niacin (B$_3$), pantothenic acid (B$_5$), pyridoxine (B$_6$), folic acid (B$_9$), and cobalamin (B$_{12}$). The B vitamins tend to be interdependent, so that excess intake of any one of them may generate a need for equivalent amounts of the others. B vitamins consumed in excess of the body's need are normally excreted in urine.

However, in severe dysplasia, there was no difference between using placebo and retinoids.

Vitamin A and HIV. HIV-infected mothers who are deficient in vitamin A while pregnant are much more likely to transmit the virus to their babies. A survey of 338 pregnant, HIV-infected women in Malawi, as reported by Fugh-Berman, found that the HIV transmission rate among mothers with severe vitamin A deficiency was 32% versus 7% among women with healthy levels.

Vitamin A and Pregnancy. Malnourished pregnant women often suffer from anemia because they lack the nutrient iron that is crucial for carrying oxygen in the blood. A 1993 study suggests that pregnant women have a much better chance of combatting anemia by ingesting vitamin A and iron supplements, instead of iron pills alone. The study, conducted in West Java, Indonesia, included 251 malnourished women who were between 16 and 24 weeks pregnant. One group of women received 2.4 mg of vitamin A and 60 mg of iron; a second group was given vitamin A and a placebo; a third group received iron and a placebo, and a fourth took two dummy pills. Anemia was eliminated in 97% of the women who received both vitamin A and iron pills. By comparison, anemia was eliminated in 68% of those who took only iron, 35% who took vitamin A alone, and 16% who took only the placebos. Dr. D. Suharno, writing in the November 27, 1993, issue of *Lancet*, warned that extremely high doses of vitamin A can be toxic, however, and cause fetal malformations during the first three months of pregnancy.

Recommended Daily Allowance (RDA) for Vitamin B$_1$ (Thiamine)

	mg
Infants (0-1 year)	0.4
Children (1-10 years)	0.8
Males (11-24 years)	1.4
Males (25-51+ years)	1.4
Females (11-24 years)	1.1
Females (25-51+ years)	1.1
Pregnant Females	1.5
Breastfeeding Mothers	1.6

Vitamin B$_1$

Vitamin B$_1$ (thiamine), is a water-soluble nutrient important for growth, digestion, and normal functioning of the nervous system, muscles, and heart. Vitamin B$_1$ keeps mucous membranes healthy and replaces deficiency caused by alcoholism, cirrhosis, overactive thyroid, infection, breastfeeding, absorption diseases, pregnancy, prolonged diarrhea, and burns.

Natural sources of vitamin B$_1$ include brewer's yeast, rice, bran, brown rice, wheat germ and whole-grained products, oatmeal, beef kidney and liver, dried beans (garbanzo, navy, and kidney), salmon, soy beans, and sunflower seeds.

People deficient in vitamin B_1 commonly experience a loss of appetite, weakness and lassitude, nervous irritability, insomnia, weight loss, muscle aches and pains, mental depression, and constipation. Alcoholics are usually deficient in most of the B vitamins, including B_1.

Vitamin B_1 has been used to treat certain types of depression associated with alcoholism. One study conducted in New Zealand concluded that alcoholics, who exhibit many of the symptoms of beriberi (including fatigue, diarrhea, weight loss, and paralysis), also may benefit from vitamin B_1 supplements containing at least 200 mg of thiamine. The study concluded that thiamine is a therapeutic agent that "is literally lifesaving in a significant proportion of patients," according to J. Cade's report in the February 1986 *Australian-New Zealand Journal of Psychiatry.*

Vitamin B_2

Vitamin B_2 (riboflavin) aids in the release of energy from food and preserves the integrity of the nervous system, eyes, and skin. It acts as a component in two co-enzymes (flavin mononucleotide and flavin adenine dinucleotide), both of which are needed for normal tissue growth. Vitamin B_2 maintains healthy mucous membranes lining the respiratory, digestive, circulatory, and excretory tracts when used in conjunction with vitamin A. In their *Encyclopedia of Natural Medicine,* Murray and Pizzorno report that vitamin B_2 appears to decrease a craving for sugar and thus may help prevent diabetes, and improves vision, especially in elderly people. It aids in treating infections, stomach problems, burns, alcoholism, and liver disease.

Recommended Daily Allowance (RDA) for Vitamin B_2 (Riboflavin)

	mg
Infants (0-1 year)	0.4
Children (1-10 years)	1.1
Males (11-24 years)	1.6
Males (25-51+ years)	1.5
Females (11-24 years)	1.3
Females (25-51+ years)	1.3
Pregnant Females	1.6
Breastfeeding Mothers	1.8

Natural sources of vitamin B_2 include almonds, liver, kidney, beef, brewer's yeast, cheese, chicken, and most B_1 sources. Vitamin B_2 deficiencies may result in itching and burning of the eyes, cracking of the skin, inflammation of the mouth, and bloodshot eyes. A deficiency of riboflavin is also believed to be linked with cataract formation.

The use of oral contraceptives has been associated with inducing several nutrient deficiencies, including riboflavin, pyridoxine, ascorbic acid, and zinc, while iron, copper, and vitamin A levels typically are increased. These findings suggest decreased liver metabolism of riboflavin. Females who suffer from premenstrual syndrome, or PMS, may benefit from B_2 supplements administered under the care of a health practitioner.

The administration of large doses of B vitamins, especially riboflavin, has been shown to be quite effective in the treatment of acute acne (rosacea), according to the *Encyclopedia of Natural Medicine.*

Recommended Daily Allowance (RDA) for Vitamin B₃ (Niacin)

	mg
Infants (0-1 year)	6
Children (1-10 years)	12
Males (11-24 years)	19
Males (25-51+ years)	17
Females (11-24 years)	15
Females (25-51+ years)	14
Pregnant Females	17
Breastfeeding Mothers	20

Vitamin B₃

Two chemicals have vitamin B₃ properties: nicotinic acid (niacin) and niacinamide (nicotinamide adenine dinucleotide). Both are necessary for releasing energy from foods, for the utilization of fats, and for tissue respiration. Niacin helps control blood fat levels and is important for the proper functioning of skin and nerves. It also promotes growth, maintains normal functioning of the gastrointestinal tract, and is necessary for metabolism of sugar. Vitamin B₃ reduces cholesterol and triglycerides in the blood; dilates blood vessels; treats vertigo (dizziness), pellagra, and ringing in the ears; and prevents premenstrual headaches. Niacinamide is generally used in treatment because, unlike niacin, it does not cause burning, flushing, or itching of the skin.

Niacin can be made in the body from the amino acid tryptophan. Natural sources of vitamin B₃ include chicken, beef liver, lean meat such as turkey or veal, brewer's yeast, wheat products, yeast, green vegetables and beans, halibut, salmon, swordfish, tuna, peanuts, pork, and sunflower seeds. Strict vegetarians who eat no animal foods must rely on nuts and legumes for niacin. Niacin found in some cereals and in vegetables such as corn may be present in chemically unusable forms.

Signs of vitamin B₃ deficiency include pellagra, inflammation of the skin and tongue, gastrointestinal disturbances, nervous system dysfunctions, muscle weakness, headaches, fatigue, mental depression, irritability, loss of appetite, neuritis, nausea, dizziness, weight loss, and insomnia.

Vitamin B₅

Vitamin B₅ (pantothenic acid) is another B vitamin essential for normal growth and development. It aids in the release of energy from foods and helps synthesize numerous body materials.

Vitamin B₅ is found in blue cheese, brewer's yeast, corn, eggs, lentils, liver, lobster, peanuts, peas, soybeans, sunflower seeds, wheat germ, whole-grain products, and meats of all kinds.

There are no known deficiency symptoms for vitamin B₅ alone. However, a deficiency in one B vitamin is usually associated with an overall lack of B nutrients. Pantothenic acid is usually given with other B vitamins if symptoms of any vitamin B deficiency exist, including excessive fatigue, sleep disturbances, loss of appetite, and nausea. Anyone with inadequate caloric or nutritional dietary intake may be vitamin B₅-deficient. Vitamin B₅ is recommended by physicians for people with a chronic wasting illness, those suffering excess stress for long periods, or those who have recently undergone surgery. Vitamin B₅ supplements are sometimes recommended for those who participate in vigorous physical activities, such as athletes and manual laborers. No RDA has been established for vitamin B₅.

Vitamin B₆

Vitamin B_6 (pyridoxine) is a water-soluble B vitamin critical for the metabolism of amino acids. Along with niacinamide, vitamin B_6 aids in the absorption of proteins, helps the body use fats, and assists in the formation of red blood cells. It helps the normal functioning of the brain, maintains chemical balance among body fluids, regulates excretion of water, and helps in energy production and resistance to stress.

Vitamin B_6 can be found in avocados, bananas, bran, brewer's yeast, carrots, whole-wheat flour, hazelnuts, lentils, rice, salmon, shrimp, soybeans, sunflower seeds, tuna, and wheat germ. A pyridoxine deficiency results in depressed immunity, noted by a reduction in the quantity and quality of antibodies produced, shrinkage of lymphatic tissues including the thymus gland, decreased thymic hormone activity, and a reduction in the number and activity of lymphocytes. Factors contributing to a vitamin B_6 deficiency include low dietary intake, excess protein intake, and alcohol and oral contraception use.

Vitamin B₆ and Asthma. Vitamin B_6 may be of direct benefit to asthmatic patients since it is involved in the synthesis of all major neurotransmitters. In one study, plasma and red cell pyridoxal phosphate (the active form of vitamin B_6) levels in 15 adult patients with asthma were significantly lower than in 16 controls. In his 1975 book, *Meganutrients for Your Nerves,* H. Newbold states that all patients reported a dramatic decrease in frequency and severity of wheezing and asthmatic attacks while taking the supplements.

Vitamin B₆ and Cancer. Vitamin B_6 is one of the most promising B vitamins for cancer treatment. Robert Reynold, Hans Ladner, and Richard Salkeld conducted a clinical trial treating cancer patients with vitamin B_6 in addition to radiotherapy. Three hundred

Recommended Daily Allowance (RDA) for Vitamin B₆ (Pyridoxine)

	mg
Infants (0-1 year)	0.5
Children (1-10 years)	1.4
Males (11-24 years)	2.0
Males (25-51+ years)	2.0
Females (11-24 years)	1.5
Females (25-51+ years)	1.6
Pregnant Females	2.2
Breastfeeding Mothers	2.1

milligrams of B_6 were given over a seven-week period to 105 endometrial cancer patients, aged 45-65. These patients had a 15% improvement in five-year survival rates compared to 105 patients who did not receive the B_6 supplements. No side effects from the B_6 supplementation were observed. Another study suggested that B_6 supplementation to correct metabolic abnormality might prevent recurrence of bladder cancer.

Ladner and Salkeld also confirmed the beneficial effects of B_6 on radiation-induced symptoms (nausea, vomiting, and diarrhea) in gynecological patients treated with high-energy radiation. They subsequently gave B_6 to 6,300 patients with cervical, uterine, endometrial, ovarian, and breast cancers and concluded that both quality of life and survival rates significantly improved. This clinical trial was cited in 1991 by Robert D. Reynold in a chapter in *Essential Nutrients in Carcinogenesis.*

Vitamin B_6 has also proved effective in inhibiting melanoma cancer cells. One research team developed a topical B_6 pyridoxal that "produced a significant reduction in the

Recommended Daily Allowance (RDA) for Vitamin B₉ (Folic Acid)

	mcg
Infants (0-1 year)	30
Children (1-10 years)	75
Males (11-24 years)	200
Males (25-51+ years)	200
Females (11-24 years)	180
Females (25-51+ years)	180
Pregnant Females	400
Breastfeeding Mothers	280

size of subcutaneous cancer nodules and complete regression of cutaneous papules." While the results were considered preliminary, they may lead to a more successful topical B_6 treatment for several forms of skin cancer, according to Reynold.

Vitamin B₆ and Morning Sickness. A study of 59 pregnant women cited by Fugh-Berman found that vitamin B_6 was more effective than placebo in reducing severe nausea and vomiting caused by pregnancy. No difference was found for mild to moderate nausea. Although vitamin B_6 has been used for morning sickness since the early 1940s, pregnant women should ask their obstetrician before taking the vitamin because it can cause insomnia and other problems.

Vitamin B₉ (Folic Acid)

Folic acid is an acid which helps promote normal red blood cell formation. It acts as a co-enzyme for normal DNA synthesis and functions as part of a co-enzyme in amino acid and nucleoprotein synthesis. It also main-

tains nervous system integrity and intestinal tract functions. In pregnant mothers, vitamin B_9 helps regulate embryonic and fetal development of nerve cells.

Most people obtain sufficient amounts of folic acid in their daily diet. Natural sources include barley, beans, brewer's yeast, calves' liver, fruits, garbanzo beans (chickpeas), green and leafy vegetables, lentils, orange juice, oranges, peas, rice, soybeans, sprouts, wheat, and wheat germ.

Folic acid deficiency is the most common vitamin deficiency in the world. Unlike vitamin B_{12}, the body does not maintain a large surplus of folic acid; folic acid stores in the liver and kidneys will sustain the body for only one to two months.

Alcoholics frequently are deficient in B_9 because alcohol impairs folic acid absorption, disrupts folic acid metabolism, and causes the body to excrete folic acid. In addition to alcohol, anticancer drugs, drugs for epilepsy, and oral contraceptives also cause a folic acid deficiency.

Folic acid deficiency is common in pregnant women. Vitamin B_9 is vital to cell reproduction within the fetus. Without a constant source of vitamin B_9 for the fetus, birth defects will result. In November 1992, the FDA recommended that food, preferably enriched flour, be fortified with folic acid to prevent neural tube defect, a common birth defect that occurs when the spinal column fails to close completely during the first six weeks of pregnancy.

Folic acid deficiencies are frequently found in patients with chronic diarrhea, coeliac disease, and Crohn's disease. Vitamin B_9 deficiency may result in anemia, depression, and a swollen, red tongue.

Vitamin B₉ and Adenoma. A high dietary folate intake also protects against colorectal adenoma, a pre-cancerous condition that can lead to colon cancer, according to *Alternative*

Medicine: What Works. Although cervical cancer appears to be caused by a sexually transmitted virus, folate deficiency also appears to be a factor.

Vitamin B₉ and Cervical Dysplasia. Folic acid supplementation (10 mg per day) has been successfully used to regress precancerous cells in patients with cervical dysplasia. Cervical dysplasia is an abnormal condition of the cells of the cervix, which is usually regarded as a precancerous lesion. When treated with folic acid, the regression-to-normal rate was observed to be 20% in one study and 100% in another, according to the January 1985 issue of the *American Journal of Clinical Nutrition*.

Vitamin B₉ and Infertility. *Alternative Medicine: What Works* cites a small controlled study which showed that folinic acid, a type of folate, has been used successfully to treat a type of male infertility called round cell idiopathic syndrome.

Vitamin B₉ and Irritable Bowel Syndrome (IBS). Folic acid supplementation is also important for patients with irritable bowel syndrome (IDS). As appropriate, nutritional supplements are utilized to correct deficiencies, normalize the inflammatory process, and promote healing of the damaged mucosa. Botanical medicines are also used to promote healing and normalize the intestinal flora.

Vitamin B₉ and Pregnancy. Folic acid, which is known to lower homocysteine levels, dramatically lowers the rate of neural tube defects, although it must be taken very early in pregnancy to be effective. Vitamin B₁₂ may also help to lower the risk of neural tube defects.

Alternative Medicine: What Works cites a study in which elevated homocysteine levels were found in 21% of women with recurrent, unexplained miscarriages. Above-normal homocysteine levels were also found in mothers whose babies were born with neural tube birth defects such as spina bifida and anencephaly (in which the baby is born missing most of its brain.)

Unfortunately, few Americans consume enough fresh fruits and vegetables, the primary dietary source of folic acid. One study cited by Fugh-Berman found that 13-15% of American women 20-44 years of age showed biochemical evidence of folate deficiency.

Vitamin B₉ and Psychological Disorders. Folic acid deficiency is the most common nutrient deficiency in people with psychological disorders. In studies of psychiatric patients, as many as 30% have been shown to be deficient in folic acid, and in one study 67% of geriatric patients admitted to a psychiatric ward were vitamin B₉ deficient. According to the May 1973 issue of the *Journal of the American Medical Association*, patients with organic psychosis, endogenous depression, and schizophrenia who were given vitamin B₉ supplements fared much better in most clinical trials than control subjects.

Vitamin B₉ and Gum Disease. Studies have shown that folic acid, administered either topically or internally, produces significant reduction of gingival inflammation (gum disease) by binding toxins secreted by plaques. The use of folate mouthwash is particularly recommended for pregnant women, oral contraceptive users, those using antifolate drugs (e.g., phenytoinand methotrexate), and people suffering from other conditions associated with an exaggerated gingival inflammatory response.

Vitamin B₁₂

Vitamin B₁₂ maintains the health of all body cells. It also helps preserve nerve tissue

Recommended Daily Allowance (RDA) for Vitamin B_{12} (Cobalamin)	
	mcg
Infants (0-1 year)	0.4
Children (1-10 years)	1.0
Males (11-24 years)	2.0
Males (25-51+ years)	2.0
Females (11-24 years)	2.0
Females (25-51+ years)	2.0
Pregnant Females	2.2
Breastfeeding Mothers	2.6

and enhances blood formation and the production of DNA (which is found in the chromosomes of the nucleus of all cells) and RNA (which carries gene data from the nucleus to the cytoplasm).

Vitamin B_{12} is found only in animal sources such as beef and beef liver, clams, flounder, herring, liverwurst, mackerel, sardines, blue and Swiss cheese, eggs, and milk. Strict vegetarians must therefore take a B_{12} supplement such as nutritional yeast. Large amounts of folic acid can mask a B_{12} deficiency, and large doses of vitamin C are known to increase the need for B_{12}. B_{12} requires absorption of a special protein that some individuals are unable to produce, necessitating B_{12} injections.

There have been few studies of how vitamin B_{12} therapies might aid in preventing certain chronic diseases. However, research has shown that when schizophrenics with low vitamin B_{12} levels are given B_{12} supplements, their symptoms improve, according to an article by E. Reynold in the *British Journal of Psychiatry* in March 1970. Vitamin B_{12}, along with several other nutrients and plant compounds, has also been used in therapeutic trials to rebuild weak immune systems.

Although B_{12} deficiency is less prevalent in psychiatric patients than that of folic acid deficiency, determining B_{12} levels in the blood is considered a useful screening measure for psychiatric patients. Patients with severe mania and psychosis secondary to B_{12} deficiency have had complete remission after B_{12} supplementation, E. Reynold reported. An improvement is usually noted within four to seven days with virtually no side effects.

Vitamin B_{12} has other uses as well. In one study of military personnel, more than half of the subjects with tinnitus (ringing in the ears) and noise-induced hearing loss were found to be deficient in vitamin B_{12}. And a small study of asthmatic children sensitive to sulfites found that vitamin B_{12} was 80% effecive in preventing asthmatic attacks.

Vitamin C

Vitamin C, also known as ascorbic acid, is a water-soluble, white crystalline that is essential for the formation of collagen and fibrous tissue; for normal intercellular matrices in teeth, bones, cartilage, connective tissue, and skin; and for the structural integrity of capillary walls. It aids in fighting bacterial infections, interacts with other nutrients, and has been shown to relieve emotional and environmental stress and depression and to protect the circulatory system from fat deposits. Vitamin C is a key factor in many immune functions as well, including white blood cell function, interferon levels, increasing antibody levels and response, and increasing the secretion of thymic hormones. Vitamin C has been used as part of aggressive treatment programs for people with AIDS, cancer, and other diseases in which optimizing immune function is a critical therapeutic goal.

Vitamin C is present in citrus fruits, tomatoes, berries, potatoes, and fresh, green, leafy vegetables such as broccoli, brussel sprouts, collards, turnip greens, parsley, and cabbage. Relative to other nutrients, it is one of the safest substances known.

Vitamin C is also available in tablets, extended-release capsules, oral solutions, and injections. Tablets and capsules are sold in most health food stores. Vitamin C injections are available only from a physician.

Vitamin C deficiency symptoms include shortness of breath, digestive difficulties, easy bruising, swollen or painful joints, nose-bleeds, anemia, frequent infections, and slow healing of wounds. Conversely, while massive daily doses of vitamin C are not necessarily toxic, because the body expels what it cannot use, they can cause stomach upset and diarrhea.

Vitamin C and Cataracts. Cataracts are caused, in part, by changes in proteins located in the eye, and research studies suggest that vitamin C can prevent these changes. In one study, reported in the July 1992 *Environmental Nutrition,* people who took several vitamin supplements, including vitamin C, had four times less risk of developing cataracts than those who took no supplements. Research on vitamin C's role in preventing cataracts is still inconclusive, however, as other antioxidant nutrients such as vitamin E and betacarotene help prevent cataracts as well.

Vitamin C and Cholesterol. Studies have demonstrated that vitamin C lowers LDL ("bad") cholesterol levels in the blood because it attacks free radicals–the highly unstable oxygen molecules that damage (or oxidize) body tissues and blood fats. The free radicals' effect on LDL is similar to what happens to a steak when it is exposed to the air too long: it oxidizes and turns brown. Scientists now think that vitamin C and other

antioxidants prevent the oxidation process caused by free radicals. According to Jeffrey Frei, assistant professor of nutrition at Harvard School of Public Health, in the October 1991 issue of *Prevention Magazine,* "Vitamin C traps free radicals in the surrounding environment before they can attack the LDL particle. As long as there is vitamin C, free radicals cannot attack LDL because the C forms a very tight, protective shield around it." Furthermore, vitamin C strengthens HDL cholesterol (the good form) by making it more resistant to free-radical

Recommended Daily Allowance (RDA) for Vitamin C

The optimum dose level for vitamin C is 1,000-5,000 mg per day, depending upon the age and physical condition of the person taking it. To reduce the frequency and severity of colds, for example, Pauling recommended that individuals take at least 3,000 mg per day, although it has been estimated that an average of 8,000 mg per day is required to prevent colds in 95% of the population.

	mg
Infants (0-1 year)	35
Children (1-10 years)	45
Males (11-24 years)	60
Males (25-51+ years)	60
Females (11-24 years)	60
Females (25-51+ years)	60
Pregnant Females	70
Breastfeeding mothers	95

damage. Lowering blood cholesterol levels is still the only proven way to reduce heart disease. As a result, many physicians now recommend foods rich in vitamin C, E, and betacarotene (such as fruits and vegetables) as a way of lowering cholesterol. In addition, many experts suggest that the current RDA for vitamins C and E may be too low, and that betacarotene (a form of vitamin A) should be added.

Vitamin C and Disease Prevention. Many studies have shown that increased vitamin C intake can produce a number of beneficial effects, including reducing the risk of cancer, strengthening the immune system, protecting against the effects of pollution and cigarette smoke, enhancing wound repair, and increasing life expectancy.

Pauling first postulated the theory that moderate doses of vitamin C (250-1,000 mg) effectively prevented the spread of viral and bacterial infections, and that large doses of one gram or more may cure those infections.

A growing body of scientists now believes that vitamin C also reduces the risk of cancer. In 1991, Dr. Gladys Block, professor of nutrition at the University of California at Berkeley, reviewed more than 100 studies linking vitamin C or vitamin C-rich foods (primarily fruit) and cancer prevention. Block found that vitamin C's protection is most convincing for cancers of the throat, mouth, pancreas, and stomach. In an article in the *American Journal of Clinical Nutrition,* published in January 1991, she also suggested that vitamin C has a protective effect against cancers of the cervix, rectum, and breast. A 1992 National Cancer Institute study, reported in the July 6, 1992, issue of *Cancer Weekly,* found that the protective effect of vitamin C against breast cancer was as great, if not greater, than the effect of reducing saturated fat intake.

Vitamin C performs several functions that explain why it may be important in preventing cancer. It acts as an antioxidant that protects cells and tissues from damage caused by free radicals, significantly influences immune function, and may inhibit the spread of tumors. Vitamin C was directly associated with "a significant protective effect" against cancer in 33 out of 46 studies that Block analyzed. Several of the studies also showed a positive correlation between fruit intake and protection against cancer. However, while these studies indicate vitamin C "reduces the risk of cancer," they do not prove that vitamin C "cures" it.

Vitamin C and Cholesterol

- Increases the rate at which cholesterol is removed by its conversion to bile acids and excretion via the intestines.

- Increases high density lipoprotein (HDL) cholesterol levels. High HDL levels are correlated with low risk of heart disease.

- Through its laxative effect, accelerates elimination of waste, thereby decreasing the reabsorption of bile acids and their reconversion to cholesterol.

Vitamin C and Disease Prevention

- Reduces the risk of some cancers.
- Diminishes the side effects of radiotherapy and chemotherapy.
- Halts the spread of viral and bacterial infections.
- Reduces the risk of developing high blood pressure.
- Lessens the risk of heart disease.
- Protects the skin against ultraviolet A (UVA) and ultraviolet B (UVB) light exposure, thereby preventing premature aging and wrinkles.
- Reduces cholesterol levels.
- Helps prevent cataracts.

The importance of vitamin C-rich diets was further confirmed in a broad-based study of esophageal cancer in China. In 1983, blood samples were collected from 100 adults (aged 25-64 years), and then analyzed. Both men and women who took vitamin C had significantly lower death rates from esophageal cancer. Death rates for people who did not take vitamin C were more than three times higher, according to a June 1984 report by Wande Guo and others in *Nutrition and Cancer.*

Vitamin C levels (as ascorbic acid) also inhibit skin tumors. A 1992 study carried out at Duke University Medical Center strongly suggests that vitamin C protects the skin against ultraviolet A (UVA) and ultraviolet B (UVB) light exposure. This study, reported in the January 1992 *Harvard Health Letter,* concluded that vitamin C acts as an antioxidant and prevents UVA and UVB oxidative damage to collagen, elastin, proteoglycan, and cell membranes. Some scientists now think that vitamin C will eventually be shown to prevent premature aging, wrinkles, and skin cancer.

Vitamin C and Hypertension. Medical surveys have found that people whose vitamin C levels are low tend to have high blood pressure. A recent study published in *Environmental Nutrition* found that 1,000 mg a day of supplemental vitamin C significantly reduced systolic blood pressure (the top number in a blood pressure reading) in a group of 20 women, 12 of whom had borderline hypertension.

Vitamin C and Increased Longevity. Adding substantially larger amounts of vitamin C to ordinary diets may prolong life by lessening the risk of heart disease and cancer. A large U.S. survey conducted by the National Center for Health Statistics (NCHS) demonstrated a strong correlation between vitamin C intake and decreased mortality. Between 1971 and 1974, the NCHS collected extensive diet and nutrition information from 11,348 adults aged 25-74. Investigators at the

Recommended Daily Allowance (RDA) for Vitamin D

	mcg
Infants (0-1 year)	10
Children (1-10 years)	10
Males (11-24 years)	10
Males (25-51+ years)	5
Females (11-24 years)	10
Females (25-51+ years)	5
Pregnant Females	10
Breastfeeding mothers	10

UCLA School of Public Health subsequently reviewed the participants' estimated daily vitamin C intake and divided them into three groups: less than 50 mg; 50 mg or more from dietary sources; and 50 mg or more from food, plus regular vitamin C supplementation, usually in the form of pills containing several hundred milligrams.

For men with the highest vitamin C intake, the total number of deaths was 35% lower than predicted; mortality due to cardiovascular diseases was 42% lower, and cancer deaths were 22% less. Benefits were not as apparent for women in the high-C group: there was an overall drop in expected mortality of 10%, with a 25% decline in deaths caused by heart disease, and a 15% reduction in those due to cancer, according to a report published in the July 1992 issue of *Environmental Nutrition*. Many of the participants also took vitamins A and E, which act to block the oxidation of cholesterol and other molecules thought to play important roles in the development of cancer and heart disease. Although the UCLA study does not prove that

vitamin C supplements will guarantee a longer life, the findings do suggest that substantial amounts of vitamin C provide greater protection against fatal diseases.

Vitamin D

Vitamin D is a fat-soluble vitamin chemically related to steroids. It is essential for the normal formation of bones and teeth and for the absorption of calcium and phosphorus in the gastrointestinal tract. Vitamin D is also called cholecalciferol and is available from both natural and synthetic sources.

Small amounts of vitamin D are present in natural foods, especially milk and dairy products. Other natural foods containing vitamin D include saltwater fish, especially salmon, sardines, and herring; organ meats; fish-liver oils; and egg yolks. Vitamin D is also obtained through exposure to sunlight. Ultraviolet rays activate a form of cholesterol in an oil of the skin and convert it to a type of vitamin D, which is then absorbed. In some cases, vitamin D cannot be absorbed without the presence of other foods such as fat.

Ten micrograms per day, or 400 International Units (IU), is the recommended amount of vitamin D to ensure normal development in babies. When a normal diet does not supply sufficient vitamin D, supplements are often recommended.

Vitamin D deficiency can result in osteoporosis and osteodystrophy. Lack of vitamin D may also lead to rickets, especially in children, weakening bones and teeth. In adults, a vitamin D deficiency may cause osteomalacia, in which calcium is lost from bones, causing chronic pain in the ribs, lower spine, pelvis, and legs.

Like vitamin A, vitamin D can accumulate in the body, causing such serious side effects as kidney failure and kidney stones. Symptoms that indicate a person has consumed too much vitamin D include nausea, weakness, and widespread aches, usually followed by more serious problems, such as high blood pressure and irregular heartbeat.

Vitamin D and Disease Prevention. Vitamin D analogs may offer a potential endocrine therapy for breast cancer. In a study reported in the September 23, 1991, issue of *Cancer Weekly*, patients with advanced breast cancer were treated daily with one gram of calcitrol ointment for six weeks; 21% subsequently showed partial slowing of the spread of cancer. Several other studies have shown that colon cancer is less common in people who have high levels of vitamin D in their blood. One study, conducted over a 19-year period, reported that a daily intake of more than 3.75 micrograms of vitamin D reduced the incidence of colon cancer by 50%. A daily intake of at least 1,200 mg of calcium was reported to reduce the risk of colon cancer by 75%. Based on the results of these studies, daily intakes of 1,500 mg of calcium for women and 1,800 mg of calcium for men, as well as at least 5 mcg of vitamin D, are recommended to reduce the risk of colon cancer, according to an article by Frank Garland in the July 1991 *American Journal of Clinical Nutrition*.

Vitamin D and the Elderly. Food and sunlight are primary sources of vitamin D, and because many elderly people do not get enough of either one, they are often vitamin D-deficient. Older people also manufacture vitamin D more slowly, and the resulting deficiency can cause their bones to weaken and grow brittle. As a result, researchers have urged that the RDA for vitamin D be raised for this age group. Some preliminary findings suggest that taking vitamin D supplements may delay bone mass loss.

The importance of vitamin D in the bone formation of infants and bone preservation in the elderly is directly related to its role in con-

trolling the body's ability to absorb phosphorous and calcium. Apparently, the human requirement for calcium changes dramatically throughout the life cycle. The need for calcium rises during growth in childhood, pregnancy, lactation, and menopause, and is lower between the ages of 25 and 51–thus the daily dietary requirement ranges from 5-10 mcg.

Vitamin D Supplements. Dihydrotachysterol, a form of vitamin D, is used to treat hypoglycemia, which occurs when there is insufficient calcium in the blood or when calcium is not used properly by the body. Calcitrol, another form of vitamin D available only by prescription, is used to treat hypoglycemia and certain types of bone disease that occur in patients who are undergoing renal dialysis for kidney disease. A third form of vitamin D, calciportiol, has been shown to be an effective topical treatment for psoriasis, according to L. May in *Drug Information*, published in 1993.

Vitamin E

Vitamin E is a co-factor in many enzymes that promote normal growth and development, including the formation of red blood cells. Along with vitamin C, it helps

Recommended Daily Allowance (RDA) for Vitamin E

	mg
Infants (0-1 year)	4
Children (1-10 years)	7
Males (11-24 years)	10
Males (25-51+ years)	10
Females (11-24 years)	8
Females (25-51+ years)	8
Pregnant Females	10
Breastfeeding Mothers	12

Note: One mg equals 1 IU (International Unit), and labels may list either.

prevent the corrosive oxidation of free radicals in the body.

Natural sources of vitamin E include wheat germ, liver, sunflower seeds, whole grains, walnuts, hazelnuts, almonds, butter, eggs, turnip greens, asparagus, spinach, peas, peanuts, cashews, soy lecithin, and vegetable oils. Salad oils, margarine, and shortening provide about 64% of vitamin E in the average U.S. diet, fruits and vegetables about 11%, and grains and grain products about 7%.

A diet high in polyunsaturated fats is a major cause of vitamin E deficiency. In *How To Live Longer and Feel Better,* Pauling suggests that "a diet high in unsaturated fatty oils, especially the polyunsaturated ones, can destroy the body's deposits of vitamin E, and cause muscular lesions, brain lesions, and degeneration of blood vessels. Care must be taken not include a large amount of polyunsaturated oil in the diet without a corresponding intake of vitamin E."

Vitamin E and Alzheimer's Disease. Patients with Alzheimer's disease have been found to have high levels of two enzymes linked to damage of nerve cells, and vitamins A, E, and betacarotene may slow down the disease's progression. Researchers at Central Middlesex Hospital in London measured serum levels of vitamins A and E and four major carotenoids (any of various yellow to red pigments found in foods) in 10 patients with Alzheimer's disease, 10 with dementia, and 20 control elderly individuals. Plasma concentrations of vitamin E and betacarotene were significantly lower in patients with Alzheimer's and dementia than in the control group. Since vitamins A and E and carotenoids act as free radical scavengers, their deficiency may accelerate the degenerative processes in the brain that cause Alzheimer's disease, according to an article in the June 1992 *Nutrition Research Newsletter.*

Vitamin E and Angina. A study conducted in Edinburgh, Scotland, tested the hypothesis that low plasma concentrations of vitamin E may be related to the risk of angina. Plasma concentrations of vitamins A, C, E, and betacarotene were measured in 6,000 Edinburgh men aged 35-55. Plasma concentrations of vitamins C, E, and carotene were inversely related to the risk of angina, while vitamin A showed no relationship. The researchers emphasized that their findings, obtained in a population with a high heart disease risk and low intakes of fruit and green vegetables, may not apply to other communities but their evidence strongly suggests that populations with a high incidence of coronary heart disease may benefit from eating diets rich in natural antioxidants, particularly vitamin E. The study was reported by R.A. Riemersma and others in the January 5, 1991, issue of *Lancet.*

Vitamin E and Bypass Heart Surgery.
Vitamin E may prevent the formation of free radicals during the final phase of bypass surgery—an operation to improve blood flow to the heart. Free radicals often form while surgeons briefly flood the heart with richly oxygenated blood, but until recently surgeons had no way of shielding the heart from this process. Dr. Terrence Yau of the University of Toronto reported that presurgical supplementation with vitamin E improved the heart's ability to pump during the risky five-hour postoperative period. He and his colleagues gave 14 patients 300 mg of highly purified vitamin E daily for two weeks prior to their bypass operations, and achieved successful, though preliminary, results, according to an article by Kathy A. Fackelmann in *Science News* of November 24, 1990.

Vitamin E and Cancer. Several studies conducted in Finland found that, on average, patients who developed cancers had less vitamin E in their bloodstreams than did healthy patients. The Finnish studies of 21,172 men and 15,093 women preliminarily support the premise that higher vitamin E levels in the blood help reduce the risk of cancer, according to an article in the June 1992 *Nutrition Research Newsletter.*

A 1992 National Cancer Institute study involving more than 1,100 patients found that, while several supplements appeared to lessen the risk of oral cancers, only vitamin E cut the risk in half. The study, reported in the July 6, 1992, *Cancer Weekly,* confirmed that vitamin E helped protect the fatty acids in cell membranes against free radicals.

Vitamin E and Cardiovascular Disease.
Vitamin E helps prevent cardiovascular ailments including blood clots, protects against cell damage by oxidation, and guards lungs against air pollutants such as ozone, nitrous oxide, and cigarette smoke.

Vitamin E and Disease Prevention

- Prevents cardiovascular ailments, including blood clots.
- Guards lungs against air pollutants such as ozone, nitrous oxide, and cigarette smoke.
- Prevents the breakdown of the immune system in older people, decreasing the likelihood of infectious disease and tumors.
- Reduces the risk of cataracts, cardiovascular disease, and other problems associated with aging.
- Helps prevent epileptic seizures.
- Reduces the risk of cancer.
- Reduces the risk of heart disease, especially ischemic heart disease (IHD).
- May slow down Alzheimer's disease.
- Prevents the formation of free radicals during the final phase of bypass surgery.
- Relieves joint inflammation in rheumatoid arthritis.

Approximately 80 studies have found that children of smokers are more prone to bronchitis, pneumonia, hospitalizations, and missed school days. When they are given a daily intake of at least 5,000-10,000 IU of vitamin A, along with 400-800 IU of vitamin E, their lungs and mucous membranes were less prone to damage, reports S. Langer in the September 1990 issue of *Better Nutrition.*

It is now widely accepted that vitamin E keeps the blood free-flowing without causing profuse bleeding by exerting a powerful anticlotting effect in veins and arteries. A study described by Frank Murray in the

Benefits of Vitamin E

- Protects against heart disease.
- Maintains adequate pulmonary capacity.
- Helps prevent blood clots in the arteries and veins.
- Dissolves existing clots.
- Increases available oxygen in the blood.
- Increases the heart's efficiency by reducing its need for oxygen.
- Prevents undesirable, excessive scarring of the heart after a myocardial infarction, while simultaneously promoting a strong patch scar during the healing process.
- Facilitates circulation by dilating capillaries and developing collateral blood vessels.

August 1990 *Better Nutrition* showed that 1,476 patients with general arteriosclerosis (thickening of the lining of the arteries, which limits blood flow) who were given vitamin E for 10 years had a significantly higher survival rate than patients who had not taken this vitamin. Dr. Gnut Haeger, a prominent Swedish surgeon, has successfully used high doses of vitamin E to treat elderly patients with poor blood circulation in the legs, according to the same article.

Vitamin E and Chemotherapy. Patients receiving chemotherapy often develop ulcers in the mouth or other parts of the digestive tract. In a controlled trial of 18 cancer patients reported in *Alternative Medcine: What Works,* six out of nine patients receiving vitamin E oil experienced reversal of their ulcers within five days, compared to only one out of nine subjects receiving a placebo.

Vitamin E and Epilepsy. Preliminary evidence suggests that vitamin E may be helpful in preventing epileptic seizures. Using controlled dosages of vitamin E, doctors at the University of Toronto reduced the frequency of seizures by more than 60% in 10 of 12 children who took 400 IU daily for three months in addition to their regular medication. When children taking a placebo were switched to vitamin E, seizure frequency was reduced 70-100%. A 1989 report in *Epilepsia* states that no adverse side effects were noted. Because the results are based on only one study, however, additional research is needed to confirm whether vitamin E supplements can help reduce or prevent epileptic seizures.

Vitamin E and Ischemic Heart Disease (IHD). According to a 1991 World Health Organization (WHO) study, low blood levels of vitamin E are the most important risk factor in deaths from IHD. IHD is known to occur when blood circulation to the heart is inadequate, usually because of coronary artery damage, resulting in pains or spasms. While not conclusive, this study tentatively suggests that vitamin E may play a protective role against IHD.

The WHO study also showed that vitamin E blood levels were more significant in predicting death than high cholesterol, elevated blood pressure, or smoking. The study involved 40 men aged 40-49 from 16 European cities; some of the men were smokers. Low blood levels of vitamin E were linked with death in 62% of the cases. The highest death rate occurred when patients had a combination of low vitamin E, low vitamin A, high total cholesterol, and high blood pressure, as reported by J. de Keyser in the June 27, 1991, issue of *Lancet*.

Two major studies conducted by the Harvard School of Public Health, and reported in the November 19, 1992, *New York Times,* concluded that taking daily doses of vitamin E may cut the risk of heart disease by one-third to one-half. The studies lend further support to the theory that vitamins and other substances that retard oxidation are good for the heart. In the first study, 87,245 female nurses in the U.S. were surveyed, 17% of whom took vitamin E. After eight years of follow-up, the researchers found that nurses who had taken vitamin E for at least two years had a 46% lower risk of heart disease than those who did not take the supplement. The other study surveyed 51,529 male health professionals. A 37% lower risk of heart disease was reported among the men who took regular vitamin E supplements. Both studies concluded that the amount of vitamin E in vitamin-rich food such as lettuce was not sufficient to produce the benefit. That occurred only when people took at least 100 IU of vitamin E daily, the amount in a single vitamin supplement.

Vitamin E and Longevity. As discussed earlier, free radicals contribute to the gradual development of chronic diseases, such as hardening of the arteries, cancer, cataracts, Parkinson's disease, Alzheimer's disease, arthritis, and other complications of aging. Vitamin E is now believed to reduce the damage caused by free radicals and to help prevent or delay the onset of these diseases, thereby potentially increasing life span.

Langer's article in *Better Nutrition* also quotes Dr. Jeffrey Blumberg of the USDA Human Nutrition Research Center on Aging: "If we really want to increase our life span, we need to decrease our caloric intake, add vitamin E, vitamin C and betacarotene supplements to our diet, and pay closer attention to the protein, fatty-acid composition and trace mineral content of our diet. As to the ideal vitamin E intake, I would suggest 100, 200, or 300 mg. daily."

Blumberg adds: "Traditionally it was accepted that a decline in various body systems, such as heart, lung and immune functions, was a natural part of aging. But new evidence leads us to believe that the rate of decline may be governed more by environmental factors, that is, nutrition and lifestyle, than by aging per se. Age-related losses in lean body mass and bone, as well as increases in fat, may be slowed or even reversed, regardless of a person's age."

Murray also describes a study of the nutritional status of more than 1,000 volunteers by Dr. Judith Hallfrisch, principal investigator for the Gerontology Nutrition Study at the National Institute on Aging. Hallfrisch found that even those volunteers who ate healthy foods "had inadequate intakes of vitamins E and B_6, magnesium, zinc, iron and calcium." Along with adequate intake of vitamin E and other nutrients, Hallfrisch believes that healthy, low-stress lifestyles will eventually lead to longer lifespans. "For those committed to extending their life span and remaining in relatively good health," she concludes, "an adequate intake of such antioxidants as vitamin E, vitamin C, and betacarotene is essential."

Vitamin E supplements may also prevent the breakdown of the immune system in older people, thereby decreasing the likelihood of infectious disease and tumors. The antioxidant defense system remains strong in most people throughout youth and the middle years, but the body's ability to produce antibodies decreases with aging. Additional research is required to determine if people who take vitamin E supplements develop more antibodies.

Vitamin E and Ozone Protection. Vitamin E may also protect humans against the dangerous effects of ozone, which causes a stiffening and accelerated aging of lung tissue. In preliminary studies, vitamin E has been shown to protect humans against the effects of ozone in smog. According to the research, described by W. Pryor in the March 1991 *American Journal of Clinical Nutrition,* ozone interacts with polyunsaturated fatty acids to form free radicals, and vitamin E apparently delays this reaction.

Vitamin E and Parkinson's Disease.

Parkinson's disease is a progressive disease of the brain that results in tremor, joint rigidity, muscle weakness, and slow movement. As the disease progresses, higher brain functioning is disabled and motor control deteriorates. It is believed to be caused by the pathological destruction of specific cells in the basal ganglia of the brain, particularly in the substantia nigra. These cells are responsible for a particular neurotransmitter, dopamine, which in turn controls communication between cells.

Currently, patients with Parkinson's disease are treated with levodopa and other compounds related to dopamine. Unfortunately, levodopa has severe side effects and many physicians prescribe it only as a last resort. According to a report in the November 16, 1989, *New England Journal of Medicine,* one form of vitamin E, tocopherol, seems to postpone the disability of Parkinson's disease, thereby delaying the need for treatment with levodopa. Results are preliminary, however, and more research is needed to determine if tocopherol is effective as a long-term therapy.

Vitamin E and Rheumatoid Arthritis.

Patients with rheumatoid arthritis (RA) have derived significant relief from inflammatory pain when given fish oil rich in vitamin E. In one European study, described by Jacob E. Tulleken, Pieter C. Limberg, and Martin van Rijswijk in their 1990 book, *Arthritis and Rheumatism,* RA patients who received fish oil for three months suffered substantially less joint inflammation. The results suggest, however, that this effect may have been more related to fatty acid consumption than vitamin E intake, although vitamin E probably enhances the effects of the fish oil.

Summary

Vitamins, like minerals, herbs, and food supplements, are medicines, and people need to be aware of their effects and the minimum and maximum amounts recommended for optimal health. A balanced, natural diet of healthy foods normally provides an adequate supply of the daily recommended dose of vitamins. Not everyone, however, receives the RDA for each vitamin, and a number of diseases are associated with vitamin deficiencies. For this reason, people diagnosed with any of these diseases (or having symptoms associated with them), or who think their diet is not nutritionally adequate, should consult a physician to determine if vitamin supplements are advisable.

Resources

References

Block, Gladys. "Vitamin C and Cancer Prevention: The Epidemiological Evidence." *American Journal of Clinical Nutrition* (January 1991).

Bower, M. "Topical Vitamin D Analogs in Advanced Breast Cancer." *Cancer Weekly* (September 23, 1991): 20.

Cade, J. "Massive Thiamine Dosage in the Treatment of Acute Alcoholic Psychoses." *Australian-New Zealand Journal of Psychiatry* (February 1986).

"Calciportiol: Advice for the Patient." *Drug Information in Lay Language* (1990): 294.

"Can Vitamins Protect Your Arteries?" *Prevention* (October 1991): 33.

de Keyser, J. "Serum Concentrations of Vitamins A and E and Early Outcome after Ischaemic Stroke." *The Lancet* (June 27, 1991): 1562.

"Depressed Plasma Peridoxal Phosphate Concentration in Adult Asthmatics." *American Journal of Clinical Nutrition* (1985): 684-88.

"Effect of Deprenyl on the Progression of Disability in Early Parkinson's Disease." *New England Journal of Medicine* (November 16, 1989): 1364.

Epilepsia 30, no. 1 (1989).

Fackelmann, Kathy A. "Vitamin E May Safeguard Bypass Hearts." *Science News* (November 24, 1990): 333.

Fugh-Berman, Adriane. *Alternative Medicine: What Works.* Tucson, AZ: Odonian Press, 1996.

Garland, Frank, and Edward D. Gorham. "Can Colon Cancer Incidence and Death Rates be Reduced with Calcium and Vitamin D?" *American Journal of Clinical Nutrition* (July 1991): 193.

Guo, Wande, et al. "Correlations of Dietary Intake and Blood Nutrient Levels with Esophageal Cancer Mortality in China." *Nutrition and Cancer* (June 1984): 121-27.

Harvard Health Letter (January 1992).

Langer, S. "Vitamin E: The Anti-Clogging Antioxidant." *Better Nutrition* (September 1990).

May, L. *Drug Information.* St. Louis, MO: Mosby Year Book, Inc., 1993.

Murray, Frank. "Vitamin E May Delay Aging." *Better Nutrition* (August 1990).

——. "Vitamin A Fights Cancer." *Today's Living* (October 1992): 8.

Murray, Michael, and Joseph Pizzorno. *Encyclopedia of Natural Medicine.* Rocklin, CA: Prima Publishing, 1991.

New York Times (November 19, 1992): A10.

Newbold, H. *Meganutrients for Your Nerves.* New York: Peter H. Wyden, 1975.

Pauling, Linus. *Vitamin C and the Common Cold.* New York: W.H. Freeman and Co., 1971.

——. *How to Live Longer and Feel Better.* New York: W.H. Freeman and Co., 1986.

Pryor, W. "Can Vitamin E Protect Humans against the Pathological Effects of Ozone in Smog?" *American Journal of Clinical Nutrition* (March 1991): 702.

Reynold, E. "Folate Deficiency in Depressive Illness." *British Journal of Psychiatry* (March 1970): 121, 287-92.

Reynold, Robert D. "Vitamin B_6 Deficiency and Carcinogenesis," in *Essential Nutrients in Carcinogenesis.* New York: Plenum Press, 1986.

Riemersma, R.A., et al. "Risk of Angina Pectoris and Plasma Concentrations of Vitamins A, C, and E and Carotene." *The Lancet* (January 5, 1991): 337.

Rivard, C. "Folate Deficiency among Institutionalized Elderly, Public Health Impact." *Journal of American Geriatric Society* (1986): 211-14.

Soharno, D., et al. "Supplementation with Vitamin A and Iron for Nutritional Anaemia in Pregnant Women in West Java, Indonesia." *The Lancet* (November 27, 1993): 1325-28.

Tulleken, Jacob E., Pieter C. Limburg, and Martin van Rijswijk. *Arthritis and Rheumatism* (September 1990).

U.S. National Cancer Institute. *Cancer Weekly* (July 6, 1992): 12.

Vijayaraghavan, K. "Effect of Massive Dose Vitamin A on Morbidity and Mortality in

Indian Children." *The Lancet* (December 1, 1990): 1342-43.

"Vitamin A Strengthens Pregnancy." *Associated Press* (November 26, 1993).

"Vitamin C: A Secret to a Long Life and a Healthy Heart." *Environmental Nutrition* (July 1992): 3.

"Vitamin E Prevents Oral Cancers." *Cancer Weekly* (July 6, 1992): 12.

"Vitamin Levels in Alzheimer's Disease." *Nutrition Research Newsletter* (June 1992): 77.

"Vitamins and Minerals." *Nutrition Research Newsletter* (June 1992): 77.

Whitehead, N., F. Reyner, and J. Lindebaum. "Megaloblastic Changes in the Cervical Epithelium Association with Oral Contraceptive Therapy and Reversal with Folic Acid." *Journal of the American Medical Association* (1973): 226.

Zimmerman, David. *Zimmerman's Complete Guide to Nonprescription Drugs.* Detroit: Gale Research, 1993.

Additional Reading

Chopra, Deepak. *Quantum Healing: Exploring the Frontiers of Body, Mind, Medicine.* New York: Bantam Books, 1993.

Davidson, Michael. "Vitamin E and Cardiovascular Disease." *Vitamin E Symposium* (June 1990).

Gannon, Kathi. "The Role of Free Radicals in the Aging Process." *Drug Topics* (February 18, 1991).

Hallfrisch, Judith. "Nutrition Components of the Baltimore Longitudinal Study in the Aging Process." *Harvard Health Letter* (January 1992).

Kutsky, Roman J. *Handbook of Vitamins, Minerals and Hormones.* New York: Van Nostrand Reinhold Co., 1973.

London, R.S., et al. "Vitamin E: Healing for PMS." *Journal of the American College of Nutrition* (February 1983).

Muller, D.P.R., et al. "Vitamin E in Brains of Patients with Alzheimer's Disease and Downs Syndrome." *The Lancet* (May 10, 1986).

Riggs, Maribeth. *Natural Child Care: A Complete Guide to Safe & Effective Herbal Remedies & Holistic Health Strategies for Infants & Children.* New York: Crown Publishing Group, 1992.

Siegel, Bernie. *Love, Medicine & Miracles.* New York: Harper & Row Publishers, Inc., 1986.

——. *Peace, Love & Healing.* New York: Harper & Row Publishers, Inc., 1989.

Sokol, Ronald J. "Improved Neurologic Function after Long-Term Correction of Vitamin E Deficiency in Children with Chronic Cholestiasis." *New England Journal of Medicine* (December 19, 1985).

Sommera, Tarwotjo, G. Hussaini, and D. Susanto. "Increased Mortality in Children with Mild Vitamin A Deficiency." *The Lancet* (1983): 585-88.

Tbac, Deborah. *Everyday Health Tips: 2000 Practical Hints for Better Health and Happiness.* Emmaus, PA: Rodale Press, 1988.

"Vitamin A and Malnutrition/Infection Complex in Developing Countries." *The Lancet* (December 1, 1990): 139.

RESOURCES

Chapter 4

MINERALS AND TRACE ELEMENTS

Minerals and trace elements are essential parts of enzymes involved in many of the body's biochemical and physiological processes, including the transportation of oxygen to the cells. If the human body requires more than 100 milligrams of the element daily, the substance is labeled a mineral. If less than 100 milligrams are needed each day, the substance is termed a trace element.

Unlike most vitamins, minerals are inorganic substances that usually are not destroyed by cooking, food processing, or exposure to air or acid. However, they sometimes combine with other substances in food to form insoluble salts that cannot be absorbed by the human digestive tract. The body utilizes at least 84 minerals and trace elements. If there is a deficiency or an absorption interference for any one of the 84, malfunctions may result in the part of the body that depends on that mineral.

Most minerals and trace elements are widely available in foods, especially fresh fruits and vegetables, and severe deficiencies are unusual. However, as noted below, iron deficiency occurs frequently in infants, children, and pregnant women. Zinc and copper deficiencies are also common among the elderly.

In the following sections, each essential mineral and trace element is discussed, including its chemical composition, physiological functions, availability in natural foods or supplements, and current Recommended Daily Allowance (RDA), as issued by the Food and Nutrition Board of the National Academy of Sciences. The RDA for minerals and trace elements, as in the case with vitamins, represents the best current assessment of safe and adequate intakes.

Recommended Daily Allowance (RDA) for Calcium

	mg
Infants (0-1 year)	500
Children (1-10 years)	800
Males (11-24 years)	1,200
Males (25-51+ years)	800
Females (11-24 years)	1,200
Females (25-51+ years)	800
Pregnant Females	1,200
Breastfeeding Mothers	1,200

Symptoms of deficiencies and excessive intake also are described. Mineral supplements should be used only with the approval of a physician or health practitioner. Like vitamins, some minerals in excessive doses are known to cause side effects, adverse interactions with other drugs, and other problems.

Minerals

Calcium

Calcium, the major constituent of the structural framework of bones, is the body's most prevalent mineral. Approximately three pounds of a 160-pound man's weight are calcium. For both men and women, 98% of the body's calcium is found in the bones, 1% in the teeth, and the remaining 1% in soft body tissues, where it performs a variety of essential functions.

In addition to supporting the growth and continued strength of bones and teeth, calci-um helps maintain cell membranes and the "cement" that holds cells together. It is essential to proper blood clotting, and it assists in regulating the transport of ions in and out of cells, thus making muscular contractions and relaxation possible.

The bones act as a calcium deposit for the rest of the body. Although they are commonly thought of as fixed, solid objects, bones continually lose and regain calcium. A network of hormones keeps the calcium level in blood and other bodily fluids at a constant level, depositing temporary excesses in the bones and removing calcium from the bones if it is needed elsewhere.

The richest food sources of calcium are milk and dairy products, including yogurt and hard cheeses. Canned sardines and salmon, caviar, almonds and Brazilian nuts, molasses, shrimp, soybeans, tofu, and green, leafy vegetables (particularly collard and dandelion greens and spinach) also are good sources, but oxalic acid in spinach renders much of the vegetable's calcium insoluble and nonabsorbable.

A persistent calcium shortage leads to distorted bone growth in children and a softening and deterioration of bones in adults. Osteoporosis, a weakening of the bones, affects one in four women after menopause. An inadequate calcium supply occurs when too little is consumed, too much is lost, or not enough is absorbed. At the other extreme, an excess of calcium in the body has been shown to depress nerve function, cause drowsiness and extreme lethargy, and decrease iron levels.

A vitamin D deficiency interferes with the absorption of calcium through the intestinal tract. Calcium absorption is also impaired by excessive dietary fat and continued use of corticosteroids, the synthetic equivalent of hormones made in the adrenal gland. Patients with irritable bowel syndrome (IBS), for example, have been shown to be at risk of developing calcium deficiency due to malabsorption, cortisoid use, and vitamin D deficiency. As a result, IBS patients are at risk for metabolic bone diseases.

Lack of dietary calcium in adults can result in a condition known as osteomalacia, or softening of the bone. In contrast, those suffering from osteoporosis have a deficiency of both calcium and other minerals, as well as a decrease in the nonmineral framework (organic matrix) of bone. Taking calcium supplements has proved effective in reducing age-related bone loss. Currently, calcium citrate appears to be the best form of calcium supplement, both in terms of better absorption and decreased risk of developing kidney stones.

Calcium deficiencies also may be indirectly related to hypertension. Several studies show that people with hypertension consume a smaller amount of daily calcium than nonhypertensive people, and may benefit from calcium supplementation. Clinical studies have demonstrated that calcium supplementation may also lower blood pressure. According to Dr. Leon Chaitow in *The Mind/Body Purification Program,* people living in areas with a soft-water supply (water with increased lead levels) are at risk for hypertension, and this may be partly due to the fact that soft water is normally low in calcium and magnesium. Coffee, alcohol, and smoking reduce calcium levels in the body and are associated with an increased risk of developing osteoporosis.

Along with other nutrients, calcium has been used with moderate success to reduce the risk of angina and heart disease. It also is routinely prescribed by naturopaths for mild allergies. In addition, calcium has been used to reduce cholesterol. In one study, reported in the *Encyclopedia of Natural Medicine,* a daily administration of two grams of calcium carbonate (800 milligrams of elemental calcium) resulted in a 25% decrease in serum cholesterol in men with high cholesterol levels, over a period of one year.

Chloride

Chloride, which enters the body primarily through table salt, is a constituent of acid in the stomach (hydrochloric acid). It interacts with sodium, potassium, and carbon dioxide to maintain an acid-base balance in body cells and fluids and is vital for normal health.

Most people consume more than adequate amounts of chloride in salt substitutes (potassium chloride), sea salt, and table salt (sodium chloride). Only people on a severely salt-restricted diet need to be concerned about how much chloride they consume, and should consider using potassium chloride as a salt substitute. As noted, excessive consumption of dietary sodium chloride in ordinary table salt, coupled with diminished dietary potassium, may increase the risk of hypertension.

Magnesium

Magnesium catalyzes hundreds of metabolic reactions in the body's soft tissues. It plays an essential role in the release of energy from glycogen (stored muscle fuel), the manufacture of proteins, the regulation of body temperature, and the proper functioning of nerves and muscles. Its specific physiological function is to aid bone growth and the proper functioning of nerves and muscles, including regulation of a normal heart rhythm. It also strengthens tooth enamel, keeps metabolism steady, and, in larger doses, works as a laxative.

Good sources of magnesium include nuts (particularly almonds and cashews), fish, molasses, soybeans, sunflower seeds, wheat germ, and green, leafy vegetables.

Magnesium deficiency has been linked to several forms of mental illness. In a February 1992 article in *Prevention Magazine,* Mark

Recommended Daily Allowance (RDA) for Magnesium

	mg
Infants (0-1 year)	500
Children (1-10 years)	120
Males (11-24 years)	350
Males (25-51+ years)	350
Females (11-24 years)	290
Females (25-51+ years)	280
Pregnant Females	320
Breastfeeding Mothers	345

Bricklin reported that doctors at the Albert Einstein College of Medicine had found that patients who displayed symptoms of depression, agitation, and hallucinations were deficient in magnesium. A follow-up study revealed that antipsychotic medications often decrease magnesium levels in patients. It is now believed that some patients who do not respond well to medication show mental symptoms that may be caused partly by low magnesium levels. Replication studies will be necessary to confirm if magnesium supplements can improve mental functioning, and, in severe cases, help treat schizophrenia and depression.

Magnesium supplementation also may help people with osteoporosis, who typically have lower magnesium levels than people without this condition. Magnesium deficiency is cross-linked with high intakes of dairy foods fortified with vitamin D. People with osteoporosis may therefore require higher levels of magnesium, as well as calcium supplements that are not derived from dairy products.

Magnesium deficiency has been linked to premenstrual syndrome (PMS). Red blood cell magnesium levels in women with PMS have been shown to be significantly lower than in women who do not have PMS. In one clinical trial, magnesium supplements given to PMS patients resulted in a reduction of nervousness (in 89%), of breast tenderness (96%), and of weight gain (95%), according to R.S. London in the October 1991 issue of the *Journal of the American College of Nutrition.*

A magnesium deficiency is common in alcoholics, due primarily to alcohol-induced loss of this mineral through the kidneys, a process that continues during alcohol withdrawal.

Magnesium deficiency may play a major role in some cases of angina. It has been observed that men dying suddenly of heart attacks have significantly lower levels of magnesium, as well as potassium, than matched controls. Magnesium supplements have proven helpful in the management of irregular heartbeats, and several studies suggest that it could be a partial treatment for angina caused by coronary artery spasm, according to a report by P. Turlapaty in the March 1980 issue of *Science.*

Dr. Dean Ornish's Program for Reversing Heart Disease reports a study involving 930 patients who showed substantial benefits in taking magnesium to treat acute heart attacks. The magnesium-treated group showed 49% fewer serious arrhythmias, 58% fewer cardiac arrests, and 54% fewer deaths than the control group. As this study suggests magnesium given after a heart attack helps people live longer. In a later, larger study of 2,316 subjects, who had suffered suspected heart attacks four weeks prior, there were 24% fewer deaths among those who had been given magnesium. A long-term follow-up of the same group found that the mortality rate of magnesium-treated subjects was reduced by 16%, and the reduction for ischemic (oxygen-deprived) heart disease was 21%.

Ornish also states that magnesium helps to lower high blood pressure, especially in patients who are magnesium-deficient. Magnesium may also help prevent migraine headaches, particularly those associated with the menstrual cycle. In a study of 20 women, those who took magnesium found a significant reduction in headaches and other premenstrual complaints.

Magnesium is also beneficial in treating patients experiencing acute attacks of bronchial asthma. One clinical study, reported by E. Brunner in the September 1985 *Journal of Asthma,* confirmed that magnesium significantly improves breathing in asthmatics. The degree of improvement directly correlates with serum magnesium levels.

Magnesium deficiency is prevalent in patients with irritable bowel syndrome. Patients with low magnesium levels often have symptoms of muscle weakness, anorexia, low blood pressure, confusion, and hyper-irritability. Magnesium levels are significantly lower in diabetics, and magnesium supplements are commonly used in treatment, according to A. Careiello in *Diabetes Care,* published in 1982.

Phosphorus

Phosphorus acts with calcium as a partner in bone and teeth formation and is found in every cell of the body as a component of nucleic acids. It is vital for the metabolism of carbohydrates and the functioning of several B vitamins, and is used to transport fats throughout the body.

Good sources of phosphorous include meat, fish, poultry, milk, nuts, legumes, and whole-grain cereals and breads. Most people take in more than enough phosphorus from the large amount of meat they eat and from

Recommended Daily Allowance (RDA) for Phosphorus	
	mg
Infants (0-1 year)	400
Children (1-10 years)	800
Males (11-24 years)	1,200
Males (25-51+ years)	800
Females (11-24 years)	1,200
Females (25-51+ years)	800
Pregnant Females	1,200
Breastfeeding Mothers	1,200

phosphorus salts used in processed foods. Prolonged use of antacids can lead to a harmful loss of phosphorus, and frequent consumption of carbonated drinks (which contain phosphorus) can distort the crucial ratio of calcium and phosphorus. If a diet contains too much phosphorus, calcium is not utilized efficiently.

A low-calcium, high-phosphorus diet has been linked with the development of osteoporosis, a condition in which the bones lose mass and become brittle. In contrast, vegetarian diets are associated with a lower risk of osteoporosis, although bone mass in vegetarians does decrease in the fourth and fifth decades. Several factors probably account for this slower decrease in bone mass. Most important is a lowered intake of protein and phosphorus. A high-protein diet or a diet high in phosphates is associated with increasing the excretion of calcium in the urine.

Potassium

Potassium is important for the proper

functioning of muscles, including the heart. Potassium is a crucial regulator of the amount of water in cells, which determines their ability to function properly. It helps in the transmission of nerve impulses, is a buffer for body fluids, and catalyzes the release of energy from carbohydrates, proteins, and fats. Potassium also may help prevent high blood pressure.

Natural sources include avocados, bananas, citrus fruits, dried fruits, lentils, milk, molasses, nuts, parsnips, potatoes, raisins, canned sardines, fresh spinach, and whole-grain cereals. No Recommended Daily Allowance for potassium has been established. However, too much sodium in the diet can compromise the body's supply of potassium, and potassium deficiencies can occur following severe diarrhea and the use of diuretics.

Symptoms of potassium deficiency include weakness, paralysis, low blood pressure, and irregular or rapid heartbeat that can lead to cardiac arrest and death.

People with low levels of potassium may be susceptible to high blood pressure. Dr. Gopal Kirshna of Temple University found that putting male patients on a potassium-deficient diet for only nine days led to significant increases in blood pressure. Similar experiments in Japan have confirmed Kirshna's findings. High blood pressure is even more common in Japan because of the culture's typically high sodium diet. According to Kirshna, quoted in Bricklin's article in the February 1992 issue of *Prevention Magazine,* Americans should consume at least three grams of potassium every day. "And there is some experimental evidence that taking more would be better. The best thing to do is to incorporate potassium-rich foods into the diet. The ideal way is to choose sources that do not give you too many calories, or too much fat or cholesterol. The most desirable sources are fruits and vegetables."

The loss of potassium ions through stress may contribute to fatigue and exhaustion. When the body's cells lose potassium, they function less effectively and eventually die. The effects of stress also can be reduced by maintaining and supplementing potassium levels. Exercise and relaxation techniques such as meditation, biofeedback, and self-hypnosis are probably more important components of a stress management program, however.

Sodium

Sodium is present in all the cells of the body. Its most important function is to regulate the balance of water inside and outside the cells. Sodium also plays a crucial role in maintaining blood pressure, aids muscle contraction and nerve transmission, and regulates the body's acid-base balance.

Natural sources of sodium include bacon and ham, beef, milk, margarine and butter, bread, clams, green beans, and canned sardines and tomatoes. Most people consume sodium as sodium chloride in ordinary table salt.

No RDA for sodium has been established, although nutritionists suggest that 3,000 milligrams is adequate for normal body function. Sodium deficiencies occur almost entirely in people ill with dehydration, patients recovering from surgery, or persons experiencing excessive sweating due to overexercising in a hot climate. Symptoms of a sodium deficiency include muscle and stomach cramps, nausea, fatigue, mental apathy, and appetite loss.

A typical American diet contains 3,000 to 12,000 milligrams of sodium a day. People who consume more than 3,000 milligrams of sodium run the risk of high blood pressure and hypertension. Excessive intake of sodium chloride (salt), coupled with diminished dietary potassium, has been shown to increase blood fluid volume and result in hypertension in susceptible individuals. Conversely, a low-sodium, high-potassium diet reduces the rise in blood pressure during periods of mental stress by reducing the blood-vessel constricting effect of adrenaline. However, sodium restriction alone does not improve blood pressure control; there must be a high intake of potassium as well, writes F. Skrabal in the October 1981 issue of *The Lancet*.

Sulfur

Sulfur is important because it binds protein molecules, and therefore is a crucial constituent of proteins in hair, fingernails, toenails, and skin. It also plays a role in oxidation-reduction reactions and aids the secretion of bile in the liver. No recommended daily dietary amount has been established, and deficiencies in humans are unknown since sulfur is widespread in protein foods. The best natural sources include cabbage, clams, dried beans, eggs, fish, lean beef, milk, and wheat germ.

Trace Elements

Chromium

Chromium is necessary to maintain normal metabolism of glucose (blood sugar) and may be important in preventing diabetes. A small amount of chromium helps insulin regulate blood sugar and improves glucose tolerance of some people with maturity-onset diabetes.

Only a small amount of dietary chromium is absorbed by the body. Beef, fish, dairy products, whole-grain products, fresh fruits, chicken, potatoes, oysters, and brewer's yeast are good sources of chromium. Some

Americans, particularly the elderly, pregnant women, and malnourished people, are often chromium deficient.

No RDA for chromium has been established, although 0.05-0.20 milligrams has been established as a safe amount to take daily. A basic high-quality multivitamin and mineral supplement high in B-complex vitamins normally contains the daily requirement for chromium.

Chromium and Disease Prevention. Chromium is believed to prevent some forms of dental cavities and may help protect against cancer of the esophagus. Chromium chloride supplementation (200 milligrams per day) results in a decrease in serum triglycerides and total cholesterol, while increasing HDL levels and improving glucose tolerance.

Cobalt

Cobalt, a trace element stored primarily in the liver, is necessary to manufacture vitamin B_{12} in the body. It helps promote normal red blood cell formation and acts as a substitute for manganese in the activation of several enzymes. It also replaces zinc in some enzymes.

Natural sources of cobalt include beet greens, cabbage, clams, figs, kidney, lettuce, liver, milk, oysters, spinach, and watercress.

Cobalt deficiencies can lead to anemia, with symptoms including weakness (especially of the arms and legs), a sore tongue, nausea and appetite loss, bleeding gums, numbness and tingling in the hands and feet, difficulty maintaining balance, shortness of breath, depression, headache, and poor memory.

Excessively toxic amounts of cobalt can cause goiter (by blocking iodine intake) and a red blood cell disorder called polycythemia.

No RDA has been established for cobalt, but deficiencies of this trace element are extremely rare.

Copper

Copper is an essential component of several respiratory enzymes and is needed for the development of normal red blood cells. It acts as a catalyst in the storage and release of iron to form hemoglobin for red blood cells and promotes connective tissue formation and central nervous system function. It is normally used as a nutritional supplement for anyone who is undergoing prolonged intravenous feeding.

The richest dietary sources of copper include barley, nuts, honey, lentils, mushrooms, mussels, oats, oysters, salmon, and wheat germ. No daily requirement for copper has been established, but most diets exceed needed amounts. Copper deficiencies contribute to health problems such as anemia; faulty development of bone and nervous tissue; loss of elasticity in the tendons and major arteries, possibly causing rupture of the blood vessels; abnormal development of the lung's air sacs, possibly predisposing people to emphysema; and abnormal pigmentation and structure of the hair. There is preliminary evidence that a copper deficiency may eventually lead to senility.

A deficiency of copper has been linked to marked elevation of cholesterol levels, and it has been suggested that the deficiency plays a role in the development of arteriosclerosis. Copper supplements may be helpful for patients with rohn's disease, an inflammatory disease of the small intestine. In studies reported by C.O. Morain in the 1984 *British Medical Journal,* patients with Crohn's disease have been found to display one or more nutrient deficiencies, including copper, vitamin K, niacin, and vitamin E.

Adult psychotic patients have an excess of copper that may produce a schizophrenic syndrome or depression. Copper excess is also connected to learning and behavior disorders in children.

High copper levels appear to have the same toxic effects as other heavy metals such as cadmium, lead, and manganese. Several studies have associated high copper levels with learning disabilities in children. High levels of copper also have been directly associated with periodontal (gum) disease.

Fluoride

Small amounts of fluoride, starting before birth and continuing throughout life, are essential for the development and maintenance of strong, decay-resistant teeth. Fluoride contributes to solid bone and tooth formation by helping the body retain calcium. In addition, it interferes with the growth of bacteria that cause dental plaque.

Food sources of fluoride include tea, apples, cod, eggs, kidneys, canned salmon and sardines, and plants grown in areas where fluoride is present in the water. There is no reliable evidence to support contentions that water fluoridation causes or contributes to cancer. However, in high doses, fluoride is just as toxic as the other trace elements and may cause mottling of the teeth.

No RDA for fluoride has been established, and most humans consume adequate amounts in their daily diet.

Fluoride and Osteoporosis. Fluoride may help prevent bone loss in the elderly and the debilitating fractures which often accompany it. There is also some evidence that fluoride, along with calcium and vitamin D, helps in treating osteoporosis, according to H. Winter Griffiths in the 1988 book, *Vitamins.* However, its use should be carefully monitored by a physician.

Germanium

Organic germaniumis naturally found in sea algae, aloe vera, Siberian ginseng, garlic, and comfrey. Its properties have been extensively analyzed in Japan. In *Miracle Cure: Organic Germanium,* Dr. Kazuhiko Asai reports that organically bound germanium acts as a biological transmitter between the brain and the nervous system. Clinical case studies in Japan, where the use of germanium is widespread, have shown it to be effective in the controlled reversal of chronic allergies, hepatitis, cancer, leukemia, cataracts, and cardiovascular disorders, according to R. Ornstein's publication, *The Human Ecology Program.*

Germanium also has been used successfully to treat numerous ailments ranging from headaches to allergies. The compound is considered an "immunostimulant," a substance that activates the body's defense system. A number of animal experiments conducted by Asai strongly indicate that Ge-132 (one form of germanium) inhibits tumors in a variety of cancers in mice.

Iodine

Iodine is an integral component of two important thyroid hormones (thyroxinand tri-iodothyronine) that regulate metabolism. It is essential for normal reproduction and cell functioning. Iodine keeps skin, hair, and nails healthy, and prevents goiter.

Seafoods, including cod, herring, lobsters, oysters, canned salmon, seaweed, and shrimp, are nature's richest sources of iodine. However, the majority of iodine is derived from the use of iodized salt (70 micrograms of iodine per gram of salt). Except for seafood and seaweed, most foods contain extremely small amounts of iodine. Some foods contain substances that prevent the utilization of iodine, such as turnips, cabbage, mustard, cassava root, soybeans, peanuts, pine nuts, and millet.

Foods high in iodine should be eliminated from the diets of those who are iodine-sensitive. At one time, it was necessary to add

Benefits of Germanium

- Increases the production of gammainterferon, a potent antiviral, anticancer agent.
- Dramatically increases the oxygen capacity of the blood.
- Helps reverse chronic allergies, hepatitis, leukemia, cataracts, and cardiovascular disorders.

iodine to salt to help prevent goiter in certain parts of the U.S. where little seafood was consumed and the soil was iodine-deficient. However, because iodine is now in many processed foods, most Americans receive the minimum RDA.

Iodine deficiency leads to a shortage of thyroid hormones and goiter (an enlargement of the thyroid gland). If this deficiency occurs before or shortly after birth, it may result in cretinism, or retarded growth.

Recommended Daily Allowance (RDA) for Iodine

	mg
Infants (0-1 year)	45
Children (1-10 years)	80
Males (11-24 years)	150
Males (25-51+ years)	150
Females (11-24 years)	150
Females (25-51+ years)	150
Pregnant Females	175
Breastfeeding Mothers	200

Recommended Daily Allowance (RDA) for Iron

	mg
Infants (0-1 year)	8
Children (1-10 years)	10
Males (11-24 years)	12
Males (25-51+ years)	10
Females (11-24 years)	15
Females (25-51+ years)	15
Pregnant Females	30
Breastfeeding Mothers	15

Hypothyroidism and/or iodine deficiency are associated with a higher incidence of breast cancer. Research has shown that thyroid supplementation decreases breast pain, serum prolactin levels, and breast nodules in thyroid patients. These results suggest that unrecognized hypothyroidism and/or iodine deficiency may be a factor in fibrocystic breast disease (FBD). Iodine may be very important in the treatment and prevention of FBD because it has significant anti-inflammatory and antiscarring effects.

According to *Alternative Medicine: What Works* molecular iodine appears to be the most effective since other types have various side effects. One study compared 23 subjects receiving molecular iodine with 33 subjects receiving placebo. In the treatment group, 65% had subjective and objective improvement, while in the control group only 33% had subjective but not objective improvement.

Iron

Iron is an essential ingredient in all cells, particularly the oxygen-carrying cells of the blood and muscles, which use two-thirds of the iron requirement. Without iron, hemoglobin (the oxygen transport pigment of red blood cells) and myoglobin (the hemoglobin of muscle cells) cannot be formed, nor can certain vital enzymes.

Iron found in animal foods such as beef, liver, fish, and poultry is more readily absorbed than that found in milk, eggs, cheese, or vegetables such as spinach. Eating foods containing iron along with foods rich in vitamin C, such as citrus fruits, tomatoes, or green peppers, can enhance iron absorption. Several foods and beverages contain substances that inhibit iron absorption, including tea, coffee, wheat bran, and egg yolks. Overuse of antacids and calcium supplements also decreases iron absorption. These items should be restricted in the diets of individuals with iron deficiencies.

Iron deficiency, or anemia, can produce such symptoms as fatigue, listlessness, irritability, pallor, and shortness of breath, which reflect a lack of oxygen being delivered to tissues and a build-up of carbon dioxide. The problem most commonly occurs in infants, young children, adolescents, and women of child-bearing age, some of whom may need to take iron supplements.

Iron supplements are routinely given to pregnant and nursing women. However, they should not be taken without a physician's recommendation based on one or more blood tests. Since iron is stored in the body and lost only through bleeding, it is possible to accumulate an excess of iron that can damage the liver, pancreas, and heart.

A 1986 study by the U.S. Department of Agriculture (USDA) has found that women who have below-normal iron supplies may start feeling cold before they experience tiredness, the usual side effect of iron-deficiency anemia. The USDA study concluded that all women of child-bearing age (roughly ages 19-50) have iron intakes of only 61% of the

Recommended Daily Allowance. Additionally, E. Pollitt, in the April 1976 *Journal of Pediatrics,* noted that iron deficiency is the second most common nutritional problem for all Americans after obesity.

Iron and Risk of Chronic Disease. According to National Institute of Health studies reviewed by Fugh-Berman, there is evidence that high iron levels can contribute to some chronic diseases. Some people have difficulty metabolizing iron (a condition called hemochromatosis), which can be dangerous in normal adult men. Using data from the extensive National Health and Nutrition Examination Survey, researchers found that large stores of iron in the body increased men's risk of cancer, although the connection was not as clear in women.

Another study found that men with high iron levels had a higher risk of colonic adenomas, which increase their risk of colon cancer. Several preliminary studies have also linked excessive iron to an increased risk of cardiovascular disease, although more conclusive research is needed in this area. So far it has been assumed that iron supplementation–common in children's foods–is beneficial. Nevertheless, one study of 47 healthy children found that those receiving iron gained weight more slowly than those given placebo. The researchers noted, however, that iron excesses can easily be reduced by exercising or giving blood.

Iron and Detoxification. Iron supplements are included in most detoxification diets. This is because iron, along with many other nutrients, helps combat heavy metal poisoning. Normally a high potency, multivitamin supplement is recommended, along with minerals such as iron, calcium, magnesium, zinc, copper, and chromium. Iron deficiency can contribute to immune dysfunction, due to the body's diminished ability to produce T-cells that fight off infection.

Iron is an important nutrient for bacteria as well as humans. During infection, one of the body's defense mechanisms to limit bacterial growth is to reduce plasma iron. There is much scientific evidence to support the conclusion that iron supplementation is not recommended during acute infection, especially for young children. However, in patients with impaired immune function, chronic infections, and low iron levels, adequate supplementation is essential.

Iron and Learning Disabilities. Virtually any nutrient deficiency can result in impaired brain function, and insufficient iron is the nutrient deficiency found most often in American children. Iron deficiency is associated with markedly decreased attentiveness, shorter attention span, decreased persistence, and decreased voluntary activity–all of which are usually responsive to iron supplementation, according to D. Wray, writing in the May 1975 *British Medical Journal.*

Iron and Mouth Ulcers. A study of 330 patients with recurrent mouth ulcers found that 47 (14.2%) were deficient in iron, along with folic acid or vitamin B_{12}. A. Hoffer states in *Orthomolecular Nutrition* that these deficiencies were corrected by iron and vitamin B supplementation, and the majority experienced complete remission.

Lithium

Lithium has no known role in the body's internal metabolism. Lithium ointment, however, is used topically to treat certain types of herpes (such as herpes zoster), as reported by G. Skinner in *Medicine, Microbiology and Immunology,* published in 1980.

Large doses of lithium (approximately 1,000 milligrams per day) has also been successfully used to treat manic-depressive psychosis. Physicians regularly use up to 300 milligrams of lithium per day to increase energy levels, diminish fatigue, eliminate depression, and alter mood changes associated with multiple food allergies, according to Skinner.

Manganese

Manganese is concentrated in cells of the pituitary gland, liver, pancreas, kidney, and bones. It stimulates production of cholesterol by the liver and helps many body enzymes generate energy. It is essential for blood clotting, bone formation, development of other connective tissues, cholesterol synthesis, and the metabolism of proteins, fats, carbohydrates, and nucleic acids.

Good natural sources of manganese include avocados, barley, dried beans, blackberries, bran, buckwheat, nuts, coffee, ginger, oatmeal, peas, seaweed, and spinach. Symptoms of manganese deficiency include difficulty in walking, blurred speech, tremors of the hands, and involuntary laughing.

Manganese functions in the antioxidant enzyme superoxide dismutase (manganese SOD), which is deficient in patients with rheumatoid arthritis (RA). Manganese supplementation has been shown to increase SOD activity (increased antioxidant activity).

Manganese and Disease Prevention.
Manganese may be useful in treating diabetes because of its important co-factor role in glucose metabolism. Diabetics tend to have only half the manganese found in normal individuals. Low magnesium levels also appear to be a significant risk factor in the development of cardiovascular disease, particularly coronary artery spasm. Magnesium supplementation may be warranted for these diseases, according to A. Mooradian in the October 1987 *American Journal of Clinical Nutrition.*

Manganese and Epilepsy.
Hoffer, who studied the role manganese may play in epileptic seizures, found that one group of people with epilepsy had abnormally low manganese blood levels. Certain substances in the diet, including magnesium, calcium, and iron, may prevent manganese from being absorbed properly. Women with PMS, for example, also have low manganese levels (77% less than normal), and manganese supplements may provide temporary relief.

Molybdenum

Molybdenum forms part of the enzyme system responsible for the development of bones, liver, and kidneys. It helps convert nucleic acid to uric acid, a waste product eliminated in the urine.

Natural sources of molybdenum include beans; cereal grains; dark green, leafy vegetables; organ meats (liver, kidney, sweetbreads); peas and other legumes. It should be noted that dietary concentration of molybdenum may vary according to the status of the soil in which grains and vegetables are grown.

No RDA for molybdenum has been established. A balanced natural diet of unprocessed foods provides all the molybdenum necessary for a healthy child or adult. However, most American diets are thought to be deficient in molybdenum as they are in chromium because modern food processing tends to remove this mineral nutrient from the average diet.

Selenium

Selenium is a trace element that even in small amounts enhances the immune system by helping to prevent free radical formation. It acts synergistically with vitamin E and possibly with vitamin A.

Dietary sources of selenium include seafood, chicken, egg yolks, milk, garlic, wheat germ and whole-grain products, and vegetables such as broccoli, cabbage, celery, cucumbers, mushrooms, and onions.

In *Selenium in Biology and Medicine,* published in 1991, Larry Clark reports that researchers suggest that large doses of selenium are safe and may prove effective in cancer prevention. For example, researchers in Finland found that people whose diets are low in selenium increase their risk of developing cancer, especially of the stomach and lungs. This conclusion was based on blood samples from nearly 40,000 people whose health had been tracked for 10 years.

Even the best planned diets may be selenium deficient, depending partially on where the food is grown. In China, selenium is virtually absent in the soil, and, as a result, children commonly suffer from a heart condition called Kershan's disease. In the early 1970s, Chinese physicians studied more than 36,000 children whose diets were supplemented with selenium. Of these, only 21 developed Kershan's disease. Among 9,642 other children from the same area who did not receive any selenium supplement, 107 contracted the disease and 53 died, according to an article by J. Mitchell in the July/August 1991 issue of *Health News & Review.*

Selenium and Disease Prevention. Selenium is currently prescribed to treat *Candida albicans* (yeast infection). It may help treat cataracts, several forms of skin cancer, and cervical dysplasia. Because food allergies have been associated with immune system dysfunction, selenium–along with zinc, B-complex vitamins, and thymus extract–has been prescribed to treat specific allergies. Selenium functions synergistically with vitamin E in the treatment of gout. It has been used (200 micrograms a day along with cod liver oil and vitamin E) to treat multiple sclerosis, reports J. Wikstrom in *Acta Nerulogie Scandinavia,* published in 1976.

Recommended Daily Allowance (RDA) for Selenium

	mg
Infants (0-1 year)	15
Children (1-10 years)	25
Males (11-24 years)	60
Males (25-51+ years)	70
Females (11-24 years)	50
Females (25-51+ years)	55
Pregnant Females	65
Breastfeeding Mothers	75

The antioxidant activities of selenium and vitamin E also deter periodontal disease (as free radicals are extremely damaging to the gums), as well as psoriasis.

Serum selenium levels are low in patients with rheumatoid arthritis (RA), probably because selenium serves as a mineral co-factor in the free radical scavenging enzyme glutathione peroxidase, the enzyme important in reducing the production of inflammatory prostaglandins and leukotrines. Free radicals, oxidants, prostaglandins, and leukotrines cause much of the damage to tissues observed in RA. Clinical studies have not yet clearly demonstrated that selenium supplementation alone improves the signs and symptoms of RA; however, one clinical study indicated that selenium combined with vitamin E had a positive effect, according to an article by U. Tarp in the September 1985 *Scandinavian Journal of Rheumatology.*

Selenium and Heart Disease. Selenium appears to have an effect on cardiovascular disease. One Danish study cited in *Alternative*

Benefits of Selenium

- Protects against the toxic effects of the heavy metal poison cadmium, predominantly found in cigarette paper and paint.
- Protects against high mercury content taken into the body through seafood and other sources.
- Increases the effectiveness of vitamin E, thus improving the oxygen-carrying capacity of the blood.
- Prevents chromosomal damage that causes birth defects and cancer.
- Reduces the risk of stomach and lung cancer and heart disease.

Recommended Daily Allowance (RDA) for Zinc

	mg
Infants (0-1 year)	5
Children (1-10 years)	10
Males (11-24 years)	15
Males (25-51+ years)	15
Females (11-24 years)	12
Females (25-51+ years)	12
Pregnant Females	15
Breastfeeding Mothers	17

Medicine: The Definitive Guide found that men with the lowest selenium levels in their blood were 1.7 times as likely to suffer a cardiovascular event.

Silicon

Silicon plays an important role in connective tissue, especially bones and cartilage. Vegetal silica, a form of silicon, is extracted from the herb horsetail and sold in health food stores. Silica (silicon dioxide), the most abundant silicon compound, is also available in supplement form. No RDA has been established for this trace element.

Zinc

Zinc is a component of the molecular structure of nearly a hundred human enzymes involved in major metabolic processes, most of which work with the red blood cells to move carbon dioxide from the tissues to the lungs. Zinc functions as an important antioxidant; promotes normal growth and development; aids in wound healing; enhances cell division, repair, and growth; maintains normal levels of vitamin A in the blood; and helps synthesize DNA and RNA.

Natural sources include lean beef, egg yolks, fish, lamb, milk, oysters, pork, sesame and sunflower seeds, soybeans, turkey, wheat bran and germ, and whole-grain products. Diets heavily dependent on grains, which contain large amounts of phytates that block zinc absorption, may result in zinc deficiencies. Symptoms of zinc deficiency include retarded growth, rashes and multiple skin lesions, psoriasis, low sperm count, delayed wound healing, and diminished learning capacity. Prenatal zinc deficiency also interferes with the maturation of the brain.

Zinc deficiencies have been linked to prostatic hypertrophy (prostate enlargement) and prostate cancer. Dr. Andre Voison, in his 1988 book *Grass Productivity,* claims that when a 35% drop in normal zinc levels occurs, a mild enlargement of the prostate is observed. A 38% drop in zinc levels leads to chronic prostatitis. Cancer often develops when zinc levels are reduced by 66%.

Benefits of Zinc

- Promotes recovery from serious head injury.
- May play an important role in cognition and neurotransmission.
- Helps maintain normal glucose levels in the blood.
- May help treat hypoglycemia and diabetes.
- May help relieve inflammation from rheumatoid arthritis.
- Used to treat advanced hardening of the arteries.
- May help relieve PMS symptoms.

Voison's work is cited by Ornstein in *The Human Ecology Program,* published by the San Francisco Medical Research Foundation in 1987.

Prostate problems are virtually unknown in areas where pumpkin seeds are regularly eaten, such as eastern Europe. Pumpkin seeds are high in zinc, essential amino acids, magnesium, and the polyunsaturated fatty acids found in lecithin.

Zinc and AIDS. Both zinc and copper are known to be important in the functioning of the immune system, and deficiencies in either may predict vulnerability to AIDS. In one study, zinc and copper levels were examined in 54 homosexual men who were infected with the human immunodeficiency virus (HIV) and later developed AIDS. Zinc blood levels were lower in men who were infected and progressed to AIDS compared with those who were infected but did not develop AIDS. Zinc deficiency predicted the progression to AIDS independently of other factors, such as the number of CD4+ lymphocyte levels or age, reports A. Sherman in *History of Nutritional Immunology,* published in March 1992.

Zinc and Diabetes. Zinc deficiencies may play a role in diabetes because it is essential for the production of insulin, the hormone responsible for maintaining normal glucose levels in the blood. Abnormally fluctuating glucose levels, called hypoglycemia, lead to unstable mental and emotional conditions due primarily to overconsumption of refined sugar. As a result, the pancreas must produce greater amounts of insulin to balance an inordinate amount of sugar absorbed into the bloodstream. Zinc appears to help restore normal insulin levels and is being used to help treat hypoglycemia and diabetes.

Zinc and Head Injuries. A study reported by Bricklin in the February 1992 issue of *Prevention Magazine* found that zinc is effective in promoting recovery from serious head injury. A medical group at the University of Kentucky conducted a three-year study in which 60 head-injury patients were given either the normal amount of zinc found in intravenous formulas and hospital food, or about five times that much in zinc supplements. A standard test, the Glasgow Coma Scale, was used by neurosurgeons to assess mental functioning after head injury. Results revealed that a month after their accidents, the zinc-supplemented patients scored significantly higher on the test, indicating faster recovery from injury. The results suggest that zinc may play an important role in several areas of cognition and neurotransmission.

Zinc is highly concentrated in the hippocampus of the brain, which is responsible for the coordination of thoughts, feelings, and emotions. Extensive research by orthomolecular (nutritional) physicians has demonstrated that sufferers of schizophrenia and manic depression are depleted in zinc, L-ascorbic acid, vitamin B, and essential amino acids.

Adequate levels of these substances appear to be prerequisites for proper neurological functioning, according to Bricklin's article.

Zinc and Immune System Diseases. Zinc is instrumental in many immune system processes, thymus gland function, and thymus hormone action. When zinc levels are low, the number of T-cells (which kill bacteria and viruses) is significantly reduced. Thymic hormone levels also are lower and many white blood cell functions critical to the immune response are severely impaired. All of these effects are reversible with adequate zinc absorption. In addition, zinc has been shown to inhibit the growth of several viruses including herpes simplex.

Adequate zinc levels are particularly important in the elderly and young children. Zinc supplementation in the elderly results in the production of a higher number of T-cells and enhanced cell-mediated immune responses. Children prone to upper respiratory tract infections typically have low levels of zinc and other trace minerals.

Zinc and Premenstrual Syndrome (PMS). Many women experience anxiety, bloating, and other premenstrual symptoms. Several tentative experiments show that zinc may help relieve PMS by regulating the secretion of several key hormones, including progesterone, during menstruation. Dr. C. James Chuong of the Baylor College of Medicine found significantly lower zinc blood levels in women with PMS than in control samples, according to a report by K. Fackelmann in the October 27, 1990, issue of *Science News.* Chuong emphasizes that further work needs to be done to confirm the proposed link between PMS and zinc.

Zinc and Rheumatoid Arthritis (RA). Some preliminary evidence suggests that zinc supplements may relieve rheumatoid arthritis. In *Wellness Medicine,* published in 1990, Dr.

Robert Anderson reports on one study in which 220 milligrams per day of zinc were added to existing therapy for 12 weeks in 24 patients with rheumatoid arthritis. According to Anderson, "There were significant improvements in flexibility (less stiffness), their sense of well-being, and increasing walking time with decreased swelling." Anderson cites another study in which 24 patients with advanced hardening of the arteries received 150 milligrams of zinc daily, which resulted in a distinct improvement in 18 of the patients.

Summary

Despite the documented role minerals and trace elements play in ensuring the healthy functioning of the body, many people still underestimate the importance of consuming enough of them in the daily diet. The small amounts of the essential minerals needed for human health can be obtained from foods, especially fresh fruits and vegetables. It is important that people monitor whether they are consuming adequate amounts through their diet alone by following the RDAs. If individuals believe they are deficient in a particular mineral or trace element, they should consult their physician or health practitioner to determine whether or not supplements are advisable.

Resources

References

Anderson, Robert A. *Wellness Medicine.* New Canaan, CT: Keats Publishing, Inc., 1990.

Asai, Kazuhiko. *Miracle Cure: Organic Germanium.* Tokyo, Japan: Japan Publications, Inc., 1978.

SUMMARY

Bricklin, Mark. "New Respect for Nutritional Healing." *Prevention* (February 1992): 3.

Brunner, E. "Effect of Parenteral Magnesium on Pulmonary Function, Plasma cAMP, and Histamine in Bronchial Asthma." *Journal of Asthma* (September 1985): 3-11.

The Burton Goldberg Group. *Alternative Medicine: The Definitive Guide.* Payallup, WA: Future Medicine Publishing, Inc.,1993.

Careiello, A. "Hypomagnesium in Relation to Diabetic Retinopathy." *Diabetes Care* (1982): 558-59.

Chaitow, Leon. *The Body/Mind Purification Program.* New York: Simon & Schuster, Inc., 1990.

Clark, Larry. *Selenium in Biology and Medicine.* New York: Van Nostrand Reinhold Co., 1991.

Fackelmann, K. "PMS: Hints of a Link to Zinc." *Science News* (October 27, 1990): 263.

Fugh-Berman, Adriane. *Alternative Medicine: What Works.* Tucson, AZ: Odonian Press, 1996.

Griffith, H. Winter. *Vitamins.* Tucson, AZ: Fisher Books, 1988.

Hoffer, A. *Orthomolecular Nutrition.* New Canaan, CT: Keats Publishing, Inc., 1978.

London, R.S. "Effect of a Nutritional Supplement on Premenstrual Symptomatology in Women With Premenstrual Syndrome: A Double-Blind Longitudinal Study." *Journal of the American College of Nutrition* (1991): 494-99.

Mitchell, J. "Many Riches from Selenium." *Health News & Review* (July/August 1991): 7.

Mooradian, A. "Micronutrient Status in Diabetes Melitus." *American Journal of Clinical Nutrition* (October 1987): 646-53.

Morain, C.O. "Elemental Diet as Primary Treatment of Acute Crohn's Disease." *British Medical Journal* (September 1984): 1859-62.

Murray, Michael, and Joseph Pizzorno. *Encyclopedia of Natural Medicine.* Rocklin, CA: Prima Publishing, 1991.

Ornish, Dean. *Dr. Dean Ornish's Program for Reversing Heart Disease.* New York: Random House, 1992.

Ornstein, R. *The Human Ecology Program.* San Francisco: San Francisco Medical Research Foundation, 1987.

Pollitt, E. "Iron Deficiency and Behavior." *Journal of Pediatrics* (April 1976): 372-81.

Sherman, A. "Zinc, Copper and Immunity." *History of Nutritional Immunology* (March 1992): 604.

Skinner, G. "The Effect of Lithium Chloride on the Replication of Herpes Simplex Virus." *Medicine, Microbiology and Immunology* (1980): 139-48.

Skrabal, F. "Low Sodium/High Potassium Diet for Prevention of Hypertension." *The Lancet* (October 1981): 895-900.

Tarp, U. "Selenium Treatment in Rheumatoid Arthritis." *Scandinavian Journal of Rheumatology* (September 1985): 249-55.

Turlapaty, P. "Magnesium Deficiency Produces Spasms of Coronary Arteries." *Science* (March 1980): 199-200.

Voison, Andre. *Grass Productivity.* Washington, DC: Island Press, 1988.

Wikstrom, J. "Selenium, Vitamin E and Copper in Multiple Sclerosis." *Acta Nerulogie Scandinavia* (1976): 287-90.

Wray, D. "Recurrent Apthatae: Treatment with Vitamin B_{12}, Folic Acid and Iron." *British Medical Journal* (1975): 490-93.

Additional Reading

American Dietetic Association. *Handbook of*

Clinical Dietetics. New Haven, CT: Yale University Press, 1981.

American Medical Association. *Drug Evaluations.* Chicago, IL: American Medical Association, 1986.

Butler, Kurt, and Lynn Rayner. *The Best Medicine: The Complete Health and Preventive Medicine Handbook.* New York: Harper & Row Publishers, Inc., 1985.

Edmunds, Marilyn. *Nursing Drug Reference.* Bowie, MD: Brandy Communications Company, 1985.

Hendler, Sheldon. *The Complete Guide to Anti-Aging Nutrients.* New York: Simon & Schuster, Inc., 1985.

Lerch, Sharon. "Memory Booster (Iron and Zinc)." *American Health* (March 1992): 129.

Marshall, Charles W. *Vitamins and Minerals: Help or Harm?* Philadelphia, PA: George F. Stickley Company, 1983.

Mills, Collins. "Zinc in Human Biology." *Journal of the American Dietetic Association* (May 1990): 756.

Murray, Frank. "Zinc Helps the Immune System." *Better Nutrition for Today's Living* (May 1991): 10.

Neil, M., et al. "Relationship of Serum Copper and Zinc Levels to HIV-1 Seropositivity to AIDS." *Journal of Acquired Immune Deficiency Syndromes* (October 1991): 976.

"Nutrition and Your Health: Dietary Guidelines for Americans." *Home and Garden Bulletin.* U.S. Department of Agriculture, 1992.

Chapter 5

BOTANICAL MEDICINES

Botanical (plant) medicines have been the basis of all medical traditions since the dawn of civilization. Throughout history, various cultures have handed down their accumulated knowledge of botanical medicines to successive generations. In the last 150 years, chemists and pharmacists have isolated and purified the "active" compounds in many plants in an attempt to produce reliable pharmaceutical drugs. Approximately 5,000 botanical plants have now been extensively tested for possible use as medicines. Currently, 25% of all prescription drugs are directly or indirectly derived from herbs, shrubs, or trees. Some pharmaceutical drugs are extracted directly from plants, while others are synthesized to duplicate the properties of natural plant compounds.

A wide range of research is currently being conducted in the United States, Europe, and Asia to investigate the chemical properties of another 5,000 botanicals for possible use in treating cancer, AIDS, diabetes, heart disorders, and many other diseases. This chapter discusses the more widely used botanical medicines whose effects have been studied in clinical trials. The English common name or popular name in the U.S. is given first, followed by the plant's botanical name.

Although botanical medicines have proven medicinal benefits, and are used throughout the world to treat many disorders, botanical medicines in the U.S. are currently not regulated by the FDA–which requires drugs to meet stringent testing and labeling requirements before they can be sold. Over-the-counter botanical medicines are offered in many different forms, and because their manufacture and labeling are not federally regulated, the only guarantee of their safety is to consult a knowledgeable expert. Some botanicals may contain toxic compounds in addition to the

Choosing a Botanical Medicine

Encapsulated   Many botanical medicines are finely ground into powder and enclosed in capsules. These capsules can be easier to use and are probably the best form for people who need to know the precise dosage. However, they can be less potent than whole dried herbs because once they are powdered, their components are exposed to air and degrade faster.

Fomentation   Fomentation is an external application of herbs, generally used to treat swelling, pain, colds, and flu. Fomentations are usually prepared by soaking a towel or cloth in the desired botanical tea and then applying the towel (as hot as possible) over the affected area.

Fresh Plants   The fresh plant may be an ideal form of botanical medicine, although people should first consult with an herbalist to identify the right species and to understand all the chemical properties of an herb or plant. The potency and toxicity of each plant species varies according to what part of the plant is used–the leaves, roots, or flowers–and what combination of chemical compounds it contains.

Infusion   Infusion was once the most common way of preparing herbs. A teaspoon of leaves, blossoms, or flowers is boiled in water and steeped for three to five minutes. Honey is often added as a sweetener.

Plaster   A plaster is similar to a poultice, except that the herbal materials are placed between two pieces of cloth and applied to the affected surface. This is a desirable alternative when the skin is irritated, as plasters help prevent the herb from coming in direct contact with the skin.

Poultice   A poultice is usually used to reduce swelling by applying a warm paste of powdered herbs directly to the skin.

Solid Extracts   Some botanical medicines are available in solid extract forms that are made by first preparing a tea or tincture and then evaporating it until a gummy residue remains. The residue is mixed with other substances and sold as capsules. This is the most expensive of all botanical medicine forms, as well as the most reliable and potent.

Teas   Many botanical medicines are now available as teas–either as single plants or in combinations of several plants. Teas lose some of the properties of whole plants because any constituents that are not soluble in water are lost. Heating also evaporates some of the plant's medicinal components.

Tincture   A tincture is an extract of a plant in a solution of water and alcohol that is easy to use and can retain its potency for several years or more. The disadvantage is its alcohol content which, taken in high doses, can present a risk for alcoholics or anyone with a liver or digestive disease.

pharmacologically useful substances. Therefore, it can be harmful to take a botanical unless all of its potential side effects are fully known and understood. An additional problem is that certain people are at high risk of intoxification, including chronic users, children, the elderly, the sick, the malnourished or undernourished, and those on long-term medications. For these reasons, botanical medicines should only be taken under the supervision of a physician, herbalist, or health practitioner who will evaluate a patient's specific case, provide advice on dosage, and monitor the herb's effectiveness.

Chaste Tree (*Vitex agnus-castus*)

Vitex agnus-castus is a deciduous tree common to southern Europe and countries of the Mediterranean. It is called the chaste tree because of its reputed power to reduce sexual desire in both women and men. Chaste tree berries are thought to contain progesterone-like compounds. German research cited by E. Wallenweber in a 1983 issue of *Planta Medica* showed that chaste berry extracts stimulate the release of luteinizing hormones (LH) and inhibited the release of follicle stimulating hormone (FSH). Other research has shown that chaste tree berries help regulate disturbed female hormonal action, reduce menstrual and menopausal symptoms, especially PMS, amenorrhea, dysmennorhea, and endometriosis. One study on PMS by Wollenweber reported that symptoms such as anxiety, nervous tension, insomnia, and mood changes were the most reduced after taking dried *V. agnus-castus* tablets.

Algae (Spirulina)

Algae and micro-algae have been growing wild in oceans (seaweed) and alkaline lakes (blue-green algae) for thousands of years. According to Helen C. Morgan and Kelly J. Moorhead's *Spirulina: Nature's Superfood*, blue-green algae, or spirulina, grew wild in the great lakes of Central Mexico and was prized by the Aztecs as a food source. The Aztecs collected spirulina from the surface of the lakes with fine-meshed nets, dried the plant in the sun, and made it into a thick paste which they then formed into cakes.

There are more than 30,000 known species of algae. Blue-green algae, the most primitive, are the most commonly used as food. They contain no nucleus and the cell walls are soft and easily digested, unlike other algae plants that contain hard cellulose. In the last 10 years, seaweed and blue-green algae have been harvested and made commercially available as food sources because they contain extremely high concentrations of calcium, potassium, manganese, copper, silicon, zinc, and lithium.

Spirulina is now sold in powder, tablet, or supplement fruit drink forms. Robert Henrikson, president of the Earthrise Company in San Rafael, California (which produces Earthrise spirulina), documents in *The Ultimate Guide to Health & Fitness* that spirulina is currently being used in Third World countries to treat malnutrition. In Togo, for example, spirulina is called "green medicine." Malnourished infants taking 3-15 grams of spirulina per day showed rapid weight gain. In China, Nanjing Children's Hospital uses spirulina in a baby-nourishing formula to help infants recover from a variety of nutritional deficiencies. Spirulina's high protein level, easy digestibility, and concentration of vitamins, minerals, and essential fatty acids make it ideal for therapeutic feeding.

According to Henrikson, spirulina has a higher concentration of protein (60%), amino acids, betacarotene, vitamin B_{12}, gamma-lineolenic acid (GLA), trace minerals, and natural pigments than any other natural food source. Morgan and Moorhead state that spirulina is the only natural food that contains all the essential and nonessential amino acids. With extra iron and trace minerals added to commercial growing ponds, spirulina has been found to have an iron concentration 10 times higher than any other conventional food–and

Henrikson claims studies have shown that iron in spirulina is 60% more absorbable than a typical iron supplement such as iron sulfate. Spirulina-growing projects are currently underway in Peru, India, Senegal, Vietnam, China, Mexico, Thailand, Japan, southern California, Oregon, and Hawaii.

According to Henrikson, spirulina also contains RNA and DNA nucleic acids, chlorophyll, and phycocyanin, a blue-green pigment (found only in blue-green algae) that may help prevent some cancers. He cites a Japanese patent application which states that daily ingestion of a small dosage of phyco-cyanin accelerates normal cell growth and inhibits the growth of malignant tumors in cancer patients. M. Boyd reports in the 1989 *Journal of the National Cancer Institute* that clycolipids extracted from blue-green algae have been found to inhibit the AIDS virus in experimental studies.

Henrikson also cites a 1986 Japanese study which found that men with hyperten-sion and hyperlipidemia had lower serum cholesterol, triglyceride, and LDL levels after consuming nine spirulina tablets daily for eight weeks. He suggests that the cholesterol reduction may be partially due to the very high gamma GLA content in spirulina. According to J. Belch, writing in the *Annals of the Rheumatic Diseases*, spirulina and breastmilk are the only natural foods that con-tain GLA that have successfully treated sever-al degenerative disorders, including arthritis.

Spirulina also increases the strength of the immune system. Henrikson cites a 1987 Japanese research study which proved that taking spirulina supplements increased *Lactobacillus* flora in laboratory animals. He suggests that humans consuming spirulina supplements can improve their digestion and stimulate their immune systems as well. Because spirulina improves the absorption of minerals and maintains proper intestinal flora which prevent some types of infections, this

botanical is currently being extensively stud-ied in clinical trials. Its unproven medical benefits include treating obesity, colitis, and diabetes mellitus.

Aloe Vera

There are at least 120 known species of aloe, many of which have been used as botan-ical medicines. The sap and rind portions of the aloe vera leaf contain healing components such as analgesics, anti-inflammatory com-pounds, minerals, and beneficial fatty acids. According to Michael Murray and Joseph Pizzorno in the *Encyclopedia of Natural Medicine*, aloe vera contains anthraquinones, which reduce the growth rate of urinary calci-um crystals that contribute to the formation of kidney stones. Once kidney stones form, as reported by K. Riley in the 1981 edition of the *Journal of John Bastyr College of Natural Medicine*, aloe vera extracts can help reduce the size of stones and subsequently eliminate them.

Aloe vera is widely known as a skin moisturizer and healing agent, especially in treating cuts, burns, insect stings, bruises, acne, poison ivy, welts, ulcerated skin lesions, eczema, and sunburns. It has also been used, according to James Balch and Phyllis Balch in *Prescription for Nutritional Healing*, to treat stomach disorders, ulcers, colitis, and many colon-related disorders. They suggest that aloe vera juice may be used to treat food aller-gies, varicose veins, skin cancer, and arthritis as well.

Aloe vera may help stop the spread of some viruses. Researchers at the University of Maryland in Baltimore tested the antiviral activity of a number of plant extracts, includ-ing aloe vera emodin. The results, according to R. Sydiskis in the December 1991 issue of *Antimicrobial Agents & Chemotherapy*, showed that aloe emodin inactivated herpes simplex virus type 1 and 2, varicella-zoster virus, pseudorabies virus, and the influenza virus.

Astralagus

Chinese astralagus, also known as "huang chi," belongs to the family of peas which have pharmacological effects on digestion. Other ingredients include the triterpenoid saponins which are analogous to animal steroid hormones. Astralagus also contains polysaccharides that enhance the immune system by increasing NK and T cell functions as well as interferon production. Dr. Daniel Mowrey reports in *The Scientific Validation of Herbal Medicine* that astralagus is widely used to increase resistance to disease and infections, to restore depressed immunity, to treat hepatitis, AIDS, and other viral conditions, and to treat peripheral vascular diseases and restore peripheral circulation. According to Mowrey, astralagus extracts have also been used experimentally for myasthenia gravis and immune depletion in cancer patients.

Bilberry Extract (*Vaccinium myrtillus*)

Bilberry extract is believed to help prevent or treat fragile capillaries, which can cause fluid or blood to leak into the tissues, leading to hemorrhage, stroke, heart attacks, or blindness. Less serious effects include a tendency to bruise easily, varicose veins, poor night vision, coldness, numbing, and leg cramping. Bilberry extract appears to protect capillaries and other small blood vessels by increasing the flexibility of red blood cell membranes. This action allows capillaries to stretch, increasing blood flow, and red blood cells can be formed into a shape that easily moves through narrow capillaries.

European clinical trials reported by Dr. S. Corsiand L. Gatta have shown the effectiveness of bilberry extract for venous insufficiency of the lower limbs in 18- to 75-year-old

subjects. It has been used to treat varicose veins in the legs, where it significantly improves symptoms of varicose syndrome such as cramps, heaviness, calf and ankle swelling, and numbness.

Black Currant Seed (*Ribes nigrum*)

Black currant seeds are a rich source of gamma linolenic acid (GLAs), an Omega-6 essential fatty acid that is a critical precursor to series 1 prostaglandins and other important hormones. The PGE1 series prostaglandins along with the PGE3 series protect the body against the deleterious effects of PGE2 series prostaglandins, such as high blood pressure, sticky platelets, inflammation, water retention, and lowered immune function. Numerous clinical trials cited by R. Chapkin in a 1992 issue of *Lipid* suggest that black currant seed oil is effective in treating atherosclerosis, diabetes mellitus, eczema, multiple sclerosis, and PMS.

Black Walnut Husks (*Juglans nigra*)

Expert gardeners know better than to plant under the black walnut tree because walnuts contain a chemical that kills anything in its proximity. American Indian tribes recognized black walnut bark's destructive power and used it to treat ringworm, a fungal skin infection. It apparently binds directly with the infected cells, and is able to quickly eliminate stubborn fungal problems such as athlete's foot and jock itch. Black walnut husks may also be effective against cancer, and German researchers have obtained a patent to use black walnut husks for anti-cancer treatments.

Preliminary studies conducted during the 1960s revealed that large doses of the chemicals in walnuts may help lower blood pressure. More recent studies of the English walnut have documented its effectiveness in helping lower cholesterol as part of a heart-healthy diet.

Black walnut supplements are also one of the highest concentrated sources of natural serotonin, the neurotransmitter that performs a variety of functions. Ample amounts of serotonin in the nerve cells, for example, help regulate sleep, mood, food intake, and pain tolerance, while low serotonin levels produce insomnia, depression, food cravings, increased sensitivity to pain, aggressive behavior, and poor body temperature regulations. The discovery of a possible link between low levels of serotonin and some cases of major depression has already led to the development of more precisely targeted antidepressant medications that boost serotonin to normal levels. Further research may find a new role for black walnut husks as a natural, non-addictive source of serotonin to treat mental disorders such as anorexia nervosa, kleptomania, self-mutilation, schizophrenia, and aggressive behavior.

Bitter Melon (*Momordica charantia*)

Bitter melon, also known as balsam pear, is a tropical vegetable widely cultivated in Asia, Africa, and South America. According to Murray and Pizzorno, bitter melon is composed of several compounds, including charantin. Charantin, which acts as a hypoglycemic agent, is composed of mixed steroids that are more potent than the prescription drug Tolbutamide in treating some cases of diabetes. Bitter melon also contains polypeptide-P, which lowers blood sugar levels when injected in patients with Type 1 diabetes. Since it appears to have fewer side effects than insulin, Murray and Pizzorno suggest that it can be used as an insulin substitute for some patients.

S. Lee-Huang, writing in the October 15, 1990 issue of *FEBS Letter*, reports that an isolated, purified extract of bitter melon seeds and fruits (*Momordica charantia* or MAP 30) formed an essential basic protein that inhibited cell-free HIV-1 infection and replications in animal experiments. No severe side effects have been identified. Lee-Huang concludes: "This data suggests that MAP 30 may be a useful therapeutic agent in the treatment of HIV-1 infections."

Capsicum (Hot Chili Peppers and Sweet Bell Peppers)

The fruit of hot chili peppers and sweet bell peppers contain high levels of capsaicin, the chemical that provides the "heat" and vitamin C. The health benefits, according to the March 1995 issue of *UC Berkeley Wellness Letter*, include weight loss, treating indigestion, ulcers, hemorrhoids, cancer, blood cholesterol, and blood clotting.

Cat's Claw (*Uncaria tomentosa Willd*)

Cat's claw is a woody vine, typically two or three inches or more in diameter, that grows in the Amazonian region of Peru. The extract is made from the bark of the woody stem that contains quinovic acid glycodes, catechins, D-catechol, and several alkaloids. According to Philip Steinberg's articles in the August/September issue of *Townsend Letter for Doctors*, cat's claw activates T-lymphocytes and macrophages and normalizes immunoglobulins. It is an antioxidant, antiviral, anti-mutagenic, hypotensive, anti-edemic, and an effective contraceptive.

The bark extract has been used, according to Steinberg, to treat AIDS patients in Austria and Germany. It has also been used successfully to treat arthritis, neurobronchitis, allergies, rheumatism, diverticulosis, Crohn's disease, peptic and gastric ulcers, gastritis, para-sites, colitis, leaky bowel syndrome, dysentery, hemorrhoids, cancer (along with other herbs that moderate the side effects of chemotherapy and radiation), herpes (herpes genitalis, stomatitis aftesa, and varicella zoster), diabetes, and inflammation.

Co-Enzyme Q-10

Co-enzyme Q-10, according to Dr. Keith Folker's 1985 article in the *Proceedings of the National Academy of Sciences*, is extracted from tobacco leaves by a special technique that eliminates any adverse ingredients related to tobacco smoking. Co-enzyme Q-10 is found in the mitochondria of cells and is key electron carrier in the cellular electron transport process which generates chemical and electrical energy. Adequate co-enzyme Q-10 levels are essential for the health of all human tissues. Current research being conducted by Folkers and others are investigating its role in cardiovascular health, cancer management, chemotherapy, infections, periodontal disease, and aging.

Green Tea (*Camellia sinensis*)

Green tea is made from the leaves of *Camellia sinensis*, an evergreen plant. Both green and black teas are derived from *Camellia sinensis*, but the black tea leaves are fermented before drying and lose their beneficial polyphenols. According to David Steinman, writing in the March/April 1994 issue of *Natural Health*, dietary surveys of the Japanese, the world's leading green tea drinkers, show that people who drink four to six cups daily have a much lower incidence of liver, pancreatic, breast, lung, esophageal, and skin cancers than people who drink less green tea or none. Steinman hypothesizes that green tea prevents cancer (and possibly other diseases) by acting as an antioxidant.

The Medical Benefits of Green Tea

1. Drinking green tea lowers the risk of liver, pancreatic, breast, lung, esophageal, and skin cancers.
2. Green tea lowers the risk of cardio-vascular disease by inhibiting the production of platelets, which form atheromas (blockages) of the coronary arteries.
3. Green tea reduces the risk of stroke.
4. Green tea lowers blood sugars. Animal experiments have shown that animals who maintain moderate blood sugar levels live longer.
5. Green tea and its active components combat viruses.

Japanese researchers recently found the main physiologically active polyphenol in green tea extract, (-)epigallocatechin gallate (EGCG), appears to inhibit the growth of tumors. A. Komori, writing in the June 1993 issue of the *Japanese Journal of Clinical Oncology*, states that EGCG inhibits protein kinase C activation by teleocidin, a tumor promoter. Komori claims that EGCG prevents the growth of lung and breast cancer. Dr. N. Ito in a 1992 issue of *Teratogeneis, Carcinogensis, & Mutagenesis*, theorizes that green tea may have a sealing effect–it may block the interaction of tumor promoters, hormones, and growth factors with their receptors.

Chamomile

Chamomile, one of the best-selling herbs in the United States, is actually two herbs with the same name: German or Hungarian chamomile (*Matricaria chamomilla*), and Roman or English chamomile (*Anthemis nobilis* or *Chamaemelum nobile*). Both have flowers with yellow centers and white rays, and both produce a light blue oil that has medicinal properties.

Chamomile has traditionally been used as a digestive aid. According to Murray and Pizzorno, several chemicals in chamomile oil, including bisabolol, relax the smooth muscle tissue that lines the digestive tract. W. Mitchell, in his book *Naturopathic Applications of the Botanical Remedies*, claims that chamomile oil has been shown to relax the gastrointestinal tract as well as or better than the prescription drug Pavabid.

J. Duke, in the *Handbook of Medicinal Herbs*, states that German researchers have also discovered that chamomile oil kills several bacteria, including *Candida albicans*, the fungus responsible for vaginal yeast infections. Chamomile is licensed in Germany as an over-the-counter drug for internal use against gastrointestinal spasms and inflammatory diseases of the gastrointestinal tract. It is also approved as a topical treatment for skin and mucous membrane inflammations, bacterial skin diseases of the mouth and gums, and inflammation of the throat and airways.

Chinese Skullcap (*Scutellaria baicalensis*)

Chinese skullcap has confirmed anti-arthritic and anti-inflammatory actions, similar in effect to the prescription drugs Phenylbutazone and Indomethacin. As reported by M. Kuba in a 1984 issue of *Chemical Pharmacology Bulletin*, Chinese skullcap does not appear to have any adverse side effects. Kuba hypothesizes that its effectiveness is due to its high content of flavonoid molecules.

Chinese skullcap may also prove useful in the treatment and prevention of HIV infections. Dr. B. Li, writing in a 1993 issue of *Cellular & Molecular Biology Research*, states that baicalin (BA), a purified extract of Chinese skullcap, inhibits infection and replication of HIV-1 in vitro. In addition, Dr. Li claims that Chinese skullcap shows no side effects. He concludes: "This data suggests that BA may serve as a useful drug for the treatment and prevention of HIV infections."

Dr. T. Nagai reported in the May 1990 issue of *Chemical & Pharmaceutical Bulletin* that of 103 species of flavonoids tested in Japan, Chinese skullcap was the most potent in inhibiting several influenza viruses.

Chinese skullcap has been used to nontoxically treat minimal brain dysfunction. Dr. H. Zhang reports in the May 1990 issue of *Traditional & Western Medicine* that 100 Chinese patients with minimal brain dysfunction were randomly divided into two groups: one group was treated with Traditional Chinese Medicine (TCM); the other with Western Medicine (WM). Patients ranged in ages from 7-14 years old. The TCM group (80 cases) was treated with bupleurum root and *Scutellaria baicalensis*. The WM group of 20 cases was treated with Retalin, a prescription drug. In the TCM group, 23 cases were cured, 46 cases were improved, and 11 cases were unchanged. The effective rate for the TCM group was 86.5%. In the WM group, six cases were cured, 12 cases were unchanged, and two cases were ineffective for an overall effective rate of 90 percent. Although both TCM and WM treatments were effective, Dr. Zhang states that the side effects of the TCM were considerably less and "the TCM group had more beneficial effects to improve intelligence."

Cranberries (*Vaccinium macrocarpon*)

Cranberries have long been used to treat bladder and urinary tract infections. In one study reported by Murray and Pizzorno 16 ounces of cranberry juice per day produced beneficial effects in 73% of the subjects (44 females and 16 males) with active urinary tract infections. Furthermore, withdrawing the cranberry juice from the people who benefitted resulted in recurrence of bladder infection in 61% of the cases. Several components in cranberry juice appear to reduce the ability of bacteria to adhere, or stick, to the lining of the bladder and urethra. In order for bacteria to infect they must first adhere to the mucosa, and by interfering with adherence, cranberry juice greatly reduces the likelihood of infection and helps the body fight off infection.

Significant variations of urinary pH are now known to cause urinary tract disorders and infections. B. Walsh suggests in the July-August 1992 issue of *Journal of Nursing* that urinary tract disorders are due to high alkaline levels in the urine. According to Dr. Walsh, ingesting cranberry juice and ascorbic acid is the "least risky method to promote the production of acidic, diluted urine."

Dandelion (*Taraxacum officinale*)

Many Americans are familiar with dandelions, those stubborn weeds that often spoil a cultivated lawn. According to Murray and Pizzorno, dandelion contains more vitamins, iron, other minerals, protein, and nutrients than any other herb. Dandelion has been used in traditional medicine to treat anemia. It is extremely high in carotenoids, even higher than carrots (14,000 IUs of vitamin A per 100 grams compared with 11,000 IUs for carrots).

A. Leung, in the *Encyclopedia of Common Natural Ingredients Used in Food, Drugs, and Cosmetics*, reviews several studies conducted in China, Russia, and India in which dandelion was used to treat breast problems, liver diseases, appendicitis, and digestive ailments. According to Leung, dandelion enhances the flow of bile which alleviates liver congestion, bile duct inflammation, hepatitis, gallstones, and jaundice. Dandelion stimulates bile secretion by the liver (as opposed to expulsion of bile by the gallbladder). It has been clinically used to treat gallstones, and may be a substitute for antacids in treating indigestion.

Dong Quai (*Angelica sinensis*)

According to a Medieval legend, the medicinal benefits of angelica were revealed to a monk by an angel during a terrible plague–and thus the plant's horticultural name became "angelica"–or "root of the Holy Ghost." Several varieties have been identified, including *Angelica norvegical* in Scandinavia, *Angelica sativa* in Holland and France, and *Angelica refractu* and *Angelica japonica* in Japan. The botanical is popularly known in the United States as dong quai.

Dong quai contains angelic acid, valeric acid, and a resin called angelicin. The Chinese have used it for many disorders, and herbalists consider it safe and nontoxic. However, its strong flavor can cause gastric acidity (gas) in some people, and as a result, it is usually mixed with other herbs. Dong quai is not recommended for use during menstruation or pregnancy.

According to Murray and Pizzorno, dong quai has been used to relieve osteoporosis, hay fever, asthma, and eczema. They suggest that dong quai selectively inhibits the production of allergic antibodies (IgE) that cause inflammation. Japanese researcher Y. Ozaki, writing in the April 1992 issue of *Chemical & Pharmaceutical Bulletin*, reports that *Angelica sinesis* contains tetremethylpyrazine (TMP) and ferulic acid (FA), both of which exert an anti-inflammatory effect during the early and late stages of inflammation.

Gotu Kola

Gotu kola is an herb found in many parts of Asia. Its active substances include asiaticoside and triterpenes which stimulate the reticuloendothial system where new blood cells are formed and old ones destroyed, where fatty materials are stored, iron is metabolized, and immune response and inflammations originate. Murray and Pizzorno report that the primary mode of action of gotu kola appears to be on the various phases of connective tissue development, which are important parts of the healing process. Gotu kola also increases keratinization, the process of creating new skin in infected areas such as sores and ulcers. Asiaticosides also stimulate the synthesis of lipids and proteins necessary for healthy skin, and strenghten the veins by repairing the connective tissues surrounding veins and decreasing capillary fragility. Gotu kola has also been found, according to Daniel Mowrey, to have important healing effects on tissues, including lymph tissues and mucous membranes.

Horsetail (*Equisetum arvense*)

Horsetail grass is a plant made up of bunches of leafless tubular stems. The plant grows in moist soil and concentrated minerals, particularly silica. Its primary element, silica, is essential for growth and healing, being a major constituent of bones, cartilage, cognitive tissue, and skin. The degeneration of tissue with age corresponds with decreasing levels of silica in the tissue. Silicic acid also stimulates an increase in white blood cells, helping to increase resistance to infection. Horsetail grass has proven effective, according to Mowrey, in treating tuberculosis. A second major class of ingredients, the saponins, have a mild diuretic effect. Horsetail has been widely used for genitourinary problems, including inflammations, kidney stones, enuresis, nephritis, gout, and prostate problems.

Purple Coneflower (*Echinacea angustifolia* or *purpurea*)

Purple coneflower, commonly known in the U.S. as echinacea, is a perennial plant native to the midwestern states. It was used by American Indian tribes as a blood purifier, analgesic, antiseptic, and snake bite remedy. It contains several chemicals, including betaine, echinacin, echinoside, fatty acids, inulin, resin, and sucrose.

According to Murray and Pizzorno, echinacea is "the most widely used herb for enhancement of the immune system." Echinacea has long been prescribed by homeopaths and allopaths to treat infections and inflammation of the stomach and bowels. Its pain-relieving properties, along with its antibiotic, anti-inflammatory nature, also make it effective in treating wounds, poison bites, ulcers, infected sores, and other skin conditions, including boils, eczema, and psoriasis. It has been used to treat bronchitis and pneumonia because it helps stimulate the immune system and supports respiratory tract drainage.

Recent research conducted in Germany suggests that echinacea has interferon-like properties that may protect some types of cells from viruses and cancer tumors. The 1989 German Ministry of Health monograph *Echinacea Purpurea Leaf* reports that echinacea contains inulin, which neutralizes some viruses and destroys bacteria. The resultant effect, according to the monograph, is enhanced T-cell mitogenesis (reproduction), macrophage phagocytosis (the engulfment and destruction of bacteria or viruses), antibody binding, natural killer cell activity, and increased levels of circulating neutrophils (white blood cells primarily responsible for defense against bacteria).

Ma Huang (*Ephedra sinica*)

Commonly called ephedra in the West, ma huang is now included in many herbal formulas. It has been grown in China for more than 5,000 years and, according to Murray and Pizzorno, has been used to relieve allergies, asthma, hayfever, colds, and inflammatory conditions. The plant contains two primary alkaloids, ephedrine and pseudo-ephedrine. Ephedrine stimulates the circulatory system, increases cardiac contractions and pumping, and stimulates blood flow to the brain. It has similar effects as adrenaline, although it can be taken orally and is less toxic.

Ephedra's effect diminishes if used over a long period of time due to weakening of the adrenal glands caused by ephedrine. It is therefore often necessary to use ephedra in combination with adrenal gland supportive herbs such as licorice (*Glycyrrhiza glabra*) and *Panax ginseng*, as well as nutrients that support the adrenal glands such as vitamin C, magnesium, zinc, vitamin B_6, and pantothenic acid.

Garlic (*Allium sativum*)

Garlic has played an important medicinal role for centuries, according to Dr. J. Dausch of the National Cancer Institute. Writing in the May 1990 issue of *Preventive Medicine*, Dr. Dausch states: "It is now known that garlic contains chemical constituents with antibiotic, lipid-lowering, detoxification, and other medicinal effects in the body."

Steven Foster in a 1991 monograph entitled *Garlic*, published by American Botanical Council, reports that garlic has been effectively used to prevent common colds and flus, intestinal worms, dysentery, sinus congestion, gout, rheumatism, and some ulcers.

Alternative Medicine: The Definitive Guide reports that garlic also has important cardiovascular benefits, including lowering blood pressure levels, thinning the blood, and reducing platelet aggregations which cause blood clots. It has been shown to strengthen the immune system by increasing natural killer cells' activity.

Recently published studies in China and Italy, cited by Dr. E. Dorant in the March 1993 issue of *British Journal of Cancer*, suggest that consuming garlic may also help prevent certain types of cancer tumors. Dr. Dorant emphasizes that the available evidence "warrants further research into the possible role of garlic in the prevention of cancer in humans."

Ginger (*Zingiber officinale*)

Ginger is a tropical perennial herb that can grow to a height of 2-3 feet. It produces a yellow flower, and its underground roots (tubers) are used to make the familiar spice. Ginger is believed to have originated in India, and was one of the first spices to reach Europe from Asia.

Ginger has a very long history of use in the treatment of a wide variety of intestinal ailments, including many different types of flu. It promotes the elimination of intestinal gas and relaxes and soothes the intestinal tract. Ginger is also very effective in preventing the symptoms of motion sickness, and many consider it superior to Dramamine, a commonly used over-the-counter drug. Dr. S. Phillips, writing in the August 1993 issue of *Anaesthesia*, cites a study that compared the effect of powdered ginger root with Metoclopramide and a placebo in relieving nausea and vomiting in 120 women who had undergone elective laparoscopic gynecological surgery. Twenty-one percent of the women receiving ginger became nauseated, compared with 27% who took Metoclopramide, and 41% who took the placebo. The ginger powder did not cause the usual side effects of prescription drugs, however, such as abnormal movement, itching, or visual disturbance.

Michael Murray states in *The Healing Powers of Herbs* that ginger has been shown to lower cholesterol levels and inhibit platelet aggregation. Ginger (along with cinnamon, thyme, balm, and rosemary) contain powerful *Candida*-killing substances as well.

Ginkgo Biloba

Ginkgo biloba is an ancient Chinese tree whose leaves contain flavonoids that appear to enhance functioning of the adrenal and thyroid glands and the central nervous system. Ginkgo flavonoids are extremely potent antioxidants that are also capable of improving the flow of blood to the brain. In one clinical trial, reported by Dr. G. Rai in a 1991 issue of *Current Medical Research & Opinion*, 112 elderly patients with chronic cerebral insufficiency were daily given 120 milligrams of *Ginkgo biloba* extract (GBE). The extract significantly regressed the major symptoms of vascular insufficiency. Rai believes that a reduced blood and oxygen supply to the brain may be the major causative factor of the so-called age-related cerebral disorders (including senility), rather than a true degenerative process of nerve tissue. *Ginkgo biloba* extract, by increasing blood flow to the brain and improving glucose utilization, offers relief from these presumed side effects of aging. Rai concludes that *Ginkgo biloba* extract may be helpful in treating senility, including Alzheimer's disease.

Another extract of *Ginkgo biloba* (Egb), produced in Austria, has been shown to be a free radical scavenger. It also decreases platelet aggregation, protects against ischemia, inhibits cerebral edema, and enhances cerebral blood flow. Dr. G. Hitzenberger, writing in a 1992 issue of *Wiener Medizinische Wochenschrift*, states: "Clinically EGb has proven favorable effects on intellectual deficiency, equilibrium disturbances and peripheral artery occlusions."

Ginseng (*Panax ginseng*)

Widely regarded as the "king of herbs," ginseng is perhaps the best known of all botanical medicines. There are at least five types of ginseng plants, each of which has different chemical properties. *Panax ginseng* has been grown in China for several thousand years. The genus name *Panax* is derived from the Latin word *panacea* meaning "cure all." American ginseng (*Panax quinquefolium*) grows throughout the woods of eastern North America from Canada to the Carolinas. Ginseng root is now available as a whole root, powdered extract, liquid extract, tea granules, tinctures, tablets, and capsules.

Recent research in China, summarized by Dr. C. Liu in the February 1992 issue of the *Journal of Ethnopharmacology*, indicates that *Panax ginseng* has 28 different ginsenosides that "act on the central nervous system, cardiovascular system and endocrine secretion, promote immune function, and have effects on anti-aging and relieving stress." Ginseng appears to help regulate the amount of adrenaline secreted by the adrenal glands. It also improves adrenal gland function and prevents the shrinkage of the adrenal gland due to aging, prolonged stress, or corticosteroid drugs.

Michael Murray in *The Healing Powers of Herbs* suggests that ginsenosides also increase nerve fiber growth and prevent nerve damage by radiation. They also protect the liver against damage by increasing cell growth in the liver. In addition, ginseng lowers total cholesterol, especially low density lipoproteins ("bad" cholesterol) while increasing HDL ("good") cholesterol.

Goldenseal (*Hydrastis canadensis*)

Goldenseal is a perennial herb native to eastern North America. It was used by American Indians for a wide variety of conditions, including infections. Goldenseal is considered a blood purifier and an antiseptic tonic for the digestive tract and mucous membrane.

According to *Alternative Medicine: The Definitive Guide*, the medicinal benefits of goldenseal are due to its high content of biologically active alkaloids–berberine, hydrastine, and canadine. Berberine has proven a potent activator of macrophages, cells that digest waste matter in the blood. Berberine has been used to effectively combat bacteria, protozoa, and fungi, including *Giardia lamblia*, *Candida albicans* and *Streptococcus* spp.

According to Murray and Pizzorno, goldenseal is effective in treating many acute diarrheas. It is usually included in most detoxification formulas because it increases splenic blood flow, improves liver function, and increases white cell activity in patients with the Epstein-Barr virus.

Hawthorn Berry (*Crataegus spp.*)

The leaves, berries, and blossoms of hawthorn contain many active flavonoid compounds, including anthocyanin-type pigments, cratagolic acid, glycosides, purines, and saponins.

Hawthorn berry and its flower extracts have been effective in clinical trials in reducing blood pressure and angina attacks, as well as in lowering serum cholesterol levels and preventing the deposition of cholesterol on arterial walls. C. Hobbs reviewed several studies in the 1990 issue of *HerbalGram*, which documents that hawthorn extracts are widely used by European physicians to lower blood pressure. The beneficial effects of hawthorn extracts in treating high blood pressure appear to be a result of dilating the larger blood vessels. In excessive amounts, however, hawthorn can be dangerous because it constricts the bronchial tubes and depresses respiration and heart rate. Hobbs also reports that studies show hawthorn berry increases blood flow to the coronary muscle and decreases heart rate and oxygen use of the myocardium (the middle layer of the heart muscle). Hawthorn extracts are currently approved by the German Ministry of Health for people with declining heart performance and mild forms of bradyarrhythmia (slow heart beat).

Kombucha Mushroom

Kombucha is a tea fungus composed of a symbiosis of bacteria, yeast, and other microorganisms derived from lactic acid. The mushroom consists of a gelatinoid and tough mushroom-web membrane in the form of a flat disk. It lives in a nutrient solution of green or black tea and sugar, in which it constantly multiplies through germination. The fungal disk at first spreads over the entire surface of the tea and gradually thickens. When the mushroom is treated properly, it thrives and multiples over a lifetime. During fermentation, the mushroom feeds on sugar and, in exchange, produces glucuron-acid, lactic acid, vitamins, amino acids, and antibiotic substances. The tea-mushroom, in effect, acts as a tiny biochemical factory.

Kombucha is reported to have potential benefits for gastro-intestinal disturbances, headaches, constipation, rheumatism arteriosclerosis, nervous disturbances, gout, high blood pressure, high cholesterol diabetes, aging problems, tonsillitis, dysentery, and cancer. Many of its components are said to have antibiotic, antiseptic, and detoxifying characteristics. Dr. Veronika Carstens of Germany, according to Dr. David Orman's essay "The Kombucha Beverage" in the

December 1994 issue of the *Townsend Letter for Doctors*, has investigated its anti-cancer properties. According to Carstens, former President Ronald Reagan used kombucha as a key part of his cancer-fighting nutrient program.

Licorice (*Glycyrrhiza glabra*)

Most Americans are familiar with licorice as the sweet black candy, but in the perennial temperate zones in Asia where it grows, licorice root has been used for its medicinal properties for several thousand years. It was originally used as an expectorant, or a medicine that helps moisten the mucous membranes when a person has a dry cough, bronchitis, or a sore throat.

Recent scientific evidence indicates that licorice is useful in combating bacteria and viruses. Its major components produce interferon which binds to cell surfaces and stimulates the synthesis of proteins that have been shown to inhibit the growth of several human viruses in cell cultures, including herpes simplex type 1. W. Lu reports in the June 1993 issue of the Chinese journal *Chung-Kuo Chung Hsi i Chieh Ho Tsa Chih* that a licorice extract inhibited HIV activity in 35% of 60 HIV-infected patients. Licorice apparently prevents the suppression of immunity by stress and cortisone, and has displayed antibiotic activity against *Staphylococcus*, *Streptococcus,* and *Candida albicans.*

Double-blind clinical studies have shown that a licorice component (SNMC) is effective in treating viral hepatitis. Dr. S. Acharya, writing in the April 1993 issue of the *Indian Journal of Medical Research*, reports that 12 of 18 patients with the disease survived after being given SNMC. He cautions, however, that further studies are necessary to standardize the dosage and duration of SNMC therapy.

Milk Thistle (*Silybum marianum*)

Milk thistle is a biennial plant that grows in the Mediterranean region of southwest Europe, and parts of the eastern United States and California. It has been cultivated for centuries as a medicinal remedy. Milk thistle contains silymarin, which Murray and Pizzorno note has been used to treat cirrhosis, chronic hepatitis, and gallbladder inflammation. *Alternative Medicine: The Definitive Guide* states that milk thistle effectively shortens the course of viral hepatitis, minimizes post-hepatitis complications, and protects the liver from complications resulting from liver surgery. Steven Foster notes in the November/December 1993 issue of *Natural Healing* that silymarin has also been used to treat gallstones. Silymarin concentrations vary in milk thistle capsules, pills, and teas, and should only be taken upon the advice of an herbalist or physician.

Mistletoe (*Viscum album*)

As N. Bloksma reports in a 1979 issue of *Immunobiology*, the mechanism underlying the long-known anti-hypertensive action of mistletoe has not yet been clarified. Although mistletoe contains a large number of biologically active substances, it appears that the healing effect is not produced by any one of its components. Rather it is produced by the whole complex of biologically active substances contained in the plant.

Mistletoe is believed to function as a regulator of blood pressure, exerting a healing effect in both hypertension and hypotension. In Europe, mistletoe has often been combined with other herbs to treat hypertension. As Murray and Pizzorno emphasize, this potentially toxic herb should not be used in high dosages or for extended periods of time except under the supervision of a physician.

E. Mueller reports in a 1992 issue of *Cancer, Immunology, Immunotherapy* that mistletoe was first used to treat cancer in 1917. Mistletoe contains lectins, polysaccharides, and polypeptides, which researchers believe may indirectly kill cancer cells by stimulating a nonspecific immune reaction. Unlike chemotherapy drugs, mistletoe kills only cancerous cells and does not damage healthy cells. Mistletoe extracts have low toxicity, and no fatal side effects have been reported. More than 40 clinical studies have been carried out, mainly at the Lukas Klinik in Arelesheim, Switzerland, and the Ludwig Boltzmann-Institute in Austria.

Mueller adds that European mistletoe has been used at the Lukas Klinik to boost the immune system and transform cancer cells into normal cells when injected beneath the skin or taken orally. German researchers have also used a *Viscum album* preparation called Helixor to prolong the survival rates of patients with colorectal and liver cancer, both of which are extremely difficult to treat with chemotherapy. Mueller reports that the average one-year survival rate for Helixor-treated patients is 40.3%, compared with 6.6% for untreated control patients.

Experiments at the University of Heidelberg substantiate the ability of mistletoe extracts (ABNOB Aviscum) and pure mistletoe lectins to prevent the growth of tumor cells. Dr. O. Janssen reports in the November 1993 issue of *Arzneimittel-Forschung* that ABNOB Aviscum and pure mistletoe lectins administered to human tumor cell lines in vitro inhibit tumor cell growth. The mechanisms of growth arrest were due to the induction of programmed cell death (apoptosis). Janssen argues that mistletoe extracts and lectins should be further studied for their possible cytogenic effects.

Nettles (*Urtica dioica*)

Stinging nettles derive their name from the presence of stinging hairs on their leaves and stems which, when touched, inject histamines into the skin and cause urticaria, or irritation, and inflammation. According to Dr. C. Baraiba's 1983 article in the *Annals of Bromotalogy*, nettles are a rich source of trace elements, and contain formic acid and the neurotransmitters acetycholine 5-hydroxyl tryptamine, and histamine, which are believed to have anti-arthritic and anti-rheumatic properties.

Nettles, because of their rich nutritional content, have traditionally been given to anemic, exhausted, debilitated, or recuperating patients in soup or tea form. Nettles have also been used as hair and skin tonics because the high quantity of silicon makes them useful for stimulating hair growth, improving hair and skin tone, and eliminating dandruff. Nettles have also been used internally and externally to treat eczema, and nettle juice is an astringent or styptic, which effectively stops bleeding and infections. The best known use, however, is in the treatment of gout and other rheumatoid conditions. Expressed nettle juice and extracts have been shown to effectively mobilize uric acid from the joints and eliminate it through the kidneys.

Pokeweed (*Phytolacca americana*)

Pokeweed has traditionally been used to treat upper respiratory infections, pharyngitis, rheumatism, and lymphatic disease. The July-August 1993 issue of *European Cytokine Network* reports that pokeweed extracts are commonly used in research and laboratory investigations (as pokeweed mitogen or PWM). PWM is a nontoxic yet potent agent that stimulates the production of T lymphocytes. Pokeweed also appears to stimulate antiviral activity against herpes simplex.

Shiitake Mushrooms (*Lentinus edodes*)

The shiitake mushroom has been used in traditional Chinese medicine to strengthen immune resistance to disease. The Chinese regard shiitake mushrooms as one of the most beneficial botanical medicines. Chinese legends refer to it as a plant that gives eternal youth and longevity.

Shiitake mushrooms contain a polysaccharide complex, lentinan, which stimulates the production of T lymphocytes and macrophages, specifically interleukin. Interleukin (a compound that destroys cancer cells and viruses) and interferon are currently being tested as possible treatments for AIDS and other diseases of the immune system. Balch and Balch state in *Prescription for Nutritional Healing* that shiitake mushroom extracts have also been used effectively to prevent high blood pressure and heart disease, and to lower blood cholesterol levels.

Nutritionist Donald Brown writes in the April 1994 *Townsend Letter for Doctors* that an extract of *Lentinus edodes* has been shown to have marked antitumor activity, to suppress viral chemical and viral oncogenesis, and to prevent cancer recurrence (metastasis) after surgery. Results of clinical trials indicate that it prolongs the lifespan of patients with advanced and recurrent stomach, colorectal, and breast cancer with minimal side effects.

Lentinus edodes also increases resistance to several bacterial, viral, and parasitic infections. An extract of *Lentinus edodes* has been used to block the development of herpes simplex. Dr. S. Sarkar, writing in the April 1993 issue of *Antiviral Research*, suggests that *Lentinus edodes* mycelia (JLS-S001) may block the replication of the virus in late stages.

Maitake Mushrooms (*Grifola frondosa*)

The maitake mushroom is native to northeastern Japan and has been prized in Japanese herbology for hundreds of years because of its ability to strengthen the body and improve overall health. According to Anthony Cichoke, writing in the May 1994 *Townsend Letter for Doctors*, maitake mushrooms have inhibited some tumor formation in animal experiments. Currently, research is being conducted by Dr. Dennis Miller of the Cancer Treatment Centers of America on its effects in stabilizing stage IV colorectal cancer in human patients.

Cichoke also suggests that maitake mushrooms may help prevent the destruction of T-helper cells by HIV. Dr. Joan Priestley, a world-renowned AIDS specialist, has used the mushrooms to improve Kaposi's sarcoma patients, especially those who received radiation. Many symptoms of AIDS were generally improved after taking the mushrooms. Cichoke further reports that Dr. Ber, a homeopathic physician practicing in Phoenix, Arizona, has used maitake mushrooms to treat HIV/AIDS patients. Ber has been able to maintain T-lymphocyte cell counts and inhibit further infections characteristic of AIDS patients. Ber believes the mushrooms improve immune function and maintain CD-4 cell levels. Cichoke emphasizes that more comprehensive controlled studies are needed, however, to substantiate maitake's use in treating AIDS-related diseases.

Pygeum (*Pygeum africanum*)

Pygeum is a large evergreen tree that grows in southern Africa and whose bark has been traditionally powdered to make a tea treatment for genito-urinary complaints. Dr. P. Bassi, writing in a 1987 issue of *Minerva Urologica*, cites numerous double-blind clinical trials that found pygeum to be effective in treating a wide range of prostatic hyperplasias. Efficacy was determined by measuring the effects of pygeum extracts on dysuria, nycturia, frequent urination, abdominal heaviness, residual urine, prostate volume, and peak flow. Consumption of pygeum extract resulted in signficant amelioration of symptoms, reduction in prostate size, and clearance of bladder and urethral obstruction.

Schisandra (*Schisandra chinensis*)

Schisandra has been widely used in folk medicine in China and Tibet to increase immune resistance. It contains various lignans, mainly schisandrins, which have been found to prevent liver damage and stimulate liver repair and normal liver functioning. Schisandra further helps in digestion, regulating gastric acid release. *Weiner's Herbal* states that schisandra also stimlates the central nervous system. M. Weiner also reports that schisandra has been shown to quicken reflexes, control anger, and relieve headaches, insomnia, dizziness, and palpitations. Other reports have mentioned increased cognitive function and increased memory. Schisandra may also be useful in reversing depression, particularly that due to exhaustion. In Oriental medicine, schisandra is prescribed to help tonify the lungs, liver, and kidneys, and as an aphrodisiac. Schisandra is also a registered medicine in Russia for vision problems since it appears to prevent eye fatigue and increase visual acuity.

St. John's Wort (*Hypericum perforatum*)

According to *Weiner's Herbal*, St. John's wort is a perennnial plant with regular flowers that has been used for centuries for a wide variety of ailments, including nervous disorders, depression, neuralgia, wounds and burns, kidney problems, and for its anti-bacte-

rial and anti-inflammatory actions. Recently attention has focused on the herb's two main active ingredients, hypericin and pseudohypericin, which have been shown to inhibit the AIDS virus.

According to Christopher Hobb's 1984 *HerbalGram* entitled "St. John's," St. John's wort contains dianthone derivatives (hypericin and pseudohypericin), flavonoids and tannins (hyperoside, quercetin, rutin, and catetchin), xanthrones, monoterpenes and sesquiterpenes, and phytosterols (beta-sitosterol). The xanthrones and hypercin in St. John's have been shown to have monoamineoxidase (MAO)-inhibiting abilities. A standard treatment for depression uses MAO inhibitors to retard the breakdown of neuro-transmitters such as serotonin and thus increase their concentration in the central nervous system. A clinical study involving standardized hypericin extract showed improvement in depressive symptoms, including anxiety, apathy, insomnia, depression, and feelings of worthlessness. A red oil made from macerating the flowers in vegetable oil has been used to dress wounds, heal deep cuts, soothe burns, and ease the pain of neuralgias. Taken internally, the oil has effectively relieved ulcers and gastritis. An infusion of the herb has also been used as an expectorant for bronchitis and as a diuretic for the kidneys and as an easing agent for menstrual cramps.

Suma (*Pfaffia paniculata*)

Suma, also known as Brazilian ginseng, is native to the Atlantic rain forest region of Brazil. According to *Weiner's Herbal*, scientists have discovered several anti-cancer and anabolic effects of the three principle active ingredients in Suma: pfaffic acid, phytosterols, and pfaffosides (saponins). Other trace elements have been found in the herb, including germanium, allantonin, and various vitamins, minerals, and amino acids.

The suma root has been used by native Brazilians for centuries as a tonic, aphrodisiac, and as a remedy for diabetes, ulcers, cancer, and general wound healing. *Weiner's Herbal* states that suma extracts have been used for muscle-building and for treating chronic fatigue syndrome. Suma is also known as an adaptogen because of its ability to promote endurance and increased vitality.

Wild Yams (*Dioscorea villosa*)

According to *Alternative Medicine: The Definitive Guide*, wild yams contain progesterone, identical to that made in the human body. Wild yams, along with about 5,000 other plants, contain a compound called dios-

genin, which is essentially a progesterone molecule with a small molecule addition. People who eat wild yams will gain some of progesterone's benefits.

Progesterone is not just vital to a successful pregnancy. It's also a precursor of other hormones, and it has important intrinsic biological properties, some of which involve opposing the actions of estrogen. In addition to its benefits to bone, postmenopausal hot flashes are improved. Progesterone can also be used in the treatment of premenstrual syndrome, uterine fibroids, urinary tract infections, ovarian cysts, endometriosis, and fibrocystic breasts, all of which are aggravated by estrogen.

Saw Palmetto (*Serenoa repens*)

The berries of the saw palmetto plant have been used extensively to treat benign prostatic hypertrophy (BPH). The standardized extract has no side effects, and costs 30% less than the main prescription drug marketed in the U.S. for BPH, according to Dr. G. Champault's 1984 article in the *British Journal of Clinical Pharamacology*. Another effective herbal drug for treating BPH is made from *Pygeum africanum* and is widely prescribed in France.

Chinese Herbs

Many herbs in China have been extensively studied using scientific verification methods acceptable to Western standards. For example, a 1992 article in the *Journal of Ethnopharmacology* reported that during the preceding 10 years more than 300 original papers on *Panax ginseng* had been published in Chinese and English. Ginseng is one of the world's most thoroughly researched herbs. According to the *Chinese Herbal Medicine: Materia Medica* (revised edition), compiled by Dan Benskyand Andrew Gamble (1993), the following herbs have also proven helpful in treating human disorders.

Chinese Foxglove Root (*Rehmannia glutinosa*) Sheng Di Huang. A preparation of Chinese foxglove root and Chinese licorice root (gan cao), *Glycyrrhiza uralensis* was used to treat 50 cases of hepatitis in various stages. Within 10 days, 41 cases showed improved symptoms, reduced liver and spleen size, and improved liver function tests. Japanese studies, according to Bensky, indicate that the herb is useful in treating experimental hyperglycemia. In other studies, decoctions of sheng di huang have been used to treat rheumatoid arthritis in adults and children. In one uncontrolled study, 12 subjects all showed reduced joint pain and swelling, increased functioning, improved nodules and rash, and lowered temperature. Follow-up over 3-6 months showed only one relapse, which was treated successfully with the same preparation.

Coptis Rhizome, Or Yellow Links (*Coptis chinensis*) Huang Lian. According to Adriane Fugh-Berman's *Alternative Medicine: What Works,* huang lian and berberine, one of its active ingredients, have broad effects against many microbes. Huang lian strongly inhibits many bacteria that are believed to cause dysentery. It is more effective, in fact, than sulfa drugs but less effective than streptomycin or chloramphenicol. Huang lian preparations have also been effective against some bacteria that developed resistance to streptomycin and other antibiotics.

Huang lian preparations also have strong inhibitory effect against many pathogenic bacteria. In one study capsules of powered huang lian were given to patients with typhoid fever, with good results. In another report, two cases that were resistant to antimicrobials responded to this herb, while in another study, 30 cases of pulmonary tuberculosis were treated with huang lian for 3 months, with all showing improvement.

A 10% solution of huang lian was also used to treat 44 patients with scarlet fever. It proved as effective as penicillin or a combination of penicillin and a sulfa drug. Huang lian has also been successfully used to treat diphtheria. In one study, the fever subsided in 1-3 days. Huang lian ointments or solutions promoted healing and reduced infections in first- and second-degree burns. It also has positive effects on blood pressure, smooth muscle, lipid metabolism, and the central nervous system. It is effective as an anti-inflammatory, and has been used successfully, according to Fugh-Berman, in gynecology, ophthalmology, and dermatology.

Wood Leaf or Woad (*Isatis tinctoria*) Da Qing Ye. Da qing ye kills some kinds of bacteria, including some strains resistant to sulfa drugs. According to Fugh-Berman, it has proven effective in treating encephalitis B, with cure rates of 93-98%. In most cases the fever subsided in 1-4 days, and symptoms disappeared 3-5 days later. Da qing ye has also been effective in treating upper respiratory infections. In one study of 100 subjects, also reported by Fugh-Berman, only 1% of the group given a da qing ye formula twice a day had upper respiratory infections after treatment. A mixture of da qing ye and herba taraxaci mongolici cum radice (pu qong ying) was given to 150 children with measles, and signs and symptoms disappeared in 4-5 days. In 68 of 100 cases, da qing ye was used successfully to treat infectious hepatitis.

Wild Chrysanthemum Flower (*Chrysanthemum indicum*) Ye Ju Hua. Ye ju hua has been used to treat hypertension, either alone as an infusion or with Japanese honeysuckle flowers (*Lonicera japonica*) (jinyin hua) and herba taraxaci mongolici cum radice (pu gong ying) in a decoction. Ye ju hua preparations have an inhibitory effect against some bacteria and viruses. Preparations given orally or as injections lowered blood pressure. In one study of 1,000 subjects reported by Fugh-Berman, 13.2% of a control group taking wild chrysanthemum flower reduced their high blood pressure. At the same time, in another study of 119 cases of chronic bronchitis, 38% reduced the incidence of acute attacks.

Bletilla Rhizome (*Bletilla striata*) Bai Ji.

Bai ji, in powered form or in a powder made from starch and a formula of bai ji, has been used to treat ulcers. In one study reported by Fugh-Berman, powdered bai ji was used to treat 69 cases of bleeding ulcers, and in all patients, bleeding stopped within six days. In another series of 29 patients with perforated ulcers, the powdered herb was successful in 23 patients. Only one patient required surgery, while the other four died. One went into hermorrhagic shock while under treatment, and three were in precarious condition on admission.

In another study, powdered bai ji was given to 60 chronic tuberculosis patients who did not respond to normal therapy. After taking bai ji for 3 months, 42 patients were clinically cured, 13 significantly improved, and only two showed no change. A sterile ointment made from bai ji and petroleum jelly was used in another study to treat 48 cases of burns and trauma (less than 11% of total body area). Dressings were changed every 5-7 days and all patients recovered within 1-3 weeks.

Salvia, Or Cinnabar Root (*Salvia miltiorrhiza*) Dan Shen.

In one study 323 patients, suffering from coronary artery disease, were given a dan shen preparation for 1-9 months; 20.3% markedly improved their symptoms, while 62% showed general improvement. Results were best when patients had coronary artery disease and no history of myocardial infarction. In a clinical series of more than 300 patients with angina pectoris, a combination of dan shen and the heartwood of *Dalbergia odorifera* (jiang xiang) given intramuscularly or intravenously improved symptoms in 82% of the cases.

Szechuan Aconite Root (*Aconitum carmichaeli*) Fu Zi.

Fu zi causes blood vessels to dilate in lower extremities and coronary vessels to improve circulation of blood. In normal dosages for humans, fu zi slightly lowers blood pressure, while a large overdose can cause rapid heartbeat or ventricular fibrillation. Fu zi seems to have a regulatory effect on heart rhythm, and according to Fugh-Berman, in all reported cases, including one of cardiogenic shock, fu zi stimulated cardiac output while decreasing breathing difficulty, liver swelling, and general edema. A few cases showed temporary side effects of flushing and slight tremors.

Ayurvedic Herbs

Ayurvedic medicine is the oldest existing medical system recognized by the WHO, and many of its botanical medicines have been used to treat chronic disorders for more than 2,000 years. The government of India recently increased research on traditional Ayurvedic herbal medicine after international studies showed that they are as effective for many conditions as conventional pharmaceuticals. The following Ayurvedic herbs have been studied in India and proven effective.

Gugulgum (*Commiphora mukul*).

According to the *Sushruta Samhita*, the ancient Sanskrit text on Ayurvedic medicine written more than 2,000 years ago, *Commiphora mukul* was useful in treating obesity and conditions such as hyperlipidemia, which involve increased concentrations of cholesterol in the body. In a recent study cited by Fugh-Berman, the crude gum from *Commiphora mukul* significantly lowered serum cholesterol with no adverse side effects. The Indian government has approved the marketing of *Commiphora mukul* for treatment of hyperlipidemia.

Eclipta alba. In Ayurvedic medicine, *Eclipta alba* is said to be the best drug for treating liver cirrhosis and infectious hepatitis. *Eclipta alba* and *Wedelia calendulacea* have been extensively used in India to treat jaundice and other liver and gall bladder ailments. One study conducted by Dr. D. Wagner and reported in a 1986 issue of *Planta Medica* showed that a liquid extract from fresh *Eclipta* leaves was effective in vivo in preventing acute carbon tetrachloride-induced liver damage. The powdered drug has also proven clinically effective in treating jaundice in children.

Indian Gooseberry or Amla (*Emblica officianalis*). An article by Dr. A Jacob in the 1988 issue of the *European Journal of Clinical Nutrition* reported that Indian gooseberry (amla) dramatically reduced serum cholesterol levels in men aged 35-55 years. The supplement was given for 28 days in raw form, and normal and hyper-cholesterolemic subjects showed decreased cholesterol levels. Two weeks after the supplement was withdrawn, total serum cholesterol levels of the hypercholesterolemic subjects rose almost to initial levels.

Picorrhiza kurroa. *Picorrhiza kurroa* rhizomes are partial ingredients of a bitter Ayurvedic tonic used to treat fever and dyspepsia (indigestion). Powdered rhizomes are used as a remedy for asthma, bronchitis, and liver diseases. Other research summarized by Fugh-Berman suggests that a *Picorrhiza kurroa*-derived mixture called kutkin helps protect the liver against toxins and that *Picorrhiza kurroa* acts as a bile enhancer. It may also have antiasthmatic effects in patients. A. Bedi speculates that *Picorrhiza kurroa*, an Ayurvedic herb, may also prevent some cancers. He also suggests that *Picorrhiza kurroa* boosts the immune system and may help patients with vitiglio, a skin disease that causes discoloration spots.

Articulin-F. Articulin-F is an Ayurvedic herbal formula that, according to Dr. R. Kulkalni, contains roots of *Withania somnifera*, stems of *Boswellia serrata*, rhizomes of *Curcuma longa*, and a zinc complex. Kulkalni has performed randomized, double-blind, placebo-controlled crossover studies of articulin-F and found that it effectively treated osteoarthritis, a common progressive rheumatic disease characterized by degeneration and eventual loss of articular cartilage.

Neem (*Azadirachta indica*) and Turmeric (*Curcuma longa*). In Ayurvedic medicine, neem and turmeric are used to heal chronic ulcers and scabies. According to an article by Dr. V. Charles in the 1986 issue of the *Journal of Tropical Medicine*, neem and turmeric were used as a paste to treat scabies in 814 people. Ninety-seven percent of cases were cured within 3-15 days. The researchers found this to be an inexpensive, easily available, effective, and acceptable mode of treatment for villagers in developing countries, with no adverse reactions.

Summary

Various components of plants have been used for thousands of years by traditional healers as botanical medicines. Modern research has yielded a great deal of information about the complex chemical structure of plants and how certain plant chemicals can be used to treat or prevent a variety of human medical disorders. More than 370 botanicals, for example, are currently being investigated in China for their possible effect in delaying the aging process. Botanical medicines show great promise for offering low-cost and safe treatments for many disorders. Nevertheless, a great deal more research needs to be conducted on the pharmaceutical and toxic effects of botanical medicines at the molecular level.

Hopefully, in the near future, governments and research institutions around the world will establish common nomenclatures for botanical medicines and coordinate research on the chemical and molecular structure of their many subspecies. P. D. Semt, writing in the March 1993 issue of the *Journal of Ethnopharmacology*, urges governments to improve the timely detection and quantification of adverse reactions to the many different botanical medicines, and develop modern testing procedures to ensure their safety. He and others have advocated that biologists and chemists form international networks to document the effects of different botanicals. Their first task would be to develop an internationally accepted botanical drug classification system, or a special set of herbal classification codes.

Resources

References

Acharya, S. "A Preliminary Open Trial on Interferon Stimulator (SNMC) Derived from *Glycyrrhiza glabra* in the Treatment of Subacute Hepatic Failure." *Indian Journal of Medical Research* (April 1993): 69-74.

Baisi, F. "Report of a Clinical Trial of Bilberry Anthocyanocides in the Treatment of Venous Insufficiency in Pregnancy and of Postpartum Hemorrhoids." *Presidio Ospedaliero di Livorno,* Livorno, Italy. 1987

Balch, James F., and Phyllis Balch. *Prescription for Nutritional Healing.* Long Island: Avery Publishing, 1993.

Baraiba, C. "Acute Chronic Toxicity Studies on Nettle." *Annals of Bromotalogy* 35 (1983): 99-103.

Bassi, P. "Standardized Extract of *Pygeum africanum* in the Treatment of Benign Prostate Hypertrophy." *Minerva Urologica* 39 (1987): 45.

Bedi, A. "*Picorrhiza kurroa*, An Ayurvedic Herb, May Potentiate Photochemotherapy In Vivo." *Journal of Ethnopharmacology* 27 (1989): 347-52.

Belch, J. "The Effects of Altering Dietary Essential Fatty Acids on Requirements for Non-Steroidal Anti-Inflammatory Drugs in Patients with Rheumatoid Arthritis: A Double-Blind Placebo Controlled Study." *Annals of the Rheumatic Diseases* 47 (1991): 94-104.

Bensky, D., and A. Gamble. *Chinese Herbal Medicine: Materia Medica.* Rev. ed. Seattle: Eastland Press Inc., 1993.

Bergner, Paul. "How to Use 12 Powerful Herbs." *Natural Health* (September/ October 1993): 92-96.

Beuscher, N. "Stimulatin der Immunanwort durch Inhaltsstoffe aus Baptisia Tinctoria." *Planta Med* 5 (1985): 381-84.

Bloksma, N. "Cellular and Humoral Adjuvant Activity of a Mistletoe Extract." *Immunobiology* 6 (1979): 309-19.

Bordia, A. "Effect of Garlic Oil on Fibrinolytic Activity in Patients with CHD." *Atherosclerosis* 28 (1977): 155-59.

Boyd, M. R., et al. "AIDS Anti-Viral Sulforlipids from Cyanobacteria (Blue-Green Alga)." *Journal of National Cancer Institute* 16 (1989): 1254.

Brown, Donald. "Phytotherapy Review & Commentary." *Townsend Letter for Doctors* (April 1994): 406-07.

RESOURCES

Brown, J. "The Use of Botanicals for Health Purposes by Members of a Prepaid Health Plan." *Research in Nursing & Health* (October 1991): 339-50.

The Burton Goldberg Group. *Alternative Medicine: The Definitive Guide*. Payallup, WA: Future Medicine Publishing, Inc., 1993.

Champault, G. "A Double-Blind Trial of the Extract of the Plant *Sereno repens* in Benign Prostatic Hyperplasia." *British Journal of Clinical Pharmacology* 18(1984): 461-62.

Chang, H. *Pharmacology and Applications of Chinese Materia Medica*. Teaneck, NJ: World Scientific Publishing, 1987.

Charles, V. "The Use and Efficacy of Neem and *Curcuma longa* (Turmeric) In Scabies." *Tropical and Geographical Medicine* (November 1991): 178-81.

Cichoke, Anthony. "Maitake–The King of Mushrooms." *Townsend Letter for Doctors* (May 1994): 432-34.

Corsi, S. "Report on Trial of Bilberry Anthocyanosides in the Medical Treatment of Venous Insufficiency of the Lower Limbs." *Casa di Cura S. Chiara*, Florence, Italy. 1989.

Culbreth, D. A. *Manual of Materia Medica and Pharmacology*. Portland, OR: Eclectic Medical Publications,1983.

Dausch, J. "Garlic: A Review of Its Relationship to Malignant Disease." *Preventive Medicine* (May 1990): 346-61.

De Semt, P. "An Introduction to Herbal Pharmacoepidemiology." *Journal of Ethnopharmacology* (March 1993): 197-208.

Dorant, E. "Garlic and Its Significance for the Prevention of Cancer in Humans." *British Journal of Cancer* (March 1993): 424-29.

Duke, J. *Handbook of Medicinal Herbs*. Boca Raton, FL: CRC Press, 1985.

Duker, E. "Effects of Extracts from *Cimicifuga racemosa* on Gonadotropin Release in Menopausal Women and Ovariectomized Rates." *Planta Med* (October 1991).

Folker, K., S. Vadhanavikit, and S. Mortensen. "Biochemical Rationale and Myocardial Tissue Data on the Effective Therapy of Cardiomyopathy with Co-Enzyme Q-10." *Proceedings of the National Academy of Sciences* 82 (1985): 901-04.

Foster, Steven. *Feverfew*. Botanical Series 310. Austin, TX: American Botanical Council, 1991.

————. *Garlic*. Botanical Series 310. Austin, TX: American Botanical Council, 1991.

————. "Herbal Antioxidants." *Herbal Renaissance* (November/December 1993).

Fugh-Berman, Adriane. *Alternative Medicine: What Works*. Tucson, AZ: Odonian Press, 1996.

Furusawa, E. "Antileukemic Activity of Viva-Natural, a Dietary Seaweed Extract." *Cancer Letters* (March 1991): 197-205.

Gelderloos, P. "Influence of a Maharishi Ayurvedic Herbal Preparations on Age-Related Visual Discrimination." *International Journal of Psychosomatics* 37 (1990): 25-29.

German Ministry of Health. *Echinacea Purpurea Leaf*. Monographs for Phytomedicines. Bonn, Germany: German Ministry of Health, 1989.

Griffith, H. Winter *Complete Guide to Vitamins, Minerals & Supplements* Tucson, AZ: Fisher Books, 1988.

Heptinstall, S. "Extracts of Feverfew Inhibit Granule Secretion in Blood Platelets and Polymorphonuclear Leucocytes." *Lancet* (1985): 1071-74.

Hitzenberger, G. *Wiener Medizinische Wochenschrift* 17 (1992): 371-79.

Hobbs, Christopher. "St. John's." *HerbalGram* 18 (1989): 19-24.

———. "Hawthorn: A Literature Review." *HerbalGram* 21 (1990): 19-33.

Ito, N. "Strategy of Research for Cancer Chemoprevention." *Teratogeneis, Carcinogensis, & Mutagenesis* 12 (1992): 79-95.

Jacob A. "Effect of the Indian Gooseberry (Amla) on Serum Cholesterol Levels in Men Aged 35-55 Years." *European Journal of Clinical Nutrition* 42 (1988): 939-44.

Janssen, O. *Arzneimittel-Forschung* (November 1993): 1221-27.

Jons, K. "Uta De Gato: Life-Giving Vine of Peru." *HerbalGram* 10 (1994): 4.

Kast, A. "Iscucin–Mistletoe Preparations for the Pre- and Postoperative Treatment of Malignancies." *Schweizerische Rundschau fur Medizin Praxis* 14 (1990): 427-29.

———. "Helixor–Mistletoe Preparation for Cancer Therapy." *Schweizerische Rundschau fur Medizin Praxis* 10 (1990): 291-95.

Komori, A. *Japanese Journal of Clinical Oncology* (June 1993): 186-90.

Kuba, M. "Studies on *Scutellariae radix*." *Chemical Pharmaceutical Bulletin* 32 (1984): 724-29.

Kulkalrni, R. R. "Treatment of Osteoarthritis with a Herbomineral Formulate." *Journal of Ethnopharmacology* 33 (1991): 91-95.

Lee-Huang, S. "MAP 30: A New Inhibitor of HIV-1 Infection Replication." *FEBS Letter* (October 15, 1990): 12-18.

Leung, A. *Encyclopedia of Common Natural Ingredients Used in Food, Drugs, and Cosmetics*. New York: John Wiley & Sons, 1980.

Li, B. "Inhibition of HIV Infection by Baicalin–A Flavonoid Compound Purified from Chinese Herbal Medicine." *Cellular & Molecular Biology Research* 39 (1993): 119-24.

Liu, C. "Recent Advances on Ginseng Research in China." *Journal of Ethnopharmacology* (February 1992): 27-38.

Louria, D. "Onion Extract in Treatment of Hypertension and Hyperlipidemia." *Cur. Ther. Res.* 37 (1985): 127-31.

Lu, W. B. "Treatment of 60 Cases of HIV-Infected Patients With Glyke." *Chung-Kuo Chung Hsi i Chieh Ho Tsa Chih* (June 1993): 340-42.

Mahajan, V. "Antimycotic Activity of Berberine Sulfate." *Sabouraudia* 20 (1982): 79-81.

Marti, James. *Serotonin*. San Francisco: Holistic Medical Research Foundation (HMRF), 1996.

———. *Consumer's Guide to Diets and Nutrition*. Boston: Houghton Mifflin, Inc., 1997.

Morgan, Helen C., and Kelly J. Moorhead. *Spirulina: Nature's Superfood*. Kailua-Kona, HI: Nutrex Inc., 1993.

Morton, J. *Major Medicinal Plants*. Springfield, IL: Charles C. Thomas, 1977.

Mowrey, Daniel. *The Scientific Validation of Herbal Medicine*. Dunvegan, ON, Canada: Cormorant Books, 1986.

———. "The Major Scientific Breakthroughs of the 90s: Reducing Body Fat through Thermogenesis." *Health Store News* (October/November 1994): 1-5.

Mueller, E. "A Viscum Album Oligosaccharide Activating Human Natural Cytotoxicity Is an Interferon Gamma Inducer." *Cancer Immunology Immunotherapy* 4 (1990): 221-27.

Murray, Michael. *The Healing Powers of Herbs*. Rocklin, CA: Prima Publishing, 1992.

——, and Joseph Pizzorno. *Encyclopedia of Natural Medicine*. Rocklin, CA: P r i m a Publishing, 1991.

Nagai, T. "Inhibition of Influenza Virus Sialidase and Anti-Influenza Virus Activity by Plant Flavonoids." *Chemical & Pharmaceutical Bulletin* (May 1990).

O'Brien, Jim. "The Herbal Cure for Migraine Pain." *Your Health* (October 19, 1993): 11-12.

Orman, David. "The Kombucha Beverage." *Townsend Letter for Doctors*. (December 1994): 1381.

Ozaki, Y. "Anti-Inflammatory Effect of Tetramethypyrazine and Ferulic Acid." *Chemical & Pharmaceutical Bulletin* (April 1992).

Petkov, V. "Plants with Hypotensive, Antiatheromatous and Coronary Dilating Action." *American Journal of Chinese Medicine* 7 (1979): 197-236.

Phillips, S. *"Zingiber offinale* (Ginger)–An Antiemetic for Day Case Surgery." *Anaesthesia* (August 1993).

Rai, G. "A Soluble-Blind, Placebo Controlled Study of *Ginkgo biloba* Extract ('Tanakan") in Elderly Outpatients with Mild to Moderate Memory Impairment." *Current Medical Research & Opinion* 6 (1991): 350-55.

" Red Hot Chili Peppers." *UC Berkeley Wellness Letter* (March 1995): 6.

Riley, K. "The Biological Efficacy of Aloes." *Journal of John Bastyr College of Natural Medicine* 2 (1981): 8-27.

Sarkar, S. "Antiviral Effect of the Extract of Culture Medium of *Lentinus edodes* Mycelia on the Replication of Herpes Simplex Virus Type 1." *Antiviral Research* (April 1993): 293-303.

Shanmugasundaram, E. "Brahmighritham, an Ayurvedic Herbal Formula for the Control of Epilepsy." *Journal of Ethnopharmacology* (July 1991): 269-76.

Sharma, H. M. "Inhibition of Human Low-Density Lipoprotein Oxidation in Vitro by Maharishi Ayurveda Herbal Mixtures." *Pharmacology, Biochemistry & Behavior* (December 1992): 1175-82.

Steinberg, Philip. "Cat's Claw Update." *Townsend Letter for Doctors*. (August/September 1995): 70-72.

Steinman, David. "Why You Should Drink Green Tea." *Natural Health* (March/April 1994).

Sydiskis, R. "Inactivation of Enveloped Viruses by Anthraquinones Extracted from Plants." *Antimicrobial Agents & Chemotherapy* (December 1991): 2463-66.

Wagner, H. "Coumestans as the Main Active Principles of the Liver Drugs." *Planta Medica* (1986): 370-77.

Walsh, B. "Urostomy and Urinary pH." *Journal of Nursing* (July-August 1992): 110-13.

Weiner, M. *Weiner's Herbal*. Mill Valley, CA: Quantum Books, 1990.

Welihinda, J., et al. "The Insulin-Releasing Activity of the Tropical Plant *Momordica Charantia*." (German) *Acta Biol. Med.* 41 (1982): 229-40.

Wollenweber, E. "Flavonoids from the Fruits of *Vitex agnus-castus*." *Planta Medica* 48 (1983): 26-27.

Zhang, H. "Preliminary Study of Traditional Chinese Medicine Treatment of Minimal Brain Dysfunction: Analysis of 100 Cases." *Traditional & Western Medicine* (May 1990): 278-79.

Organizations

American Association of Acupuncture and Oriental Medicine.
433 Front St., Catasauqua, PA 18032. (610) 266-1433.

American Association of Naturopathic Physicians.
2366 Eastlake Avenue, Suite 322, Seattle, Washington 98102. (206) 323-7610.

American Botanical Council.
P.O. Box 201660, Austin, Texas 78720. (512) 331-8868.

The American Herbalists Guild.
P.O. Box 1683, Soquel, California 95073. (408) 464-2441.

Additional Reading

Duke, J. *Handbook of Medicinal Herbs*. Boca Raton, FL: CRC Press, 1988.

Editors of Prevention Magazine Health Books. *The Complete Book of Natural and Medicinal Cures*. New York: Berkley Books, 1994.

Hoffman, David. *The New Holistic Herbal*. Rockport, MA: Element Books, 1992.

Holmes, Peter. *The Energetics of Western Herbs*. Artemi Publishers, 1989.

Simon, Harvey B. *Staying Well*. Boston: Houghton Mifflin Co., 1992.

Thomson, William. *Medicines from the Earth*. New York: McGraw-Hill Books, 1978.

Tierra, Lesley. *The Herbs of Life*. Freedom, CA: Crossing Press, 1992.

RESOURCES

Chapter 6

EXERCISE

In 1991, public health specialists at the University of Michigan invited 75 men and women, most of whom were 75 years of age or older, to take part in a very unusual experiment. The majority of the participants, according to Alan Rees and Charlene Willey's *Personal Health Reporter* were overweight and had never exercised regularly. Many of them also reported suffering from three out of four chronic health problems: arthritis, hypertension, heart disease, or diabetes.

Despite their particular infirmities, the men and women were asked to exercise for 30 minutes a week under the supervision of specialists at the University of Michigan's School of Public Health. The exercises were not strenuous and included neck and shoulder rolls, spinal twists and side stretches, arm and leg extensions, and pelvic rotations. Slow deep-breathing exercises were also part of their routine.

At the end of the trial, all subjects reported that they felt better and had lost weight. Even minor physical improvements were noticeable. Participants said they could "get around and move faster" and "felt less stiff in the joints," or "had more energy and were able to walk longer distances."

To the many Americans who exercise, these findings are not surprising. An increasing number of Americans of all ages are making exercise a part of their daily routine and for a good reason. More and more studies show that by not exercising, people put their health at risk. The same studies show that conversely, even moderate exercise can help prevent many diseases. The American Cancer Society, for example, has suggested that exercise alone can lower the risk of cancer for both men and women.

In one study of 10,000 men and 3,000 women conducted by the Institute for Aerobics Research in Dallas, men who were most fit on a treadmill test had four times lower cancer rates over an eight-year period than nonexercisers. Women who were physically fit on the same treadmill test were 16 times less likely to get cancer. Exercise, particularly in a woman's teenage and young adult years, directly lowers the rates of breast cancer and various hormone-related cancers of the reproductive tract. Non-athletes almost always have higher rates of cancers of the uterus, ovary, cervix, and vagina. Exercise appears to reduce cancer risk in women because exercise lowers a woman's lifetime exposure to estrogen, which can stimulate growth of cells in the breasts and reproductive organs.

In a Harvard School of Public Health study summarized by Michele Wolf in the October 1993 issue of *American Cancer*, 5,400 women who had graduated from college between 1925 and 1991 were asked about their diet, health, and reproductive and exercise histories. Half the subjects were non-athletes; the other half had been college athletes, and 75% of this latter group reported that they had continued to exercise. After eliminating factors such as smoking and family history of cancer, "we found that the former athletes had a significantly lower rate of breast cancer and cancers of the reproductive system," claims Dr. Rose Frisch, an Associate Professor who headed the research. Frisch also noted that with the exception of skin cancer, the athletes had markedly less of all types of cancer–including nonreproductive-tract cancers–than sedentary subjects.

The Centers for Disease Control and Prevention (CDC) and the American College of Sports Medicine now recommend that every adult engage in at least 30 minutes of moderate physical activity throughout the day, at least five times a week, to prevent car-diovascular illness. These guidelines, reported in the December 1990 issue of the *The University of California at Berkeley Wellness Letter,* can be met by participating in sports or walking, or by adding physical activities such as gardening and climbing up stairs to a daily routine. The guidelines are aimed at increasing the proportion of adults who get enough exercise to achieve worthwhile health benefits. Currently, 54% of Americans over the age of 18 need more physical activity.

This chapter discusses the many physiological benefits of exercise. Clinical trials in which exercise has proven effective are analyzed, and general guidelines for measuring the effects and benefits of different forms of exercise are suggested. The major forms of exercise are then described, along with specific exercises for different groups: children, the elderly, and people with disabilities. Understandably, not everyone has the leisure time or inclination to exercise regularly out of doors or at a local health club. Yet anyone can find the time to do simple calisthenics at home which gently exercise the muscle and tissue systems of the body.

Physiological Benefits of Exercise

Professional athletes, marathon runners, or people who exercise regularly tend to look healthier than those who do not exercise. Their bodies are slim, their muscles are firm, and they have more energy. Physiologists have long been struck by the similarities between the effects of sedentary living and aging, so much so that many researchers have concluded that many of the "normal symptoms of aging" may be, in part, symptoms of inactivity. Such effects include changes in the cardiovascular and respiratory system, cholesterol levels, bone mineral mass, joint flexibility, bowel function, immune system function, sleep patterns, sensory abilities, and intellectual capacity.

Exercise Helps Maintain Heart and Lung Fitness. The most important physiological benefit of exercise is that it helps maintain heart and lung fitness. The heart's function is to pump blood (most adults have slightly more than a gallon of blood in their bodies) through more than 60,000 miles of blood vessels. Each day the heart beats approximately 100,000 times, depending on the body's activity. In a 70-year lifetime, an average human heart beats more than 2.5 billion times. The respiratory system, including the lungs, provides the body with oxygen and removes carbon dioxide via tiny air sacs in the lungs called alveoli (which number approximately 300 million).

The heart's ability to pump blood drops an average of 58% between the ages of 25 and 85. By age 70, lung capacity can decrease by 40-50% and muscle strength by 20%. In fact, scientists now think that by the time most people turn 20, their cardiovascular and respiratory functions have already begun to decline, a trend that accelerates throughout life. As the heart becomes less efficient with age, oxygen is thus delivered to the muscles more slowly. Exercise increases the size of the heart muscle and its chamber volume, and greatly improves its efficiency.

Exercise Lowers Hypertension (High Blood Pressure). Diastolic blood pressure rises with age by as much as 10% between the ages of 60 and 70. Poor nutrition, a sedentary lifestyle, and an increasing intake of medications generally combine to increase blood pressure in the elderly. As a result, the heart has to pump harder than normal because of an excess of fluid in the bloodstream combined with narrowed or constricted arteries. Both the pumping of the heart and the functioning of the arteries affect blood pressure.

Along with stress reduction therapies such as yoga, meditation, hypnosis, and biofeedback, regular sustained exercise effectively lowers blood pressure. People with hypertension should consult their physician before starting any form of exercise because even mild exercise temporarily raises blood pressure. The best exercises, according to clinical trials, are those that reduce the level of stress hormones in the bloodstream that constrict the arteries and veins. Progressive weight lifting, walking or jogging three times a week for 20 minutes, stationary bicycling, and a combination of walking, jogging, and bike riding have all been found to lower blood pressure.

Exercise Prevents Loss of Muscle Mass. As people age, they can lose as much as 10-12% of their muscle mass with no appreciable loss in overall body weight. In fact, they normally gain weight. Men in their 80s can lose another 20 pounds of muscle mass, while continuing to gain body fat.

A 1990 Tufts University study cited in *The Exercise Bible: The Medical Benefits Of Exercise* showed that working out can build muscle mass in elderly people. Ten nursing home residents at the Hebrew Rehabilitation Center for the Aged in Boston, between the ages of 87 and 96, completed two months of high-intensity resistance training using weights. The participants nearly doubled their leg muscle strength, increased thigh muscle size by 9% and improved performance on mobility tests. The researchers concluded that strength training effectively helps people of advanced age with multiple chronic diseases, functional disabilities, and nutritional inadequacies build muscle mass.

Exercise Reduces Body Fat and Helps Maintains Ideal Body Weight. The benefits of exercise in helping people lose weight or maintain their ideal body weight have been extensively documented in many

Exercises to Lose Weight

The following forms of exercise have been shown to burn a significant number of calories in only a 30-minute period. The figures are calculated for a 130-pound woman.

Aerobic Exercise (intense)	Calories Expended
Badminton	360
Bowling	300
Cleaning windows	240-300
Cross-country skiing (walking speed)	252
Cycling	420
Cycling (9.4 mph)	177
Downhill skiing	600
Golf, pulling cart	300
Handball or squash	660
Ice or roller skating	400
Jogging (5 mph)	480
Paddleball	600

Aerobic Exercise (intense)	Calories Expended
Rowing machine	210
Running (8-minute mile)	375
Scrubbing floors	360
Sitting, conversing	72-84
Stair climbing (moderate pace)	285
Step aerobics (6-inch step)	175
Step aerobics (8-inch step)	208
Strength training (free weights)	150
Swimming (crawl)	228
Table tennis	360
Tennis, singles	480
Volleyball	400
Walking (on pavement)	141
Walking (treadmill at 3 mph)	132
Walking (2 mph)	120-150
Water skiing	480

studies. Exercise burns calories consumed as food, and raises the basal metabolic rate (BMR). In order for an individual to lose weight, energy intake must be less than energy expenditure. This can be done by decreasing calorie intake (dieting) or by increasing the rate at which the calories are burned (exercising). To lose one pound, people must consume 3,500 fewer calories than they expend in a typical week–or 500 calories per day. Most individuals will begin to lose weight if they decrease their calorie intake below 1,500 calories per day and engage in aerobic exercise for 15-20 minutes three to four times per week.

Physical energy expenditure (PEE) has the greatest impact of any other variable on total caloric requirements. Whereas the average sedentary person usually expends only 300-800 calories a day in physical activity, athletes in training or workers engaged in heavy manual labor may expend as many as 3,000 calories.

Exercise Improves Glucose Tolerance and Reduces Insulin Resistance. Exercise not only helps control weight gain, but it also plays an important role in improving glucose tolerance and reducing insulin resistance–both significant factors in the development of diabetes. Glucose tolerance is a measure of the body's ability to metabolize glucose as it is released into the bloodstream. This ability usually declines with age. Since insulin's ability to convert glucose in the cells is also reduced, glucose can gradually increase to dangerous levels in the bloodstream.

Increased muscle activity, however, accelerates the transport of glucose into muscle cells regardless of the presence of insulin, thereby helping to compensate for insulin resistance. Consequently, exercise can sometimes be a useful tool for controlling type II diabetes and may even help prevent it in some cases. It may also forestall the serious complications of the disease.

Exercise Helps Maintain Bone Mass and Prevent Bone Loss. Bone is constantly being formed and reabsorbed throughout a person's life. Until the age of 35, more bone is deposited than removed, leading to a net gain in bulk and strength. After 35, however, the trend gradually begins to reverse.

According to the June 1994 *Tufts University Diet & Nutrition Letter*, 24 million Americans, 80% of them women, suffer from osteoporosis, a progressive condition in which bones lose mass and become extremely brittle and prone to injury. Osteoporosis begins when the body cannot make new bone fast enough to replace bone loss. Both men and women lose some bone mass as they age, but the rate of loss is much slower in men (who have denser bones to begin with) than in women, and osteoporosis is rarely a problem for men. Conversely, according to Kurt Butler and Lynn Rayner, women who live to the age of 80 usually lose a third to two-thirds of their entire skeletons and up to six inches of their height.

The process of bone loss typically begins in a woman's mid-30s, some 10-15 years before the onset of menopause, at a rate of 0.5-1% a year. This loss increases to 2-5% in the first 10 years following menopause, and then tapers off to about 1% per year. In the decade after menopause, women typically lose 5-10% of the bone-sustaining minerals in their spines alone. As a result, according to the National Osteoporosis Foundation, one-third of American women over 65 suffer spinal fractures and 15% break their hips because of osteoporosis.

Exercise appears to stimulate bone mineralization. Even though women who exercise regularly tend to have lower estrogen levels and be thinner (two states associated with higher risk for osteoporosis), the effect of exercise more than compensates for those factors, giving these women denser and stronger bones than women who do not exercise regularly. A study at the Queen Elizabeth Hospital in Toronto, Ontario, compared bone densities of sedentary women between the ages of 50 and 62 with those of women who engaged in aerobic exercise and others who did both aerobic and strengthening exercises. The active women of both groups experienced similar significant gains in bone mass, while the sedentary women showed a loss.

After puberty, the only way women can increase their bone mass is to continually exercise. It is still unclear whether women in their 70s can significantly increase their bone mass. It also appears that those bones most directly stressed by exercise increase in size the most. Nancy Lane, a rheumatologist at the University of California in San Francisco, has extensively researched the bone density of older female runners. She suggests that exercise can slow the rate of bone loss during menopause, while the benefits from gains in strength and balance help to prevent falls.

A study at Washington University School of Medicine in St. Louis suggests that lifting weights is the best way to build bone mass. The Bone Mineral Mass (BMM) was significantly higher for those participating in a weight-bearing program (more than six hours per week of rigorous weight lifting) combined with aerobic exercise (more than 40 miles per week of running or more than six hours per week of aerobic dance classes) than for sedentary people or people participating only in aerobic exercise. Other studies have shown that competitive master swimmers have greater bone mineral content than non-athletes.

Exercise Helps Maintain Joint Flexibility.
Joint flexibility is also a special concern of the elderly because the aging process gradually diminishes the amount of fluid in the joints. Rheumatoid arthritis, the most common disorder of the joints, is caused by inflammation of the lining of the synovial capsule (the fiber tissue surrounding bones and cartilage). Exercises for rheumatoid arthritis sufferers help maintain cartilage, mineralize underlying bone, strengthen shock-absorbing muscles and ligaments around joints, and increase joint flexibility. Several new programs at the University of Michigan Medical Center, for example, suggest that weight lifting in water helps distribute synovial fluid around the cartilage and throughout entire joint spaces.

Exercise Reduces Depression and Negative Moods.
With aging, a reduced cerebral blood flow causes a depletion of neurotransmitters (biochemicals in the brain that send instructions from neuron to neuron), which may affect memory, attention span, concentration, and learning function. The neurotransmitters norepinephrine, serotonin, and dopamine require oxygen for their synthesis and metabolism, and regular endurance exercise is an excellent way to supply this oxygen to the brain.

Depression is linked to disturbances in these neurotransmitter levels—a major reason why aerobic exercise is now being prescribed for depressed patients. The mood improvement experienced after vigorous exercise may

also be related to a better biochemical balance in the brain.

Exercises which require the least expenditure of energy produce the least amount of change on depression and mood levels. Any exercise to lower depression must be progressive because people who start with high intensity workouts are most likely to quit and therefore will not realize the benefits of exercise.

Exercise Helps Increase Life Expectancy.
Can regular exercise lengthen life expectancy? Dr. Ralph Paffenbarger's study of 1,700 Harvard alumni whose weekly energy output in walking, stairclimbing, and active sports totaled at least 2,000 calories had a 28% reduction in all-cause death rates. For those expending 3,500 calories a week in exercise, death rates were an astonishing 50% lower. Life expectancy was 2.15 years greater for those who expended more than 2,000 calories than for those who expended less. In practical terms, because even sedentary people burn 1,000 calories a week in physical activity, this improvement in longevity can be gained by walking or jogging 8-10 miles a week. In general, regular physical activity has a beneficial impact on life expectancy by reducing the likelihood of chronic diseases such as heart disease, obesity, and diabetes. However, there is no evidence to support the contention that physical activity can actually lengthen lifespan (the maximal obtainable age of a particular person).

The physiological benefits of exercise are perhaps most evident in coronary artery disease (CAD). Hypertension (high blood pressure) is considered a major risk factor for CAD and is less likely to develop in people who are physically fit. Exercise, whether it is accompanied by weight loss, also raises the body's production of high-density lipoprotein (HDL), an effect associated with a lower risk of CAD. Both elderly and young men appear to exhibit similar HDL rises, with the degree of benefit apparently commensurate with the intensity of exercise. Even brisk walking for 2.5-4 hours per week, however, is sufficient to raise HDL levels. HDL is especially important to men over 50, for whom it is the single most important cardiac risk factor.

In Paffenbarger's long-term study of the health and lifestyles of approximately 17,000 male Harvard alumni between the ages of 35 and 74, those who exercised relatively strenuously for 4.5-8 hours per week reduced their chances of coronary disease by approximately 50%.

Exercise Reduces Back Pains. Back pain is almost always associated with muscular weakness. Regardless of whether this weakness is a cause or an effect of pain, exercise can usually produce increased strength and function of the back muscles and decrease pain. Dr. Richard A. Deyo, Professor of Medicine and Health Services at the University of Washington School of Medicine, uses exercise to reduce the number of days back-pain patients spend in the hospital. According to an article by Joel Posner in the March 15, 1992 issue of *Patient Care*, Deyo prescribes a minimum bed rest period for back-pain patients, normally no more than two days if necessary (most doctors recommend two weeks in bed). Dr. Deyo suggests that prolonged bed rest may increase later back pains because it contributes to bone loss, general weakness, and blood clots in the legs. Light weight lifting, preferably with hydrotherapy; swimming; rowing machines; stretching; and yoga have all been found to be effective in relieving back pain.

Choosing the Right Exercise Program

The basic components of a good exercise program are discussed in the following section. Each form of exercise is evaluated and the reader may choose among any appropriate exercise or combination. The basic guidelines every person should consider before choosing an exercise program include:

- Current health status.
- Desired goals to be accomplished through exercise (such as living longer, losing weight, or increasing mental functioning).
- Maximum pulse rate and optimal exercise training range.

Current Health Status. Before starting an exercise program, it is important that people determine their current health status. Those who have been inactive for a number of years or have a diagnosed illness should consult their physician first. Individuals over 30 who have been sedentary for several months or years should be especially careful to work up to higher levels of exercise very gradually. Some experts recommend that all potential exercisers undergo a complete physical examination before embarking on a regular training program.

Exercise Goals. While people of all ages should exercise to maintain good health, the type of exercise varies for different age groups. Not all forms of exercise are equally beneficial for every individual. In general, exercises are either aerobic or isometric. In aerobic exercises such as walking, running, swimming, and cycling, rhythmic contraction and relaxation of flexor and extensor muscle groups occur, which promotes blood flow through the arteries to and from the heart. At the right pace, such activities can be continued for long periods. In isometric exercises (in which muscles are held in contraction for prolonged periods, such as in weight lifting), the sustained contraction limits blood flow by compressing the small arteries, and fails to help pump blood back to the heart. Moreover, the acute increase of blood pressure associated with isometrics can be very hazardous to people with heart disease or high blood pressure.

Maximum Pulse Rate and Optimal Exercise Training Range. The safety and effectiveness of any exercise is partially determined by measuring heart rate (number of heartbeats per minute). Exercise physiologists recommend training at a level of between 70% and 80% of maximum heart rate; under no circumstances should the rate exceed 85%.

To determine maximum heart rate, simply subtract your age from 220. To determine your training range, multiply this number by 70-80%. If you are 50 years old, for example, your maximum heart rate would be 170, and your training range 119-136. You should never exceed a heart rate of 145 beats per minute. A minimum of 30 minutes of exercising at your training heart rate at least three times a week is necessary to gain significant benefits from exercise.

Taking Precautions. It is important to remember that people should never exceed their capacity for exercise, or serious injury can result. Exercising at a level that makes the heart beat at or near its maximum capacity forces the muscles into more anaerobic metabolism that quickly uses up available glucose and increases the breakdown of muscle tissue. Normally, the lost tissue from exercise is more than replaced during the recommended rest period of approximately 20 hours after exercise. If exercise is resumed before full recovery, a net loss of muscle tissue–rather than a gain–may result.

Overexercise can result in significant loss of muscle mass and fat-burning capacity. The older a person is, the more likely this is to occur because tissue repair rate slows down with age. People who consistently overexercise can become sore and tired, and actually end up in worse condition than before they started.

Most importantly, many experts now warn that overexercise can precipitate a heart attack, even in apparently healthy individuals. Exercisers should monitor their heart rates while exercising and not ignore symptoms such as tightness or pain in the chest, dizziness, light headedness, stomach pain, or breathing difficulties. Remember that exercises which cause pain can also lead to severe injuries. In the moderate-to-intensive aerobic training programs, which are more beneficial to cardiovascular fitness and general health, there is no reason to experience pain in order to gain fitness.

Another precaution to keep in mind is to drink water or other non-sugar liquids while exercising, particularly during hot weather when the body loses fluids most rapidly. Perspiring excessively can lead to dehydration (with symptoms including increased body temperature, dizziness, and weakness), which in turn can cause heat stroke. Most experts suggest that if you begin to feel thirsty, drink a glass of water or a non-carbonated sports beverage which also provides small amounts of sodium and potassium (carbonated or sugary drinks can upset the stomach if people are dehydrated). Check the label for serving sizes and calorie counts. Drink 8-12 ounces of fluid at least 15 minutes before exercising, and do not wait until you become thirsty to replenish your body's supply of liquids.

According to *Food Insight,* the bulletin of the International Food Information Council, "drinking enough fluid is certainly key to maximum athletic performance. But it is even more basic than that. It can make the difference between feeling great or drained after exercise." *Food Insight* says that the average adult needs 64 ounces (eight cups) of fluid a day. The fluid can come from water, milk, meat, or vegetables. Even dry cereal or bread contains from 8-35% water.

Approximately 12-15% of Americans suffer from exercise-induced asthma (EIA).

There is a danger that someone might have this problem without knowing it as EIA typically occurs in people who have no history of asthma or allergies. The symptoms usually include early signs of difficulty such as a drop in performance or post-exercise fatigue. During heavy exercise, an athlete normally breathes in 18-20 times more air than when at rest. If the body cannot consume and humidify this large volume of air, spasms or constriction of the airways may occur. Colds, pollution, and recent upper respiratory tract infection can also trigger this reaction.

During exercises such as running, swimming, and cycling, people can monitor for EIA by noting their breathing response and lowering intensity, if necessary. Swimming is the ideal sport for athletes with EIA because the warm, moist air decreases the incidence of spasms or constriction of the airways. Sports that involve intermittent exertion, such as baseball and volleyball, are usually low risk as well. People with EIA who exercise regularly should use medication, if prescribed, 30-60 minutes before starting, and warm up at 50% of maximum heart rate for 10-15 minutes. They should also cool down by walking or stretching after exercising for 10-20 minutes and should, in all cases, stay well hydrated.

Proper exercise can be beneficial even for people with a number of illnesses, including hypertension and diabetes, but a vigorous exercise program should not be undertaken without first consulting a physician or health practitioner. Individuals susceptible to EIA should discuss the problem with their physician as well. There may be reasons why an individual, due to genetic factors, age, sex, and prior activity levels, should not perform a certain exercise.

How Much Exercise Do You Need? The amount you personally need will depend on your goals. In order to achieve a training

How Can You Keep Exercise from Becoming Boring?

About 50% of people who are concerned enough with their health to begin exercise programs drop out within six months to a year–even cardiac patients who stand to benefit the most from exercise drop out at a rate as high as 70%. Studies show that those who withdrew from exercise programs reported that their workout routines were boring or the facilities were expensive and inconvenient.

The most important factor when starting an exercise regimen is to set realistic, attainable goals. If you're out of shape, don't try to run several miles or swim 30 laps in the first week or two. You're better off concentrating on the length of time you exercise, not on distance. Researchers have found that runners who aim for 30 minutes during an exercise session, for example, are more likely to keep running than those who go for mileage.

Testing yourself will help you monitor your progress and enable you to stick to your activity once you see your fitness improve. Exercising with other people can also increase your enjoyment, and entering amateur races is yet another tool for motivation.

effect and thereby cardiorespiratory fitness, you'll need to perform aerobic exercise three to five times a week, according to the American College of Sports Medicine. Depending on how fit you already are and how intensely you exercise, each session should last 20-60 minutes, in addition to the warm-up and cool-down activities you perform. You also should exercise at your target heart rate.

Exercising less than this will not help you achieve an adequate training effect for fitness. However, experts have recently found that if you simply want to improve your health and increase your odds of living longer, you don't necessarily have to engage in a rigorous exercise program to achieve the training effect. What's important is simply being physically active.

Most people could expend 2,000 calories if they simply jogged for 30-40 minutes five days a week, or walked 5-8 hours per week. Paffenbarger's study also showed that simply walking nine miles a week will significantly reduce one's chances of developing heart disease.

Aerobic Exercises

Aerobic exercise is defined as any form of movement that conditions the heart and lungs to work more efficiently. When the body is working harder than it is accustomed, the muscles demand more oxygen. The capacity of the lungs increases and the heart becomes stronger (and larger) as it works to pump oxygen-rich blood through the arteries.

Exercising aerobically less than three times a week does not increase aerobic capacity or help in attaining or maintaining weight loss. At the same time, exercising aerobically more than five times per week does not provide a significant increase in fitness and may result in injury if the exercise is too strenuous.

Aerobic exercise includes any activity that uses large muscle groups in a rhythmic, continual motion that increases oxygen consumption. A three-mile daily walk is the most simple aerobic exercise. Hiking, bicycling, swimming, dancing, rowing, skating, and cross-country skiing are other good aerobic

exercises. Indoor exercises include cross-country ski machines, aerobic dance and step aerobics, weight training, and indoor climbing.

Which Aerobic Exercise Is Best?

The answer depends on your exercise goals and preferences, and the shape you're in. Virtually every aerobic activity can provide a training effect. The one possible exception is walking, which may not elevate the heart rate sufficiently for people who are already quite fit. On the other hand, recent studies have indicated that it isn't necessary to exercise at a high training intensity to reap certain health benefits. In several studies of walking, including one involving postal workers who'd been walking an average of 25 miles a week for 15-28 years, a researcher found a link between walking and increased levels of HDL cholesterol.

Such findings are significant because many exercise physiologists have reported that, in order to increase HDL levels significantly, you need to run or perform some other intense aerobic exercise. These studies, however, appear to indicate that walking or other low-intensity exercise, when done regularly, may provide the same benefit.

Walking. Walking is the fastest growing form of exercise among Americans and also the most popular. More than 68 million Americans walk regularly to satisfy their exercise needs. According to a study in the *British Medical Journal*, reported in the December 12, 1992 edition of the San *Jose Mercury News*, those who participate in moderate physical activity such as walking have a 40% lower risk of stroke than inactive people. Walking has also been shown to bolster the body's defense against colds. Joel Posner reports in the March 15, 1992 issue of *Patient Care* that walking strengthens the specific components of the immune system

Walking Guidelines

1. To maintain basic health and minimize risk of disease, walk at least 20 minutes at least three times a week. Walking at 2.75 miles per hour or less is considered strolling and offers minimal fitness benefits. Any type of stop-and-go walking has far fewer benefits than continuous walking.

2. To maintain a moderate level of health and fitness, walk briskly for 30-45 minutes. Walking at 3-3.5 m.p.h. is considered a normal, comfortable pace. Many beginners can maintain a 17-minute mile, a pace sufficient to metabolize body fat.

3. To achieve a generally good level of health and fitness, walk briskly for 30-60 minutes every day. Walking at 3.75-4 m.p.h. is considered brisk walking. The goal of most brisk walkers is to attain a 15-minute mile and be able to walk two miles in 30 minutes. At this pace, the arms are partially bent and swinging.

4. To achieve optimal health and fitness, expend a minimum of 2,000 calories per week by walking briskly for 60 minutes every day. Walking at 4-4.75 m.p.h. is considered speed walking. At 4 m.p.h., most people swing their arms, breathe deeply, and sweat mildly. Pumping the arms vigorously burns approximately 7% more calories than brisk walking alone. Speed walking is therefore a whole-body aerobic exercise: it tones the buttocks, legs, and arms, while trimming fat, flattening the abdomen, and improving posture.

5. To achieve the ultimate in health and fitness, expend up to 3,500 calories per week by walking briskly six miles every day. Walking at 5 m.p.h. or more is considered race walking. The aim is to walk a mile in 12 minutes or less and three miles in 36 minutes. Race walking sets a faster pace, uses more energy, and requires faster breathing. Walking at 5 m.p.h. for one hour is equivalent to bicycling 14 miles, and burns more calories than running.

that fight cold viruses. Test subjects who walked did not always avoid colds, but when they got them, the colds were less severe and lasted only half as long as those suffered by physically inactive people. According to the American College of Sports Medicine, regular, moderate-intensity endurance exercises such as 30 minutes of walking every other day can also reduce mild to moderate hypertension, and help people avoid getting high blood pressure.

Walking requires no special skills or equipment and can be stopped at any time without danger. A good pair of walking shoes is absolutely essential. Any comfortable, well-cushioned athletic shoe that fully supports the sole of the foot is adequate.

Susan Johnson, author of *The Walking Handbook,* suggests that beginners start with a simple 10-minute walk at any speed, five minutes out and five minutes back. During the second week, build up to 15 minutes a

Safe Running Tips

Dr. R. James Gregg of the International Chiropractor's Association recommends the following injury-prevention guidelines for people who jog.

1. Wear a running shoe with ample heel padding. Air-cushioned shoe inserts help absorb shock.

2. Run on surfaces that "give," such as grass, pathways, and dirt roads.

3. Run on alternate sides of the road. Running continually in the same direction on the same side of the road may cause a muscle imbalance in the lower back because the grade of the road surface may slope towards the sides of drainage.

4. Stretch at least five minutes before and after the jog; stretch both leg and back muscles.

5. Avoid running downhill frequently. With gravity pulling you on a downgrade, your normal three-foot stride can become five feet long. To compensate for a longer gait, the body leans backwards, which increases the curve of the lumbar spine and may tighten back muscles.

6. Measure your heart rate and do not exceed your training range.

day. By the third week, increase to 20 minutes a day. And by the fourth week, continue to walk 20 minutes a day, but after warming up with a slow stroll for five minutes, pick up the pace until eventually you are walking briskly, as if you are late for an appointment. End the exercise by slowing your pace back

down to a stroll, then cool down with passive stretching, and drink an 8-12 ounce glass of water.

According to Johnson, walkers will see immediate results in three to four weeks in the form of more strength and firmness in their legs. By the end of eight weeks, they will begin to lose body fat. At that time, walkers can concentrate on strengthening calf and hamstring muscles by pushing off their back foot rather than reaching with the front, or by developing a long, even rhythmic stride which will tone the buttocks.

Brisk Walking. In the last 10 years, brisk walking has become one of America's favorite exercises, particularly for women. Research now indicates that brisk walking may offer virtually the same health and fitness benefits as running or jogging, but without stress to the joints and risk of injury. Physicians recommend brisk walking as an efficient and safe form of exercise for almost everyone. Many participants achieve a level of fitness in which they are able to easily walk a 13-minute mile or ascend a 2,000-foot hill.

Running (Jogging). Running is a high-impact sport and should only be undertaken by people in good health who have no ankle, knee, or back problems. Individuals who can comfortably walk two miles in 30 minutes without dangerously increasing their heart rate are good candidates for running. Sports physicians normally advise that people beginning to run first alternate between walking and jogging for 20 minutes, doing 2-3 minute stretches of each, and slowly build up to 30 minutes of uninterrupted running.

As a high-risk aerobic exercise, running can be quite stressful to the body and lead to injuries. Butler and Rayner cite one survey of 1,000 runners that found that "60 percent had been injured for considerable periods of time. The most common injuries are of the knee, shin, Achilles' tendon, forefoot, hip, thigh, heel, ankle, arch and groin." As with any form of exercise, injury can be avoided by choosing appropriate shoes, proper running surfaces, practicing good running habits, and by consulting a trainer or sports physician.

Aerobic Dancing. Aerobic dancing is a special type of exercise that is scientifically designed to maximize aerobic respiration. Sessions vary in length and degree of difficulty. A session should include at least 10 minutes of stretching and warming-up exercises, followed by 15-30 minutes of nonstop aerobic movements at a pace determined by a person's fitness level (beginner, intermediate, advanced). At least five minutes of cooling-down activities such as walking and stretching should conclude the program.

Aerobic dancing has proven effective in improving fitness and reducing weight. The workouts popularized on television videos provide significant benefits, but exercisers should remember that to be of real value, any aerobic dance workout should increase heartbeat up to 75% of its maximum rate for at least 15 minutes. Many aerobic injuries can result from prior foot, leg, or back injuries, and good shoes and a resilient surface should always be used.

Step Aerobics. Step aerobics (or bench aerobics) is an increasingly popular form of aerobics that utilizes a small platform approximately the height of a stair-step. Working to music, aerobicizers step on and off the bench in routines that give them a cardiovascular workout while toning legs and buttocks. Since this form of aerobics is low in impact, because one foot is always on the floor or on the step, it is less likely to result in exercise-related injuries typically associated with dance aerobics.

Researchers at San Diego State University found that working at a rate of 120 steps per minute while pumping the arms was as exerting as running at seven miles per hour. However, impact forces were similar to those created by walking at only three miles per hour. In a second study at the University of Pittsburgh, subjects working at a rate of 80 steps per minute burned almost 300 calories in 30 minutes. The calorie expenditure increased 19% when one-pound hand weights and a pumping arm motion were added.

As with any aerobic exercise, it is important to warm up and stretch before the cardiovascular session and cool down after the exercise is concluded.

Rowing. Rowing is both an intensely demanding physical activity and a competitive sport. Noncompetitive rowing is an excellent aerobic exercise, although it is normally used in combination with running or bicycling as part of a total fitness program. Adaptive rowing is a popular exercise in the U.S., and many different types of rowboats have been marketed to appeal to different age groups Many homes now also have gyms equipped with a rowing machine. Rowing is an ideal form of exercise for the disabled. One variant of the rowing machine is the landrower, a rowing bicycle that propels the upper body forward as the rower pulls on the oars.

Cross-Country Skiing. Butler and Rayner recommend cross-country skiing as one of the best aerobic exercises because it provides all the benefits of running without the jarring stresses that accompany it. The large leg muscles are used more than in swimming, and very high levels of oxygen consumption can be reached by the fit cross-country skier. Unfortunately, the sport is not accessible or affordable for all people, although it is much less expensive than downhill skiing. Some exercise devices now mimic cross-country skiing very well and are excellent for skiers and nonskiers alike.

Exercising at Work

Americans spend an average of 11-12 hours a day working and commuting to and from work, which often results in a lack of time or inclination to exercise. For people who cannot exercise before, during, or after work, the following gentle exercise is recommended to effectively stretch various body muscles.

Door Stretch Exercise

1. Find a narrow doorway.

2. Lay your forearms up against each side of the doorway, with one foot behind the other and begin to lean forward.

3. As you lean forward, your shoulders should be pulled back.

4. Done correctly, this exercise will fully stretch your chest muscles as well as the muscles around your shoulders. You can control the force of the stretch by moving your front leg farther forward.

5. As you move your leg forward, you should feel a strong stretch along your calves and hamstrings. This also stretches out the hip flexors, the muscles surrounding the hipbone.

6. Now turn to one side as you lean forward. This helps stretch the serratus interior, the rippled muscles above the rib cage.

7. Put your other foot forward and repeat the exercise.

There are two different techniques involved in cross-country skiing, both of which provide excellent exercise for the legs and heart. In the skating technique, the skier pushes off from the rear ski in a motion similar to ice skating. These lateral pushes on the skis result in a skating movement when performed from side to side. The pushing portion is known as the propulsive phase and occurs between pole plant and toe off. The remainder of the cycle is the stride phase. The skating technique is a slightly more effective form of aerobic exercise.

Swimming. Swimming is considered by many experts to be the safest form of exercise and also uses more muscles than most other aerobic alternatives. It is an excellent choice for people of all age groups and physical fitness levels because swimmers can pace themselves, both in terms of duration and intensity (speed) of the workout. Swimming has been shown to help relieve varicose veins by increasing circulation in the legs. And, as will be discussed later in this chapter, it is ideal for people with physical disabilities. However, a person must swim for at least 15 minutes nonstop to derive the benefits of other forms of aerobic exercise. Because swimming entirely immerses the individual in water, all of the cells of the skin are stimulated, and relaxation is induced.

Bicycling. Bicycling provides an excellent aerobic workout, and an increasing number of Americans now bicycle to work, school, or shops or use a stationary cycle at home or at the gym.

In bicycling, the peak oxygen load is not as great as with running or cross-country skiing. It is also much less physically stressful than running or aerobic dancing. To produce positive benefits, a person must bicycle hard enough to increase heart rate for at least 15 consecutive minutes. In order to burn 300-360 calories, it is necessary to cycle at least eight miles per hour. To burn 350-420 calories, a person must cycle at least 10 miles per hour.

Other Sports. Other sports such as tennis, basketball, and volleyball can be very tiring, although they often consist of standing around between short bursts of action, and are not as aerobically valuable as sports with nonstop movements. It has been estimated that jogging at a rate of at least 3 m.p.h. for 15 minutes is equivalent to an hour or more of most other sports, including tennis, racquetball, and ping pong. This, of course, depends on how fast and vigorously the latter games are played.

Although these sports tend to be less aerobically effective, an exception is two-on-two volleyball, which can be extremely demanding, especially between players good enough to keep long volleys in play. Baseball and football players often keep in shape by jogging, sprinting, and other exercises which combine nonstop smooth movements of all major muscle groups.

Exercises for Children

One of the most valuable gifts parents can give their children is the motivation to stay physically fit. If children's early years are physically active, they will lay a solid foundation for a healthier adult life. Unfortunately, an estimated 25 million American children are not fit, and more than half of the children who participate in organized athletics cannot pass a basic fitness test, according to the American Physical Therapy Association (APTA).

The National Exercise for Life Institute in Excelsior, Minnesota, further claims that 50% of all American children are not getting enough exercise to develop healthy cardiorespiratory systems; 67% of children have at least three heart risk factors; and obesity figures are 54% higher than in the 1960s. One study found that typical gym classes give chil-

Are Your Children Physically Fit?

The Prudential Life Insurance Company lists the following guidelines to help parents determine if their children are physically fit:

- 11-year-old boys should be able to run one mile in 11 minutes; 11-year-old girls should be able to do the same in 12. Boys over 17 should be able to run one mile in 8 1/2 minutes; girls should be able to do the same in 10.
- 11-year-old boys should be able to perform eight consecutive push-ups; 11-year-old girls should be able to do seven. Boys over age 14 should be able to perform 14 consecutive push-ups; girls over 14 should be able to do seven. Older teens and adult men should strive for 18 consecutive push-ups; women should hold steady at seven.
- The percentage of body fat in boys and young men should not exceed 25%; the percentage of body fat in girls and young women should not exceed 32%.

dren only one to three minutes of vigorous exercise per class. However, the U.S. Public Health Service and the National Exercise for Life Institute recommend that children ages six through 17 exercise vigorously for 20 minutes three times a week.

The APTA publishes a 13-page activity booklet for children in grades one through four to encourage fitness through illustrations, games, and puzzles. (For a copy of APTA's booklet, write to "Fit Kids," P.O. Box 37257, Washington, D.C. 20013.)

Exercise for the Elderly

Only one of four elderly persons regularly maintains the level of physical activity recommended by medical specialists. Yet research has conclusively demonstrated both the conditioning and rehabilitative effectiveness of physical activity for this age group. As noted, vigorous physical activity, especially if it is recreational, has been linked to increased longevity.

Water exercises are especially beneficial for the elderly. Water-based programs allow seniors to gain full benefits of aerobic exercise without exerting strain or pressure on their joints. With the aid of water walkers (buoyancy devises that attach easily around the waist), exercisers have total freedom of movement and can participate at their own pace.

Water exercise has been shown to have similar cardiovascular and musculoskeletal benefits for older people as "on the ground" aerobic exercise. The American College of Sports Medicine now recommends aquatic aerobic activity involving large muscle groups for elderly patients with rheumatoid arthritis (RA) because of the soothing and salubrious effects of warm water. A further benefit of water-based exercises is that they cause less exercise-induced asthma than other forms of exertion. Traditional low-impact and chair aerobic programs geared for seniors have also proven popular.

The Optimal Aging Program at the Medical College of Pennsylvania uses a variety of exercises to help elderly patients stay physically fit. The most important part of the program is lifting weights three times a week for 40 minutes. The weight lifting programs are individually tailored, and the smallest weights are only two pounds. One set of 10

repetitions may be enough for the beginning exerciser. When three sets of 10 repetitions can be done easily, the weight loads are increased. Lower body work includes exercising the quadriceps, hamstrings, and legs. Exercises for the hip are important, especially for women, in preventing falls and hip fractures. A weight-stack machine or ankle weights gently tones the knee joints.

Upper body weight lifts, including shoulder work (overhead presses and/or lateral raises on the weight-stack machine), pectoral work, upper and lower back exercises, abdominal work, and trunk exercises are also included in the Optimal Aging Program. People in their 70s can increase upper body strength by approximately 20% after six months. In addition, lower back pain is often alleviated by strengthening the lower back and abdominal muscles. The fitness program amounts to a total commitment of 1 1/2 hours three times a week.

Exercise Programs for the Disabled

There are many people with physical or emotional disabilities who are nevertheless able to exercise parts of their bodies and even compete in athletic competition. An increasing number of physically challenged people now regularly participate in sporting events such as the Special Olympics that recognize their physical abilities. Many disabled athletes try to keep their bodies in shape, and for these athletes, exercise is not only good for their health, it is part of the recovery process that in some cases allows them to live independently.

Many disabled people have learned to swim, ski, bicycle, and lift weights. With recent advances in equipment and techniques, exciting new exercise programs are available for people who are physically challenged. The Idaho State University's Senior Enhancing Lifelong Fitness program, for example, has been very successful in tailoring chair aerobic exercise programs for seniors confined to wheelchairs. Adaptive rowing is especially helpful for people confined to wheelchairs or on crutches. Water-based exercise is probably the most beneficial for the disabled because it allows them a great range of movement and physical exertion without fighting the forces of gravity. Disabled people now water walk, play water polo, snorkel, and scuba dive. Rowing has become one of the most popular sports for the disabled, who now hold their own regattas each year in the U.S. and Europe.

Calisthenics. Everyone, despite their age or health status, should exercise regularly each day. And it is not necessary to belong to a sports gym, exercise facility, or sports team to do so. The Centers for Disease Control and Prevention has, in fact, stated that most Americans can achieve the physiological benefits of exercise by doing simple tasks around the house, such as walking up and down stairs and doing yardwork.

One of the easiest and most systematic methods of gently exercising all parts of the body is calisthenics. The purpose of calisthenics is to gently exercise all the muscle groups of the body and increase aerobic breathing. People suffering from stress tend to take shorter breaths and, as a result, not enough oxygen reaches their lungs. Physical exercises such as calisthenics or yoga can be an excellent way of coping with stress.

Calisthenics are practiced in most societies of the world, as virtually all cultures recognize the importance of regularly moving all parts of the body. In India, exercise includes practices such as yoga, which combines movement with deep breathing and mental exercises. In China, exercise has been practiced for 2,500 years using martial arts such as Tai Chi Chuan (TCC), and a series of 108 slow, fluid, spherical movements intended to increase the body's agility and calm the mind.

The Chinese maintain that exercises such as Tai Chi not only tone the muscles and tissues, but also supply energy to the body that must be kept circulating. One important purpose of Tai Chi is, through movement and concentration, to find your center or "chi" that the Chinese believe is health itself.

Summary

In both Eastern and Western cultures, exercise is a vital component of maintaining good health. Studies consistently show that exercise improves circulation, increases energy, stimulates digestion, strengthens bones, helps regulate hormones, and provides increased stamina for responding to both physical demands and emotional stress. Regular activity is also essential for maintaining a healthy body weight and increasing longevity.

Perhaps a well-known Chinese adage best sums up the importance of exercise: "The body is like a hinge on a door. If it is not swung open, it will rust." Or, as maintained by Dr. Ralph Paffenbarger, Jr., a Professor of Epidemiology at the Stanford University School of Medicine: "Exercise seems to improve quality of life, as well as longevity. People who exercise regularly and live healthy lifestyles consistently look and feel younger than their years."

Resources

References

Adams, G. "Physiological Effects of Exercise Training Regimen upon Women Aged 51 to 79." *Journal of Gerontology* (1973): 50-55.

Allison. M. "Improving the Odds: Aging and Exercise." *Harvard Health Letter* (February 1991): 4.

"The Bare-Bones Facts for Avoiding Osteoporosis." *Tufts University Diet & Nutrition Letter* (June 1994): 3-6.

Brody, Jane. "Personal Health." *The New York Times* (July 14, 1993): B6.

Butler, Kurt, and Lynn Rayner. *The Best Medicine: The Complete Health and Preventive Medicine Handbook.* San Francisco: Harper & Row, 1985.

Doyne, E. "Running Versus Weight Lifting in the Treatment of Depression." *Journal of Consultative Clinical Psychology* (1987): 748-55.

"Exercise Found to Benefit Even the Very Old." *The New York Times* (June 23, 1994): A12.

Guiton, Arthur. *Textbook of Medical Physiology.* Philadelphia, PA: Harcourt Brace Jovanovich, 1991.

"Health Worries? Take a Hike." *San Jose Mercury News* (December 23, 1992).

Heyden, S. "Can Regular Exercise Prolong Life Expectancy?" *Sports Medicine* 6 (1988): 63-71.

Hoeger, W. "Effect of Low-Impact Aerobic Dance on the Functional Fitness of Elderly Women." *Gerontologist* 3 (1990): 189-92.

"How Risky Is Physical Exercise?" *Harvard Health Letter* (May 1994): 13.

Johnsgard, Keith. *The Exercise Prescription for Depression and Anxiety.* New York: Plenum Publishing, 1989.

"Let Your Feet Do the Walking to Lower Blood Pressure." *Associated Press* (October 31, 1993).

Marti, James. *The Exercise Bible: The Medical Benefits of Exercise.* San Francisco: Holistic Medical Research Foundation (HMRF), 1996.

——. *Consumer's Guide to Diet and Nutrition.* Boston: Houghton Mifflin Inc., 1997.

Morey, M.C. "Evaluation of a Supervised Exercise Program in a Geriatric Population." *Journal of the American Geriatric Society* 3 (1993): 348-54.

Murray, Michael, and Joseph Pizzorno. *Encyclopedia of Natural Medicine.* Rocklin, CA: Prima Publishing, 1991.

Nehlsen-Cannarella, S. "The Effects of Moderate Exercise on Immune Response." *Medical Science Sports Exercise* (1991): 64-70.

"The Next Step in Aerobics." *The University of California at Berkeley Wellness Letter* (December 1990): 6.

Nieman, David. *Fitness and Sports Medicine: An Introduction.* Palo Alto, CA: Bull Publishing, 1990.

——. *Fitness & Your Health.* Palo Alto, CA: Bull Publishing, 1993.

Norris, R. "The Effects of Aerobic and Anaerobic Training on Fitness, Blood Pressure and Psychological Stress and Well-Being." *Journal of Psychosomatic Research* (1990): 367-75.

Paffenbarger, Ralph S. "Physical Activity, All-Cause Mortality and Longevity of College Alumni." *New England Journal of Medicine* 314 (1986): 605-13.

Peck, W.A. "Research Directions in Osteoporosis." *American Journal of Medicine* 84 (1988): 275-82.

Posner, Joel. "Optimal Aging: The Role of Exercise." *Patient Care* (March 15, 1992): 35-39.

"Progress in the War against Heart Attacks." *Harvard Health Letter* (April 1994): 1-5.

RESOURCES

Rees, Alan, and Charlene Willey. *Personal Health Reporter*. Detroit, MI: Gale Research Inc., 1993, p. 215.

Schatz, Mary. *A Doctor's Gentle Yoga Program for Back and Neck Pain Relief*. Berkeley, CA: Rodmell Publishers, 1992.

Sheppard, R.J. "The Scientific Basis of Exercise Prescribing for the Very Old." *JAMA* 314 (1990): 3862-70.

Stamford, B. "Exercise and the Elderly." *Sport Science Review* 16 (1988): 341-79.

Stevenson, J. "A Comparison of Land and Water Exercise Programs for Older Individuals." *Medical Science Sports Exercise* 6 (1988): 537.

Walford, Roy. *Maximum Life Span*. New York: W.W. Norton & Company, Inc., 1983.

Wolf, Michel. "Can Exercise Ward Off Cancer?" *American Cancer* (October 1993): 77.

"You Can Prevent Many of the So-Called By-Products of Aging–or Even Reverse Them by Doing One Thing: Weight Lifting." *Healthy Woman* (Winter 1993): 42-45.

Organizations

American Heart Association.
7320 Greenville Avenue, Dallas, TX 75231.

American Physical Therapy Association (APTA).
P.O. Box 37257, Washington, D.C. 20013.

President's Council on Physical Fitness and Health.
450 Fifth Street, N.W., Washington, DC 20001.

Pamphlets

American Heart Association. *Statement on Exercise*. 1990. 2 pp.

California Medical Association. "Exercise and Heart Disease." *Health Tips Index*. April 1989. 2 pp.

"Exercise during Pregnancy." *Health Tips Index*. June 1990. 2 pp.

Additional Reading

Awbrey, B. "Chronic Exercise Induced Pressure." *American Journal of Sports Medicine* (1988): 391-97.

Challis, S. "Treating Arthritis the Holistic Way." *Professional Nurse* (May 1991): 448-51.

Cumming, M. *Rowing beyond Handicaps*. U.S. Rowing Association, 1989.

Dorsen, P. "Overuse Injuries from Nordic Ski Skating." *Physician Sports Medicine* (1986): 34.

Harkcom. T. "Therapeutic Value of Graded Aerobic Exercise Training in Rheumatoid Arthritis." *Arthritis Rheumatism* (1985): 32-39.

Simon, Harvey B., and Steven R. Levisohn. *The Athlete Within: A Personal Guide to Total Fitness*. Boston: Little, Brown, 1987.

Chapter 7

STRENGTHENING THE IMMUNE SYSTEM

In the course of a single day, the average American is typically exposed to a multitude of potentially harmful toxins. This exposure takes place while driving to and from work, inside the office or factory, when eating meals or shopping, and while carrying out simple household chores. In the home alone, there are hundreds of toxins in the walls, floors, building materials, carpets, paints, cleaning materials, drinking water, and even in the food.

Some people are exposed to high levels of these toxins and rarely get sick. Yet their friends or neighbors may be exposed to the same toxins at much lower levels and become ill far more frequently. What accounts for the difference in the way our bodies fight off the toxins that can cause infection and illness?

The answer to this question has a great deal to do with how each person's immune system eliminates toxins. It is the immune system that prevents infectious and chronic diseases and is most responsible for guaranteeing optimal holistic health. However, a balanced natural diet and adequate amounts of vitamins, minerals, herbal supplements, and exercise–which all play a critical role in maintaining the health of the immune system–may not necessarily protect everyone from dangerous toxins in the air, food, and water. And, depending on the amount of toxins absorbed, it may be necessary for some people to regularly eliminate dangerous toxins from their bodies. This chapter discusses the major toxins as well as how the body's immune system attempts to eliminate them, and outlines the components of a basic, gentle detoxification program.

The Dangers of Carbon Monoxide Poisoning

Carbon monoxide poisoning is a major health problem that most people do not even consider because symptoms mimic those of the flu. A Yale University study estimates that up to 700,000 American homes are affected. Exposure causes nausea, sexual dysfunction, headaches, dizzy spells, premature menopause, and even death.

Chemical and Metal Toxins

What are environmental toxins? Basically, they are substances in the environment that can cause physiological or psychological disorders and even death. These toxins can be in the air we breathe, the water we drink, the food we eat, and even inside homes and offices.

Polluted air contains the most potentially dangerous toxins. Gordon Edlin and Eric Golanty (*Health and Wellness*) explain that clean air, which is essential for all living things to function normally and maintain health, consists of approximately 21% oxygen, 78% nitrogen, and trace elements of seven other gases. The human body must have a constant source of pure oxygen, and if the oxygen content of air drops below 16%, body and brain functions are adversely affected.

The air in many industrialized countries is now severely polluted. Air pollution limits the amount of pure oxygen available and forces the body to breathe in hundreds of chemical toxins that are harmful to the lungs, blood, and body tissues. This can be particularly disasterous for people who already suffer from cardiovascular or respiratory diseases. According to Edlin and Golanty, the American Lung Association estimates that one out of every five Americans now suffers from some kind of pulmonary disease, including asthma, emphysema, bronchitis, and chronic coughing. Equally ominous is a survey reported by the American Lung Association in the September/October 1993 issue of *Natural Health,* which revealed that 66% of the U.S. population lives in counties and cities that violate the federal clean air standards for ozone, carbon monoxide, and lead.

Unfortunately, everyone is familiar with smog, the grey or yellow haze produced when gases from automobiles, electricity-generating plants, furnaces, or oil refineries mix with sunlight. According to the Natural Resources Defense Council, long exposure to smog may cause irreversible cell damage, reduced lung functioning, higher susceptibility to respiratory illness, and accelerated lung aging. Children are particularly vulnerable to the effects of air pollution because their bodies are still growing and much of their day is spent outdoors. The Council claims that in southern California, 90% of children under the age of 14 live in areas that do not meet U.S. air quality standards.

Virtually every day, anyone in a modern industrialized nation can be exposed to any of an estimated 100,000 new chemicals or byproducts that have been invented in the past 50 years. Many of these substances have not been studied to determine if they are toxic or dangerous. Several, however, have already been proven to cause disease. For example, asbestos and cigarette smoke have been shown to cause cancer. Lead and pesticides such as DDT have been linked to birth defects and mental retardation. Other toxins have been linked to mood changes, allergies, visual and mental disturbances, rashes, flu-like symptoms, nervous system disorders, and respiratory diseases.

Soot, the tiny particles emitted from industrial plants and the exhaust of diesel vehicles, is another dangerous toxin. Several studies have concluded that as many as 60,000 deaths are caused by soot in the U.S. each year, a figure that rivals the death toll from some cancers. These deaths occur mostly among children with respiratory problems, people of all ages suffering from asthma, and elderly Americans who have bronchitis, emphysema, or pneumonia. While soot particles do not cause heart or lung disease, long-term exposure to soot particles, according to an article in the July 19, 1993 issue of *The New York Times*, worsens existing cases, and short-term exposure may reduce the odds of surviving medical crises brought on by the diseases.

Most new heavy metals result from environmental contamination. Common sources include lead from the solder in tin cans, pesticide sprays, cadmium and lead from cigarette smoke, mercury from dental fillings, contaminated fish, cosmetics, and aluminum from antacids and cookware. According to Michael Murray and Joseph Pizzorno, heavy metals tend to accumulate within humans in the brain, kidneys, and immune system, where they can severely disrupt normal functioning.

Lead, for example, is now linked to high blood pressure, strokes, heart attacks, and kidney disease. Since the 1920s, millions of tons of lead have been added to gasoline to improve engine performance. Lead has also been used widely in paints, although some countries now limit this use. Studies show that adults who suffer from acute lead poisoning may become alcoholics and suffer mental depression. According the U.S. Centers for Disease Control (CDC), "children are particularly susceptible to lead toxic effects." It is now estimated that from three to four million American children under six years of age have high enough levels of lead in their blood to suffer neurological damage or a reduced intelligence quotient (IQ). Studies have also

Natural Ways to Combat Heavy Metal Poisoning

People can effectively combat heavy metal poisoning by including certain foods and nutritional supplements in their diet. These include:

- A high potency multiple vitamin and mineral supplement.
- Minerals such as calcium, magnesium, zinc, iron, copper, and chromium.
- Vitamin C and B-complex vitamins.
- Sulfur-containing amino acids (methionine, cysteine, and taurine).
- High sulfur-containing foods such as garlic, beans, onions, and eggs.
- Water-soluble fibers such as oat bran, pectin, and psyllium seeds.

documented that women who work with lead in factories suffer higher rates of sterility, miscarriage, premature birth, and birth defects. Dr. R. Wedden suggests in his book *Poison in the Pot: The Legacy of Lead* that brain damage, comas, and convulsion can result in severe cases of lead poisoning.

Immunotoxins

Newer chemicals are being released into the environment that are immunotoxic–that is, poisonous to the human immune system. Young children, whose immune systems are still in development, and persons with chronic illnesses such as asthma, are especially vulnerable. Unfortunately, one danger of these new immunotoxins is that scientists do not know their long-term effects.

Natural Protectors Against Lead

Dr. Steven Schecter, a leading authority on allergies, suggests that supplementing diets with the following vitamins and minerals can help the body combat daily lead exposure.

- Optimal amounts of zinc, iron, and copper protect against the absorption of lead in the body.
- Optimum levels of calcium prevent the absorption of lead into the intestinal tract. Deficiencies of calcium can result in higher lead levels in the blood, bones, and soft tissues.
- Megadoses of vitamin B_1 (thiamin), along with a high potency whole B complex, may counteract lead poisoning.
- Vitamin C neutralizes the toxic effects of lead, increases its elimination, and specifically protects muscle tissue from lead damage.
- Several forms of fiber (particularly algin and pectin) are natural chelating agents–they attack the lead in the intestinal tract and eliminate it quickly from the body.

Scientists studying the immune system have identified more than two dozen immune-damaging chemicals, including sulfur dioxide and nitrogen dioxide emitted from power plants and automobiles. The most dangerous immunotoxic chemicals are industrial gases which many people breathe every day. Inhaled gases readily find their way into the human bloodstream. Although the lungs are coated with cells that normally eliminate toxic particles, some pollutants (such as asbestos and silica) cannot be eliminated by the human body.

Extremely Low Frequency (ELF) Electromagnetic Fields

Modern society is dependent on electricity, and people who live near electric power lines are being exposed to high and potentially dangerous levels of ELF radiation. In 1989, researchers at John Hopkins University first began classifying the effects of ELF radiation. They found surprisingly high rates of cancer among workers employed in the electrical power industry, especially the cable-splicers for New York Telephone Company. Yet, as Edlin and Golanty detail, these cable splicers were exposed to only about three times the amount of ELF radiation that is found in the average American home. Recent studies in Sweden have proven that direct exposure to electromagnetic fields generated by high voltage power lines causes leukemia in children. As a result, Edlin and Golanty state that the Swedish government now strictly enforces more stringent safety requirements.

Sunlight

Sunlight also contains harmful radiation, and too much exposure to the sun's rays over time can cause squamous-cell carcinoma, a skin cancer developed by more than 100,000 people in the U.S. each year. While only about 2% of patients die from the disease, which is the second most common skin cancer after basal-cell carcinoma, it can prove lethal if allowed to spread. The cancer is often preceded by actinic keratoses–red, rough, and scaly spots that appear on the face, the top of the hands, or other locations where the skin is frequently exposed to the ultraviolet light from sun.

Once the skin is burned by high levels of the sun's radiation, the body becomes more susceptible to immunotoxic chemicals. Relatively small doses of ultraviolet light, for example the amount received from a mild sunburn, can suppress the immune response against bacteria and yeast infections. Sunscreen lotions containing the B vitamin PABA, and the antioxidant vitamins A, C, and E, provide the best protection against radiation from the sun.

Radioactive Gases

Exposure to high concentrations of radioactive gases can also cause cancer. The most dangerous radioactive gas in the U.S. is radon, a naturally occurring gas that is contained in certain rocks (especially granite) and building materials such as concrete, bricks, and tiles. Radon is believed to be the second leading cause of lung cancer, resulting in 7,000-30,000 deaths annually, according to the EPA. Because several cities in the U.S. recently had radon scares, the EPA now advises people to contact their local authorities or enviornmental groups to determine if they live in a radon area. Since approximately 6% of American homes have elevated radon levels, it may be advisable for people who live in a radon area to assess the toxicity in their home by buying a radon detector.

Water Toxins

More than 100 potentially toxic chemicals have been introduced in drinking water supplies in the U.S. Some are compounds that seep into underground water supplies adjacent to industrial complexes or toxic waste dumps. Several are carcinogenic (cancer-causing), including benzene, carbon tetrachloride, dioxin, ethylene dibromide (EDB), polychlorinated biphenyls (PCBs), and vinyl

chloride. Studies show that children are especially vulnerable to these toxins.

Tap water in some areas of the U.S. may also carry toxins. Ordinary drinking water stored in wells may be contaminated by wastes, pesticides, or other toxins. Well water can leach heavy metals from copper or lead pipes, and drinking water contaminated with these heavy metals can result in mental retardation in children and nervous system disorders. The drinking water of some American cities also contains small amounts of chlorine to control bacteria, which may also be toxic if it exceeds recommended levels. A National Cancer Institute survey cited by Edlin and Golanty showed that in 10 areas of the U.S., regular consumption of chlorinated tap water was responsible for between 12 and 27% of bladder cancers. People who are worried about water contamination should drink only pure spring or filtered water, or buy a water purifier.

Food Toxins

Even the foods purchased at the local grocery store probably contain some toxins. For example, fruits and vegetables that are not grown organically often contain dangerous chemical residues from pesticides, insecticides, larvicides, and herbicides. These substances kill rodents, insects, molds, and weeds that interfere with agricultural crop production. Unfortunately, they also bury themselves in the soil and water and remain in food products which, once eaten, enter the human body. The danger is that human tolerance levels for insecticides and pesticides are extremely low. Dr. Leon Chaitow claims in *The Body/Mind Purification Program* that the U.S. National Academy of Sciences estimates that one million cases of cancer over the next decade will result from pesticide poisoning in food alone, not taking into account pesticide

Natural Ways to Protect Against Toxic Chemicals in Food

People can strengthen the liver's ability to detoxify itself after exposure to toxic chemicals (including food additives, solvents, pesticides, and herbicides) by consuming the following:

- Amino acid methionine.
- Antioxidants such as vitamins A, C, and E and betacarotene.
- Choline.
- Botanicals such as dandelion root, milk thistle, artichoke leaves, and curcuma root.

Fighting Food Contamination

- Grow your own vegetables or buy organic produce, meat, and fish.
- Remove the outer leaves of leafy vegetables, and peel the waxy coating off fruits and vegetables.
- Wash all hard-skinned produce in well-diluted, washing-up liquids.
- Lower consumption of dairy products.
- Eat live yogurt, which will reduce vulnerability to viruses, including *Salmonella* and *Listeria*.
- Avoid out-of-season fruits and vegetables which carry double the risk of pesticide and fungicide contamination. Ninety percent of fungicides are carcinogenic.
- When washing your hands before handling food, be sure to clean under your fingernails.
- Vegetable oils can become rancid with exposure to oxygen, heat, and light. It is better to store oils in small, dark bottles rather than in partially empty large bottles to reduce the oils' exposure to oxygen.

exposure from water and atmospheric contamination.

Meat and fish are increasingly dowsed with chemical insecticides and toxic artificial hormones. In fact, today's meat contains as much as 30 times more saturated fats and artificial hormones than 40 years ago. Chaitow cautions that meats that are produced from animals raised on hormones can cause infertility, impotence, behavioral disorders, and cancer in humans.

Many people mistakenly assume that meat, fish, and dairy product toxins are not dangerous to human health. Yet recent studies indicate that 95-99% of all food poisoning comes from meat, fish, dairy products, and eggs. Furthermore, most of the poisons found in meat and dairy products are carcinogenic at the lowest levels tested in laboratory animals. They have been shown to suppress the human immune system, according to Chaitow, and

cause birth defects, sterility, and neurological disorders.

Microbial Toxins

Toxins can also be produced inside the human body by the bacteria and yeast in the intestines. Examples of these toxins include endotoxins, exotoxins, toxic amines, toxic derivatives of bile, and various carcinogenic substances. Murray and Pizzorno suggest that intestinal toxins have been linked to a wide variety of diseases, including liver disease, Crohn's disease, ulcerative colitis, thyroid disease, psoriasis, allergies, asthma, and many immune disorders. One of the dangers of these internal toxins, they add, is that they prevent the development of natural antibodies that normally fight infections. In effect, microbial toxins form antigens which cross-react with the body's own tissues, thereby causing autoimmunity–that is, the body's immune system cannot protect itself. Autoimmune diseases that have been associated with cross-reacting antibodies include rheumatoid arthritis, diabetes, and autoimmune thyroiditis.

Office Toxins

Inside a typical office building are likely to be at least 50 (possibly as many as 500) volatile organic compounds and gases that are emitted by everything from caulk to carpeting. The EPA ranks indoor pollution in offices as one of the five most urgent environmental issues in the U.S. Thirty to 75 million workers, according to Edlin and Golanty, are estimated to be at risk of developing an illness due to office pollution. Most office pollution results from harmful gases that are usually highest in newly constructed or recently renovated buildings. Some gases, however, cannot be detected by odor. This is complicated by the fact that many gases and chemicals mix with each other to form even more dangerous toxins. Edlin and Golanty state that Danish researcher Lars Molhave, for example, found that more than 40 common office chemicals irritate the eyes, nose, and throat. Some forms of indoor air pollution are known to cause asthma and a severe lung inflammation called hypersensitivity pneumonitis. A small percentage of office workers develop "multiple chemical sensitivity" which cripples

Indoor Toxins

- Some textiles are potential sources of pollutants.
- Padded partitions, curtains, and carpets may be toxic.
- Office machinery contributes to indoor pollution. Some photocopying machines give off ozone–detectable by its metallic odor–which may cause nosebleeds, irritate the eyes and throat, and make it difficult for contact lens wearers.
- Machines that duplicate an executive's signature emit butyl methacrylate, which can trigger allergic reactions.
- Blueprint copiers give off ammonia and acetic acid vapors, causing the eyes, nose, and throat to burn.
- Shredders release irritating particles of paper into the air. Proper ventilation minimizes such hazards.
- Ventilation systems that collect moisture when air is cooled harbor molds, fungi, and bacteria. If these systems are not kept clean, the biological agents proliferate, traveling through the building in the air currents.
- Water leaks may cause mold or fungus to build up in carpets and ceiling tiles.

their immune system. People who suffer from indoor toxicity have one or several of the following symptoms: dizziness, headaches, nausea, burning eyes, and nosebleeds. In addition, people may find themselves unusually tired, suffer from coughing and sneezing, or have itchy skin and throats.

Common Sources of Toxins in the Home

In the Kitchen

- Paper towels fortified with formaldehyde can cause skin rashes, nausea, and menstrual irregularities.

- Air fresheners (carbolic acid or formaldehyde) can cause nausea and eye and lung irritation.

- Oven cleaner formulas contain lye, phenols, formaldehyde, benzene, or ammonia that can cause blisters and rashes.

- Some deep frying, hydrogenated oils are carcinogenic. People should use their ventilator when cooking with these oils.

In the Bathroom

- Antiperspirants contain aluminum chlorohydrate which blocks skin pores.

- Commercial toothpastes contain ammonia, ethanol, formaldehyde, mineral oil, or saccharin.

- Furniture and tile polish contain sodium phosphate or turpentine, which can burn the skin and is dangerous when inhaled as a vapor.

- Toilet cleaners contain cresol, which is easily absorbed through the skin and can damage major organs.

Clothes

- Spot removers often contain benzene, sulfuric acid, or toluene, which can cause skin rashes and nervous system complications.

- Leather dyes in shoes contain nitro-benzene, which can turn skin blue, affect breathing, and induce vomiting.

Recommendations

- Avoid using bleached paper containing dioxin.

- Use all natural, non-toxic products such as corn flour or arrowroot instead of talc; bicarbonate of soda; peppermint oil; or natural herb toothpastes.

- Use essential oils deodorants instead of the strong chemical deodorants.

- Use natural, non-toxic, anti-dandruff shampoos.

Contact lens wearers may suffer eye irritation. Some building-borne pollutants can also be fatal, as tragically demonstrated in 1991 when an outbreak of Legionnaire's disease at the Social Security Administration building in Richmond, California, killed two workers.

Toxins in the Home

The home may also be full of toxins–even from innocent sources. Ordinary building materials used for house walls, floors, insulation, roofing treatments, paints, and plastic tiles are often toxic. Even something as seemingly innocuous as new carpeting has been linked to a variety of respiratory and nervous ailments. According to the U.S. Consumer Products Safety Commission report cited in the November 3, 1993, issue of the *Associated Press*, these ailments have flu-like symptoms such as weakness, aching joints, congestion, nosebleeds, and even dementia. Many people now have their homes professionally examined for toxins and replace toxic materials with non-toxic substitutes where possible.

Measuring Toxicity Levels

With so many toxins in the air, water, home, and office, how can people prevent infections and diseases caused by these substances? The answer is regular elimination of toxins from the body. The first step is to be alert to the symptoms of toxicity and, if necessary, measure toxicity levels. A number of special laboratory techniques are useful in detecting toxins in the body. To determine exposure to other toxic chemicals, a detailed medical examination by an experienced physician may be necessary, or laboratory analysis that involves measuring blood and fatty tissue for suspected chemicals. It is extremely important to measure the toxicity of the liver because it is responsible for eliminating most toxins from the body. The serum bile acid assay test is primarily used to measure liver toxicity.

Natural Ways to Strengthen the Immune System

It is virtually impossible for people to effectively avoid toxins. As discussed, toxins are in the air, soil, water, and many foods, and once they enter the body, they must be eliminated. The rest of this chapter describes how the immune system eliminates toxins and how it can be strengthened through detoxification programs. The most important components of the immune system are discussed below, along with vitamin, mineral, and herbal supplements that have proven effective in detoxification programs.

The skin, the body's largest organ, is also the first line of defense against external toxins because it can prevent the entry of most microorganisms, while the mildly acidic surface of the skin neutralizes harmful bacteria. A number of toxins are also eliminated

through the skin, principally through sweat. The skin needs to be strong, supple, and moist. Natural supplements which detoxify the skin include PABA (ointment) and beta carotenes. The herb dandelion root is used in Europe as a skin detoxicant and to treat various skin problems.

The mucous membranes of the eyes, nose, throat, and lungs also protect against toxic substances. These membranes secrete enzymes that degrade toxins and eliminate them naturally from the body. Tears wash away toxins from the eye, and ear wax protects the ear canal.

As Murray and Pizzorno explain, "the spleen is the largest mass of lymphatic tissue in the body. In addition to producing lymphocytes which engulf and destroy bacteria and cellular debris, the spleen is responsible for destroying worn-out blood cells and platelets. The spleen also serves as a blood reservoir," and during emergencies such as hemorrhage, releases stored blood to prevent shock. Goldenseal improves spleen function by enhancing blood flow through this important organ.

The liver performs more than 1,500 different functions, many of which directly maintain the body's immune system. Except for some fats, the liver processes all foods absorbed by the intestines before they are released into the bloodstream. It filters the blood by removing, deactivating, or reprocessing wastes, toxins, and bacteria. The liver also helps eliminate the byproducts of alcohol and pesticides. Perhaps most importantly, it helps produce interferon, the special chemical agent that activates white blood cells to destroy and eliminate disease-causing microbes and toxins. Several nutrients are known to enhance the liver's production, including zinc, manganese, and vitamin C. Lipotropic formulas or silymarin from milk thistle (*Silybum marianum*) and vitamin C help detoxify the liver, as do echinacea and goldenseal.

The kidneys are important because they remove toxins from the blood for elimination in the urine and reabsorb valuable nutrients which are recycled for further use in the body. The kidneys gradually decline in efficiency with age and excessive toxicity due to diet, drugs, or pollutants that place stress on them. Cranberry juice has been used to treat bladder infections by toning the kidneys. Several compounds isolated from rubia, cassia, and aloe vera also help maintain healthy kidneys. Murray and Pizzorno recommend the following nutritional supplements to detoxify the kidneys: vitamin B_6 and K supplements, glutamate, magnesium citrate, and potassium citrate.

A healthy, intact intestinal lining allows properly broken down particles of fats, proteins, and starches to be assimilated into the blood. When the intestinal lining becomes disturbed, it loses its effectiveness as a filter, and allergies and food sensitivities can develop, along with chronic infections and inflammation. Shortages of beneficial bacteria can damage the intestinal lining. Caprylic acid, a naturally occurring fatty acid, has been reported to be an effective intestinal compound. *Lactobacillus acidophilus*, the type of bacteria found in natural yogurt, also strengthens the intestine's natural microflora and retards the growth of *Candida*, a dangerous bacteria linked to AIDS. Garlic has proven effective in preventing fungi from growing in the intestine. The common barberry plant has been used to prevent a wide range of harmful bacteria in the intestines, including *Candida albicans*.

The colon probably contains most of the dangerous toxins in the body, many of which lead to the production of free radicals that may be responsible for systemic degenerative autoimmune conditions such as cancer, arthritis, arteriosclerosis, and possibly AIDS.

Many of these diseases can be prevented by continually eliminating toxins that collect in the colon. Herbs that help eliminate toxins from the colon include alfalfa, bentonite, goldenseal, and echinacea. Buckthorn has long been used as a laxative to increase the peristalsis (the muscular activity of the colon). *Cassia senna* leaves are also commonly used for their laxative properties, as is psyllium seed powder mixed with a full glass of water.

When bacteria, viruses, pollen, microorganisms, or dangerous chemicals enter the body, the organs discussed above attempt to neutralize them. The result of this process is the production of specific protein molecules called antibodies and special blood cells called lymphocytes. In a strong immune system, antibodies and lymphocytes inactivate the toxins, which are then removed by macrophages and phagocytic cells in the blood. Macrophages and phagocytic cells are transported throughout the body by lymphatic vessels, which run parallel to arteries and veins and drain waste products from tissues. Important nutrients that detoxify the lymph are vitamins A, B_6, and C, and the trace mineral zinc. Herbs recommended by Murray and Pizzorno that enhance lymphatic function include goldenseal, echinacea, Korean ginseng, Siberian ginseng, and licorice. Picrorrhiza (*Picrorrhiza kurosa*) has also been used for treating liver ailments and strengthening the immune system.

Exercise. Aristotle seemed to anticipate the discoveries of modern immunology when he wrote more than 2,000 years ago, "A man falls into ill health as a result of not caring for exercise." Today, according to the National Institute of Mental Health (NIMH), more than 85% of physicians prescribe exercise as an aid in treating stress or immune system-related disorders. Researchers disagree on how much exercise is enough to maximize immunity. Dr. David Nieman, in his book *Fitness & Your Health*, states that "while the risk of

NATURAL WAYS TO STRENGTHEN THE IMMUNE SYSTEM

infection may decrease when one engages in moderate exercise training, risk may rise above average during periods of excessive amounts of high-intensity exercise." A sedentary lifestyle, however, is not immunity-inducing because non-exercisers in Nieman's studies reported twice as many infections as moderate exercisers. Those who maintained aerobic activity, strength training, and even flexibility programs enhanced their immunity. Whatever the regimen, three variables, according to Nieman, dictate moderation: duration, frequency, and intensity. *Duration* refers to how long exercise lasts. The American College of Sports Medicine officially recommends that all people exercise for 20-60 minutes three to five days per week (*frequency*). Two days of rest are suggested for allowing the immune system to adapt to the stress of exercise.

Intensity refers to how hard an exerciser works. Moderately intense exercise means that an exerciser is working out somewhat hard, but not overdoing it (most people can carry on a conversation, for example). At least six weeks of regular training are required, according to Nieman, to attain an increase in the number and activity of immunostimulatory cells.

Nutritional Therapies. According to Charles Simon's *Cancer and Nutrition*, nutritional deficiencies decrease a person's capacity to resist infection and its consequences and decrease the capability of the immune system. This is especially true in elderly people. In old age, Simon states, there is a decrease in skin hypersensitivity reaction, a decreased number of T cells, and impairment of some phagocytic functions. Surveys of elderly Americans, for example, have disclosed that the gradual impairment of immune functioning with aging may be due to one or more nutrient deficiencies. Poor nutrition adversely affects all components of

Fighting Can Make You Sick

Harsh words and name-calling between a husband and wife not only result in hurt feelings, but also weaken the immune system. A study conducted by Janice Kiecolt-Glaser, an Ohio psychologist, and her immunologist husband Ronald Glaser found that the immune systems of married couples who became hostile toward one another were weakened more dramatically than those of couples whose disagreements were milder. Although exploding with anger can significantly weaken the immune system, not dealing with important conflicts can damage a marriage as well, the researchers claimed.

immune functioning, including T cell function, the ability of B cells to make antibodies, the functioning of the complement proteins, and phagocytic function. Simon cites 1989 research conducted at the Shriner's Burn Institute in Cincinnati that showed that administration of a special liquid diet to severely burned patients the day they were burned reduced the risk of infection by 50%. The special diet consisted of protein vitamins, including A and E, minerals, and iron, as well as omega-3 fatty acids.

Nutritionist Ann Louse Gittleman agrees with Simon that supporting the immune system with foods rich in vitamins C, E, and betacarotene, as well as zinc and selenium, is a good first line of defense against infections, especially parasitic infection. She notes in *Guess Who's Coming to Dinner* that additional vitamin and mineral supplements may be prescribed in specific cases, along with botan-

Foods to Enhance Your Immune System

- **Foods rich in vitamin C**. The best food sources of vitamin C are broccoli and citrus fruits.

- **Foods rich in betacarotene and vitamin A**. Betacarotene, a substance from which the body makes vitamin A, is thought to trigger the anti-tumor activity of macrophages, the white blood cells that engulf and destroy bacteria and other invaders. Some researchers suggest that betacarotene can also protect macrophages from deterioration and enhance T and B-lymphocytes. Good sources of vitamin A and betacarotene include deep yellow, orange, or green vegetables (such as beet, mustard, and turnip greens; carrots; chili peppers; pumpkins; spinach; and winter squash) and fruits such as apricots, cantaloupes, mangoes, papayas, and peaches.

- **Foods rich in vitamin E.** Vitamin E makes the immune system more vigorous. Immune cells need a special chemical, prostaglandin E2, to turn them off after they've finished fighting a specific threat to the body. Vitamin E supplements help reduce the production of prostaglandin E2, thus enabling the immune system to stay "turned on." Scientists are also now discovering that vitamin E increases interleukin-2, the naturally occurring substance necessary for a healthy, disease-preventing immune system. Nuts, sunflower seeds, wheat germ, and vegetables oils are excellent sources of vitamin E.

- **Foods rich in zinc.** Zinc is the best known activator of the thymus gland, which helps produce T-cells. Zinc deficiency, for example, is especially common in AIDS patients. Seafoods, especially oysters, are excellent sources of zinc.

- **Foods rich in iron, selenium, folate, and vitamin B$_6$**. A deficiency of vitamin B$_6$, for instance, depresses overall immune function, while an iron deficiency often increases susceptibility to infections. Selenium is important as a fuel for antibodies responding to infection, and folate boosts immune function. Animal meats and fish are the best natural sources of iron. Dried beans are one of the best vegetable sources, while iron-enriched cereals are excellent breakfast choices. Bananas, cantaloupes, lemons, oranges, and strawberries are good fruit sources of folate. Good vegetable sources include asparagus, broccoli, lima beans, and spinach. The best sources of selenium are high protein foods such as meats, cereal, and dairy products. White meats such as chicken and fish are the richest sources of vitamin B$_6$, along with whole grains and potatoes.

icals such as echinacea, ginseng, and astralagus. These vitamins, minerals, and botanicals, she states, have been shown in numerous studies to enhance immunity.

Vitamin C Therapy. Vitamin C is probably the most important vitamin in building a strong immune system because it binds with toxins in the body and helps eliminate them.

Vitamin and Mineral Therapies

James Balch and Phyllis Balch provide a comprehensive list of vitamins, minerals, enzymes and other nutrients that are essential for the functioning of the human immune system. Specifically, they recommend the following:

Vitamin A	15,000 IU daily
Betacarotene	10,000 IU
Vitamin B complex	100 mg in tablet form
Vitamin B$_6$	50 mg capsules, 3 times daily
Vitamin B$_{12}$	1,000 mg
Vitamin C	3,000-10,000 mg daily
Vitamin E	400 IU daily
Multivitamin & mineral complex	Follow instructions on label
Zinc chelate	50-80 mg daily
Copper	3 mg daily
Protein (free-form amino acids)	As directed on label
Proteolytic enzymes	2 tablets between meals and with meals
Raw thymus plus	As directed on label
Selenium	200 mcg daily
L-Cystein	500 mg each; take twice daily
L-Methionine	As directed on label
L-Lysine	As directed on label
L-Ornithine	As directed on label
Acidophilus (or Megadophilus)	As directed on label
Co-enzyme Q-10	100 mg daily
Garlic capsules	1 capsules 3 times daily
Germanium	200 mg daily
Kelp	8 tablets daily; use instead of salt

If people are deficient in vitamin C, they become much more susceptible to environmental pollutants; conversely, exposure to various toxins, such as lead or benzene, directly depletes their vitamin C stores. Evidence also suggests that vitamin C deficiency hampers the body's own detoxification process.

According to *Alternative Medicine: The Definitive Guide*, Dr. Robert Cathcart, III, of Los Altos, California, has successfully treated over 11,000 immune deficient patients with vitamin C therapy. Cathcart's vitamin C therapy involves taking controlled, large doses of vitamin C supplements daily, along with vitamin C-rich foods.

Chelation Therapy. Chelation therapy involves intravenously administering EDTA (ethylene diamine tetraacetic acid) which binds to various toxic metals in the blood such as lead, cadmium, and aluminum. The toxins are quickly eliminated though the kidneys, and according to *Alternative Medicine*, "many doctors have found that EDTA can remove the calcium and plaque present in the walls of arteries in atherosclerosis." Chelation therapy has been used safely and effectively for more than 30 years on more than 500,000 patients.

Hydrotherapy. According to Dr. Zane Gard, quoted in *Alternative Medicine*, hydrotherapy can also remove calcium deposits from the blood vessels and break down scar tissue from their walls. She also notes that hydrotherapy can remove chemicals such as DDE (a metabolite of DDT), PCBs, and dioxin from fat cells. According to Gard, many studies show that hydrotherapy can affect numerous body systems, including the cardiovascular, endocrine, neurological, neuromuscular, bronchopulmonary, blood, skin, and immune.

Dr. Erich Rauch, director of a health spa in Austria specializing in holistic therapies, has also effectively used hydrotherapy to strengthen the immune systems of patients with chronic disorders. A review of his book *Naturopathic Treatment of Colds and Infectious Disease* in the December 1993 issue of *Townsend Letter for Doctors* details how Rauch uses warm baths to facilitate sweating, extraction baths to eliminate toxins, dry brushing, and inhalations of chamomile or sage fragrances. Botanical and homeopathic remedies are also used at his spa. Rauch also recommends taking herbal teas, including lilac tea and elder blossoms, to induce perspiration; licorice tea and horsetail for catarrh; and rose hip tea, high in ascorbic acid, to promote the eliminatory function of the kidneys.

Colon Therapy. Colon therapy, one of the most effective ways to cleanse the large intestine of accumulated toxins and waste products, can be used in combination with massage, fasting, and special diets. With the help of a trained professional and a colonic machine, purified water (which sometimes contain vitamins, herbs, friendly bacteria, or oxygen) is introduced directly into the rectum.

Fasting. Partial or total fasts are two inexpensive and effective methods of strengthening the immune system through detoxification. Fasting is often combined with enemas and bowel stimulation to help rid the body of bacteria and toxins trapped in the bowels. One by-product of fasting is weight loss. It is generally advisable to consult with a doctor or qualified holistic health professional before initiating a fast. Long fasts require medical supervision as well as prior assessment of nutrient status, such as vitamins and minerals, to insure that deficiency does not occur. Short weekend fasts are safe for most people, although consulting a specialist is recommended.

Juice Fasts. Juice fasts have become a popular and effective way of strengthening the immune system. Dr. Evarts G. Loomis, founder of Meadowlark, one of the first live-in health and growth retreat centers in the U.S., pioneered the juice fast. His fasting program, outlined in *Alternative Medicine*, prescribes vegetable juices (equal parts of carrot–diluted with water 1:1–and celery) for detoxification. Green vegetables, including green beans, zucchini, watercress, and parsley, can be added if desired. He also prescribes a "detoxifying cocktail" combining garlic, lemon juice, grapefruit juice, and olive oil. This is normally taken at bedtime because the liver, a major immune system organ, is most active, according to Traditional Chinese Medicine, between 11:00 P.M. and 1:00 A.M.

Breathing Exercises. *Alternative Medicine: The Definitive Guide* cites a study conducted by Dr. Jack Shields, a lymphologist in Santa Barbara, California, that demonstrated that simple breathing exercises can help build immune response. Using cameras inside the body, Shields found that deep, diaphragmatic breathing stimulates the cleansing of the lymph system by creating a vacuum effect that sucks the lymph through the bloodstream. This increased the rate of toxic elimination by as much as 15 times the normal rate of elimination.

Lymphatic Massage, Osteopathy, and Chiropractic Lymphatic Draining.
According to Jared Zeff, a naturopath cited in *Alternative Medicine: The Definitive Guide*, lymphatic circulation can be enhanced by lymphatic massage, osteopathy, and chiropractic lymphatic drainage techniques. According to Zeff, massage builds immune response by accelerating the flow of lymph throughout the body. Other techniques he uses with patients include light beam generators (LBG), which emit photons of light and high-frequency electrostatic fields to correct the electromagnetic charge on cells. He notes that Rena Davis, of Davis Nutrition Consultants in St. Helen, Oregon, has successfully employed LBGs to stimulate the lymph system of patients by breaking open sealed and calcified blood vessels, increasing blood circulation, reducing edema, and transporting waste products in tissue out of the body.

Basic Detoxification Programs.
As discussed above, the immune system can naturally eliminate most external toxins to which everyone is exposed to varying degrees. However, if people are exposed to high levels of certain toxins, or lower levels of other toxins over an extended period of time, their immune system may be weakened. Given that more than 100,000 new potentially toxic chemicals have been released into the environment during the past 50 years, it is important for everyone to consider regularly detoxifying their bodies.

Possible Side Effects of Detoxification Programs

1. Headaches may occur during the first 48 hours. To alleviate a headache, use the acupressure points or self-massage.
2. Nausea, especially if fasting. Nausea can be relieved by drinking a light herbal tea such as chamomile.
3. Loss of body heat.
4. Inability to focus.
5. Constipation due to fluid loss.
6. Diarrhea.
7. Weight loss due to reduced food intake.
8. Rashes and blemishes.
9. Loss of amino acids.

The most important components of any detoxification program are the organs specifically targeted for detoxification; the diet, vitamins, minerals, herbal supplements, and botanical medicinal formulas prescribed; and the exercise regime (aerobics, meditation, yoga, visualizations) incorporated. People should contact a holistic physician for recommendations about a specific diet for their program, whether to fast, and which vitamins, minerals, and botanical supplements will most efficiently and gently detoxify their bodies.

Before starting a detoxification program, it is important to be aware of the possible side effects. These side effects are not dangerous, but may cause slight discomfort. Before taking any vitamins, herbs, or supplements, it is important to consult with a physician.

Summary

Many people today have less than optimal health because their bodies contain potentially dangerous toxins. While a normally functioning immune system can eliminate most toxins, if the body has an excess of these substances, the immune system may become depressed and unable to function effectively. The best protection against the adverse effects of toxins is to regularly eliminate toxic debris through gentle detoxification programs that rejuvenate the immune system. Given the right proportions of nutrients; vitamin, mineral, and botanical supplements; exercise; meditation; and relaxation, the body has the miraculous ability to maintain the health of all its systems. This ability of the body to detoxify largely determines an individual's life energy ("chi" or elan vital) and health.

Resources

References

Balch, James F., and Phyllis Balch. *Prescription for Nutritional Healing.* Long Island: Avery Publishing, 1993.

Bone, Kerry. "Picrorrhiza." *Townsend Letter for Doctors.* (May 1996).

"Book Corners." *Townsend Letter for Doctors.* (December 1993): 124-25.

The Burton Goldberg Group. *Alternative Medicine: The Definitive Guide.* Payallup, WA: Future Medicine Publishing, Inc., 1993.

"Carpet Industry Will Adopt Cautionary Label." *Associated Press* (November 3, 1993).

Chaitow, Leon. *The Body/Mind Purification Program.* New York: Simon & Schuster Inc., 1990.

Edlin, Gordon, and Eric Golanty. *Health and Wellness.* Boston: Jones and Bartlett Publishers, 1992, p. 373.

Gittleman, Anne. *Guess Who's Coming to Dinner?* New York: Putnam & Sons, 1994.

Hilts, P. "Studies Say Soot Kills Up to 60,000 in U.S. Each Year." *The New York Times* (July 19, 1993).

"Indoor Air Pollution." *Mayo Clinic Health Letter.* (November 1993): 4.

Murray, Michael, and Joseph Pizzorno. *Encyclopedia of Natural Medicine.* Rocklin, CA: Prima Publishing, 1991, p. 32.

Nieman, David. *Fitness & Your Health.* Palo Alto, CA: Bull Publishing, 1993.

"Report Tells How Smog Affects Kids." *Associated Press.* (October 28, 1993).

Simon, Charles. *Cancer and Nutrition.* Garden City Park, NY: Avery Publishing Group, 1992.

"Two-Thirds of the U.S. Population Breathes Polluted Air." *Natural Health* . (September/October 1993).

Wedden, R. *Poison in the Pot: The Legacy of Lead.* Carbondale, IL: Southern Illinois University Press, 1984.

Organizations

Consumer Product Safety Commission. 5401 Westbard Avenue, Bethesda, MD 20207.

Environmental Protection Agency (EPA). 401 M Street, S.W., Washington, DC 20460.

Food and Drug Administration (FDA). 5600 Fishers Lane, Rockville, MD 20857.

National Institute for Occupational Safety and Health (NIOSH). 1600 Clifton Road N.E., Atlanta, GA 30333.

Occupation Safety and Health Administration (OSHA).
200 Constitution Avenue,
Washington, D.C. 20210.

Additional Reading

Agency for Toxic Substances and Disease Registry. *The Nature and Extent of Lead Poisoning in Children in the United States: A Report to Congress.* 1988. EPA, Office of Air and Radiation.

Brown, Lester, et al. *State of the World.* New York: W.W. Norton, 1988.

Bunyard, Peter. *Health Guide for the Nuclear Age.* London, UK: Macmillan, 1988.

Chaitow, Leon. *The Radiation Protection Plan.* London, UK: Thorstens, 1989.

Cook, Judith. *Dirty Water.* London, UK: Unwin Hyman, 1989.

Dudley, Nigel. *The Poisoned Earth.* London, UK: Piatkus Publishers, 1987.

Greeley, Alexandra. "Getting the Lead Out of Just about Everything." *FDA Consumer Reports.* (July/August 1991): 26-31.

Haddy, R.I. "Aging, Infections, and the Immune System." *Journal of Family Practice.* (October 1988): 409-13.

Jaroff, Leon. "Controlling a Childhood Menace: Lead Poisoning Poses the Biggest Environmental Threat to the Young." *Time.* (February 25, 1991): 68-69.

Marwick, C. "As Immune System Yields Its Secrets, New Strategies Against Disease Emerge." *JAMA.* (November 24, 1989): 2786-87.

Nossal, G.J.V. "The Basic Components of the Immune System." *New England Journal of Medicine.* (May 21, 1987): 1320-25.

Pearson, David. *The Natural House Book.* New York: Simon & Schuster, 1989.

Stanway, Andrew. *The Natural Family Doctor.* New York: Simon & Schuster, 1987.

Chapter 8

COPING WITH STRESS

In 1990, as reported in Alan Rees and Charlene Willey's *Personal Health Reporter*, the London School of Hygiene and Tropical Medicine invited 192 men and women between the ages of 35 and 64 to experiment with managing their stress levels. Each of the participants had two or more of the following risk factors: high blood pressure, high cholesterol, and a smoking habit of 10 or more cigarettes a day. The volunteers were then divided into two groups; one group took eight one-hour lessons in relaxation, meditation, stress management, and breathing exercises, while the other group received no instruction.

After eight weeks, the doctors discovered that blood pressures were significantly lower for those in the group who were taught to relax and breathe correctly compared with those who were given no instruction. Four years later, those who had taken the lessons still showed lower blood pressure readings. Compared with those who had no instruction, they were less likely to be in treatment for hypertension and were also less apt to show symptoms of heart disease, or to have died of a heart attack–medical conditions that have been linked to stress.

Most people experience some stress in their lives. The December 1993 issue of *New Body* magazine, for example, states that a 1993 U.S. Public Health Survey estimates that 70-80% of Americans who visit a physician suffer from a stress-related disorder. Job-related stress costs U.S. businesses $60 million a year, and stress-related disability cases have doubled since 1981.

This chapter discusses how the body responds to stress and the various holistic therapies for reducing stress and its effects, including nutritional, vitamin, and mineral therapies; exercise;

guided imagery; yoga; mediation; biofeedback; massage; and group support.

What Is Stress?

In 1925, Hans Seyle, a European physician trained at the German University in Prague, noticed that all his patients displayed the same symptoms, including fatigue, aching bones and joints, fever, and appetite and weight loss. He subsequently developed the concept of "stress"–and the body's adaptive reactions to any demand, or "the rate of wear-and-tear caused by life." In his book *Stress Without Distress,* Seyle explains how a number of agents can cause stress, including intoxification, trauma, nervous strain, heat, cold, muscular fatigue, polluted air, and radiation.

According to Seyle, the body reacts to stress in the same way it reacts to danger–by going through a series of biochemical changes which he called the General Adaptation Syndrome (GAS). In the first stage, which he termed "the alarm reaction," the body mobilizes its defenses against the stressor agent. Nerve impulses from the brain stimulate the adrenal medulla to secrete adrenalin and other stress-related hormones such as cortisol. This is known as the "fight or flight" response: the heartbeat is accelerated, blood pressure levels are elevated, an increased amount of blood flows to the muscles, and the lungs dilate to increase respiratory effort.

Seyle called the second stage of the General Adaptation Syndrome the "resistance" phase–the phase during which the body continues to fight the stress or long after the effects of the "fight or flight" response have worn off. If the stress is induced by infectious agents, the body's immune system activity increases. If the stress is physical, the neuroendocrine system converts protein to energy. If the stress is psychological, a combination of responses may occur.

Prolongation of the resistance reaction or continued stress can lead to "exhaustion," the third stage of the General Adaptation Syndrome. During this stage, glucocorticoid reserves become depleted and some body cells do not receive sufficient amount of glucose or other nutrients.

Exhaustion may manifest itself in a total collapse of body functions or a collapse of specific organs. Prolonged stress can overwork many organ systems, especially the heart, blood vessels, adrenals, and immune system. When stress is overwhelming, the response is general depression, low blood pressure and heart rate, increased cortisol (natural steroid hormone), and low sex steroid hormone secretions. Failure to cope with stress can lead to stress-related disorders such as headaches, hypertension, heart disease, stroke, and ulcers.

Measuring Stress Levels. Many people may not be aware that they are undergoing stress. To help people assess their own stress levels, Drs. Thomas Holmes and Richard Rahe developed a list of potential stressors that have been linked to medical disorders. The Social Readjustment Rating Scale (see below) ranks stressful life events. The highest value, 100 points, is attached to the most grievous loss, the death of one's spouse. The scale demonstrates that stress is cumulative. For some people, it may take only a few significant events, or a number of smaller events, to overload the adaptive system of the body.

Coping with Stress

Successfully coping with stress involves using therapies that are designed to counteract the effects of the "fight or flight" response by inducing its opposite reaction–the "relaxation response." The term was coined by Dr. Herbert Benson of Harvard Medical School, who found that people undergoing stress

The Social Readjustment Rating Scale

Read the list of life events below and enter the score for each event that has occurred in your life over the past year. If any event occurred more than once, multiply the point value by the number of times the event occurred. Then total your score.

Life Event	Point Value	Your Score
1. Death of spouse	100	——
2. Divorce	78	——
3. Marital separation	65	——
4. Detention in jail or other institution	63	——
5. Death of a close family member (other than spouse)	63	——
6. Major personal injury or illness	53	——
7. Marriage	50	——
8. Dismissal from job	47	——
9. Marital reconciliation	45	——
10. Retirement	45	——
11. Major change in health or behavior of a family member	44	——
12. Pregnancy	40	——
13. Sexual difficulties	39	——
14. Gain of a new family member (through birth, adoption, mother moving in)	39	——
15. Major business readjustment (merger, reorganization, bankruptcy)	39	——
16. Major change in financial status	38	——
17. Death of a close friend	37	——
18. Change to a different line of work	36	——
19. Major change in number of arguments with spouse	35	——
20. Taking out a mortgage/loan for a major purchase (home, business)	31	——
21. Foreclosure of mortgage/loan	30	——

→

The Social Readjustment Rating Scale (continued)

Life Event	Point Value	Your Score
22. Major change in responsibilities at work	29	____
23. Son or daughter leaving home (college, marriage)	29	____
24. Trouble with in-laws	29	____
25. Outstanding personal achievement	28	____
26. Wife begins or ceases work outside the home	26	____
27. Beginning or ceasing formal schooling	26	____
28. Major change in living conditions (new home, remodeling, moving)	25	____
29. Revision of personal habits (dress, manners)	24	____
30. Trouble with boss	23	____
31. Major change in working hours/conditions	20	____
32. Change in residence	20	____
33. Change in schools	20	____
34. Major change in usual type/amount of recreation	19	____
35. Major change in church activities	19	____
36. Major change in social activities	18	____
37. Taking out a loan for a lesser purchase (car, TV, freezer)	17	____
38. Major change in sleeping habits	16	____
39. Major change in family get-togethers	15	____
40. Major change in eating habits	15	____
41. Vacation	13	____
42. Christmas/holiday season	12	____
43. Minor legal violations (traffic or jaywalking ticket)	11	____
TOTAL		____

→

The Social Readjustment Rating Scale (continued)

What Your Score Means

The higher your score (i.e., the more changes occurring in your life over the past year), the more likely you are to develop a stress-related illness.

Below 150 Points: Statistically, you have a 30% chance of experiencing a significant health problem in the near future.

Between 150 and 300 Points: You have a 50% chance of experiencing a significant health problem in the near future.

More than 300 Points: You have an 80% chance of developing a significant health problem in the near future.

could control their reaction to it by relaxing. In his book, *The Relaxation Response*, Benson suggests that a variety of techniques can induce the relaxation response, including yoga, meditation, progressive relaxation, autogenic training, self-hypnosis, and biofeedback.

Progressive Relaxation. Progressive relaxation, according to Benson, is an effective therapy for inducing the relaxation response. People are first taught to contract and relax their face and neck muscles. These muscles are tensed for one to two seconds and then relaxed. This simple procedure helps patients experience the difference in blood flow to a muscle when it is stressed–and away from the muscle when it is relaxed. The procedure is repeated progressively from the face and neck to the upper chest and arms, the abdomen, hips, buttocks, thighs, knees, calves, and feet. The whole process is repeated two or three times, and produces a deep state of relaxation.

Spiral Relaxation. Spiral relaxation is a variation of progressive relaxation. The procedure begins by the person lying comfortably on a bed with the palms of the hands facing up. With the eyes closed, the person imagines a point of light or heat which begins a series of three clockwise spirals around the top of the head and moves down around the face, neck, upper chest, each arm, the abdomen, waist, hips, thighs, knees, calves, and feet. Each part of the body relaxes as the series of three spirals encircles it.

Another variation of the relaxation technique involves a person imagining her body being filled from the top of her head to the tip of her toes with healing energy. The energy enters through an opening at the top of the head and moves through the frontal lobes to the lower brain stem. The person relaxes the cranium, skull, ears, eyes, mouth, cheeks, throat, nose, and ears. This energy moves down the body and relaxes the arms, chest, abdomen, hips, buttocks, thighs, knees, calves, and feet.

Nutritional Therapies. According to Dr. Serafina Corsello, executive medical director of The Corsello Centers for Nutritional Medicine in New York, the link between stress and diet is indisputable. She states in the March 1994 issue of *Delicious*: "Stress depletes the body's energy reserves while food supplies the body with fuel it needs to produce energy. How much energy you have also depends on the quality of the food you ingest and the distribution of food in the digestive system that works properly. If you're under stress, you can't properly digest food. Therefore, you are not getting all the nutritional benefits of the food you eat."

Corsello recommends a diet high in complex carbohydrates (which provide a steady supply of slow-burning fuel as well as protective antioxidants) and low in animal fat. "The best diet includes raw or steamed fresh vegetables, whole-grain foods such as brown rice, oatmeal and whole wheat pasta, and a small amount of oily fish such as salmon, which contains essential fatty acids," she counsels. Corsello also suggests avoiding coffee and other caffeine-containing substances which "in the long run contribute to adrenal fatigue."

Vitamin and Mineral Therapies. As noted, the adrenal glands play a critical role in how most people respond to stress. Michael Murray and Joseph Pizzorno in the *Encyclopedia of Natural Medicine* suggest that vitamin C, vitamin B_6, zinc, magnesium, potassium, and pantothenic acid are necessary nutrients for the normal functioning of the adrenal glands. Supplementation of all these nutrients may be appropriate during high periods of stress for people who need adrenal support. However, one should consult a physician or a nutritionist before taking vitamin and mineral supplements.

Botanical Therapies. Many people experiencing milder stress symptoms treat themselves with sedatives and sleeping pills. This can result in chemical addictions, however, and holistic physicians emphasize that natural medicinal herbs can be used effectively to reduce stress, with fewer or no side effects.

Murray and Pizzorno claim that a number of botanical medicines have proven effective in calming nerves, reducing tension, and relieving stress-related symptoms. These herbs are typically used in conjunction with recommended changes in nutrition and lifestyle. Although herbs can be effective in treating stress and anxiety, people are best advised to have a complete physical examination and only take botanical or herbal stress relievers recommended by a licensed physician. Anyone with chronic symptoms of anxiety, for example, or who has a history of heart disorder, should also consult a physician.

Ginseng. Ginseng (especially Korean or Chinese ginseng) has been shown to enhance adrenal gland function and improve reactions against a variety of stresses. Ginseng is regarded as an "adaptogen," or an herb that protects against both mental and physical fatigue and helps the body maintain its natural equilibrium. Murray and Pizzorno cite 10 studies that document how ginseng improves adrenal functions and helps the body withstand extremely stressful conditions.

Valerian Root. Valerian root has been used throughout recorded history as a sedative, and in several studies it was found to be as effective as benzodiazepines or barbiturates in the treatment of insomnia. Valerian can have unpredictable effects, however, and should only be used under the supervision of a physician. Also, it should not be taken daily in high doses for more than a few weeks because overuse can cause the same symptoms that the herb was intended to relieve in the first place.

Hops. Hops is an effective substitute for people who cannot take valerian. Bitter in taste (responsible for the bitter flavor of beer), it acts as a digestive stimulant, and is especially effective in treating stress-related digestive disorders, including irritable bowel syndrome (IBS). The active ingredients in hops break down rapidly after being harvested, and the herb must therefore be ingested fresh to be most effective. Hops is more stable in tincture form than in a dried form.

Passion Flower, Skullcap, and Chamomile. The use of passion flower dates back to the Aztecs. One of its constituents, harmine, was originally called telepathine because of its ability to induce a contemplative state. Passion flower is a sedative, anti-spasmodic, and a natural painkiller. Because of its gentleness, passion flower is especially well suited for the treatment of nervousness in children and insomnia in the elderly resulting from stress.

Skullcap is employed as a sedative in China and Europe because it is mild and does not induce drowsiness, unless a person is already sleepy. Skullcap can be taken for long periods of time (up to six weeks) without becoming toxic or addictive.

Chamomile, one of the most popular herbs in the U.S., is a potent sedative when taken for short-term use in doses of as much as a gram in powder form. It also aids in digestion, but can cause allergic reactions, and should be taken under the advice of a physician.

Lemon Balm. Lemon balm has long been used to relax the nervous system. Some nutritionists believe it also improves digestion, reduces heart palpitations, eliminates headaches, calms anxiety, and alleviates depression.

Aromatherapy. According to *Alternative Medicine: The Definitive Guide*, therapeutic use of oils, known as aromatherapy, has also proven effective in relieving anxiety, depression, fatigue, insomnia, and stress. Because the nose is the closest sense organ to the brain, inhaling aromas effectively stimulates the limbic system. Aromas are first detected by the olfactory receptor cells, which in turn send information to the olfactory bulb, which then sends it directly to the limbic system of the brain. Research has shown that pleasant aromas subconsciously trigger relaxation and positive emotions. Several companies market aromas, which when inhaled, helps to reduce stress. One company, for example, markets an inhaler and a gentle blend of pure lavender oil, laurel, and thyme to relax facial skin.

Biofeedback. Michael Murphy states in his book *The Future of the Body* that biofeedback has been extremely successful in reducing stress levels. Using biofeedback machines, patients can voluntarily relax specific muscles, reduce their blood pressure and heart rate, and improve digestion. Biofeedback is often used in conjunction with other relaxation therapies such as meditation, yoga, visualization, or guided imagery.

Exercise. A growing body of evidence suggests that regular exercise boosts the body's ability to withstand stress. Exercise is one of the best techniques for reducing stress because physical activity allows the body to "throw off" tension. Anyone who runs, walks, or swims regularly knows how the body feels after exercising–tired, even drained, but relaxed. Exercise can also help protect the cardiovascular and immune systems from the consequences of stressful events. Psychologist Jonathan Brown of the University of Washington, for example, studied the stress and fitness levels of approximately 500 college students as part of three studies over a five-year period. According to Brown, quoted in the July 7, 1993 edition of the *San Jose Mercury News*: "There is a general tendency for stress to have a detrimental effect on well-being. My research suggests you can escape or minimize those effects if you stay physically fit."

Stress Reduction Exercise Hints

- Start slowly, progress gradually, and do not overexercise.
- Work out with friends or as part of an exercise class. Social support makes exercise more fun and decreases the tendency to stop exercising.
- Start with an activity involving repetitive motion, such as running or brisk walking. Running and brisk walking prompt a meditative effect from the sound of feet hitting the pavement.
- Exercise regularly.
- Don't rush from exercising back to a normal routine. Take at least a few minutes to enjoy feeling relaxed.

As noted, exercise relieves muscle tension and helps dissipate the hormones that can build up in response to stress. The primary psychological benefit of exercise may be that it helps people regain control of their health. One aspect of stress is the sense of feeling out of control, or of not being able to respond to a stressor. When people are afraid and lose their sense of control, their heart races and their blood pressure increases. But exercise, along with relaxation, helps to reverse this process.

Qi Gong. Qi gong, a Chinese meditative exercise, also effectively relieves stress. There are several variations of the exercise. In one form, practitioners sit in a relaxed pose and use their mental concentration to channel chi energy to specific parts of the body. In the movement form of qi gong, practitioners combine graceful, rhythmic movements while meditating on the movement of chi throughout their bodies. According to an article by R. Jahnke in the January-February 1991 issue of the *Townsend Letter for Doctors*, qi gong initiates the "relaxation response," which reduces stress, decreases heart rate, lowers blood pressure, and increases tissue regeneration.

Tai Chi. Tai chi, moving meditation, is also effective in post-stress recovery. According to Dr. Herbert Benson (*The Relaxation Response*), both tai chi and qi gong produce "exactly the same physiological responses as passive relaxation techniques like meditation. Practiced properly, they are thoroughly relaxing." Tai chi and qi gong share characteristics such as gentle, fluid movements performed in synchrony with slow, carefully controlled breathing.

Dance Therapy Stress is often exacerbated by poor diet, lack of exercise, and social isolation. Exercise increases respiration and circulation, and deep breathing increases the flow of oxygen to the organs and stimulates the endorphins, which help produce positive mental states. Dancing not only stimulates the endorphins, it also puts one in contact with others. Dance therapy, according to the *People's Folk-Dance Directory*, may even help people express and resolve their personal problems.

Yoga. Daniel Goleman, in his book *The Meditative Mind*, states that more than 1,000 studies have proven that yoga along with meditation effectively reduces stress and anxiety, lowers blood pressure, relieves addictions, and improves metabolic and respiratory functioning. He notes that because meditation has proven highly effective in reducing stress and tension, the National Institutes of Health recommends that it replace prescription drugs as the first treatment for mild hypertension. Yoga schools can be found in many parts of the United States, and each school offers its own variation. All forms of yoga involve gentle movements and regular breathing exercises. Some yoga practices also include visualization, progressive relaxation exercises, and meditation.

Meditation. There are several different forms of meditation, but all share the common goal of quieting the mind. In some traditions, such as Buddhism, meditators sit comfortably in silence and think no thoughts. In transcendental meditation, practitioners silence their minds by internally reciting a mantra, or holy sound. In qi gong, tai chi, and other Chinese disciplines, practitioners perform gentle, dance-like movements while meditating on the flow of chi energy through their bodies. In *The Relaxation Response* Dr. Herbert Benson details a number of studies which show that meditation helps slow the breathing rate and increases oxygen consumption and blood flow to the brain, which produce a more relaxed brain wave rhythm.

Dr. Jon Kabat-Zinn, founder of the Stress Reduction Clinic at the University of Massachusetts, has used meditation to help people suffering from chronic diseases as well as stress-related disorders, including abdominal pain, ulcers, and chronic diarrhea. In his book, *Full Catastrophic Living: Using the Wisdom of Your Body and Mind to Face Stress, Pain, and Illness*, he details how a majority of his patients reduced the pains associated with stress and improved their health by meditating.

Mindful Exercise (Exercise Plus Meditation). A University of Massachusetts Medical School study recently showed that mindful exercise (exercise combined with meditation) elicits immediate, positive emotions such as enthusiasm, alertness, and increased self-esteem. The research, reported by Suzanne Hildreth in the January/February 1994 issue of *Natural Health*, was done in

Zen Breathing

The following Zen breathing exercise can help turn anxious mental states into tranquillity.

- Find a quiet, comfortable place to sit where you will not be disturbed.

- Breathe in slowly and through your nose.

- With each breath you take, concentrate on the feelings, sensations, and changes you experience through breathing. Listen to your breath. This process helps you to tune out other sounds and to forget distracting, left-brain thoughts.

- After about 15 minutes, take one last deep breath and end the session. You should feel completely relaxed and refreshed. As you become more proficient with this technique, it'll take you progressively less time to become relaxed because your nervous system has learned the relaxation conditioned response. Just two or three breaths will bring you the benefits of a longer period of meditation.

collaboration with the Center for Balance and Fitness and Dr. Herbert Benson's Mind/Body Medical Institute at the New England Deaconess Hospital in Boston. Researchers examined four groups of exercisers, as well as a control group that read quietly. During the course of the study, one group followed a low-intensity walking program; one group walked while listening to a relaxation tape developed by Dr. Benson. The third group practiced a combination of visualization and tai chi movements, while the fourth walked at a higher intensity than the others. Those who walked while listening to the tape, participated in the t'ai chi and visualization class, or exercised more briskly reported less irritability, guilt, fear, and hostility, along with increased feelings of excitement and strength, than the low-intensity walking group.

Acupuncture. Acupuncture is also effective in relieving stress. Acupuncture, as noted in Chapter 1, is based on the theory that the body contains a vital energy force called chi that circulates freely in a healthy body. Chi is altered when a body is undergoing stress, and an unbalanced chi force can cause disease. Acupuncture treatments rebalance the chi force, and the physical symptoms associated with stress are alleviated.

Shiatsu. Practitioners of acupressure (also known as shiatsu) use their thumbs, fingers, and elbows to stimulate the body's 361 tsubos, or acupuncture points. The technique involves repetitively pressing the tsubos for three to five seconds, and then releasing pressure. Acupressure is most useful for rebalancing energy blockages associated with stress, rather than curing specific diseases.

Massage. Massage is another useful stress-relieving therapy. Tui na, a Chinese form of massage, uses a combination of gentle hand pats and stretches to redistribute the chi flow throughout the body. Tui na is based on the same model of the body as acupuncture and acupressure, although it is more forceful and focuses on broader areas rather than specific points.

Visualization. Another way of inducing the relaxation response is to use a visualization exercise or guided imagery. In these therapies, summarized by Gerald Epstein in *Healing Visualizations,* people imagine themselves in an environment they associate with relaxation—a peaceful beach, seashore, lake, or favorite mountain. After closing their

eyes and taking a few deep, easy breaths, they remember the details of the setting—the sights, smells, and sounds—and focus on feeling peaceful and relaxed.

Humor and Laughter. Doctors have observed that patients with a well-developed sense of humor have better chances of recovering from a serious disease. In *Anatomy of an Illness*, Norman Cousins, former professor at the UCLA Medical School, recounts how laughter helped to cure him of an unexplained illness. Cousins relates that he stopped taking medication and began watching reruns of Marx Brothers films and Candid Camera. According to Cousins, the resulting laughter, sustained and heavy, was the key to his recovery. Cousins also cites research studies by Dr. William Fry of Stanford University that show that a good laugh—like a good workout—produces an overall sense of well-being. Laughter flexes the diaphragm, chest, and abdominal muscles, causing deep breathing to take place. It helps relax the shoulders, neck, and facial muscles, as well as aid in digestion, stimulate the heart, and increase the production of endorphins which help relieve pain.

Psychologically, humor is a form of transcendence—it removes us from our self-absorbed ego. It helps people balance their perspectives on painful experiences, and enables them to deal with difficulties in a healthy way. Being humorous is also a way of releasing negative thoughts.

Many medical experts are beginning to appreciate the benefits of humor and laughter in reducing stress, and are recommending laughter-provoking activities such as cultivating friends and acquaintances who smile and joke and putting playfulness into relationships.

Music. In the ancient cultures of China, Greece, and India, music was understood to have healing power. The Greek philosopher

Tonal Massage

One stress-reduction exercise, tonal massage, detailed in *Music and the Brain*, involves visualizing musical tones massaging the body:

1. Turn on a favorite piece of music and concentrate on the sounds while clearing your mind of worries.

2. Imagine the tones, starting at your feet, and moving up your legs and into the abdomen.

3. Visualize the tones relaxing your heart and lungs, slowing down and regularizing their rhythms.

4. Visualize the tones relaxing your shoulders and neck, jaw, eyeballs, and forehead.

Pythagorus taught his students to cleanse themselves of worry, sorrow, fear, and anger through daily singing and music making. In the ancient temples of India, China, and Tibet, healing through sound was a highly developed science, based on the belief that vibration emanating from a spiritual source could have physiological effects. Buddhist and Hindu monks used prolonged chants, ecstatic rhythms, and ancient melodies to awaken their chakras, believed to be powerful centers of energy in the body.

According to M. Citchley's *Music and the Brain*, three neurophysiological processes are triggered by music. First, because music is nonverbal, it directly stimulates the center of the limbic system that governs emotional responses as well as basic metabolic processes such as body temperature, blood pressure, and heart rate. Second, music triggers the flow of stored memory across the left and

On the Job Stress Reduction

In *Whole-Brain Thinking*, Jacquelyn Wonder and Priscilla Donovan recommend these quick relaxation excrcises at the work place:

1. **Eye Exercises**. Turn your face to the wall or look out the window (whatever is less conspicuous). Close your eyes and roll your eyeballs upward. Take two deep breaths.

2. **Mini push-ups**. Put your arms at your side, hands pointed forward. Now bend your hands backward as far as possible and hold them rigid. Count to 20 (if you have time) and release. Put your hands in your lap for a few seconds and enjoy the feeling of release.

3. **Roll-arounds**. Roll your head in a circle several times and then reverse direction. Repeat for as long as you can comfortably, each time rolling more slowly and fully.

4. **Lean-to's**. Lean from side to side in your chair until your hands are touching the floor with each lean.

5. **A mini mind-vacation**. Close your eyes and visualize yourself in your favorite place. Stay there until your body feels it's there, too. If you have cold hands or feet, visualize yourself in a warm, friendly place and warm those extremities.

6. **Standing room only**. If you must stand for extended periods, shift from foot to foot, exaggerating the movements by bending your knees and ankles.

Summary of Stress-Relieving Therapies

- Relaxation Exercises: Practice progressive relaxation, spiral relaxation, or guided imagery and visualization exercises.
- Exercise: Start a moderate exercise program such as brisk walking or running, which combines aerobic exercise, repetitive motion, and social interaction.
- Yoga and Meditation: Practice yoga and meditation to reduce stress and anxiety, lower blood pressure, and improve metabolic and respiratory functioning.
- Biofeedback: Use biofeedback to voluntarily relax specific muscles, reduce blood pressure and heart rate, and improve digestion.
- Nutritional Therapies: Eat a diet high in complex carbohydrates, raw or steamed fresh vegetables, whole-grain foods, and fish such as salmon, which contains essential fatty acids.
- Vitamin and Mineral Therapies: Ask a physician or nutritionist about adding vitamin C, vitamin B_6, zinc, magnesium, potassium, and pantothenic acid supplements to your nutritional program.
- Botanical Therapies: Ask a physician, nutritionist, or herbalist about adding ginseng, hops, chamomile, or lemon balm as supplements to your diet.

right hemispheres of the brain via the corpus callosum. Finally, music stimulates the endorphins, the natural opiates secreted by the hypothalamus that produce a feeling of relaxation.

According to an article in the October 30, 1995 *Marin Independent Journal*, the National Institutes of Health is spending $30,000 on a pilot study to measure the effects of music on patients with stress disorders and brain injuries. Currently, there are more than 4,000 music therapists in the U.S.

Social Support and Stress Reduction. Psychosocial processes often mediate the relationship between stressful events and how the body reacts to stressors. A 1993 Swedish study reported by Daniel Goleman in the December 7, 1993 issue of *The New York Times* suggests that stress is easier for individuals to cope with if they have the support of close friends or family. In the study, a random sample of 50-year-old men living in Goteborg were given a physical examination and psychological evaluation in 1986. Seven years later, researchers analyzed official records and found that the men who were socially isolated and identified themselves as lacking emotional support were three times as likely to die from stressful events than men who were not socially isolated.

Research on the effects of social isolation, stressful events, and death rates began in the 1970s when Dr. Lisa Berkman, an epidemiologist at the Yale University School of Medicine, and Leonard Syme, an epidemiologist at the University of California at Berkeley, first conducted a study of more than 7,000 men and women in Alameda County, California. They reported in a 1979 issue of the *American Journal of Epidemiology* that between 1970 and 1979, people with the fewest social ties were twice as likely to die as those with the strongest ties. Scientists are still uncertain as to precisely how social support decreases a person's likelihood of dying from a stress-related experience. In commenting on the Swedish study, Dr. Berkman states in Daniel Goleman's article in *The New York Times* that "there's ample evidence now that having a rich social network protects health somehow." She suggests that people with social ties may have healthier habits in general–or that such ties help strengthen a person's neuroendocrine and immune systems.

Psychotherapy. Psychotherapy is also effective in relieving stress. Talking with a therapist helps many patients understand how stress impairs both their physical and mental health. Psychotherapy, for example, is an important component in treating stress-related disorders such as irritable bowel syndrome (IBS). Psychologist William Whitehead at Johns Hopkins University School of Medicine uses biofeedback, along with cognitive-behavioral therapy and regular exercise, to help his IBS patients curb anxiety. He suggests that other therapists have successfully employed a three-part therapy to relieve stress disorders. First, patients clench and relax a series of muscles throughout their body (progressive relaxation), so that they become aware of how they feel when they're tense. Second, the therapist then uses guided imagery to teach patients to relax. Third, patients learn to recast their negative, stress-producing thoughts into positive, healing images.

Summary

Some stress is unavoidable in normal living, and can provide an opportunity for growth and development. Excessive, prolonged stress is harmful, however, and increases the risk of medical disorders such as atherosclerosis, headaches, hypertension, and ulcers. More important than the stress level itself is how efficiently a person converts the stress into useful energy, and is able to successfully manage it. Recognizing the early signs of stress and doing something positive through exercise, relaxation, and other techniques can make an important difference in a person's quality of life and sense of well-being.

Resources

References

Arnold, Kathryn. "Energy!" *Delicious* (March 1994): 18-20.

Balch, James F., and Phyllis Balch. *Prescription for Nutritional Healing*, Long Island, NY: Avery Publishing, 1993.

Benson, Herbert. *The Relaxation Response*. New York: William Morrow, 1975.

Berkman, L.F., and S.L. Syme. "Social Networks, Host Resistance, and Mortality: A Nine-Year Follow-Up Study of Alameda County Residents." *American Journal of Epidemiology* 2 (1979): 186-204.

Chapman, A. "The Use of Humor in Psychotherapy." *Archives of Neurosis.* (March 1995): 153-56.

Citchley, M. *Music and the Brain*. New York: Simon & Schuster, 1992.

Cousins, Norman. *Anatomy of an Illness*. New York: Random House, 1992.

Epstein, Gerald. *Healing Visualizations*. New York: Bantam, 1989.

Goleman, Daniel. *The Meditative Mind.* Los Angeles, CA : Jeremy P. Tarcher, Inc., 1988.

——. "Stress and Isolation Tied to a Reduced Life Span," *New York Times* (December 7, 1993): B8.

Hildreth, Suzanne. "The New Body/Mind Workout." *Natural Health* (January/February 1994): 54-56.

Jahnke, R. "The Most Profound Medicine–Part II and Part III: Physiological Mechanisms Operating in the Human System during the Practice of Qigong and Yoga Pranayama." *Townsend Letter for Doctors* (January-February 1991): 124-30; 281-85.

Kabat-Sinn, J. *Full Catastrophic Living: Using the Wisdom of Your Body and Mind to Face Stress, Pain, and Illness* . New York: Delacorte Press, 1990.

Krucoff, C. "Personal Fitness." *San Jose Mercury News* (July 7, 1993): 7D.

Murphy, Michael. *The Future of the Body*. Los Angeles: Jeremy P. Tarcher, Inc., 1992.

Murray, Michael, and Joseph Pizzorno. *Encyclopedia of Natural Medicine*. Rocklin, CA: Prima Publishing, 1991.

"Music Can Influence Feelings, New NIH Research Confirms." *Marin Independent Journal*. (October 30, 1995): 10.

Rees, Alan, and Charlene Willey. *Personal Health Reporter*. Detroit: Gale Research, 1993.

Scofield, M. *Work Site Health Promotion*. Philadelphia: Hanley & Belfus, Inc., 1990.

Seyle, Hans. *Stress without Distress*. New York: New American Library, 1975.

"Stress Can Make You Sick, But Can Managing Stress Make You Well?" *Consumer Reports Health Letter* 2 (January 1990): 1-3.

"Stress Is Sickening." *New Body* (December 1993).

Wilkinson, Greg. "Stress: Another Chimera." *British Medical Journal* (January 26, 1991): 191-92.

Wonder, Jacquelyn, and Priscilla Donovan. *Whole-Brain Thinking*. New York: Basic Books, 1993.

Yagi, Y. "An Experimental Study of the Determinants to the Effects of Self Affirmation." *Japanese Journal of Psychology*. (August 1992): 170-80.

Organizations

American Heart Association.
7320 Greenville Avenue, Dallas, TX 75231.

The American Institute of Stress. Department U.
124 Park Avenue, Yonkers, NY 10703.

National High Blood Pressure Education Program. 120/80.
4733 Bethesda Avenue, Bethesda, MD 20814.

The National Institute of Mental Health. Consumer Information Center.
Department 563Z, Pueblo, CO 80033.

People's Folk-Dance Directory.
P.O. Box 8575, Austin TX 78713.

Additional Reading

Benson, Herbert, and William Proctor. *Beyond the Relaxation Response*. New York: Berkeley, 1987.

Girdano, Daniel, and George Everly. *Controlling Stress and Tension: A Holistic Approach*. Englewood Cliffs, NJ: Prentice-Hall, 1986.

"How to Fend Off Stress." *Good Housekeeping* (February 1991): 106, 130.

Kirsta, Alix. *The Book of Stress Survival*. New York: Simon & Schuster, 1986.

Mason, L. *Guide to Stress Reeducation*. New York: Celestial Arts, 1985.

Shimer, Porter, and Sharon Ferguson. "Unwind and Destress (Part 1)." *Prevention* 42 (July 1990): 75-92.

RESOURCES

Chapter 9

STRESS-RELATED DISORDERS

As discussed in the previous chapter, certain experiences are so physically or emotionally stressful that they can severely compromise the immune system's ability to ward off disease. Prolongation of stress can exhaust specific organ systems, especially the heart, blood vessels, and adrenal glands. This chapter discusses the alternative prevention and treatment of medical disorders associated with chronic stress: headaches, hypertension (high blood pressure), irritable bowel syndrome (IBS), ulcers, and atherosclerosis.

Atherosclerosis

Arteriosclerosis is the general term for the thickening and hardening of the arteries that occurs as part of the aging process. Atherosclerosis, one form of arteriosclerosis, is caused by hypertension and other risk factors including high cholesterol levels, a rich diet (with large amounts of meat, butter, whole milk, eggs, and calories), genetics, diabetes, poor physical fitness, and cigarette smoking. Atherosclerosis, according to Kurt Butler and Lynn Rayner in *The Best Medicine: The Complete Health and Preventive Handbook*, causes or contributes to more deaths in the U.S. than all other diseases or accidents combined.

People with atherosclerosis have deposits of fatty substances of cholesterol, cellular waste products, calcium, or fibrin (a clotting material) on the inner linings of their arteries. These substances combine to form arterial blockages called plaque. Plaque may partially or totally block the blood's flow through an artery and cause bleeding (hemorrhaging) in the plaque, or blood clots (thrombi) on the plaque's surface. If a coronary artery becomes blocked, less blood is supplied to the heart, and a heart attack can occur. If the arteries supplying blood to the brain are occluded, a stroke can occur. The clogging of arteries feeding the kidneys can lead to kidney failure.

Treatments for atherosclerosis include removal of the fatty substances or plaque by surgery or laser, widening of affected arteries using small balloons (angioplasty), and the use of various drugs. Therapies also include diet, treating hypertension, and not smoking.

Alternative Treatments for Atherosclerosis

Ayurvedic Medicine. Ayurvedic physicians use herbal food supplements, detoxification, and purification techniques to reduce free radicals and lipid peroxides that are believed to contribute to atherosclerosis. Sodhi states in *Alternative Medicine: The Definitive Guide* that one hospital in Bombay, India, has treated more than 3,000 cases of coronary heart disease using herbals and detoxification and purification therapies that eliminate toxins from the blood and reduce stress. The hospital's stress reduction program combines yoga and meditation.

Botanical Medicines. Michael Murray and Joseph Pizzorno cite several studies in the *Encyclopedia of Natural Medicine* that indicate garlic oil, alfalfa leaf, and hawthorn berry may help lower cholesterol levels and inhibit the formation of plaque. Garlic oil increases the breakdown of fibrin and inhibits atherosclerotic platelets from forming. Alfalfa leaf appears to exert a "shrinkage" effect on atherosclerotic plaque. Hawthorn berry and its flower extracts have been widely used in Europe in clinical trials to lower serum cholesterol levels and to prevent the deposition of cholesterol in arterial walls. Hawthorn berry

can be toxic in excessive amounts, however, and should be taken only under the supervision of a physician or nutritionist.

Chinese physicians have used an herbal extract from the plant mao-tung-ching (*Ilex puibeceus*) to treat coronary atherosclerosis. The extract, according to Chung San Yuan in an article that appeared in the 1973 *Chinese Medical Journal,* helps dilate blocked blood vessels and increase blood flow to the heart. Of a total of 103 cases, 101 patients showed significant improvement.

Exercise. Regular aerobic exercise such as walking or cycling raises HDL ("good") cholesterol blood levels and lowers triglycerides. A study reported in the April 1993 issue of *Archives of Internal Medicine* suggests that resistance exercise helps lower both total cholesterol and LDL ("bad") cholesterol levels, at least in premenopausal women. In the study, inactive women with normal cholesterol levels were assigned to either an exercise group or a control group. The participants were told to continue their usual eating patterns. Those in the exercise group were placed on a supervised program of strength-training–12 resistance exercises for one hour three times a week. At the end of the five-month period, the exercise group showed significant declines in cholesterol levels. As a group, the women who trained with weights lowered their total cholesterol by 13% and their LDL cholesterol by 14 points.

Nutritional Therapies. In his best-selling book *Dr. Dean Ornish's Program for Reversing Heart Disease,* Ornish outlines a combination of alternative treatments he has used successfully to reverse coronary atherosclerosis. A diet of vegetables, fruits, and dietary fiber (including flax seed, oat bran, and pectin) is a key component. Ornish suggests that patients with coronary atherosclerosis must totally avoid saturated fats, cholesterol, sugar, and animal proteins.

To prevent atherosclerosis and heart disease, he recommends that people limit their fat consumption to 20% of calories consumed. To reverse heart disease caused by coronary atherosclerosis, he counsels his patients to limit their fat intake to 10% of calories.

Butler and Rayner claim that dietary fibers such as cellulose, pectin, lignin, and other indigestible components of whole grains, legumes, fruits, and vegetables appear to reduce cholesterol (a key risk factor in atherosclerosis). They report one study in which participants who ate a quarter-pound of raw carrots for breakfast for three weeks reduced serum cholesterol levels by an average of 11%. The effect lasted for three weeks after patients stopped eating the carrots. Butler and Rayner theorize that the fiber may decrease intestinal absorption of cholesterol.

They also note that vegetarians are known to be less susceptible to atherosclerosis, which traditionally was linked to their lower fat and cholesterol intake. However, as Butler and Rayner suggest, it also could be the result of their higher consumption of vitamin B_6 (pyridoxine), which is abundant in plant foods. By comparison, meat eaters (especially those who also eat a lot of processed and sugary foods and little fresh produce) usually consume very little vitamin B_6.

Vitamin and Mineral Therapies. Several studies summarized in Chapter 3 have shown that vitamins C, E, and B help prevent atherosclerosis. Vitamin C dissolves cholesterol, aids in fat metabolism, and helps restore the integrity of the arterial walls. Supplemental vitamin E helps prevent atherosclerosis by inhibiting platelet aggregation and elevating HDL cholesterol levels. Niacin also has been used to lower cholesterol levels, although its use should be supervised by a physician because it can lead to liver damage and glucose intolerance.

Pantetheine lowers LDL cholesterol levels and increases HDL cholesterol levels.

Magnesium and calcium supplementation (see Chapter 4) also increases HDL cholesterol levels, decreases platelet aggregation, and prolongs the time it takes plaque and blood clots to form. According to Murray and Pizzorno, carnitine, a vitamin-like compound, stimulates the breakdown of long-chain fatty acids and can help prevent fatty plaques from forming in the blood. Lecithin increases the solubility of cholesterol and helps remove cholesterol from tissue deposits. Onions and bromelain, an enzyme found in pineapples, also decrease platelet aggregation, they claim.

Butler and Rayner report that studies have confirmed the ability of lecithin to increase HDL cholesterol and inhibit platelet clumping or aggregation. It is found in unbleached soy flour, seeds, nuts, whole grains, and cold-pressed vegetable oils, all of which contain other important nutrients as well.

Headaches

Nine out of ten people in the U.S. experience at least one headache a year, while as many as 45 million Americans suffer from chronic or severe headaches that seriously interfere with their lives, according to studies cited in a November 1990 article in *The University of California, Berkeley Wellness Letter*. Headaches now account for 150 million lost work days and 80 million visit to doctors' offices each year in the U.S. More than $400 million is spent annually on over-the-counter pain relievers.

Headaches almost always are due to dilation, constriction, spasm, irritation, or inflammation of arteries or muscles of the head and neck. Sometimes more than one factor is involved. There are several types of headaches, each overlapping in symptoms and

Types of Headaches

Tension headaches are caused by sustained constriction of scalp, neck, and face muscles, with symptoms of tightness and pressure in the forehead and the back of the head and neck.

- **Migraine headaches** are caused by constriction of the arteries with symptoms that include flashing lights, extreme pain in one side of the head, and numbness.

- **Cluster headaches** are characterized by piercing pain around and behind one eye, and may occur in clusters of several a day with recurrences every few weeks.

- **Food sensitivity headaches** are caused by chocolate, red wines, cheeses, excessive salt, preservatives such as monosodium glutamate (MSG), and other foodstuffs.

- **Alcohol headaches** occur hours after drinking and often are the main aspect of a hangover.

- **Smoking headaches** are caused by inhaling nicotine.

- **Toxic headaches** are caused by exposure to chemicals such as benzene, gasoline, formaldehyde, paints, glue, or carbon dioxide.

- **High blood pressure headaches** (which occur in 10% of hypertension cases) resemble migraines and usually necessitate antihypertensive drug therapy.

- **Bruxism headaches** are caused by excessive clenching and grinding of the teeth, excessive gum chewing, or jaw disorders.

- **TMJ headaches** are caused by abnormal temporomandibular joints (where the jaws meet the skull) due to arthritis, biting on hard objects, excessive gum chewing, or malocclusion (bad bite).

response to treatment. The triggering factors and modes of relief vary from person to person. The majority of primary headaches (those caused by stress and lifestyle factors such as smoking or drinking, and not by other diseases) fall into three categories: tension headaches, migraine headaches, and cluster headaches.

Nine out of ten headaches are tension-related, caused by the sustained constriction of scalp, neck, and face muscles and characterized by tightness and pressure in the forehead and the back of the head and neck. Poor posture on the job, with prolonged flexing of the neck, can trigger such a headache. Depression, fatigue, mental tension, and emotional distress also can be factors. Tension

headaches affect men and women in equal numbers.

According to Butler and Rayner, migraines affect approximately 8% of the U.S. population and tend to run in families. In migraine headaches the pain usually is limited to one side of the head and is pounding and often incapacitating. It often is accompanied by nausea and vomiting. Certain neurological symptoms may occur 10 to 30 minutes before an attack, such as flashing lights, blind spots, blurred vision, or a tingling, numbing sensation on one side of the body. Other vague symptoms beforehand include mental fuzziness, mood changes, fatigue, and unusual retention of fluids. Migraines, which affect three times as many women as men, are believed to be caused by several factors, including emotional stress, depression, unstable levels of the brain chemical serotonin, alcohol, allergies, nitrates, excessive sun, motion sickness, fluctuating levels of female hormones, and genetics. Migraine pain can last several hours to several days. These headaches strike as often as several times a week or as rarely as once every few years.

Cluster headaches occur when the blood vessels on the surface of the brain widen excessively; they usually last between 30 and 45 minutes. Although some specialists consider them migraine variants, cluster headaches are distinguished by a knifelike, piercing pain around and behind one eye, which is tearing and red, and by a runny nose and accelerated heartbeat. The pain is very severe but non-throbbing, and both the onset and cessation are sudden. These headaches tend to occur in clusters of several a day, with recurrences every few weeks. They are much less common than migraines (only 1% of the U.S. population suffers from them), affect men much more often than women (especially those who are heavy smokers and heavy drinkers), and do not run in families. They seem to be linked to seasonal changes in the amount of daylight, according to the October 1993 issue of the *Mayo Clinic Health Letter*.

Treatments for Headaches

Acupuncture.   In the last 20 years, acupuncture has become a respected therapy in many American hospitals. It is widely used to reduce pain in patients with migraine headaches. A 1980 study conducted at the University of California at Los Angeles found that acupuncture reduced the frequency and severity of migraines in more than 20,000 patients. In another study, 74% of 204 patients suffering from chronic migraines experienced significant pain relief for more than three months after being treated by

acupuncture. Acupuncture may be useful in relieving other types of headaches as well, although few clinical double-blind trials have been conducted.

Bach Flower Remedies.   Dr. Julian Barnard reports in *Alternative Medicine: The Definitive Guide* that he has effectively relieved migraines with a combination of flower remedies, including gentian, water violet, walnut, and Bach's emergency stress formula.

Biofeedback.   Biofeedback is very successful in treating headaches caused by muscle contraction, according to Fugh-Berman, especially for patients whose muscle contraction headaches are chronic and/or severe. Biofeedback is also effective for migraine headaches caused by dilated blood vessels. One technique involves helping patients warm their hands by dilating their blood vessels, which increases blood flow to the head and reduces pain.

Bodywork Therapies.   Many stress-related headaches occur when the muscles that run between the base of the skull and along the top of the shoulders become tight or go into spasm. Massage therapy, rolfing, or other techniques such as the Feldenkrais method, the Alexander technique, the Trager approach, or polarity therapy help relax these tensed muscles as well as the neck, and can relieve some headaches.

Botanical Medicines.   Feverfew, a perennial composite herb, has a long folk history in the treatment of fever, arthritis, and migraine headaches. Steven Foster, in a 1991 pamphlet entitled *Feverfew* published by the American Botanical Council, states that feverfew's effectiveness in relieving migraines apparently is due to its ability to inhibit the secretion of serotonin and to reduce the size of inflamed blood vessels in the brain that cause throbbing pain in sufferers. Canada's

Health and Welfare Department has approved the sale of feverfew for migraine prevention. Approval was based on two clinical trials conducted in the United Kingdom in 1985 and 1988, as reported by Jim O'Brien in the October 19, 1993, issue of *Your Health.* He quotes Dr. D. Awang, head of the Natural Products Bureau of Drug Research, as saying that feverfew "effectively reduced the incidence and severity of migraine attacks." Approximately 70% of patients in the 1988 study had fewer migraines after they took the equivalent of two medium-sized feverfew leaves daily. By comparison, only 50% of a group of control patients derived benefits from prescription migraine drugs. Canadian health officials currently advise consumers not to take feverfew continuously for more than four months without the advice of a physician.

Brush Massage. *The 1992-1993 Holistic Health Directory* reports that poor circulation in the cerebral lobes often causes headaches, and that self-massages using hair or bath brushes can relieve symptoms by increasing circulation. The entire surface of the scalp should be gently brushed, stroking downward from the top of the head.

Chiropractic Therapy. Headaches caused by a misalignment of the neck sometimes can be relieved with chiropractic therapy. In a six-month clinical trial conducted in Australia, as reported by G. Parker in a 1978 issue of the *Australian/New Zealand Journal of Medicine*, 85 patients reduced the severity of their migraine headaches through cervical spine manipulation by a chiropractor. Another study found that five treatments every month, given over a period of six months, decreased recurrences of headaches in 45% of patients.

Exercise. Dr. Joseph Primavera, co-director of the Comprehensive Headache Center at Germantown Hospital and Medical Center in Philadelphia, uses moderate exercise to treat patients suffering from headaches. According to Primavera, as quoted in the January 1994 issue of *American Health,* 20 minutes of aerobic exercise three times a week–running, brisk walking, bicycling, or swimming–can help prevent headaches. Primavera suggests that exercise improves cardiovascular functioning, reduces stress, and produces endorphins, the body's natural pain relievers.

Regular sexual activity also may relieve tension and migraine headaches. According to Kristin Von Kreisler, writing in the January 11, 1994, issue of *Your Health,* researchers at Southern Illinois School of Medicine studied the effect of regular sexual activity in 52 female migraine sufferers. Eight patients who made love during the headache reported that their headaches were eliminated, while 16 experienced some relief.

Homeopathic Remedies. According to Maesimund Panos and Jane Heimlich in *Homeopathic Remedies for Everyday Ailments and Minor Injuries*, homeopathic therapies have successfully treated many types of headaches. Homeopaths prescribe individualized remedies based on the patient's symptoms and overall mental and physical condition. The most frequently used homeopathic remedies include aconitum nappellus, arnica montana, belladonna, bryonia, gelsenium, iris versicolor, kali bichronicum, nux vomica, and sanguinaria canadensis.

In *Everybody's Guide to Homeopathic Medicine,* Dr. Stephen Cummings and Dana Ullman cite 107 controlled studies in which homeopathic therapies effectively treated a variety of medical disorders, including headaches. They list several homeopathic remedies such as belladonna, bryonia, nux vomica, pulsatilla, gelsenium, and sanguinaria.

Self Massage

Hands On Healing suggests the following simple self-massage to relieve tension headaches:

1. Place your fingers of both hands on either side of the spine just under your skull.

2. Keep your fingers straight and, pointing your elbows up, apply pressure to your neck muscles through the balls of your fingertips.

3. Stroke forward and apply pressure deep into the muscle. Exhale and let your head fall back into your fingers as your elbows descend, pulling your hands forward. Massage individual muscle fibers with your fingers as your hands glide forward.

Nutritional Therapies. James F. Balch and Phyllis Balch suggest in *Prescription for Nutritional Healing* that most stress-related headaches can be relieved by avoiding salt and acid-producing foods. They recommend that people who suffer frequent headaches consult a nutritionist who can design a customized rotation diet that will eliminate fried, fatty, and greasy foods. Some people may benefit from eliminating dairy products, yellow cheese, and cherries. The nitrate preservatives found in hot dogs and luncheon meats should be avoided as well.

Murray and Pizzorno claim that food allergies are a major cause of migraine headaches. They suggest that migraine sufferers adopt a food elimination diet that avoids alcoholic beverages, cheese, chocolate, citrus fruits, and shellfish. The diet should be low in animal fats and high in foods that inhibit platelet aggregation, including fish oils, vegetable oils, garlic, and onion. Butler and Rayner also identify certain foods as possible precipitating factors for migraine headaches. These include cheeses, wine, beer, chocolate, vinegar, pickles, organ meats, preserved fish and meat, soy beans, lima beans, onions, spinach, and foods with MSG or nitrates.

Stress Reduction Therapies. Biofeedback, yoga, meditation, and hypnosis help prevent migraines, although they are not effective in all cases. Simeon Margolis and Hamilton Moses III report in *The Johns Hopkins Medical Handbook* that biofeedback therapy teaches patients how to consciously raise their hand temperature, which can reduce the number and intensity of headaches including migraines. In this therapy, while the patient tries to warm his or her hands, a computer monitor provides a reading as the temperature increases. In another type of biofeedback, called electromyographic or EMG training, patients learn to control muscle tension in the face, neck, and shoulders. Both types of biofeedback sometimes are combined with relaxation training techniques that help patients mentally reduce their tension levels without the use of biofeedback machines. Dr. Andrew Weil, quoted in the October 19, 1993, issue of *Your Health,* recommends that people who get frequent headaches combine biofeedback with other relaxation methods such as yoga, meditation, visualization, and guided imagery.

Vitamin and Mineral Therapies. Several vitamins, minerals, and amino acids improve brain oxygenation and relieve migraine headaches. Murray and Pizzorno recommend that people who suffer recurring migraine headaches consult a physician who may recommend vitamin B_3 (niacin), magnesium, or quercetin supplements. Nia-

Dangerous Headache Symptoms

While headaches generally are not life threatening, they can signal a serious medical disorder such as a blood clot, brain tumor, or weakened blood vessel that could burst (aneurysm). People experiencing any of the following symptoms should consult a physician immediately:

- Abrupt, severe headache, often like a thunderclap.

- Headache with fever, stiff neck, rash, mental confusion, seizures, double vision, weakness, numbness, or speaking difficulties.

- Headache after a recent sore throat or respiratory infection.

- Headache after a head injury, even if it is a minor fall or bump, especially if the pain gets worse.

- Chronic, progressive headache that worsens after coughing, exertion, straining, or a sudden movement.

- New headache pain after age 55 (which could signal temporal arteritis, an inflammation that affects arteries in the scalp, brain, and eyes).

cin dilates blood vessels and helps prevent premenstrual headaches. Niacinamide is generally used in treatment because, unlike niacin, it does not cause burning, flushing, or itching of the skin. Evening primrose oil capsules and MaxEPAS, a form of fish oil, are sources of essential fatty acids that supply the body with anti-inflammatory agents and help prevent constriction of cerebral blood vessels.

Hypertension (High Blood Pressure)

Hypertension (excessive and sustained blood pressure against the walls of the arteries) is the most common stress-related disorder in the U.S., and a major cause of death. According to a September 1989 article in the *Johns Hopkins Medical Letter,* approximately 60 million Americans (or one in four) have blood pressure that is high enough to require treatment. Only half of the 60 million know they have the condition, however, and only 25% of those 30 million receive adequate medical care. Chronic hypertension (called a "silent killer" because of its lack of symptoms) can damage the kidneys, heart, brain, and retinas if left untreated. The article goes on to claim that hypertension is a factor in 75% of strokes and 68% of first heart attacks in the U.S. Butler and Rayner point out that because hypertension is so harmful, blood pressure is the most important factor life insurance companies use to predict life expectancy and to determine premiums.

There are two main types of hypertension: that resulting from other medical disorders such as diabetes; and essential hypertension, for which the cause has not been fully established. Factors that have been tentatively linked to essential hypertension include obesity and inactivity; excess salt, sugar, and licorice intake; heredity; smoking; coffee; alcohol; prolonged stress; and drugs, including estrogens, indomethacin, phenylpropanolamine (the appetite suppressant), amphetamines, and cocaine. Long-term studies have shown that chronic high blood pressure typical of essential hypertension increases the risk of heart disease, stroke, atherosclerosis, and kidney disease. Anxiety, heart palpitations, increased pulse rates, or feeling "all wound up" are not necessarily reliable indicators of high blood pressure. The only way to detect abnormal pressure and to minimize the risk of hypertension is to have an annual blood pressure examination.

Treatments for Hypertension

Acupuncture. According to the December 1992 *National Acupuncture Detoxification Association Newsletter (NADA)*, acupuncture effectively relieves symptoms of high blood pressure. A six-month study conducted by Dr. Tom Atwood cited in *Alternative Medicine: The Definitive Guide* found that 16 patients were able to reduce their blood pressure, sleep better, and become "more productive" after acupuncture treatments. According to Atwood, other benefits included less agitation and calmer behavior, improved clarity of thought, reduced aggression, and improved social interaction.

Ayurvedic Medicine. Dr. Virender Sodhi, director of the American School of Ayurvedic Sciences in Bellevue, Washington, states in *Alternative Medicine: The Definitive Guide* that Ayurvedic medicine has helped patients suffering from hypertension. Patients are treated with diets low in sodium, cholesterol, and triglycerides; yogic breathing; relaxation, and Ayurvedic herbs. According to Sodhi, Ayurvedic herbs such as convolvulus pluricaulis, ashwaganda, and rauwolfia help lower blood pressure levels. Herbs often are used in combination, depending on the patient's individual needs, along with calcium, magnesium, silicon, and zinc.

Biofeedback. Biofeedback, according to Fugh-Berman, is effective in treating some patients with mild hypertension, although it does not work for everyone. It appears most successful in relieving moderate symptoms of hypertension.

Bodywork Therapies. *Alternative Medicine: The Definitive Guide* suggests that one or several of the following bodywork

Alternative Therapies for Hypertension

- **Lose excess weight.** An estimated 20-30% of hypertension cases result from excess body weight, which, if lost, results in a commensurate drop in blood pressure.
- **Reduce sodium intake.** Recent studies show that approximately half of those people who have hypertension can lower their blood pressure by making a moderate reduction in dietary sodium consumption.
- **Reduce dietary fats** to 20% of caloric intake. Dr. Ornish's research proves that hypertension can be greatly reduced through a totally vegetarian diet that has less than 20% of its calories from fats.
- **Increase calcium.** Increased calcium intake may slightly lower blood pressure.
- **Increase potassium.** Potassium lowers blood pressure, although the benefit is modest.
- **Reduce alcohol intake.** Curtailing alcohol consumption has corresponded to decreases in blood pressure in limited trials.
- **Exercise.** Exercise helps to lower blood pressure.
- **Relaxation.** Relaxation routines such as deep breathing, meditation, and progressive muscle relaxation relieve muscular tension and lower blood pressure.
- **Stop smoking.** Nicotine constricts the arteries and increases blood pressure.

therapies may be appropriate for treating hypertension: acupressure, reflexology, shiatsu, massage, rolfing, the Feldenkrais method, the Alexander technique, the Trager approach, and polarity therapy. Although these techniques are popular in the U.S. and have been used for 20 years to treat a variety of medical problems, their effectiveness has not been proven conclusively in clinical trials.

Botanical Medicines. Seaweed preparations have been shown to lower blood pressure more effectively than prescription medicines. Dr. M. Krotkiewski, writing in the June 1991 issue of the *American Journal of Hypertension,* reports that Swedish scientists reduced the blood pressure of 62 middle-aged patients suffering from mild hypertension by giving them seaweed fiber. This decrease, according to Krotkiewski, "was dependent on the decreased intestinal absorption of sodium and increased absorption of potassium released from the seaweed preparation." He concluded that seaweed fiber is a useful treatment for mild hypertension.

Murray and Pizzorno report that hawthorn berry extracts are widely used in Europe to lower blood pressure. The extracts appear to work by dilating the larger blood vessels, increasing intracellular vitamin C levels, and decreasing capillary permeability and fragility. The extracts also may help ward off angina attacks by lowering serum cholesterol levels and preventing the deposition of cholesterol on arterial walls.

Mistletoe is used by European physicians (combined with *Crataegus*) to treat hypertension. The berries, leaves, and stems of the plant contain beta phenyethylamine and tyramine, which help regulate blood pressure. However, as mistletoe is toxic, it should not be used in high doses or for extended periods of time except under the supervision of a physician. Balch and Balch report that alfalfa, barley, spirulina, and wheatgrass, all of which

are sources of concentrated chlorophyll, help lower blood pressure as well.

Patricia Hausman's *The Healing Foods: The Ultimate Authority on the Curative Power of Nutrition* reports that Pacific oyster extract is effective in normalizing blood pressure in some patients. Hausman cites several studies which suggest that it not only lowers blood pressure but may correct cardiac arrhythmia, normalize blood sugar levels in diabetics, and alleviate liver disturbances due to poor fat metabolism and alcohol consumption. She also notes that the passion flower plant *Chlorella* (a micro algae high in betacarotene, iron, zinc, and vitamin B_{12}) and maitake mushrooms lower high blood pressure and cholesterol levels.

Diet Pills and Recreational Drugs. Dr. Marvin Moser, author of *Lower Your Blood Pressure and Live Longer,* warns that an overdose of diet pills containing amphetamines can cause severe elevation in blood pressure and increase the chance of a stroke. He cautions patients with high blood pressure to take diet pills only prescribed by their physician. He further warns that the use of cocaine or street drugs can cause extreme elevations of blood pressure.

Exercise. Moderate exercise has been shown to directly reduce both stress and blood pressure. However, people with hypertension should consult a physician before starting any form of exercise, because even mild exercise can temporarily raise blood pressure. The best exercises, according to clinical trials, reduce the level of stress hormones in the bloodstream that constrict the arteries and veins. For example, a Johns Hopkins University Medical Center study cited by Margolis and Moses in *The Johns Hopkins Medical Handbook* found that progressive weightlifting reduced blood pressure 13 to 14 points in a group of 52 men, while intensive heavy lifting raised systolic blood pressure by

5 to 7 points. To lower blood pressure, a person should lift light weights three times a week at 40% of maximum strength in conjunction with aerobic exercise. The same study also found that walking or jogging three times a week for 20 minutes reduced blood pressure by approximately 6 points. Researchers are not certain how weightlifting reduces blood pressure, but researchers suggest that exercise relaxes the blood vessels so blood flows through them more efficiently.

Mineral Salt Substitutes. One excellent way of restricting table salt consumption is to use a mineral salt substitute. J. M. Gelcijnse reports in the August 13, 1994 issue of *British Medical Journal* that Dutch physicians reduced high blood pressure levels in 100 men and women between the ages of 55 and 75 with a low-sodium, high-potassium diet supplemented with high-magnesium mineral salt and foods. The researchers concluded that replacing mineral salt substitutes "offer a valuable non-pharm-acological approach to lowering blood pressure in older people with mild to moderate hypertension."

Nutritional Therapies. Many nutritional factors, according to Murray and Pizzorno, have been linked with high blood pressure, including sodium to potassium ratios, high cholesterol, and low fiber consumption. People who consume large quantities of salt are at risk of developing hypertension, and reducing dietary sodium directly lowers high blood pressure in some patients. The chloride present in table salt, along with sodium, may affect hormonal regulation of fluid and salt retention and contribute to hypertension. A calcium deficiency may also contribute to hypertension because people who decrease their calcium intake usually experience increased blood pressure. A high-calcium diet helps counteract the harmful effects of a high-sodium diet, and sodium may be indirectly related to hypertension by its direct effect on calcium metabolism. For maximum benefits, Murray and Pizzorno recommend that people with high blood pressure adopt a diet that is low in sodium and high in potassium and calcium.

Ornish notes in *Dr. Dean Ornish's Program for Reversing Heart Disease* that people with hypertension often have low levels of magnesium. Elevated blood pressure returns to normal levels when magnesium-rich foods are added to the diet, and magnesium is believed to help the heart and blood vessels contract and relax. People who think they might have hypertension should also reduce their dietary fats. When dietary fats are reduced to 20% of total calories, blood pressure declines by as much as 10%. Ornish notes that vegetarians generally have lower blood pressure, and lower incidences of hypertension and other cardiovascular diseases, than do nonvegetarians. Vegetarian diets typically contain more potassium, complex carbohydrates, polyunsaturated fat, fiber, calcium, magnesium, vitamin C, and vitamin A, all of which lower blood pressure.

According to both Ornish and Murray and Pizzorno, high-fiber diets effectively prevent and treat hypertension. The best fiber diet includes oat bran, apple pectin, psyllium seeds, guar gum, and gum karaya. This diet reduces cholesterol and promotes weight loss, which helps lower blood pressure. Ornish further recommends that table sugar be eliminated because it elevates blood pressure, and claims that garlic and onions decrease both systolic and diastolic blood pressure levels.

Stress Reduction Therapies. Elmer and Alyce Green of the Menninger Foundation claimed in a 1980 issue of *Primary Cardiology* that four out of five people with essential hypertension can restore and maintain normal blood pressure without drugs, through biofeedback and stress reduction ("psychophysiological") training.

W.S. Agras reported in the May 1983 issue of *Hospital Practice* that biofeedback, yoga, meditation, visualization, and hypnosis are clinically proven, effective therapies for lowering blood pressure in hypertensive patients.

In one study of 20 hypertensives using yoga relaxation and biofeedback, reported by Butler and Rayner, 16 showed great improvement. The average blood pressure dropped from 160/102 to 134/86, and most of the group were able to reduce or eliminate the drugs they had been taking for hypertension. Butler and Rayner go on to say that other studies of people using meditation regularly, and attaining a deep relaxation one to four times a day, showed significant blood pressure reductions. These reductions lasted over a period of weeks, not just for the duration of the session, as long as the sessions continued.

Tai Chi. Dr. P. Jin reports a study in the May 1992 issue of the *Journal of Psychosomatic Research* that tai chi, moving meditation, is also effective in lowering blood pressure levels. In Jin's study, 48 male and 48 female patients were taught tai chi, brisk walking, and meditation. After treatment, salivary cortisol levels were measured, and tai chi and brisk walking were found to effectively lower heart rates and blood pressure levels in all subjects.

Traditional Chinese Medicine (TCM). Hypertension is viewed in TCM as a problem in the circulation of energy (chi) in the body. According to *Alternative Medicine: The Definitive Guide,* Chinese physicians have treated it successfully with acupuncture, herbs, exercises such as qi gong, meditation, and a diet high in vegetables and low in fat, sugar, and alcohol.

Vitamin, Mineral, and Botanical Therapies. Dr. Robert Atkins, director of the Atkins Center in New York City, claims in the May/June 1994 issue of *Well Being Journal* to have helped thousands of patients lower their blood pressure by using nutrient combinations. Atkins recommends pantetheine, chromium picolinate, GLA, hexanicotinate, calcium, lecithin, magnesium, garlic, olive oil, avocado, gum guggulu, DHEA, fenugreek seed powder, psyllium husks, guar gum, and vitamin C.

Weight Loss. Many hypertensives are overweight, and weight loss is often prescribed to lower high blood pressure. Moser, however, cautions that "weight loss does not always bring blood pressure down to normal levels, but many hypertensive patients who lose at least some excess weight will also achieve reduced blood pressure." Moser advises patients to begin by cutting portions in half and limiting cakes, candies, cookies, and bread and increasing intake of fruits, vegetables, and other high-nutrition, low-calorie foods.

Irritable Bowel Syndrome (IBS)

Irritable bowel syndrome is a chronic disorder in which the muscle of the lower portion of the colon functions abnormally and produces exaggerated contractions. Put another way, IBS is a disorder of the natural conveyer-belt mechanism of the bowels, the mechanism that helps move waste products through the body. Approximately 15% of Americans suffer from IBS, and twice as many women as men have the disorder. While doctors have been unable to pinpoint its organic cause, IBS often is linked to emotional conflict or stress. Patients usually complain of lower abdominal pain, gas, bloating, constipation, or diarrhea, or alternating constipation and diarrhea. Although IBS can cause a great deal of discomfort, it is not serious, nor does it lead to any serious disease such as ulcerative colitis or cancer. With attention to proper diet, stress management, and, in some cases, medications, most people with IBS can keep their symptoms under control.

Treatments for Irritable Bowel Syndrome

Botanical Therapies. Murray and Pizzorno recommend peppermint oil capsules, ginger, and herbal antispasmodics as botanical medicines that reduce the overgrowth of *Candida albicans*, a common yeast, and sometimes offer relief for IBS sufferers. Ginger has a long history of use in relieving digestive complaints. Other herbs that have proven effective include chamomile, valerian, rosemary, and balm. David Hoffman recommends in *Alternative Medicine: The Definitive Guide* a combination mix of tinctures of bayberry, gentian, peppermint, and wild yam.

Balch and Balch's *Prescription for Nutritional Healing* reports that lobelia, pau d'arco, rose hips, and cascara sagrada are also effective in treating IBS. They add that alfalfa tablets containing vitamin K (needed to build the intestinal flora for proper digestion) may be helpful in relieving mild symptoms. They further recommend that IBS sufferers add acidophilus to their diets in order to replenish beneficial bacteria. Some patients may also benefit from drinking one-half cup of aloe vera juice three times daily, which keeps the colon walls clean of excess mucus and slows down food reactions. Garlic aids, primrose oil, free-form amino acids and proteolytic enzymes low in hydrochloric acid and high in pancreatin may also provide relief.

Colonic Therapy. IBS disorders sometimes are characterized by the inability of the colon to effectively eliminate wastes, which can then be passed into the lymph glands, bloodstream, and intestines. Colonic therapy, which irrigates the colon with water, helps dislodge fecal material and restores normal bacteria flora. A single session normally lasts 30 to 45 minutes. Another option suggested by Balch and Balch is to take regular enemas to keep the colon clean.

Exercise. In *Gastrointestinal Health*, Dr. Steven R. Peikin claims that daily exercise improves bowel function, reduces stress, and relieves IBS. He states that the best exercises are swimming, walking, and bicycling.

Food Intolerances. In *The I.B.S. Wellness Diet,* dietian Deralee Scanlon cites research published by the Clymer Health Clinic that suggests that food intolerances and sensitivities may cause some cases of IBS. Intolerances occur when a person's body lacks a specific enzyme needed to break down particular food substances. People deficient in lactase, for example, often develop adverse physical reactions to milk or milk products—and may experience typical reactions such as gas, diarrhea, nausea, or bloating.

Foods that Scanlon suggests may cause intolerances include (listed in descending order): milk and dairy products, colas, chocolate, corn, eggs, legumes (soybeans and peanuts), citrus fruit and related fruits, tomatoes, wheat, cinnamon, pork, beef, onions, garlic, white potatoes, fish, coffee, shrimp, bananas, walnuts, and pecans.

Hydrotherapy. According to *Everyday Health Tips*, full body sitz baths are extremely effective in relieving symptoms of IBS, including infections of the uterus, ovaries, vagina, bladder, and prostate. Digestive problems such as stomach cramps are also alleviated by sitz baths.

Dietary Recommendations for IBS

1. Identify food allergens, sensitivities, or intolerances.
2. Avoid offending foods, including milk and dairy products (lactose intolerance), gas-forming foods and beverages, foods containing high amounts of fructose and raffinose, and dietetic foods containing Sorbitol.
3. Eat regular, small, frequent, and low-fat meals.
4. Gradually increase dietary fiber to 15-25 grams daily.
5. Limit caffeine and alcohol intake.
6. Exercise regularly and practice stress reduction techniques.
7. Drink eight or more cups of fluid a day.

Hypnosis. IBS is often caused by psychological stress, and hypnosis has proven effective in reversing symptoms in some sufferers. *Alternative Medicine: What Works* documents one uncontrolled study in which 11 of 33 patients with IBS reversed their symptoms after seven weeks of hypnotherapy. Twenty-seven percent reported lessening of symptoms, while 39% found no benefit. Another uncontrolled trial found that hypnosis was 80% effective in reversing IBS complaints, while a follow-up, randomized, controlled trial of 30 subjects found hypnotherapy was more effective than psychotherapy in eliminating incidences of gas pains. Another study found that patients younger than 50 with classic IBS symptoms had 100% response rate to hypnosis, while the rate for those over 50 was only 25%.

Nutritional Therapies. Because of the variable nature of the disorder, IBS patients must be treated on a case-by-case basis. In general, however, consuming a diet rich in complex carbohydrates and dietary fiber (present in whole grain breads and cereals, fruits, and vegetables) often is curative. Fiber supplements such as guar, pectin, psyllium seed, or oat bran also help eliminate waste from the colon.

The National Institute of Diabetes and Digestive and Kidney Diseases further counsels IBS sufferers to eat smaller meals more frequently, or to eat smaller portions of foods, especially if they are low in fat and rich in carbohydrates and proteins. Foods high in carbohydrates and low in fat include pastas, rice, breads, cereals, fruits, and vegetables. Those high in protein and low in fat include chicken and turkey without the skin, lean meats, most fish, and low-fat dairy products such as skim milk and low-fat cheeses.

Murray and Pizzorno cite a study in which approximately two-thirds of the patients with IBS had at least one food intolerance, and some had multiple intolerances. When IBS symptoms were caused by food sensitivities, sufferers who used a food elimination diet normally experienced improvement within five or six days. For this reason, IBS sufferers should first determine whether or not they have any food intolerances and, if so, begin to follow a diet that eliminates these foods.

Stress Reduction Therapies. Many patients with IBS complain of psychological symptoms such as anxiety, fatigue, hostile feelings, depression, and sleep disturbances. It is not known whether these are a cause or a result of bowel disturbances. According to Murray and Pizzorno, psychological stress reduction techniques such as biofeedback, progressive relaxation, deep breathing, massage, and hypnosis are often quite helpful in alleviating IBS symptoms.

Vitamins and Mineral Supplements. Scanlon documents that the following daily vitamin and mineral supplements can relieve IBS by healing irritated areas of the gastrointestinal tract:

- Pantothenic acid: 500 milligrams.
- *Lactobacillus acidophilus* or *Lactobacillus bifidus*: one gram, four times daily.
- Metamucil: one tablespoon daily in an eight-ounce glass of water.
- Oat bran: two tablespoons, three times a day, in soup, stew, cereal, or juice.
- Vitamin B_6: one to two tablets of 50 milligrams.
- Vitamin A: a maximum of 25,000 units, starting with 5,000 units per day and increasing only with a doctor's approval.
- Hypo-allergenic vitamin B complex: one tablet.
- Buffered vitamin C: 500 milligrams.
- Calcium lactate: one to two tablets daily, taken between meals.
- L-Arginine: 2 to 10 grams.

Peptic Ulcers

According to the National Digestive Disease Information Clearinghouse, one out of every ten Americans develops a peptic ulcer, although many will go unnoticed. Butler and Rayner warn, however, that even ulcers that have been treated tend to recur. Care and watchfulness are required throughout life to avoid hemorrhage, surgery, and even–in extreme cases–removal of the stomach.

Peptic ulcers are sores, usually one-quarter to three-quarters of an inch in diameter, that form in the lining (mucosa) of the stom-ach or the first part of the small intestine below the stomach, called the duodenum. Peptic ulcers that occur in the lining of the stomach are called gastric ulcers, and those in the lining of the duodenum are called duodenal ulcers. As Margolis and Moses point out in *The Johns Hopkins Medical Handbook,* duodenal ulcers are more common than gastric ulcers in the U.S., while the reverse is true in Japan.

Both the stomach and the duodenum secrete hydrochloric acid and the digestive enzyme pepsin, which help break down foods. If too much hydrochloric acid or pepsin is secreted, it begins to erode the mucosa of the stomach or duodenum and causes an ulcer–hence the name "peptic" ulcer. The linings of the stomach and duodenum also lose their ability to resist erosion as people age, and peptic ulcers sometimes occur in older people with low acid levels. Butler and Rayner and others claim that sustained emotional stress–such as anxiety, anger, and fear–can contribute to excessive acid production and sometimes is the main factor; even noise can be a problem. In some cases, there are no identifiable causes.

The most common symptom of a gastric ulcer is a burning pain in the stomach, which may be temporarily relieved by food or antacids. The most common symptom of a duodenal ulcer is a burning pain in the abdomen between the navel and the lower end of the breastbone. Other symptoms include lower back pain, headaches, choking sensations, and itching. A physician should be consulted if these pains persist, because serious complications may develop. If they are not treated, ulcers can erode blood vessels and cause bleeding into the digestive tract. If the damaged blood vessels are small, the blood may seep out slowly and the patient can become anemic. If the damaged blood vessels are large, the patient may vomit blood or collapse suddenly. If the ulcer erodes through the wall of the stomach or duodenum, partially digested food and bacteria from the digestive tract can inflame the abdominal cavity. This condition, called a "perforated ulcer," produces sudden, severe pain and usually requires hospitalization and corrective surgery.

Treatments for Ulcers

Acupuncture. William Cargile, chairman of research for the American Association of Acupuncture and Oriental Medicine, reports in *Alternative Medicine: The Definitive Guide* that acupuncture can aid some patients with ulcers. He suggests that ulcers be treated by using acupuncture points associated with stress, anxiety, and stomach gastrointestinal problems (especially the stomach meridian). Some patients who receive acupuncture treatments for ulcers no longer need to use prescription drugs such as Tagamet.

Antacids. As Butler and Rayner note, antacids–best taken between meals and at bedtime–have long been standard medication for ulcers. They relieve the burning pain, and studies have shown that they speed healing. Since antacids can be harmful, however, if taken in large doses or over a prolonged period of time, they should be used with caution and awareness of side effects such as constipation or diarrhea.

Anti-Inflammatory Medications. The December 1990 issue of the *Johns Hopkins Medical Letter* suggests that elderly people who take nonsteroidal anti-inflammatory drugs (NSAIDs) for arthritis–such as aspirin, ibuprofen (Motrin, Advil, Nuprin), naproxen (Naprosyn, Anaprox), or piroxicam (Feldene)–are especially susceptible to stomach ulcers. Therefore, one of the first steps in alternative treatment of ulcers is to help patients reduce or eliminate their need for these drugs.

Aromatherapy. In *Alternative Medicine: The Definitive Guide*, lemon oil, chamomile, and geranium are recommended as effective oil essences for relieving ulcers.

Ayurvedic Medicine. According to Dr. Sodhi, licorice, taken half a teaspoon in powder form three times a day, can reverse some ulcers. He also recommends bananas, coconut (the milk and fruit), and the herb ashwagandha. A mixture of cinnamon, cardamom, and cloves, ground into one quarter teaspoon of powder, also can be helpful.

Botanical Medicines. Paul Bergner, editor of *Medical Herbalism: A Clinical Newsletter for the Herbal Practitioner,* states in the September/October 1993 issue of *Natural Health* that licorice may be helpful in treating ulcers. He cites several studies that found licorice to be "as effective in preventing recurrence of ulcers as anti-ulcer drugs like Tagamet."

Murray and Pizzorno confirm that licorice can prevent and heal both gastric and duodenal ulcers. As noted earlier, however, licorice can be toxic and should be taken under the supervision of a physician. Other botanicals recommended in *Alternative Medicine: The Definitive Guide* to relieve ulcer symptoms include marshmallow, calendula, chamomile, goldenseal, meadowsweet, and cayenne pepper.

Balch and Balch suggest bayberry, catnip tea, myrrh, sage, slippery elm, and cayenne (also known as capsicum). Soothing herbal teas such as chamomile, anise, fennel, and flax seed are recommended by Butler and Rayner. However, they warn against certain herbs that are likely to irritate the stomach lining, such as peppermint, spearmint, and such stimulating herbs as gotu kola (which contains caffeine), desert tea, and damiana.

Juice Therapy. *Alternative Medicine: The Definitive Guide* recommends that ulcer sufferers drink fresh fruit and vegetable juices, including wheatgrass juice. Raw cabbage juice is recommended for duodenal ulcers, which can be mixed with carrot or celery. Raw potato juice is advisable for peptic ulcers.

Nutritional Therapies. Alternative treatments for ulcers focus on neutralizing acid and pepsin levels while regenerating the integrity of the lining of the stomach and gastrointestinal tract. The first stage of treatment usually involves eliminating foods that cause allergies, quitting cigarette smoking, and reducing stress. Allergies are a primary factor in peptic ulcers, according to Murray and Pizzorno, and food elimination diets often are effective. People who develop ulcers are advised to stop smoking, because smoking slows the healing of ulcers and makes them more likely to recur. It may also be necessary to reduce consumption of alcohol; alcoholic cirrhosis has been linked to an increased risk of ulcers, and heavy drinking has been shown to delay the healing of ulcers.

Butler and Rayner warn that alcohol, caffeine (coffee, tea, and cola), and cigarettes can provoke and aggravate ulcers. They point out that while decaffeinated coffee can be easier on the stomach, it sometimes stimulates as much acid flow as regular coffee, either by a conditioned reflex association with the flavor or by the action of oils or other substances in the coffee.

Diets rich in fiber help prevent duodenal ulcers because they promote mucus secretion and delay gastric emptying, counteracting the rapid movement of food into the duodenum that normally occurs in ulcer patients. Raw cabbage juice also has been documented to help heal peptic ulcers. Murray and Pizzorno claim that one liter per day of fresh cabbage juice, taken in divided doses, can heal an ulcer in an average of 10 days. Not only do fiber-rich foods such as fruits, vegetables, and whole grain breads protect against the formation of ulcers and promote healing, they also prevent relapses once ulcers develop. It is believed that the fiber somehow slows down or buffers stomach acid.

Balch and Balch recommend a diet of easy-to-digest, nutritious, and chemical-free foods, which they claim has produced excellent results after 30 days. It includes well-cooked millet, cooked white rice, raw goat's milk, and soured milk products such as yogurt, cottage cheese, and kefir. If symptoms are severe, soft foods such as avocados, bananas, potatoes, squash, and yams should be eaten daily. They advise putting all vegetables through a blender or processor, and consuming well-steamed vegetables such as broccoli and carrots occasionally. Balch and Balch counsel those with bleeding ulcers to eat baby foods, and to add nonirritating fiber such as guar gum and psyllium seed.

Dr. Braly's Diet & Nutrition Revolution recommends that patients with ulcers reduce fat in their diet to less than 10% of daily calories, and restrict their consumption of alcohol, caffeine, and aspirin. He also advises patients to add linseed oil to their daily diet, and drink three ounces of concentrated aloe vera juice 20 minutes before meals. Bismuth in doses recommended by a physician can relieve ulcers caused by *Helicobacter pylori*.

Stress Reduction Therapies. Some nutritionists, including Murray and Pizzorno, believe there may a link between stress and peptic ulcers. However, the chemical mechanisms by which stress promotes the development of ulcers have not been identified. It seems likely that a stressful lifestyle works in combination with food allergies, diets high in animal fat, cigarette smoking, alcohol, and NSAIDS to cause the growth of ulcers. Stress reduction therapies that are effective in relieving hypertension, such as yoga, meditation, biofeedback, and hypnosis, also may help with the symptoms of ulcers.

Vitamin and Mineral Therapies. Butler and Rayner recommend that certain vitamins and minerals may be especially useful in treating ulcers. Supplementary vitamin A seems to help by maintaining the healthy functioning of the mucus-producing cells that line the stomach and protect it from the powerful pepsin acid. Zinc and vitamin E also may be beneficial, they advise, but large doses (more than three times the RDA) should not be used without consulting a physician or health practitioner.

SUMMARY

Summary

Everyone experiences some stress in the course of daily living. Over the last few years, many studies have documented that stress is a major factor in the development of atherosclerosis, headaches, hypertension, irritable bowel syndrome, and ulcers. Repeated incidences of stress can interfere with digestion, increase heart rates and blood pressure, alter brain chemistry, and affect metabolic immune functioning. The holistic treatment for stress-related disorders emphasizes a whole-body approach that includes nutritional therapies; vitamin, mineral, and botanical therapies; and stress-reduction techniques such as exercise, massage, yoga, meditation, hypnosis, biofeedback, and relaxation. While some stress cannot be avoided, it can be managed using alternative biological and psychoimmunological therapies that induce the "relaxation response."

Resources

References

Agras, W.S. "Relaxation Therapy in Hypertension." *Hospital Practice* (May 1983): 129-37.

Altman, Nathaniel. *Oxygen Healing Therapies.* New York: Health Sciences Press, 1994.

Atkins, Robert C. "Lower Cholesterol: Seventeen Natural Ways to Bring Cholesterol Under Control." *Well Being Journal* (May/June 1994): 1, 5.

Balch, James F., and Phyllis Balch. *Prescription for Nutritional Healing.* Garden City Park, NY: Avery Publishing Group, 1993.

Benson, Herbert. *The Relaxation Response.* New York: William Morrow, 1975.

Beverly, Cal, ed. *Natural Health Secrets Encyclopedia.* Peachtree City, GA: FC&A Publishing, 1991.

Braly, James. *Dr. Braly's Diet & Nutrition Revolution.* New Canaan, CT: Keats Publishing, 1992.

Butler, Kurt, and Lynn Rayner. *The Best Medicine: The Complete Health and Preventive Medicine Handbook.* New York: Harper & Row Publishers, Inc., 1985.

Chaitlow, Leon. *The Body/Mind Purification Program.* New York: Simon & Schuster, Inc., 1990.

Cummings, Stephen, and Dana Ullman. *Everybody's Guide to Homeopathic Medicine.* New York: St. Martin's Press, 1991.

Eliasson, K. "A Dietary Fiber Supplement in the Treatment of Mild Hypertension." *Journal of Hypertension* (February 1992): 195-99.

Feinstein, Alice. *Symptoms: Their Causes & Cures.* Emmaus, PA; Rodale Press, Inc., 1993.

Foster, Steven. *Feverfew.* Botanical Series 310. Austin, TX: American Botanical Council, 1991.

Fugh-Berman, Adriane. *Alternative Medicine: What Works.* Tucson, AZ: Odonian Press, 1996.

Geleijnse, J. "Reduction in Blood Pressure with a Low Sodium, High Potassium, High Magnesium Salt in Older Subjects with Mild to Moderate Hypertension." *British Medical Journal* (August 13, 1994): 233-37.

Green, Elmer, and Alyce Green. "The Ins and Outs of Mind-Body Energy." *Science Year* (1974): 137-47.

——. "Self-Regulation Training for Control of Hypertension." *Primary Cardiology* 6(1980): 126-37.

Hands on Healing. Emmaus, PA: Rodale Press, 1989.

Hausman, Patricia. *The Healing Foods: The Ultimate Authority on the Curative Power of Nutrition.* Emmaus, PA: Rodale Press, 1989.

"Headache." *Mayo Clinic Health Letter* (October 1993): 1-8.

"Heading Off Headaches." *The University of California, Berkeley Wellness Letter* 7 (November 1990): 4-5.

Hoffman, David. *The New Holistic Herbal.* Rockport, MA: Element Books, 1992.

"Irritable Bowel Syndrome–Can Medication Help?" *Harvard Medical School Health Letter* (January 1989).

Jin, P. "Efficacy of Tai Chi, Brisk Walking, Meditation and Reading In Reducing Mental and Emotional Stress." *Journal of Psychosomatic Research* (May 1992): 361-70.

Kirchheimer, Sid. *The Doctor's Book of Home Remedies.* Emmaus, PA: Rodale Press, Inc., 1993.

Krotkiewski, M. "Effects of a Sodium-Potassium Ion-Exchanging Seaweed Preparation in Mild Hypertension." *American Journal of Hypertension* (June 1991): 483-88.

Lenhard, L., and P. Waite. "Acupuncture on the Prophylactic Treatment of Migraine Headache: Pilot Study." *New Zealand Medical Journal* 96 (1983): 663-66.

Malagelada, Juan. "About Stomach Ulcers." *National Digestive Disease Information Clearinghouse Fact Sheet.* NIH Pub. No. 87-676 (January 1987): 1-3.

Margolis, Simeon, and Hamilton Moses III. *The Johns Hopkins Medical Handbook.* New York: Medletter Associates, Inc., 1992.

Marti, James. *Ultimate Consumer Guide to Diets and Nutrition.* Boston: Houghton Mifflin Inc., 1997.

Moser, Marvin. *Lower Your Blood Pressure and Live Longer.* New York: Random House, 1989.

Murray, Michael, and Joseph Pizzorno. *Encyclopedia of Natural Medicine.* Rocklin, CA: Prima Publishing, 1991.

NADA Newsletter Committee. *National Acupuncture Detoxification Association Newsletter* (December 1, 1992): 1-6.

National Digestive Disease Information Clearinghouse. *Fact Sheet about Stomach Ulcers.* Bethesda, MD: National Digestive Disease Information Clearinghouse, 1993.

O'Brien, Jim. "The Herbal Cure for Migraine Pain." *Your Health* (October 19, 1993): 11-12.

Ody, Penelope. *Complete Medicinal Herbal.* London, England: Dorling Kindersley, 1993.

Ornish, Dean. *Dr. Dean Ornish's Program for Reversing Heart Disease.* New York: Ballantine Books, 1990.

Panos, Maesimund B., and Jane Heimlich. *Homeopathic Medicine at Home.* Los Angeles: Jeremy P. Tarcher, Inc., 1980.

Parker, G. "A Controlled Trial of Cervial Manipulation for Migraine." *Australian/New Zealand Journal of Medicine* 8 (1978): 589-93.

Peikin, Steven. *Gastro Intestinal Health.* New York: HarperCollins, 1991.

Petkov, V. "Plants with Hypotensive, Antiatheromatous and Coronary Dilating Action." *American Journal of Chinese Medicine* 7 (1979): 197-236.

Radetsky, Peter. "You Don't Have to Suffer Anymore: How to Handle Headaches." *Your Health* (January 11, 1994): 64-69.

Rowan, Robert L. *How to Control High Blood Pressure without Drugs.* New York: Ballantine Books, 1986.

Scanlon, Deralee, and Barbara Cottman Becnel. *The Wellness Book of I.B.S.* New York: St. Martin's Press, 1989.

Singh, R. "Dietary Modulators of Blood Pressure in Hypertension." *European Journal of Clinical Nutrition* (1990): 319-27.

Tbac, Deborah. *Everyday Health Tips: 2000 Practical Hints for Better Health and Happiness.* Emmaus, PA: Rodale Press, 1988.

"Ulcers: New Thinking on Causes and Cures." *Johns Hopkins Medical Letter: Health after 50* (December 1990): 4.

Von Kreisler, Kristen. "Sexual Healing." *Your Health* (January 11, 1994): 30-31.

Weil, Andrew. *Natural Health, Natural Medicine.* Boston: Houghton Mifflin, 1990.

Yuan, Chung San. "Treatment of 103 Cases of Coronary Disease with Ilex pubescens." *Chinese Medical Journal* 6 (1973): 6-7.

Organizations

American Heart Association.
7320 Greenville Ave., Dallas, TX 75231.

Chronic Fatigue and Immune Dysfunction Syndrome Association.
PO Box 220398, Charlotte, NC 28222-0398.

Chronic Fatigue Immune Dysfunction Society.
PO Box 230108, Portland, OR 97223.

National Chronic Fatigue Syndrome Association.
919 Scott Ave., Kansas City, MO 66105.

National Digestive Disease Information Clearinghouse.
Box NDDIC, Bethesda, MD 20892.

National Foundation for Colitis.
444 Park Ave. S., New York, NY 10016.

National High Blood Pressure Information Center.
4733 Bethesda Ave., Bethesda, MD 20814.

Additional Reading

Altman, Nathaniel. *Everybody's Guide to Chiropractic Health Care.* Los Angeles: Jeremy P. Tarcher, Inc., 1989.

American Heart Association. *About High Blood Pressure.* Dallas, TX: American Heart Association, 1986.

Chopra, Deepak. *Perfect Health: The Complete Mind/Body Guide.* New York: Harmony Books, 1991.

"Hypertension: Lower Your Blood Pressure without Drugs." *Mayo Clinic Nutrition Letter* (May 1990): 2-3.

Moser, M. "Controversies in the Management of Hypertension." *American Family Physician* (May 1990): 1449-60.

RESOURCES

National High Blood Pressure Information Center. *High Blood Pressure and What You Can Do About It*. Bethesda, MD: National High Blood Pressure Information Center, 1987.

Newberry, Benjamin H., Janet Madden, and Thomas Gertsenberger. *A Holistic Conceptualization of Stress & Disease*. New York: AMS Press, Inc., 1991.

Porkett, Manfred. *Chinese Medicine*. New York: Henry Holt & Co., 1992.

Reid, Daniel. *Chinese Herbal Medicine*. Boston: Shambhala Publications Inc., 1993.

Santillo, Humbart. *Natural Healing with Herbs*. Prescott, AZ: Hohm Press, 1991.

Schwartz, Harry. "Initial Therapy for Hypertension–Individualizing Care." *Mayo Clinic Proceedings* (January 1990): 73-87.

RESOURCES

Chapter 10

DRUG ABUSE AND ADDICTION

Most people at one time or another have taken drugs to relieve unpleasant symptoms such as headaches, indigestion, tension, cramps, fatigue, or anxiety. Many different types of drugs exist, each differentiated by the effect it has on the body. Medical (pharmaceutical) drugs, for example, contain chemicals that can prevent, cure, or aid in the recovery from certain diseases. These drugs include vaccines which help protect the human body against viral infections and antibiotics which can destroy dangerous pathogenic microorganisms.

This chapter discusses another class of drugs which people take, not to prevent an illness or eradicate symptoms, but to stimulate pleasurable feelings. These drugs are sometimes referred to as "psychoactive drugs" because they psychologically alter a person's thoughts, feelings, perceptions, or moods. Some of these drugs can easily become addictive, and alternative medicine treatments for various addictions are described.

Many people tend to associate psychoactive drugs with illegal substances such as marijuana, LSD, and cocaine. However, a number of drugs such as alcohol, nicotine, caffeine, amphetamines, and tranquilizers are legal in the United States and abroad. In fact, according to Gordon Edlin and Eric Golanty's *Health and Wellness,* more than 25% of all legal drugs sold in the U.S. (and virtually all illegal drugs) are psychoactive drugs.

Many psychological factors contribute to a person initially taking a psychoactive drug. Using a drug infrequently is usually not dangerous or habit forming. In fact, most people are able to tolerate and eliminate small quantities of most drugs without harmful side effects.

Some individuals, however, become habituated or addicted to a drug. "Drug habituation" is defined as use of a drug to the point where a person becomes psychologically dependent on it. "Drug addiction," on the other hand, is defined as a physiological dependence on a drug, the removal of which can cause a severe or even fatal physiological reaction.

In the early stages of habituation, each use of the drug increases feelings of pleasure and reduces anxiety, fear, or stress. Eventually, however, habituation can lead to subtle changes in people's rational judgment and their ability to perceive how the drug is affecting their behavior. Their personality may become altered under the influence of the drug, and as a consequence, they may put their relationships, jobs, or families at risk.

Drug Abuse in Children and Adolescents

Drugs have become a fact of life for some American children. Some children are more vulnerable to the temptation of using drugs than others. The most salient risk factor is a family history of alcohol or drug abuse extending even beyond the parents to grandparents, uncles and aunts. Other predictors of drug use include learning disabilities, low grades or poor school performance, aggressive or rebellious behavior, excessive peer influence, lack of parental warmth, support, or guidance, and behavior problems at an early age.

Adolescent drug use usually starts with legal substances, such as alcohol, the most abused drug. Young substance abusers, particularly during the early stages of drug experimentation, typically feel invulnerable, as if nothing could ever harm them or make them lose control. Psychoactive substances affect judgment, and can lead children to do things they otherwise wouldn't do. With chronic drug use, their schoolwork may suffer, and they may develop psychological problems which increase their risk of pregnancy, suicide, or contacting sexually transmitted diseases.

Children's use of drugs may indicate an underlying physical or emotional disorder such as depression. The earlier parents recognize a problem and seek treatment for their child, the brighter the prognosis for the child. Treatment must always be based on the particular child and his or her circumstances. In some cases, individual, group, or family therapy can be effective. In others, children or teens may have to be placed in a residential or day treatment center.

Alcoholism

Alcoholism is a leading cause of disease, physical disorders, and death throughout the world. Current estimates indicate that alcoholism affects at least 22 million people in the United States and causes 200,000 deaths each year, making it one of America's most serious health problems. As many as 88 million people in the U.S. are adversely affected by an alcoholic parent, family member, friend, or associate. A 1992 Gallup poll cited in the October 24, 1993 edition of the *New York Times* reported that approximately 81 million Americans have been directly or indirectly hurt by someone else's drinking problem.

Alcoholism is a complicated disease, partly because it involves several progressive stages, and because drinking (even excess drinking) is still socially acceptable. In the first stage, people develop a tolerance for alcohol and are able to drink it in great quantities without appearing to be drunk. In the second stage, their tolerance increases, and they require more alcohol to achieve the desired effect. During this stage, they often become sick from alcohol but deny that they have a problem. In the third stage, people

Effects of Alcohol Abuse

Cell Damage. Alcohol causes some metabolic damage to every cell.

Birth Defects. Birth defects can occur in offspring of female alcoholics. Some babies are born with abnormally small heads or mental deficiencies. Some babies may also be born with an addiction and experience withdrawal symptoms within the first week of life.

Malnutrition. Because alcoholics receive more than half of their total calories from alcohol, they are more likely to develop eating disorders. Many develop food addictions (especially to sweets) and become obese.

Liver Disease. Many alcoholics develop liver diseases, including alcoholic hepatitis and liver cirrhosis, which can be fatal.

Heart Disease. Alcohol directly poisons the heart muscles and can cause alcoholic cardiomyopathy.

Stomach Disease. Alcohol can cause gastritis and ulcers.

Lung Disease. Alcohol has been linked with greater incidences of tuberculosis, pneumonia, and emphysema.

Nerves. Alcohol increases the risk of polyneuritis (loss of sensation).

Blood and Marrow Disease. Alcohol increases the coagulation of blood, which can lead to anemia and blood and bone marrow defects.

Muscle Disease. Alcohol increases muscle weakness, cramping, and alcoholic myopathy (painful muscle contractions).

Cancer. Alcoholics tend to smoke more, which increases the risk of cancer of the mouth, esophagus, pancreas, and breast.

Sexual Impotence. Alcohol directly damages the nerves of the penis and causes atrophy of the testes in males. Because alcohol also damages the liver, the liver produces less testosterone and more estrogen.

cannot go without alcohol without experiencing severe withdrawal symptoms, and are at risk of developing several severe physiological disorders. Third-stage alcoholics often black out (alcoholic amnesia) for several minutes to several days during a prolonged drinking binge.

Physiological Effects of Alcohol. The alcohol that humans drink contains a chemical called ethyl alcohol. Most alcohols, including ethyl alcohol, are toxic (poisonous) in small amounts. The human liver, however, is able to metabolize (break down) ethyl alcohol into carbon dioxide and water, which can be then eliminated. Excessive alcohol, however, does considerable damage to many different parts of the body before it exits. The specific damage varies with each individual and how much alcohol is consumed.

Alcohol is probably most damaging to the human brain because chronic drinking can cause the impairment of memory and degeneration of white brain matter, as well as brain damage and premature senility. Obvious signs of alcohol intoxication are drowsiness, judgment errors, loss of inhibitions, poorly articulated speech, uncoordinated movement, and involuntary, rhythmic movements of the eyes.

At one time, it was believed that chronic drinking killed nerve cells in the brain which, once dead, could not regenerate or be replaced. A 1993 study in Denmark cited in *Alternative Medicine: The Definitive Guide*, however, found that alcohol does not actually kill the nerve cells, but simply disconnects them. The Danish scientists compared the brains of 11 severely alcoholic men with those of 11 other men who were not alcoholics. Using a sophisticated technique, the scientists counted precisely the number of nerve cells in tissue-thin slices of the neocortex, the outermost region of the brain. The number of nerve cells, according to Dr. Bente Pakkenberg, director of the Neurological Research Laboratory at the Bartholin Institute in Copenhagen, was "almost identical in the two groups." Nevertheless, the alcoholics did show significant damage to their white matter–the cells and fibers that support and nourish neurons, which carry signals throughout the brain. In the Danish study the alcoholics' white matter was reduced by 11% in the outer brain region and 30% in a deeper area that contains the memory center. The findings suggest that cerebral damage caused by heavy drinking may be potentially reversible.

Symptoms of Alcoholism. Dependence on alcohol can be either psychological or physical. If you're psychologically dependent, you turn to it fairly continuously, as the main means to find relief. Some people abuse alcohol but are not dependent on it. For instance, if you usually don't drink, but every few weekends go on a drunken binge that makes you miss work for a day or two, or you drink even when a physician has told you it worsens some medical condition, then you are abusing alcohol.

Alcoholism also creates unhealthy patterns of communicating and relating. It can destroy a family, and separation and divorce rates are quite high among alcoholics. A common occurrence is "codependence," the pattern by which close family members or friends encourage an alcoholic's problem by defending, rationalizing, or justifying it. Such behavior is harmful because it reinforces denial. Alcoholic individuals do not experience the full ramifications of their problem because members of their family often protect them from the consequences of their drinking.

Codependents often need help in acknowledging their own feelings and needs. National self-help organizations such as Al-Anon help adult family members recognize codependent behaviors in their relationships. Self-help groups such as Alateen, Adult Children of Alcoholics, and Adult Children of Dysfunctional Families provide a mutually supportive group setting in which family members can discuss their childhood experiences with alcoholic parents and the emotional consequences they carry into adult life. Through such groups or other forms of therapy, individuals may learn to move beyond anger and blame, to see the part they themselves play in their current unhappiness, and to create a healthier and happier future.

Children of Alcoholics. Children who grow up with alcoholic parents normally must assume certain roles to cope. The adjuster or "lost child" does whatever the parent says. The responsible child or "family hero" typically takes over many household tasks and responsibilities. The acting-out child or "scapegoat" causes problems at home or in school. The "mascot" disrupts tense situations by focusing attention on himself or herself, often by clowning. Regardless of which roles they assume, these children of alcoholics are prone to learning disabilities, eating disorders, and addictive behavior themselves.

The consequences of a parent's drinking

Advice for Children of Alcoholics

- Talk about your feelings with a close friend, relative, or teacher. Talking to someone will help you feel less alone.
- Try to get involved with fun things at school or near where you live.
- Don't feel guilty or ashamed about the problems at home. Alcoholism is a disease, and diseases are nobody's fault.
- Don't pour out or try to water down your parent's alcohol. You didn't cause the drinking problem, and you can't make it stop. What your parent does is not your responsibility or your fault.

Advice for the Nonalcoholic Parent

- When children go off to be alone during or after a parent's drinking episode, seek them out and comfort them. Try to avoid letting them go to sleep under upsetting conditions. If this does occur, talk to them at the first opportunity.
- Avoid putting your oldest child in the position of being a confidant or surrogate parent. This places too much strain on a youngster and may anger your spouse.
- Avoid pressuring children, either verbally or with your actions, to take sides in conflicts with your spouse.
- Don't use your children's opinions about drinking or the alcoholic parent to "get at" your partner. This approach places youngsters in a difficult position, in which they may not be willing to share their feelings with you in the future.

may affect the child long after he's grown up. Adult children of alcoholics, for example, are more likely to have difficulty in solving problems, identifying and expressing feelings, trusting others, and forming intimate relationships. In addition to being at increased risk for addictive behaviors and disorders themselves, they are more likely to marry individuals with a substance abuse problem and to keep on playing the roles assumed in childhood.

Treatments for Alcoholism

Conventional medicine has traditionally treated alcoholic patients with aversive drugs. According to Steven Schroeder's *Current Medical Diagnosis & Treatment*, Disulfiram (Antabuse) has proven helpful in deterring binge drinking by blocking the metabolism of alcohol. People who have alcohol in their blood and take Disulfiram generally experi-

ence headaches, flushing, and nausea within 30 minutes. While Disulfiram effectively discourages people from drinking, it can lead to a buildup of toxic substances and may have potentially dangerous side effects such as impotence, liver damage, drowsiness, and fetal anomalies in pregnant women. Disulfiram cannot be used by persons with thyroid, liver, or kidney problems or diabetes. Emetine, another aversive drug, has also proven successful in clinical trials by causing severe nausea and vomiting.

Alternative Treatments for Alcoholism

Holistic treatments for alcoholism focuses on treating the underlying psychological factors that cause alcoholics to drink in excess. In the first stage of treatment, patients are forced to acknowledge that they have a chemical or psychological dependence on

Professional Therapies for Alcoholism

- Cognitive therapy.
- Family therapy.
- Psychodynamic therapy.
- Organizations such as AA have been the most successful in reversing alcoholism. Support groups provide a sense of "family"; the patient becomes part of the group, helping others while helping himself. More importantly, the group provides a safe environment in which to acknowledge one's powerlessness over the addiction and to ask "higher powers" for help.

alcohol. Social support for both the patient and family is very important during this stage, and patients usually choose to join support groups such as Alcoholics Anonymous (AA). Successful programs such as AA always prohibit drinking, and although strict abstinence is not always followed, it has proven the safest and most effective treatment. This is largely because of the support, encouragement and acceptance offered by those in the group.

Diet and Nutrition. Michael Murray and Joseph Pizzorno suggest that alternative medicine practitioners have also successfully treated alcoholism with different diets. These diets focus on stabilizing blood sugar levels by eliminating simple sugars and foods containing added sucrose, fructose, or glucose. Alcoholics increasingly crave calorie-rich, nutrient-poor foods, especially sugars which increase their desire for more alcohol. Therefore, foods which increase the desire for alcohol must be avoided. These

include all sweets, dried fruit, low-fiber fruits (grapes and citrus fruits), white flour, and instant potatoes, among others. Meat is normally restricted (to keep protein and fat levels low) and substituted with brown rice, whole grains, vegetables, and legumes.

Holistic physicians have also used vitamin and mineral supplements to treat alcoholism. The type and amounts of supplements used vary with each patient, and most treatment regimens are supervised by a licensed physician or nutritionist.

Durk Pearson and Sandy Shaw's *Life Extension* lists the following vitamin and minerals for "people who enjoy alcohol" (to minimize the effects of alcohol) and to quit drinking:

Vitamin A	10,000 to 20,000 IU
Vitamin B_1	1 gram
Vitamin B_2	100-200 milligrams
Vitamin B_3 (niacin)	600 milligrams to 3 grams
Vitamin B_5	2 grams
Vitamin B_6	500 milligrams
Vitamin B_{12}	500 micrograms
Vitamin C	3 to 10 grams
Vitamin E	1000 to 2000 IU
Choline	3 grams
Cysteine (not cystine)	2 grams
Zinc (chelated)	50 milligrams
Selenium	250 micrograms

Botanical Medicines. Holistic practitioners may also prescribe botanical medicines which have been successfully used in limited clinical studies. According to an article in the September 21, 1993 issue of *Your Health*, XJL, an ancient Chinese herbal hangover remedy, may help reduce the desire for alcohol and limit excess drinking. In clinical trials conducted at the University of North Carolina, researchers found XJL reduced

Vitamin, Mineral, and Botanical Treatments for Alcoholism

Zinc. Zinc supplementation, combined with vitamin C, greatly increases alcohol detoxification.

Vitamin A. Vitamin A deficiency, along with zinc deficiency, appears to be linked to alcoholism. Vitamin A supplementation inhibits alcohol consumption in experimental animals.

Amino Acids. Serum amino acid levels are abnormal in alcoholics, and restoration to normal levels generally helps alcoholic patients.

Vitamin C. Supplemental vitamin C helps reduce the effects of acute and chronic ethanol toxicity. Vitamin C increases white blood cell count, helps eliminate alcohol from the blood, and detoxifies the liver.

B Vitamins. Most alcoholics have a vitamin B deficiency. B vitamin supplements, especially thiamine (B_2), may be helpful.

Selenium. Selenium, an important antioxidant, works synergistically with vitamin E to prevent alcohol-induced lipoperoxidation.

Fats. Alcohol induces essential fatty acid deficiency, particularly of the omega-6 series. Omega-8 supplements may be helpful.

Glutamine. Glutamine supplementation has been shown to reduce voluntary alcohol consumption in several studies.

---

cravings for alcohol by up to 60%. Previous studies have shown that it effectively reduces hangover symptoms and inebriation levels. Investigators speculate that because of the way the herb interacts with the brain, XJL may be capable of reducing cravings for other illegal drugs as well.

Kudzu, an Asian vine, has been used widely in China and Japan since 200 A.D. to treat alcohol abuse. It is available in those countries in pill form, and consumed as tea. According to an article in the November 2, 1993 issue of *The Wall Street Journal* , Dr. Bert Vallee at the Harvard Medical School has used an extract from the plant, its active ingredient daidzin, to reduce voluntary alcohol consumption in laboratory animals by more than 50%. Daidzin produces no significant change in food intake or body weight, and Vallee hopes the drug will be ready for clinical testing in humans by late 1994.

Acupuncture. In 1989, the British medical journal *The Lancet* documented a study noting that when acupuncture was added to the treatment program of chronic alcoholics, it significantly increased the percentage of those who completed the program. Furthermore, it reduced their need for alcohol, with fewer relapses and readmissions to a detoxification center.

Two other controlled studies on treatment of alcoholic recidivism cited by the National Acupuncture Detoxification Association (NADA)–one with 80 patients and the other with 54 patients–found that acupuncture treatment at fixed points was more effective than sham points in reducing expressed need for alcohol, drinking episodes, and hospital admissions for detoxification.

Exercise. Holistic treatments for alcoholism usually also incorporate an exercise program,

Caffeine's Effects on the Body

Immune System Suppression. Overconsumption of caffeine (and alcohol) depresses the immune system, and increases risk of chronic disorders.

Depression. Caffeine intake increases the risk of depression in patients treated for psychiatric problems.

Heart Problems. Caffeine increases cholesterol levels, heart palpitations, and aggravates hypertension.

Cancer. Coffee contains many roasted hydrocarbons that may be potent carcinogens. Research has shown a correlation between overconsumption of caffeine (along with theophyline and theobromine) and fibrocystic breast disease and cancer of the bladder.

Blood Pressure. Caffeine raises blood pressure even when consumed in moderate amounts. One study of 6,321 adults demonstrated a small but statistically significant elevation in blood pressure when comparing those who drank five or more cups a day to non-coffee drinkers.

Smoking. Caffeine and alcohol consumption can lead to a dependence on nicotine.

as regular exercise helps alleviate the anxiety and depression caused by alcoholism. Improved physical fitness also reduces a person's likelihood of resorting to alcohol. It is recommended that alcoholic patients exercise 20-30 minutes, five to seven times a week, at an intensity sufficient to raise their heart rate to 60-80% of maximum capacity for the given age group.

Homeopathy. According to Lauri Aesoph, homeopathy complements nutrition, stress management, exercise, and support groups in treating psychological and physical addictions such as alcoholism. *Arnica* (Leopard's bane) and *Stramonium* (thorn-apple) help relieve the convulsions and hallucinations typical during withdrawal. *Chelidanium majus* (greater celandine) assists those with jaundice, and helps detoxify the liver of excess alcohol. *Carduus mariana* (St. Mary's thistle) is also effective in reducing liver disorders caused by alcohol. *Zincum metallicum* (zinc) relieves twitching, irritability, depression, and restlessness which often accompany alcoholism. *Nux vomica* is used for compulsive patients who tremble and twitch during withdrawal from alcohol.

Biofeedback. E. Saxb reports a study in the September 1995 issue of the *Journal of Clinical Psychology* in which 14 alcoholic outpatients used biofeedback brainwave treatment for alcohol abuse. After temperature biofeedback pretraining, the subjects completed two 40-minute sessions of alpha-theta brainwave neurofeedback training (BWNT). A 21-month follow-up study indicated sustained prevention of relapse in alcoholics who completed the biofeedback therapy.

Caffeine

Caffeine is the most widely used drug in American society. The average American consumes an estimated 150-225 milligrams of caffeine daily, 75% of which comes from coffee. A typical cup of coffee contains approximately 50-150 mg, while a cup of tea contains 50 mg and a 12-ounce can of cola contains approximately 35 mg. Murray and Pizzorno report that some Americans consume an excess of 7,500 mg of caffeine per day.

Caffeine is a natural substance that is found in a variety of plants. In addition to coffee, tea, and cola drinks, it is also found in kola nuts, chocolate, many nonprescription stimulants, pain relievers, cough medicines, cold remedies, alertness tablets, and weight control pills.

In moderate doses, caffeine increases alertness and physical and mental endurance. In high doses, however, it can produce nervousness, insomnia, tremors, and restlessness. In the early 1990s, it was believed that caffeine-containing foods, such as tea and coffee, cola drinks, and chocolate, might be responsible for the premenstrual breast pain and tenderness some women experience, because these substances contain methylxanthines. However, various studies have yet to prove an association between methylxanthine and the development of these symptoms. Nevertheless, women with these symptoms who consume large amounts of coffee or chocolate should consult with a physician.

Alternative Treatments for Caffeinism

Nutritional Therapies. "Caffeinism" is a clinical syndrome in which people develop a mild psychological dependence on caffeine, and must consume increasing amounts to maintain their mental alertness. In *Staying Healthy with Nutrition*, Dr. Elson Haas states that a diet of alkaline foods, especially fresh fruits and vegetables, helps reduce cravings for caffeine. He also recommends taking potassium bicarbonate tablets to increase the body's alkalinity, and drinking at least eight glass of water daily to flush out toxins. To nourish the adrenal glands, Haas recommends eating six light meals each day that are low in sugar and fat. Since caffeine is a laxative, discontinuing can cause constipation, and

Haas recommends consuming a diet high in fiber and carbohydrates (65-70% of the total diet) to replace depleted glycogen stores.

Coffee Substitutes. Holistic physicians usually encourage patients to drink coffee substitutes such as green tea, which is not roasted and therefore less toxic than coffee. Green tea is also rich in flavonoid compounds and may have antioxidant and anti-allergy properties. The choice of which green tea to substitute for coffee should be made after consulting with a health practitioner, as some teas contain ephedra, camellia, or cola, which can produce insomnia, anxiety, and hypertension. Coffee substitutes are usually prescribed in conjunction with a diet and exercise program.

Haas recommends drinking roasted grain beverages such as Postum, Roma, or Cafix, or herbal tea, broth, hot cider, or water. He cautions people to avoid chocolate, caffeinated soft drinks, certain drugs (Anacin has 30 mg of caffeine, Dristan 16.2 mg, and No Doz 100 mg), and herbal products such as guarana, kola, or mate.

Vitamin and Mineral Supplements. Before eliminating caffeine altogether, take vitamin and mineral supplements to replace depleted nutrients, support the adrenal glands, and ease withdrawal. Dr. Haas recommends vitamin C, B complex vitamins, calcium, potassium, magnesium, and zinc. Other helpful nutrients include co-enzyme Q-10 and octacosanol to increase immune resistance.

Botanical Medicines. Haas advises coffee drinkers to take valerian capsules or drink chamomile tea to withdraw from caffeine. Willowbark extracts or caffeine-free pain killers such as hops capsules help relieve the headaches that often accompany withdrawal from caffeine.

Massage. According to Haas, several types of massage (including self-massage) have also proven effective in relieving the symptoms of caffeine withdrawal. He suggests that patients have their neck, temples, forehead, and shoulder massaged to relieve the headaches of withdrawal. Massage also helps eliminates toxins, and strenghten the immune system.

Acupuncture and Acupressure. Acupuncture, according to Haas, can ease withdrawal, eliminate cravings, and improve body functions, all of which help keep caffeine addicts from relapsing. Acupressure, by harmonizing the body's energy flow, also speeds up healing, helps to expel toxins, and restores muscles, nerves, organs, and glands. Stroking the front of the face, from the bridge of the nose to the temples, and rubbing the back of neck and base of the skull have also proven effective.

Exercise. By improving the body's ability to deliver and process oxygen, Haas argues that exercise enhances overall stamina and energy so that patients have an easier time cutting out caffeine. Aerobic exercise also helps to reduce tension and eliminate toxins through the skin. Haas cites several studies which suggest that yoga, tai chi, meditation, and breathing exercise all help relieve tension and the perception of the need for caffeine. Deep breathing exercises also help induce the relaxation response which revitalizes muscle and nerve fibers, and helps detoxify the liver, kidneys, bladder, and colon.

Amphetamines

College students who stay up all night to write term papers, and truck drivers who drive without sleeping for 24-hour stretches, may well be familiar with amphetamines. Amphetamines are chemical compounds that stimulate the sympathetic and central nervous systems and act as euphoriants. People using amphetamines experience increased alertness and elevation of mood, and are able to do strenuous physical work. Most amphetamines, including Dexedrine, Benzedrine and Methedrine are taken orally, although some can be injected with a needle.

Amphetamines were originally developed by chemists to help people lose weight, overcome depression, and increase their mental alertness. Very few of these benefits, however, have been clinically proven. Excessive intakes of amphetamines can produce headaches, irritability, dizziness, insomnia, panic, confusion, and delirium. In addition, users often experience a rebound crash after several hours, during which they sleep for long periods, and may become very tired or in some cases, progress to depression.

Holistic Treatments for Amphetamines

Amphetamines are not physically addictive. People using amphetamines, however, can become psychologically dependent on the euphoric moods which the drugs produce, as do people who use amphetamines to lose weight. In some cases, the dependency is difficult to treat because of the so-called "Yo-Yo cycle." People first use the drugs to stimulate their nervous system and stay awake. Later, they may take a depressant to go to sleep. After they wake up, they need to take more of the stimulant to become alert again. Prolonged use can produce amphetamine psychosis in which people experience auditory or visual hallucinations or delusions.

The holistic treatment for amphetamine abuse first substitutes natural stimulants for amphetamines to break the first stage of the Yo-Yo cycle. If the abuser has a normal heart rate, aerobic exercise is then used as a substitute for drug depressants to naturally tire the muscle system. Through diet, exercise, botanical supplements, and psychological counseling, patients can gradually stimulate their natural endorphins so that they no longer require the amphetamines.

Cocaine

Joseph Treaster states in his July 16, 1993 article in the *New York Times* that more than 25 million people in the U.S. have tried cocaine, 10 million regularly use the drug, and half of them suffer serious problems. Each day, 5,000 Americans are reported to try cocaine for the first time. Twenty percent (more than one million) of those who continue to use it eventually become addicted.

Cocaine is derived from the leaves of the coca plant which grows primarily in South America. After the plant is grown, the coca leaves are made into either a paste or a powder. Coca paste is popular in South America, and is smoked with tobacco or marijuana cigarettes. Most cocaine found in the U.S. is a white powder (cocaine hydrochloride) which is sniffed through the nose or mixed with water and injected.

"Freebase" is a purified, concentrated form of cocaine paste which is heated and smoked. It is chemically stronger than cocaine powder because the powder is usually mixed ("cut") with baking soda or other solvents. People addicted to cocaine powder usually progress to freebase because it contains more pure cocaine. "Crack" is a rock form of freebase which is sold in vials or sticks and is easier to sell and smoke—either in a water pipe or after being added to tobacco or marijuana cigarettes.

Cocaine Withdrawal. Because cocaine is physically addictive, people attempting to withdraw from it often experience sweating, muscle tremors, accelerated heart rate, weight loss, malnutrition, sexual dysfunction,

Cocaine's Effect on the Body

- Stimulates the central nervous system.
- Produces a short-lived high followed by depression and craving.
- Depletes the brain's supply of natural chemicals such as norepinephrine and dopamine.
- Acts as a local anesthetic to relieve pain and numb tissues.
- Constricts the blood vessels.
- Increases temperature, heart rate, and blood pressure.
- Depresses appetite.
- Relaxes and anesthetizes the throat, larynx, and lower respiratory tract.

anxiety, panic, insomnia, paranoia, and hallucinations, according to Alan Rees and Charlene Willey (*Personal Health Reporter*). As they report, even more serious side effects of withdrawal can include psychosis, coma, strokes, seizures, liver damage, heart failure, and respiratory arrest. Withdrawal symptoms usually occur within 24-48 hours of the last dose and may continue for 7-10 days.

Several conventional treatments have proven partially successful in either curing addiction or alleviating withdrawal symptoms. Buprenorphine, a pain killer, produces abstention in some addicts. Desipramine, an anti-depressant, reduces cravings and helps abstention in many difficult-to-treat patients. Flupenothixol, also an anti-depressant, promoted abstinence for an average of 24 weeks in one clinical trial. Edlin and Golanty suggest that arbamazapine, an anti-seizure drug, can reduce craving and prevents seizures brought on by chronic cocaine use.

Dangers of Cocaine Addiction

- Snorting cocaine can cause perforated septums (tiny holes in the nasal membranes).
- Intravenous users (IU) suffer the risk of hepatitis, AIDS, and other diseases.
- Smoking cocaine can seriously damage the lungs.
- Chronic use can produce affective disorder, schizophrenia, and personality disturbances.
- Other side effects include tremors, twitching, malnutrition, sexual dysfunction, insomnia, paranoia, auditory or visual hallucinations, psychosis, coma, strokes, seizures, liver damage, heart failure, and respiratory arrest.
- Sudden death can occur in otherwise healthy people.

Holistic Treatments for Cocaine Addiction

Holistic treatment for cocaine addiction, similar to that for alcoholism, focuses on rebuilding the addict's immune system and preventing the depression which occurs during the withdrawal period. Normally the addict is offered group and family therapy and minimal dosage of anti-depressants.

A key component of treatment is denying the patient access to more cocaine. Some physicians may decide to control all of the addict's funds and require routine urine testing for cocaine. If patients find it impossible to stay away from cocaine, they may be temporarily hospitalized. As any treatments must prevent relapse, most therapists try to prevent the cues which trigger cravings. Long-term treatment necessarily focuses on helping the patient build a full and satisfying life without cocaine while coping with the stresses which could trigger relapse. Recovery for cocaine addicts almost always requires intensive psychological support, and groups such as Narcotics Anonymous have been very effective.

Acupuncture (Auriculotherapy). The December 1, 1992 issue of the *National Acupuncture Detoxification Association (NADA) Newsletter* states that acupuncture can reverse some cases of cocaine addiction. It cites a study conducted at the Lincoln Substance Abuse/Acupuncture Clinic in New York City in which 68 pregnant women addicted to crack or cocaine received acupuncture treatments in conjunction with a detoxification regimen, counseling, and daily urinalysis tests. Women who attended the program for 10 visits or more showed significantly higher infant birth weights than those who attended less than 10 times.

Dr. Jeffrey Holder, founder and director of Exodus, a residential treatment for addictions based in Miami, Florida, believes that every drug of choice has a receptor site mechanism located in the ear. What acupuncturists do is satisfy the needs of that receptor site by supplying and directing the endorphins or enkephalins. Using auriculotherapy, Dr. Holder reports success rates of over 80% for nicotine, alcohol, cocaine, heroin, and other mood-altering substances among addicts. Holder was the first American to be awarded the Albert Schweitzer prize in medicine for his pioneering research.

In 1989, auriculotherapy was officially recognized by the WHO as a viable medical modality. In the U.S. auriculotherapy is currently used in the treatment and control of pain, dyslexia, and other functional imbalances. It is applied through needles, ear massage,

Risks of Marijuana Use

Increased Potency. Marijuana products have become increasingly stronger. In 1975 the average sample of confiscated marijuana contained 0.4% of THC (tetrahydrocannabinol). By 1990, cultivated forms contained 7% THC.

Brain Impairment. Marijuana interferes with memory, learning, speech, reading, comprehension, problem solving, and the ability to think. Driving skills are impaired, along with general intellectual performance. The long-term intellectual affects are still not fully understood.

Affected Social Behavior. Some researchers have observed amotivational syndromes among marijuana smokers, who, with frequent use, tend to lose interest in school friends and sexual intercourse.

Affected Psychomotor Functions. Like alcohol, marijuana interferes with psychomotor functions such as reaction time, coordination, visual perception, and other skills important for driving and operating machinery safety. Tests of marijuana-intoxicated drivers show that their driving is impaired, yet they think they are driving better than usual.

Psychological Dependence. While marijuana is not considered physically addicting, it is known to aggravate existing emotional problems. The most common adverse emotional effect is acute panic reactions, in which users became terrified and paranoid and require hospitalization.

Lung Damage. Marijuana cigarettes are normally unfiltered, and smokers tend to inhale deeply, exposing sensitive lung tissue to potent, irritating chemicals. One study among marijuana smokers showed that five marijuana cigarettes a week were more damaging to the lungs than six packs of cigarettes smoked over the same period.

Toxins. Marijuana smoke contains 150 chemicals in addition to THC, and the effects of most are not yet known. One ingredient, benzopyrene, is a known carcinogen that is 70% more abundant in marijuana smoke than in tobacco smoke. Marijuana cigarettes also contain more tar than tobacco cigarettes.

Impaired Heart Function. Marijuana has a greater effect on heart function than tobacco. It can raise the heart rate by as much as 50%.

Hormone and Reproductive Effects. Several studies suggest that marijuana smoking can lower the level of the male sex hormone testosterone in the blood. Sperm abnormalities, including reduced numbers of sperm and abnormal sperm movement and shapes, have also been observed in male marijuana smokers. Preliminary studies suggest an adverse effect on the menstrual cycle in 40% of women who smoke marijuana at least four times a week. The result may be infertility—as the female sex hormones estrogen and progesterone are reduced in female marijuana smokers.

Pregnancy Risks. Marijuana can cross the placenta and reach the developing fetus, and miscarriages are more common among pregnant female marijuana smokers.

Immune System Impairment. Human studies have shown that marijuana damages basic body defense against disease by weakening the immune system.

and, in certain cases, electrical stimulation or infrared treatment.

Recent Research Discoveries. Guilford Pharmaceuticals of Baltimore, Maryland, announced in early 1997 the production of their new patented compound which in animal studies effectively blocks the effects of cocaine without interfering with normal brain functions. The Guilford drug, GPI Compound 2138, shows great promise and more research is currently underway.

Marijuana and Hashish

Marijuana and hashish are products of the *Cannabis sativa* plant and have been used as medicines in many different cultures. Marijuana, the leaves of the sativa plant, are smoked or added to foods (especially brownies) and teas. Hashish is a concentrated form of marijuana which is made by burning cannabis leaves and collecting the left-over resins into a brown gummy powder.

Tetrahydracannabiol (THC) is the psychoactive constituent of marijuana. When the plant is smoked, the THC is inhaled into the lungs, absorbed into the blood, and transported throughout the body. A small amount of THC in the bloodstream produces a euphoric-like state. Many people experience a sense of relaxation, and occasionally an altered perception of space and time. Some speech impairment may also occur along with short-term memory loss. Different subspecies of marijuana vary substantially in THC content. Female plants (sensimilla marijuana), for example, have no seeds and are reported to have 10 times the concentration of THC as either male or hermaphrodite plants.

Physiological Effects. High doses of THC have been known to produce anxiety, panic, hallucinations, and paranoia. Marijuana and hashish may also complicate prior mental health problems or negative mood swings.

Nevertheless, long-term use has not been proven to cause permanent changes in brain function or chemistry, nor has either marijuana or hashish been found to lead inevitably to the use of other drugs, according to the National Academy of Sciences' report "Marijuana and Health."

Opiates

Opiates are a class of compounds extracted from the opium poppy, *Papaver somniferum*, which contains several different chemicals that are isolated or mixed together to produce heroin, morphine, codeine, or opium. All opiates can cause physical dependence and produce serious withdrawal symptoms.

Heroin, derived from morphine, is a semi-synthetic narcotic which was first manufactured in 1889 by the Bayer pharmaceutical company. It was originally marketed as a pain reliever for chronic coughs and was later used to treat opium, alcohol, and morphine addictions. Heroin is now illegal in the U.S., although it is still grown illegally in the Southwest. It is either inhaled, smoked, or injected, and is often cut with dangerous substitutes. The heroin typically sold on American streets, for example, often contains only 1% heroin–the rest consists of cornstarch, cleansing agents, or strychnine.

Heroin affects the body as soon as it enters the bloodstream and reportedly produces extreme states of euphoria. Unfortunately, prolonged use leads to addiction and large doses can result in death. Heroin does not cause any fatal diseases and does not directly damage any internal organs. Rather, it triggers a reaction in the brain's respiratory center which can cause a person to stop breathing. Many users die as a result of injecting it, because they either destroy their veins or contact serum hepatitis or the HIV virus through contaminated needles. Heroin is converted to morphine in the body, which is subsequently excreted in the urine. A mother addicted to heroin can transfer the drug to the fetus in her womb who will become addicted even before it is born.

Withdrawal from heroin usually begins four to eight hours after the last dose and usually lasts about a week. The physical discomforts of withdrawal typically involve insomnia, diarrhea, cramps, nausea, vomiting, and painful involuntary muscle spasms.

Treatments for Heroin Addiction

There is no known cure for heroin addiction. The current way to treat it is with methadone, a synthetic narcotic that eliminates the desire for heroin, but is itself also addictive. Once on a methadone maintenance program, however, heroin users can overcome their addiction and eventually live without heroin.

Holistic medical therapies have been successfully used to help people undergoing methadone treatment strengthen their immune systems. Nutrition, vitamins, and botanicals can be used to alleviate the heroin withdrawal symptoms.

Acupuncture. Several studies cited in the 1992 *National Acupuncture Detoxification Newsletter* document the effectiveness of acupuncture in aiding withdrawal symptoms from opium and heroin addictions. As a result, the National Institute of Drug Abuse conducted several clinical trials using acupuncture on heroin addicts in New York City outpatient drug detoxification programs. Detoxification from chronic use of prescribed opiates (morphine, Demeral, etc.) usually takes from 3-6 months. Even "brief" detoxification programs take more than a month. One uncontrolled trial found that after electrical stimulation at ear acupuncture points, 12 out of 14 patients (86%) were able to completely withdraw from narcotics in 2-7 days. They also experienced fewer or no side effects.

Several studies cited in *Alternative Medicine: The Definitive Guide* suggest that acupuncture was equal to or better than methadone in helping people withdraw from heroin. Methadone treatment programs substitute a less expensive, longer-acting, government-sanctioned drug. Researchers now think that acupuncture, in combination with a relapse prevention program, can eliminate the heroin addict's need for both methadone and heroin.

A controlled study of real versus sham acupuncture in heroin detoxification found that addicts receiving the real treatment attended the acupuncture clinic more days and stayed in treatment longer. The treatment seemed to be most effective in addicts with lighter habits. Acupuncture also claims good success rates with cigarette addiction, where a newly discovered acupoint called "Tien Mi" is used in conjunction with other traditional acupoints, particularly those located in the ear.

According to *Alternative Medicine: The Definitive Guide*, Dr. Michael Smith of Lincoln Hospital in the Bronx has successfully used acupuncture for nearly two decades to help heroin, opium, and tranquilizer addicts overcome their addictions. According to Smith, "Methadone and Valium are so addictive that they create problems of their own. And there is no pharmaceutical treatment effective in quelling the cravings for cocaine." Acupuncture treatments, on the other hand, are not threatening, help patients immediately feel better, and enable dialogue with the therapist to take place during the sessions in a relaxing way.

Psychedelic Drugs

Drugs which produce changes in a person's psychological perception of reality are defined as psychedelic drugs. These drugs often result in visual hallucinations–and are also called "hallucinogens." People under the influence of one of these drugs are usually aware that their hallucinations are caused by the drug and will eventually disappear. The most potent psychedelic is lysergic acid diethylamide, or LSD. Other psychedelic drugs include Mescaline (peyote), STP, DMT, DET, PCP, and Psilocybin mushrooms.

A wide variety of hallucinogens are either extracted from more than 100 different kinds of plants, or synthetically produced in laboratories. Psychedelic plants include datura, harmine, kava, morning glory seeds, and nutmeg. Plant psychedelics are usually ingested orally while the synthetics are taken in powder or pill form.

Hallucinogens normally take effect in 45-60 minutes, and can result in sweating, nausea, increased body temperature, and dilation of the pupils. Although many hallucinogens have not been fully researched, most of the available studies suggest that they are not addictive. They can, however, produce a psychological dependence. Hallucinogens do not appear to produce any withdrawal symptoms, and no conclusive evidence exists that they cause permanent physiological or genetic damage or birth defects.

Mescaline, the active component of the peyote plant, is grown largely in Mexico. It is sold dried and sliced or sometimes purified into a powder called mescaline sulfate. Most so-called mescaline sold in tablets and capsules is LSD, PCP, or both. Mescaline has a bitter taste which often causes nausea or vomiting. Peyote is stronger than mescaline and contains other alkaloids, some of which are toxic. Psilocybin and psilocin are the active components of several species of mushrooms which grow in many areas of the world, and are very powerful drugs with effects comparable to those of LSD. They are not illegal and are sold without a prescription.

Angel dust, also known as PCP, was originally developed as an anesthetic. According to Edlin and Golanty, PCP either stimulates or depresses the central nervous system, depending on its dosage and in what form it is taken, and can trigger hallucinations in some people. Users normally take it to elevate their mood or relax. Pure PCP is not physiologically addictive, according to Edlin and Golanty, although the PCP sold on the streets is often mixed with other drugs and can be lethal.

Central Nervous System (CNS) Depressant Drugs

CNS depressants constitute the largest class of prescription drugs sold in the U.S. and many are dangerous. Virtually all of them carry some potential for physical or psychological dependency, and some can be lethal in high doses Unfortunately, a large number have not been fully tested, according to Edlin and Golanty, and many of their side effects are still unknown.

The most widely used legal CNS drugs in the U.S. are tranquilizers. Valium, the best-selling drug in the world at one time, can cause ataxia (the loss of equilibrium and muscle coordination), vertigo (dizziness), and drowsiness. It also decreases blood pressure and decreases sexual potency. Halcion, a legal sleeping pill, can cause serious side effects, including confusion, hallucinations, and amnesia.

Psychologically, CNS depressants can produce a mild state of euphoria which helps some people relax and lose their inhibitions. With continued use, many people become addicted to one or more tranquilizers or antihistamines, and it can often take them years to cure their dependency. Withdrawal can be extremely painful, and users may experience deep depression and hallucinations.

Holistic Treatments for CNS Depressants

Holistic practitioners treat patients with CNS depressant dependency with vitamin and mineral supplements, botanical medicines, and diet programs. The holistic treatment for each CNS depressant varies with the chemical nature of the particular drug. Initial stages of treatment usually include substituting a natural, non-toxic tranquilizer for the synthetic drug tranquilizer. Holistic physicians also use nutrition, exercise, and group therapy to alleviate the psychophysiological factors underlying dependence on drug tranquilizers. The initial stages of withdrawing from a tranquilizer addiction can be quite difficult and are eased most effectively when undertaken with medical advice and the assistance of a support group or counselor.

Nicotine

Approximately 400,000 Americans die each year as a result of smoking tobacco, while another 10 million suffer from diseases related to smoking. Cigarette smoking is responsible for 85% of lung cancers in the U.S, and heavy smokers suffer 20 times the rate of lung cancer than nonsmokers. Nevertheless, Edlin and Golanty state that more than 50 million Americans continue to smoke cigarettes.

Even non-smokers, especially children, can get lung cancer by being exposed to tobacco smoke. According to the EPA, children exposed to secondhand tobacco smoke are more likely to suffer lower respiratory tract infections, reduced lung function, and more ear infections. The EPA and the Centers for Disease Control estimate that secondhand smoke causes 3,000 deaths annually from lung cancer, 150,000-300,000 cases of bronchitis and pneumonia in youngsters, and asthma attacks in more than twice that number.

Physiological Effects of Nicotine

- Nicotine increases heart rate and the release of adrenalin.
- Nicotine can cause nausea and vomiting.
- Nicotine and carbon monoxide contribute to heart and blood vessel disease.
- Nicotine, along with other chemicals in tobacco, contributes to the development of cancer and respiratory tract diseases.
- Babies born to mothers who smoke have lower birth weights and a higher risk mortality.
- Pregnant mothers who smoke are more likely to have spontaneous abortions.

Nicotine is the principal component of tobacco products, although as many as 4,000 other chemical substances are released and carried in tobacco smoke, including carbon monoxide, methanol, nitrous dioxide, traces of mineral and radioactive elements, acids, and insecticides. There are several different species of the tobacco plant, and the toxicity of particular brands of cigarettes or pipe tobacco varies depending on the soil and climate in which they are grown and the chemicals with which they are treated.

Alternative Treatments for Nicotine Addiction

People who smoke tobacco can become either psychologically or physiologically addicted to nicotine. Fortunately, there are many therapies for treating nicotine addiction, and each year approximately 20% of the 50 million smokers in the U.S. attempt to give up smoking. More than 85% of all smokers who quit do so on their own, without the aid of smoking cessation programs or products, according to Rees and Willey (*The Personal Health Reporter*). Most people who quit indicate in surveys that they did so because they were worried about cancer or other diseases which they knew were linked to smoking.

Nicotine Gum. The best way for people to permanently stop smoking depends on the nature of their addiction. People who are chemically addicted to nicotine often need a chemically based therapy, such as nicotine gum or a nicotine-like drug which satisfies their dependence on nicotine. As many as 20% of American smokers successfully quit each year using nicotine gum therapies. Chewing gum, when combined with psychological counseling, is successful in 38% of cases where addiction is cured. Other chemical aids for smoking cessation, such as the nicotine patch, nicotine aerosol, or nasal nicotine solutions, are currently being studied.

Nicotine Patches. The side effects of nicotine patches—which release a constant low-level stream of nicotine into the blood stream—are controversial. In 1992, for example, a Massachusetts hospital claimed it treated five heart attack victims who had been smoking while using the patches. Also, nicotine patches apparently do not supply a powerful enough jolt to overcome the need to smoke. After a person inhales a cigarette, nicotine reaches the brain in only seven seconds, faster than injecting nicotine directly into a vein. In contrast, patches take nearly four hours to reach peak strength. For this reason, some manufacturers have begun to double the nicotine in patches to 42 mg, the same amount found in a pack of cigarettes. Nasal inhalers and sprays appear to be more

successful. In one British study, reported by Eben Shapiro, 26% of smokers using a nasal spray to administer nicotine quit smoking. Whatever alternatives are used, however, the key to success appears to be a strong desire on the part of the user to stop smoking–a habit that is about 75% psychological.

Of those smokers who attempt to quit, only 6% are able to do so "cold turkey." Nevertheless, a 1993 study conducted at the University of California, San Diego, showed that when smokers are encouraged to smoke less and quit intermittently, rather than making the difficult choice of stopping immediately, they have a good chance of eventually dropping the habit for good. Of those taking part in the study, 26.7% were able to stop smoking, approximately twice the rate of those trying to quit without the program. The study also found that restriction of smoking at home and at the workplace is a factor contributing to successful quitting. The study, reported in November 14, 1993 *Associated Press*, was based on interviews with 4,624 Californians who were asked about their smoking habits and history, and interviewed again 18 months later.

One small study conducted at the Mayo Clinic and reported in the July 1994 issue of the *Mayo Clinic Health Letter* indicates that nicotine patch plus a doctor's advice and weekly counseling is the most effective way of quitting smoking. Adults who took part in the study smoked at least a pack of cigarettes a day. Half received a maximum-strength nicotine patch (22 mg) and half wore an inactive patch. As part of their eight weeks of patch therapy, both groups had an initial visit with a physician and met weekly with nurse for counseling. After a year, 27% of those who had worn the nicotine patch remained nonsmokers compared to 14% of the inactive patch group–a significant improvement over "cold turkey" withdrawal programs or physician counseling alone. Patients in the study had the best long-term success when the level of nicotine in their patch closely matched the level of nicotine in their blood when they entered the study. The researchers who conducted the study concluded that the average amount of nicotine in currently available patches may be not be strong enough for most people, especially heavy smokers.

Vitamin and Mineral Therapies. Holistic treatments for nicotine addiction, as with other substance dependencies, incorporate vitamins and botanical supplements, nutrition, and exercise. If a person has a chemical addiction, a holistic physician may use nicotine gum in the early stage of treatment along with vitamin supplements, which help the lungs recover from the adverse effects of nicotine and also ease withdrawal symptoms. Dr. Leon Chaitow's detoxification program as detailed in his book *The Body/Mind Detoxification Program* recommends the following vitamin supplements: vitamin A, vitamin C, vitamin E, and one high potency B-complex vitamin. The herb obeline (oats), according to Barbara Yoder, is also reported to be of great value in helping patients stop smoking.

Pearson and Shaw list the following basic vitamins and minerals for smokers who want to quit:

Selenium	250 micrograms
Vitamin A	10,000 to 20,000 IU
Vitamin E	1,000 to 2,000 IU
Zinc (gluconate)	50 milligrams
Vitamin B_1	1/2 to 1 gram
Vitamin B_2	100 to 200 milligrams
Vitamin C	3 to 10 grams
Cysteine	1 to 3 grams
Vitamin B_3 (niacin)	300 milligrams to 3 grams
Vitamin B_5	250 to 1,000 milligrams
Vitamin B_6	250 to 500 milligrams
Choline	1 to 3 grams
PABA (a B vitamin)	500 milligrams to 1 gram
Betacarotene	20,000 to 60,000 IU

Acupuncture and Acupressure. Chaitow also claims that acupuncture and acupressure have been helpful in clinical trials in which patients successfully quit smoking. Edlin and Golanty point to other holistic therapies which have also proven successful for many people. These therapies include hypnosis, group therapy, and stress reduction techniques such as biofeedback and meditation.

Hypnosis. Hypnosis is commonly recommended for smoking cessation, although the evidence concerning its efficacy is controversial. Hypnosis and smoking studies have been criticized for relying on the patients' own reporting of how often they smoke (substance abusers are notoriously inaccurate about how much of a substance they abuse) and for the lack of long-term follow-up. One review of 17 smoking studies cited by Bowers found that the percentage of people treated by hypnosis who still weren't smoking after six months ranged widely from 4-88%. However, in programs that offered several hours of hypnosis, intense interpersonal interaction, individualized suggestions, and follow-up treatment, success rates of quitting smoking were above 50%. 226 smokers were treated with self-hypnosis and 52% achieved complete smoking abstinence only one week after the intervention, according to Bowers.

Lifestyle Changes. In general, holistic therapies attempt to help patients quit smoking by focusing on changing their lifestyle habits. The American Heart Association (AMA) now claims that smokers who quit dramatically reduce the risk of heart attacks and strokes. In particular, the AMA stresses that diet and vitamin supplements can

Optimal Combined Holistic Therapies for Quitting Smoking

Surveys have shown that almost half of those who reported ever smoking have successfully quit. Here are a few tips:

Set a Date. Name the specific day when you intend to quit smoking. The American Cancer Society suggests that the day be no more than three weeks in the future.

Quit on Your Own. Most quitters, according to the NIH, quit on their own with little outside help, and they are almost twice as likely to success as those who seek help from a smoking cessation program. But self-quitters may succeed because they're lighter smokers in the first place (less than 25 cigarettes a day). Heavy smokers, the researchers say, may still benefit from professional help.

Count Down Gradually. Taper off a few cigarettes a day for a week or so before quitting cold turkey.

Join a Program. Sign up with a local smoking cessation program where you'll receive guidelines and group support to see you through physical or psychological difficulties.

Aversion Therapy. Nicotine aversion therapy usually employs a drug which makes smokers sick within 15 minutes of smoking a cigarette. Research has shown that this technique, when used in conjunction with other anti-smoking therapies, is helpful for approximately half of all smokers who eventually quit.

Nicotine Gum. Chewing nicotine gum helps relieve withdrawal symptoms and temporary weight gain. The gum also eliminates the tar and carbon monoxide, two of the deadliest substances in tobacco, and releases lower levels of nicotine than cigarettes. As you get accustomed to being a nonsmoker, you gradually cut back on chewing the gum, until you stop altogether, usually within three to six months.

Wear a Nicotine Patch. Over a period of 6-8 hours, nicotine contained in a small, bandage-like patch is gradually absorbed through the skin. Heavy smokers usually need to put a fresh patch on in the late afternoon. A one-month supply of nicotine patches is available by prescription, and helps approximately 50% of patients quit.

Counter Cravings. Virtually all heavy smokers experience intense cravings during the first weeks of quitting–which usually disappear after two or three weeks. Each craving actually lasts no more than 20 seconds. Distract yourself during a craving by: touching your toes 10 times; jogging in place while you count to 30; or practice deep breathing, which can help the cravings pass and diminish its intensity. Inhale deeply, expanding your abdomen fully. Then exhale, taking at least twice as long as inhalation. Repeat this procedure for 2-3 minutes to feel totally relaxed.

Eliminate Caffeine. Caffeine is known to increase the symptoms of tobacco withdrawal during the stressful first few days after quitting.

Exercise. Exercise not only burns up calories but helps relieve stress and improves your mood. Many people smoke to relieve stress, and by dealing with tension more effectively, exercise counteracts feelings of depression, gives smokers more energy, and helps them feel better about themselves.

Optimal Combined Holistic Therapies for Quitting Smoking (cont.)

Drink Water. Water speeds up the elimination of nicotine from the body. It also helps with weight loss and improves self-esteem–both of which appear to help people stop smoking.

Cinnamon Sticks. Cinnamon is an oral substitute for nicotine, which resembles cigarettes in shape and size and has a refreshing flavor that makes smoking tasteless by comparison.

Reward Yourself. You can use positive reinforcement rewards for quitting smoking. Stick to calorie-free indulgences such as buying new clothes or sleeping late on Saturday when you successfully resist smoking.

Choose the Most Convenient Method. No particular smoking cessation method is appropriate for everyone. Surveys show that 90-95% of all smokers prefer to quit on their own or by using printed instructions, guides, or videos. Others need informal group support or counseling. But those who show the highest success rates not only reflect the highest levels of determination, but are also committed to personal change and are well aware of the reason why they want to quit. Studies show that these people are open to trying any one of a variety of cessation programs rather than being prejudiced toward a particular method. It's essential that the smoker plan ahead and choose the method that most closely conforms to his or her personal needs.

help former smokers avoid the fatal diseases associated with smoking. In 1993, the AMA released a study in which female survivors of heart attacks or strokes cut their risks of further trouble by eating spinach, carrots, and other fruits and vegetables which contain vitamins C, E, B$_2$, and betacarotene. In the study, reported in the November 9, 1993 *Associated Press*, researchers found that those whose diets included the highest quantities of these vitamins had a 33% lower risk of heart attack and a 71% lower risk of strokes.

Summary

Drug abuse has become a serious problem in the U.S. A study conducted by researchers at Brandeis University cited in the October 24, 1995 edition of the *New York Times*, for example, concluded that drug abuse was America's "number one health problem." According to the study, more than 520,000 Americans die each year as a result of substance abuse, particularly cigarettes, alcohol, or drugs. Drugs taken under a physician's supervision may be helpful in treating some psychological and physical disorders. However, many drugs can have hidden side effects and result in physiological or psychological dependency. Psychoactive drugs are especially dangerous because they contain substances that can lead to addiction.

The physical and psychological addictions caused by most drugs can be successfully treated with holistic medical therapies which combine nutrition, exercise, vitamin and botanical supplements, and lifestyles changes. In fact, the importance of using holistic treatments for drug addictions was highlighted in the Brandeis study which concluded that many drug-related deaths "could be reduced, if not eliminated, by changing people's habits."

Resources

References

Aesoph, Lauri. "Homeopathy." *Delicious.* (Novemer 1996): 31.

"Alcoholism." *Your Health* (September 21, 1993).

American Council on Science and Health. "Cocaine: Facts and Dangers." (April 1990): 32-33.

Barrios, A. A. "Hypnotherapy: A Reappraisal." *Psychotherapy: Theory, Research and Practice* 1 (Spring 1970): 2-7.

Becker, R. O. *Cross Currents. The Promise of Electro-Medicine.* Los Angeles: Jeremy P. Tarcher, Inc., 1990.

Beinfield, Harriet. *Between Heaven and Earth: A Guide to Chinese Medicine.* New York: Ballantine Books, 1991.

Bowers, Kenneth S. "The Use of Hypnosis to Enhance Recall." *Science* 22 (1983): 184-85.

————. "Hypnosis." In *Personality and Behavioral Disorders*, Norman Endless, ed. 2nd ed. New York: Wiley, 1984.

Bullock, M. "Controlled Trial of Acupuncture for Severe Recidivist Alcoholism." *The Lancet* 8652 (June 1989):1435-39.

Burton Goldberg Group. *Alternative Medicine: The Definitive Guide.* Payallup, WA: Future Medicine Publishing, Inc., 1993.

Dicke, William. "Ancient Chinese Herbal Remedy Found to Curb Desire for Alcohol." *Wall Street Journal* (November 2, 1993).

DiGregorio, D. "Cocaine Update: Abuse and Therapy." *American Family Physician* (January 1, 1990): 250.

Edlin, Gordon, and Eric Golanty. *Health and Wellness.* Boston: Jones and Bartlett Publishers, 1993, p. 293.

Eisenberg, D. *Encounters with Qi: Exploring Chinese Medicine.* New York: Penguin Books, 1987.

Fugh-Berman, Adriane. *Alternative Medicine: What Works.* Tucson, AZ: Odonian Press, 1996.

Gaura, Maira Alicia. "Drug Addicts Treated with Acupuncture." *San Francisco Chronicle* (November 1, 1993).

Gerber, R. *Vibrational Medicine.* Sante Fe, NM: Bear & Company, 1988.

Hau, D. "Effects of Electroacupuncture on Leukocytes and Plasma Protein." *American Journal of Chinese Medicine* (1980): 354-66.

Holder, J. *New Auricular Therapy.* State of Florida Department of Health and Rehabilitative Services, 1991.

Huard, P. *Chinese Medicine.* New York: McGraw-Hill, 1968.

Jayasuraiya, A. *Textbook on Acupuncture.* Colombo, Sri Lanka: Open University, 1987.

Kaptchuk, Ted. *The Web That Has No Weaver: Understanding Chinese Medicine.* New York: Congdon and Week, 1992.

Mitchell, Ellinor. *Plain Talk about Acupuncture.* New York: Whalehall, Inc., 1987.

Murray, Michael, and Joseph Pizzorno. *Encyclopedia of Natural Medicine.*

Rocklin, CA: Prima Publishing, 1991, p. 264.

NADA Newsletter Committee. *National Acupuncture Detoxification Association Newsletter* (December 1, 1992): 1-6.

National Academy of Sciences. "Marijuana and Health." 1991.

Pearson, Durk, and Sandy Shaw. *Life Extension.* New York: Warner Books, 1984.

Rees, Alan, and Charlene Willey. *Personal Health Reporter.* Detroit: Gale Research, 1993, p 149.

Saxb, E. "Alpha Theta Brainwave Neurofeedback Training: An Effective Treatment for Male and Female Alcoholics with Depressive Symptoms." *Journal of Clinical Psychology.* (September 1995): 685-93.

Schroeder, Steven. *Current Medical Diagnosis & Treatment.* Norwalk, CT: Appleton & Lange, 1992, pp. 819-20.

Shapiro, Eben. "After Nicotine Patches: Sprays, Pill, Inhalers?" *Wall Street Journal* (November 8, 1993).

"Smoking Doubles Smoke Risk, Study Find." *Associated Press* (November 9, 1993).

"Snuffing Out Secondhand Smoke." *New York Times* (November 7, 1993).

"Study: Alcohol Doesn't Kill Cells in Brain." *Associated Press* (November 12, 1993).

"Substance Abuse Is Blamed for 500,000 Deaths." *New York Times* (October 24, 1993).

"Tapering Off Proves Better Way to Quit Smoking." *Associated Press* (November 14, 1993).

Treaster, Joseph. "Drug Use Making Comeback, Study Says." *New York Times* (July 16, 1993).

Ulman, Dana. *Hypnotherapy.* Glendale, CA: Westwood Publishing Co., 1984.

Worsley, J. R. *Acupuncture: Is It for You?* New York: Harper & Row, 1973.

Yoder, Barbara. *The Recovery Resource Book.* New York: Simon & Schuster, 1990, p. 129.

Organizations

Al-Anon.
1372 Broadway, New York, NY 10018.

Alcoholics Anonymous.
P.O. Box 459, Grand Central Station, New York, NY 10163.

American Cancer Society.
4 East 35th Street, New York, NY 10001.

American Council for Drug Education.
204 Monroe Street, Rockville, MD 20850.

American Council on Alcoholism.
8501 LaSalle Road, Suite 301, Towson, MD 21204.

American Lung Association.
1740 Broadway, New York, NY 10019.

Hazelden Foundation
Box 11, Center City, MN 55012.

Johnson Institute of Rehabilitation,
509 South Euclid Avenue, St. Louis, MO 63110.

National Clearinghouse for Alcohol and Drug Information.
P.O. Box 2345, Rockville, MD 20852.

National Council on Alcoholism.
12 W. 21st Street., New York, NY 10010.

Nic-Anon.
511 Sir Francis Drake Boulevard, Greenbrae, CA 94904.

Office on Smoking and Health.
Public Information Branch, Park Building. 5600 Fishers Lane, Rockville, MD 20857.

Pamphlets

Al-Anon. *Al-Anon Is for Adult Children of Alcoholics.* 1987.

American Council on Alcoholism. *The Most Frequently Asked Questions about Drinking and Pregnancy.* 1988.

Johnson Institute. *Alcoholism: A Treatable Disease.* 20 pp.

National Clearinghouse for Alcohol and Drug Information. *Alcohol and the Body.* 1988. *Facts about Alcohol.* 1988.

National Institute on Drug Abuse. *Cocaine/Crack: The Big Lie.* 1989. 9 pp. *When Cocaine Affects Someone You Love.* 1989. 11 pp.

Additional Reading

Alcoholics Anonymous. *Twelve Steps and Twelve Traditions.* New York: Alcoholics Anonymous, 1953.

Barringer, F. "Youthful Drinking Persists: With Teens and Alcohol, It's Just Say When." *New York Times* (June 23, 1991): Section 4.

Baum, Joanne. *One Step Over the Line: A Non-Nonsense Guide to Recognizing and Treating Cocaine Dependency.* New York: Harper & Row, 1985.

Fisher, Edwin B., Jr., et al. "Smoking and Smoking Cessation." *American Review of Respiratory Disease* (1990): 702-20.

Gold, Mark. *800-COCAINE.* New York: Bantam Books, 1984.

———. *The Facts about Drugs and Alcohol.* New York: Bantam Books, 1987.

Goodwin, Donald W. *Is Alcoholism Hereditary?* New York: Ballantine, 1988.

Gordis, Enoch, et al. "Finding the Gene(s) for Alcoholism." *JAMA* (April 18, 1990): 2094-95.

Hannan, Deborah J., and Alan G. Adler. "Crack Abuse: Do You Know Enough About It?" *Postgraduate Medicine* (July 1990): 141-43, 146-47.

Jeanne, E. *The Twelve Steps for Tobacco Users.* Center City, MN: Hazelden, 1984.

McGinely, Laurie. "Zeroing In on Cure for Cocaine Addiction." *Wall Street Journal.* (January 6, 1997).

Mumey, Jack. *The Joy of Being Sober.* Chicago, IL: Contemporary Books, 1984.

Pike, Ronald F. "Cocaine Withdrawal: An Effective Three-Drug Regimen." *Postgraduate Medicine* (March 1989): 115-16,121.

Rogers, Jacqueline. *You Can Stop Smoking.* New York: Pocket Books, 1987.

Weiss, Roger D. *Cocaine.* Washington, D.C.: American Psychiatric Press, 1987.

Wolf, Phillip A., et al. "Cigarette Smoking as a Risk Factor for Stroke." *JAMA* (February 19, 1988): 1025-29.

Chapter 11

MENTAL HEALTH DISORDERS

Everyone periodically experiences emotional stress, and most people develop ways to cope successfully with these episodes. Some people, however, cannot control their own thoughts, moods, fears, or emotional reactions to stressful life experiences. These people suffer from a variety of mental health disorders, each of which is distinguished by unique symptoms. This chapter discusses causes of, and holistic treatments for, the most common of these disorders, including anxiety, depression, panic disorders and phobias, schizophrenia, compulsive disorders, and insomnia.

Early diagnosis and treatment of mental disorders can help many people return to fulfilling and productive lives. People seeking guidance from a mental health professional should ask the therapist about his or her educational training, professional licenses, areas of specialty (some offer only marriage and family counseling, others work only with children), and approach to therapy before starting treatment. The costs and length of therapy programs vary, and should be discussed with the therapist before counseling begins.

Anxiety

A fashion model is so frightened of performing in front of an audience that she cancels a lucrative contract. A famous professional football player is haunted by a fear of snakes. A biologist refuses a prestigious award because of the overwhelming anxiety he feels in any group. A popular singer becomes paralyzed with terror before every performance. These people all suffer from

Symptoms of Anxiety

- Excessive unrealistic worries. Typically these worries are widespread, not just focused on one or two issues, and may persist for months.

- Physical tensions, which manifest as twitching or trembling, restlessness, or fatigue. The body shows signs of the "fight or flight" reaction: clammy hands; racing heartbeat or palpitations; shortness of breath or a sense of being smothered; dizziness or lightheadedness; stomach troubles such as nausea or diarrhea; hot flashes or chills; trouble swallowing.

- Edginess, over-vigilance, as though dreading something that is about to happen; easily irritated; trouble sleeping.

anxiety, a state of apprehension and psychic tension which is common in many mental disorders.

Anxiety takes many forms, the best known of which are generalized anxiety, phobias, post-traumatic stress, and panic attacks. Like physical pain, anxiety often functions as a warning sign that precedes some action. Everyone suffers from anxiety, and most people relieve their anxiety by taking rational, productive steps to diminish their worry. It's only when anxiety becomes chronic and prevents productive problem-solving, that problems arise. What sets anxiety problems apart from ordinary worries are their intensity and persistence.

People who suffer prolonged anxiety attacks often have histories of early loss or extreme stress. Physical factors such as anemia, diabetes, menopause, premenstrual syndrome, thyroid disorders, low blood sugars (hypoglycemia), pulmonary disease, endocrine tumors, and various heart problems may all contribute to feelings of anxiety. Drugs such as cocaine, amphetamines, diet pills, and caffeine can also contribute to anxiety.

Traditional Treatments for Anxiety

Few primary care doctors treat serious anxiety problems. Most refer patients to psychiatrists, psychologists, clinical social workers, or other mental health therapists.

Psychotherapy. Psychotherapy focuses on examining the underlying issues that trigger the anxiety. It explores possible unconscious meanings behind panic attacks. It's especially helpful for anxieties caused by losses or post-traumatic stress. In the latter, a key element involves retelling the traumatic events and coming to terms with the stress they cause. Some psychotherapists offer specialized group sessions for people suffering from particular anxiety problems. Group therapy is generally less expensive than individual therapy, and group participants can provide support and feedback and share coping strategies.

Cognitive Therapy. Cognitive therapy helps eliminate feelings of vulnerability and apprehension by correcting faulty thoughts and reasoning. People often view the problems in their lives inaccurately or distort the facts. For example, some people "overgeneralize"–that is, if one thing goes wrong, they decide everything in their life is wrong. Others engage in "all or nothing thinking." For instance, the idea that if they're not the best, they must be the worst. Or they "jump to conclusions," which can be negative and destructive.

Self-Help Therapies for Anxiety

- Cut out caffeine. It is a major, often overlooked, contributor to anxiety. In fact, in high doses, caffeine produces caffeinism, with symptoms identical to those of serious anxiety problems.

- Get adequate rest and exercise. Any exercise helps, although aerobic exercise works best. Aerobic exercise releases endorphins, the body's natural pain and anxiety-relieving chemicals. If you already exercise regularly, increase the frequency and duration of your workouts. If not, and you're not physically limited by a chronic illness or disability, start by taking a brisk 20-minute walk, swim, or bike ride three times a week. After a few weeks, most people notice new feelings of clear-headedness and energy, with decreased tension and anxiety.

- Breathing. One of the most common symptoms of anxiety attacks is hyperventilation, or very rapid breathing. Hyperventilation affects the flow of oxygen and blood to the brain and can cause dizziness and confusion. Controlled breathing and relaxation training, involving the tensing and relaxing of various muscle groups, and biofeedback are all very helpful.

- Meditation, visualization, music therapy, and progressive relaxation can help you release tension and relieve anxiety.

- Talk to a friend or family member. Talking things out with someone you know well can defuse anxiety and reorder fragmented emotions.

- Journal writing. Some people find solace writing down their anxious thoughts and feelings. Instead of simply focusing on how bad you feel, think about possible causes and what you might reasonably do about them.

- Modeling. In an anxiety-provoking situation, act as someone you admire would act.

Participating in therapy or group support sessions can help people identify how their chronic anxiety prevents them from taking effective actions in their lives. Both peer- and professionally-led groups can help people with specific anxiety problems.

Behavioral Therapy. Behavioral therapy focuses on strategies that alter the undesired behavior. It's a particularly effective treatment for phobias. The specific approach is desensitization, whereby the person is gradually exposed to the dreaded object or situation and trained to react without anxiety. For example, a person who is afraid of flying may first receive instruction about the principles of flying, sit in an airport waiting area, then on a parked airplane, then on a plane that taxis without taking off, and finally, on a plane that goes up for a short flight.

Costs of Depression

According to the U.S. Department of Health and Human Services, nearly one in 20 Americans (more than 11 million people) suffers from depression in a given year, and for nearly two-thirds it goes undiagnosed and untreated. The annual cost of depression in America is an estimated $43.7 billion, including suicide, days lost from work, and productivity impairment on the job from poor concentration and memory, indecisiveness, apathy, and a lack of self-confidence. Dr. Frederick Goodwin, the director of the National Institute of Mental Health, stated in the December 3, 1993 edition of *The New York Times* that among major diseases, clinical depression ranks second only to advanced coronary heart disease in the total number of days patients spend in the hospital or disabled at home.

Medication. Psychiatrists may prescribe such mood-altering drugs as imipramine, phenelzine, buspirone, and alprazolam, particularly for agoraphobia and severe anxiety attacks. If you and your doctor opt for drug therapy, you should discuss the potential side effects, including the possibility of addiction, among others.

Depression

Many life events can cause depression and, in fact, transitory feelings of sadness or discouragement are perfectly normal, especially during difficult times. Ordinarily, most people are able to "snap out" of a temporary depression within several weeks. People who cannot boost their spirits, however, experience a continuous cycle of depression in which they think increasingly negative thoughts. They often withdraw from their friends (social withdrawal) and lose interest in activities that once brought them pleasure. This withdrawal reinforces their feelings of worthlessness, helplessness, gloom, and futility. Many depressed people are also afflicted with vague physical symptoms or complaints such as stomach aches or joint pain. Untreated, the disorder normally lasts six months or longer.

Three types of depression have been identified by the National Institute of Mental Health in its 1989 publication *Plain Talk about Depression*. People with major depression are defined as those who have difficulty working, sleeping, eating, or enjoying once pleasurable activities. This form of depression is episodic, and usually occurs only once, twice, or several times in a lifetime. Dysthymia is a less severe type of depression and involves long-term chronic symptoms that do not disable a person from working, but nevertheless prevents them from feeling good about themselves or their life. The third type of depression is now called bipolar disorder (formerly known as manic depression). Bipolar disorders involve cycles of depression (lows) followed by elation (mania). The mood switches are often quite dramatic and rapid–and a person's judgment and thinking abilities may become irresponsible. This is the most serious form of depression and is often a chronic, recurring condition. Major depressive disorders are not caused by a single factor. They are instead caused by a combination of biochemical, genetic, or psychological factors. Certain life conditions, such as extreme stress or grief, may trigger a natural psychological or biological tendency toward depression. In some people, depression occurs even when life is going well.

The three major forms of conventional treatment for depression are anti-depressant medicine (which corrects brain chemistry imbalances), psychotherapy (which is most helpful for those whose personality and life experiences are the main causes of their illness), and a combination of anti-depressant medicine and psychotherapy. There are now more than 20 anti-depressants currently available, the most popular of which–Prozac–is already prescribed to more than five million Americans.

It is now thought that a disruption in the normal interplay between certain chemicals in brain cells and the neurotransmitters (natural substances that facilitate the passage of impulses from one nerve cell to another) plays an important role in the onset of depression. Of the 100 neurotransmitters scientists have thus far identified, two of them–norepinephrine and serotonin–appear to be most closely tied to depression. Depression also appears to be partly genetic, and scientists hope that once they identify the genes that are associated with depression, they can design more effective therapies to treat it.

Psychological traumas such as the loss of a parent during childhood, chronic stress, rejections, and failures can also contribute to depression. People with certain types of personalities–those with low self-esteem or those who tend to be dependent on others, for example–are also more vulnerable to depression.

Medical problems can trigger depression in some people. Persons who suffer strokes, thyroid disorders, hepatitis, viral pneumonia, or cancer, for example, are more likely to become depressed. Specific vitamin and mineral deficiencies may also trigger depression in some people. Medications, including barbiturates, tranquilizers, drugs for heart problems, blood pressure medications, pain killers, arthritis drugs and even some antibi-

Symptoms of Depression

According to the American Psychiatric Association (APA), if a person has five of these symptoms, she is diagnosed as depressed; if she has four, she is likely to be suffering from depression. The APA advises that people who continue to experience these symptoms for at least one month seek professional help.

- Poor appetite with weight loss, or increased appetite with weight gain.
- Insomnia.
- Physical hyperactivity or inactivity.
- Loss of interest or pleasure in usual activities, or a decrease in sexual drive.
- Loss of energy and feelings of fatigue.
- Feelings of worthlessness, self-reproach, or inappropriate guilt.
- Diminished ability to think or concentrate.
- Recurrent thoughts of death or suicide.

otics, have been linked to depression, as has chronic alcohol use, according to an article in the November 1990 issue of *The Johns Hopkins Medical Letter: Health After 50* entitled "Depression: Lifting the Cloud."

Depression in the Elderly

Cerebral circulation gradually declines as people get older, which can cause symptoms of depression and mental confusion in the elderly. This is often complicated by the fact that elderly people tend to exercise less and may not be able to maintain a healthy diet of natural, unprocessed foods. As a result, they become more susceptible to the adverse psychological side effects of any medications they may be taking for such conditions as high blood pressure, cancer, or arthritis. Their low moods of depression are sometimes misdiagnosed as Alzheimer's disease or senility and, as a result, appropriate therapy is not sought or provided. For older adults who feel depressed (and for people who have older relatives who are acting depressed), it is advisable to consult a doctor who may want to re-evaluate the medications they may be taking.

Holistic Treatments for Depression

Depression is one of the most treatable mental disorders, and between 80 and 90% of all depressed people respond to treatment, according to the National Institute of Mental Health. The holistic approach to treating depression is to first determine what nutritional, environmental, social, and psychological factors may be related to the depressive cycle. A complete medical examination is usually given to help identify the overall health of clients, whether they are suffering from illnesses such as hypothyroidism or hypertension that can bring on depression, or whether they are taking any medications that may contribute to their condition. The evaluation should also include a psychiatric history to outline a patient's emotional background, and a medical examination to uncover changes in mood, thoughts, patterns of speech, and memory that are symptomatic of depression.

Nutritional Therapies. Nutritional therapies may help some individuals because unbalanced diets, food sensitivities, nutrient deficiencies, and food allergies have all been linked to depression. Many patients who complain of depression, according to Dr. Harvey Ross, an orthomolecular psychiatrist in Los Angeles quoted in *Alternative Medicine: The Definitive Guide,* also have hypoglycemia, or an excess of sugar in their blood. Hypoglycemia may "be the sole cause of their depression." The same patients may also experience low energy, irritability, or suffer from attacks of anxiety or fear, sometimes to the point of developing phobias.

Dr. Ross suggests that depressed people who think they might be hypoglycemic start an individualized diet plan which eliminates simple sugars. He recommends a high-protein, low-carbohydrate diet. In addition to three meals daily, he advises patients to eat smaller snacks every two hours between meals until bedtime. After four months on this diet, Dr. Ross recommends that people suffering from depression begin a maintenance diet that avoids processed foods and sugars and adds no more than three servings of fruit a day.

Leon Chaitow, author of *The Stress Protection Plan*, suggests that one common cause of depression is the excessive use of aspartame, the artificial sweetener widely used in diet colas and foods. He claims that aspartame can cause an allergic or food sensitivity which leads to depression. Chaitow adds that because of the documented link between artificial food colors, flavors, and preservatives and depression, many European countries now officially prohibit their use in common foods.

James Balch and Phyllis Balch stress in *Prescription for Nutritional Healing* that patients suffering from depression, especially bipolar disorder (manic depression), should follow a dietary plan which consists of vegetables, fruits, nut, seeds, beans, and legumes. Foods that contain sugar or its byproducts should be avoided, along with alcohol, soda, caffeine, and dairy products. All foods which contain nitrates such as additives or food colorings, as well as processed foods, should also be eliminated.

Vitamin and Mineral Therapies. A substantial amount of research has shown that deficiencies in vitamins B_{12} (thiamine), B_6, niacin (B_3), folic acid, and vitamin C may be specifically linked to depression. Several mineral deficiencies, including magnesium and zinc, may also contribute to depression. As a result, some holistic physicians and nutritionists now believe that sufferers of depression may benefit from vitamin, mineral, and amino acid supplements. However, vitamin and mineral supplements should always be supervised by a physician or holistic health practitioner.

Botanical Therapies. St. John's wort (*Hypericum perforatum*) appears to effectively relieve minor depression. Researchers have discovered that components in St John's wort alter brain chemistry in a way that improves mood. In one clinical study of 15 women with depression, cited by Michael Murray and Joseph Pizzorno in *Encyclopedia of Natural Medicine*, a standardized extract of St. John's wort significantly reduced symptoms of anxiety, depression, and feelings of worthlessness. The extract also greatly improves the quality of sleep because it effectively relieves both insomnia and hypersomnia (excessive sleep). Additionally, ginkgo biloba extract has been effective in treating insufficient blood and oxygen supply in the brain associated with common symptoms of depression.

Increasing serotonin levels can also help reduce the symptoms of manic depression. Dr. Hugh Riodin, director of the Center for the Improvement of Human Functioning International, suggests in *Alternative Medicine: The Definitive Guide* that people who experience recurring cycles of depression may benefit from drinking walnut tea, which is high in serotonin, an amino acid believed to elevate moods.

Homeopathic Therapies. According to Dana Ullman in *Discovering Homeopathy*, homeopaths treat both depression and anxiety disorders using a holistic approach. A homeopath will prescribe individually tailored medicines. When appropriate, they provide basic information on nutrition, exercise, stress management, and lifestyle changes. The may also provide psychological counseling. Because homeopaths view human nature as basically creative, they attempt to help the "bodymind adapt to and deal creatively with internal and external stresses."

Exercise. Exercise is extremely important in preventing and treating depression. A 1988 study by C. E. Ross and D. Hayes, summarized by Murray and Pizzorno, found that regular exercise reduces stressful emotions associated with depression, reduces muscle tension and anxiety levels, and increases self-confidence and emotional stability. This effect is due to enhanced cerebral circulation resulting from general cardiovascular improvement. As a result, many psychiatrists now encourage their patients to take up moderate aerobic exercises such as jogging. Regular exercise not only alleviates depression, but also improves concentration, memory, creativity, and mental agility. Physicians normally advise depressed patients to exercise three times a week at a level which elevates their heart rates by 50%.

Massage Therapy Massage therapy has been used to treat depression resulting from trauma. The Touch Research Institute (TRI) at the University of Miami Medical School studied the effect of massage on patients whose depression arose from trauma. The researchers, according to an article by Meredith Ruch in the November/December 1993 issue of *Natural Health,* found that depressed patients had consistently lower levels of stress-related hormones–specifically cortisol and norepinephrine–and were more alert, less restless, and better able to sleep after a 30-minute massage.

Deep Breathing Exercises. Dr. Riodan, director of the Center for the Improvement of Human Functioning International, also uses deep breathing exercises to prevent the depressive stage of bipolar disorder. He claims that many studies show that a nondepressed person breathes in six times the amount of air as a depressed person. Deep breathing exercises increase oxygen levels in the brain and appear to elevate moods.

Depression in Children

The causes of depression in children are complex. Some may inherit a biological pre-disposition, and depressed children often live with a depressed parent, usually their mother. Negative life events, such as abuse, lack of secure relationships, parental divorce, a close relative's death, or a major financial setback for the family can lead to deep feelings of helplessness and hopelessness in the child.

Preschoolers who are depressed may have trouble separating from their parents, appear hyperactive, and show learning dis-abilities. In the elementary grades depressed children commonly complain about a host of physical and emotional hurts. They may be self-deprecating or overly sensitive, and have trouble forming relationships with their peers. Some may have difficulty getting up in the morning and plead to stay home from school; at night they may become obstinate. Depressed children may also evidence a loss of appetite or binge eat. Some may have hal-lucinations or obsessions about death, or experience feelings of guilt, hopelessness, failure, humiliation, or worthlessness.

Psychotherapy Treatments for Childhood Depression

It was once thought that childhood and adult depression were unrelated—that a child who was regularly depressed would not nec-essarily become depressed as an adult. However, a recent study conducted by Dr. Maria Kovacs, a psychologist at Western Psychiatric Institute and Clinic in Pittsburgh, and reported in the January 11, 1994 issue of *The New York Times,* found that 75% of chil-dren between the ages of eight and 13 who were depressed had recurrences of depression in their adult years. According to Dr. Kovacs, one of the symptoms of depression in children is their inability or unwillingness to talk about their sadness. They are typically irritable, impatient, cranky, and angry, especially towards their parents.

The best therapy for children suffering from depression usually involves helping them learn new, more positive ways of react-ing to their difficulties. Dr. Gregory Clark, a psychologist at Oregon Health Sciences University, found that 25% of students in one high school had low-level depression. Seventy-five students subsequently attended eight-weeks of after-school classes in which they learned to change the thinking patterns that lead to depression, improve their skills in making friends and reducing conflict with their parents, and find enjoyable social activi-ties. By the end of the sessions, 55% had recovered from their mild depression (about twice as many as in a comparison group that did not attend the classes)–and of those, only 14% later became seriously depressed.

Group therapy also appears to be success-ful in preventing children from becoming depressed. One experiment led by Dr. Martin Seligman of the University of Pennsylvania proved that it is possible to prevent the emer-gence of depression in children who are not yet depressed but who are at risk. In the pro-gram, 69 children from 10-13 years old met in small groups once a week for 12 weeks in special afternoon classes. They learned to handle interpersonal disputes, understand moods such as anxiety, sadness, and anger and how to control them, and alter their pessimistic beliefs which lead to depression. A year later, 44% of the children who did not take the classes developed depression, compared with only 22% of the children who attended the classes.

Panic Disorders and Phobias

Margie, a 23-year-old California woman, first experienced a panic attack when she was 19. She'd gone off to college at a large state university, her first venture away from the small town where she grew up. Suddenly she began experiencing attacks of shaking, heart beatings, and fainting. Two or three times a week at the most unpredictable times she would suddenly find herself suffering an attack, sometimes during class. Her doctor diagnosed her as suffering from panic attacks.

Panic attack sufferers like Margie are often convinced that they're having a heart attack. A majority of patients to hospital emergency rooms for heart attacks are actually found to be suffering panic attacks. Since some symptoms resemble heart attacks–for instance, chest pain and heart palpitation–the fear of dying is not unreasonable. Because many of the symptoms of panic attacks mimic medical problems (or at least seem to) the person who suffers from them may spend months or years fruitlessly seeking a medical diagnosis for what is actually a psychological problem.

Everyone is occasionally frightened by something, and most people learn to overcome common fears or learn to live with them. Some people, however, suffer from intense fears (phobias) or panic disorders which they cannot control, and which can seriously disrupt their lives. According to the National Institute of Mental Health pamphlet *Useful Information on Phobias and Panic*, panic disorders afflict approximately three million Americans. Victims usually report

Therapies for Childhood Depression

Some doctors prefer to try mild antidepressant medications for several weeks, particularly if the child is very depressed or has expressed suicidal wishes. In most cases, psychotherapy and family therapy are usually necessary. A child who is actively suicidal may require temporary hospitalization.

- Individual or family pyschotherapy is the primary treatment for adolescent depression.
- Family therapy is especially helpful if other family members also suffer from depression.
- Interpersonal therapy, which has proven effective in adults, also holds promise for children by helping them express feelings and communicate better with others, particularly their parents. Generally, the earlier in life depression develops, the more severe its course over a lifetime. The prognosis is almost always better if it's recognized and treated quickly.

experiencing intense, overwhelming terror for no apparent reason. The fear is accompanied by sweating, heart palpitations, hot or cold flashes, trembling, choking, shortness of breath, chest discomforts, and dizziness. People suffering such an attack for the first time often rush to a hospital, convinced that they are having a heart attack.

People who suffer from simple phobias have fears of specific objects or situations. Common examples include fear of heights (acrophobia), fear of open spaces (agoraphobia), fear of enclosed spaces (claustrophobia), fear of dirt and germs (misophobia), fear of snakes (ophediophobia), and fear of animals (zoophobia). Simple phobias, especially animal phobias, are common in children, but they are known to occur at all ages. The recognition by most phobics that their fears are unreasonable does not make them feel any less anxious, although their phobias normally do not interfere with daily life.

People with social phobias are intensely afraid of being watched and judged by others and manifests as shyness or avoidance of social situations such as public speaking, eating in public, or going to parties. Social phobias usually begin between the ages of 15 and 20 and, if left untreated, continue through much of a person's life. Sufferers may have difficulty breathing in such situations, or fail to remember what to say or how to act appropriately.

Scientists do not agree on what causes panic disorders. They appear to run in families, which suggests the disorder is partly genetic in origin. Psychotherapists believe that disordered thinking in some people produces an anxiety level that can trigger panic attacks. Biochemical theories point to possible physical defects in a person's autonomic nervous system. General hypersensitivity in the nervous system, for example, can increase arousal. Chemical imbalances created by caffeine, alcohol, or other agents can also trigger these symptoms.

Treatment for Panic Disorders and Phobias

Psychotherapy. Psychotherapy helps people think and act appropriately by making the feared object or situation less threatening through group support and desensitization. Group therapy, with or without individual therapy, is valuable for those with low self-esteem because criticism or guidance offered by group members may be easier to accept

than from a therapist. Family members and friends can play an important role in the treatment process if they provide support, assistance and encouragement.

Homeopathic Therapies. Dana Ullman describes two psychotherapeutic treatments which he considers homeopathic in their approach to treating phobias: "paradoxical intention" and "therapeutic double-blind." Both approaches aim at dislodging the symptoms and setting the natural healing process of the brain in motion. The homeopathic therapist encourages the patient to pretend to experience the problematic emotional state. If the patient has a phobia of snakes, for example, the therapist asks her to pretend to see a snake and to pretend to feel afraid. Ullman states that this method is considered effective if the client is unable to produce the fear at will and afterwards, as a result, is less susceptible to having the phobia at other times.

Biofeedback and Relaxation. Many people who suffer from anxiety, panic attacks, and phobias show patterns of hyperventilation and shallow breathing. Dr. Leon Chaitow notes in his book *The Stress Protection Plan* that these people often report a sense of oppressive pressure on the chest and an inability to take a full breath. According to Chaitow, biofeedback, relaxation exercises such as yoga, meditation, or tai chi, and visualizations can help stimulate the relaxation response. Once sufferers are relaxed, they can retrain their breathing habits, decrease their hyperventilation, and stimulate a more positive mental state. These techniques, Chaitow relates, are being widely used in Europe to treat chronic phobias and anxiety.

Schizophrenia

The National Institute of Mental Health in its pamphlet entitled *Schizophrenia:*

Questions and Answers estimates that at least two million Americans suffer from the disabling symptoms of schizophrenia. The economic costs of the disease, in terms of patient care and lost productivity, are now estimated to run as high as $20 billion a year.

Schizophrenia, according to the NIMH, can be one psychotic disorder or many different disorders. To be psychotic means to be out of touch with reality, or unable to separate real from unreal experiences. There are several degrees of schizophrenia, ranging from mild schizophrenic disorder (paranoia) to severe chronic, deteriorating schizophrenia. People with mild schizophrenia have infrequent psychotic episodes and can lead relatively normal lives during the interim periods. Chronic schizophrenics, on the other hand, tend to suffer from prolonged depression, personality problems, fatigue, mental derangement, or hallucinations. They usually cannot lead normal lives and require long-term treatment, which often necessitates institutionalization and controlled medication to alleviate the symptoms. Some schizophrenics suffer from hallucinations or sense things that in reality do not exist, such as hearing voices.

Another group of schizophrenics experiences delusions, or false personal beliefs that are not subject to reason or contradictory evidence. These people feel they are being persecuted, watched, or followed by their neighbors, or they have delusions of grandeur. Another class of schizophrenics suffers from disordered thinking. They may not be able to think clearly, or may experience thoughts which they cannot control. Schizophrenics also sometimes exhibit what is called "inappropriate affect"–that is, they show emotions which are inconsistent with their own speech or thoughts. For example, schizophrenics may say they are being persecuted by demons and then laugh. Some may also exhibit prolonged extremes of elation or depression. In these cases, the National Institute of Mental Health urges physicians to determine whether the patient is schizophrenic or suffering from bipolar disorder.

According to the National Institute of Mental Health's pamphlet *Useful Information on Paranoia*, paranoid schizophrenia is characterized by suspiciousness (or mistrust) that is either highly exaggerated or not warranted at all. Extreme paranoid schizophrenics often experience bizarre delusions or hallucinations. They may claim to hear voices that others cannot hear, or believe that their thoughts are being controlled or broadcast aloud. In contrast, people with milder paranoid disorders may experience delusions of persecution or delusional jealousy, but not hallucinations. These people can usually live a relatively normal existence because, apart from occasional delusions, their thinking remains clear and orderly.

Causes of Schizophrenia. Scientists do not know precisely what causes schizophrenia. It was once thought that dysfunctional family relationships caused the disorder. Recently, genetic scientists have speculated that schizophrenia is hereditary. A study by the National Institute of Mental Health seems to indicate it is not. As related in the March 22, 1990 issue of *The New England Journal of Medicine*, scientists used sophisticated scanning devices to examine the brain structure of 15 pairs of identical twins (one schizophrenic, the other normal) and discovered subtle anatomical differences. In the mentally ill twins, the fluid-filled brain cavities called ventricles were consistently found to be enlarged, indicating that the tissue had either shrunk or developed abnormally. Regions of the brain responsible for thinking, memory, concentration, decision-making, and higher mental abilities were also abnormally smaller in the schizophrenic twins. Since the genetic material of identical twins is identical molecule for molecule, researchers concluded that the development of the illness must be nongenetic. It is not known whether schizophrenia is caused by a virus, chemical exposure to a toxin, or a metabolic defect, although some experts postulate that it could be partially induced by complications during birth or due to a head injury.

Whatever the origin of the disorder, scientists agree that altered brain structure and chemistry play a role in schizophrenia. For this reason, holistic physicians usually give schizophrenic patients a complete physical examination, including laboratory tests, to determine the underlying cause (or causes) of their specific disorder.

Treatment for Schizophrenia

Vitamin and Mineral Therapies. Dr. Abraham Hoffer, president of the Canadian Schizophrenia Foundation, has successfully treated schizophrenics with megavitamins. Writing in a 1993 issue of the *Journal of Orthomolecular Medicine*, he demonstrates that vitamin B_3 (nicotinic acid or nicotinamide) can double the recovery rate of acute schizophrenics. After 10 years of vitamin treatments, 11 of Hoffer's 26 schizophrenic patients are working, two are married and looking after their families, two are single mothers caring for their children with difficulty, and three are managing their own businesses.

The orthomolecular treatment of schizophrenia developed by Hoffer and others appears remarkably more successful than traditional psychiatric treatment. A follow-up study of schizophrenics treated by psychiatrists, for example, reported by E. Johnstone in a 1991 issue of *The British Journal of Psychiatry,* showed that only 5% of schizophrenics treated by psychiatry showed significant recovery. Dr. Hoffer now believes that nutritional and orthomolecular therapies combining nutritious foods, vitamins, minerals,

and amino acids will soon become the standard treatment for schizophrenia.

Dr. William Walsh of the Carl Pfeiffer Treatment Center in Naperville, Illinois, reports in *Alternative Medicine: The Definitive Guide* that schizophrenia may be related to histamine levels in the blood. He has found that schizophrenics with low histamine levels are much easier to treat with nutritional therapies than those with elevated histamine levels. His medical staff gives folate and nutrients which eliminate excess copper and lower histamine levels. Nervousness, depression, and hallucinations often disappear after several months of treatment. Paranoid symptoms, however, often take as long as a year to subside.

For schizophrenic patients with elevated histamine levels, Dr. Walsh's treatments focus on megadoses of calcium which help release excess histamines from body cells. Megadoses of the amino acid methylamine also help eliminate unnecessary histamines. Schizophrenics with high levels of histamines must avoid niacin, folic acid, and green leafy vegetables. In each case, he recommends individual nutritional counseling. Some adult psychotic patients have an excess of copper that may produce a schizophrenic syndrome. Copper excess has been linked to learning and behavioral disorders in children, and Walsh advises that copper levels be decreased in schizophrenic patients.

Botanical Therapies. Dr. Q. Ma reports in the April 1991 issue of the *Chinese Journal of Integrated Traditional & Western Medicine* that Sin Shen Ling (XSL) may prevent relapses of schizophrenia. Thirty Chinese patients suffering from chronic schizophrenia were given a Chinese immunological herbal formula, XSL, rather than neuroleptic medications because these had not proved effective. Sixty-seven percent of the patients

Professional Therapies for Schizophrenia

1. The majority of psychotherapists recommend supportive therapy for both acute and long-term treatment. During the acute phase, behavioral or psychotherapy is usually recommended.

2. During long-term treatment, family and behavioral approaches are often recommended.

3. Acute episodes of schizophrenia usually require hospitalization and treatment with antipsychotic drugs. Most drugs help schizophrenics feel more in control of themselves, organize chaotic thinking, and reduce or eliminate delusions or hallucinations, allowing fuller participation in normal activities. Even those who do not improve significantly on medication usually do worse without it.

4. Clozapine (Clozaril) can help to relieve both positive and negative symptoms in individuals who do not improve with standard antipsychotic medications or who develop intolerable side effects. In one study, 30% of patients who were not helped by other antipsychotics improved with Clozapine.

5. Clinical trials indicate that risperidone (Risperdal), which blocks receptors for serotonin and dopamine, significantly reduces both positive and negative symptoms of schizophrenia, produces fewer side effects than Clozapine, and does not require intensive and expensive weekly blood monitoring.

6. Electroconvulsive therapy (ECT) has been used on schizophrenic individuals who show no improvement after several months of drug therapy and on those with catatonia or depression. Although it relieves depressive symptoms and reverses catatonia, there have been few reports on its long-term effectiveness.

7. The use of other types of medication, including lithium, benzodiazepines, and antidepressants, together with antipsychotics, is currently being studied by investigators around the world.

clinically improved after six weeks of herbal treatment with XSL.

Medications. One promising treatment for schizophrenia is the antipsychotic drug Clozapine, which has been approved by the FDA for nationwide use. Designed only for schizophrenics who fail to respond to the standard antipsychotic drugs, or who suffer from negative side effects such as anxiety or insomnia, Clozapine appears to counteract excess dopamine in the brain which is associated with the disorder's symptoms. Clozapine, however, can cause a potentially fatal condition called agranulocytosis in which the body's ability to produce infection-fighting white blood cells is impaired, as reported by David Perlman in the March 2, 1990 edition of the *San Francisco Chronicle*. Because of that risk, all doctors prescribing the drug must require patients to undergo a white blood cell count every week while taking the medication so that the medication

Examples of Compulsive Disorders

- Excessive hand washing. Someone who washes his hands 100 times a day until they are red and raw.
- Checking and rechecking. Someone who locks and relocks the door each day for 30 minutes before leaving the house.
- Collecting. Someone who stores every newspaper in the garage.
- Repetition. A student who must tap the door frame of every classroom before entering.
- Arranging. Someone who spends hours alphabetizing every item in the kitchen cabinets, or have all clothing organized by color.

can be stopped if white blood cell levels drop dangerously low.

Compulsive Disorders

Diane Sands, 42, suffers from a compulsive disorder. As a child, while doing her homework, she often erased her writing over and over, until there were holes in the paper from her trying to make it perfect. As she grew up, Diane developed other compulsions that she learned to hide. Finally, at the age of 35, Diane consulted a behavior therapist who helped her overcome her compulsions.

For a long time, psychiatrists thought compulsive disorders like Diane's were rare conditions that affected only about one out of 10,000 people. But a large survey in the 1980s revealed that it's much more common—1-2% of the American population has the disorder.

People express their obsessive-compulsive disorders in different ways. Some fill their garages with food because they fear running out of food. Others have such strong fears of contamination that they can't ride subways or buses or sit among crowds.

Compulsive disorders should not be confused with common quirks that many people have, such as a husband who insists on stacking the dishwasher his way every time. Compulsions are far more severe than quirks, sometimes causing people to lose their jobs or alienate loved ones. Their repetitive behavior is often the expression of anxiety over an underlying obsession. The obsession itself might be a fleeting mental image of a violent scene, or a sexual violation. Some women, for example, have an image of killing their young children. Others can't pick up a kitchen knife because they're afraid they might stab something. They never do; nevertheless, they're tormented by the idea that they might, and their anxiety leads them to perform repetitive rituals as a way to relieve stress and inhibit their underlying impulse. Underneath their anxiety is the fear that if they don't do this, something terrible could happen to somebody they love or upset their lives.

People with compulsions are helped by psychotherapy, which helps the patient identify the fears underlying the behavior, such as the fear of not being good enough. Many compulsives are also helped with either behavior therapy or medication. Systematic desensitization techniques, utilizing deep muscle relaxation and Transcendental Meditation, are also effective during the treatment phase.

Insomnia

Sleep patterns vary widely among individuals, and although insomnia is not a psychotic disorder like schizophrenia, it has become a chronic mental health problem for an increasing number of Americans. Dr. Sanford Auerback, director of the Sleep Disorders Center at Boston University, estimates in the July/August 1993 issue of *Natural Health* that as many as 15-17% of Americans suffer from chronic, untreated sleep disorders such as insomnia. A pamphlet compiled by the American Sleep Disorders Association entitled *How Much Sleep Do You Need?* claims that accidents and loss of productivity due to sleep deprivation cost the U.S. $50 billion per year. As a result of these disturbing trends, President Clinton has signed legislation creating a new National Center for Sleep Disorders at the National Institutes of Health.

Most researchers now think that few people can subsist regularly on less than seven hours a night–the minimum amount of sleep needed to promote continuous daytime alertness. By this definition, many Americans are sleep deprived. Coffee, tea, chocolate, soft drinks, and other foods or drugs containing caffeine are believed to be important factors that prevent people from obtaining an adequate amount of sleep. Nicotine is also a stimulant that prevents normal sleeping behavior.

Treatments for Insomnia

Botanical Therapies. Several plants have sedative effects, including passion flower (*Passiflora incarnata*), hops (*Humulus lupulus*), skullcap (*Scutellarea latriflora*), chamomile (*Matricaria chamomilla*), and valerian (*Valeriana officinalis*). In a large double-blind study involving 128 subjects, reported in a 1992 issue of *Psychopharmacology,* valerian root improved the patients' subjective ratings for sleep quality and sleep latency (the time required to get to sleep), and did not leave them feeling lethargic the following morning.

Homeopathic Therapies. Dr. Stephen Cummings and Dana Ullman in *Everybody's Guide to Homeopathic Medicine* suggest that homeopathic formulas can be very helpful for occasional insomnia, including *Nux vomica, Coffea Pulsatilla, Passiflora, Arnica,* and *Chamomilla.* They advise patients with recurrent or chronic insomnia to seek professional homeopathic care.

Hormone Therapy. Melatonin is a hormone produced by the pineal gland in the brain which regulates the body clock and induces sleep. As reported in the April 1994 issue of *Your Health*, a synthetic version of melatonin has been successfully used to treat insomnia. Neuroscientist Richard Wurtman of the Massachusetts Institute of Technology gave subjects either melatonin or an inert placebo substance, placed them in a dark room at midday, and told them to close their eyes for 30 minutes. In the stressful environment of having to sleep on demand, it took the volunteers with the placebo 25 minutes to fall asleep. Yet those who took melatonin were able to fall asleep within five to six minutes. Judith Vaitukaitis of the National Center for Research Resources is quoted in the article as suggesting that melatonin may be a natural, nonaddictive agent that could improve sleep for millions of Americans.

Sleep Therapy. Sleep therapy may be able to help insomniacs sleep better. An experimental study at the Medical College of Virginia, reported in the September/October issue of *Natural Health,* placed 24 adults (with an average age of 67) who had suffered from insomnia for an average of 13 years on an eight-week program of sleep therapy. Before, during, and after the study, participants kept a sleep diary in which they recorded their sleep patterns and their emotional reactions to sleep. During the eight-week program, researchers instructed participants to use their beds only for sleep and sex, and to forego reading, watching television, or eating while in bed. After the eight weeks, more than half of the participants reported that they were sleeping better with fewer awakenings. Although almost 50% had used sleeping pills before the study, none resumed these medications in the year following therapy.

Exercise. When the body is exercised, it becomes naturally fatigued and people who exercise regularly find it much easier to fall asleep naturally. H. Kaplan, in his book *Modern Synopsis of Comprehensive Textbook of Psychiatry*, cites several studies which indicate that regular aerobic exercise helps promote healthy sleeping patterns. However, exercise should not be performed just before bedtime. It should be of moderate intensity and last a minimum of 20 minutes at the target heart rate.

Summary

Like all other body organs, the human brain is composed of molecules and cells whose functioning is influenced by many different factors. Brain tissues can be affected by injury, infectious disease, inherited genetic errors, chemical toxins, and stressful or tragic events. When, as a result of one or a combination of these factors, the brain becomes biochemically unbalanced, depression, phobias, and psychotic disorders such as schizophrenia can result.

Mental disorders can pose tragic problems for both their sufferers and their families. Fortunately, major advances have been made in noninvasive treatment of these disorders. Scientists have begun to map the brain and identify the specific neurotransmitters that are responsible for emotions and mental disorders such as depression, schizophrenia, anxiety, and panic disorders. This chapter has suggested that holistic therapies such as nutrition, vitamins, minerals, amino acids, hormones, botanical medicines, exercise, and massage, when used in a combination with psychotherapy, behavioral therapy, or cognitive therapy, can help treat psychological disorders. The goal of holistic treatment is to return the patient to natural, total mind/body health as quickly as possible in the least invasive way.

Resources

References

American Psychiatric Association. *Diagnostic and Statistical Manual of Mental Disorders (DSM-IV)*. 4th ed. Washington, D.C.: APA, 1994.

Balch, James F., and Phyllis Balch. *Prescription for Nutritional Healing*. Long Island: Avery Publishing, 1993.

Burns, David. *Feeling Good*. New York: Signet, 1980.

The Burton Goldberg Group. *Alternative Medicine: The Definitive Guide*. Payallup, WA: Future Medicine Publishing, Inc., 1993.

Chaitow, Leon. *The Stress Protection Plan*. San Francisco: Harper, 1992.

"Depression: Lifting the Cloud." *The Johns Hopkins Medical Letter: Health after 50* (November 1990): 4-5.

Freudenheim, Milt. "The Drug Makers Are Listening to Prozac." *The New York Times* (January 9, 1994): 7.

Goleman, Daniel. "Scientists Trace Voices in Schizophrenia." *The New York Times* (September 22, 1993): 7.

———. "Depression Costs Put at $43 Billion." *The New York Times* (December 3, 1993): A9.

———. "Childhood Depression May Herald Adults Ills." *The New York Times* (January 11, 1994): D7.

Hoffer, Abraham. "Chronic Schizophrenic Patients Treated Ten Years or More." *Journal of Orthomolecular Medicine* 8 (1993).

"How Much Sleep Do You Need?" *Natural Health* (July/August 1993): 21.

"How to Get a Better Night's Sleep." *Natural Health* (September/October 1991): 21.

Johnstone, E. "Disabilities and Circumstances of Schizophrenic Patients: A Follow-Up Study." *The British Journal of Psychiatry* 159, 13 (1991): 3-46.

Kaplan, H. *Modern Synopsis of Comprehensive Textbook of Psychiatry*. Baltimore, MD: Williams & Wilkens, 1985.

Lader, M. "Rebound Insomnia and Newer Hypnotics." *Psychopharmacology* 108 (1992): 248-55.

Ma, Q. "Immunological Study of Inefficiency Schizophrenics with Deficiency Syndrome Treated with Xin Shen Ling." *Chinese Journal of Integrated Traditional & Western Medicine* (April 1992).

Margolis, Simeon, and Hamilton Moses III. *The Johns Hopkins Medical Handbook*. New York: Medletter Associates, Inc.,1992.

Mesulam, Marsel. "Schizophrenia and the Brain." *The New England Journal of Medicine* (March 22, 1990): 842-45.

Murray, Michael, and Joseph Pizzorno. *Encyclopedia of Natural Medicine*. Rocklin, CA: Prima Publishing, 1991.

Perlman, David. "New Study, New Drug for Schizophrenia." *San Francisco Chronicle* (March 22, 1990): A17

Posner, M. "Depression among Women Is Widespread, Survey Says." *Reuters* (July 15, 1993).

Rees, Alan, and Charlene Willey. *Personal Health Reporter*. Detroit: Gale Research, 1993.

Ross, E.E., and D. Hayes. "Exercise and Psychological Well-Being in the Community." *American Journal of Epidemiology* 127 (1988): 762-71.

Ruch, Meredith. "Feeling Down? Study Show Massage Can Lift Your Spirits." *Natural Health* (November/December 1993): 48-49.

Tollespson, G. "Recognition and Treatment of Major Depression." *American Family Physician* (November 1990): 655.

U. S. Department of Health and Human Services. *Depression Is a Treatable Illness: A Patient's Guide.* April 1993.

Waldholtz, M. "Study of Fear Shows Emotion Can Alter Wiring of the Brain." *Wall Street Journal* (October 29, 1993).

Wartik, Nancy. "Depression." *American Health* (December 1993): 40-45.

"What Twins Tell Us about Schizophrenia." *U.S. News & World Report* (April 2, 1990): 13-14.

RESOURCES

Organizations

American Psychiatric Association,
1400 K Street N.W., Washington, DC 20005.

Disabled American Veterans,
807 Maine Ave, S.W., Washington DC. 20024.

National Alliance for the Mentally Ill.
1901 North Fort Myer Drive, Suite 500, Arlington, VA 22209.

National Depressive and Manic Depressive Association.
Merchandise Mart, Box 3395, Chicago, IL 60654.

National Foundation of Depressive Illness.
245 Seventh Avenue, 5th Floor, New York, NY 10001.

National Institute of Mental Health.
Parklawn Building 15C-05, 5600 Fishers Lane, Rockville, MD 20857.

National Mental Health Association.
1201 Prince Street, Alexandria, VA 22314-2971.

Phobia Society of America.
P.O. Box 2066, Rockville, MD 20852-2066.

Pamphlets

American Psychiatric Association: *Manic-Depressive Disorder.* 1990. *Let's Talk Facts about Panic Disorder.* 1989.

National Alliance for the Mentallyl Ill: *Mood Disorders: Depression and Manic Depression.* n.d. 12 pp.

National Institute of Mental Health: *Useful Information on Paranoia.* 1989. 10 pp. *Bipolar Disorder: Manic-Depressive Illness.* ADM 89-1009. 1989. *Depressive Disorders: Treatments Bring New Hope.* ADM 89-1491. 1989. 25 pp. *Helpful Facts about Depressive Disorders.* ADM 87-1536. 1987. 8 pp.

Additional Reading

Griest, J. *Anxiety and Its Treatment: Help Is Available.* Washington, DC: American Psychiatric Press, 1986.

Sheehan, D. *Anxiety Disease and How to Overcome It.* New York: Scribner, 1984.

Torrey, Fuller. *Surviving Schizophrenia: A Family Manual.* Revised Edition. New York: Harper & Row, 1987.

Wilson, R. *Don't Panic: Taking Control of Anxiety Attacks.* New York: Harper & Row, 1987.

Chapter 12

COMMON MALE HEALTH PROBLEMS

The most common male health problems involve disorders of the genitourinary system, which includes the bladder, urethra, prostate gland, penis, and testicles. These disorders may encompass infections, weakening of organs, and sexual diseases. For that reason, special attention must be paid to the health of the genitourinary system in order to maintain normal sexual functioning, proper elimination, and sustained immune resistance. This chapter discusses holistic treatments for common male problems, including andropause, low sexual energy and impotence, premature ejaculation, enlarged prostate (benign prostatic hypertrophy), and prostatitis.

Andropause

Although its onset in men is more subtle than in women, male menopause, called andropause, can cause such symptoms as impotence, weakness, stiffness, pain, nervous exhaustion, loss of muscle tone, irritability, and profuse sweating with heat intolerance. According to Ann Louse Gittleman's *Super Nutrition for Men*, these problems will likely disappear with proper holistic therapy.

Diet and Nutrition. Diet and nutrition play a role in increasing physical performance, including sexual performance, and a man's ability to handle stress. Gittleman speculates that adopting a diet of predominantly unprocessed whole foods will have a stabilizing effect on blood sugar, mood swings, attention span, focus and long-term energy. She recommends a 40/30/30 eating program, in which 40% of total calories derive from carbohydrates such as bread and pasta, 30% from natural and unprocessed fats such as

Vital Nutrients for Men

Nutrient	Dose	Action	Food Source
Vitamin A	2,500 IU	Helps maintain testicular tissue.	Liver, yellow fruits & vegetables, fish liver oil and dairy foods
B complex	50 mg (each)	Influences testosterone production.	Brewer's yeast, liver, whole-grain cereals.
Vitamin C	300 mg	Insufficient amounts diminish sex drive as sex gland function decreases or stops.	Citrus fruits, cantaloupe, strawberry, broccoli, tomatoes, green pepper.
Vitamin E	200 IU	Works with selenium as an antioxidant.	Peanuts, cold-pressed oils, eggs, organ meats, wheat germ, desiccated liver sweet potatoes, leafy vegetables.
Selenium	200 mcg	Antioxidant mineral needed to offset free radical damage to cells and preserve oxygen. Aids fertility.	Tuna, butter, wheat germ, Brazil nuts, brewer's yeast, whole grains, sesame seeds.
Manganese	5 mg	Deficient in impotent men.	Whole-grain cereals, nuts, seeds.
Zinc	25 mg	Vital to testosterone	Organ meats, brewer's yeast, soybeans, mushrooms, herring, eggs, wheat germ, meats.
Phosphorous		Important for sex drive.	Chutney, hot sauces, brewer's yeast, curry, pumpkin, squash, sunflower seeds.

butter and olive oil, and 30% from protein such as turkey, fish, and lean beef.

Consuming whole foods, especially essential fatty acids (EFAs), will help the body produce hormone-like substances called prostaglandins that regulate many physiological functions, including sexual response. An insufficient supply of prostaglandins–due to lack of the omega-6 EFAs, gamma linolenic acid (GLA)–can produce such sexual dysfunctions as insufficient ejaculation and infertility.

Vitamins and Minerals. Gittleman notes that vitamin B_6, along with evening primrose oil, spirulina, and borage oil have been clinically effective in treating impotency, lack of libido, and premature ejaculation. Vitamin E and zinc, she adds, also help nourish the sexual glands, vitamins A, C, and B_2 indirectly increase potency by stimulating the adrenal glands. Iodine, vitamin B_1, and pantothenic acid help recharge the thyroid glands, which is beneficial in some cases.

Impotence

As reported by Lawrence Altman in the December 22, 1993 edition of *The New York Times*, the largest study of impotence since the Kinsey report more than 40 years ago suggests that 19 million men from 40-70 years of age in the U.S. may either be impotent or have experienced the problem. That is almost double the current estimate of 10 million, according to the study's senior author, Dr. John McKinlay, who directs the New England Research Institute in Watertown, Massachusetts.

The frequency of impotence steadily increased with age in the study. At the age of 40, 5% of respondents reported complete impotence. By age 70, the prevalence of complete impotence tripled to 15%.

Impotence (technically called male erectile dysfunction), or the inability to sustain an erection, once was linked solely to emotional causes or a natural decline in sexual energy due to aging. However, according to McKinlay, it is now thought that the condition has many other causes as well, including medical conditions such as heart disease, diabetes and high blood pressure, smoking, alcohol consumption, lack of exercise, depression, and repression of anger.

For example, McKinlay notes that men who take drugs for high blood pressure have experienced varying degrees of impotence. However, two classes of antihypertensive drugs are less likely to cause this condition. One group is known as ACE inhibitors, including captopril (Capoten), enalapril (Vasotec), and lisinopril (Prinivil, Zestril). The other group, called calcium channel blockers, includes diltiazem (Cardizem), nacardipine (Cardene), nifedipine (Procardia), and verapamil (Calan, Isoptin).

Other factors contributing to impotence include neurological disorders from injury or brain disease, high blood cholesterol, or low levels of the male hormone testosterone. In addition, it can result from using heroin and other recreational drugs. About 25% of impotence cases are a result of taking medications for other conditions. More often, however, impotence problems are caused by a fear of sexual performance (including anxiety about the ability to get an erection), or the wish not to be sexually intimate with a particular partner.

Treatments for Impotence

Each case of impotence varies with the individual's environment, age, sexual history, diet, and level of exercise. An holistic physician may prescribe a low fatty acid diet, aerobic exercise, and vitamin, mineral and botanical supplements to try and correct the condition. Current psychological treatments include sensate focus exercises; cognitive-behavioral therapy relaxation training; hypnosis and guide imagery; and group therapies. Specific techniques, such as directed self-stimulation, the stop-start and squeeze techniques, the sexological examination, systematic desensitization, and Kegel exercises are all appropriate. Marital therapy to improve communication and resolve conflict is also part of standard therapy.

Botanical Therapies. Botanical medicines, in some cases, may offer many of the same therapeutic benefits for impotence as prescription drugs–and without severe side effects. In *Alternative Medicine: The Definitive Guide*, naturopath Dr. Tom Kruzel of Gresham, Oregon, reports that the botanicals coryanthe yohimbe and ginkgo biloba are often used to treat impotence due to their ability to stimulate vascular flow to the penis. Coryanthe yohimbe also increases libido and decreases the latency period between ejaculations.

Kruzel cites a study in the December 1991 *Townsend Letter for Doctors* which found that ginkgo biloba extract increased penile blood flow in a group of patients who had not responded to traditional drug therapies. Half the group regained potency within six months.

N. Farnsworth, writing in *Economic and Medicinal Plant Research*, reports that Siberian ginseng or *Panax ginseng* has been used in Chinese medicine as an aphrodisiac. Its American counterpart, *Eleutherococcus senticosus*, does not appear to possess the same stimulating properties, but according to Farnsworth, it is safer to use over an extended period of time.

H. Felter, in the *Eclectic Materia Medica,* reports on several studies which suggest that unicorn root (*Aletris farinosa*) is an effective botanical medication for impotence in men. It has also been used to promote fertility in both females and males.

According to Michael Murray and Joseph Pizzorno, marapuama, along with catuaba, suma, guarana, and damiana have been used as energizers, adaptogens, nervine tonics, aphrodisiacs, and remedies for impotence.

Saw palmetto (*Serenoa repens*) may also be used to treat impotence and prostate problems, according to Felter, especially when it is combined with other botanical medicines. This herb inhibits the enzyme that converts one type of testosterone to another, a process thought to be important in the development of both enlargement of the prostate and prostate cancer. Saw palmetto is considered an aphrodisiac by herbalists.

Dong quai, ginseng, goldenseal, and licorice have also been used in Europe as aphrodisiacs, although the FDA has not approved them for use in the U.S.

Cell Therapy. Dr. Peter Stephan of the Stephan Clinic in London reports in *Alternative Medicine: The Definitive Guide* that cell therapy has successfully treated impotence in clinical trials in England. Stephan removes cells of erectile tissue from patients' testicles, prostate, or pituitary glands and injects them into the penis. A study using his procedure was conducted with 3,500 men (ranging in age from 22-76 years of age) suffering from sexual disorders, and resulted in a 76% success rate.

Exercise. Exercise, especially aerobic exercise, is an important part of maintaining a healthy sexual response. By increasing blood flow to the heart, exercise boosts sexual energy. Jane Brody in the August 4, 1993 edition of *The New York Times* cites several large studies of men and women which have demonstrated the positive effects of regular exercise on sexual energy. As a relaxant, body toner, energy booster, antidepressant, and confidence builder, exercise is one of the most accessible, safest, and effective treatments for impotence. Many holistic physicians use exercise to build sexual confidence in their patients.

According to Kirsten Olsten's *The Encyclopedia of Alternative Health Care*, tai chi provides improved balance and physical stamina, generating chi and helping reverse impotence.

Homeopathic Therapies. F. Ellingwood, writing in *American Materia Medica, Therapeutics and Pharmacognosy*, describes several homeopathic treatments for male impotence. He suggests that *Nux vomica* is especially effective in cases where patients have an excess of alcohol, cigarettes, or dietary indiscretions. Male patients with symptoms of impotence should consult a licensed homeopath since this formula contains small amounts of strychnine alkaloids which are toxic.

Nutritional Therapies. According to James Balch and Phyllis Balch in *Prescription for Nutritional Healing*, diet is one of the most critical factors in male sexuality because androgen levels depend on the type and amounts of foods eaten. A diet that reduces calories and increases sexual vigor normally includes whole grains and beans, fresh vegetables and fruit, fish, seeds, and nuts. These foods are rich in vitamin E (essential for sexual hormone production and normal erections), as well as minerals such as zinc (which maintains hormonal balance) and the trace elements critical to a normal sex drive.

One important dietary measure for preventing and treating impotence is reducing the percentage of calories men consume as fats. High LDL ("bad') cholesterol levels contribute to both heart disease and high blood pressure, conditions directly associated with impotence problems. Conversely, McKinlay found that low levels of high-density lipoprotein (HDL), the "good" form of cholesterol, correlated significantly with impotence.

Psychotherapy. Psychological factors, including depression, low self-esteem, anger, anxiety, childhood sexual abuse, and communication problems with one's sexual partner, often contribute to impotence. A diagnostic evaluation for emotional problems, along with a full physical examination is the first step in therapy.

Traditional Chinese Medicine (TCM). Impotence and premature ejaculation are considered by Chinese physicians to be caused primarily by stress and nutritional imbalances. According to Kruzel, quoted in

Psychological Therapies for Impotence

- **Support groups** are very effective in helping males whose impotence may have been caused by childhood sexual abuse.
- **Brief sex therapy**. Moderate sexual problems in an otherwise sound relationship usually respond well to brief sex therapy.
- **Psychotherapy**. Sexual problems stemming from serious psychological difficulties, such as personality problems or deep-seated conflicts about sex, respond best to long-term individual psychotherapy. Along with psychoanalysis and behavioral therapy, it's also helpful in healing sexual problems resulting from abuse, such as frigidity, impotence, and the inability to become intimate.
- **Couple or marital therapy**. Sexual problems that stem from emotional tension may be symptomic of destructive interactions between partners. These respond best to couple therapy.
- **Behavioral therapy** is beneficial for abuse victims who become impotent or develop addictions.

Alternative Medicine: The Definitive Guide, "impotence due to low hormone output is considered a deficiency of kidney yang, while premature ejaculation is viewed as an inability to withhold the semen and is considered a deficiency of the kidney storage vessel."

TCM uses acupuncture and botanical medicines to enhance blood flow. As noted,

Panax ginseng has long been regarded as an aphrodisiac in Chinese medicine. However, *Panax ginseng* is not recommended for long-term use, and *Eleutherococcus senticosus* is often substituted for it. S. Dharmananda notes in his book *Your Nature, Your Health–Chinese Herbs in Constitutional Therapy* that lyceum berries are also used to treat sexual dysfunctions, including impotence. Other botanicals such as cascata and lotus seed also enhance sexual function and eliminate premature ejaculation.

Vitamin and Mineral Therapies. Balch and Balch state that vitamin supplements also play an important role in increasing and maintaining sexual energy. Vitamin A, for example, is necessary for regulating healthy testicular tissue and sex hormone production, and helps prevent cancer of the sexual organs. Good sources include liver, eggs, fortified milk, carrots, tomatoes, apricots, cantaloupe, fish, and dark-green leafy and yellow vegetables.

Vitamin B_5 (pantothenic acid) found in whole grains, beans, eggs, nuts, organ meats (liver), peanuts, and broccoli regulates the adrenal cortex and increases sexual secretions. Vitamin C is also required for sexual stamina.

Magnesium found in whole grains, raw leafy vegetables and nuts (especially cashews and almonds) plays a major role in sex organ sensitivity, healthy ejaculation, and orgasm. Copper and zinc deficiencies may lead to impotence or sexual dysfunction and/or infections. Good natural sources include oysters, nuts, beans, eggs, raisins, corn oil, margarine, crab meat, liver, and whole wheat bread.

Other Treatments. Simeon Margolis and Hamilton Moses III report in *The Johns Hopkins Medical Handbook* that if nutrition, exercise, or psychological counseling do not produce results, physicians may prescribe other procedures, including vacuum suction devices or injections as a last resort. A vacuum or mechanical suction device is placed around the penis. As air is drawn out of the chamber of the instrument, it creates a vacuum that draws blood into the penis, causing an erection. This procedure is relatively safe, inexpensive, noninvasive, and has no documented side effects. Papaverine injection therapy may be prescribed in chronic impotence cases. Papaverine is an experimental drug that increases blood flow to the penis and keeps it firm for several hours. However, as papaverine may have adverse side effects, its use should be supervised by a physician.

Premature Ejaculation

According to David Zimmerman, in Zimmerman's *Complete Guide to Nonprescription Drugs*, about 10% of American males suffer from premature ejaculation, which means that orgasm occurs when the penis first enters a woman's vagina, or even before. The majority of men, in contrast, climax about two minutes after entering the vagina. Males who consistently reach climax too soon should consider counseling to discover any psychological factors that may be contributing to this condition.

According to Bernie Zilbergeld, author of *The New Male Sexuality*, premature ejaculation is the most common sexual problem among men and the easiest to cure. "With the right treatment," Sheldon Burman, founder and director of the Male Sexual Dysfunction Institute in Chicago, states in Zilbergeld's book, "the cure rate is near 100%." Burman adds that the right holistic treatments are usually painless, inexpensive, and relatively easy.

Treatments for Premature Ejaculation

Ejaculation is a reflex that a man can learn to control in a manner similar to controlling bladder function. The key lies in recognizing the bodily sensations that signal the onset of ejaculation and in modulating arousal. Holistic physicians usually begin treatment by trying to identify the physical or psychological factors that have been linked to premature ejaculation. Some patients may have a history of practicing coitus interruptus for birth control and may be conditioned to ejaculate outside the vagina. In other men, early ejaculation can be caused by anxiety and fear about their sexual adequacy.

According to Zimmerman, the FDA has approved benzocaine and lidocaine as safe, over-the-counter treatments for premature ejaculation. Benzocaine temporarily diminishes penile sensation and thereby enables men to delay orgasm. Lidocaine is usually sold in an aerosol spray dispensed from a dose-metered container that delivers measured amounts. Repeated use, however, may irritate the skin. Condoms also help delay orgasm by reducing sensitivity.

Botanical Therapies. In *Your Nature, Your Health–Chinese Herbs in Constitutional Therapy*, S. Dharmananda reports that lyceum berries, cascata, and lotus seed are natural botanicals which have been found to reverse premature ejaculation.

Nutritional Therapies. Premature ejaculation is often caused by diet-related problems such as obesity, diabetes, and high-fat, high-cholesterol diets. The problem normally results from an inadequate blood supply to the penis. When the arteries in the penis become partially blocked with fat and cholesterol, maintaining an erection becomes more difficult. When this occurs, the brain tells the body that it must ejaculate quickly. Thus, many overweight men quickly lose their erection. According to Zilbergeld, males can increase their sexual potency by adopting a low-fat, low-cholesterol diet, exercising

regularly, not smoking or drinking, and maintaining their ideal body weight.

Physical Techniques. In certain cases, a physician may prescribe the "squeeze technique." In this procedure, the partner manually stimulates the penis just before the point of ejaculation. To stop the ejaculation, she presses her thumb against the underside of the penis with sufficient pressure to deter ejaculation. Zilbergeld also points out that men are most easily aroused when they are on top of their partner. Men with premature ejaculation may want to reverse sexual positions so that the partner controls the movements.

Kegel Exercises. Zilbergeld also advises clients with premature ejaculation to perform Kegel exercises, the same pelvic muscle strengthening exercises that women practice during pregnancy and childbirth. Kegels involve contracting the buttocks for one second as though trying to delay a bowel movement. Men should start by repeating the exercise 15 times in a row, working up to 60-75 contractions twice daily. By strengthening the pelvic muscles, kegels enable men to contract or relax as they near orgasms, delaying ejaculation. Zilbergeld adds that some men may delay ejaculation when squeezing the muscles, and others when relaxing them.

Prostate Enlargement

The prostate, the male sex gland beneath the urinary bladder, is the most common site of disorders in the male genitourinary system. A doughnut-shaped gland, the prostate encircles the urinary outlet, or urethra. Contraction of the muscles in the prostate squeezes fluids into the urethral tract during ejaculation.

According to Balch and Balch in *Prescription for Nutritional Healing*, one third of American men over the age of 50 develop a prostate enlargement (BPH). An enlarged prostate is not cancerous but can cause disability and even serious illness if left untreated. When the prostate becomes too large, it presses against the urethral canal and interferes with normal urination. As a result, urine may back up in the kidneys, subsequently damaging them by excessive pressure and contaminated urine. Bladder infections such as cystitis commonly occur as well.

Symptoms of BPH typically include progressive urinary frequency, night-time awakening to empty the bladder, pain, burning, difficulty in starting and stopping urination, and an inability to empty the bladder fully.

Treatments for Prostate Enlargement

Antibiotics and analgesics are sometimes prescribed for BPH. In addition, a new drug, finasterid (Proscar), shrinks the prostate by interfering with the production of the hormone that stimulates growth. In one controlled clinical trial involving 1,645 men, as cited in *Consumer Reports Health Answer Book*, about one-third experienced greatly improved urinary flow after a year on the drug, while another third had at least some relief. Side effects, including impotence, decreased libido, and decreased volume of ejaculation, were minimal (occurring in only approximately 4% of participants).

Balch and Balch note that another drug, leuprolide, may shrink enlarged prostates. However, they warn that side effects can include impotence, decreased libido, and even hot flashes, and counsel men not to take the drug if they are concerned about potency.

Acupuncture. Acupuncture treatment for BPH has been developed by naturopath Rick Marinelli of Beaverton, Oregon, as described in *Alternative Medicine: The Definitive Guide*. Marinelli uses acupuncture, herbal medicines, and TCM to reduce prostate swelling. Marinelli claims that some patients experience improvement within the first three to six weeks of combined therapy.

Amino Acid Therapy. According to Murray and Pizzorno, the combination of glycine, alanine, and glutamic acid (in the form of two 6-grain capsules administered three times daily for two weeks and one capsule three times daily thereafter) has been shown in several studies to relieve many of the symptoms of BPH. In one controlled study of 45 men, night-time urination was relieved or reduced in 95%, and urgency reduced in 81%.

Ayurvedic Medicine. Dr. Virender Sodhi, director of the American School of Ayurvedic Sciences in Bellevue, Washington, claims that Ayurvedic medicine has proved effective in treating BPH. In *Alternative Medicine: The Definitive Guide*, he advises patients to practice exercises such as the ashiwin mudra, which is the squeezing and relaxing of the anal sphincter, to help relieve congestion and aid in circulation in the prostate gland. His patients also take several Ayurvedic botanical medicines, including triphala, amla, neem, and shilajit.

Botanical Therapies. Berries from the saw palmetto plant relieved BPH symptoms and stimulated immune function in clinical studies, as reported by Morton Walker in the February/March 1991 *Townsend Letter for Doctors*. Berries from the plant contain approximately 15% saturated and unsaturated fatty acids, which significantly reduce prostatic swelling in BPH patients.

The bark of the *Pygeum africanus* tree, taken in powder form, has been used in Europe for centuries to treat urinary disorders. Clinical trials in humans, according to Kruzel in the August 1991 issue of *Health Review Newsletter*, have shown clearly that this herb can reduce prostate swelling with no toxic side effects, even when administered in large doses and for prolonged periods of time.

In *Alternative Medicine: The Definitive Guide*, Kruzel reports one case in which a 68-year-old man with BPH and a bladder stone reduced prostatic swelling within 10 days using a formula including saw palmetto extract, prostate glandulars, *Pygeum africanus*, horsetail, and corn silk. According to Kruzel, this formula can also decrease blood in the urine and increase urinary flow.

Balch and Balch report that flower pollen has been used to treat prostatitis and BPH in Europe since the early 1960s. It is not known how bee pollen reduces prostate swelling, although it has been shown to be quite effective in treating BPH in several double-blind clinical studies.

Balch and Balch also claim that drinking teas made from equal quantities of gravel root, sea holly, and hydrangea root will reduce the discomfort of urination in BPH sufferers. Marshmallow leaves may be added to this mixture to relieve burning and pain. Other beneficial teas can be made from the diuretic herb buchu (which should not be boiled, however), and from corn silk.

Murray and Pizzorno report that ginseng eases BPH by increasing testosterone levels and decreasing prostate weight. Increased testosterone levels appear to improve intestinal zinc absorption, while decreased prostatic size usually alleviate the symptoms of BPH.

Hydrotherapy. Murray and Pizzorno state that sitz baths, one form of hydrotherapy in which male patients are immersed in hot, cold or netural bath water up to the pelvic region, effectively relieve some cases of BPH. In some cases, the feet are immersed in a separate tub of hot water before or during the bath.

A hot sitz bath is first taken for 3-10 minutes at 105°-115°F (40.5°-46°C). A hot foot bath at 110°-115°F (43°-46°C) is then taken, followed by cool sponging of the pelvic area. Hot sitz baths are not recommended in cases of acute inflammation or infection of the prostate.

Neutral sitz baths are more appropriate for situations of acute inflammation of the prostate. They are given at 92°-97° F (33°-35° C) for 15 minutes to two hours. It is necessary to provide adequate coverings during this period to avoid chilling.

Nutritional Therapies. An increasing number of nutritionists and allopathic physicians now believe that most prostate problems, including BPH, result from dietary imbalances that can be reversed with low-fat diets. Kruzel advises men with BPH to avoid spicy foods, foods high in fat and carbohydrates, caffeine, alcohol, and tobacco. These can serve as irritants and negate the effects of essential vitamins and minerals such as vitamins C and E and zinc, which are necessary for the production of semen.

Kurt Butler and Lynn Rayner suggest in *The Best Medicine: The Complete Health and Preventative Medicine* that inadequate intake of essential fatty acids such as linoleic acid promotes prostate enlargement and recommend consumption of whole grains, nuts, seeds, and vegetables. Balch and Balch claim that eating one ounce of raw pumpkin seeds or taking pumpkin seed oil capsules on a daily basis is helpful for almost all prostate disorders because of their high zinc content.

Vitamin and Mineral Therapies. *Alternative Medicine: The Definitive Guide* claims that vitamin and mineral supplementation is also beneficial. Vitamin C is a major component of the seminal vesicles and prostate gland, and high amounts are found in prostatic secretions. Vitamin E is also present and, due to its fat solubility, acts as an antioxidant and stabilizes membranes and lipids. Vitamin B and magnesium may

Therapies for Prostate Enlargement

- **Botanical Medicines**: Ask your physician or herbalist about taking saw palmetto, ginseng, flower pollen extracts, pygeum bark, horsetail, or corn silk supplements.
- **Nutrition**: Avoid spicy foods, foods high in fat and carbohydrates, caffeine, alcohol, and tobacco. Consume whole grains, nuts, seeds (especially pumpkin seeds), and vegetables.
- **Vitamins and Minerals**: Take vitamins C and B, magnesium, zinc, garlic, or primrose oil supplements.
- **Other Remedies**: Consult an Ayurvedic physician who may recommend yoga postures (especially the ashiwin mudra), or botanicals such as triphala, amla, neem, and shilajit.

relieve BPH, as these appear to be deficient in most BPH patients. Garlic can also help supply the body with vitamins and minerals and prevent infection of the prostate.

Zinc supplements may reduce dihydro-testosterone levels in the prostate and help shrink the gland. According to Murray and Pizzorno in the *Encyclopedia of Natural Medicine*, zinc picolinate and zinc citrate are the best supplemental forms of zinc to use. However, Butler and Rayner warn that men should not take large doses of zinc indefinitely.

According to *Alternative Medicine: The Definitive Guide*, essential fatty acids such as fish oils, olive oil, evening primrose oil, and eicosapentaenoic acid (EPA) are needed in large amounts for normal functioning of the prostate gland. Used as supplements, these acids can help normalize prostatic functioning.

Prostatitis

Many males between the ages of 20 and 50 suffer acute or chronic inflammation of the prostate gland–or prostatitis. The condition usually results from a bacterial infection from another area of the body which has invaded the prostate. Noninfective forms of prostatitis may be associated with autoimmune disorders. Prostatitis can partially or totally block the flow of urine out of the bladder, resulting in urine retention. This causes the bladder to become distended, weak, tender, and susceptible to infection due to the increased amount of bacteria in the retained urine.

Some symptoms of acute prostatitis detailed by Butler and Rayner include fever, chills, frequent urination accompanied by a burning sensation, pain between the scrotum and rectum, fatigue, and blood or pus in the urine. Symptoms of chronic prostatitis include a burning sensation while urinating, the presence of blood in the urine, lower back pain, and impotence. As prostatitis becomes more advanced, urination is increasingly difficult.

It is important for men who suffer from any of these symptoms to see a physician because the condition may progress to more severe complications, including kidney infection, orchitis (painful swelling of the testicles), and epididymitis (inflammation of the epididymis, a tube along the backside of the testicles). Bladder outlet obstruction and prostate stones may also occur if chronic prostatitis remains untreated.

Treatments for Prostatitis

Ayurvedic Medicine. Sodhi describes a typical Ayurvedic treatment for prostatitis in *Alternative Medicine: The Definitive Guide* that combines three procedures. First, he advises patients to reduce sexual activity if their infection is caused by sexual overstimulation. Second, he counsels them to drink large amounts of water so that they urinate more frequently. He also suggests they practice the ashiwin mudra exercise and soak their testicles in cold water. Finally, Sodhi recommends taking antibiotic botanicals such as neem, amla, and shilajit. In certain cases, he also prescribes a berberine extract and zinc supplements.

Botanical Medicines. H. Felter reports in the *Eclectic Materia Medica* that an evergreen plant, pipsissewa (*Chimaphilia umbellata*), effectively treats urinary tract disorders, including prostatitis. The plant contains arbutin, the active ingredient in uva ursi, which combats infections of the urinary tract and increases blood flow to the prostate gland. He also suggests that horsetail relieves the pain of acute prostatic infections. Purple coneflower has been used against prostatitis and is often combined with *Delphinia staphysagria*, *Thuja occidentalis*, and Anemone pulsatilla. According to Felter, these botanical agents decrease pain, irritation, prostate swelling, and impotence associated with prostatitis.

Balch and Balch also agree that horsetail, an astringent, may eliminate blood in the urine and may help alleviate frequent urination at night. Other herbs that help treat these symptoms are goldenseal, parsley, juniper berries, slippery elm bark, and ginseng.

Homeopathic Therapies. Kruzel reports in *Alternative Medicine: The Definitive Guide* that homeopathy has been used to treat all forms of prostatitis, especially chronic prostatitis that is unresponsive to antibiotic treatments. For example, he treated one 38-year-old man with severe aching pains in his hips, thighs, testicles, and prostate gland who had been given antibiotics and later

nonsteroidal anti-inflammatory medication over the course of several years without experiencing any pain relief. After one month of homeopathic treatment with berberis 30C, the patient was 60% better—and after three months, he was pain free.

Hydrotherapy. Balch and Balch claim that in some cases, hydrotherapy can increase circulation in the prostate region, and recommend several treatments. One treatment is to sit in a tub filled with the hottest water tolerable for 15-30 minutes once or twice a day. Men may also stand in a shower and spray their lower abdomen and pelvic area with warm water for three minutes, then cold water for one minute. A third treatment is to sit in hot water while putting the feet in cold water for three minutes, and then sit in cold water while immersing the feet in hot water for one minute. They also recommend drinking two to three quarts of spring or distilled water daily to stimulate urine flow, which helps prevent retention, cystitis, and kidney infection.

Nutritional Therapies. Kruzel advises men with prostatitis to avoid caffeine in any form—coffee, tea, chocolate or soft drinks—because it tends to tighten the bladder neck, making it more difficult to pass urine. Patients should also avoid spicy foods, foods high in fat and carbohydrates, alcohol, and tobacco.

Ozone Therapy. Ozone therapy involves removing 50-100 milliliters of blood, bubbling ozone and oxygen into the blood sample for several minutes, and then reintroducing the ozonated blood back into the patient through a vein. This method, according to Nathaniel Altman's *Oxygen Healing Therapies*, has been successful in Cuba in treating a wide variety of health problems, including atherosclerosis and

SUMMARY

Male Checkups for Prostate Cancer

In 1994, an estimated 165,000 American men were diagnosed with cancer of the prostate gland, which produces fluid that carries sperm out of the testicles. Of these, one in four was likely to die from the disease. Many such deaths could be prevented, however, if the cancer was discovered at an early stage.

In order to ensure early detection, the American Cancer Society, Prostate Cancer Education Council, and The American Urological Association now officially recommend that all men between the ages of 50 and 70 undergo an annual checkup for the disease, which involves two procedures. In the first, a digital rectal exam, a physician inserts a gloved finger into the rectum to feel for lumps or growths on the prostate. The second, a new procedure called a Prostate Specific Antigen (PSA) test, measures the level of PSA, a substance produced by the prostate gland. High PSA levels may mean the patient is at risk for prostate cancer.

prostatitis. Edward McCabe's *Ozone and Oxygen Therapy* documents that ozone therapy has also been used effectively in Germany to treat prostatitis.

Traditional Chinese Medicine (TCM). Kruzel states in *Alternative Medicine: The Definitive Guide* that prostatitis is regarded in TCM as a condition of damp heat in the prostate and urinary tract, and thus acupuncture has not been effective in treating it. However, Chinese botanical medicines

that contain polyporus, akebia, or the cephalanoplos or dainthus formulas have neutralized prostatic infection.

Vitamin and Mineral Therapies. Murray and Pizzorno prescribe the following supplements for prostatitis:

- Zinc (picolinate), 60 mg per day (maximum of 6 months).
- Pyridoxine (vitamin B_6), 100-250 mg per day.
- Linseed oil (essential fatty acid source), 1 teaspoon twice daily.
- Glycine, 200 mg per day.
- Glutamic acid, 200 mg per day.
- Alanine, 200 mg per day.

Summary

Prevention of common male health problems is extremely important for men of all ages. Periodic examinations combined with blood tests provide the best method of early detection for prostate enlargement, prostatitis, and other genitourinary problems. Lifestyle changes, especially those associated with sexual habits, are also crucial in preventing genitourinary problems. If these problems do occur, changes in dietary habits, along with vitamin, mineral, and botanical supplements, homeopathic therapies, hydrotherapy, Traditional Chinese Medicine, and Ayurvedic therapies may be effective methods of treatment.

The long-term prognosis of the sexual dysfunction varies with the type of disorder and its causes. Generally good results (80-95% satisfaction) are obtained when treating impotence, male erectile disorder. Long-term results are modestly successful (40-80%) when treating inhibited male orgasm and premature ejaculation. Current holistic treatments include sensate focus exercises, cognitive-behavioral therapy relaxation training, hypnosis and guide imagery, and group therapy. Specific techniques, such as directed self-stimulation, the stop-start and squeeze techniques, the sexological examination, systematic desensitization, and Kegel exercises are also effective in some cases.

Resources

References

Altman, Lawrence. "A Study of Impotence Suggests Half of Men Over 40 May Have Problem." *The New York Times* (December 22, 1993): B9.

Altman, Nathaniel. *Oxygen Healing Therapies.* New York: Health Sciences Press, 1994.

———. "Ozone in Medicine." *Townsend Letter For Doctors.* (June 1995): 34-44.

Balch, James F., and Phyllis Balch. *Prescription for Nutritional Healing.* Long Island, NY: Avery Publishing, 1993.

Brody, Jane. "Science Finds No Magic in Age-Old Aphrodisiacs." *New York Times* (August 4, 1993): B7.

Brown, D. "Literature Review–Ginkgo Biloba: Phytotherapy Review & Commentary." *Townsend Letter for Doctors* (December 1993).

The Burton Goldberg Group. *Alternative Medicine: The Definitive Guide.* Payallup, WA: Future Medicine Publishing, Inc., 1993.

Butler, Kurt, and Lynn Rayner. *The Best Medicine: The Complete Health and Preventative Medicine.* New York: Harper & Row, Publishers, Inc., 1985.

Dharmananda, S. *Your Nature, Your Health–Chinese Herbs in Constitutional Therapy.* Portland, OR: Institute for Traditional Medicine and Preservation of Health Care, 1986.

Editors of Consumer Reports with Jonathan Leff. *Consumer Reports Health Answer Book.* Yonkers, NY: Consumers Union of United States, Inc., 1993.

Ellingwood, F. *American Materia Medica, Therapeutics and Pharmacognosy.* Portland, OR: Eclectic Medical Publications, 1983.

Farnsworth, N. "*Eleuthrococcus senticosus*: Current Status as an Adaptogen." *Economic and Medicinal Plant Research* (1985): 156-215.

Felter, H. *The Eclectic Materia Medica.* Portland, OR: Eclectic Medical Publications, 1983.

Gittleman, Ann. "Is There Male Menopause?" *Delicious.* (September 1996): 44.

Gittleman, Anne Louise. *Super Nutrition for Men.* Sante Fe, NM: Evans , 1997.

Halvorsen, J. "Sexual Dysfunction. Diagnosis, Management and Prognosis." *Journal of American Board of Family Practice* (March 1992): 177-92.

Kruzel, T. "What Is the Prostate and Why Is It Doing This to Me?" *Health Review Newsletter* (August 1991): 8-10.

Margolis, Simon, and Hamilton Moses III. *The Johns Hopkins Medical Handbook.* New York: Medletter Associates, Inc., 1992.

McCabe, Edward. *Ozone and Oxygen Therapy.* New York: The Family News, 1994.

Murray, Michael, and Joseph Pizzorno. *Encyclopedia of Natural Medicine.* Rocklin, CA: Prima Publishing, 1991.

Olsten, Kirsten. *The Encyclopedia of Alternative Health Care.* New York: Pocket Books, 1989.

Walker, Morton. *"Seronoa epens* Extract (Saw Palmetto) Relief for Benign Prostatic Hypertrophy." *Townsend Letter for Doctors* (February/March 1991): 67.

Zilbergeld, Bernie. *The New Male Sexuality.* New York: Bantam Books, 1991.

Zimmerman, David. *Zimmerman's Complete Guide to Nonprescription Drugs.* Detroit, MI: Gale Research, 1993.

RESOURCES

Organizations

Alan Guttmacher Institute.
11 Fifth Avenue, New York, NY 10003.

Association for Voluntary Sterilization Inc., 112 East 42nd Street, New York, NY 10168.

National Institute of Allergy and Infectious Diseases,
9000 Rockville Pike, Bethesda, MD 20205.

Chapter 13

COMMON FEMALE HEALTH PROBLEMS

In 1900, the average life expectancy for a woman in the United States was 50 years. Today, that life expectancy has increased to almost 80, which means that American women can expect to live a third of their lives after menopause. Since 40 million Americans are now in or past menopause, with another 20 million due in the next decade, the subject has become one of increasing national concern. In addition to menopause, this chapter discusses holistic therapies for preventing and treating common female health problems, including PMS, dysmenorrhea, vaginitis, and fibrocystic breast disease.

While conventional practitioners have often used invasive medical procedures (for example, breast removal and hysterectomies) to treat symptoms and diseases affecting women's health, holistic medicine offers a variety of therapeutic and preventive approaches. Diet, vitamin and mineral supplementation, exercise, and stress management are holistic approaches intended to help women regain their health and maintain overall well-being.

Fibrocystic Breast Disease (FBD)

Fibrocystic breast disease (FBD), also known as cystic mastitis, is a noncancerous condition marked by the presence of nodules or cysts (sacs filled with fluid), which may or may not be accompanied by pain and tenderness. It can occur in one or both breasts, with the cysts spread throughout the breasts or located in one general area. The lumps can be either firm or soft, and may change in size. FBD is typically cyclical, and usually disappears during pregnancy and nursing.

Dr. Susan Love, associate professor of clinical surgery at UCLA and director of the Breast Center in Los Angeles, estimates in *Alternative Medicine: The Definitive Guide* that FBD occurs in 80% of premenopausal women. While it can develop at any age, it is most likely to appear between the age of 30 and menopause.

The cause or causes of FBD are unknown, but according to James Balch and Phyllis Balch, the Medical College of Pennsylvania claims that an iodine deficiency is a common reason. Other factors include an imbalance of the female sex hormones and abnormal breast milk production (caused by high amounts of the hormone estrogen).

The benign cysts that develop in women with FBD are tender and move freely, unlike cancerous lumps which usually do not move freely, are generally not tender, and do not go away. FBD is considered a low risk factor for breast cancer.

To diagnose FBD, a physician extracts fluid from the cysts with a needle. A mammogram is usually taken to rule out cancer. If FBD is diagnosed, treatment focuses on relieving pain and tenderness, and reducing or eliminating the cysts. Conventional options for severe symptoms include hormonal therapies (including birth control pills, Danocrine, Bromocriptine, and tamoxifen, an anti-estrogen drug), which can have undesirable side effects such as weight gain, growth of facial and bodily hair, headaches, fatigue, blood clots, depression, and nerve problems.

The drug Danazol, a hormone, has been successful in shrinking FBD lumps, according to Balch and Balch. Approximately 60% of women users report less pain and tenderness within several weeks. However, Danazol is not effective for all women and may have some side effects.

Treatments for Fibrocystic Breast Disease

Botanical Therapies. Balch and Balch indicate that echinacea, goldenseal, mullein, pau d'arco, poke root, and red clover may be helpful in treating FBD, and report good results with primrose oil in reducing the size of the cysts. They also recommend daily supplementation of germanium and kelp. Hoffman suggests in *Alternative Medicine: The Definitive Guide* that herbal squaw vine, mullein, pau d'arco, and red clover can reduce swelling. In addition, dandelion is used for breast sores, tumors, and cysts, while parsley reduces swollen breasts.

Tori Hudson, academic dean at the National College of Naturopathic Medicine in Portland, Oregon, reports in the May 1994 *Townsend Letter for Doctors* that she has successfully used several botanical diuretics to treat FBD, including taraxacum leap, foeniculum, angelica, macrotys, and arctium. She claims never to have had a FBD patient who did not respond to natural botanical therapies. She also recommends evening primrose oil, iodine, flax seed oil, and methionine.

Michael Murray and Joseph Pizzorno detail a clinical trial of 414 women which found that evening primrose (EPO) was just as effective as the prescription drug bromocriptine in relieving breast pains, but not as effective as the prescription drug danazon. However, since EPO had fewer side effects than either drug, they suggest it should be the first holistic treatment for FBD.

Hormone Therapy. Dr. John Lee, a physician and educator in Sebastopol, California, recommends in *Alternative Medicine: The Definitive Guide* that applying natural progesterone cream directly to the skin usually causes breast cysts to disappear.

He advises women to use progesterone cream starting on the fifteenth day of their monthly cycle and continuing until the twenty-fifth day.

Lee states that wild yams contain a compound called diosgenin, which is essentially a progesterone molecule with a small molecule addition. The natural progesterone in wild yams has many of synthetic progesterone's (progestin) benefits, and none of its harmful side effects. Natural progesterone, by countering estrogen in the body, can help heal premenstrual syndrome, uterine fibroids, urinary tract infections, ovarian cysts, endometriosis, and fibrocystic breasts, all of which are aggravated by estrogen. Lee states that wild yams also increased the bone density of several of his female patients with osteoporosis (in one women, by 40%)–while *decreasing* fibrocystic breast symptoms. Several hypothyroid women also began to get better and no longer needed supplementation.

Massage. Bill Moyers' "Healing and the Mind" PBS series documents the case of a 37-year-old Chinese woman who reversed fibrocystic disease with massage. Instead of recommending surgery, her Chinese physician massaged her breast to move the blocked chi energy down her stomach and out through the bottom of her feet. After a few treatments, the woman's cysts began disappearing and she reported feeling virtually no pain. The doctor interviewed by Moyers reported that he had cured 25 of 27 patients suffering from fibrocystic disease.

Nutritional Therapies. Balch and Balch recommend that women consume a low-fat, high-fiber diet of raw foods, beans, seeds, nuts, and whole grains to treat FBD. They advise eating bananas, grapes, grapefruit, apples, yogurt, and fresh vegetables at least three times a day. They also suggest avoiding animal fats, cooking oils, fried foods, salt, sugar, white flour, tobacco, and caffeine.

There is no conclusive data to suggest that a caffeine-free diet relieves FBD symptoms. However, one study by Dr. John Peter Minton of the Department of Surgery at Ohio State University College of Medicine, cited by Balch and Balch, found that women suffering from FBD who eliminated caffeine-containing substances from their diets had a high rate of disappearance or elimination of breast cysts.

Vitamin and Mineral Therapies. Hudson suggests in the May 1994 *Townsend Letter for Doctors* that vitamin E regulates the synthesis of specific proteins and enzymes required to prevent and treat FBD. Hudson advises women with FBD to start a combined supplementation program of vitamin E, betacarotene, vitamin B complex, choline, and methionine. Improving dietary habits to decrease estrogen sources, increasing fiber, and consuming low-fat foods are also therapeutic.

Balch and Balch also recommend daily doses of vitamin E, and further suggest taking co-enzyme Q-10 (an antioxidant similar to vitamin E in action but more potent), and vitamins A, B complex, and C.

Murray and Pizzorno recommend vitamin A supplements. They cite a study in which five out of 12 women had complete or partial remission of their FBD after three months of vitamin A supplementation. However, some patients developed mild side effects, resulting in two of the original 12 withdrawing due to headaches (an early sign of vitamin A toxicity), and one patient reducing her dosage.

Iodine Supplements. Iodine may be an effective treatment for fibrocystic breast disease. Of the several types of iodine in current use, molecular iodine is prescribed most frequently because other types have various side effects. In one study cited in *Alternative Medicine: What Works* 23 subjects received molecular iodine while a

Health Guidelines for Women

- Stop smoking. One out of every four American women currently smokes cigarettes, which is one of the primary risk factors for lung and breast cancer, and the leading cause of cancer mortality among women.
- Maintain good nutrition by reducing fat in the diet and taking calcium supplements to prevent osteoporosis.
- Get an annual Pap smear to test for cervical cancer.
- Get a yearly clinical breast examination in a doctor's office, combined with self-breast examinations each month.
- If over the age of 50, get an annual mammogram.
- Protect yourself against sexually transmitted diseases.

control group of 33 subjects received a placebo (no medication whatsoever). In the treatment group, 65% had both subjective and objective improvement. In the control group, 33% had subjective—but not objective—improvement.

Fibroids

Fibroids are nonmalignant tumors that grow within the uterine wall. If detected early enough, fibroids can be treated with holistic therapies. Experts do not know what causes fibroids, although it is well known that black women have a 75% chance of developing fibroids, compared with a 33% chance for white women. The first step in prevention is to have your gynecologist perform uterine examination each year. Shafia Monroe, founder of Boston's Traditional Childbearing Groups, Inc., asserts in the December 1991 issue of *Essence*: "Problems like fibroids could be averted if women were educated by their gynecologists."

Treatments for Fibroids

Botanical Medicines. In an *Essence* article, herbalist William LeSassier of Manhattan recommends several botanical medical formulas that have successfully shrunk fibroids in his patients. One 30-year-old women had four plum-size uterine fibroids which produced severe backaches and heavy bleeding for seven to nine days of her menstrual cycle. LeSassier augmented nutritional therapy with botanical supplements of chaste berry, raspberry leaf, and wild yam. After three months of treatment, two of the fibroids had dispappeared, while the two remaining had shrunk to the size of a pea. LeSassier also notes that the patient's periods decreased to four days and were much more manageable.

Nutritional Therapies. As noted, herbalist LeSassier reversed fibroids in a 30-year-old patient by changing her meat-packed gourmet diet to a macrobiotic regimen. The diet eliminated red meat, chicken, dairy products, and eggs, replacing them with beans, brown rice, tofu, granola, couscous, soy-milk products, and fresh seasonal vegetables.

LeSassier suggests that a vegetarian diet helps avoid and shrink small fibroids. He, along with other researchers, believe that tumors may partially be caused by the build-up of estrogen which is a prevalent hormone in meat products.

Daya, a holistic health consultant and director of Daya Associates, also employs nutritional therapies, asserting that "70 percent of my female clients (most of whom are black) have fibroids, which I believe are an accumulation from high-cholesterol diets. Black women need to spend their money on juicers and organic vegetables." Daya advises fibroid sufferers to cut down on red meat, fried and sugary foods, whole milk dairy products, and processed foods. In addition, women at risk for fibroids should eliminate coffee, tea, chocolate, and cola drinks, and to consume more beans, rice, soy products, fresh vegetables, fruit, and fish. Daya also reports that colonic irrigations may effectively shrink fibroids by clearing the bowel tract of the impurities that may cause the disorder.

Surgery. Botanical, nutritional, and colonic therapies are less effective for the treatment of large fibroids. Surgery is normally recommended in severe cases, although each women should inquire about alternatives to hysterectomy, the removal of the entire uterus. While hysterectomy is a common procedure in removing fibroids, experts estimate that 600,000-700,000 of these operations are unnecessary. Evelyn White cites a University of Maryland study concluding that a disproportionate number of hysterectomies are performed on black women, who have twice the mortality rate from the operation than white women. White also notes that the Hysterectomy Education Resources and Services (HERS) foundation recommends laser or scalpel myomectomy as alternatives to conventional hysterectomies.

Menopause

Menopause occurs when a woman no longer menstruates (because she no longer ovulates) and, as a result, can no longer bear children. The average age of occurrence is 48-52, although it occasionally happens several years earlier or later. Even after menopause, a woman's body continues producing

estrogen, though far more slowly. Women undergoing menopause report experiencing sudden and severe hot flashes, while their vaginal walls may become thinner and lose moisture, and sexual intercourse may cause bleeding and pain. Vaginal itching and burning can also occur, and women are more susceptible to yeast and bacterial infections, due to menopausal hormone changes which disrupt the delicate pH of the vagina. In addition, menopause can be accompanied by a loss of muscle tone in the pelvic region, resulting in stress incontinence (urine leakage when coughing, laughing, or exercising vigorously), and a drop of the pelvic organs. As estrogen production declines, the relative increase in testosterone (also produced in the ovaries) may trigger growth of facial hair and thinning of scalp hair.

The National Institute on Aging warns in *The Menopausal Time of Life* that mood changes can also occur during menopause. Other common symptoms include fatigue, nervousness, excessive sweating, breathlessness, headaches, loss of sleep, joint pain, depression, irritability, and impatience. These symptoms may partially stem from hormonal imbalances and other factors such as heredity, general health, nutrition, medications, exercise, stressful life events (such as grown children leaving home or the need to care for parents who are ill), and attitude. The Institute counsels women to develop a positive attitude towards menopause, and to regard it simply as a normal life change (rather than the end of a useful life) and continuing to participate in satisfying activities.

Treatments for Menopause

Botanical Therapies. Botanicals recommended for menopause by Murray and Pizzorno include dong quai, licorice, unicorn root, black cohosh, fennel, and false unicorn root. These botanicals are regarded as uterine tonics. The Chinese regard dong quai as the most important herb for the female hormonal system before, during, and after pregnancy. Hoffman also asserts that red raspberry leaves, sarsaparilla, wild yam, sassafras, and ginseng help lower blood pressure and increase energy in menopausal women.

Balch and Balch suggest that black cohosh, damiana, licorice (which stimulates estrogen production), raspberry, sage, Siberian ginseng (which helps relieve depression and stimulates estrogen production), and squaw vine ease menopausal symptoms. They also claim that gotu kola and dong quai relieve hot flashes, vaginal dryness, and depression.

In *The Healing Foods,* Patricia Hausman reports that the passion flower plant, a woody vine whose flower reminded early Jesuit travelers of the passion of Christ, produces a small berrylike fruit called granadilla or water lemon. This fruit contains low levels of serotonin, which has been used to calm nerves of menopausal women and to lower blood pressure by expanding heart coronary vessels.

Deep Breathing Exercises.
One study reported by Greg Gutfeld in the March 1993 issue of *Prevention* suggests that slow, deep breathing can relieve some of the symptoms of menopause, including hot flashes. A group of 33 women experiencing frequent hot flashes practiced one of three options: slow, deep breathing, muscle relaxation, or brainwave (EEG) biofeedback. Muscle relaxation and biofeedback had no effect, while deep breathing reduced hot flashes by 50%. Slow, deep abdominal breathing probably arrests hot flashes by relaxing the central nervous system, which is aroused by the onset of menopause. This technique may be useful for women suffering hot flashes whose health precludes hormone replacement therapy.

Estrogen Replacement Therapies (ERT).
Conventional physicians sometimes prescribe synthetic estrogen to help alleviate hot flashes, nausea, bone loss, mood swings, reduced vaginal lubrication, and other symptoms associated with menopause. Synthetic estrogen can be prescribed in several forms: pill, cream or ointment, or as a skin patch. The effectiveness of different forms of estrogen vary, and both synthetic and natural estrogens–like all medication–may pose a health risk. To minimize ERT's degree of risk, doctors prescribe minimal yet effective doses of estrogen, to which a synthetic form of the hormone progesterone has been added. As ERT is still controversial, women considering long-term estrogen use should discuss the benefits (such as a lower risk of cardiovascular disease, stroke, and Alzheimer's disease, as well as reduction of postmenopausal bone loss) with their physician or gynecologist.

An alternative to using synthetic progesterone is a natural form of this female hormone found in wild yam (not to be confused with the tuberous sweet potato yam) which, according to herbalist Rosemary Goldstar in *Herbal Healing for Women*, is "the most widely used herb in the world today." More than 200 million prescriptions that contain its derivatives are sold each year. New York City obstetrician Neils Lauersen, author of *PMS: Premenstrual Syndrome and You*, advocates the use of wild yam as well, claiming that–unlike synthetic progesterone–"natural progesterone (from the wild yam) does not cause masculinization and is known to reduce sodium and fluid retention." Wild yam progesterone is available as a cream, oil, tablet, or capsule through physicians or over-the-counter in pharmacies.

Holistic physicians use natural estrogenic substances from plants (phytoestrogens) in place of synthetic estrogen products. Phytoestrogens are components of many medicinal herbs with a historical use in conditions which are now treated by synthetic estrogens. They may be suitable alternatives to estrogen therapy to prevent osteoporosis and other common symptoms of menopause. While generally effective, synthetic estrogens may pose significant health risks, including increasing the risk of cancer, gall bladder disease, and thromboembolic disease (strokes, heart attacks, etc.). Phytoestrogens do not produce these side effects, and exert the same estrogenic effects, according to Murray and Pizzorno.

Botanicals which possess both proven estrogenic activity and a long historical use in treating various female complaints include dong quai (*Angelica sinensis*), licorice (*Glycyrrhiza glabra*), unicorn root (*Aletris farinosa*), black cohosh (*Cimicifuga racemosa*), fennel (*Foeniculum vulgare*), and false unicorn root (*Helonias opulus*).

Exercise. For women who do not wish to use estrogen replacement therapy (ERT), exercise may help reduce the symptoms of menopause. A University of Illinois trial reported in the April 1994 issue of *American Health* studied the effects of exercise on 279 women aged 37-64. Over the course of a year, participants filled out questionnaires describing their menopausal status and level of physical activity. They monitored symptoms of hot flashes and night sweats, fatigue, irritability, depression, vaginal dryness, urinary incontinence, loss of sex drive, and general health. Women who spent the most time in exercise activities, such as ballroom dancing and tennis, experienced less of all the symptoms. Dr. JoEllen Wilbur, a family nurse practitioner who conducted the study, concludes that exercise may prove an effective substitute for ERT. She cautions that although ERT may help prevent heart disease and osteoporosis in women, it may also increase the risk of breast and endometrial cancer. Dr. Ernst Bartisch, an obstetrician/gynecologist at New York City's New York Hospital-Cornell Medical Center, commenting on Wilbur's study, suggests that active menopausal women may not have to take estrogen as soon as inactive women, or may be able to take less of it.

Nutritional Therapies. According to Murray and Pizzorno, women who experience continual unpleasant symptoms during menopause, including hot flashes, will benefit from adopting a diet high in vegetables and fruits and low in fat and animal products. Balch and Balch claim that dairy products, sugar, and meat cause most hot flashes. They suggest that menopausal women consume at least 50% raw foods and protein supplements (to avoid low blood sugar). Refined carbohydrate and alcohol intake should be minimal, and caffeine should be completely eliminated. Blackstrap molasses, broccoli, dandelion greens, kelp, salmon with bones, sardines, and low-fat yogurt are beneficial additions to the diet.

Vitamin and Mineral Therapies. There is no unanimous agreement on which vitamins and minerals will help all women with menopausal symptoms. Balch and Balch claim that vitamin E may relieve hot flashes. Calcium and magnesium chelate help alleviate the nervousness and irritability accompanying menopause. Germanium, L-arginine, and L-lysine relieve the symptoms as well. Vitamin C and potassium may prevent severe hot flashes and heavy perspiration. Evening primrose oil, an excellent source of essential fatty acids, is also recommended.

Vitamin K. Vitamin K is required for the production of osteocalcin, a protein found only in bone which attracts calcium to bone tissue and enables calcium crystal formation to occur. Osteocalcin is the protein matrix upon which mineralization occurs, providing the structure for bone tissue. During menopause women usually retain less vitamin K, even though the hormonal changes of menopause generally increase their need for this essential vitamin. As a result, many menopausal women become deficient in vitamin K, and it is therefore important to take supplements of 150-500 micrograms a day. For best absorption, vitamin K should be ingested with meals. Women taking coudamin or warfarin should not take these supplements because the vitamin interferes with the effect of those drugs.

Menstruation

Each month, from puberty until menopause, a woman's body prepares to conceive, nurture, and give birth to a new human being. The ovaries begin to manufacture estrogen, which triggers the thickening of the uteral lining (the endometrium) with blood vessels, glands, and cells in anticipation of new life. Simultaneously, an egg begins to develop in the ovaries. Within 10 days to three weeks, the lining and the egg are ready for conception, and the egg is released–a process called ovulation (which is when pregnancy can occur). After ovulation, the ovaries increase production of a second hormone, progesterone, which stimulates the uterine lining to complete its development in anticipation of the egg's fertilization by the sperm. If conception does not occur, all hormone levels drop, and some of the endometrial layer is released or shed (menstruation). The cycle then starts over.

Although a normal menstrual cycle has traditionally been defined as 28 days, the length of the lunar cycle, Alan Rees and Charlene Willey claim in *Personal Health Reporter* that only one out of six women has a 28-day cycle. Anywhere between 23 and 35 days is considered normal, even if the cycle is irregular. During the average menstrual period, a woman loses only two tablespoons to one-half cup of blood. The rest of the discharge (almost two-thirds) is fluid released from cells that have either shrunken or died as the lining of the uterus breaks down.

Dysmenorrhea (Menstrual Cramps)

According to the American College of Obstetricians and Gynecologists, as many as 70% of women experience some form of menstrual cramps (dysmenorrhea) during their period, and 15% have cramps severe enough to be disabling. This discomfort results primarily from hormones called prostaglandins that cause contractions of the uterus, and most women who have menstrual cramps do not have any underlying illness. Other symptoms of dysmenorrhea, in addition to cramping pelvic pain, include nausea, vomiting, diarrhea, headaches, dizziness, and fatigue.

For mild cramps, the best therapy may be aspirin, over-the-counter medications containing ibuprofen, or acetaminophen. Low-dose antiprostaglandin pain relievers are also available without a prescription. Felicia Stewart reports in *Understanding Your Body: Every Woman's Guide to a Lifetime of Health* that at least 80% of women treated for cramps with antiprostaglandin medication experience good results. Several closely related drugs called prostaglandin synthetase inhibitors have similar effects. All of them decrease production of the prostaglandin hormone within normal body cells, including the cells lining the uterus.

Treatments for Dysmenorrhea

Acupuncture. *Alternative Medicine: The Definitive Guide* reports that acupuncture is widely used to reduce pain in patients with dysmenorrhea, hysterectomies, chronic back disorders, and migraine headaches.

Botanical Therapies. Herbal tonics for both menstrual cramps and heavy bleeding are now widely available in natural food stores. In *Alternative Medicine: The Definitive Guide*, David Hoffman, past president of the American Herbalist Guild, recommends combining tinctures of skullcap, black haw, and black cohosh in equal parts and taking this mixture as needed. If a woman suffers from excess water retention, Hoffman suggests taking a tincture of dandelion or drinking dandelion tea. Dr. Susan Lark, in her book *PMS Self-Help Book: A Woman's Guide*, recommends ginger, white willow bark, red raspberry leaf, cramp bark, chamomile, hops, ginkgo biloba, and chaste tree berry. Bromelain extract from the pineapple plant has been documented as relieving menstrual cramping by decreasing spasms of the contracted cervix.

Consultation with an herbalist or naturopathic physician can help determine which herbs are most appropriate. Herbalists normally use herb treatments for a minimum of three months. However, if a woman has suffered from hormonal imbalances for a long period of time, it may take six months or more to see results.

Chiropractic. *Alternative Medicine: What Works* reviews three uncontrolled studies divulging that chiropractic manipulation may provide substantial relief for dysmenorrhea. In one study, chiropractic manipulation alleviated menstrual cramps and discomfort twice as much as sham (fake) manipulation. Another small trial provided chiropractic manipulation to eight women, while three controls went untreated. Seven of the eight women treated with manipulation at least twice a week experienced decreased pain and disability, while none of the controls did.

Nutritional Therapies. Menstrual cramps are caused by a variety of nutritional, vitamin, mineral, and hormonal factors. The nutritional therapies recommended by Murray and Pizzorno for PMS symptoms may prove helpful for women with dysmenorrhea. They advise women to limit consumption of refined carbohydrates (sugar, honey, and white flour) and other concentrated carbohydrates such as maple syrup, dried fruit, and fruit juice. Consumption of milk and dairy products should be decreased, along with natural and synthetically saturated fats–which should be substituted with vegetable oils rich in linoleic and linolenic acids. Protein intake from vegetable sources such as legumes should be increased, with green leafy vegetables (except cabbage, brussels sprouts, and cauliflower) and fish replacing red meats. Alcohol, tobacco, coffee, tea, chocolate, and other caffeine-containing foods and beverages should also be restricted.

Osteopathic Therapy. Dysmenorrhea can produce low-back pain and an electromyographic (EMG) pattern typical of trauma-induced, low-back pain. Dr. D. Boesler describes one trial in a February 1993 monograph published by the Health Sciences College of Osteopathic Medicine in Des Moines, Iowa: twelve dysmenorrheic subjects were assigned to a group receiving osteopathic treatment, to a group not receiving osteopathic treatment, or both. Eight women participated in both groups, the other four women being equally distributed between groups. Osteopathic manipulative treatment significantly decreased EMG activity during extension of the lumbar spinae erector muscles, abolished the spontaneous EMG activity, and alleviated low-back pain and menstrual cramping.

Traditional Chinese Medicine (TCM). Honora Lee Wolfe, a TCM practitioner in Boulder, Colorado, states in *Alternative*

Medicine: The Definitive Guide that menstrual cramps are usually due to chi stagnation (when the vital energy is unable to move freely through the body) in the lower abdomen, blood stasis, or a combination of both. She claims that both acupuncture and Chinese herbs restore a balanced chi flow to the lower abdomen.

Menorrhagia

Menorrhagia, excessive menstrual bleeding, is a common female complaint that can be prevented by taking proper nutritional measures. Menorrhagia, blood loss greater than 80 ml, occurring at regular menstrual cycles (cycles are usually, but not necessarily, of normal length), can be caused by uterine fibroids, endometrial polyps, endometrial hyperplasia, and endometriosis. According to Murray and Pizzorno, the cause of functional menorrhagia is currently believed to involve abnormalities in the biochemical processes of the endometrium. The endometrium (lining of the uterus) of women with menorrhagia contains abnormally large concentrations of arachidonic acid, which results in increased production of series 2 prostaglandins, which are thought to be the major factor both in the excessive bleeding seen at menstruation, as well as in menstrual cramps.

Other factors believed to contribute to menorrhagia are iron deficiency, hypothyroidism, vitamin A deficiency, and intrauterine devices.

Treatments for Menorrhagia

The first step in treating a woman with menorrhagia is to rule out serious causes. As excessive menstrual blood can reflect a serious condition, any woman experiencing excessive menstrual blood loss should immediately consult a physician. When the excessive bleeding has been determined to be functional, i.e., not due to any disease, the following therapies may be beneficial.

Botanical Medicines. Numerous botanicals, Murray and Pizzorno document, have been used in the treatment of menorrhagia, including spotted cranesbill (*Geranium maculatum*), birthroot *(Trillium pendulum)*, blue cohosh (*Caulophyllum thalictroides*), witch hazel (*Hamamelis virginiana*), and shepherd's purse (*Capsella bursa-pastoris*). Shepherd's purse has proven effective in clinical trials in treating both menorrhagia and hemorrhage.

Nutritional Therapies. Because Murray and Pizzorno suggest that a heavy period may be caused partially by high blood levels of arachidonic acid, they recommend a diet that restricts the consumption of animal fats, and substitutes vegetable oil sources of linolenic and linoleic acids such as green leafy vegetables, which also contain vitamin K.

Murray and Pizzorno also state that chronic iron deficiency can be a cause of menorrhagia, and they recommend women supplement their diet with vegetable sources of iron. They also advise taking 100 milligrams of daily iron supplements, because one double-blind placebo-controlled study found that 75% of menorrhagic women who took iron supplements decreased their menstrual bleeding, compared with 32.5% for the placebo group.

Thyroid Hormones. Minor thyroid dysfunctions, as determined by basal body temperature or thyroid stimulation (TRH test), may be responsible for menorrhagia and other menstrual disturbances. Murray and Pizzorno cite several studies in which patients with mild hypothyroidism and menorrhagia dramatically reduced menstural bleeding by taking thyroid hormone supplements.

Vitamin and Mineral Therapies. Murray and Pizzorno also suggest that some women develop menorrhagia because they have extremely thin or fragile uterine capillaries. For such cases, they recommend that women take vitamin C supplements (200 mg three times a day) and bioflavonoids, since one small study showed that such a regimen reduced menorrhagia in 14 out of 16 patients. Because vitamin C is known to increase iron absorption significantly, its therapeutic effect could derive also from enhanced iron absorption. In addition, vitamin E supplements (100 IU every two days) have been clinically proven to decrease heavy bleeding. The use of vitamin K (historically in the form of crude preparations of chlorophyll) and vitamin A have also been clinically effective. In one study, serum vitamin A levels were found significantly lower in 71 menorrhagic women than in healthy controls. After 40 of these women were given 25,000 IUs of vitamin A twice a day for 15 days, 92.5% had either complete relief or significant improvements.

Premenstrual Syndrome (PMS)

Premenstrual syndrome (PMS) is the term used to describe the physical or behavioral changes that many women undergo 7-10 days before their monthly periods begin. About seven million American women experience some symptoms of PMS, while 3-5% are affected by "premenstrual dysphoric disorder (PDD)," the most severe PMS, which now is classified by the American Psychiatric Association as a depressive disorder in its *Diagnostic and Statistical Manual of Mental Disorders* (DSM IV). Although there is no unanimous agreement on the causes of PMS, it is believed now to be related to hormonal changes that occur before menstruation.

The principal physical and emotional symptoms of PMS include water retention (edema), weight gain, abdominal bloating, breast tenderness, headaches, swollen hands and feet, constipation, feelings of depression, irritability, tension and anxiety, mood swings, a change in sex drive, and inability to concentrate. The symptoms, which reappear at about the same time each month, usually disappear once a woman's menstrual period begins.

Treatments for Premenstrual Syndrome

Botanical Therapies. Balch and Balch report that dong quai relieves PMS symptoms, particularly bloating, vaginal dryness, and depression. Siberian ginseng (for those who are not hypoglycemic), cayenne, blessed thistle, kelp, raspberry leaves, squaw vine, and sarsaparilla may also alleviate PMS, but should be taken only after consulting a physician or herbalist.

Tori Hudson reports in the December 1995 issue of the *Townsend Letter for Doctors* that *Glycyrrhiza glabra* root, *Arctium lappa* root, *Dioscorea villosa* root, *Angelica sinensis* root, and *Leonurus cardiaca* leaf all have been used to treat PMS. She conducted a three-month, double-blind, placebo-controlled pilot study of 13 women with PMS symptoms. After three months, all participants that took equal parts of the five powdered botanicals inserted into gelatin capsules (weight per capsule: 770 mg) twice daily reported a reduction in their symptoms, versus 6% in the placebo group; 71% of the test group reported fewer symptoms versus 17% in the placebo group. Hot flashes, insomnia, mood changes, and vaginal dryness diminished in 71% of the test group.

Vitex agnus-castus (chaste berry), a deciduous tree common to southern Europe and countries of the Mediterranean, contains berries composed of progesterone-like compounds. German research cited in the 1983 issue of *Planta Medica* has shown that chaste berry helps regulate disturbed female hormonal action, reduces menstrual and menopausal symptoms, especially PMS, amenorrhea, dysmennorhea, and endometriosis. One study on PMS by E. Wollenweber reported that symptoms such as anxiety, nervous tension, insomnia, and mood changes were the most reduced after taking dried *agnus-castus* tablets.

Black currant seeds are a rich source of gamma linolenic acid (GLAs), an Omega-6 essential fatty acid which is a critical precursor to series 1 prostaglandins and important female hormones. Clinical trials cited by R. Chapkin in a 1992 issue of *Lipid* suggest that black currant seed oil is effective in treating PMS. Borage oil, black currant oil, and evening primrose contain botanical sources of essential fatty acids (EFAs) obtainable in supplement form, according to the July/August 1993 issue of *Natural Health*. However, high amounts of these supplements should be taken only under professional supervision. Unicorn root has been used in folk medicine for women with poor ovarian function, and its estrogen-like activity may be useful in treating PMS.

Carol Hart suggests in *The Secrets of Serotonin* that black walnut husk (*Juglans nigra*) supplements may relieve PMS discomforts. Many mood-enhancing drugs such as Prozac achieve their effects by increasing the brain's suppy of serotonin. Black walnuts contain the most concentrated source of natural serotonin and may be helpful for PMS, although no clinical trials have investigated their use.

Exercise. Women with PMS have low beta-endorphin levels (which suppress pain), increased water retention in their bowels, and breast tenderness, among many other possible symptoms. Aerobic exercise has been effectively used to stabilize beta-endorphin

levels, improve mood, and reduce anxieties associated with PMS.

In one clinical trial conducted by exercise physiologist Jody Weizman at George Washington University and reported in the September/October 1994 issue of *Fitness*, 14 women with chronic PMS worked out on treadmills, bikes, stair-climbers, and rowing machines for 45-minute sessions three times a week for three months. The women kept daily diaries to chart their moods, and by the end of the experiment, their PMS symptoms (specifically anxiety and depression) were on average only half as severe than before they began exercising.

A larger study by the University of Kansas involving 968 women over the age of 30 found that exercise greatly benefits menstrual cycle function. The study, cited in the December 1993 issue of *New Body*, showed that women who worked out at least three times a week reported fewer negative symptoms—such as bloating, food cravings, irritability, and breast tenderness—than those who exercised infrequently or not at all.

Hot Baths. According to the *Encyclopedia of Natural Medicine*, taking a hot bath can be helpful in relieving PMS symptoms because it temporarily raises the body temperature, increasing drowsiness. For prolonged pain, Murray and Pizzorno suggest taking a natural sedative such as chamomile tea before a hot bath.

Homeopathic Therapies. In *Discovering Homeopathy*, Dana Ullman lists the following homeopathic therapies which have been used successfully to treat women with occasional acute symptoms of PMS: deadly night shade (Belladonna), phosphate of magnesia (Agnesia phosphorica), bitter cucumber (Colocynthis), black snake root (Cimicifuga), chamomile (Chamomilla), blue cohosh (Caulophyllum), windflower (Pulsatilla), cuttlefish (Sepia), and salt (Natrum mur).

Nutritional Guidelines for Relieving PMS

1. Avoid caffeine and alcohol which cause abnormal increases and decreases in blood sugar levels. Also avoid sugar, citrus juices, fructose, white flour, white rice, candy, cake, soft drinks, pastries, ice cream, sherbet, artificial sweeteners, and highly refined foods.

2. Avoid simple carbohydrates such as refined sugars and flours which raise glucose levels in the blood too rapidly.

3. Eat complex carbohydrate and high protein products which provide the body with a constant supply of glucose to the bloodstream.

4. Eat magnesium-rich foods such as whole grain breads and cereals, fresh green vegetables, and peanut butter.

5. Eat potassium-rich foods, including fresh fruits (not juices), especially bananas, tomatoes, oranges, and apricots.

6. Eat calcium-rich foods such as dairy products (skim milk and low-sodium cheeses) and dark green and yellow vegetables, including zucchini, broccoli, and asparagus.

7. Most importantly, do not fast or skip meals, or go longer than three hours without eating a small amount of complex carbohydrates such as grains or pasta. Consume low-fat foods.

Nutritional Therapies. The vast majority of PMS cases result from biochemical imbalances that are manageable through nutritional intervention. PMS is believed to be partly the result of prostaglandin imbalances, food allergies, blood sugar disturbances, and hormonal fluctuations. PMS sufferers also usually have high levels of estrogen, progesterone, and prolactin, which may account for fluid retention and cause smaller blood vessels to contract and spasm. Changing hormone levels during the menstrual cycle affect carbohydrate metabolism and the production of corticosteroids by the adrenal glands.

Nutritionists generally advise PMS patients to limit their consumption of refined carbohydrates (sugar, honey, and white flour) and other concentrated carbohydrates such as maple syrup, dried fruit, and fruit juice.

Murray and Pizzorno recommend in *Encyclopedia of Natural Medicine* that women with PMS increase their protein intake, particularly from vegetable sources such as legumes. Milk and honey fats (especially natural and synthetically saturated fats) should be decreased and vegetable oils rich in linoleic and linolenic acids substituted. Women with PMS should also decrease salt intake, and restrict alcohol and tobacco use, as well as coffee, tea, chocolate, and other caffeine-containing foods and beverages.

Hudson advises in *Alternative Medicine: The Definitive Guide* that women suffering from PMS adopt a diet that includes fresh fruits, whole grains, legumes, nuts, fish, seeds, and vegetables. She suggests avoiding foods containing refined sugars and high amounts of protein or fat, along with dairy products, caffeine, and tobacco.

In *Prescription for Nutritional Healing,* Balch and Balch recommend a diet of fresh fruits and vegetables, cereals and breads, whole grains, beans, peas, lentils, nuts and seeds, and broiled chicken, turkey, and fish. They also advise that drinking one quart of distilled water daily, starting one week before the menstrual period and ending one week after, may also provide relief.

Essential fatty acids (EFAs), which cannot be made by the body and must be obtained from food sources or supplements, are helpful in the treatment of PMS symptoms. The July/August 1993 issue of *Natural Health* cites research studies in Europe and Canada which have shown that EFA supplements reduce PMS symptoms by as much as two-thirds. Food sources of EFAs include walnuts, pumpkin, flax, sesame and sunflower seeds, soybeans, water fish such as salmon, trout, and sardines.

Progesterone Therapy for PMS. Conventional physicians often use progesterone to alleviate severe PMS symptoms such as migraine headaches and depression. However, this treatment has not been shown to help all women, and side effects may include blood clotting and cancer. Although progesterone is the most widely used treatment for PMS, studies have not proven that it is more effective than a placebo, according to the February 8, 1994 issue of *Your Health.*

Qi Gong. According to Morton Walker, qi gong therapy effectively relieves PMS, and includes a modified diet, herbs, relaxation, breath manipulations, acupuncture, and qi gong physical exercises. The most important dietary regimen emphasizes the avoidance of foods that irritate the liver, including alcohol, coffee, fatty red meats, cooking grease of any kind, fried foods, spicy and hot foods, and pungent foods. Overeating and eating foods that are hard to digest also irritates the liver.

Since most women with PMS gain several pounds from fluid weight during the two weeks prior to their period, they should also eliminate salty foods. Nicotine, a brain stimulant, can magnify PMS symptoms and should be avoided. Complex carbohydrates such as whole grains, beans, fresh fruit and vegetables help to maintain the body's essential nutrients and should be included.

Qi gong exercise produces positive results in moderating PMS symptoms, according to Walker, while also improving general health. A monthly workout plan rotating activities designed to strengthen muscles, reduce fat, relieve tension, and provide overall relaxation is highly beneficial. Vigorous exercise like running, biking, swimming, aerobics, or racquet sports have been shown to elevate mood and improve alertness as well. Most beneficial, however, is a program that combines vigorous cardiovascular exercise during the first seven days of the menstrual cycle with stretching and flexibility exercises such as yoga, tai chi, and qi gong. Walker advises women to engage in less vigorous cardiovascular work such as walking on days when they are prone to PMS symptoms. Combined exercise programs increase the heart-lung capacity and improve overall physical condition, while reducing the strain on breasts, thighs, and abdomen during PMS.

Sexual Intercourse. Regular sexual intercourse may also help relieve the symptoms of PMS. Dr. Alfred Franger, associate professor at the Medical College of Wisconsin in Milwaukee, states in the February 8, 1994 issue of *Your Health* that the bloating feeling which can accompany PMS is caused by an increased blood flow to the pelvis five to seven days before a woman's period. Muscle contractions during orgasm force the blood to flow rapidly away from the pelvic region. Franger contends that regular sexual activity before a menstrual period may

How Exercise Relieves PMS Symptoms

- Boosts metabolism and helps burn fuel (food) more effectively.

- Simulates the smooth muscle of the intestines to contract and relax more efficiently, preventing or relieving a sluggish bowel, constipation, and a bloated abdomen.

- Decreases psychological tension and relieves some forms of anxiety.

- Increases muscle density (the ratio of muscle to fatty tissue), which enhances energy and stamina.

- Produces biochemical changes that relax muscles and elevate mood.

- Prevents the build-up of lactic acid in the muscles which can make them feel tender or painful.

be a more effective treatment for PMS than diet or hormone therapies.

Vitamin and Mineral Therapies. According to *Alternative Medicine: The Definitive Guide*, vitamin A relieves bloating (it is a diuretic) and is beneficial in reducing PMS symptoms in the second half of the menstrual cycle. Vitamin B_6 helps combat depression, and also relieves bloating. Vitamin E relieves nervous tension, headaches, fatigue, depression and insomnia. Martorano reports in the December 1993 issue of *New Body* that taking magnesium supplements may relieve cravings for certain foods such as chocolate, which are common in PMS sufferers.

Magnesium helps prevent migraine headaches, particularly those associated with the menstrual cycle. *Alternative Medicine: What Works* cites one study which found that 20 women who took magnesium found a significant reduction in PMS complaints such as headaches. Another study of migraine patients found that magnesium levels with red blood

cells were lower in patients who never experienced migraines.

Walking, Jogging, Tennis, and Yoga. Dr. Susan Lark indicates in *Premenstrual Syndrome Self-Help Book* that women who used a combination of exercises effectively decreased PMS symptoms, including fluid congestion in their breasts and abdomens. Dr. Lark's program also incorporates the "child" and "sponge" yoga poses, which alleviate menstrual cramps.

Spotting between Periods

Dr. Mona Shangold, professor of obstetrics and gynecology at Hahnemann University in Philadelphia and co-author of *The Complete Sports Medicine Book for Women*, warns that between-period spotting—even after strenuous exercise—is not normal and should be discussed with a gynecologist. Spotting could signal polyps, fibroids, infections, hormonal problems, or cancer. She advises women to use a calendar to record every episode of spotting to help determine whether they are spotting at certain times during each of their menstrual cycles.

Vaginitis (Yeast Infections)

Vaginitis, or yeast infection, is one of the most common reasons women visit a physician. More than 20 million American women report this inconvenience each year and, according to Rees and Willey, for an estimated 10% of women, it is a recurring problem.

The symptoms of vaginitis include frequent, moist vaginal discharges, vaginal odor, vulval or vaginal itching, burning or irritation, and painful urination after intercourse. The skin around the vagina may also become sore and red. Women with these symptoms should see a physician because untreated vaginal infections have been linked to endometritis (inflammation of the uterus), inflammation of the pelvis (pelvic inflammatory disease), and cancer.

Several factors increase a woman's susceptibility to vaginitis. These include the use of antibiotics (which eliminate certain protective bacteria) and oral contraceptives, diabetes, pregnancy, obesity, excessive, improper douching, a vitamin B deficiency, menopausal thinning of the vaginal wall, and cuts or abrasions in the genital area.

Yeast infections traditionally have been treated with prescription antifungal medications inserted into the vagina, including suppositories, tablets, creams, and gels. In 1993, two new antifungal drugs, Gyne-Lotrimin and Monistat 7, were introduced as over-the-counter treatments. No side effects or toxicity have been reported. However, Rees and Willey urge women who are pregnant (or think they may be pregnant), or who have had more than four yeast infections in the past

Preventing Vaginitis

- Avoid oral contraceptives if vaginitis is a persistent problem.
- Avoid routine douching, feminine hygiene sprays, and bath products that contain chemicals which may irritate the vagina.
- Avoid tight undergarments, girdles, and pantyhose, especially when wearing tight jeans or pants.
- Wear cotton underpants, or underpants with a cotton crotch, and loose clothing.
- Carefully wipe the rectum after urinating to prevent bacteria from spreading to the vagina.

year to use the product under a doctor's supervision.

Treatments for Vaginitis

Acidophilus. The intake of various prescription drugs, especially antibiotics, destroys the natural intestinal flora and can cause constipation, diarrhea, and vaginitis. The intestinal tract of normal, healthy adults contains approximately three-and-one-half pounds of bacteria. *Lactobacillus acidophilus* accounts for most of the friendly bacteria found in the small intestine. These friendly bacteria are critical for proper nutrient absorption, help prevent bacterial and yeast overgrowth, and also produce B-complex vitamins and vitamin K.

According to *Zimmerman's Complete Guide to Nonprescription Drugs*, Dr. Eileen Hilton and colleagues at the Long Island Jewish Medical Center in New York put 33 women with recurring yeast infections on one of two diets–with yogurt containing acidophilus, and without–for six months. Women on the yogurt diet had only a third (0.4 attacks per six months) the number of yeast infections than those who were not consuming yogurt (2.5 attacks per six months). Dr. Hilton and her colleagues concluded that eight ounces of *L. acidophilus*-rich yogurt daily "decreased candidal colonization and infection."

Women with yeast infections need to increase *Lactobacillus acidophilus* in the bowels, intestines, and vagina. *Lactobacilus acidophilus* may either be eaten in yogurt form, swallowed in capsules or tablets, or applied externally as a topical treatment. Douches which include apple cider vinegar, acidophilus, and garlic may relieve some symptoms, although there is no clinical evidence that douches are effective.

Botanical Therapies. Botanical medicines can prevent both the spread of *Candida albicans* and soothe the vaginal membranes. Balch and Balch suggest that black walnut and tea tree oil combined with pau d'arco may be effective. One botanical douche described in *Alternative Medicine: The Definitive Guide* includes antiseptic herbs such as St. John's wort, goldenseal, echinacea, fresh plantain, and garlic, all of which strengthen the immune system to suppress the infection. The douche also includes comfrey leaves which soothe the membranes. The douche may be alternated with one containing acidophilus, and is most effective when patients avoid eating fats, sugars, and refined foods.

Hudson has developed a botanical capsule for yeast infections, as described in *Alternative Medicine: The Definitive Guide*. Her formula consists of powdered boric acid mixed with berberis, hydrastis, and calendula. Calendula both neutralizes the infection and heals the vaginal membranes. According to

Hudson, "This works so well that I no longer prescribe douches for this condition."

Homeopathic Therapies. Dana Ullman in *Discovering Homeopathy* suggests that homeopaths have successfully treated vaginitis using pulsatilla, sepia, and *Natrum mur*. Rather than using medicines that attack a specific infectious microorganism, Ullman suggests homeopaths prescribe remedies that stimulate the woman's immune system to eliminate the infectious agent. Homeopathic medicines are prescribed individually based on the woman's nutritional, physical, and mental state.

Ozone Therapy. According to Nathaniel Altman's *Oxygen Healing Therapies*, ozone gas added to olive oil and applied as a balm or salve effectively treats yeast infections. In Cuba it is made with sunflower oil, and applied exernally to treat a wide variety of problems, including fungal infections such as herpes simplex, hemorrhoids, and vaginitis. Cuban gynecologists also use capsules filled with ozonated oil to treat gastroduodenal ulcers, gastritis, giardia, and peptic ulcers.

Nutritional Therapies. In *Textbook of Natural Medicine*, Murray and Pizzorno advise women with yeast infections to test for possible allergies. They recommend a basic diet low in fats, sugars, and refined foods. Hudson suggests in *Alternative Medicine: The Definitive Guide* that women follow a yeast-free diet, avoid fermented foods and sugar that feed yeast growth, and increase their intake of acidophilus yogurt and garlic, both of which control the spread of the yeast-like fungus *Candida albicans*.

Vitamin and Mineral Therapies. Depending on the patient's symptoms, holistic physicians may prescribe vitamins A, B complex, C and E, betacarotene, and the bioflavonoids. Lithium, lysine, acidophilus, and iodine may also be helpful.

Balch and Balch warn women to avoid zinc and iron supplements until the infection disappears, since bacterial infections require iron for growth. They claim that the body actually stores iron in compartments of the liver, spleen, and bone marrow when a bacterial infection is present in order to prevent further growth of bacteria. To relieve the itching that accompanies vaginitis, they suggest opening vitamin E capsules and applying them to the inflamed area, or using vitamin E or enzyme cream.

Summary

Women have unique hormonal response patterns which can make them vulnerable to sexual organ disorders and infections of the genitourinary tract. As more women enter the obstetrics and gynecology professions, new clinical programs will increasingly focus on safe, long-lasting, noninvasive, nutritional, botanical, and hormonal therapies to prevent, treat, and reverse common female health problems. The holistic approach to female health challenges women to be well informed and to form an equal partnership with health care professionals in exploring a variety of therapeutic approaches.

Resources

References

Altman, Nathaniel. *Oxygen Healing Therapies*. New York: Health Sciences Press, 1994.

———. "Ozone in Medicine." *Townsend Letter for Doctors* (June 1995): 34-44.

American College of Obstetricians and Gynecologists. *Gynecological Problems: Dysmenorrhea*. Washington, DC: American College of Obstetricians and Gynecologists, 1985.

American Psychiatric Association. *Diagnostic and Statistical Manual of Mental Disorders (DSM-IV)*. Washington, D.C.: APA,1994.

Balch, James F., and Phyllis Balch. *Prescription for Nutritional Healing*. Long Island: Avery Publishing, 1993.

Beil, Laura. "New Brain Drug that Beats PMS." *Your Health* (February 8, 1994): 18-19.

Boesler, D. "Efficacy of High-Velocity Low-Amplitude Manipulative Technique in Subjects with Low-Back Pain during Menstrual Cramping." Monograph. (February 1993): 213-14. Des Moines, IA: Health Sciences College of Osteopathic Medicine.

The Burton Goldberg Group. *Alternative Medicine: The Definitive Guide*. Payallup, WA: Future Medicine Publishing, Inc., 1993.

"Drugs Used to Treat PMS Found Ineffective." *Health Facts* (August 1990): 5.

Edlin, Gordon, and Eric Golanty. *Health and Wellness: A Holistic Approach*. Boston: Jones and Bartlett Publishers, 1992.

"EFA for PMS." *Natural Health* (July/August 1993): 3.

"Exercise and Menstrual Cycle." *New Body* (December 1993): 13.

Fugh-Berman, Adriane. *Alternative Medicine: What Works*. Tucson, AZ: Odonian Press, 1996.

Gilman, Eleanor. "Waltzing through Menopause." *American Health* (April 1994): 98.

Goldstar, Rosemary. *Herbal Healing for Women*. New York: Simon & Schuster, 1993.

Gutfeld, Greg. "Relax the Flash." *Prevention* (March 1993): 18.

Hart, Carol. *The Secrets of Serotonin.* New York: St. Martin Press, 1996

Hausman, Patricia. *The Healing Foods: The Ultimate Authority on the Curative Power of Nutrition.* Emmaus, PA: Rodale Press, 1989.

Hudson, Tori. "Fibrocystic Breast Disease...Or Is It?" *Townsend Letter for Doctors* (May 1994): 549.

———. "A Pilot Study Using Botanical Medicines in the Treatment of Menopause Symptoms." *Townsend Letter for Doctors* (December 1995): 1372.

Lark, Susan. *PMS Self-Help Book: A Woman's Guide.* Berkeley, CA: Celestial Arts, 1984.

Lauersen, Neils. *PMS: Premenstrual Syndrome and You.* New York: Simon & Schuster, 1983.

Love, Susan. *Doctor Susan Love's Breast Book.* Palo Alto, CA: Addison-Wesley, 1990.

Martorano, Joseph. "Overcoming PMS." *New Body* (December 1993): 30-31.

McVeigh, Gloria. "Mastering Menopause: A Plan of Action for Every Symptom and Side Effect." *Prevention* (April 1990): 51-52.

Murray, Michael, and Joseph Pizzorno. *Textbook of Natural Medicine.* Volumes 1-2. Seattle, WA: John Bastyr College Publications, 1989.

———. *Encyclopedia of Natural Medicine.* Rocklin, CA: Prima Publishing, 1991.

National Institute on Aging. *The Menopausal Time of Life.* NIH Pub. No. 86-2461. July 1986. pp. 13-15.

Rees, Alan, and Charlene Willey. *Personal Health Reporter.* Detroit: Gale Research, 1993.

Rubin, Sylvia. "Women's Health Goes Mainstream." *San Francisco Chronicle* (March 21, 1994): E9.

Shangold, Mona. *The Complete Sports Medicine Book for Women.* New York: Simon & Schuster, 1992.

Stewart, Felicia. *Understanding Your Body: Every Woman's Guide to a Lifetime of Health.* New York: Bantam, 1987.

Ullman, Dana. *Discovering Homeopathy.* Berkeley, CA: North Atlantic Books, 1988.

Wagner, H. "Coumestans as the Main Active Principles of the Liver Drugs." *Planta Medica* (1986): 370-77.

White, Evelyn. *The Black Women's Health Book–Speaking for Ourselves.* New York: The Seal Press, 1991.

———. "More on Fibroids (Uterine Fibroids)". *Essence* (December 1991): 26.

Wollenweber, E. "Flavonoids from the Fruits of *Vitex Agnus-Castus.*" *Planta Medica* 48 (1983): 26-27.

"Working Off the PMS Blues." *Fitness* (September/October 1993): 45.

Zimmerman, David. *Zimmerman's Complete Guide to Nonprescription Drugs.* Detroit: Gale Research, 1993.

Organizations

Hysterectomy Educational Resources and Services (HERS) Foundation.
422 Bryn Mawr Avenue, Bala Cynwyd, PA 19004. (215) 667-7757.

National Institute of Allergy and Infectious Diseases.
9000 Rockville Pike, Bethesda, MD 20205.

National Women's Health Network.
1325 G Street N.W., Washington, DC 20005.

Planned Parenthood Foundation of America. 810 Seventh Avenue, New York, NY 10014.

Additional Reading

Bender, Stephanie, and Kathleen Kelleher. *PMS: A Positive Program to Pain Control.* Tucson, AZ: The Body Press, 1986.

Burnett, Raymond. *Menopause: All Your Questions Answered.* Chicago, IL: Contemporary Books, 1987.

Ody, Penelope. *The Complete Medicinal Herbal.* London, UK: Dorling Kindersley, 1993.

Stein, Diane. *The Natural Remedy Book for Women.* Freedom, CA: The Crossing Press, 1992.

RESOURCES

Chapter 14

HOLISTIC PREGNANCY AND CHILDBIRTH

Holistic Keys of Pregnancy and Childbirth

This chapter profiles important holistic keys to making child-birth one of the most beautiful and spiritual events of a woman's life. It outlines a medically safe and clinically proven program for conception, pregnancy, labor, childbirth, and childcare currently being practiced in the U.S., China, Japan, and Europe. These techniques focus on making pregnant women feel more relaxed, more beautiful, and in full control of the process of delivering a healthy baby.

Fertilization

Many cultures have recognized the need to cleanse and "tonify" the body prior to conception to ensure the optimum health of the sperm and egg—and to maximize the chances that an egg will be fertilized. A preconception checkup should include personal and family medical history, present lifestyle, and an assessment of both partners' health. This normally includes a complete physical examination and screening for breast and cervical cancer and sexually transmitted diseases.

Holistic Key: Detoxification. Both the mother and father should adopt healthy lifestyle habits a year before they attempt to have a child—and the mother should carefully avoid toxins that have been linked with both infertility and birth defects. She should consult a holistic gynecologist/obstetrician who will develop with her a complete mind/body program for conception. The gynecologist/obstetrician will also monitor the couple's exposure to: 1) alcohol, cigarettes, marijuana, cocaine, heroin,

Holistic Keys of Pregnancy and Childbirth

- Nutrition
- Traditional Chinese Medicine (TCM)
- Yoga Asanas
- Nadi Shodhana
- Progressive Relaxation
- Botanical Medicines
- Positive Thinking
- Hydrotherapy

- Guided Imagery
- Chiropractic
- Acupressure
- Fetal Stimulation
- Hypnosis
- Physiotherapy

- Acupuncture
- Biofeedback
- Pranayama Yoga
- Meditation
- Spiral Relaxation
- Intimacy Exercises
- Physical Activity
- Craniosacral Therapy
- Therapeutic Massage
- Visualization
- Receptive Imagery
- Qigong
- Homeopathy
- Music Therapy
- Mother-Baby Bonding
- Vitamin and Mineral Therapy

and LSD; 2) medications such as lithium and tetracycline which have been linked to birth defects; 3) pesticides, petroleum products, and heavy metals such as lead and mercury; and 4) over-the-counter medications such as aspirin, which can harm the fetus, and should be avoided throughout pregnancy.

Holistic Key: Nutrition. It's important for women who are planning to become pregnant to understand that her and her partner's nutritional status *prior* to conception will affect the chances of her egg being fertilized by a healthy sperm. Both mother and father therefore should work closely with the obstetrician to design a nutritional program that maximizes the mother's ability to conceive.

Her diet prior to fertilization will also affect her fetus' development once she becomes pregnant. Several famous studies of hospital births in Holland and Leningrad during World War II (where pregnant women were starving before or during their pregnancies), for example, showed that poor nutrition *prior* to pregnancy caused more birth defects and stillbirths than poor nutrition *during* pregnancy. General guidelines for optimum nutrition several months prior to conception include: Consume at least five daily servings of fresh fruits and vegetables, especially dark orange or green vegetables and citrus fruits; consume at least six servings of whole grain breads and cereals each day; consume between 25 and 35 grams of fiber daily; limit dietary fat intake to less than 30% of total calories, saturated fat to less than 10% , and cholesterol to less than 300 milligrams per day.

Holistic Key: Acupuncture. Acupuncture is the ancient Chinese technique of inserting tiny needles into the surface of the skin to stimulate the vital energy called "chi." Several clinical trials have demonstrated that acupuncture can be more effective in helping infertile women become pregnant than hormone injections.

Options for Infertility

One in every five couples who want to have children are unable to do so. Nevertheless, several recent breakthroughs have given new hope to childless couples, including:

- Surgical procedures which can repair a woman's damaged fallopian tubes, reconnect the sperm ducts of men who have had vasectomies, or correct vein disorders which impair sperm production.

- Artificial insemination in which active male sperm are deposited directly into the woman's cervix.

- In vitro fertilization (IVF) in which several ova are fertilized with active sperm and placed into the woman's uterus.

- New acupuncture treatments which have proven more effective than hormonal drug therapy in helping infertile women become pregnant.

- New Traditional Chinese Medicine (TCM) therapies which are more effective than Western pharmaceuticals in keeping the fallopian tubes open following recanalization therapy.

Dr. I. Gerhard, for example, reports a fascinating study in the September 1992 issue of *Gynecological Endocrinology* in which researchers compared the effectiveness of auricular acupuncture and hormone treatments in stimulating ovulation in 45 infertile woman with hormone imbalances. Twenty-five of the women who were treated exclusively by acupuncture subsequently became pregnant. Fifteen additional women became pregnant after being treated with acupuncture combined with hormone therapy.

Holistic Key: Traditional Chinese Medicine (TCM). Chinese obstetricians believe that a couple should prepare six months to a year in advance of the time they wish to conceive. Several TCM protocols for fertilization have been developed by Dr. Maoshing Ni and colleagues at the University of Traditional Chinese Medicine in Santa Monica, California. The TCM program includes a vegetarian diet and herbal supplements which help the sperm fertilize the egg.

Some women cannot become pregnant because of obstructions in their fallopian tubes, the tubes through which the egg travels on its way from the ovary to the uterus. These women often have pelvic inflammatory disease (PID), which either inflames their tubes or forms scar tissue that blocks the egg's passage.

In some cases, a woman's fallopian tubes can be reopened by a surgical procedure called recanalization. Nevertheless, after surgery the tubes often close up again. Western physicians normally use drugs such as Gentamyclin to keep the tubes open after recanalization, although drug treatments can have side effects such as stimulating extreme menstrual irregularities.

Two small clinical trials suggest that Chinese botanical medicines can be as effective as drug therapy in keeping the tubes open following recanalization. In one study conducted at the Affiliated Hospital of Shandong

FERTILIZATION

College of Traditional Chinese Medicine, 50 women with fallopian tube obstructions were initially treated by catheter recanalization, and then divided into two groups. The Chinese Medicine Group (CMG) was treated with two Chinese botanical formulas: tongjingbao and *Angelicae* complex injection. The Western Medicine Group (WMG) was treated with the Western drugs Gentamyclin, Dexamethasone, and Chymotrypsin. All of the women in the CMG subsequently became pregnant, compared with 50% in WMG.

Holistic Therapies during Early Pregnancy

Fertilization normally takes place within 24 hours after a sperm encounters an egg inside the fallopian tube. Only one of the millions of sperms will pass through the membrane of the ovum (female egg). Once the sperm has fertilized the ovum, enzymes in the egg alter the inner membrane and make it impossible for more sperm to enter. Once introduced, the nucleus of the sperm and egg, each containing 23 chromosomes, unite to form one fertilized egg. The fertilized egg then travels to the womb where it embeds itself in the lining of the uterus, and begins to grow.

The fertilized egg in the wall of the uterus soon divides into many cells and begin to form the embryo's organs. Five weeks after fertilization, the embryo develops a nervous system, skin, muscles, and internal organs. By the eighth week, the 3-centimeter long embryo has a complete nervous system, a beating heart, a fully formed digestive system, and the beginnings of facial features. By the sixteenth week, its heart and brain are well developed; and by the twenty-sixth week, its lungs are functional.

Holistic Key: Nutrition during First Trimester. A mother's diet during the first days of pregnancy is crucial because the only

---

General Nutritional Guidelines: First Trimester

1 Keep your weight gain during pregnancy between 25 and 35 pounds because underweight women tend to deliver low birth-weight babies.

2 Consume at least 2,000 calories a day.

3 Consume fruits and vegetables, which are excellent sources of fiber, minerals and vitamins.

4 Eat at least three nutritious snacks a day in addition to three balanced meals.

---

way the embryo in her womb can receive the nutrients and oxygen it needs for growth is through her bloodstream. Each organ and tissue of the fetus has its own specific time for cell division. By the time an organ such as the heart begins to grow in size, the important events are probably already over. This is why her nutrition during the five weeks following conception is extremely important. This means that if her diet is lacking in essential nutrients, it can have irreversible effects that may not fully become apparent until her child reaches maturity, including: delayed sexual development during early adolescence; poor dental health; and smaller number of brain cells, which researchers believe affect a baby's learning ability.

How can a woman be sure that the foods she consumes provides the fetus with the essential nutrients it requires? The safest method is to have an obstetrician regularly monitor her intake of essential nutrients.

Holistic Key: Nutrition during Second Trimester. Many pregnant mothers

---

experience heartburn and constipation, either due to the slowing of digestion or due to the size of the uterus, which will begin crowding the stomach and intestines. An obstetrician may recommend that the mother introduce a blander diet consisting of unprocessed and unseasoned foods. The obstetrician or naturopath may also prescribe natural antacids for heartburn and herbal laxatives for constipation. Prescription drugs should be avoided as they may have toxic effects on the fetus.

More than 50% of pregnant women complain of morning sickness at some time during their pregnancy. Typical symptoms include nausea and vomiting, especially in the morning, but which can occur at any time. Mothers should ask their obstetrician or nutritionist whether taking vitamin and mineral supplements will help prevent these symptoms. Vitamin B_6 supplements, for example, reduce nausea and vomiting during pregnancy. Vitamins K and C, when used together, have also been shown in clinical trials to be helpful. In one study, 91% of patients who took daily vitamin K and C tablets showed complete remission within 72 hours.

Women might also consider consuming natural herbs which have proven effective in relieving morning sickness. Eating a small amount of fresh ginger, for example, has proven effective in alleviating morning sickness. In one study, ginger was shown to be far more effective than Dramamine, a popular prescription drug used to relieving nausea and vomiting.

Holistic Key: Nutrition during Third Trimester. Approximately 10% of American women develop hypertension (high blood pressure) during pregnancy, most often in the third trimester. In most cases, the elevation is mild and produces no adverse symptoms. If it is not stabilized, however, it can result in kidney failure, liver damage, and seizures in the mother.

A 1992 study conducted at Brown University in Providence, Rhode Island, reported that low calcium intake (along with low magnesium and potassium intake) during pregnancy increases the risk of elevated blood pressure in the newborn. When pregnant women consumed 1,000 to 2,000 milligrams of calcium daily, however, they as well as their fetuses had significantly lower risks of high blood pressure. A calcium-rich diet of foods such as low-fat milk, dairy products, sardines, salmon, caviar, almonds, and Brazil nuts effectively prevents high blood pressure. Calcium supplements may also help prevent premature deliveries and low birth weight babies. Calcium supplements, however, can have side effects, including constipation. The best advice is to consume all the recommended absorbable calcium through a balanced diet.

Holistic Key: Stress Reduction. Today, virtually everyone knows what "stress" is, although it is especially important for a pregnant mother to understand how it affects her body and her fetus. During pregnancy, labor, and childbirth, she'll experience a variety of stresses, some of which will be unavoidable. In addition, she'll also undergo substantial hormonal changes which will affect how she reacts to stressful situations. For example, she may feel more irritable, anxious, or fatigued as her baby becomes larger in the womb. In his book, *The Relaxation Response*, Herbert Benson explains how a variety of holistic therapies can induce the "relaxation response," including biofeedback, yoga, meditation, visualizations, hypnosis, guided imagery, and progressive relaxation exercises. These stress-reducing therapies are essential "keys" in the holistic approach to a comfortable pregnancy and natural childbirth.

Holistic Key: Biofeedback. Biofeedback training is a method of learning how to consciously regulate brain waves, breathing rhythm, heart rate, and blood pressure. Biofeedback machines are simply computers with wires that attach to a patient's skin which measure important biological processes such as the heart beat.

How is biofeedback beneficial for a pregnant woman? Research has shown that when a mother is overstressed, her stress hormones are transferred to her baby's blood supply. One result is that her baby's movements in the womb will increase several hundred percent—even if the mother's stress lasts only for several minutes. The baby's hyperactivity, however, often continues for several hours. If the mother continues to be stressed for several weeks, her baby will remain hyperactive throughout that entire period.

Is this necessarily dangerous for the fetus? Research has documented contradictory results. It appears that a certain amount of short-term stress may be beneficial because moderately active fetuses tend to be more alert and creative following birth. Mothers who experience extreme chronic stress during pregnancy, however, tend to have babies with lower birth weights. These babies also tend to be more irritable, colicky, and cry more. Researchers have suggested that one reason this occurs is because chronic stress decreases the mother's ability to absorb important nutrients that she and her fetus need, especially phosphorous, calcium, and nitrogen.

Chronic stress, as noted, also increases the mother's heartbeat—and when her heart beats faster, so does her baby's. This influences the baby's development while inside the womb—and also affects the baby's heart rate after birth. This was demonstrated by a very interesting experiment conducted with a group of newborn babies. In the experiment, researchers played several tape recordings of a mother's heartbeat. When they played a tape of a normal heartbeat—the babies became quiet, breathed evenly, ate well, and gained weight. When the recording of the heartbeat was speeded up above normal, the same babies became restless and began to cry.

The experiment suggested to the researchers that unborn babies in the uterus seem to recognize when the mother is anxious or frightened, because they, in turn, become anxious. Other research has confirmed that the heart rhythms which a fetus develops in the womb persist long after birth. Researchers have found, for example, that unborn babies whose heart rates were accelerated due to their mother's stress showed similar cardiac variations at 20 years of age.

Biofeedback has many beneficial uses during pregnancy. In the latter part of her pregnancy, for example, a mother may find that her legs and feet become painful, or that she develops varicose veins—swollen leg veins caused by increased blood pressure due to the weight she has gained. In some cases, these symptoms result because she places a disproportionate amount of weight to one side of the body.

Dr. Marjorie K. Toomim, director of the Biofeedback Institute of Los Angeles, uses a biofeedback machine to help pregnant mothers detect muscle imbalances caused by improper weight distribution. When they are connected to an EMG feedback machine, her patients can see which weaker muscles need to be exercised to rebalance their weight. Biofeedback has also helped pregnant women with back problems by showing them how to relax specific muscles to prevent muscle spasms and back pains.

Holistic Key: Yoga. The meaning of the word yoga is "union," the integration of physical, mental, and spiritual energies. Yoga involves many different forms of physical (stretching), breathing, and mental exercises.

Some yoga practices also include visualization, progressive relaxation exercises, and meditation.

In *The Relaxation Response*, Benson details a number of studies which show that yoga induces deep breathing, decreases the heart rate, and increases blood flow to the brain, which produces more relaxed brain wave rhythms called "alpha and theta state." Each of these is important for a mother and her baby.

Deep breathing is important because it produces the "relaxation response." A pregnant mother undergoing emotional stress tends to breath faster (shallow chest breathing) and may also hyperventilate. Shallow or hyperventilated breathing, in turn, increases her heart rate, which can cause her fetus to become hyperactive—or to be born with cardiac irregularities.

Yoga and biofeedback are the two most effective therapies in lowering heart rates. Benson also documents how women who practice yoga also produce "alpha and theta" brain waves which are associated with positive thinking. One type of yoga, hatha yoga—which combines deep breathing exercises with a gentle form of calisthenics is especially effective in lowering a person's heart rate. Dr. F. Schell reports in the January 1994 issue of the *International Journal of Psychosomatics* that women who practiced hatha yoga showed "markedly lower scores in heart rates, excitability, aggressiveness, emotionality and somatic complaints." They also had significantly higher scores in positive thinking.

Pranayama ("prana"=life force; "yama"=regulation) is also effective in regulating heart rates and lowering blood pressure levels. "Prana" is similar to what the Chinese call "chi"—and both Indian and Chinese physicians believe that when a person is stressed, the vital life energy which normally flows throughout their body becomes blocked.

Pranayama exercises help remove these blockages and promote a steady, even flow of prana throughout the body. According to *Alternative Medicine: The Definitive Guide*, pranayama yoga can also help relieve indigestion and morning sickness.

One form of pranayama yoga, Nadi Shodhana, employs alternate nostril breathing. Indian Ayurvedic physicians believe that slow, meditative breathing through alternate nostrils acts as a kind of acupuncture—that is, it purifies the nadis (channels) along which the prana "flows." In *Quantum Healing*, Dr. Deepak Chopra suggests that this technique helps the brain produce its own natural pain-killers ("endorphins") which are actually several hundred times stronger than prescription drugs.

The best known form of yoga, the asanas (asana means "ease" in Sanskrit), uses physical postures and deep breathing to align the vertebrae of the spine, which in turn helps relieve back, neck, and joint pains which pregnant women often experience. By performing these gentle postures, a mother can automatically regulate her heartbeat and breathing.

Three to five percent of all pregnant women develop diabetes during pregnancy, usually during the second trimester. Pregnant women with diabetes will find practicing asanas especially beneficial. Dr. Mary Schatz, president of the Medical Staff at Centennial Medical Center in Nashville, Tennessee, has found that alternate nostril breathing can help diabetic mothers decrease their insulin dependency. Her book *Back Care Basics* also details case studies in which yoga has helped pregnant women with cardiovascular arrhythmias and thyroid disorders.

Practicing yoga will also help to keep the mother's pelvic muscles and ligaments strong and supple, which will enable her pelvis to expand more easily when the baby moves through the birth canal. Yoga will also relieve lower back stiffness and soreness in the front joint of the pelvis (symphysis pubis).

Holistic Key: Meditation.   Meditation is a state of focused concentration that produces a heightened sense of inner peace and awareness. Daniel Goleman, in his book *The Meditative Mind*, states that more than 1,000 studies have proven that meditation effectively reduces stress and anxiety, lowers blood pressure, relieves addictions, and improves metabolic and respiratory functioning. He notes that meditation has proven so effective in reducing stress and tension that the National Institutes of Health (NIH) now recommends it in place of prescription drugs as the first treatment for mild hypertension.

Why is maintaining a normal blood pressure important for a mother and her baby? Many healthy women develop a mild form of hypertension when they become pregnant. One reason is that as her fetus grows it presses on veins in her pelvis, which increases the pressure in the veins that bring blood up from her legs. This increased pressure may cause her leg veins to enlarge (to become "varicose"). The pressure can also cause fluid to leak from the veins into the tissues, in which case her feet and ankles will become swollen.

The impact of hypertension on a baby can be severe. Several studies have suggested, for example, that babies tend to be born with higher blood pressure levels if their mothers had high blood pressure in their third trimester. Dr. A. Himmelmann reports a study in the October 1994 issue of *Blood Pressure* which showed that babies born to hypertensive mothers tend to have higher blood pressure levels during their first year. They also tend to maintain high levels through their later childhood. In addition, the same study suggested that babies born with high blood pressure tend to have lower birth weights.

Holistic Key: Progressive Relaxation. Progressive relaxation, according to Benson, is another effective therapy for inducing the "relaxation response." In each form of exercise, expectant mothers first contract (or tense) a muscle group such as the back and neck muscles for several seconds—and then relax them. This is a particularly effective way to relax the womb. The procedure can be repeated progressively from the face and neck to the upper chest and arms, the abdomen, hips, buttocks, thighs, knees, calves, and feet. The whole process is repeated two or three times, and produces a deep state of relaxation.

Holistic Key: Spiral Relaxation.   Spiral relaxation is a variation of progressive relaxation in which a person imagines a point of light or heat circling three times around the top of the head—and slowly spiraling down around the face, neck, upper chest, arms, abdomen, waist, hips, thighs, knees, calves, and feet. Each part of the body relaxes as the series of three spirals encircles it.

The third relaxation exercise for pregnant women involves imagining their body being filled with healing energy which enters through the top of their head and progressively moves from the frontal lobes down the rest of the body. Although these exercises are imaginary, they effectively relax tensed muscles (especially in the womb), and they also lower the heart rate and blood pressure and slow down breathing.

Holistic Key: Deep (Dream State) Sleeping. Sleep requirements and patterns will vary throughout pregnancy. Many women find that they go to bed earlier, sleep more, and take frequent naps.

The most obvious benefit of sleep is that it replenishes the mother's energy. Deep sleep patterns are very important for the baby. Researchers have found that when the mother sleeps in a deep dream state, essential hormones are transferred across the placenta to her baby. These hormones appear to stimulate her baby's brain growth and differentiation. Consequently, if a woman is chronically stressed and do not sleep in deep sleep cycles, her baby will receive less growth hormones and more stress hormones, which can be harmful.

Holistic Key: Intimacy with Partner.
The mother's feelings of intimacy with the baby's father can also affect her fetus' development because it can sense her emotions at a physiological level. Arguments and conflicts with the father, or lack of support from an absent father, for example, can produce a sense of loneliness in the mother which stimulates "stress hormones" that are transferred to her fetus. Researchers have found that mothers who are emotionally stressed due to marital adjustment or the absence of the father tend to have babies who develop colic.

If a woman feels intimate with her partner, on the other hand, this will help her maintain the "relaxation response"—and also strengthen her immune system. Researchers have noted, for example, that mothers who feel loved and supported by their partners tend to develop healthier holistic habits such as resting and relaxing more, and maintaining a more nutritious diet. As a result, pregnant women who feel loved have been shown to maintain stronger immune systems throughout pregnancy and develop fewer illnesses and infections.

One problem many pregnant women report is a fear of sexual intimacy while they are pregnant. A mother's sexual desire often flows in different rhythms during each trimester. She may become anorgasmic for a period, or the symptoms and discomforts of pregnancy may dampen her sexual drive. During the latter months, she may also feel awkward about her body which may inhibit her lovemaking.

A mother need not be concerned that intercourse even in the third trimester will harm the fetus. In fact, developmental researchers suggest that unless there is a danger of abortion or premature labor, sexual intimacy beneficially stimulates the fetus and also increases her the mother's self-esteem. Sex also relaxes the mother, and nourishes her body because her partner's semen is rich in prostaglandins, natural chemicals that help soften her cervix. Gentle intercourse can also help initiate uterine contractions.

Holistic Key: Exercise. Regular, moderate exercise is also essential for the baby's health. A two-year study of 463 women at the Columbia School of Public Health in New York City, for example, found that expectant mothers who worked out for 30 minutes five days a week gave birth to bigger, healthier babies. Other studies have also shown that pregnant women who exercise have a heightened sense of well-being and experience fewer complications and less pain during labor.

Even if a woman has not exercised regularly before, she can safely begin this workout program. The safest, most beneficial physical activities for first-time mothers are swimming, yoga, and brisk walking because they can usually be continued safely until almost the day of delivery and involve little risk of injury. Swimming, walking, yoga, and gentle stretching are ideal for maintaining circulation and supple muscle and relieving back pain.

The type of exercise which is best for each woman will depend on her pre-pregnancy health status and how much weight she has gained during pregnancy. Expectant mothers should discuss their exercise program with an obstetrician, and be careful to avoid strenuous exercise because it may deprive the fetus of blood and nutrients. Several studies have suggested that strenuous exercise in the third trimester is associated with low birth weight babies.

Holistic Key: Hydrotherapy. Hydrotherapy is a stress reduction therapy which is especially beneficial for pregnant mothers when it's combined with water-based exercises. Water is an ideal exercising environment because its buoyancy makes movement easier and safer. Its viscosity also provides the right amount of resistance to allow a pregnant woman to maintain her muscle tone and aerobic capacity without jarring her fetus. In addition, the circumferential pressure of water enhances blood circulation.

Hydrotherapy has proven effective in relieving many discomforts associated with spinal stress and hypertension in late stages of pregnancy. Dr. Dean Edell notes that hydrotherapy also help lower heart rates and high blood pressure. He describes one study conducted by researchers at the University of North Carolina at Chapel Hill in which 11 healthy women in their third trimester were immersed in 92°F water (50 minutes a day) for five days. At the end of the study, all of the women urinated more and experienced safe declines in their heart rates and blood pressure levels. The researchers also discovered that in several of the women hydrotherapy relieved edema, the normal but uncomfortable swelling that results from water retention during pregnancy. Every mother should consult with her obstetrician before starting any program of water immersion. Mothers should not immerse themselves in water (including baths) which are hotter than 96°F.

Holistic Key: Kegel Exercises. Virtually all pregnancy books and childbirth classes recommend gentle exercises called Kegels that strengthen a mother's back, pelvic, and abdominal muscles. Along with yoga, these are the best exercises to offset the mechanical strain and postural changes that result from the weight gained during pregnancy. Doing daily Kegel exercises can prevent backaches and help with bladder control and sexual enjoyment after pregnancy.

Holistic Key: Therapeutic Massage. A massage is certainly relaxing, and many people fall into a deep, restful sleep after receiving one. In fact, massage is an excellent way of inducing the deep (dream) sleep state. Massage is also an ideal way for a mother and her partner to be intimate together. Some mothers report that they can feel their baby moving when they massage their womb.

Dr. John Yeat, in his book *A Physician's Guide to Therapeutic Massage*, details a number of studies which have demonstrated that therapeutic massage can help relieve common discomforts of pregnancy, including muscle spasms, swelling of the legs and feet, and migraine headaches.

Massage is also an excellent way to prepare for labor. Most childbirth classes teach pregnant women to massage their perineum (the small space between the anus and the vagina) before delivery in order to prevent perineal trauma during delivery. Several studies conducted by physicians at the Hospital du Saint-Sacrement in Quebec City found that pregnant women who practiced perineum massage at least four times a week for three weeks or longer subsequently experienced less difficulties (including no episiotomies) during childbirth.

Holistic Key: Visualization and Imagery. Visualization is another excellent therapy which induces the "relaxation response" and creates more positive, pleasurable images about childbirth. Studies have documented that mothers who have the most positive images before birth have the closest, most satisfying relationships with their child after birth.

Receptive imagery involves relaxing and

letting subconscious images rise into the conscious in order to silently observe any fears a mother might have about childbirth. Once she has identified her anxieties, she'll be able to focus on taking practical steps to ensure a healthy pregnancy and birthing experience. By visualizing the best birth outcome for herself and her baby, she'll increase her sense of empowerment and self-control.

The more women talk with their obstetricians or midwives, the better they'll be able to visualize what happens during labor and childbirth. Visualizations also stimulate what is called the "nesting instinct." Most pregnant women spend a good deal of time in the final months of pregnancy creating a loving and stimulating environment for their baby. This can be heightened during imagery if she visualizes holding and nursing her newborn baby.

Tuning into the "nesting instinct" is a good example of using one's intuition to prepare for a pleasurable, relaxed childbirth. The results are both practical and psychological. Each mother receives many intuitive messages during her pregnancy and the more she's in tune with them, the more relaxed her baby will be. If she has subconscious fears about how she'll feel in labor, she can use programmed imagery to intentionally picture herself experiencing contractions in a calm, relaxed manner.

Holistic Key: Chiropractic. Many mothers experience back pains during pregnancy and labor which are usually caused by minor misalignments of the spine. Sometimes, they occur if they sleep in an uncomfortable position. A chiropractor can relieve these pains by gently realigning the neck and spine. In one trial reported by Dr. P. Diakow, researchers at Canadian Memorial Chiropractic College in Toronto found that 170 women who received a gentle back manipulation prior to their labor experienced less pain during labor and childbirth.

Benefits of Qigong during Pregnancy

- Produces endorphins in the mother's brain which relieve pain and discomfort during labor.
- Induces alpha and theta brain wave states which reduce heart rates and blood pressure levels.
- Reduces depression and addictive cravings during pregnancy.
- Enhances the mother's immune system by increasing the flow of lymphatic fluids and eliminating toxins from interstitial spaces in tissues, organs, and glands.
- Improves cellular metabolism and tissue regeneration through increased circulation of oxygen and nutrient-rich blood to the brain, organs, and tissues.

Holistic Key: Qigong. Qigong (chi-kuang) is an ancient Chinese exercise which combines calisthenics-type movements with breath coordination to stimulate the flow of qi ("chi")—the vital life energy which flows through the acupuncture meridians (energy pathways). Several variations of qigong exercise are beneficial for pregnant mothers. In the first form, a mother sits in a relaxed pose and uses her mental concentration to channel "chi" energy to specific parts of her body, especially her womb. In the movement form of qigong, she integrates meditation with graceful, dance-like movements which also circulates "chi" through the meridians. Today, most hospitals in China include qigong as part of their pregnancy heath care programs.

Holistic Key: Acupuncture and Acupressure. Both acupuncture and acupressure stimulate the flow of "chi" energy. In acupressure, the therapist uses her fingers and thumbs rather than needles to press different "chi" points on the surface of the body. The specific benefits of both therapies for pregnant mothers is that "chi" point stimulation triggers the release of "endorphins," the neurochemicals that relieve pain—especially during labor and childbirth.

Both therapies also relieve muscular tension, which enables more blood, oxygen, and nutrients to be carried to tissues throughout the body. Both have also proven effective in relieving headaches, stiff necks and shoulders, nausea, vomiting, morning sickness, and pelvic pain in pregnant mothers.

Holistic Key: Homeopathy. Approximately 10% of pregnant women suffer from anemia and fatigue, especially during the third trimester. These symptoms can be alleviated by taking iron supplements. Homeopathic remedies, which have been used in obstetrics in Europe for more than 100 years, can also relieve anemia. In some cases, homeopathic remedies have proven slightly more effective than conventional drug treatments in treating pregnant women with anemia. Homeopathic treatments may also be beneficial during labor and childbirth. One study by Dr. B. Hochstrasser found that pregnant women with anemia experienced "fewer hemorrhages and decreased abnormal contractions" when they were given homeopathic remedies instead of conventional drugs.

Holistic Key: Fetal Stimulation. In the last 10 years, researchers have learned a great deal about what the baby experiences in the womb. For example, researchers now know that a baby already "thinks" and "perceives" by the sixth month of development. As noted, the mother's movements, heartbeat, and breathing all affect her growing fetus. Her baby's sense of touch, for instance, is stimulated when she exercises. Her heartbeat and breathing stimulates her fetus' sense of hearing.

Many parents have discovered the benefits of playing relaxing music to their babies while still inside the womb. Music, like meditation, appears to stimulate the endorphins. British osteopaths, for example, frequently use sound and music to transmit specific frequencies (healing vibrations) to specific diseased organs. In a like manner, soothing music appears to transmit a healing, stimulating vibration to the fetus.

Therapeutic music can also be beneficial during labor. Listening to music during the birthing process enhances the mother's sense of comfort and security. *Alternative Medicine: The Definitive Guide* adds that "the best long-term results, in terms of the health and well-being of the newborn, are coming from births that provide soothing, nurturing soundtracks."

Many mothers have noticed that their unborn baby is especially sensitive to sound. They will often kick, for example, in response to sudden loud noises. They also respond when the mother talks to them because they can sense love from the vibration of her words. Dr. Mike Samuels suggests in *The Well Baby Book* that one way of enhancing this verbal communication is to give the unborn baby a name (which is a vibration).

Holistic Therapies during Labor

Labor is the period during the ninth month of pregnancy when contractions of the uterus begin opening the cervix and forcing the baby through the birth canal. During labor, a woman's uterus will contract as few as 25 times or as many as 300 times. Labor can last a few hours or as long as 36 hours. Shorter labors are normally easier for the

Popular Childbirth Classes

- **The Grantly Dick-Read Method.** Grantly Dick-Read, an English obstetrician, believed that a woman's *fear* of childbirth disturbs nerve-muscle interactions during labor and produces tension which is perceived as pain. He developed a method which: 1) educates pregnant women in the physiology and anatomy of childbirth; 2) teaches relaxation methods, physical conditioning, and breathing exercises to use during their contractions; and 3) stresses the importance of the relationship between the expectant mother and her birth attendant.

- **Psychoprophylaxis.** Similar to the Dick-Read method, psychoprophylaxis was developed in Russia in the 1940s. Preponents believe that pain is a learned reflex and that women can be reeducated not to focus on their pain during labor. Mothers are also taught anatomy, breathing techniques, relaxation, pushing methods, and positions to use during labor.

- **Lamaze.** The Lamaze technique was developed by Frederick Lamaze, a French obstetrician who modified the method of psychoprophylaxis. Lamaze educated women to replace pain and fear with joyful expectation and redefined contractions as sensations instead of birth pains. Lamaze classes now teach breathing, relaxation, and delivery exercises such as pant-blow breathing to help with pushing in labor.

- **The Bradley Method.** This program, developed by an American obstetrician, combines Lamaze and Dick-Read methods. Women are trained in relaxation exercises for labor, and the role of the father or intimate partner as labor coach is strongly emphasized.

mother and baby, and are likely to result in less complications. Most women, except those with unusually small pelvises, are usually able to deliver their babies naturally without drugs or special medical procedures.

Which women have the shortest labors with the least pain? In the *Motherhood Report*, Dr. Louis Genevie suggests that the best indicator is a woman's stress level during her pregnancy. Women who report more psychological stress during the third trimester of pregnancy, for example, tend to have more painful labors. Interestingly, researchers have discovered that a mother's stress level in the 32nd week is the best predictor of labor pains.

Holistic obstetrics focuses on mind/body therapies which prepare the mother psychologically and physiological for an optimum birthing experience. The following sections discuss holistic therapies which have proven clinically effective during labor.

Holistic Key: Self-Hypnosis. How does self-hypnosis help to relieve labor pains? Several English obstetricians have suggested that it produces a natural state of anesthesia. Like biofeedback, yoga, meditation, visualizations, and positive thinking, self-hypnosis can trigger the release of endorphins, the body's natural pain killers.

Dr. Gowri Mothad, an English obstetrician who supervises a holistic "pain-free" pregnancy clinic in northeast London, uses self-hypnosis to help mothers focus exclusively on positive, peaceful thoughts during labor. Her staff also provides reflexology, massage, osteopathy, yoga, and other holistic healing methods to help women have pain-free, pleasant birthing experiences. Mothad's clinic delivers the majority of babies in water, and many of her patients labor for less than six hours.

Holistic Key: Childbirth Classes. Both conventional and holistic medicine stress the importance of childbirth classes because numerous studies have shown that preparation classes reduce a pregnant woman's anxiety and increase her positive images about labor and delivery. The information offered in a prenatal course will help eliminate some of the doubt and fear that surrounds childbirth, as well as provide practical information on prenatal exercise and nutrition. Childbirth classes also offer a first-time mother the opportunity to discuss the safest and least invasive birthing options with childbirth educators and midwives.

Holistic Key: Responsive Caregiver. Perhaps the most important holistic "key" to minimizing pain and complications during labor is for the mother to choose a caregiver with whom she is comfortable. Ideally, this caregiver should be he obstetrician, a nurse, or nurse-midwife. Joyce Roberts, a certified nurse-midwife, conducted a study in 1989 at the University of Colorado School of Medicine in which she and her colleagues analyzed videotapes of the labor and delivery process of hundreds of women. Roberts discovered that when mothers felt that their caregivers were "responsive," they and their newborns were healthier after delivery. The mothers surveyed by Roberts defined a "responsive" caregiver as a person who allowed them to choose their delivery positions and to push when they felt the urge.

Penny Simkin, a birth attendant, also found that women who felt that their caregivers were sensitive to their emotional needs had shorter labors, less pain, fewer complications, and less postpartum depression than those who did not have a sensitive caregiver. Pregnant women who told Simkin that they felt in control of their childbirth also recalled more positive memories about their labor and childbirth. Simkin suggests that a positive relationship a caregiver will also increase the mother's sense of self-esteem during postpartum. She notes that mothers who had negative memories of their childbirth reported more postpartum pain and depression.

Holistic Key: Certified Nurse-Midwives. An increasing number of American mothers now use certified nurse-midwives (CNMs) as their caregivers. The American College of Nurse-Midwives (ACNM), for example, estimates that within five years 10% of all births in the U.S. will be attended by CNMs.

Several large studies have shown that when midwives assisted in the delivery of a baby, mothers were more relaxed, their labors were shorter, and they required fewer drugs or medical procedures. A five-year NIH study, for example, found that 13% of the mothers attended by a CNM used epidural anesthesia during labor, compared to 41% attended by a conventional obstetrician; 36% of CNM patients received continuous electronic fetal monitoring compared to 74% of regular patients; 32% CNM patients, compared to 59% of regular patients, received episiotomies; and only 8% of CNM patients required Cesarean section, while 19% of regular patients received one.

These findings confirmed an earlier 1987 NIH study which found that mothers cared for by CNMs were significantly less likely to experience postpartum hemorrhage, infection, and major perineal damage than patients treated by a nonholistic physician. The study also revealed that women assisted by nurse-midwives fared as well as doctors' patients and were less likely to have intravenous fluids, Pitocin induction, artificially ruptured membranes, sedatives, or anesthesia.

Holistic Key: Mother-Father Intimacy. A mother's sense of intimacy with her partner may also influence how long she will be in labor. Several studies have shown that women who felt supported in their labor by their husband or partner have shorter labors, and fewer birth-related complications, including Cesarean sections. Psychologist Katherine Nuckolls, for example, surveyed pregnant mothers and found that those who had strong support from their partners experienced one-third fewer complications during pregnancy and childbirth. According to Nuckolls, being supported during their labor made women feel more loved, increased their self-esteem, and made them feel part of something larger than themselves.

Holistic Key: Perineal Massage. The importance of perineal massage throughout pregnancy has already been discussed. It's particularly important to massage the perineum prior to labor to prepare it for stretching during childbirth. For some women, this reduces their need to have an episiotomy—the small surgical cut in the perineum which facilitates the emergence of the baby. Massage can also prevent the perineum from tearing or scarring, even if an episiotomy is necessary. Massage should be delayed if there are any vaginal problems, such as an active herpes sore or vaginitis. It can be resumed once the vagina is healed.

Holistic Key: Acupuncture. Acupuncture has been used in Russia since the 1940s to relieve labor pains. There have been several Russian clinical trials in which acupuncture was effectively used as a form of reflex analgesia during labor. One clinical trial,

reported by Dr. O. Oberg, investigated the effectiveness of reflex analgesia via electrical acupuncture in 46 patients with an abnormal preliminary labor periods. Oberg concludes "that acupuncture was found to effectively reduce preliminary pain sensation, to normalize central nervous function, autonomic reactions, uterine contractility, reduce the need for pharmacological agents and result in better deliveries."

Acupuncture appears to be a less invasive pain-relieving therapy during labor than drugs. Dr. Jack Pritchard, author of "Analgesia and Anesthesia" in *William's Obstetrics*, cautions mothers not to indiscriminately take pain relief drugs during labor—unless they feel it is absolutely necessary—because some drugs reach the baby through the placenta. He notes that Pethidine, for example, sedates newborns to the point of disturbing their early suckling patterns and may inhibit successful breastfeeding.

Newer analgesic drugs appear to have less severe side effects. Epidural analgesia is a "local" pain medication which is injected close to the spine. The proponents of epidurals claim that in extreme cases, it can make the difference between a terrible experience and a tolerable one. They also suggest that it has few long-term effects on the mother or her baby. Holistic obstetricians, however, caution that most epidurals weaken the mother's bearing down reflex which sometimes delays the second stage of labor, and can lead to early surgical interventions, including forceps and vacuum extractions. It is important for all women to decide in advance whether they wish to have a natural labor without medications. Should complications develop, they should discuss pain relief options with their obstetrician or caregiver before they're administered.

Holistic Key: Progressive Relaxation and Imagery. Total body relaxation helps relieve pain during labor and childbirth. The more familiar a mother is with relaxation exercises during labor, the easier it will be for her to maintain the relaxation response for longer and longer periods. If she steadily relaxes her uterus during labor, she has a better chance of having fewer and less painful contractions. Like relaxation, imagery is a skill that needs to be practiced, and becomes easier with use.

Holistic Therapies during Childbirth

The holistic approach to childbirth focuses on providing the mother with the safest and most relaxing environment in which to quickly deliver her baby with a minimum of pain. Where the mother chooses to have her baby will determine the alternatives that will be available to her during childbirth. The most important thing for her is to select an environment that makes her feel safe, comfortable, and fully in control.

Holistic Key: Choose a Safe, Relaxing Birthing Environment. The increasing demand for holistic approaches to labor and delivery has motivated many hospitals to provide comfortable, more private birth rooms. Should a mother wish to have her baby in a hospital, but still want to have a natural birth, she should arrange for this option with her obstetrician. Options currently available in the U.S. include:

• Free-Standing Birth Centers. Free-standing birth centers (FSBCs) offer a holistic compromise between having a hospital and a home birth. FSBCs often provide a home-like setting in which the mother's friends and relatives may be present during the birth. They are generally staffed by experienced midwives trained in prenatal care and birthing. The obstetrician may also agree to be on call during labor. Approximately 15-20% of first-time mothers who choose a FSBC birth need

to be transferred to a hospital during labor or after delivery.

• Home Births. The proponents of home births argue that home births are as safe, if not safer than hospital births in terms of interventions, birth injuries, and maternal hemorrhaging. However, it is important that all women consult their obstetrician before choosing this option. Women with hypertension, heart and kidney disease, anemia, diabetes, or epilepsy should only give birth in a hospital. Women who have had previous Cesareans, and first-time mothers over the age of 35 are also usually advised to have a hospital birth.

• Water Births. Water births were pioneered in France by Dr. Michel Odent and have become increasingly popular in the U.S. Women who have experienced water births report that they felt more relaxed during their labor because the weightless feeling of the water eased their pain. Others noted that birthing in water reduced the risk of perineal tearing. Advocates of water birthing claim that it is the least stressful way to give birth for both a mother and her baby because it shortens labor and makes pushing easier.

Holistic Key: Birthing Positions. The birthing position(s) the mother uses should be determined by what feels comfortable and most suitable for her body. Standing and walking can enhance the dilation of the cervix, and aid the baby's descent through the birth canal. Some women report that they needed fewer pain medications when they remained physically active during labor. Staying in bed during labor tends to impair breathing, compress major blood vessels, reduce circulation, and decrease uterine blood flow. Some women find it helpful to squat during birthings because it also increases the pelvic opening by half to a full centimeter. Other mothers report that they found it helpful to sit in warm water during labor. Each mother should discuss all of these alternatives with her obstetrician or nurse-midwife.

Holistic Key: Vaginal Births. The holistic method of childbirth stresses that women should plan to have a vaginal birth without an episiotomy, vacuum or forceps extraction, or a C-section. Contrary to popular belief, pregnant women can have a vaginal birth even if they previously had a Cesarean.

Most experts agree that the best way to minimize pain during labor is for the mother to be fully conscious of what is occurring in her body. They recommend that women continue to perform yoga, massage, or other relaxation exercises during labor that gently induce the "relaxation response." In the end, every mother will need to trust her own body's wisdom. The most successful births are by women who have confidence in themselves and their birthing team.

Medical technology has its place in emergency childbirths, although holistic physicians do not recommend the standard interventions typically used in hospitals, such as pain medications, Cesarean sections, and episiotomies. Currently, approximately 90% of American women have episiotomies. A holistic obstetrician will not recommend this procedure except in cases of severe fetal distress or if the mother is unable to deliver her child without help. According to *Alternative Medicine: The Definitive Guide,* episiotomies do not, as previously thought, prevent perineal tears or trauma, enhance later sexuality, or benefit the baby. In addition, they are not necessary for deliveries which require the use of forceps or vacuum extractions.

Holistic obstetricians do not recommend the use of forceps to pull the baby through the birth canal because infant deaths have been caused by forceps delivery. Forceps deliveries have also been associated with impairing a baby's vision and causing foot problems. Vacuum extractions, in which the baby is sucked through the canal, are also not practiced because they have recently been associated with decreased oxygen delivery and internal bleeding of the fetus during birth. In addition, they have resulted in leg problems in newborns.

Approximately 25% of all births in the U.S. are performed by Cesarean-section, the surgical operation for delivering a baby by cutting through the mother's abdominal and uterine walls. In some emergencies, a C-section delivery may be the only alternative. But it should only be used as a last resort because it increases the risk of maternal complications, including infections, bleeding, a longer recovery period, and less initial bonding with the newborn baby. According to the Public Citizens Health Research Group, Cesareans are necessary in only 12% of deliveries.

Holistic Therapies for Postpartum

Holistic therapies immediately following childbirth focus on mother-baby bonding, and naturally healing the mother's uterus and perineum. It is extremely important that mother and baby bond before the umbilical cord is cut, and the mother nurse her newborn baby before it is given eyedrops. Placing the baby on the mother's breast will normally initiate suckling, which is important to future breast-feeding. Most infants will imitate crawling motions toward the breast immediately after delivery and suckle in less than an hour if they're not drugged or disturbed.

Holistic Key: Mother-Baby Bonding. Holistic physicians also recommend that a mother nurse her baby before it is given vitamin K injections. If the mother has consumed vitamin K-rich foods or vitamin K oral supplements during the last month of pregnancy, her baby will usually not need injections. There have been several studies

Benefits of Breastfeeding for the Baby

- Enhances bonding with mother
- Provides optimum nutrition
- Supplies lactoferrin, lysozyme, secretory immunoglobulins A, T, and B lymphocytes, and macrophages which strengthen the immune system
- Increases survival rate for low birth weight newborns
- Decreases gastrointestinal infections
- Protects against necrotizing enterocolitis, a serious intestinal disorder common in premature or low birth weight babies.

Benefits of Breastfeeding for the Mother:

- Stimulates contractions of the uterus and helps control postpartum blood loss
- Increases strength of immune system
- Increases mother's confidence in parenting skills.

---

released linking intramuscular vitamin K shots with childhood cancer, whereas no such ties were found when vitamin K was administered orally.

Bonding with the baby is not only an important spiritual event, it also has immediate medical benefits. The May 1986 issue of *Pediatrics* reported a study in which doctors at the University of Miami Medical School divided 40 premature babies who had been delivered after 31 weeks of pregnancy. One group was given normal treatment in the hospital's intensive care unit. The other received 15 minutes of daily special attention, in which someone reached in through the portholes of their sealed cribs to stroke them and gently wiggle their arms and legs.

The results of such a simple bonding-like touch therapy were striking. Although fed on demand with the same formula, the stroked babies gained 47% more weight each day than the control group. They were more alert and started to act like normally delivered babies. They also left the hospital a week ahead of schedule, resulting in a savings of $1,000.

Massaging the baby will reduce both the baby and the mother's stress levels. Researchers at the Touch Research Institute (TRI) at the University of Miami Medical School conducted a study investigating the effects of massage on adolescent mothers and their newborn infants. They found that after a 30-minute massage, both the mothers and their babies had lower levels of cortisol and norepinephrine (stress hormones) and were more alert, less restless, and better able to sleep.

Holistic Key: Breastfeeding. The holistic method of childbirth recommends that women breastfeed their babies whenever possible. Breastfeeding has many advantages extensively documented in clinical trials, the most important of which is that it stimulates the development of the newborn baby's immune system. Breastfed babies, for example, have been shown to have lower rates of allergies, diarrhea, colic, stomachaches, dental problems, ear infections, respiratory infections, and meningitis than bottle-fed infants.

Holistic Key: Uterine Massage. It is important that the mother's uterus remain contracted after birth to prevent excess bleeding. Most women lose about one cup of blood at the time of birth, and nursing the baby often causes the uterus to contract. Nursing is the most natural way of healing the uterus—and it has the added benefit of helping to establish the mother's milk supply. Uterine massage should be continued for several days until it stays naturally contracted, and begins to shrink to the size of a tennis ball.

A small number of pregnant women experience postpartum hemorrhaging. Dr. M. Varner reports one trial in the October 1991 issue of *Critical Care Clinics* in which massage effectively reduced minor hemorrhaging and pelvic pulse pressure. Women whose hemorrhaging was due to a rupture of their uterus, however, required surgery.

Holistic Key: Perineal Massage. The mother's perineum may be sore and swollen for several days after birth, due to stretching during delivery. The first day following childbirth, she can reduce swelling by massaging the perineum with ice packs (covered with a cloth) at half hour intervals. On the second day, holistic obstetricians normally recommend replacing the ice pack with a hot water bottle or heating lamp (not ultraviolet or sunlamp). Taking a warm water sitz baths at 20-minute intervals is also helpful. Witch hazel or essential oil of lavender applied to a sanitary napkin can also help reduce swelling. Douching and tampons should be avoided during this period.

Many mothers find it difficult or painful to urinate the first week following childbirth. This is normally caused by tight sphincter muscles which can be relaxed by performing gentle yoga exercises and visualizations. It's also important to keep the perineum clean after urination; an excellent method is to spray warm water using a peri bottle. Some mothers experience constipation and painful bowel movements immediately following childbirth. One way to keep stools soft is to eat high-fiber foods such as bran and fresh vegetables, and drink more fluids.

Holistic Key: Nutrition. During childbirth, the mother's body is depleted of many essential nutrients which must be replaced as soon as possible during her postpartum recovery. Obstetricians normally advise mothers who breastfeed to consume at three to four servings of calcium-rich foods each day, including whole grains, fruits and vegetables, lean meat, or cooked dried beans and peas. Low-fat milk is an excellent source of nutrients, including protein, calcium, vitamin B_2, and magnesium. Mothers who cannot tolerate milk (lactose intolerant) should consume foods similar in nutrient composition such as cheese, soy milk, dark green vegetables, and yogurt.

Holistic Key: Exercise. It's also important for every mother to resume Kegel exercises as soon as she feels comfortable to regain pelvic strength. Each mother should be guided by her own body, and resume her preferred form of exercise when she feels ready. Lack of sleep, nursing, and child care will place extra demands on her body—and the fastest way for her to recover her physical energy is to resume safe, gentle exercises such as yoga, qigong, or tai chi.

Holistic Key: Yoga. Yoga is the safest restorative therapy that women can begin immediately after birth. Yoga will quickly normalize their heart rate, blood pressure and breathing, and gently exercise their pelvic and abdominal muscles so they do not become sore or tight. A study by Dr. P. Raju indicates that practicing yoga effectively restores aerobic fitness in new mothers without raising their blood lactate levels (which cause muscle soreness). This, in turn, according to Raju, gives new mothers more energy to nurse their babies.

Yoga also helps mothers regain their normal, pre-pregnancy body weight and shape. Dr. T. Bera reports in the July 1993 issue of the *Indian Journal of Physiology and Pharmacology* that when new mothers practice yoga they experience a "significant improvement in ideal body weight, body density, cardiovascular endurance and anaerobic power."

Holistic Key: Physiotherapy. European mothers commonly undergo physiotherapy immediately following childbirth to heal their pelvic muscles. First-time mothers may find it difficult to walk without pain, and physiotherapy exercises retrain women to walk in a relaxed and comfortable way. Physiotherapy also restores the circulation of blood in abdominal muscles and reduces swelling and pain. The most restorative physiotherapy programs combine exercise, massage, relaxation, and other treatments.

Holistic Key: Craniosacral Therapy for the Baby. Difficult deliveries, extended periods of engagement (the time the baby's head is in the birth canal), or the incorrect application of forceps and vacuum suction can pinch a newborn baby's cranial tissues. This can cause ear aches, sinus congestion, vomiting, irritability, and hyperactivity. In some cases, these symptoms occur if part of the baby's neck was compressed during birth—especially by an extreme backward extension of the baby's head during delivery. According to *Alternative Medicine: The Definitive Guide,* newborn babies can be treated immediately after birth by craniosacral therapy which gently readjusts baby's soft neck and spine cartilage, and eases the symptoms of a difficult delivery.

Holistic Key: Guided Imagery. Many mothers suffer postpartum depression often because of a painful delivery, medical complications, an insufficient postpartum diet, or stress. Dr. B. Reese reports a clinical study in the September 1993 issue of the *Journal of Holistic Nursing* which found that "anxiety and depression declined and self-esteem increased" in women who were trained in relaxation and guided imagery.

Holistic Key: Nursing and Relaxation Exercises. The way a mother touches, nurses, and communicates with her newborn baby directly affects the development of its nervous system. Mothers who nurse their infants in a relaxed manner tend to develop fewer diseases and infections—and so do their babies.

Several studies by Dr. Roger Mayer, a pediatric researcher, for example, compared the sickness rates of babies nursed by relaxed or stressful mothers. In one study, he found that babies with strep throats were four times as likely to have been nursed by nervous mothers. Other studies have also shown that the duration of upper respiratory illnesses is prolonged in babies who undergo stress during nursing and early development.

Summary

Becoming a parent is truly one of life's great moments, and it should be approached with a plan to do everything possible to ensure that the new infant is healthy and will enjoy a natural, peaceful development. The expectant mother and child are one biological organism until the moment of birth, and whatever the woman puts into her body will most likely be passed to her baby. Therefore, it is extremely important that the pregnant woman eat properly and avoid consuming any drugs or toxins that could harm the fetus. Starting and maintaining an exercise routine has been strongly linked in several studies with good health during pregnancy, an easier delivery, and larger, healthier babies. Childbirth should be a natural process except in cases of emergency, and the baby should be bonded to the mother as soon as possible. Women who breastfeed significantly increase the chances that their babies will enjoy healthy physiological and psychological development. The most important factor in ensuring a safe and successful pregnancy is a woman's confidence in her obstetrician and nurse-midwife and her awareness of her own body.

Resources

References

Aleksandrina, E. "The Acupuncture Prevention of Anomalies in Labor Strength in Pregnant Women of a Risk Group." *Akuehrstvo i Ginekologiia* (Russian) (August 1992): 22-24.

Anonymous. "Diagnosis and Management of Postpartum Hemorrhage." *International Journal of Gynecology & Obstetrics.* (October 1991): 159-63.

Banerud, B. "Pelvic Relaxation and Physiotherapy Prevention and Treatment." *Tidsskrift for Den Norseke Laegeforening* (Norwegian). (January 30 1992): 349-51.

Bellumini, J. "Acupressure for Nausea and Vomiting of Pregnancy: A Randomized, Blinded Study." *Obstetrics & Gynecology* (August 1994): 245-48.

Berger, B. "Mood Alternation with Yoga and Swimming: Aerobic Exercise May Not be Necessary." *Perceptual & Motor Skills* (December 1992): 1331-43.

Chopra, Deepak. *Quantum Healing.* New York: Bantam Publishing, 1991.

De Aloysia, D. "Morning Sickness Control in Early Pregnancy by Neiguan Point Acupressure." *Obstetrics & Gynecology* (November 1992): 852-54.

Edell, Dean. "Medical Journal." *San Jose Mercury News* (July 22, 1993).

Gerhard, I. "Auricular Acupuncture in the Treatment of Female Infertility." *Gynecological Endocrinology* (September 1992): 171-81.

Graf, F. "Nongenetic Perinatal Anemias: Conventional, Herbal, and Homeopathic Treatments." *Clinical Issues in Perinatal & Women's Health Nursing* 3 (1991): 357-63.

Himmelmann, A. "Blood Pressure and Left Ventricular Mass in Children and Adolescents: The Hypertension in Pregnancy Offspring Study." *Blood Pressure* (October 1994): 1-46.

Hochstrasser, B. "Homeopathy and Conventional Medicine in the Management of Pregnancy and Childbirth Review." *Schweizerische Medizinische Wochenschrift.* (Swiss)

Jain, S. "A Study of Response Pattern of Non-Insulin Dependent Diabetics to Yoga Therapy." *Diabetes Research & Clinical Practice.* (January 1993): 69-74.

Jordan, Sandra. *Yoga for Pregnancy.* New York: St. Martin's Press, 1987.

Labrecque, M. "Prevention of Perineal Trauma by Perineal Massage during Pregnancy: A Pilot Study." *Birth* (March 1994): 20-25.

Lian, F. "Clinical Study of the Treatment of Fallopian Tube Obstruction with Catheter Recanalization and Blood Statis Removing Drugs." *Chug-Kuo Chug Hsi i Chieh Ho Tsa Chih* (Chinese). (February 1994): 80-82.

Oberg, O. "Feflektornaia Analgeziia." *Akusherstvo i Ginekologiia* (Russian). (February 1991): 37-39.

Parsons, C. "Back Care in Pregnancy." *Modern Midwife* (October 1994): 16-19.

Raju, P. "Comparison of Effects of Yoga & Physical Exercise in Athletes." *Indian Journal of Medical Research* (August 1994): 81-86.

Reese, B. "An Exploratory Study of the Effectiveness of a Relaxation with Guided Imagery Protocol." *Journal of Holistic Nursing* (September 1993): 271-76.

Rosenthal, Elisabeth. "Study Says Calcium Helps High Blood Pressure in Pregnancy." *The New York Times* (September 13, 1993): 1.

Samuels, Mike, and Nancy Samuels. *The Well Baby Book*. New York: Summit Books, 1991.

Schell, F. "Physiological and Psychological Effects of Hatha-Yoga Exercise in Healthy Women." *International Journal of Psychosomatics*. (January 1994): 46-52.

Telles, S. "Breathing through a Particular Nostril Can Alter Metabolism and Autonomic Activities." *Indian Journal of Physiology & Pharmacology* (April 1994): 133-37.

Varner, M. "Postpartum Hemorrhage." *Critical Care Clinics* (October 1991): 883-97.

Webb, K. "Effects of Acute and Chronic Maternal Exercise on Fetal Heart Rate." *Journal of Applied Physiology* (November 1994): 2207-13.

Organizations

American Association of Naturopathic Physicians.

2366 Eastlake Avenue, Suite 322, Seattle, Washington 98102.

American College of Nurse Midwives.
1522 K Street NW, Suite 100, Washington, D.C. 20005.

American Holistic Medical Association.
4101 Lake Boone Trail, Suite 201, Raleigh, North Carolina 27607.

Doulas of North America (DONA).
110 23rd Avenue East, Seattle, Washington 98112.

Informed Birth and Parenting.
P.O. Box 3675, Ann Arbor, Michigan 48106.

International Association of Parents and Professionals for Safe Alternatives in Childbirth.
Route 1, Box 646, Marble Hill, Missouri 63764.

International Childbirth Education Association.
P.O. Box 20048, Minneapolis, Minnesota 55420.

National Association of Childbirth Assistants (NACA).
205 Copco Lane, San Jose, California 95123.

National Women's Health Network.
1325 G Street NW, Washington, D.C. 20005.

Planned Parenthood Foundation of America.
810 Seventh Avenue, New York, New York 10014.

Read Natural Childbirth Foundation.
P.O. Box 150956, San Rafael, California 94916.

RESOURCES

Chapter 15

DENTAL CARE

Many people do not appreciate the importance of dental health to their overall well-being. This is because until recently dental care was considered peripheral to general health, and cavities and eventual tooth loss were commonly regarded as inevitable. However, recent advances in conventional and holistic dental treatment now make it possible for people to maintain healthy teeth and prevent virtually all dental and oral infections. An holistic approach to dental care is critical because dentists are often the first to diagnose many types of diseases, not just those in the mouth. In fact, a recent survey of dentists cited in the November 28, 1993 Gannet News Services revealed that they often made the initial diagnosis of chronic illnesses among their adult patients. Fifty-two percent of the dentists said they had been the first to uncover oral cancer; 28% were the first to diagnose bulimia, and 26% first detected diabetes. This survey clearly suggests that dentists are increasingly concerned with the whole body health of their patients. As an example, nearly half of the 603 dentists surveyed said they now ask all patients about tobacco use and counsel smokers on how to quit smoking.

Teeth and gums, like all other parts of the body, depend on a strong immune system, and when the immune system is weakened, the teeth and gums are more likely to become infected. For this reason, a holistic approach to dental care should include eating natural whole foods which both strengthen the immune system and prevent the formation of bacteria or acids that corrode the teeth and cause gum disease and infections.

Teeth, like other bones, are affected by the foods a woman eats during her pregnancy. Because nutritional factors have a significant effect in prenatal tooth development, holistic dental care should begin by encouraging pregnant women to consume sufficient amounts of Vitamins A, B, C, and D, as well as calcium, phosphorous, and fluoride. Vitamin A is essential because a deficiency in the fetus (or during infancy) can cause abnormal tooth development, poor calcification, and reduced enamel formation. Vitamin C is important because a deficiency can result in weakening of the connective tissue of the gums and decreased formation of dentin, the bone-like bulk of the tooth. A deficiency of vitamin D, calcium, or phosphorous can cause poor tooth positioning, decreased dentine and enamel, and increased susceptibility to decay. And a mild deficiency of the B vitamins, especially folate, has been shown to weaken the soft tissues and tooth-supporting structures and increase their vulnerability to infection.

A baby's primary teeth are already formed when it is born, while the permanent teeth begin forming immediately after birth. The primary teeth usually appear through the gums by the seventh month. By the age of two or three years, most babies have all 20 primary teeth, and a full set of permanent teeth is usually formed by the age of five. Oral hygiene, fluorides, and diet are the main factors that affect the health of the primary teeth. If the primary teeth are not regularly brushed and monitored by a dentist for straightness, the permanent teeth are likely to develop problems. Jane Brody's *Guide to Personal Health* suggests that the most important oral hygiene practices for primary teeth include regularly cleaning the baby's teeth with a cotton or gauze pad, rinsing the baby's mouth daily with water, and adding fluoride liquids to the baby's food if fluoride is not present in the drinking water. Fluoride supplements should only be added upon the advice of a dentist.

Infant tooth decay can occur when a baby is given a bottle filled with milk, formula, or fruit juice at bedtime, naptime, or for long periods during the day. Extended exposure to the sugar in these liquids can cause teeth to discolor and decay. Since breast milk also contains sugar, decay can occur when a baby falls asleep when breastfeeding. To prevent damage, it is important that a child's teeth be cleaned after each feeding, and if necessary, the infant should be given a bottle filled only with water at bedtime or naptime.

Preventing Cavities

It has been estimated that half of all American children have at least one cavity by the age of two. Most people are aware that cavities are caused by bacteria which adhere to the teeth and excrete a sticky transparent film of dextran called plaque. When the plaque becomes thick enough, it produces acids which can eat away the enamel covering a tooth and eventually erode (decalsify) the underlying bone, leaving a hole in the tooth. Once this occurs, the bacteria (caries), which created the hole in the tooth, must be removed, and the hole filled.

Several factors determine whether a young child will develop cavities. First, genetic structure will partly determine how well teeth resist the bacteria. What a person eats is also an important factor because sugar and honey, when left on the surface of teeth, produce acids which eat away tooth enamel. Sweet snacks, particularly sticky foods containing caramel, such as candies, cookies, and pastries cause the most damage. Sweet drinks also produce cavities, especially colas which contain tannin acids.

Despite the role of genetic or nutritional factors in causing cavities, the American Dental Association (ADA) claims that virtually all cavities can be prevented by proper brushing. Unfortunately, most Americans, according to the ADA, fail to brush their teeth sufficiently to prevent cavities. Proper brushing is important because even if teeth are inherently weak and exposed to sugars which can cause cavities, proper brushing will neutralize and eliminate most sugars through the saliva.

To brush properly, the ADA recommends using a brush with soft, rounded bristles and a flat brush surface. The head of the brush should be small enough to reach all sides of the teeth, and should be held against the teeth with the bristles at a 45-degree angle facing into the gum. The tongue should also be brushed to remove bacteria and to freshen breath. Gum stimulators, pointed rubber tips at the end of toothbrushes, are useful for massaging gum tissue. The ADA now endorses the use of electric toothbrushes and specifically urges people to avoid abrasive toothpastes or powders. Water piks can replace toothbrushes and are useful for people with bridgework or braces.

Dental floss, either the waxed or unwaxed kind, should be used twice a day to clean under the gumline and between the teeth. An 18-inch piece of floss, held between the thumbs and forefingers of each hand, should be eased between the teeth and curved into a C shape around each tooth at the gumline. When it is moved up and down gently between the tooth and gum, the floss scrapes against the side of the tooth, and removes bacteria. Flossing should always be followed by a thorough rinsing of the mouth to wash out loosened bacteria. The ADA also recommends that people regularly monitor their brushing by purchasing a disclosing solution or tablets which contain a vegetable dye that stains plaque.

Dental Fillings. Once a tooth develops a cavity, it must be filled. The type of filling the dentist recommends depends on the size of the cavity, its location, and what the patient can afford. Several different types of fillings currently exist which vary in hardness, endurance, and cost. Most dentists prefer to

Preventing Tooth Decay

The following guidelines to prevent tooth and gum decay are recommended by the American Dental Association (ADA).

1. **Brushing**. Replace your brush often, ideally once every three months or when the bristles show wear, because a worn-out toothbrush will not clean teeth properly. Change the position of the toothbrush frequently, as it will clean only one or two teeth at time. Brush gently and with very short strokes, but use enough pressure so you feel the bristles against the gum. Only the tips of the bristles clean, so do not squash them. Be sure to brush at least twice a day to help prevent plaque damage.

2. **Toothpaste**. Some fluoride toothpastes prevent 25-30% of the decay a child might otherwise develop. However, not all fluorides are effective. The seal of the ADA Council on Dental Therapeutics guarantees the most effective paste.

3. **Mouthwashes**. A mouthwash can temporarily freshen breath or sweeten the mouth, but none remove plaque or prevent tooth decay. However, mouthwashes with fluoride provide minor protection against some tooth diseases. Do not rely on mouthwashes to relieve pain or other symptoms of gum disease.

4. **Flossing**. Floss regularly, preferably after every meal.

5. **Dental Visits**: Regular checkups and professional cleanings are also essential.

use gold or porcelain fillings because they are the strongest and last the longest. Porcelain also has the same whiteness as natural teeth, and is the obvious choice for cosmetic reasons. Composite fillings are made from several different materials including small amounts of metal oxide which dry as hard as glass. According to San Francisco dentist Gary Lindsey, "composite fillings are very technique sensitive and are not the easiest and fastest to apply. But when a composite filling is done by an expert practitioner, they wear better and polish better than amalgam fillings."

Amalgam fillings (sometimes called silver fillings) are permanent fillings which are easy to install, and fill holes in teeth quite adequately. Most Americans with fillings have had at least one amalgam filling, which lasts a long time and is less expensive than gold. Most amalgam fillings contain approximately 40-54% mercury, 35% silver, small amounts of tin mixed with copper, and a trace of zinc.

Some holistic dentists, however, have counseled their patients not to use amalgam fillings because of their high mercury content. Although mercury has been used in amalgam fillings for more than 150 years, recent evidence has shown that even in small amounts it can be quite toxic. The Occupational Safety and Health Agency (OSHA) and the Environmental Protection Agency (EPA), for example, now classify excess mercury as a toxic waste. OSHA uses 50 micrograms per cubic meter as a maximum allowable level of mercury vapor in the work place. The EPA and National Aeronautics and Space Administration (NASA) use one microgram per cubic meter as their maximum allowable level. According to the 1993 *Shared Guide*, the average level of mercury vapor measured in the mouths of people with several mercury filling varies from 50-150 micrograms per cubic meter.

Many holistic dentists now believe that the small amounts of mercury which are contained in amalgam fillings may gradually leach into the body (either as part of the saliva or as a gas), and may subsequently pass along nerve roots directly to the brain. Most crowns also have amalgam fillings under them, and the mercury can leak out through the root of the tooth and into the bloodstream. Mercury has been shown to affect the nervous system, sometimes resulting in numbness, extreme fatigue, mental incapacity, or even paralysis. As a result of the potential danger of mercury toxicity, several countries, including Sweden, have banned amalgam fillings in pregnant women, according to the February 1985 *CDA Journal*.

The ADA's official position is that the small amount of mercury that may get into a person's system from amalgam fillings does not present a health threat. Studies by Dr. T. Vaidyanathan, a dental materials expert at the New Jersey Dental School in Newark, found that the maximum amount of mercury that can be absorbed from a new filling is 0.4 micrograms per day, compared with previous estimates of more than five micrograms. According to Vaidyanathan, quoted in the January/February 1994 issue of *American Health*, "You need about 135 fillings in your mouth to even approach toxic levels of mercury." Nonetheless, until conclusive research is available on dental fillings containing mercury, holistic dentists recommend composite fillings made from silica with a plastic matrix binder.

Kinetic Cavity Preparation. A new technique is now being used instead of drilling to treat tiny cavities before they destroy larger areas of the tooth. According to the November 1993 issue of *American Health*, the technique, called "kinetic cavity preparation" (KCP), uses a high-speed stream of particles that sandblasts away superficial decay and stains. Although dentists tend to ignore discolored pits on teeth, decay can often be present particularly on the back teeth. If a cavity has not yet developed, the stain alone is removed and a sealant applied to the tooth to prevent further trouble and discomfort. Treating these areas with KCP prevents more serious damage. And, because the sandblasting device provides greater control than conventional drilling, it also removes less of the tooth's enamel. However, it does not replace drilling for more extensive work. Anesthesia is not necessary when the KCP technique is used.

Fluorides. Ninety-eight percent of all Americans have at least one cavity, and virtually all of these can be prevented by fluoride, according to the ADA. When infants and young children swallow fluoride, it is incorporated into the teeth as hard, insoluble crystals called fluorapatite. Fluorapatite replaces some of the natural outer-tooth enamel and penetrates into the deeper layers of the teeth. Fluoride in the saliva also helps to remineralize enamel by retaining calcium and phosphate. These crystals inhibit the ability of bacteria to become attached to teeth and produce the acids which cause the dentin (tooth bone) to decay.

The best sources of flouride include natural drinking water, drinking water fortified with fluoride supplements, and fluoride products available over-the-counter in mouth rinses and treatment gels. The most common source of fluoride in the United States is drinking water. Of 133 million Americans who live in communities where the public water supply contains 0.7 parts per million (ppm) of fluoride, nine million drink naturally fluoridated water, while 124 million use water that contains fluoride supplements. According to *Zimmerman's Complete Guide to Prescription Drugs*, most ground, river, and lake waters contain some natural fluoride.

Benefits of Fluoride

- Fluoride in drinking water yields a 50-65% reduction in cavities.
- Fluoride in school drinking water yields a 40% reduction in cavities.
- Fluoride drops or tablets taken at home yield a 50-65% reduction in cavities.
- Fluoride mouth rinses yield a 30-40% reduction in cavities.
- Fluoride toothpastes yield a 20-40% reduction in cavities.
- Annual fluoride applications by dentists yield a 30-40% percent reduction in cavities.

While the use of fluoride in drinking water and in various supplement forms is still controversial, it is quite clear that fluoride effectively prevents cavities. An article in the *Journal of the American Medical Association* reviewed all the literature on fluoride and concluded that community water fluoridation "yields a 50 to 65 percent reduction in cavities, while fluoride drops or tablets, mouth rinses, toothpaste and dental applications yield from 20 to 65 percent reduction in cavities."

Botanical Medicines. People who are reluctant to take fluoride supplements should consider substituting a natural spice, cardamom. Cardamon is an aromatic seed often used in cooking curries, stews, and pastries, and has been found to have significant cavity-fighting potential. The Academy of General Dentistry reports that cardamom contains more than 10 compounds that have varying degrees of cavity-fighting potential. According to Paul Stephens, president of the Academy, quoted in the Winter 1993 issue of *Healthy Woman*, "the trend of society is to go back to nature. So we can expect natural substances such as cardamom to be used instead of chemicals in toothpastes and mouthwashes to fight cavities and bad breath."

Another natural spice can be used to temporarily ease tooth pain when professional help is not available. For emergency pain relief, holistic dentists recommend an application of oil of cloves, extracted from the spice commonly used to flavor apple cider and pumpkin pie. The essential oil will temporarily numb the nerves in the tooth which signals pain. Available at natural food stores and many pharmacies, oil of cloves can be used to soak a cotton ball or swab, which is then rubbed on the painful tooth and surrounding gums. If oil of cloves is not available, the same pain-relieving effect can be obtained by soaking several whole cloves in a small amount of hot water in a covered pot for several minutes to activate the essential oils. The cloves should then be held next to the affected tooth with the tongue or cheek until pain subsides.

Natural Toothpastes. So-called natural toothpastes have acquired a large following among consumers who want to avoid the artificial sweeteners and chemicals contained in most commercial pastes. Most natural toothpastes lack fluoride, the only substances the FDA and ADA have officially approved as effective in fighting tooth deterioration. Several natural toothpastes contain a calcium base, baking soda, natural domestic peppermint oil, and no preservatives, dyes, or artificial flavorings. One brand contains vitamin E, thought to be beneficial to periodontal health. Other brands contain calcium for tooth strength and natural germicides which kill the bacteria that cause tooth decay.

According to I. Sellach, natural and homeopathic toothpastes are also effective in removing fatty films from dental surfaces and remineralizing dental bone. Sellach recommends homeopathic toothpaste formulas flavored with lemon and lime, sea salt, and baking soda.

Susan Hodges reports in the November 1990 issue of *Better Nutrition* that several dental products sold in health food stores are based on traditional ayurvedic formulae. One herbal toothpaste, contains 26 herbal extracts, including neem and triphala. Twigs from the neem tree, a large evergreen found throughout India and Africa, have long been used as a natural toothbrush and general antiseptic. Memory Elvin-Lewis, an expert on natural dental products at Washington University in St. Louis, has found that neem has antibiotic properties that help destroy plaque. Natural toothpastes manufactured by Tom's of Maine use propolis and myrrh in its non-fluoride toothpastes. Propolis, a resin found in beehives, has antibacterial properties. Hodges cites research which suggests that it also helps prevent tooth decay in rats, although no test results are yet available in humans. Myrrh is believed to relieve bleeding gums, mouth ulcers, and sore throats.

Dental products manufactured by Nature's Gate also contain sanguinaria. An FDA advisory panel is conducting a long-term review to determine whether sanguinaria is safe and effective for use in dental products. Some studies cited by Hodges show that it fights gingivitis and plaque, but others have found it to be useless. Elvin-Lewis and other plant experts hope to conduct further studies to determine whether sanguinaria has "the potential of being a carcinogen."

Tea tree oil has been used in Australia as a tooth cleanser. Its manufacturers, Desert Essence, suggests that it is a powerful antibacterial agent. Tests on tea tree oil toothpastes, however, have concentrated on its pur-

Holistic Dental Health for Children

Despite the development of new dental gadgetry, the best protection for a child's teeth is to encourage children early to practice preventive dental hygiene early:

- Cleaning should start as soon as teeth appear. Brush a child's teeth with a soft-bristled brush (without toothpaste) before bedtime. If a child resists, use a soft, wet cloth, and remove all food and drinks, especially sweet and sticky matter, to prevent cavities.

- Don't let your child take a bottle to bed. Children who sleep with a bottle containing anything but water, or who use the bottles as a pacifier, are especially susceptible to baby-bottle tooth decay.

- Avoid sugary foods during meals and snacks. Even though these are "baby" teeth and will come out, if they become diseased, the permanent teeth that follow can be affected.

- Once the child is able to rinse, usually by the age three, add a pea-size portion of fluoridated toothpaste to the toothbrush. Pediatric dentists stress the importance of waiting until the child is old enough to spit the toothpaste out. Recent studies cited in the January 4, 1994 issue of *San Jose Mercury News* show that swallowing too much fluoride may affect enamel formation.

- Even after your child starts brushing his own teeth, you need to supervise his dental hygiene. Without encouragement, young children rarely brush long enough or thoroughly enough.

- When permanent teeth emerge, they require flossing to remove trapped food bits. Children are usually coordinated enough to floss by age 8 or 9.

ported power in fighting skin disease, and its ability to prevent dental problems has not been proved.

Dental Sealants. Dental sealants were invented in the early 1980s, but they are not widely used in the United States, according to the May 1990 issue of FDA Consumer Reports. While the ADA promotes sealants, for example, only 17% of American eight-year-olds have had their permanent teeth sealed. In Finland, the figure is 85%

While some dentists seal baby teeth, most sealants are applied only to the chewing surfaces of permanent teeth to create a barrier against food and bacteria that can cause decay. The majority of dental sealants are applied to molars because their deep grooves make them difficult to brush, and they are consequently most vulnerable to cavities. After the molars are first etched with an acidic solution to help the sealant adhere, the sealant–which can be milky white or colorless–is applied and hardened with a bonding light. Chewing and brushing eventually wears away sealants, but their use gives the teeth enough time to resist decay, especially if they are used in conjunction with regular brushing. Sealants do not eliminate the need to brush and floss as cavities can still develop between teeth. And regular dental care is still necessary because sealants must be checked for wear and occasionally touched up. Sealants currently cost $25 to $50 per tooth, and many dental insurance plans now cover them. They are nearly 100% effective in preventing decay in back teeth.

Dental Chewing Gums. For the last 20 years, it was believed that chewing gums containing sugar caused cavities. But non-sugar gum, especially chewing gums with xylitol (a sweetener extracted from corn stalks), may help prevent cavities. In one recent clinical trial reported in the July/August 1993 issue of *Health*, University of Michigan researchers asked 1,000 children in Belize to chew gum containing either xylitol, sugar, or sorbitol (a natural sweetener) three to five times a day. Another 140 children chewed no gum at all. After 28 months, children who chewed sugared gum had an average of 50% more cavities than when the study began–about the same as those who did not chew any gum. Those who chewed sorbitol gum had only slightly more cavities than at the beginning of the study. The children who chewed xylitol gum, however, had a third fewer cavities than the other groups. The researchers believe that the xylitol gum generated minerals which filled shallow cavities and caused them to harden. Chewing gum has a protective effect because it simulates saliva, which washes away some cavity-causing bacteria. Regular sugar gum feeds the bacteria and neutralizes the effect of saliva. Xylitol, on the other hand, slows bacterial growth, allowing saliva to break down and eliminate the bacteria.

Gingivitis and Periodontal Disease

Periodontal disease is any form of disease affecting the periodontium, or the tissues that surround and support the teeth. These include diseases of the gums (gingivitis), the bone of the tooth socket, and the periodontal ligament (the thin layer of connective tissue that holds the tooth in its socket and acts as a cushion

between tooth and bone).

Gingivitis is an inflammation of the gum tissue caused by bacterial infection. Alan Rees and Charlene Willey report that one U.S. nationwide survey by the National Institute of Dental Research found that 40-50% of U.S. adults studied had at least one spot on their gums with inflammation that was prone to bleeding. Since gingivitis is painless in the early stages, many people do not know until it is too late that their gums have developed this potentially serious infection.

Plaque is also a major contributor to gum disease. Plaque bacteria produce toxins that inflame the gums. Once the gums are inflamed, they become swollen and start to pull away from the teeth. Plaque which causes gingivitis starts first above the gum line (it is referred to as supragingival plaque). Over time, according to the *Personal Health Reporter*, areas of supragingival plaque become covered by swollen gum tissue or spread below the gum line, and in this airless environment the harmful bacteria within the plaque proliferate. Pockets of pus and cell debris may form between the teeth under the gum line, allowing the toxins to move down along the roots of the teeth to the bones which support them. Hundreds of bacterial species may thrive in the spaces between the teeth and the gums, and at least seven or eight can generate serious infections. Eventually the bone retreats, the fibers that hold the teeth to the bone are eaten away, and the teeth loosen and fall out. Proper and frequent flossing, however, can play an important role in preventing the formation of plaque and eventual gum disease.

Tartar is the yellow mineral deposit that forms on teeth. It provides a surface for additional plaque to adhere and grow, and is also a major contributor to gingivitis. Without proper brushing and flossing, plaque and tartar can build up and extend below the gumline, accelerating the development of periodontal dis-

Stages of Periodontal Disease

1. Healthy Gums: The gums are firm and do not bleed. Tiny fibers hold the teeth tightly to the gums and underlying bone. Since the gums fit snugly around all the teeth, the best way to eliminate plaque from below the gumline is to brush and floss daily. Regular checkups and professional cleanings are also essential.

2. Gingivitis: In the early stage of gingivitis, the gums become mildly inflamed as plaque and tartar (hardened plaque) accumulate at the gumline. The gums become red and puffy and may bleed during brushing and flossing. The bone and fibers holding the teeth in place are unaffected, and with early treatment, the condition can be reversed.

3. Periodontitis: During this stage, plaque spreads to the roots of the teeth and infects the supporting bone and fibers. The gums may separate from the tooth and start to recede. A pocket forms below the gumline and traps plaque and food. Proper treatment at the beginning of this phase can prevent further damage.

4. Advanced periodontitis: In this stage, infection destroys the supporting bone and fibers, and the gums recede even more. Teeth may shift or loosen, and biting may be altered. If treatment can't save the teeth, a dentist may decide to remove them to prevent further infection and damage.

ease. Once tartar develops, only a dental hygienist or dentist can remove it by either scraping the crown and root of the tooth or by laser incision.

In their early stages, both gingivitis and periodontal disease are preventable and reversible. In early stages of gingivitis, for example, dentists can remove plaque and tartar from the crowns and roots of teeth by scaling. Scaling is usually performed with root planing, in which the rough surfaces of the root are smoothed, allowing the gum to heal. The key to preventing and treating gum disease in its early stages is for individuals to recognize the symptoms: red, puffy, tender, or easily bleeding gums, signs of pus at the gumline, evidence that gums seem to be shrinking away from the teeth, teeth that have shifted or loosened, or persistent bad breath. People with any of these symptoms should immediately visit their dentist or oral health care professional.

Scientists are now developing new procedures to detect these destructive infections at an early stage. One of them, nearing final approval by the FDA, is a test to detect an enzyme in the mouth that is released only by cells that are dead or are dying. The enzyme, called amino aspartate transferase, has long been used to uncover evidence of dying cells in heart vessels during coronary disease. Also nearing approval are new gene probe techniques that can identify genetic material in the bacteria principally responsible for periodontal infections. One such test is so straightforward that it can be completed in a dentist's office while the patient is undergoing routine cleaning. Dentists can now also detect the first signs of gum disease by noting the existence of pockets and analyzing the bacteria

Treatments for Periodontal Disease

1. Plaque Removal. Brushing, flossing, and professional cleaning help remove plaque which eventually causes gum disease.

2. Scaling. Plaque and tartar are scraped off the tooth's crown and roots. Scaling is usually performed with root planing.

3. Root Planing. The rough surfaces of the root are exposed and medicated, allowing the gum to heal. The procedure usually takes several dental appointments.

4. Flap surgery. The gum is first lifted from the tooth and bone so that infection can be removed. The infected bone may also be reshaped. After surgery the gum is repositioned and sutured to hold it in place until it heals.

5. Regeneration. In some cases destroyed tissue between teeth and roots can be partially regenerated. Once the damaged area is prepared and special membranes are inserted, new tissue can grow over a period of weeks and months.

found in them. Using periodontal screening and recording (PSR), a dentist can probe the patient's gumline with a tool that measures the depth of any existing pockets and signs of bleeding at six areas around each tooth. The result, according to an article by David Perlman in the November 9, 1993 *San Francisco Chronicle*, is a scorecard that helps the dentist decide whether gum therapy is necessary.

In severe cases, gum surgery may be required to remove shallow pockets around the teeth. When this surgery (called flap surgery) is performed, the gum is lifted from the tooth and bone so that the infection can be removed. The infected bone may also be reshaped. After surgery, the gum is repositioned and sutured to hold it in place until it heals. Advanced periodontal disease may also require reshaping grafting of bone and gum transplants. Treatment may also involve grinding or capping teeth to correct abnormal pressure points, or the use of splints to control harmful mouth habits and reduce movement of loose teeth. Conventional periodontal disease treatment can take six to eight months or longer, and cost several thousand dollars.

A prescription product called Peridex, which contains the antimicrobial chlorhexidine, was approved by the FDA in 1986 based on studies showing it reduced gingivitis by up to 41%. According to Rees and Willey, chlorhexidine mouthwashes have long been used in Europe, and chlorhexidine is now approved for use in mouthwashes in the United States. Listerine has also received approval by the FDA and ADA as a plaque deterrent.

Holistic Treatments for Gingivitis

Studies at the National Institute of Dental Research tentatively suggest that holistic treatments for gingivitis may be effective. Dental scientists have experimented with treating gingivitis patients with daily solutions of salt, baking soda, and hydrogen peroxide. Using an electric toothbrush and pulse-water irrigator (which delivers an antiseptic solution directly into the pockets between teeth and gums), along with frequent dental cleanings and antibiotic treatments, has also been successful. Nevertheless, the ADA, according to *Zimmerman's Complete Guide to Nonprescription Drugs*, has suggested that further

Holistic First-Aid for Toothaches

- Some toothaches are caused by bruxism, involuntarily grinding of teeth while one sleeps. Bruxism is a primary cause of tooth enamel erosion. It is caused by stress, and relaxation techniques such as massage, exercise, and yoga can help relieve symptoms.
- Change your brushing technique. Many people unknowingly erode the enamel on their teeth by overbrushing. Dentists recommend a soft-bristle brush which should be wetted before toothpaste is applied.
- Toothpastes for sensitive teeth usually contain strontium chloride, which, like sodium fluoride, helps draw calcium from the saliva into the tubules and the enamel. Fluoride mouthwashes also help block the tubules.
- Remove food that is trapped in a cavity. Pry gently with a toothpick, floss, or rinse the mouth with warm, salty water.
- Apply cold to deaden nerves and relieve pain. Put an ice cube in the mouth to suck on, or wrap ice in a cloth and apply it to the tooth or to the exterior of the cheek. Apply cold for 15 minutes three to four times daily. Alternating periods of cold and warmth may also help, particularly if the pain is throbbing and there's visible swelling of the cheeks. Alternate cold and hot treatment of 20 minutes each.
- Massage the area around the cheek and gums. Placing a wad of gauze between the tooth and the inside of your cheek helps relieve toothaches by lessening pressure on the tooth.
- Eat soft foods such as yogurt. The pressure of chewing hard foods aggravates a toothache.
- Apply the essential oil of clove to relieve pain. Eugenol can also be used as a pain reliever or oral disinfectant. A number of over-the-counter toothache remedies, such as Numzident, contain eugenol. Wintergreen and eucalyptus oil can also be used to relieve pain.

research is required to confirm whether this treatment can prevent irreversible periodontal disease.

Guided Tissue Regeneration. Until recently, the only way to stop gum disease from progressing was to cut away diseased tissue. In the June 1994 issue of *American Health*, Rebecca Hughes details a new experimental surgical procedure called guided tissue regeneration (GTR) which rebuilds diseased gum tissue without removing it. The procedure entails placing a thin artificial membrane in the pocket between the gum and the jawbone (the membrane is removed surgically after four to six weeks). Made of gore-tex, the membrane allows healthy cells to grow while excluding diseased ones that could interfere with the attachment of the tooth to the bone. If the teeth are already lost, GTR can regenerate supporting bone tissue, preventing further tooth loss. The procedure can also be used to build up the ridge of the jaw so it can better support a denture, bridge, or dental implant. The FDA has approved biodegradable GTR membranes.

Homeopathic Remedies to Relieve Toothache Pain

- **Magnesia phos.** This remedy, made from magnesium phosphate, works well for piercing pains along the length of a tooth's nerve.

- **Coffea.** Coffea remedy relieves toothache caused by heat and hot foods.

- **Chamomilla.** This remedy is used for severe or unbearable pain that is worse at night, or is made worse by cold air, or by warm food and drink.

- **Belladona.** Belladona relieves throbbing toothache pains, dry mouth, and swollen gums.

Toothaches

Everyone occasionally experiences fleeting pain in their teeth when they bite into something cold. These are usually caused by the loss of enamel protection in part of a tooth. Beneath the enamel lies tiny, fluid-filled tunnels called dental tubules. These tubules lead directly to the tooth's inner core, which contains pulp and the tooth's sensitive nerve. Normally saliva helps deposit calcium on the enamel to cover and protect the tubules' openings. Excessively hard brushing, especially with abrasive tooth polishes, receding gums, acidic foods, or tooth grinding can erode the protective covering, exposing the ends of the tubules. Cracks in the teeth and loose filling also expose the tubules and the sometimes the pulp itself.

Eroded enamel can cause painful reactions to hot or cold foods or drinks. In most cases, the sensitivities are caused by pus-filled inflamations (abscesses) of the pulp of the tooth. If the pain does not go away after several weeks, people should consult their dentist to ensure that the nerve in the tooth does not die.

Vitamin and Mineral Therapies. Vitamin C can assist dental healing after a tooth extraction, according to research reported by the Academy of General Dentistry, and cited in the April 1994 issue of *American Health.* Of 161 patients studied, approximately 90% of those taking 1,500 milligrams of vitamin C daily for three weeks reported less pain, no infection or swelling, and no need for antibiotics after dental surgery, compared with 63% in the placebo group. Only 1% of those taking vitamin C developed a dry socket in which the tissues failed to fill the empty socket. Ten percent of the placebo group developed dry sockets.

Botanical Medicines. Botanicals such as yarrow, echinacea, comfrey, aloe, osha, and ginger can relieve toothaches. They can be made as teas, which can be taken orally, or made as compresses and applied with a cloth to the tooth or cheek. Herbalist Christopher Hobbs, author of *Echinacea: The Immune Herb*, recommends applying drops of a tincture of echinacea and water on the sore tooth every 15 minutes to relieve pain.

Cayenne and chili peppers contain the compound capsaicin which reduces pain and inflammation. Cayenne powder, or a few drops of cayenne concentrate can be applied directly to a sore tooth. Cayenne will sting initially, but will lessen the pain. The sting of cayenne is usually reduced by adding myrrh or peppermint oil. A clove of garlic can also be placed on a tooth for approximately an hour. Dipping a cotton swab or ball in lime juice and applying it to a tooth is also effective.

Biofeedback. According to an article in the November 1996 issue of *Self*, the American Dental Association (ADA) estimates that as many as 10 million Americans are so afraid of injection that they avoid having their teeth examined at all. A growing number of dentists are using electronic anesthesia, a new therapy that gives patients control over the localized pain that often accompanies simple procedures such as fillings and cleanings— even the discomfort stemming from the prick of a Novocain injection. First used in dentistry during the late 1970s, the technique uses electronic waves to block pain signals on their way to the brain. The therapy involves the dentist placing a tiny electrode on the gum next to the tooth or teeth being worked on, and one on each of the patient's hands to complete the circuit. The electrodes are connected to a box the size of a thick paperback that sits in the patient's lap and sends a signal up each arm and into the mouth, where the patient feels a tingling sensation. The box's control center allows patients to increase or decrease the effect according to the degree of pain they feel. The electrical stimulation interferes with the transmission of pain by triggering the release of endorphins. The effectiveness of electrical stimulation varies from patients and may not provide sufficient stimulation for all patients.

Acupuncture and Acupressure. Acupuncture and acupressure also relieve toothaches. Two acupuncture points in the index finger and on the shoulder are stimulated. A rapid, circular massage in the middle of the webbing of the index finger for a few minutes on the side affected relieves pain. Pressing the arm one-third of the way down from the tip of the shoulders to the elbow also relieves pain.

Hydrotherapy. Applying wet cold packs to the feet and surrounding them with a wool blanket will also lessen the pain of most toothaches. The cold packs draw blood and irritation away from the head. This procedure is usually combined with gargling

with a 1:4 ratio solution of 3% hydrogen peroxide and salt water. Traditional Chinese Medicine uses cold packs and a solution of three fresh star fruits which the patient drinks.

Wisdom Teeth

More than 2 million impacted wisdom teeth are removed annually in the United States, according to the February 1995 *Berkeley Wellness Health Letter*. Sometimes these teeth are badly positioned in the jaw and crowd the second molars as they grow in. Other times they partially erupt, and, because they may lie under a flap of skin and are hard to clean, they quickly decay, causing pain and swelling. Occasionally cysts may develop around the impacted tooth, which can damage bone and adjacent teeth.

A study published in the 1990 issue of *International Journal of Technology Assessment in Health Care* strongly recommended against early extraction of wisdom teeth when no symptoms were present. There is no evidence that an impacted molar harms the alignment of other teeth. The risk of developing a cyst is also quite low. Athletes in contact sports were once thought to be more vulnerable to jaw fracture if they kept their wisdom teeth, but there is no evidence to support the suspicion, according to the ADA. A tooth won't change position until after the age of 25. If wisdom teeth are not persistently painful, the ADA recommends not extracting them.

Knocked-Out Teeth

Each year more than two million Americans have accidents serious enough to knock a tooth completely from its socket. Most of these accidents occur during a sporting activity or result from an auto accident.

Prompt first aid is essential for teeth and gum injuries. Teeth that are loosened by an impact to the mouth are the easiest to treat.

First Aid for Fractured, Chipped, or Knocked-Out Teeth

Dr. Joe Camp, a dental expert at the University of North Carolina, recommends immediate treatment for anyone who has a tooth fractured, chipped, or knocked out.

1. It is essential to receive treatment the same day for a fractured tooth, especially if it is fractured at the root.

2. Knocked-out teeth treated within 30 minutes have a 90% chance of being replanted.

3. If a tooth is knocked out, pick it up carefully by the crown (or top), not by the delicate roots. Rinse it gently and put it back in its socket. If that is not possible, put it in a cup of milk or glass of water to keep it wet, or wrap the tooth in a damp cloth.

4. If a tooth is chipped, find the chipped piece, if possible, as a dentist may be able to bond the piece back on to the tooth.

The ADA recommends gently biting down to help keep them in place, and taking special care not to put twisting pressure on the tooth. It's best to leave a crack filling, crown, or denture in place if it doesn't readily come out. For extra safety, a narrow strip of tape can be used to secure a denture that's broken, but not loose. The tape should be placed on the tongue side of the denture after it's been dried. The mouth should then be rinsed with warm salt water, or exposed to few drops of clove oil.

When a hard force breaks a tooth's ligament, part of the ligament usually stays attached to the root of the tooth and part remains in the tooth's socket. Anything that further injures the ligament remaining on the tooth, such as allowing the ligament to dry out or scraping it off the tooth to clean the root, prevents the tooth from being successfully reimplanted. An adult tooth that's knocked out of its socket can usually be saved by acting quickly. If the ligament can be restored to its blood-rich environment within 15-30 minutes, there's a good chance that the tooth will reattach to the socket.

If a tooth is knocked out of the mouth, it should be rinse and replaced in its socket. Do not clean, scrape, or attempt to sterilize the tooth. Once it's back in its socket, cover it with sterile gauze, and seek emergency treatment.

Botanical Medicines. Green or black tea, myrrh, and oak bark are astringent herbs which relieve pains of loose teeth and gum ailments, including sore and receding gums. These can be applied as a powder or tincture, and applied directly on the loose tooth. The powder or tincture should be held in the mouth for 30 seconds, and either swallowed or spit out.

Bromelain, a natural enzyme derived from the pineapple plant, contains anti-inflammatory and wound-healing properties which relieve pain following tooth extractions. Dental surgery often bruises the gums, cheeks, and mouth.

Bach Flowers. Oral doses of Bach flower "Rescue Remedy" helps calm the nerves surrounding the area of a tooth which has been knocked out. Three to four drops of liquid concentrate should be applied under the tongue. Rescue Remedy can also be diluted in a glass of water, tea, or juice, and consumed as a beverage.

Homeopathy. Homeopathic remedies have also been used to effectively relieve pain caused by traumas. These include hyperimum, which helps reduce nerve pain; aconite, which is normally taken before surgery to calm the nerves in the mouth; ledum, a "puncture" remedy which reduces pain after an anesthesia injection; belladonna, which is an excellent remedy for throbbing pain accompanied by a dry mouth; apis tinctures which treat stinging and burning tooth pains; and arnica 6X tablets which, when taken before dental surgery, reduce toothaches as effectively as acetaminophen tablets.

Abscesses and Mouth Infections

The mouth is one of the body's most favorable breeding grounds for bacteria. Bacteria from a cavity can pass through the pulp and into the socket of a tooth and form abscesses. Abscesses also form in the gums, usually from food particles that get trapped between the teeth. Gums infections also develop around wisdom teeth that push up through the gums.

Diet and Nutrition. Crunchy foods such as apples, carrots, and celery that need to be chewed well not only exercise the jaw muscles and increase circulation to the teeth and gums, they also help to clean the teeth's surface and prevent abscesses and mouth infections. Other foods or beverages include cashews and other nuts; teas or beverages which contain decay-preventing fluoride; seeds (especially sunflower seeds); and cheese, olives, dill pickles, and blackstrap molasses.

Vitamin and Mineral Therapies. According to James Balch and Phyllis Balch, vitamin and mineral supplements which reduce the risk of abscesses and infections include: boron (2 mg); calcium and magnesium in a 2:1 ratio (1,500 mg calcium and 750 mg

---

Tooth Traumas

Listed below are several alternative remedies to use for a variety of tooth traumas.

1. Acupressure. Apply gentle pressure to the point of the web of the hand between the thumb and index finger. Manipulating this point can calm nerves and help relieve pain.

2. To help stop gums or other mouth tissues from bleeding, apply green or black tea bag to the injury. The tannins in green and black tea contain an astringent that help constrict blood vessels and inhibit bleeding. Green or black tea bags can also be placed over a loose tooth to tighten it in place. The tannins also prevent tooth decay and gum disease. Some people have found that moist chamomile tea bags have a soothing effect when applied to tissues, perhaps because chamomile has anti-inflammatory and wound-healing properties. Chewing on a green leaf of yarrow or plantain also relieves pain caused by aching teeth or wisdom teeth.

---

magnesium); manganese and zinc in balanced mineral formulations (15-30 mg manganese and 25-50 mg zinc); niacin (50-100 mg); silicon (2 mg); vitamin A (25,000 IU in the form of betacarotene); vitamin C (2-5 g); and vitamin D (400-600 mg).

Botanical Medicines. Echinacea, myrrh, cayenne, and goldenseal can be applied as herbal compresses or poultices to relieve pain and inflammation of abscesses and infections. A clean cotton cloth is dipped into a tea of these herbs and applied to the tooth or gums. A poultice of myrrh mouthwash and goldenseal powder also relieves gum pains and swelling. Echinacea is also available as a dental salve or cream.

Propolis, a resinous substance that bees collect from plants, is also commonly used to treat abscesses and infections, including painful cold sore. A few drops is normally applied directly to the inflamed gums. Other botanical remedies which are available from health food stores include:

- Aloe gel from a freshly broken leaf, or products containing 96% pure aloe.
- Tea tree oil or fresh plantain leaves.
- Calendula in gel form: mix two full droppers of tincture of calendula in a half glass of water, and gargle.
- Black ointment, a tar-like topical ointment that contains comfrey root, plantain, goldenseal root, activated charcoal, pine, juniper tar, pine gum, beeswax, and lanolin.
- Garlic: Wrap a raw garlic clove or garlic powder in cheesecloth or a layer of sterile gauze and place between the cheeks and gum.
- Echinacea: Mix five to six drops of echinacea tincture and a vitamin E capsule. Dip a clean piece of gauze in the mixture and place between the gum and cheek so that it rests directly on the abscess or sore.

Homeopathy. Belladonna, heapar sulph, silica, and mercurius also effectively treat abscesses, inflammation, and mouth infections. Belladonna is normally taken at the first hint of an abscess or gum boil. Hepar sulph made from calcium sulfide, relieves the sharp, splinter-like pains of abscesses. Silica, made from flint, helps relieve slow-developing abscesses at the root of teeth, especially those sensitive to cold water. Made from mercury, mercurius stimulates the saliva to help relieve the pain of loose teeth.

Traditional Chinese Medicine (TCM). TCM physicians usually prescribe watermelon frost formula to relieve toothaches as well as the pain of mouth sores and ulcers. Watermelon frost crystals are usually added to other herbs to make a sweet-tasting compound formula which is taken both internally and externally. Watermelon frost, called Fu Fang Xi gua Shuang (or simply Xi gua Shuang), is sold as a powder in 2-gram vials. The powder is mixed with water to make a paste. It's also available as a lozenge or liquid spray.

Astragalus, another popular Chinese botanical, reverses the growth of mouth ulcers. A tincture of astragalus mixed with myrrh and echinacea is used in TCM to stimulate healthy gums.

Crooked Teeth (Malocclusions)

Nearly 50% of American children aged six through 11 have a normal bite with only slight abnormalities in tooth formation. However, 25% have crooked teeth (a condition known as "malocclusion"–literally, "bad bite"). At one time, crooked teeth were thought to be primarily inherited from the parents with little recourse to prevent them. The American Academy of Periodontics estimates that 50-80% of orthodontics can be avoided if problems are detected early enough. More than 15% of orthodontic patients in the United States, according to David Zimmerman, are adults who have their teeth straightened to improve their appearance and prevent tooth loss that sometimes occurs with malocclusion.

Braces. Treatments for crooked teeth vary, but in most cases the teeth are straightened by the use of orthodontic braces. Today's braces are more comfortable and flexible and require fewer adjustments than the old "train tracks" that were wrapped around each tooth and cemented in place. In the most common type today, tiny stainless steel or ceramic brackets are attached to teeth; a thin wire made of nickel and titanium runs across the front of the teeth. These devices are more comfortable and less noticeable, and are available in clear and tooth-colored versions.

Lingual braces, in which brackets are concealed behind the teeth, are an option in some cases, but treatment takes longer and costs up to twice as much–from approximately $6,500 to $9,000. According to the June 1994 issue of *American Health*, partial insurance coverage is available for about half of all patients seeking orthodontic treatment. *Jane Brody's Guide to Personal Health* identifies several types of braces. Some braces are removable, some can be worn part of the time outside the mouth, and others are permanently attached to the teeth for several years. Most braces consist of wire-connected brackets which are fitted across the teeth. Permanent braces are increasingly constructed of plastic which blends more naturally with the color of the teeth. Facial bones, as well as teeth, can be realigned to improve both bite and appearance.

All forms of braces work by pressuring the teeth to reposition themselves inside the bone socket in which they sit. In children whose bones are softer and still growing, the process of reshaping the bone through pressure is faster than in an adult. Direct pressure on facial bones can have a similar effect, with the amount and direction of pressure determining the shape the bone will assume.

Dental Magnets. The American Association of Orthodontics reports that tiny magnets implanted in the teeth can correct many common orthodontic disorders without using braces or surgery. The tiny magnets, only three to four millimeters in diameter, are made of materials such as neodymium-iron-boron, and are essentially the same type of magnets used in stereo equipment and other electronics. According to the October 19, 1993 issue of *Your Health*, magnets are used to pull teeth in a certain direction or push them apart, which can be particularly effective in treating children who traditionally required braces to correct misaligned teeth. The magnets can be bonded directly onto teeth, which eliminates the possibility of them being lost or not worn correctly. They often work more quickly than ordinary braces.

Natural Teeth Straightening Techniques. According to an article in the October 1993 issue of *Your Health*, an 8-year-old boy corrected an underbite problem by simply using pressure from his tongue and lips. The boy was given a bite-block which forced his tongue to push his top front teeth out and lips to push his bottom teeth in so that they eventually meshed properly. According to Dr. Robert Keim, assistant professor in the College of Dentistry at the University of Tennessee Health Science Center, this technique used natural forces in the mouth to correct the bad bite. The boy was instructed to wear the bite brace at all times, removing it only for cleaning. Movement of the misaligned teeth was monitored monthly. Use of the bite block helped bring the boy's teeth into alignment in one month, and results were so good that the device was discontinued in just three months.

Dentures

According to a 1985-86 survey conducted by the National Institute for Dental Research, Americans 65 years or older have lost an average of 10 teeth, and those 34-64 years old have an average of nine teeth missing. Four out of 10 (42%) Americans aged 65 or older, according to Rees and Willey, have lost all their teeth, as have 4% of those 35-65 of years of age.

One alternative to replacing missing teeth is to have dentures made. Ordinary dentures are generally made of plastic and tailored to each patient's mouth. They are normally fitted

Relieving Denture Discomfort

The Home Remedies Handbook lists the following suggestions for relieving denture discomfort:

- Eat soft foods. During the adjustment phase, the gums need time to adjust to the compression created by new dentures. Patients should consume soft foods to avoid damaging tender tissues. Some foods, such as apples and corn on the cob, should be avoided.

- Brush the dentures twice daily. Excess bacteria which remains on the dentures can infect the gums and retard healing. Toothpastes, special denture cleaners, and soap and water help keep dentures free of bacteria.

- Brush the gums. Brushing the gums, palate, and tongue daily not only stimulates the tissues and increases circulation, it also helps reduce bacteria and remove plaque.

to match and adhere to the upper or lower jaw or made to clamp on to remaining teeth with metal supports or bridges. Difficulties with dentures can result from a failure to initially detect such problems as cysts, tumors, inflammation, bone loss, tooth roots that are lodged in the jaw, and distorted positions of the jaw.

Dentists are sometimes able to save some portion of missing teeth, which serve as anchors for a partial denture. When a full denture (upper, lower, or both) is needed, the muscles of the cheeks and the tongue must be relied upon to keep it in place. Careful measurements must be made to ensure that the dentures fit correctly because an ill-fitting denture may put undue tension on the jaw muscles, irritate the gums and cheeks, and cause loss of underlying bone.

Dentists recommend that to prevent staining, dentures should be cleaned daily with special brushes and dental aids (not ordinary toothpastes) and placed in water or a cleansing solution when they are out of the mouth. In addition, the mouth should be rinsed each morning, after every meal, and before bed to clean out harmful bacteria and food particles. The dentist should exam the dentures once each year to monitor and refit them, if necessary.

Dental Implants. In the United States, 40 million people wear dentures and another 60 million Americans are missing one or more teeth, according to the December 1988 January 1989 *FDA Consumer Reports*. To avoid the problems and inconvenience of dentures, and to utilize the bone of teeth which are still in place, dental researchers have begun experimenting with new methods of implanting artificial tooth supports surgically set directly and permanently to the jaw bone. The technique is called dental implants because artificial teeth (similar to dentures) are implanted directly into the bones of the jaw to replace missing teeth. The advantage of dental implants is that they are permanent and there is no need to remove them, as with dentures.

The first dental implant was developed in Sweden in 1965 by Per-Ingvar Branewmark. His method involved drilling a hole in living bone at the implant site and inserting a tiny fixture made of titaniumwhich was screwed or pressed into place in the jawbone. After three to six months, during which time the bone was allowed to grow around the implant, the gum was reopened and an abutment attached to the titanium fixture. The new tooth, several teeth, or an entire row of teeth was then attached to the abutment. A clear plastic healing cap prevented the gum from growing into the abutment.

Today, there are four different types of dental implant procedures in use. According to the *FDA Consumer Reports* of December 1988/January 1989, the two most frequently used are one-and two-stage cylindrical implants and blade implants. The former is very similar to the method developed by Dr. Branewmark, and features channels which are cut lengthwise into the jaw bone. The blades have openings which can accept bone regrowth through their framework.

In 1992, more than 100,000 Americans underwent surgery to be fitted with titanium dental implants. Titanium's advantage is that bone tissue actually fuses to it. For reasons which are not fully understood, titanium seems to bond with successive generations of bone cells while other materials lose their bonding power over time.

In general, the chances for dental implant success are much higher in the lower jaw–about 95%–because it is a thicker bone. People considering this type of surgery should consult a specialist who will recommend the appropriate implant design. The ADA has cautioned that there is no substitute for natural teeth, and that implants will never function as well as real teeth. With today's technology, dentists can salvage even badly damaged teeth, and the ADA advises that people first try everything possible to restore their natural teeth.

There are several risks associated with dental implants, including inadvertent perforation of the nasal sinus, infection, and nerve injury. A holistic dentist will normally conduct a complete medical history of the patient before performing dental implant surgery. The use of tobacco, alcohol, and most drugs must be discontinued during dental implant surgery and post-surgery recovery. The dental implant surgery may also result in pain and swelling, and gingivitis.

Dental Implants

For people considering dental implants, the ADA suggests the following guidelines:

- First determine if it is possible to save your own natural teeth.
- Make sure you are able to keep the schedule for required implant surgery and follow-up. Some implants require many visits and a second stage of surgery.
- Make sure you are told in advance what pain, soreness, and long-term restriction to your diet are involved. You may also have to wear temporary devices.
- Ask your dentist whether your body is likely to reject the implant after several months or years.

Teeth Cleansers

All toothpastes are abrasive, and some can remove minor stains. However, only professional cleanings performed by a dental hygienist can remove the stubborn stains which accumulate near the gum line caused by coffee, tea, or smoking. Ronald Goldstein's *Change Your Smile* cautions against using commercial abrasives such as smoker's toothpastes without the guidance of a dentist. Even though smoker's toothpastes may be no more abrasive than regular toothpaste, scrubbing too aggressively with commercial abrasives can wear down the enamel.

Dental professionals scrub away stains and plaque with either powdered pumice stone or a Prophy Jet, which sandblasts the tooth surface with baking soda. Teeth are then polished to a high gloss, giving them a pearly appearance. Typically, dental cleanings only remove a few micron's depth of enamel. People who have lost considerable enamel should avoid consuming too many oranges, grapefruit juice, or other highly acidic foods and beverages which leave tiny pits or grooves that accumulate deposits. Chewing ice or hard candy can also cause hairline fractures in teeth which attract bacteria.

Stains that cannot be scrubbed away can sometimes be bleached by a dental hygienist with heat or light. Bleaching can whiten as many as 10-12 teeth at one time without anesthesia.

Teeth that have yellowed with age, according to Goldstein, can also be whitened with bleaching. Teeth that are blue-gray due to extensive silver fillings or darkened by stain ingrained in a tooth (such as those caused by taking tetracycline or other drugs) may not respond as well to bleaching. Extensive stubborn stains caused by an injured or dead nerve may require root canal treatment.

Teeth Whiteners. One way to whiten teeth is to use a bleaching system obtained from your dentist for use at home. At the office, the dentist fits a mouth guard (called splints) and gives a prescription bleaching gel which usually contains carbamide peroxide, similar to hydrogen peroxide. Over-the-counter whitening agents usually contain hydrogen peroxide. Repeated use of hydrogen peroxide may speed the development of oral cancers, especially in smokers.

Deeply stained teeth which contains pits or gaps can be treated with porcelain veneers, which cover the whole tooth, making them look natural. Dental caps, the most expensive alternative, cover the entire surface of the tooth, front and back. Dental caps must be applied by a dentists. Porcelain veneer kits for dental pits are now available as self-care kits from many pharmacies.

Bonding. If a tooth is badly discolored, pitted, or chipped, a dentist may recommend composite resin bonding. To bond teeth, the dentist normally first etches the surface with a mild acid gel or liquid, and applies a plastic veneer that covers the flows. Veneers are available in varying shades which restore the tooth's natural enamel. Newer, stronger bonding materials can also be used to reconstruct missing tooth structures and to fill in large chips, deep grooves, or gaps between teeth.

Bonded teeth stain more easily than enamel or porcelain, and need to be professionally cleaned there to four times each year. Certain foods must be avoided, including coffee, tea, soy sauce, cola drinks, blueberries, and fresh cherries.

New Dental Technologies

In the next 10 years, dental researchers believe a number of breakthroughs will help prevent or reverse common dental problems. Future DNA tests, for example, will enable patients to determine their likelihood of developing gum disease. Vaccines currently in development may help produce antibodies that isolate and kill gum-disease bacteria, preventing gum disease and its resulting tooth and bone loss. Within five years, it will be possible to chemically alter the proteins in saliva which help produce bacteria.

Many dental procedures, such as the conventional means of removing diseased gum tissue, are extremely painful. Fortunately, new laser surgical techniques have been developed for use in gum surgery that cause no apparent pain because they vaporize only a few layers of cells at a time and the body can easily repair the minimal damage to surrounding healthy tissue. Lasers have now been used in more than 100,000 dental procedures in 12 countries, including Canada, England, Japan, Mexico, and Australia. With laser surgery, dentists can clean out diseased pockets of gum tissue to the point where the body can heal itself. They can also make the teeth more resistant to future decay by sterilizing the deep crevices toothbrushes cannot reach.

However, since lasers cannot cut through the healthy enamel of teeth, dentists still need to use a drill to enlarge a hole in a tooth to get at a cavity or to shape a tooth to receive a restoration. Some reports have documented using the laser in place of a needle to anesthetize a tooth which needs to be drilled. The advantage of this procedure is that unlike a drill, the laser exerts no pressure and does not cause stress. With laser surgery, there is usually very little pain and swelling. An increasing number of holistic dentists now routinely use laser surgery because there is less trauma, bleeding, infection, and need for anesthesia, and teeth can be saved in ways that are impossible with conventional surgery. Within several years, lasers may be able to painlessly drill cavities as well.

Dental x rays are a critical component in analyzing the bone and gum structure of teeth. The only disadvantage of x-ray machines is that they emit a very slight amount of radiation. With the advent of computers, inventors have experimented with several forms of digital radiography which eliminate the need for x-ray films and film processing. The advantage of direct digital radiography is that it can deliver instantaneous computer-enhanced x-ray images with less radiation. The newest radiographic systems, detailed in the October 1993 issue of *Dental Products Report*, depend upon a charged-couple device (CCD), a small cassette-style intraoral silicon receptor with a solid-state electronic circuit embedded in the silicon which captures the x-ray signal. The x rays strike the silicon, and electrons are released and stored as a digital image which can then be sent immediately to a computer monitor and viewed. Radiation exposure doses using digital radiography are 90% less than using normal x-ray machines.

Guidelines for Choosing a Holistic Dentist

1. Prevention. Because tooth decay and tooth loss are not inevitable, the dentist should stress the importance of diet and daily home care (proper brushing and flossing) as well as periodic cleanings. The dentist should be sensitive to the health of your entire body, provide counseling to minimize any pain associated with surgery (if needed), and recommend using natural preventative measures and therapies whenever possible.

2. Examination. The dentist should provide a thorough examination, including a visual examination of the soft tissue of the mouth (cheeks, tongue, throat, gums, and tooth bite), as well as a periodontal examination to measure the depth of pockets that have formed between gums and teeth. The dental examination should include a full set of x rays.

3. Treatment. The dentist should discuss what treatment you need and why, how long it will take, how much it will cost, and what holistic alternatives might be available. If extensive work is recommended, obtain a second opinion from another dentist. If you have a serious gum disease, the dentist should refer you to a periodontist.

Summary

Dental health is imperative to whole body health because the mouth cavity is a primary site of many different types of infection. More importantly, dental abnormalities often reflect immune disorders. For both these reasons, it is important to eat a diet of natural whole foods which help prevent tooth decay and significantly enhance the maintenance of healthy teeth throughout life. Poor nutrition can result in weakening of the microstructure of the calcified tissues and vulnerability to tooth decay. Proper and frequent brushing and flossing can also play an important role in preventing cavities and the formation of plaque which can eventually lead to gum disease and tooth loss.

Resources

References

"Braces for Grown-Ups." *American Health* (June 1994): 24.

Brody, Jane. *Jane Brody's Guide to Personal Health*. New York: Avon Books, 1982.

The Burton Goldberg Group. *Alternative Medicine: The Definitive Guide*, Payallup, WA: Future Medicine Publishing, Inc., 1993.

"Chewing Away Tooth Decay." *Health* (July/August 1993).

"Dentists Report a More Holistic Approach." *Gannet News Services* (November 28, 1993).

Goldstein, Ronald. *Change Your Smile*. Long Island: Quintessence, 1992.

Griffin, Jean. "Measuring Mercury." *American Health* (January/February 1994): 24.

"Healing Vitamin." *American Health* (April 1994): 19.

"Health Update." *American Health* (November 1993).

Hobbs, Christopher. *Echinacea: The Immune Herb*. Long Island: Avery Publishers.

Hodges, Susan. "Natural Toothpastes." *Better Nutrition* (November 1990).

Hughes, Rebecca. "Growing New Bone Tissue." *American Health* (June 1994): 24.

"Kaleidoscope." *Healthy Woman* (Winter 1993).

Liles, Alan. "Mercury Free Dentistry." *Shared Guide* (1993).

"The Low-Tech Ways to Keep Kids' Teeth Healthy." *San Jose Mercury News* (January 4, 1994).

"Mercury: How Much Is Too Much?" *CDA Journal* (February 1985): 42.

Modeland, V. "Dental Implants." *FDA Consumer Reports* (December 1988/January 1989): 13.

"No More Braces." *Your Health* (October 1993).

"Pain Free Fillings." *Self* (November 1996): 90.

"Painless Cavity Fillings." *New Body* (December 1993).

Perlman, David. "S.F. Dental Conference Gives Gum Disease High-Tech Treatment." *San Francisco Chronicle* (November 9, 1993): A19.

Rees, Alan, and Charlene Willey. *Personal Health Reporter*. Detroit: Gale Research, 1993.

Reese, Diana. "Sandblasting Cavities." *American Health* (November 1993): 20.

Reis, D. "Direct Digital Intraoral Radiography Systems." *Dental Products Report* (October 1993): 22.

Renners, John. *The Home Remedies Handbook*. Lincolnwood, IL: Publications International Ltd., 1993.

Selach, I. "A New Dentrifice." *Zahnarztliche Praxis* (March 15, 1966).

Shepherd, Steven. "Brushing Up on Gum Disease." *FDA Consumer Reports* (May 1990): 9-10.

Vaughan, Don. "No More Braces!" *Your Health* (October 19, 1993): 19.

"Wise Words about Wisdom Teeth." *Berkeley Wellness Health Letter* (February 1995).

Zimmerman, David. *Zimmerman's Complete Guide to Nonprescription Drugs*. Detroit: Visible Ink Press, 1993, p. 437.

Organizations

American Academy of Implant Dentistry.
6900 Grove Road, Thorofare, NJ 08086.

American Academy of Periodontology.
211 East Chicago Avenue, #114, Chicago, IL 60611.

American Dental Association.
211 East Chicago Avenue, Chicago, IL 60611.

National Institute of Allergy and Infectious Diseases.
9000 Rockville Pike, Bethesda, MD 20205.

National Institute of Dental Research.
NIH Building 30, Bethesda, MD 20892.

National Women's Health Network.
1325 G Street N.W., Washington D.C. 20005.

Additional Reading

"Combating Periodontal (Gum) Disease." *Health News* (June 1989).

"Dental Implants: How Good They Are, How Long They Last." *Johns Hopkins Medical Letter* (March 1989).

Holland, Lisa. "Dental Implants." *Good Housekeeping* (January 1990).

Langer, Burton. "Dental Implants Used for Periodontal Patients." *Journal of the American Dental Association* (October 1990): 505-08.

McVeigh, Gloria. "High-Tech Tooth Savers from the American Academy of Periodontology." *Prevention* (May 1990).

Williams, Ray. "Periodontal Disease." *The New England Journal of Medicine* (February 8, 1990)

Chapter 16

EYE, EAR, NOSE, AND THROAT DISORDERS

The eyes, ears, nose, and throat, along with the skin and mucous membranes, serve as the body's first line of defense against external toxins and infectious organisms. They are often the first organs to decline with age, and many people assume that this is a natural process. However, physical, mental, and emotional stress, along with poor nutrition and vitamin deficiencies, can accelerate the process. This chapter focuses on holistic approaches to keeping these organs healthy and preventing chronic disorders.

Eyes

Virtually 80% of what we perceive and know about the world depends on our eyes. Like a camera, the eye has a single lens that focuses on objects and projects an image of those objects onto the retina, the light-sensitive region at the back of the eyeball. A normal clear lens allows light to pass through unobstructed. But for a number of reasons, the lens, cornea, iris, or eye muscle may develop problems and vision can become impaired.

Most common eye defects, if detected early enough, can be treated by an ophthalmologist, a specialist in diagnosing and treating eye diseases. Diagnosis normally consists of a vision test during which an ophthalmologist tests the patient's ability to focus on near and far objects. At the same time, the physician will check for signs of blood vessel damage, blank spots, and weakness of the eye muscles which can cause the retina to become detached.

A recent Gallup poll indicated that 75% of Americans value their eyesight above all other senses. Yet 85% admitted that they are not as careful in caring for their eyes as they should be. Virtually all eye injuries and half of the 50,000 cases of blindness which occur annually could be prevented, according to experts, with simple common-sense precautions.

Cataracts

Cataracts are the leading cause of impaired vision and blindness in the United States. Approximately four million Americans have some degree of vision-impairing cataract, and at least 40,000 people in the United States become blind each year as a result. A cataract is any clouding of the normally clear and transparent lens of the eye. It is not a tumor or a new growth of skin or tissue over the eye, but a yellow fogging of the lens itself. The lens, located behind the pupil, focuses light on the retina at the back of the eye to produce a sharp image. When a cataract forms, the lens becomes so opaque that light cannot easily be transmitted to the retina. If only a small part of the lens is involved, sight is not greatly impaired, and there may be no need to remove the cataract. If a large portion of the lens becomes cloudy, however, sight can be partially or completely impaired, and the cataract must be removed.

Many factors contribute to the progression of cataracts, including other eye disorders, injury, systemic diseases (such as diabetes mellitus or galactosemia), toxins, hereditary diseases, and ultraviolet and near-ultraviolet light or radiation exposure. Cataracts usually occur in elderly persons, although people of any age can develop them as well. Cataracts which appear in children are usually hereditary, or are caused by infection or inflammation which the pregnant mother transmits to her baby.

Preventing and Treating Cataracts

Cataracts develop slowly and often do not reach the point where they interfere with a person's normal vision. The most important ways of preventing cataracts are to consume nutrtional foods and supplements which maintain the integrity of the central nucleus and soft outer cortex of the lens, and prevent the lens from being damaged by chemical toxins and the sun's ultraviolet rays. The FDA is now considering adopting national regulations that will require all new sunglasses to block 99% of ultraviolet B radiation.

Nutritional Therapies. Dr. Glen Swartwout, an optometrist in Hilo, Hawaii, reports in *Alternative Medicine: The Definitive Guide* that cataracts in many of his patients directly result from nutritional imbalances and are further aggravated by smoking, drinking alcohol, and the use of some prescription drugs (especially cortisone

Preventing Eye Damage

1. Annual examinations: Adults over the age of 40 should have their eyes examined annually by a specialist.

2. Sunglasses: Always wear sunglasses with polarized lenses when out in the bright sunlight. These glasses block 95% of the sun's harmful rays, especially at the beach or in snow areas.

3. Avoid dangerous chemicals: Wear protective eyewear when handling dangerous chemicals or doing household or shop work which raises dirt or debris. Heavy polycarbonate lenses offer more protection than regular glasses and should be worn when playing racquet sports or high-impact sports such as hockey and football.

4. Be careful with makeup and facial creams: Cosmetics can also cause eye irritation and possible infection. Women should replace mascara and eyeliner every three to six months to prevent bacterial build-up, and never share makeup or applicators with anyone.

5. Contact lenses: Contact lens wearers should use makeup designated as safe for contact lenses. It is also advisable to insert lenses before applying makeup and to take them out before using makeup remover. Be sure to wash your hands thoroughly before handling your lenses and follow all cleaning and storage instructions exactly.

6. Eye drops: A variety of eye drops and other lubricating preparations are available to relieve occasional discomfort caused by common allergens such as pollen, dust, or pet dander, as well as city smog and pollution.

and other steroids). Two-thirds of his patients in one study showed improved vision within four weeks after changing their diet and adding nutritional supplements.

To prevent cataracts, Swartwout advises his patients to restrict processed, high-fat foods, along with alcohol, caffeine, sugar, and nicotine. In their place, he recommends increasing the consumption of legumes (which are high in sulphur-containing amino acids), yellow vegetables (carotenes), and vitamin E- and C-rich foods (particularly fresh fruits and vegetables).

Vitamin and Mineral Therapies. Several studies have shown a link between deficiencies of vitamins A, E, and C and the development of cataracts. Preliminary research suggests that vitamin C can prevent changes in proteins in the eye associated with cataracts. In one study reported in the July 1992 issue of *Environmental Nutrition*, people who took several vitamin supplements, including vitamin C, had four times less risk of developing cataracts than those who took no supplements. Research on vitamin C's role in preventing cataracts is still inconclusive, however, as other antioxidant nutrients such as vitamin E and betacarotene help prevent cataracts as well.

A Finnish study reported in the July 13, 1993 issue of *Your Health*, for example, found a strong link between low nutrient levels of vitamins A and E and the likelihood of needing cataract surgery. The study collected blood samples from 1,419 people between 1966 and 1972, and concluded that people with low levels of vitamins A and E were nearly "twice as likely to need cataract surgery compared to those with high levels." The investigation concluded that "free radicals contributed to the growth of cataracts and vitamins A and E appeared to neutralize free radicals." Similar results, according to the *Your Health* article, were reported in a study of 660 people in Baltimore. Those with the most vitamin E in their blood were least likely to develop the most common form of cataracts.

Many holistic physicians believe that cataracts are caused by free radical damage to some of the sulphur-containing proteins in the lens. The lens is dependent on adequate levels of superoxide dismutase (SOD), catalase, and glutathione (GSH). When a cataract begins to form, these protective nutrients are damaged by free radicals. Glutathione levels can be increased by taking cysteine, glutamine, or glycine supplements which have proven beneficial in cataract treatment.

Zinc supplements may also be helpful in treating cataracts. Zinc is a well-known antioxidant believed to be essential for normal lens functioning. In addition, betacarotene may act as a filter, protecting against light-induced damage to the fiber portion of the lens. People with cataracts also have 15% of the selenium levels of people who do not have cataracts, which suggests that taking selenium supplements may retard the progression of cataracts.

Botanical Medicines. The Chinese herbal formula hachimijiogan has been shown to increase the glutathione content of the lens and has been used in the clinical treatment of cataracts in both China and Japan. In one Japanese clinical study, 60% of the subjects who used hachimijiogan did not develop cataracts, while 20% showed no progression and 20% developed cataracts. An extract of ginkgo biloba (EGb) produced in Austria may also help prevent the formation of cataracts. It is known for its anti-aging properties, and is now being tested as a treatment for degenerative eye disorders.

Traditional Chinese Medicine. According to Maoshing Ni, vice president of Yo San University of Traditional Chinese Medicine in Santa Monica, California, acupuncture and herbs can relieve both cataracts and glaucoma. He suggests in *Alternative Medicine: The Definitive Guide* that dietary changes combined with acupuncture, Chinese herbs, and stress management can reverse the growth of cataracts in some patients.

Surgery. Severe cataracts which impair vision usually require surgery. Modern cataract surgery typically takes less than an hour and involves making a small incision through the cornea and sclera that permits the surgeon to remove the cloudy lens, leaving the lens capsule in place. In 90% of cases, according to Jane Brody, writing in the July 21, 1993 edition of *The New York Times*, an artificial lens can be slipped in to replace the one that was removed, and most patients are able to go home the same day.

Glaucoma

According to the May 1994 issue of *The Johns Hopkins Medical Letter*, more than three million Americans are visually impaired because of glaucoma. Several different types of glaucoma have been identified, including chronic open-angle glaucoma, congenital glaucoma, acute angle-closure glaucoma, and secondary glaucoma, which is caused by secondary conditions such as hemorrhages, tumors, and inflammations. People with glaucoma usually experience hazy vision, eye and head pains, nausea, and rapid loss of vision. Glaucoma can occur in people of all ages, but is more likely to develop in people over the age of 35 years who are very nearsighted or diabetic.

Glaucoma occurs when extra fluid builds up inside an eye and presses against the optic nerve at the back of the eye. The build up usually results either from genetic factors or as part of the aging process. Normally a clear, transparent liquid called aqueous humor flows continually through the structures of the inner eye. If this flow becomes blocked, liquid pressure can build up against the optic nerves, which impairs their ability to transmit visual images to the brain.

In chronic open-angle glaucoma, the drainage channels of the aqueous humor become smaller with age and clogged with deposits, which gradually increase pressure against the optic nerves. This is the most common type of glaucoma in adults, and many do not realize they have the condition because they assume it is a natural part of aging. This type of glaucoma causes a loss of peripheral vision, and if it is detected early by an opthalmologist, it can be treated with eye drops that decrease fluid build-ups in the aqueous humor.

Congenital glaucoma is caused by genetic abnormalities in the drainage openings of the eye at birth. It is quite rare and can only be reversed through surgery. Acute angle-closure glaucoma is caused by the iris pressing against the drainage canals in the inner eye. Fluid backs up and increases eye pressure which results in blurred vision, severe pain, and nausea. Patients with these symptoms should see an eye physician immediately as blindness can result within several days. Secondary glaucoma is caused by hemorrhages, tumors, or inflammations in the inner eye which block the drainage channels.

Prevention

If diagnosed promptly, the eye pressure which causes glaucoma can be stabilized and future glaucoma can be prevented. An important aspect of holistic treatment is testing patients to determine what type of glaucoma they have and whether they are taking prescription medications for other disorders which may increase their risk of glaucoma. According to *Alternative Medicine: The Definitive Guide*, more than 90 medications, including antihypertensives, steroids, and antidepressants, can lead to glaucoma if used over a prolonged period of time.

Vitamin and Mineral Therapies. Vitamin C supplements and foods which contain bioflavonoid compounds may help prevent glaucoma by protecting the optic nerves from free radical damage. Vitamin, mineral, or botanical treatments have not been shown to be effective in treating acute forms of glaucoma, however, and eye damage caused by glaucoma usually cannot be reversed.

Botanical Medicines. James Balch and Phyllis Balch cite several botanical medicines in *Prescription for Nutritional Healing* which effectively relieve glaucoma. They suggest that rutin helps reduce inner eye pressure when used in conjunction with standard drugs. They also recommend warm fennel herb eye baths, alternated with chamomile and eyebright, as helpful in relieving the pain which accompanies glaucoma. No clinical trials on the effectiveness of these botanical medicines have been reported.

Traditional Chinese Medicine. Dr. Maoshing Nireports in *Alternative Medicine: The Definitive Guide* that acupuncture and herbs can relieve both cataracts and glaucoma. Acupuncture and Chinese herbs can significantly decrease the interocullar pressure associated with glaucoma, which allows patients to reduce the amount of

Alternative Treatments for Acute Glaucoma

Approximately 10% of Americans with glaucoma suffer from the acute, sudden-onset form which is a medical emergency. Acute glaucoma typically strikes the elderly and affects only one eye at a time. If not treated within 48 hours after the onset of symptoms, it can damage the optic nerve, impair peripheral vision, and cause blindness. The sudden increase in intraocular pressure causes a person to feel severe pain in the affected eye. Since the iris is normally pushed up toward the cornea, the person experiences blurry vision and halos around light sources. In extended attacks, the person may vomit and develop a hazy cornea. Physicians usually administer sedatives and analgesics, reduce eye pressure with special eye drops, and may perform surgery or laser therapy to open up the drainage channel in the iris.

Three alternative emergency treatments are recommended by H. Mark's *Handbook of Natural First-Aid for Treating Emergencies.*

1. **Acupressure**. Apply firm pressure to the acupressure point in the middle of the web between the thumb and index finger.

2. **Homeopathy**. Take the homeopathic Belladonna 30C remedy every 15 minutes for up to one hour. Belladonna is effective for dilated pupils and pain in one eye that are caused by bright lights or acute glaucoma.

3. **Botanical Medicines**. According to Mark, naturopaths and herbalists prescribe the herb bilberry (*Vaccinium myrillus*) to prevent and treat acute glaucoma attacks. Clinical evidence suggests that the anthocyanosides in bilberry markedly affect biochemical reactions in the eye, including improving night vision. Mark suggests taking a bilberry extract with 25% anthocyanoside content three times daily.

---

medications they are taking or even postpone surgery. Ni also notes that Forskolin, a drug extracted from the coleus plant, has been used successfully at Yale University to relieve glaucoma without side effects.

Biofeedback. Dr. Steve Fahrion, director of the Center for Applied Psychophysiology at the Menninger Clinic in Topeka, Kansas, cites several studies in *Alternative Medicine: The Definitive Guide* which suggest that biofeedback can relax the forehead muscles and help reduce the pressure on the eyeball caused by glaucoma. One technique involves placing electrodes on the forehead which allow patients to monitor their own stress levels and stimulate the relaxation response.

Eye Drops. Although the eye damage caused by glaucoma usually cannot be reversed, it can be controlled with special eye drops, pills, and surgery to prevent further damage. Patients with minor chronic open-angle glaucoma can recover some visual abilities if their condition is detected early enough and they begin using eye drops. Eye drops prescribed by an ophthalmologist are usually administered two to four times daily along with prescription pills. These medications decrease eye pressure either by assisting the flow of fluid out of the eye or by decreasing the amount of fluid entering the eye.

Surgery. Simeon Margolis reports in *The Johns Hopkins Medical Handbook* that surgery is the only treatment for acute angle-closure and congenital glaucoma, as it is the only way that blocked or incorrectly formed drainage canals of the eye can be opened up. Laser surgery, the least painful and invasive surgical procedure, uses a laser beam of light to burn an opening in the iris and open the eye's drainage canals.

Refractive Eye Disorders

Myopia (nearsightedness), hyperopia (farsightedness), and astigmatism (distorted vision) are caused by differences in the length or shape of the eye. Presbyopia (aging eye) occurs when the lens inside the eye loses its focusing ability for near vision.

Biofeedback. Biofeedback can correct refractive problems. Joseph Trachtman, a New York-based optometric physician, reports in *Alternative Medicine: The Definitive Guide* that he has helped people with extremely poor vision to either eliminate or reduce their need to wear eyeglasses. Trachtman uses a machine which he invented called Accomotrac Vision Trainer to help patients retrain their eye muscles to overcome refractive problems.

Surgery. Acute refractive eye problems which cannot be treated with noninvasive treatments normally require corrective eye surgery. Radial keratotomy is the most common corrective eye surgery technique. During the procedure, a surgeon makes a series of spoke-like microscopic incisions that reshape the surface of the cornea. When the cuts heal, the cornea is slightly flattened, so

Common Refractive Eye Defects

Amblyopia. A slightly crossed or drifting eye (called lazy eye) that can lead to permanent loss of vision.

Astigmatism. Vision is partially blurred because of irregularities in the curvature of the cornea, causing haphazard focusing on the retina of both near and far images.

Farsightedness (hyperopia). People can adjust their eyes to see distant objects clearly, but develop eye strain when trying to see things nearby.

Nearsightedness (myopia). Nearby objects can be focused on the retina, but the image of distant objects focuses in front of the retina causing blurred vision. A nearsighted person needs to squint to bring distant objects into focus.

Presbyopia. With aging, people find it more and more difficult to focus on close objects. This is caused by weakening of the eye muscles that adjust the lens, as well as a loss of elasticity in the lens itself.

Strabismus. This is found mostly in children–crossed or drifting eyes that cannot focus together on the same object.

that light rays focus directly on the retina, not in front of it. This type of surgery works best with patients who have moderate myopia. As reported by David Holzman in the January 22, 1990 issue of *Insight*, 90% of patients who undergo surgery for myopia achieve vision of 20/40 or better, which enables them to pass the Department of Motor Vehicles vision test without glasses. Photoreflective keratotomy, another surgical procedure, uses a new laser device to reshape the cornea. The procedure is currently being tested by the Food and Drug Administration and is not yet available.

Vision Training. In *Total Vision*, New York opthamologist Richard Kavner states that many cases of nearsightedness are caused by the strain of close work. He cites studies of Japanese students who, after studying intensely, developed myopia. When they were given eye exercises and relaxation techniques, they reversed their myopia. Kavner, along with the International Myopia Prevention Association, prescribes the following vision training for myopia patients to prevent eyestrain:

• Relax the eyes every few hours by closing them for five minutes.

• Look out the window or at objects 30 feet away for approximately 30 seconds.

• Hold a pencil at arm's length, and pull it slowly toward you until you see double.

• Give your eyes a mini-sauna by squeezing your hands together for a few minutes to warm them and then cupping your palms over your eyes.

• Proper reading posture is also important. Sit up straight when you read, hold the material 18 inches from your face and at a 20-degree angle.

Macular Degeneration

The macula is the point of the retina in back of the eye responsible for fine vision. When the macula is damaged, images are either blocked or blurred. The condition which results, macular degeneration, is the leading cause of difficulty with reading or close-up vision in the U.S., according to Alan Rees and Charlene Willey in *Personal Health Reporter*.

Approximately 70% of macular degeneration cases occur in elderly people, and is caused by a breakdown or thinning of the tissues in the macula. Another 10% is due to blood vessels which burst and leak fluid that damages the macula. In both instances, vision becomes distorted and blurred as dense scar tissue develops which blocks a person's central vision. Other types of macular degeneration are genetic, or are caused by injury, infection, or inflammation of the macular. There are no noninvasive treatments for macular degeneration. Holistic therapies focus on preventing the condition through early detection and taking vitamin supplements which maintain the integrity of the macular tissue.

Nutritional Therapies. According to an article in the April 1988 issue of *Health Facts*, blueberry extract, bilberry, ginkgo biloba extract, and zinc sulfate have been shown in several preliminary clinical trials to be effective in retarding severe visual loss due to macular degeneration. However, patients are advised to consult an eye specialist before taking any supplements. Antioxidants such as vitamin C, selenium, and vitamin E may also be beneficial.

Biofeedback. Dr. Joseph Trachtman claims that he has helped patients suffering macular degeneration with biofeedback treatments. Using his Accomotrac Vision Trainer machine, patients have been effectively trained to use a part of the eye other than the deteriorating macula.

Surgery. Advanced macular degeneration can only be treated by laser surgery. Such surgery, however, according to Margolis in *The Johns Hopkins Medical Handbook*, can damage small parts of the retina and leave blind spots. Researchers at Johns Hopkins University have developed a new prototype laser treatment which effectively seals blood leaks in wide areas of the retina without damaging it. Tests are underway to further develop the technique.

Retinopathy (RP)

Retinopathy (RP) is a disease in which capillaries that nourish the retina leak fluid or blood that damage the rod and cone cells of the eye. At least 60% of patients suffering from diabetes for 15 years or more have some form of RP. Diabetic RP affects approximately seven million people in the U.S., and causes blindness in about 7,000 Americans annually. Patients with diabetes must make sure to undergo regular eye examinations to detect the onset of RP because laser surgery to seal leaking blood vessels can now prevent vision loss.

A new form of intensive therapy has been developed for diabetics which corrects elevations in their blood sugar levels. Dr. Ping Wang, director of a research study at the Joslin Diabetes Center in Boston, reported in the May 23, 1993 edition of *The New York Times* that this therapy significantly prevents the long-term consequences of diabetes-related eye diseases, such as RP.

Vitamin and Mineral Therapies. In a controlled study involving 601 patients with common forms of RP, Dr. Eliot Berson, professor of Ophthalmology at Harvard Medical School, found that high doses of vitamin A can slow down the loss of remaining eyesight by approximately 20% per year. In the study, reported by David Tenenbaumin the September 1993 issue of *American Health*, a typical 32-year-old embarking on this therapy, for example, could retain vision until age 70 instead of losing it at age 63. However, people taking vitamin supplements to prevent RP should be careful not to combine vitamins A and E. While high daily doses of vitamin A appeared to be effective in Berson's trials, large doses of vitamin E (400 IU) seemed to worsen the

disease. Berson urges people with RP to consult an eye specialist before beginning any treatment. He also suggests that people who take large doses of vitamin E consult an ophthalmologist to ensure they are not developing RP.

Sty

A sty is an inflamed or infected swelling of the sebaceous (oil-producing) glands on the

---

Bloodshot Eyes

The Doctor's Book of Home Remedies II suggests the following for relieving bloodshot eyes:

- Avoid known allergens. Allergies cause the eyes to become red and tear. Always wash your hands after petting pets or applying makeup and shampoo.

- Limit the use of "red-out" eye washes and eyedrops. Prescription eyedrops for eye redness should only be used occasionally, because they can become habit forming. After using them for several weeks, some people develop a "rebound" effect, and their eyes become red if they don't use the drops.

- Use only "preservative-free" contact lens cleaners.

- Try artificial tears. If bloodshot eyes sting, try soothing them with nonpreservative artificial tears.

- Use warm compress. If the eyes are red but don't itch, use warm compresses to relieve bloodshot eyes caused by fatigue. Placing a warm washcloth over closed eyes for 10-20 minutes can reduce irritation.

Self-Help Treatments for Removing Foreign Objects in the Eye

- Holding the eye open, flush the object off the cornea using a gentle stream of clean water. One way to thoroughly wash the eyes is to fill a sink or basin with water and put your face in it. Holding the eye open, move your head from side to side to allow water to flow over the cornea.

- Holding the eye open, remove the particle with the moistened corner of a piece of clean cloth or moistened cotton swab. Don't use dry cotton swabs or tissues because loose fibers may come off and stick to the eye. A drop of lukewarm milk in the eye may help isolate the foreign object.

- If the particle is under the eye's upper lid, slowly drag the upper lid down over the lower lid. Hold it there for several seconds and then gently release. This usually causes tears to flush the foreign body out of the eye.

- If the object is a contact lens, and the eye is rapidly swelling, remove the lens by holding the upper eyelid open. Use your thumb to slide the contact toward the white area at the outside corner of the eye, pulling the skin there down and out.

inner or outer surface of the eyelid. The infection is commonly caused by *staphylococcus* bacteria. An external sty appears on the surface of the skin at the edge of the eyelid. An internal sty is caused by inflammation, infection, or obstruction of a sebaceous gland on the inner surface of the eyelid. Initially, a

sty feels like a foreign object in the eye. Tearing, redness, swelling, and tenderness in or around a particular of the eye soon follow. The eye may become sensitive to light and touch. In addition, pustules (small, yellow bumps filled with pus) may develop. These pustules often burst, release the pus, and begin to heal. Once the pressure has been released, the pain usually subsides.

Treatments for a sty usually involve botanical eye drops or ointments. Applying warm, moist compresses to the eye for ten minutes three to four times daily may encourage the sty to burst. In some cases, especially for internal sties, surgical opening may be necessary to cure the condition.

Foreign Bodies in the Eye

A tiny foreign body that is allowed to remain in the eyes can cause constant pain, infection, and in some cases irreversible visual damage. Common foreign objects that get caught in the eyes include contact lenses, eyelashes, dirt or dust, and wood or metal flakes. Obvious particles can usually be removed with a moistened cotton applicator, magnet, or saline solution. A physician may also use a special fluorescent dye which highlights tiny objects and scratches. If a foreign body is superficially embedded in the cornea, the physician will normally anesthetize the eye and remove the object with the tip of a hypodermic needle.

Botanical Medicines. Eyebright (*Euphrasia officinalis*) has been used to relieve eye irritation due to the removal of foreign objects. Others herbs include goldenseal, echinacea, and fennel seeds. Compresses can be made by using one ounce of herb per pint of water. The herbs should be boiled, then strained through an unbleached coffee filter and cooled to room temperature. The liquid can then be put into a clean eyecup and slowly poured over the open eye, while

<table>
</table>

Natural Remedies for Treating Thermal Burns to the Eyes

1. Cleanse the eye by using an eyecup and flushing. Funnel-shaped eyecups are available at most pharmacies. Use the spray nozzle from the kitchen-sink hose and control the pressure so that the flow of water to the eye is slow and gentle.

2. If both eyes or other parts of the face are contaminated, quickly take off your clothes, get in the shower, and flush the eyes thoroughly.

3. Put cold chamomile tea bags or raw potato slices on the closed infected eye for 15-20 minutes. Wet and reapply every five minutes.

4. Take the homeopathic remedy Euphrasiafor watery eyes accompanied by burning pain and swollen, red eyelids.

Other Common Eye Problems

- Spots before the eyes. This condition, in which people see spots (or "floaters"), is believed to be caused by a clear gel-like fluid inside the eye which increases with age. The spots seldom interfere with vision, however, and usually disappear on their own. If they suddenly increase in number or size, especially if accompanied by pain in the retina, people should contact an ophthalmologist.

- Twitching. Some people experience frequent twitchings in their lower eyelids. These twitches usually disappear spontaneously over time and require no treatment. If they persist, a neurologist may need to be consulted.

blinking and rolling the eye. "Rue and Fennel Compound" from Herb Pharm of Williams, Oregon, which includes concentrated drops of fennel, eyebright, goldenseal, and mullein flower helps relieve eye irritation. It is available in glass bottles from many natural food stores.

An alternate treatment is to cover the eye for 20 minutes with a slice of cucumber. According to Mark's *Handbook of Natural First-Aid for Treating Emergencies*, a poultice of grated apple wrapped in a clean, damp cotton cloth also relieves eye irritation.

Homeopathy. Euphrasia, a homeopathic formula made from the eyebright plant, can also be used in eyewashes, tinctures, or pellets (orally) to relieve eye irritation. It is especially effective when there is profuse watering of the eyes with burning pain, swelling, and redness.

Ears

The ear consists of three important components: the outer ear including the ear canal leading to the tympanic membrane (eardrum); the middle ear consisting of three bones connected to the throat by the eustachian tube; and the inner ear where mechanical vibrations are converted to nerve impulses.

According to the American Speech and Hearing Association (ASHA), more than 2.1 million Americans develop hearing impairment annually in the United States. Ear disorders are extremely difficult for people to diagnose themselves and usually require medical attention by an ear specialist–either an otologist or an otolaryngologist. According to ASHA, the three most common types of hearing impairment in the U.S are those that involve conductive hearing loss, those that involve ear nerve loss, and those that involve both.

Conductive hearing loss is a condition in which sound waves are blocked as they travel through the auditory canal of the middle ear and cannot reach the inner ear. Common causes include wax blocking the ear canal, infection, or a punctured eardrum. Most problems of this nature can be easily treated.

Otosclerosis, the second most common hearing disorder, is a condition in which the bones of the middle ear soften, do not vibrate well, and eventually calcify. Once this problem occurs, it can only be corrected by surgery.

"Nerve deafness" involves either temporary or permanent damage to the hair cells or nerve fibers of the inner ear. Causes of nerve deafness include high fevers, heredity, excess noise, adverse reactions to drugs, diseases such as meningitis and head injuries.

Nutritional Therapies. Toxins such as caffeine, tobacco, aspirin, some diuretics, and chemotherapy can cause sensory hearing loss and benign tumors or ulcers in the ear. In some cases, these conditions can be prevented and treated with balanced diets low in saturated fats and cholesterol, wheat, dairy products, sugar, alcohol, and yeast. A study reported by J. Spencer in the October 1981 issue of the *Southern Medical Journal* showed that 1,400 patients with inner ear symptoms who reduced lipoprotein (proteins that carry fat) blood levels decreased pressure in their ears and improved their hearing. A small study reported by M. Strome in the February 1993 issue of *Laryngoscope* found that when several children with "fluctuating

hearing loss" were placed on a low fat diet, their hearing returned.

Ear Blockages

Children frequently push objects into the ear which either block sound or cause an outer-ear infection. If an adult decides to try to remove the object, it is important not to push the object deeper into the ear canal.

For minor build-ups of wax, physicians recommend that adults remove the wax themselves by gently pushing warm water into the ear. In *Alternative Medicine: The Definitive Guide,* nutritionist Katie Data of Fife, Washington, recommends gently washing the inner ear with lukewarm water and a few drops of vinegar or hydrogen peroxide. Virender Sodhi, an Ayurvedic physician, suggests in the same book washing the inner ear with warm herbal oils such as garlic or mullein combined with olive oil. Earwax which cannot be removed using heated water normally has to be removed by a physician.

Earwax can build up in the ear channel and occasionally interfere with hearing. The build-up is often caused by food or mold allergies. Ear specialist Dr. Constatine A. Kotsanis reports in *Alternative Medicine: The Definitive Guide* that excessive earwax in children is often caused by allergies to cow's milk.

Earaches

Earaches are common in young children, and are usually caused by an infection spreading from the nose or throat, or by sinusitis. Fever and partial loss of hearing usually accompany earaches. Earaches can also be a symptom of dental decay, teething in a young child, or an abscess or boil in the ear canal. Earaches in adults often precede the onset of mumps, which can be serious. If the pain is very severe and there is neck stiffness and

Emergency Treatments for Ear Infections

To relieve outer ear canal infections:

1. Place a few drops of an equal mixture of white vinegar and 70% isopropyl alcohol in the ears several times daily. Apply the drops by tilting the head so that the liquid stays in the canal for 30 seconds.

2. Apply a few drops of full-strength echinacea concentrate or tincture, and gently flush with a 3% hydrogen peroxide solutions.

To relieve middle ear infections:

1. Yawn. Yawning exercises the muscle that opens the tube at the back of the throat.

2. Chew gum. This helps some people open the eustachian tube.

3. Drink plenty of warm chamomile or yarrow tea. Extra liquids help thin ear secretions and promote drainage.

4. Massage. Massage the ear around the outer ear. Try pulling gently down on the earlobe, stroking the neck, and rubbing the temples–this encourages drainage and increases blood circulation in the inner ear.

5. Massage the outer ear with three to five drops of eucalyptus or lavender essence diluted in a teaspoon of olive or other vegetable oil.

To relieve inner ear earaches:

1. Botanical medicine. Put 5-10 drops of mullein oil into the ear every two to three hours. Mullein's active ingredients include mucilage and aucubin, which soothe irritated mucous membranes. Or place a few drops of garlic oil directly in the ear every two hours.

2. Homeopathy. Take an appropriate homeopathic remedy to relieve ear infections. The remedies most commonly recommend by homeopaths include:

- Pulsatilla. This is an effective remedy for earaches caused by colds.

- Belladonna. This remedy is used for throbbing or piercing ear pain which occurs during a high fever when the ear canal or drum is red.

- Chamomilla. This is helpful, especially for children who are in great pain and oversensitive to touch.

- Aconite. This is used at the onset of an earache, when the outer ear is hot and painful and the patient is sensitive to noise.

3. Acupressure. Use your index and middle fingers to press in on both sides in the hollow, sensitive area in the back of the jawbone. Complement these point massages with gentle stroking of the neck and temple.

4. Yoga. The plow and shoulder stand yoga positions increase circulation in the ears, benefit hearing, and can relieve some types of earaches.

elevated temperature, it is important to consult a doctor.

Relieving Earaches

Botanical Medicines. Feinstein's *Symptoms: Their Causes & Cures* recommends the following botanical treatment for common earaches. Feinstein suggests warming up a baby bottle with hot water and adding a few drops of olive or mineral oil. The oil should be tested to ensure that it is about room temperature and applied with an ear dropper; the oil should only coat the inner lining of the ear. A few drops of isopropyl alcohol in the ear helps dry any excess water that remains in the ear. Swim-Ear, an ear product available at most pharmacies, also helps evaporate excess water.

Otitis Media (Infections of the Middle Ear)

The middle ear is the small space between the outer and inner ear which contains three delicates bones–the hammer, anvil, and stirrup–which are essential for hearing. Air pressure is kept constant by the eustachian, or auditory, tube, which leads into the middle ear from the back of the nasal cavity. If a virus or bacteria invades the middle ear, it can cause inflammation and a build-up of fluids which are the two major symptoms of otitis media.

There are several types of otitis media, each defined by their causes. Secretory otitis media is an infection caused by an allergen which enters the middle ear through the eustachian tube. Acute serious otitis media results from a bacterial or viral infection in addition to fluid build up. Acute purient otitis media is caused by pus from a bacterial infection and may result in a ruptured eardrum. Chronic otitis media is caused by an untreated bacteri-

al infection, infected adenoids, or structural deformities of the bones of the middle ear.

Symptoms of the four types of otitis media vary substantially. Most sufferers first experience sharp, stabbing, dull, and/or throbbing pains in the ear. Some bleeding or discharge of pus may occur as well. These symptoms usually result from ruptures of the eardrum through which pus flows. Children with middle ear infections may experience nausea and vomiting. People with chronic otitis media also experience constant swelling in the middle ear. Any indication of a middle ear infection should be referred to an ear specialist. Such infections are not dangerous as long as they are treated before serious complications occur. If left untreated, otitis media can lead to severe complications such as mastoiditis, brain abscesses, or meningitis.

Treatments for Otitis Media

Nutritional Therapies. To treat ear infections caused by allergies, holistic physicians recommend diets that eliminate allergy-producing foods, including milk and dairy products, eggs, wheat, corn, oranges, and peanut butter. These diets also usually restrict concentrated simple carbohydrates (such as sugar, honey, dried fruit, and concentrated fruit juice) because they can weaken the immune system.

Garlic has been used successfully to treat ear infections caused by bacteria. Researchers at Boston University School of Medicine conducted tests in which garlic proved as effective as an antibiotic in killing 14 bacteria that cause recurrent ear infections in children. As cited in the April 1994 issue of *Your Health*, the garlic even killed some bacteria known to be resistant to common antibiotics.

Vitamin and Mineral Therapies. In addition to eliminating allergens from the diet, Michael Murray and Jospeh Pizzorno suggest in the *Encyclopedia of Natural Medicine* that betacarotene, vitamin C, zinc picolinate, bioflavonoids, and evening primrose oil have proved useful in preventing or alleviating ear infections. They also claim that some symptoms have been successfully treated with the herbs echinacea, goldenseal, and licorice.

Infections of the inner ear which are due to destroyed inner ear hair cells may be treatable by a new procedure using chemicals made from vitamins. Dr. Thomas R. Van De Water of the Albert Einstein College of Medicine in New York City has found that retinoic acid, a derivative of vitamin A, can cause the inner ear to grow new auditory hair cells. The destruction or malfunction of auditory hairs cells is believed to be the major cause of deafness for approximately 18 million Americans, according to an article entitled "Vitamin A May Be a Key Deafness Cure" which appeared in the May 4, 1993 edition of the *San Jose Mercury News*.

Botanical Medicines. Dr. John Hibbs of the Natural Health Clinic of Bastyr College in Seattle, Washington, reports in *Alternative Medicine: The Definitive Guide* that a botanical formula of goldenseal, mullein, and hypericum in a glycerine base can reduce ear pain and help drain excess fluid of the inner ear. Echinacea and goldenseal also kill bacteria which may cause inflammation.

Homeopathic Therapies. Homeopath Randall Neustaedter, director of the Classical Medicine Center in Palo Alto, California, notes that acute ear infections are a simple problem to treat with homeopathic remedies. Common homeopathic remedies which he has successsfully used include deadly nightshade (*belladonna*), windflower (*pulsatilla*), phosphate of iron (*ferrum phose*), chamomile (*chamomilla*), and Hahnemann's calcium sulphide (*Hepar sulph*).

According to *Alternative Medicine: The Definitive Guide*, Robert Milne, a Las Vegas homeopath, has successfully used two homeopathic remedies, aconite and ferrum phose, to treat the early stages of middle ear infections. For later stages, he gives his patients *Chamomilla, Hepar sulph, Lycopodium, Merc sol, Pulsatilla* and *Silicea*.

Ayurvedic Medicine. Dr. Virender Sodhi, as reported in *Alternative Medicine: The Definitive Guide*, uses neem oil to effectively kill bacteria and fungus which cause some middle ear infections. Dr. Sodhi also employs lymphatic massage outside the ears to open the eustachian tube and facilitate draining. In addition, he prescribes the herb amla, which has antibacterial and antiviral properties, to help strengthen the immune system.

Other Treatments. Locally applied heat is often helpful in reducing the discomfort of an ear infection. It can be applied as a hot pack with warm oil (especially mullein oil), or by blowing hot air into the ear. Also of value is putting hygroscopic anhydrous glycerine into the ear, which draws fluids out and reduces pressure in the middle ear.

Surgery. When ear infections cannot be cured by holistic treatments, a surgical procedure to drain excess fluids called myringotomy is necessary. The treatment involves placing a tiny plastic tube through the eardrum to assist drainage of fluid into the throat. Myringotomy is not a curative procedure, however, as demonstrated in a double-blind study published in the October 1981 issue of *Lancet* which showed that children with tubes in their ears are more likely to have further problems with ear infections. The researchers recommended that natural antibiotics such as garlic should be used first because children not receiving chemical antibiotics had fewer recurrences of infection than those receiving antibiotics.

Tinnitus

When sound waves enter the ear, they travel down the ear canal and strike the eardrum, a skin-covered tympanic membrane. The drum is shaped like a broad flat cone approximately a half-inch across and less than one-fiftieth inch thick. Prolonged exposure to loud noises can harm the organ of the inner ear called corti, which converts vibrations to nerve impulses. Teenagers, for example, who listen to music at extremely loud levels often develop tinnitus, a condition in which they experience prolonged ringing or buzzing sounds in their ears. Their ability to enjoy music or any other sound in later years is often seriously impaired.

Nutritional Therapies. Because the inner ear is supplied with blood, nutrient excesses or deficiencies can affect hearing. High levels of blood fats and cholesterol, for example, have been shown to cause poor circulation of blood in the ear, and restricting saturated fats in the diet has proved helpful. Vitamin A is highly concentrated in the inner ear, and vitamin A and B supplements have improved hearing, especially in cases of inner-ear circulation problems and ear infections, according to Kurt Butler and Lynn Rayner in *The Best Medicine: The Complete Health and Preventive Medicine Handbook*.

Botanical Medicines. Ginkgo biloba increases circulation in and around the ear and, according to Dr. Kotsanis, is commonly used to treat tinnitus. He reports in *Alternative Medicine: The Definitive Guide* of successfully restoring full hearing to a teenage girl who had lost her hearing in one ear. Dr. Hoffman also reports in the same book that tinctures of black cohosh and ginkgo biloba in equal parts can restore hearing to tinnitus patients.

Homeopathic Remedies. Several homeopathic remedies help treat tinnitus, including *Salicylicum acidum*, *Chenopodium*, and *Cinchona officinalis*. Dr. Milne of Las Vegas recommends that people suffering from the disorder see a homeopath who will prescribe a remedy dependent upon the type of noise which initially damaged the ear.

Exercise and Inner Ear Disorders. Dr. Michael Weintraub, clinical professor of neurology at New York Medical College in Valhalla, reports in the April 6, 1994 edition of *The New York Times* that 20-25% of people who regularly do high-impact aerobics may eventually develop inner ear problems. Weintraub has found in preliminary clinical studies that 80% of those with symptoms suffered damage to the parts of the inner ear involved with balance. He warns that the repeated jarring of some forms of exercise such as aerobic dancing and running loosen tiny stone-like structures called otoliths, jamming them down among the hair cells that transmit information to the brain about the body's position in space. Once otoliths are unbalanced, they send the wrong signals to the brain which can result in a persistent, off-balance sensation, dizziness, a disoriented feeling, and difficulty in navigating. Many of those with symptoms experienced motion sickness and vertigo. According to Weintraub, 67% also had ringing in their ears (tinnitus), or a sensation of ear muffling or fullness. Eighty-seven percent of the aerobics instructors studied and 67% of enthusiasts also had high-frequency hearing loss. These symptoms indicate damage to the hair cells of the cochlea, the organ that transmits nerve impulses for sound to the brain To prevent problems, Weintraub urges aerobic exercisers to wear good shoes that absorb the impact of dancing, and to avoid using loud music. A switch to a less-jarring activity, such as low-impact or step aerobics, is also recommended.

Biofeedback. According to the American Tinnitus Association, biofeedback is especially useful for tinnitus patients whose symptoms are aggravated by anxiety or tension. In one study, 40 of 51 patients with tinnitus reported significant improvement through biofeedback. All patients in the study were able to stop taking sedatives to relieve their symptoms, and their improvement lasted for a year or longer.

Relaxation Therapy. Alice Feinstein's *Symptoms: Their Causes & Cures* suggests that relaxation and visualization therapies can relieve tinnitus. She details a program developed by Dr. Bill Reid of Beaverton, Oregon, who himself suffered from the disorder. His therapy involves putting patients in a relaxed "alpha state" and having them visualize a time before they developed tinnitus. The purpose of his therapy is to access a subconscious state where patients can *feel* the natural sounds they once were able to hear. Reid has patients choose words to remind themselves of this time when they didn't have tinnitus. By using words to access the memory, patients experience two to three minutes when they're not aware of their tinnitus. According to Reid, listening to visualization and imagery tapes and developing a positive attitude are the keys to successfully managing and reversing tinnitus.

Meniere's Disease (Vertigo)

Meniere's disease (vertigo) is a disorder of the inner ear characterized by a sensation of whirling motion or ringing in the ear. Some people also experience a feeling of fullness in the ear, and fluctuating hearing loss. About 250,000 people develop Meniere's disease annually in the United States.

The cause of Meniere's disease is not known, although it has been linked to brain tumors, high or low blood pressure, allergies, lack of oxygen circulation in the brain, anemia, infections, nutritional deficiencies, neurological disease, stress, excess earwax, and poor cerebral circulation. It can also result from moving suddenly from a sitting to a standing position. Sometimes the disease results from a watery fluid build-up in the inner ear which clouds messages being sent to the brain. Dizziness is the most noticeable symptom, and can often be so severe that sufferers are unable to work or remain independent.

Treatments for Meniere's Disease

Nutritional Therapies. Michael Glasscock, president of the Ear Foundation in Nashville, Tennessee, has found that 85% of patients with Meniere's disease can be treated with a low-salt diet and diuretics, both of which reduce the amount of fluid in the inner ear. Ear specialists in Toronto have also been able to eliminate vertigo in 89% of patients using several doses of gentamicin each day for four days. Hearing was improved and vertigo eliminated in 35% of the patients; 39% remained unchanged; and 25% of the patients got worse. These findings were reported in the November 3, 1992 edition of the *San Jose Mercury News*.

According to Feinstein's *Symptoms: Their Causes & Cures*, a low-calorie, low-fat, low-sugar diet also relieves vertigo. Feinstein cites a study by ear specialist Dr. Joel Lehrer in which 100 patients with dizziness and hearing loss or ringing in the ears relieved their symptoms with a weight-loss diet. Many of the patients, according to Lehrer, were overweight and had high blood cholesterol and triglyceride levels. They were also insulin resistant, in which their cells had trouble utilizing insulin, even when normal amounts were present in their blood. Lehrer notes that most of his patients in the study remarkably improved on his diet, and for many, nutritional therapy was the only treatment they needed.

Vitamin, Mineral, and Botanical Therapies. Balch and Balch report in *Prescription for Nutritional Healing* that patients with vertigo symptoms may benefit from vitamin and mineral supplements which increase circulation of oxygen in the brain, including vitamins B_3, B_{12}, C, and A. They also suggest that coenzyme Q-10, calcium with magnesium, germanium, and kelp may be helpful. In addition, botanicals such as butcher's broom, cayenne, chaparral tea, dandelion extract or tea, and ginkgo biloba extract have been used effectively to treat vertigo. People who manifest the symptoms should also restrict their intake of nicotine, caffeine, salt, and fried foods.

Balch and Balch stress that some cases of dizziness and vertigo are caused by poor cerebral circulation. For these symptoms, they recommend the following botanicals treatments: butcher's broom, cayenne, green tea, and ginkgo biloba.

Homeopathic Therapies. Dr. Milne reports in *Alternative Medicine: The Definitive Guide* that many patients with Meniere's disease also complain of migraine headaches, which suggests that their hearing disorder is partly dietary in origin. Depending on a patient's specific symptoms, he treats Meniere's with homeopathic remedies such as *Carboneum sulphuratum* and *Salicylicum acidum*, in addition to ginkgo biloba. He also prescribes vitamin B_6 to decrease fluid build up and restricts sodium, caffeine, and chocolate intake. Finally, he determines whether the patient is sensitive to dental amalgams.

Vestibular Rehabilitation Therapy. A new type of exercise therapy has been used to successfully treat some patients suffering from Meniere's disease and other forms of dizziness caused by inner ear disorders. According to Melinda Henneberger, writing in January 26, 1994 edition of *The New York Times*, approximately 50 vestibular rehabilitation centers now treat inner ear disorders. The therapy combines several home exercise programs custom-designed for each patient, including jumping on a mini trampoline, sitting up and lying down rapidly, and turning in circles. Patients are also given eye exercises to do at home which retrain the vestibular ocular reflex (a nerve reflex of the inner ear) to allow the eyes to maintain a steady field of vision as a person moves. The eye exercises, in which patients repeatedly move their heads from side to side or up and down while focusing on specific objects, help patients steady their gaze and regain their equilibrium. Most inner ear disorders such as Meniere's disease require between six weeks and 18 months of treatment. Studies show that 85% of patients with inner ear problems achieve partial relief from the therapy, and 30% recover completely.

Ayurvedic Medicine. In *Alternative Medicine: The Definitive Guide*, Dr. Sodhi describes an Ayurvedic treatment for Meniere's disease that uses albad oil in the ear to draw out excess fluid. He also internally administers albad oil in a solution with sesame oil and ghee (clarified butter), and prescribes rest and lymphatic drainage massage.

Surgery. Patients with Meniere's disease who do not respond to noninvasive treatments may need to undergo surgery (vestibular neurectomy), which generally involves spending five to six days in the hospital. Risks of post-surgical complications include some hearing loss, infections, headaches, and small leaks of brain or spinal fluid, as reported in an article that appeared in the *San Jose Mercury News* on November 3, 1992.

Helium-Neon (HN) Laser Treatments. Homeopath Dr. Arabinda Das reports in the May 1994 *Townsend Letter for Doctors* that he has successfully used helium-neon lasers to treat Meniere's disease. A one-time application of laser for 10 minutes can effectively remove mild symptoms, while two to five treatments are needed for patients with severe symptoms. Five-year follow-up studies show no recurrences of the symptoms. He suggests that laser treatments inhibit the DNA and RNA of bacteria which causes the disorder. According to Das, laser surgery is a noninvasive holistic treatment which constitutes the "fourth generation of homeopathic remedies."

Otosclerosis

Otosclerosis is a hereditary hearing problem that primarily develops in adults. Usually the disorder is caused by an overgrowth of the tiny stirrup-shaped stapes bones in the middle ear. When the bones become overgrown, they impede the conduction of sound signals traveling through the middle ear.

There are no holistic treatments for acute otosclerosis. This hearing problem can often be completely remedied by surgery which removes the excess bone and replaces all or part of the stapes with an artificial part, and often restores complete hearing ability.

Deafness (Total Hearing Loss)

Hearing involves a complex process by which sounds outside the ear are transmitted as auditory signals through the middle and inner ear and to auditory centers in the brain. Some infants, due to genetic factors or birth abnormalities, are born deaf—that is, they are born with structural abnormalities of the three middle ear bones. Other causes of deafness include impairments of the eight nerve fibers concerned with hearing. As Margolis reports in *The Johns Hopkins Medical Handbook,* more than 4,000 infants are born deaf every year in the United States. Approximately half of these cases are due to hereditary disorders.

Deaf patients with structural abnormalities can never recover full hearing. They can, however, be given cochlear implants which stimulate partial hearing. Cochlear implants are tiny microphones which are placed behind the ear. The microphones pick up sound signals and relay them to a speech processor which the patient wears in a pocket. Gillian Weiss reports in the November 1990 issue of *American Health* that the implants may eventually be common treatment for total deafness.

People with partial deafness can benefit from using hearing aids which amplify sound signals that stimulate the cochlear hair cells. However, hearing aids can only help people who still have some hearing abilities. Their effectiveness varies according to their design and how well the aid matches the individual's needs.

Vitamin and Mineral Therapies. According to the May 4, 1993 edition of the *San Francisco Chronicle*, researchers hope to develop an eventual cure for the principal form of deafness by restoring inner-ear cells essential for hearing. Dr. Thomas Van De Water of the Albert Einstein College of Medicine in New York reported a study in the April 1993 issue of *Science* which found that retinioc acid, a derivative of vitamin A, can cause the inner ear to grow new auditory hair cells in laboratory rats. The death or malfunction of auditory hair cells is thought to be the major cause of deafness for approximately 18 million Americans. Van De Water and his colleagues are hopeful that the growth of inner ear cell tissue will be successful in humans.

Vasoconstrictors. Over-the-counter nasal sprays which contain phenylephrine help reduce swelling in the ear. The spray shrinks the lining of the nose and the area around the entrance of the eustachian tubes. Nasal sprays or nose drops containing phenylephrine, however, should not be used for more than a few days, and recommended dosages should never be exceeded.

Heat Therapy. Two forms of heat therapy, according to Feinstein, help relieve earaches. One involves setting a heating pad on medium and placing it on top of the sore ear. Another entails turning a hair dryer on the lowest warm setting and directing the warm air down the ear canal by holding the dryer 6-12 inches from the ear. The dryer should not be used for more than three to five minutes.

The Nose

The nose, the main channel for breathing, performs several critical functions. The nasal membranes that line the nasal passages secrete liquid mucus which contains lysozyme, a chemical that destroys bacteria. The nose also plays an important role in warming and humidifying the air which enters the lungs. In addition, the nose and the olfactory senses also help create appetite.

Sinusitis

The nose contains four large sinus cavities: two inside the cheekbones (the maxillary sinuses) and two above the eyes (frontal sinuses). The sinuses are lined with membranes which secrete antibody-containing mucus that protects the respiratory tract from toxins in the air.

Sinusitis is a disorder that occurs when the cavities become inflamed (swollen). Acute bacterial sinusitis results from a viral infection in the upper respiratory tract (a common cold) which fills the sinus cavities with mucus. Chronic sinusitis is an inflammation of the sinuses caused by allergies, normally food allergies. Symptoms include swelling of the sinuses, a dull pain over the involved sinus, persistent nasal congestion, and discharge, postnasal drip, and a diminished sense of smell. Sinusitis, Rees and Willey state in *Personal Health Reporter*, is the most com-

mon chronic nose disorder in the United States, affecting an estimated 14% of all Americans.

Chronic sinusitis is a circular process in which the sinuses first become inflamed, then become cracked, scarred, or swollen. Once they are scarred or cracked, they can become infected by bacteria. As a result, they can subsequently become more sensitive to allergens and even more inflamed. If not treated in its earliest stages, sinusitis can progress to asthma, bronchitis, and inflammation of the brain.

Many people develop sinus problems because of dry-air heating systems (in winter) or air-conditioning systems (in summer). As a result, many holistic physicians advise sinusitis patients to use humidifiers in their homes and offices. Salt-water sprays which are inhaled through the nose five or six times a day can also help drain a temporary inflammation.

Treatments for Sinusitis

Nutritional Therapies. If early inflammations are caused by food allergies (chronic sinusitis), a strict diet is implemented which eliminates common food allergens such as milk, wheat, eggs, citrus fruits, corn, and peanut butter. Murray and Pizzorno describe several food allergy elimination diets which have proven effective in treating sinus disorders. Most sinusitis diets require that patients drink large amounts of fluids such as diluted vegetable juices, soups, and herb teas. Simple sugar consumption (including fruit sugars) should also be limited.

Vitamin and Mineral Therapies. According to Murray and Pizzorno, both types of sinusitis can be treated with vitamin and mineral supplements, including vitamins C and A, betacarotene, bioflavonoids, and zinc lozenges. These should only be taken under the supervision of a physician, and

Murray and Pizzorno do not recommend prolonged supplement treatments. They also suggest that thymus extract has helped some patients with sinusitis. Bee pollen, and vitamin B complex with extra vitamin B_6 (pyrodoxine) and pantethenic acid (B_5), help sufferers increase their immunity to new infections and may relieve mild sinus congestion.

Botanical Medicines. Rees and Willey indicate that for some patients, heat, volatile oils, and antibacterial botanicals are helpful in draining sinuses and preventing chronic infection. Intranasal douches with goldenseal tea provide relief, as does swabbing the nasal passages with oil of bitter orange. Murray and Pizzorno also suggest that menthol or eucalyptus packs held over the sinuses are sometimes helpful. Hot botanical liquids help the mucus flow and relieve congestion and sinus pressure. Balch and Balch suggest that mild sinusitis can be alleviated with the following herbs: anise and horehound, echinacea, fenugreek, lobelia, marshmallow, mullein, red clover, and rose hips.

Hydrotherapy. Dr. Richard Barrett of the National College of Naturopathic Medicine in Portland, Oregon, states in *Alternative Medicine: The Definitive Guide* that the dry heat of a sauna or hydrotherapy is the most helpful treatment for relieving sinus congestion. In the early stages, nasal lavages of salt water and steam inhalations help loosen up sinus mucus for secretion. An alternative is applying a hot compress over the sinuses for three minutes, followed by a cold compress for 30 seconds.

Another method, according to Barrett, is to inhale hot steam. This can be easily done by boiling a quart of water, and standing over the water, covering the head with a towel while inhaling the steam. Small amounts of aromatic herbs such as mint or eucalyptus are sometimes added to the hot water.

Homeopathic Therapies. According to Stephen Cummings and Dana Ulman in *Everybody's Guide to Homeopathic Medicine*, homeopathic therapies have been used for several hundred years to treat sinus infections. Depending on the cause of sinus inflammation and the symptoms, *Arsenicum album*, *Nux vomica*, *Mercuriius iodatus* and *Silicea* have been used with some effectiveness. A trained homeopath can prescribe the right remedies according to the cause and symptoms of sinusitis and an individual's unique biochemistry.

Acupuncture. William Cargile, chairman of research for the American Association of Acupuncture and Oriental Medicine, believes that acupuncture is one of the most effective holistic therapies for sinusitis. He states in *Alternative Medicine: The Definitive Guide* that sinus problems are often related to toxins in the bowels and intestines. Acupuncture treatments which stimulate the body to detoxify almost immediately detoxify the sinus membranes as well. In some cases, the relief last for weeks or the sinusitis is cleared up completely.

In severe cases, antibiotic medicines may be necessary. Prescription drugs for sinus problems, however, can be addictive and repeated use of drugs can lead to the development of tolerance by the bacteria, according to Richard N. Podell, writing in the February 1991 issue of *Redbook*. Podell cites a number of studies which suggest that decongestants such as pseudoephedrine constrict blood vessels and may permanently shrink the sinus and nasal membranes. Those that contain antihistamines often cause drowsiness. Spray decongestants such as Afrin and Dristan are only effective for a few days, and are known to have a rebound effect: when patients stop their use, their sinuses become more congested and they need more spray to provide relief. Prescription inhalers provide temporary relief, but do not fight bacteria directly, and do not heal the inflamed sinus membrane. Antihistamines can relieve nasal itchiness and inflammation by blocking the action of histamines, but do not help drain the mucus, according to Podell.

Nasal Polyps

Nasal polyps are swollen sinus tissues that protrude into the nasal cavity. Polyps occur either singly or in grape-like clusters, and are usually caused by allergies. They can easily be removed by surgery, although the best treatment is to eliminate the allergens or bacteria which cause them, because polyps often reappear after being surgically removed.

Nutritional Therapies.   According to Balch and Balch, a diet which enhances the immune system is important, and animal fats should be reduced. As with all infections, the diet should include green vegetables and fiber, and exclude fried and highly processed foods, caffeine, tobacco, and alcohol.

Vitamin and Minerals.   Vitamin C has proved helpful for eliminating cervical polyps and may help relieve nasal polyps. Vitamin A, betacarotene, and calcium are also recommended by Balch and Balch. Vitamin E may be effective as well because the mucus membrane linings are more vulnerable to damage when a person has a vitamin E deficiency.

The Throat

The throat (pharynx) is the five-inch-long muscular tube through which both food and air enter the body. It is composed of two divisions: the trachea (windpipe) which inhales air and sends it to the lungs, and the esophagus (food passage), which helps break down foods and transport them to the stomach. The throat also conducts air through the vocal cords (larynx), which allows people to speak and sing.

Hoarseness or a change in voice quality may be early symptoms of throat disorders, and a physician should be consulted if they persist. Throat hoarseness which lasts for more than two weeks may be an early warning sign of throat cancer, for example, especially for men older than 50. Doctors at the University of Iowa studied 73 patients who had their voice boxes removed after being diagnosed with throat cancer, and found that in 75% of them, hoarseness and changes in voice quality were early symptoms of the disorder. Other early signs of throat cancer may include problems with swallowing, sore throat, and weight loss.

Throat Cankers

Small mouth ulcers, or canker sores, periodically develop inside the mouth or along the throat channel. These can be caused by infections, skin burning (eating hot foods such as pizza, for example), or emotional stress. Alternative remedies focus on neutralizing the infecting organisms and healing the sores. Carbamide peroxide, which contains glycerin and peroxide, is available in over-the-counter medications, and can provide temporary relief. Peroxide releases oxygen and kills the bacteria, while glycerin coats and protects the sore.

Vitamin and Mineral Therapies. Cankers almost always develop when the immune system is weak. Vitamin C, vitamin B complex lozenges, or vitamin B complex tablets with folic acid, and B_{12} taken with meals restrengthen the immune system. Lysine taken on an empty stomach may also prove helpful. Acidophilus will balance the intestinal flora, and zinc gluconate lozenges may provide relief as well.

Dentists sometimes recommend squeezing vitamin E oil from a capsule onto canker sores. This is a safe, natural treatment which is usually supplemented with vitamin C to restrengthen the immune system against infection. If the sores persist for more than several days, people should consult their doctor who may in severe cases prescribe a topical steroid and/or oral antibiotic.

Botanical Medicines. Dermatologists, according to Murray and Pizzorno, sometimes recommend applying a wet black teabag to a throat canker. Black tea, which contains tannin, has been used as a herbal astringent to relieve pain. Alum, the active ingredient in styptic pencils, is an antiseptic and a pain reliever, which can prevent a throat canker infection from worsening. Goldenseal, either as a tea or applied directly to a canker, mouthwashes made with sage and chamomile, or pastes made of echinacea tincture and myrrh gum are also reported by Balch and Balch to provide relief.

Sore Throats

According to Murray and Pizzorno, 90% of sore throats in adults are caused by viruses which are not serious, and they normally heal within two to three days. The other 10% are "strep throats" caused by streptococcal bacteria. Strep throats are more common in children than adults and produce a variety of symptoms including throat pain, fever, muscle aches, swollen lymph glands in the neck, and chills. Strep throats require immediate treatment because they can lead to kidney disease, rheumatic fever, and heart complications.

Vitamin and Mineral Therapies. The holistic treatment for sore throats employs diet, vitamins, and botanical medicines to treat the early stages of viral or bacterial infection. Patients with symptoms should increase their fluid intake, including filtered water, hot herbal teas, diluted fruit juices, and broths. One effective remedy is drinking warm water mixed with powdered vitamin C, along with lemon and honey. In addition, vitamin C-rich foods (especially orange juice), along with vitamin A and bioflavonoids, betacarotene supplements, and zinc lozenges have proven effective in uncontrolled clinical trials.

Botanical Medicines. According to Murray and Pizzorno, goldenseal and *Echinacea angustifolia* are natural antibiotics which prevent the spread of streptococcal bacteria.

Alternative Medicine: The Definitive Guide suggests several other botanical therapies to treat infection, including osha root (*Ligusticum porteri*), infusions of lavender or hyssop, and slippery elm, and ginger tea.

Homeopathic Therapies. Dr. Stephen Cummings and Dana Ullman, in *Everybody's Guide to Homeopathic Medicine*, list the following homeopathic remedies for sore throats: lachesis, *Ignatia*, *Arnica*, *Aconite*, *Hydrastis*, *Gelsemium*, *Merc. sol.,* and *Phytolacca*. They stress that homeopathic treatments must be individualized and that a licensed homeopath should be consulted.

Hydrotherapy. Heating compresses can provide relief and reduce swelling caused by infection. A warm, wet face cloth covered with a wool sock can be applied directly to the throat. Gargling several times a day with water and salt, or apple cider vinegar mixed with hot water, salt, lemon juice, and honey can also provide relief.

Antibiotics. Antibiotics such as penicillin, should only be given to patients who do not respond to natural holistic treatments. The danger of prolonged penicillin use is that the streptococcal bacteria develops a tolerance to it. In addition, penicillin fails in approximately 20% of cases to eliminate the streptococci. In all cases of sore throat, any treatment must eliminate the virus or bacteria by restrengthening the immune system through rest and drinking large amounts of fluids.

Dry Mouth (Xerostomia)

Dry mouth, caused by inadequate saliva, is a common problem, especially among elderly people. Besides being unpleasant, inadequate salivation can increase the frequency of tooth decay since saliva contains substances that kill tooth-destroying bacteria and the saliva itself also washes the bacteria away.

Saliva also reduces swelling inside the mouth, inflammation, pain, and persistent sores. Food tastes and oral functions such as talking, chewing, and swallowing are often affected.

Xerostomia is caused by several illnesses, including Sjogren Syndrome. X rays and drugs, including antihistamines and anticholingergics, can also dry out the mouth. Persons who feel that their mouths are drier than normal should consult a physician, who can determine appropriate remedies.

Doctors advise dry-mouth patients to drink water frequently or suck on pieces of ice. For some sufferers, chewing stimulates salivary flow. Patients are also usually encouraged to nibble on carrots, celery, and other chewy foods and to chew sugarless gum which does not cause dental cavities.

For many sufferers, saliva substitutes may be the only recourse other than frequently sipping water. Several drug preparation are available without prescription which provide transient relief. Some are water-based or glycerin-based fluids or sprays. Other contains polymers such as sodium carboxymethylcelulose or hydroxymthylcellulose that bind and hold moisture. These saliva substitutes also may contain other ingredients, including electrolytes.

Debris Removers/Wound Cleansers

Colds and other conditions that cause sore throat or irritation and soreness in the mouth may produce an accumulation of mucus, phlegm, and other secretions that stick to and build up on the mucous membranes. These secretions can be irritating and are apt to cause coughing and considerable pain.

Holistic ebriding agents act in several ways. Some release tiny bubbles of oxygen that lift the offending matter off the tissue surface. Other mineral-containing compounds act to mechanically wash the debris away. Gargling with sodium bicarbonate (ordinary baking soda), for example, increases the alkalinity of mucus, loosening it so that it's easier to swallow, cough up, or blow out through the nose. Gargling with salt water also removes debris by drawing water out of the mucous membranes, which dilutes the mucus and cleanses the membrane surface. Although these debriding agents work quite effectively, the effect is brief and they do not cure the underlying condition.

Botanical Medicines. Demulcents are lozenges, mouth rinses, and gargling solutions which protect the mucous membranes from chemicals, fluids, air, and other irritants. Some bind and hold irritating substances, thereby neutralizing them. Elm bark, derived from the dried inner bark of the slippery-elm tree produces a gluey substance with a curry-like aroma when boiled. Elm bark troches or lozenges protect inflamed and irritated mucous membranes in the throat and mouth. The FDA has recommended them as safe for occasional medicinal use.

Gelatin. Ordinary gelatin provides a protective coating over irritated or ulcerated areas of the mouth and throat. It also inhibits the ability to feel cold, warmth, pressure, or pain, although it appears to have no curative or wound-healing properties. A special dosage form called an absorbable gelatin sponge is often used to medicate the upper throat and the insides of the cheek.

Glycerin. Glycerin is a clear, colorless, syrupy liquid that is used to protect the skin as well as the mucous membranes. When applied to the mouth in a rinse, wash, spray, or on a swab, it forms a thin, protective layer that adheres to the mucous membranes. It also insulates sensory nerve endings from painful stimuli, but does not promote healing.

Pectin. Pectin, the fruit extract used to make fruit jellies, has a long record of use in food and medicines. The FDA regards it as a safe treatment for protecting raw or ulcerated mouth and throat sores. It also protects the sensory receptors from further stimulation and the tissue from further irritation. It does not, however, enhance healing or cure the soreness in the tissue it's covering. It is normally available in rinses, gargles, sprays, lozenges, or gels.

Summary

The eyes, ears, nose and throat are often considered a single medical system because their functions overlap and, in the case of the ears, nose and throat, they share the same nerve supply. An infection or imbalance in any one of the areas may manifest in the others. Because they function as the first line of defense against external infectious organisms and toxins, their disorders are often immune system-related. And, because they degenerate over time, it may be necessary for some people to take vitamin, mineral, and botanical supplements to help maintain the integrity of the immune system and supply necessary nutrients to these tissues.

Resources

References

Balch, James F., and Phyllis Balch. *Prescription for Nutritional Healing*, Long Island: Avery Publishing, 1993.

Brody, Jane. "Personal Health." *The New York Times* (July 21, 1993): B7.

The Burton Goldberg Group. *Alternative Medicine: The Definitive Guide*, Payallup,

WA: Future Medicine Publishing, Inc., 1993.

Butler, Kurt, and Lynn Rayner. *The Best Medicine: The Complete Health and Preventative Medicine.* New York: Harper & Row, Publishers, Inc., 1985.

Cummings, Stephen, and Dana Ulman. *Everybody's Guide to Homeopathic Medicine.* New York: St. Martin's Press, 1991.

Feinstein, Alice, ed. *Symptoms: Their Causes & Cures.* Emmaus, PA: Rodale Press, 1993.

"Garlic Kills Ear Infection Bacteria." *Your Health* (April 1994): 53.

"Glaucoma: Arresting This Thief of Sight." *The Johns Hopkins Medical Letter* (May 1994): 4-6.

Henneberger, Melinda. "Exercise Therapy Can Help Inner-Ear Dizziness." *The New York Times* (January 26, 1994): D7.

Holzman, David. "Test Gives a Better Vision of Future." *Insight* (January 22, 1990): 46.

Kasper, Rosemarie. "Hearing Loss and You: Hearing Impairment Is One of the Most Prevalent Disabilities in the Country." *Independent Living* (August-September 1990): 59-60.

Kavner, Richard. *Total Vision.* New York: A & W Publishers, 1992.

Kirchheimer, Sid. *The Doctor's Book of Home Remedies II.* Emmaus, PA: Rodale Books, 1993.

"Lasers Battle Blindness." *Consumer Reports Health Letter* (December 1990): 96.

Margolis, Simeon, and Hamilton Moses III, eds. *The Johns Hopkins Medical Handbook.* New York: Rebus Inc, 1993.

Mark, H. *Handbook of Natural First-Aid for Treating Emergencies.* New York: Pocket Books, 1991.

Murray, Michael, and Joseph Pizzorno. *Encyclopedia of Natural Medicine.* Rocklin, CA: Prima Publishing, 1991.

Podell, Richard. "The Cold That Won't Go Away–Sinusitis." *Redbook* (February 1991): 93-94.

Rees, Alan, and Charlene Willey. *Personal Health Reporter.* Detroit, MI: Gale Research Inc., 1993.

Strome, M. *Laryngoscope* (February 1993).

"Surgery for Vertigo Carries Chance of Some Hearing Loss." *San Jose Mercury News* (November 3, 1992): 3C.

Tennebaum, David. "Saving Sight." *American Health* (September 1993): 66-67.

Van Buchen, F. "Therapy of Acute Otitis Media: Myringotomy, Antibiotics, or Neither?" *Lancet* (October 9, 1981): 883-87.

"Vitamin A May Be a Key Deafness Cure." *San Jose Mercury News* (May 4, 1993): 5.

"Vitamin C: A Secret to a Long Life and a Healthy Heart." *Environmental Nutrition* (July 1992): 3.

"Vitamin E and Cataracts." *Your Health* (July 13, 1993): 7.

"Warding Off Diabetes Complication." *American Health* (September 1993): 13.

Weintraub, Michael. "Inner-Ear Ailments Traced to High-Impact Aerobics." *San Jose Mercury News* (April 7, 1994): C1

Weiss, Gillian. "New Hope for Deaf Children: Implant Gives Them Hearing and Speech." *American Health* (November 1990): 17.

"Zinc Retards Macular Degeneration." *Health Facts* 13 (April 1988): 5.

Organizations

American Tinnitus Association.
P.O. Box 5, Portland, OR 97207.

RESOURCES

National Eye Research Foundation.
910 Skokie Boulevard, Suite 207A, Northbrook, IL 60062.

National Institute of Allergy and Infectious Diseases.
9000 Rockville Pike, Bethesda, MD 20205

Optometric Extension Program Foundation, Inc.
2912 Robeson, Fall River, MA 02720.

Sound, Listening and Learning Center.
2701 East Camelback, Suite 205, Phoenix, AZ 85016.

Additional Reading

Cataracts: A Consumer's Guide to Choosing the Best Treatment. Washington, D.C.: Public Citizen's Health Research Group, 1981.

Maloney, William, Lincoln Grindle, and Donald Pearcy. *Consumer Guide to Modern Cataract Surgery.* Fallbrook, CA: Lasenda Publishers, 1986.

Schmidt, Michael. *Childhood Ear Infections (What Every Parent and Physician Should Know).* Berkeley, CA: North Atlantic Books, 1990.

RESOURCES

Chapter 17

CANCER

In 1993, more than five million Americans were diagnosed as having some type of cancer. Currently, one out of every five Americans is likely to develop cancer during his or her lifetime, and one person in five who develop cancer is likely to die from it. Approximately one third of all cancers result from cigarette smoking and other forms of tobacco use. It is estimated that 80% of all cancers could be prevented if people ate nutritious low-fat foods, did not smoke, and limited other unhealthy behaviors.

This chapter describes the causes and major types of cancer and outlines the holistic approach to preventing and treating them. This holistic approach is summarized best by Dr. Bernie Siegel in his book *Love, Medicine & Miracles*, who states: "A vigorous immune system can overcome cancer if it is not interfered with, and emotional growth toward greater self-acceptance and fulfillment helps keep the immune system strong."

Cancer is not one disease, but a group of diseases, all of which occur when healthy cells stop functioning and maturing properly. Normal, healthy cells grow, divide, and replace themselves in an orderly way. Sometimes, however, for reasons still not fully understood, cells lose their ability to control their growth–and begin to multiply abnormally. During this process, they can develop their own network of blood vessels which siphon nourishment away from the body's blood supply.

Every cell in the body has the ability to turn cancerous, and many do so on a daily basis. Normally, the immune system is able to either destroy these cells or reprogram them back to normal functioning. However, if the immune system is weakened (suppressed) severely, it cannot destroy or reprogram the cells, which subsequently form tumors, or masses of abnormal cells (usually more than a billion before they become detectable). If the cancer cells do not spread beyond the tissue or organ where they originated, the cancer is considered to be localized or benign. Benign tumors (such as warts and cysts) usually remain localized, can be removed by surgery, and are not life-threatening.

Malignant tumors, which can develop in any organ or tissue in the body, are composed of cells that multiply much faster than normal cells and usually have one or more abnormal chromosomes. The cells of malignant tumors do not remain localized; instead, they enter the bloodstream and migrate to vital body organs where they can form new tumors. By diverting essential nutrients from normal cells and releasing toxins into the blood and organ systems, malignant tumors interfere with the functioning of those organs so that serious illness and death ensue. If left untreated, cancer is almost always fatal.

Different types of cancers are defined according to the organ or kind of tissue in which the tumor is located. Although there are more than 100 different varieties of cancer, the five basic categories include carcinomas, sarcomas, myelomas, lymphomas, and leukemias. Carcinomas are tumors that form in tissues covering or lining internal organs. They are the most common type of cancer, accounting for 80-90% of all cancers, and typically found in the intestines, lung, breast, prostate, and skin.

Sarcomas originate in connective tissues and muscles, cartilage, or the lymph system. Though they represent the smallest number of cancer cases, they are also the most fatal. Myelomas form in the plasma cells of bone marrow. Lymphomas are cancers of the lymph glands (or nodes) found in the neck, groin, armpits, and spleen. Prevalent types include Hodgkin's disease and non-Hodgkin's lymphomas. Leukemias are tumors that form in the tissues of the bone marrow, spleen, and lymph nodes. They are not solid tumors and are characterized by an overproduction of white blood cells.

Although the precise causes of cancer are still unknown, one common feature unites all tumors: they develop as a result of changes or rearrangement of information coded in the DNA within single cells. Four of the primary causes of cancer, scientists now concur, are environmental factors (including exposure to carcinogenic substances such as air pollution, tobacco smoke, and industrial chemicals), diet, heredity, and lifestyle.

Diagnosing Cancer. Physicians use a variety of diagnostic tests to determine if a symptom is cancer-related. The American Cancer Society recommends a Pap smear, a simple test for cervical cancer, every three years for women over 20. It also recommends a pelvic exam every three years from the ages 20-40 and annually thereafter. The American College of Obstetricians and Gynecologists recommends an annual Pap smear, especially for women with genital warts or herpes. Women should also examine their breasts regularly by feeling for any areas of thickening or for lumps and, after the age of 50, have an annual mammogram. Women at high risk of breast cancer may need earlier and more frequent mammograms. Breast self-examinations should be done about one week after the menstrual period when temporary, hormonally induced changes will be minimal. Men should regularly examine their testicles for unusual lumps as well, and be examined yearly by a physician to test for prostate cancer.

Prevention of Cancer

Preventing cancer depends on avoiding the risk factors linked with cancer and maintaining a healthy immune system that efficiently eliminates abnormal cells from the body. This can be accomplished in a number of ways, including adopting a diet that ensures the optimal intake of immuno-enhancing nutrients and decreasing the intake of immuno-suppressing foods which weaken the immune system. Living a life free from continual emotional or mental stress is also important, as is avoiding carcinogenic toxins in the home and in the environment.

Nutritional Therapies. Cancer rates differ noticeably in various parts of the world depending on dietary patterns, which suggests that diet plays a major role in cancer. Diets containing foods high in carbohydrates and cholesterol are now considered risk factors for cancer, while diets high in vitamin E, vitamin C, betacarotene, fiber, and other substances may prevent certain cancers. A five-nation study of 802 patients with pancreatic cancer, reported by G. Howe in the May 1992 issue of *International Journal of Cancer*, for example, showed that cancer was directly related to intake of carbohydrates and cholesterol and inversely related to dietary fiber and vitamin C.

The Role of Fiber in Preventing Cancer. In *The Cancer Eating Recovering Plan*, Dr. Daniel Nixon cites an impressive number of studies suggesting that fiber can reduce the risk of cancer. Water-insoluble fiber has been associated with decreased cellular activity and decreased polyp formation in the gut, and thereby is thought to help prevent colon cancer. Fiber also acts as a laxative and reduces the amount of time food remains in the intestinal tract. It may also bind with carcinogens in the gut and render them harmless. A final benefit is that fiber may alter gut bacteria and acidity so that fewer carcinogens are produced. The water-soluble group (gums, pectin, and others) also tend to lower cholesterol levels in the blood, which may reduce the risk of some cancers. Nixon stresses that Americans should consume as

Symptoms of Cancer

According to the American Cancer Society, anyone with one or several of the following symptoms should be examined by a physician.

- A sore, especially in the mouth, that persists.
- A sore throat that does not heal.
- A nagging cough or hoarseness.
- A lump, white spot, or scaly area on the lip or in the mouth.
- A swollen lymph gland in the neck, armpit, or groin that last three weeks or more.
- Moles, freckles, or warts that have changed in color or shape, or that bleed.
- Unusual bleeding or discharge between periods, especially during or after menopause.
- A thickening of, or lumps in, the breast.
- A testicular lump or enlargement.
- Difficulty in swallowing or a lump on or near the thyroid gland.
- Rectal bleeding or changes in bowel habits, unexplained by dietary or other changes.
- Urinary difficulties such as pain, frequency, weak flow, or blood in the urine.

much as 35 grams of fiber daily to prevent cancer.

Charles Simone writes in *Cancer & Nutrition* that many cancer specialists have found that fiber protects against colon/rectal cancer, breast cancer, heart disease, diverticu-

The National Cancer Institute (NCI) Recommendations:

1. Reduce intake of dietary fat–both saturated and unsaturated–to a maximum level of 30% of total calories. This can be done by limiting consumption of meat, trimming away its excess fat, avoiding fried foods, and eating limited amounts of butter, cream, and salad dressings.

2. Increase consumption of fresh fruits, vegetables, and whole-grain cereals. Increase the intake of betacarotene (a vegetable precursor of vitamin A), vitamins C and E, selenium, and dietary fiber–all of which are known to have a protective effect against cancer.

3. Consume salt-cured and charcoal-broiled foods only in moderation (or not at all).

4. Drink only moderate amounts of alcoholic beverages (or none at all).

lar disease, obesity, and diabetes. A low incidence of cancer is seen in people who consume large amounts of carotene-rich foods and cruciferous vegetables such as cabbage, broccoli, cauliflower, and brussels sprouts. Fiber's protective action, Simone explains, is due to the fact that it binds bile acids, cholesterol, lipids poisons, and carcinogens. It also increase the weight and mass of stool, which dilutes carcinogens. Additionally, it decreases the gastrointestinal transit time so that the carcinogens are excreted more quickly. It also helps keep the intestinal flora healthy. Finally, high fiber intake may reduce the risk of breast cancer by lowering estrogen levels and changing the way food is absorbed in the gut.

Simone especially recommends high-fiber cereals and vegetables of the *Brassiceae* family which provide fiber and induce enzymes to destroy certain carcinogens. Dieters are advised to eat whole or lightly milled grains such as rice, barley, and buckwheat. Whole wheat bread and wheat pasta, cereals, crackers, and other grain products should also be eaten.

Carbohydrates. According to Nixon, cross-national studies have shown that high intake of carbohydrate-rich foods, especially vegetables and fruits, has a cancer-fighting effect. These foods tend to be high in vitamin and chemopreventive compounds and fiber and low in fat–all of which may prevent cancer.

Fat. Fat may act both as a promoter of cancer and as a modulator of the growth of existing cancers. Nixon presents a substantial amount of evidence that suggests that high-fat diets can cause breast and colon cancer. Conversely, he notes that a low-fat, low-calorie diet can inhibit the development of certain tumors and even slow the growth of established tumors in laboratory animals.

Scientists do not yet know which types of fat (saturated, unsaturated, omega-3 fatty acids, etc.) activate specific cancers. Therefore, Nixon recommends consuming less than 20% of calories as fat. For persons recovering from breast, colon, and prostate cancer, he emphasizes that 15% fat is even better. He also notes that most Americans consume fat that comes from animal products and that "animal fat is the major problem in our diets."

Cholesterol. A diet high in fats also increases blood cholesterol levels, although, according to Nixon, it is not clear precisely what role, if any, cholesterol might play in cancer. There is evidence, however, that farnesyl, a substance created as the liver synthesizes cholesterol, may have some role in the earliest stages of cancer development. Farnesyl may interact with oncogenes (the genes through which cancer begins) and create byproducts which trigger cancer cells to activate. If the farnesyl hypothesis is true, Nixon contends that consuming less cholesterol may reduce oncogene byproducts.

Protein. According to Nixon, the link between excess protein consumption and cancer has not been definitively established. Nevertheless, he cites several population studies which found a relationship between high consumption of animal protein (meat and dairy products) and breast cancer. He also notes that laboratory studies have shown that when breast tumors are induced by carcinogens in animals, feeding the animals more protein leads to increased tumors. Some epidemiological studies have also linked animal protein intake to colon cancer, prostate cancer, and endometrial cancer. Nixon hypothesizes that one reason cancer causes cachexia is that it interferes with the body's ability to turn food into lean protein and muscle tissue.

Meat. Nixon does not recommend a strict vegetarian diet because it lends itself to nutritional deficits; however, he does state that "limiting meat consumption to six ounces weekly has as much anticancer benefit as the total exclusion of meat from the diet." He therefore advocates at least two meat-free days a week, a routine which helps reduce total fat intake and increase fiber intake.

Caffeine. Simone notes that caffeine contains mutagens, or chemical compounds that cause heritable changes in the genetic material of cells. Some vegetables also contain mutagenic flavonoids, and mutagens are also produced in charred and smoked foods. Mutagens can also be produced at lower temperatures, such as from the normal cooking of meat. Others, like coffee and horseradish, contain quinones and allyl isothiocyanate, although the risk of developing cancer from mutagens in humans appears minimal.

Food Carcinogens. University of California Berkeley researcher Bruce Ames has found that some plants have certain molecules to protect them from microorganisms and insects–some of which are carcinogenic or mutagenic in humans. For example, black pepper contains piperine and sarole; bruised celery contains psoralen; herbal teas contain pyrolizidine; and mushrooms contain hydrazines. Foods that pose the greatest risk of cancer in humans, according to Simone, are the mycotoxins (aflatoxin) and nitrous compounds from bacteria.

Food Additives. Simone warns that there are now more than 3,000 intentional food additives, some of which are potentially carcinogenic. One of these, nitrite, for example, is sometimes converted in the body to nitrosamine, a potent carcinogen. In addition, more than 12,000 unintentional additives are found in packaging and food processing, including vinyl chloride and diethylsilbestrol, which may cause some cancers.

Obesity and Cancer. Simone also notes the increasing evidence that excess weight and obesity are directly linked to cancer. According to Simone, obesity is a major risk factor for the development of endometrial cancer (cancer of the inner lining of the uterus) in postmenopausal women. The reason, he suggests, is because obese postmenopausal women produce substantially more of the female hormone estrone. This increased production is directly related to the

Food Substitution Recommendations to Reduce Dietary Fat

1. Replace whole eggs in baking recipes with two egg whites.

2. Use nonfat yogurt instead of sour cream, heavy cream, oil, or mayonnaise. For cooked dishes that require sour cream, substitute the same amount of nonfat yogurt plus a 1/2 teaspoon of flour.

3. Use nonfat yogurt cheese and use in place of cream cheese to top bagels or to make cheesecake, or use nonfat cream cheese.

4. Use evaporated skim milk in coffee or hot tea, cream-based soups, stews, and salad dressings.

5. In baking recipes, replace whole milk with skim milk or non-fat buttermilk.

6. Substitute an equivalent portion of applesauce for oil in muffins, cakes, brownies, and sweet breads.

7. Substitute unsweetened cocoa for Baker's chocolate.

8. Reduce 1/2 cup nuts in recipes to 1 tablespoon nuts.

9. Replace ground beef with ground turkey and chicken in recipes; reduce the meat to 3 ounces per person.

number and size of the woman's fat cells, since estrone is manufactured in fat cells from another hormone called androstenedione. Estrone apparently stimulates the uterus, and this is believed to cause endometrial cancer.

Similarly, postmenopausal women who take estrogens daily for symptoms of menopause also have a higher incidence of endometrial cancer. Simone also notes that obese persons also usually consume more fats in their diet, and this, as noted, is a major risk factor for breast and colon cancer.

Phytoestrogens. According to *Alternative Medicine: What Works* Chinese and Japanese women who eat traditional foods have lower breast cancer rates than Western women, a fact that leads some researchers to speculate that the predominantly vegetarian Asian diet may lower the risk of cancer and heart disease. Asians eat less fat and protein, and more carbohydrates than Westerns, and a low-fat diet is known to protect against several cancers.

Both Chinese and Japanese women, for example, consume tofu, green soybeans, and other soy products, which contain phytoestrogens (estrogen-like compounds found in plants). Consequently, the level of phytoestrogens they excrete is quite high. One study of Chinese women in Singapore reviewed by Adriane Fugh-Berman found that the intake of soy products appeared to protect premenopausal (but not postmenopausal) women from breast cancer.

Vitamin and Mineral Therapies. Chapters 2 and 3 detail a number of clinical trials proving that vitamins and minerals have a protective effect against cancer. These include betacarotene, vitamin A, vitamin C, vitamin E, selenium, and zinc.

Vitamins A, C, and E may also help remove potentially harmful oxidative compounds from cells capable of damaging DNA, thus causing cancer. These vitamins are called "anti-oxidants" because they inhibit the harmful activity of free radicals and prevent oxidative damage. The extent of their ability to prevent cancer is still not fully known. Some vitamins and vitamin precursors such as betacarotene appear to hinder the development of skin cancer and upper digestive tract cancers, as well as cervical cancer in its earliest stages.

Vitamin A and Cervical Dysplasia. *Alternative Medicine: What Works* suggests that vitamin A supplements may lower the risk of cervical dysplasia. In a controlled study of 301 women with a precancerous condition, cervical dysplasia, derivatives of vitamin A called retinoids were applied to the cervix (the neck of the uterus). This treatment completely reversed the dysplasia in 43% of women, compared to 27% of those who used placebo cream. However, in the case of severe dysplasia, there was no difference between placebo and retinoids.

Vitamin A and Skin Cancer. Vitamin A derivations have been shown to be effective in precancerous conditions of the skin, mouth, and vocal cords, according to *Alternative Medicine: What Works*. They can also normalize some cells effected by leukemia.

Vitamin A and Breast Cancer. *Alternative Medicine: What Works* states that vitamin A may also help prevent breast cancer. In a study of the diets of 89,494 nurses, those who ingested the most vitamin A had 16% less risk of breast cancer. When vitamin A supplements were given to those needing it most, their risk also went down.

Folic Acid and Colon Cancer. Folic acid, a B vitamin, may be one of the key ingredients in fruits and vegetables that prevent colon cancer. Elyse Tanouye reports a study conducted by the Harvard Medical School in the June 2, 1993 issue of the *Wall Street Journal* which found that folic acid appears to turn cancer genes off. Analyzing information obtained from questionnaires on patient's diets during a one-year period, Dr. Edward Giovannucci and colleagues at the Harvard Medical School found that a high intake of folic acid–from fresh fruits and vegetables

and vitamin supplements–was associated with a lower risk of developing tumors. In addition, people drinking the equivalent of two alcoholic drinks a day were at an 85% higher risk of developing tumors than nondrinkers. Giovannucci hypothesized that folic acid helps transfer a compound called methyl from molecules commonly found in the body to other molecules that turn off cancer genes. When the process, called methylation, doesn't work–as, for example, when alcohol is introduced–cancer genes produce protein that appear to cause the cells to proliferate. Others researchers, including Dr. Joel Mason at Tufts University, have shown that folate contributes to normal tissue formation by guarding the integrity of the genetic messages encoded in DNA.

Dr. Gladys Block, professor at the University of California, Berkeley School of Public Health, suggested that the study indicates that many people need to take daily folic acid supplements and fortified prepared foods with folic acid to prevent cancer. Most American do not eat balanced diets, she noted, and may be deficient in folic acid.

Calcium. Nixon cites research suggesting a possible link between calcium deficiencies and cancer. Epidemiological studies, for example, have shown that the more milk a person drinks, the lower their risk of colon cancer. Calcium has also been shown in laboratory studies to decrease the cell division activity in the colon lining walls. Calcium may also bind and inactivate carcinogens in the stool. Excellent sources of calcium along with nonfat dairy products include asparagus, broccoli, Great Northern and navy beans, okra, spinach, and soybean products (tofu).

Botanical Medicine Therapies. Several botanical nutrients discussed in Chapter 5 have been shown to be effective preventive agents against cancer, including spirulina, aloe vera, green tea made from the leaves of

Optimal Anti-Cancer Vitamin and Mineral Program

	Adult Amount	Child (Age 1-4) Amount
Betacarotene	20 mg	1 mg
Vitamin A (palmitate)	5,000 IU	834 IU
Vitamin D (ergocalciferol)	400 IU	400 IU
Vitamin E (di-tocopherol)	400 IU	15 IU
Vitamin C (ascorbic acid)	350 mg	60 mg
Folic acid	400 mcg	200 mcg
Vitamin B$_1$ (thiamine)	10 mg	1.1 mg
Vitamin B$_2$ (riboflavin)	10 mg	1.2 mg
Niacinamide	40 mg	9 mg
Vitamin B$_6$ (pyridoxine)	10 mg	1.12 mg
Vitamin B$_{12}$ (cyanobalamin)	18 mcg	4.5 mcg
Biotin	150 mcg	25 mcg
Pantothenic acid	20 mg	5 mg
Iodine	150 mcg	70 mcg
Copper (cupric oxide)	3 mg	1.25 mg
Zinc (zinc gluconate)	15 mg	10 mg
Potassium	30 mg	2 mg
Selenium (organic)	200 mcg	20 mcg
Chromium (organic)	125 mcg	20 mcg
Manganese (gluconate)	2.5 mg	1 mg
Molybdenum	50 mcg	25 mcg
Inositol	10 mg	0
Para aminobenzoic acid	120 mg	0
Bioflavonoids	10 mg	10 mcg
Choline (choline bitartrate)	10 mg	5 mg
L-Cysteine	230 mg	0
L-Arginine	5 mg	0
Histidine	N/A	10 mg
Leucine	N/A	10 mg
Lysine	N/A	10 mg

Optimal Anti-Cancer Vitamin and Mineral Program (continued)

Threonine	N/A	10 mg
Calcium (calcium carbonate)	500 mg	N/A
Magnesium (magnesium oxide)	140 mg	
Silicon	2 mg	
Boron	2 mg	
L-Threonine	2 mg	
L-Lysine	2 mg	

Note: Simone recommends pregnant or lactating women to consult their physician before following this program.

Camellia sinensis, echinacea, garlic, mistletoe, shiitake mushrooms (extract of *Lentinus edodes*), and maitake mushrooms.

Exercise and Cancer Prevention

Several studies among men and women have indicated that those who are physically fit or physically active have lower death rates from cancer. In the October 1993 issue of *American Health*, Michele Wolf reports a study of more than 10,000 men and 3,000 women examined at the Institute for Aerobics Research in Dallas. She found that those deemed most fit on a treadmill test had much lower cancer death rates in the ensuing eight years. There was a four-fold difference in cancer deaths among the men and a sixteen-fold difference among the women. The strongest evidence for exercise's protective effect involves colon cancer, a leading cause of cancer deaths among Americans.

Wolf goes on to report that exercise for women, particularly during teenage and young adult years, seems to be associated with lower rates of breast cancer and various hormone-related cancers of the reproductive tract. Dr. Rose Frisch of the Harvard School of Public Health found that among nearly 45,400 female college alumnae, those who had been college athletes or who trained regularly had about half the risk of later developing breast cancer than nonathletes. Nonathletes also had higher rates of cancers of the uterus, ovary, cervix, and vagina.

The main benefit of exercise in reducing cancer risk in women is believed to be a lower lifetime exposure to estrogen, which can stimulate growth of cells in the breasts and reproductive organs. Physical activity can change the hormone ratio and reduce body fat, which itself increases the amount of cancer-stimulating estrogens in the blood. Since one-third of a woman's estrogen before menopause is produced by body fat, leaner, fitter women tend to manufacture less.

Wolf adds that exercise may also help fight other forms of cancer because of its ability to boost the performance of two types of immune system cells–natural killer (NK) cells and macrophages. Although NK cells and macrophages seem to inhibit tumor growth, exercise cannot eliminate it once it begins to spread. It may, however, prevent malignant cells from spreading. Exercise physiologists have not yet determined exactly how much exercise is needed to lower the risk of cancer.

Exercise helps decrease body fat and increase lean body mass, a process that may foster a more favorable hormone balance in early breast cancer–and perhaps other hormonally sensitive cancers as well. Several studies have also suggested that exercise helps overcome cancer cachexia, the condition by which people suffer debilitating weight loss and strength, even when they eat an adequate amount of food. Exercise may improve the body's conversion of glucose to useful energy and make it more sensitive to insulin.

According to Simone, the main benefit of exercise for cancer patients is that, in most cases, it produces a higher number of white blood cells, specifically granulocytes, that are needed to fight off infections and tumors. He states that people who exercise tend to have higher B and T killer cell counts. During exercise a person's temperature rises slightly, a condition accompanied by the production of pyrogen, an important protein produced by white blood cells that enhances lymphocyte functions. Elevated temperatures can also kill viruses–and have also been shown to kill cancer cells.

Role of Exercise in Colon, Breast, and Lung Cancer.

A Stanford study conducted by Dr. Ralph Paffenbarger found that moderately active men are 50% less likely to develop colon cancer than less active men. Exercises must be aerobic, strengthen the immune system, decrease harmful effects of stress-related hormones, and burn 1,000 calories a week. Exercises must also be monitored along with diet, as several studies show that exercise combined with a high-fat diet may accelerate tumor growth. Another study at Harvard University found that women active in swimming, running, gymnastics, and volleyball had significantly less risk of developing cancer of the breast,

uterus, ovaries, cervix, and vagina. The study also discusses exercises that have proven helpful for patients undergoing surgery, chemotherapy, radiation, or biological therapy.

Exercise during Chemotherapy.

Chemotherapy suppresses the immune system and can cause loss of energy and appetite, nausea, vomiting, or mouth sores. Cancer specialists usually advise intravenous chemotherapy patients to avoid exercise for 24 hours following therapy because heart irregularities are more frequent during this time. According to Nixon, several studies have shown that aerobic exercise 24 hours *after* treatment increases appetite, increases the body's ability to utilize food nutrients, and decreases nausea.

Stationary Bicycle.

In *Living with Exercise*, Dr. Steven Blair suggests that people at risk for cancer must burn at least 1,000 calories per week to prevent tumors. He notes that chemotherapy patients in several clinical trials were able to increase their basal metabolic rate (BMR) 4-6% while using stationary bikes, as well as increasing their energy levels and appetite. Dr. Mary Winningham of the University of Utah College of Nursing found that aerobic stationary bicycling helps cancer patients regain stamina, appetite, and muscle strength.

Cancer Treatments

Once a person is diagnosed with cancer, there are three conventional treatments: surgery, radiation therapy, and chemotherapy. Recommended treatments vary with the type of cancer, whether the cancer is localized or has begun to spread, and the general health of the patient. All three conventional treatments are invasive and have potentially severe side effects. While none of the treatments constitute a "cure" for cancer, they do prevent the cancer from spreading with varying success rates. Anyone diagnosed as having cancer should insist on a full discussion and understanding of their problem, and ask their doctor to fully evaluate the risks and benefits of any recommended therapy.

Surgery. Surgery, the most common treatment for cancer, involves removing cancerous cells from the body. For cancers that develop in areas close to the surface of the body, surgery is normally recommended first. Sometimes healthy cells must also be removed from the area surrounding the tumor in order to prevent the cancerous cells from spreading.

Radiation Therapy. During radiation therapy (also called x-ray therapy, radiotherapy, cobalt treatment, or irradiation), high-energy rays are used to damage cancer cells so that they are unable to grow and multiply. Like surgery, radiation therapy is localized and affects only the cells in the treated area. For some cancers, such as leukemia and lymphoma, the whole body may be radiated. Radiation therapy may be used before surgery to shrink the tumor, or after surgery to destroy any cancer cells that remain in the area.

The two most common types of radiation therapy are external radiation therapy and radiation implants. In external radiation therapy, a machine directs high-energy rays at the cancer cells. Patients usually receive these treatments five days a week for several weeks as outpatients. Most patients receive either x ray or cobalt gamma ray radiation, both of which gradually lose their energy as they pass through the body, damaging not only the tumorous cells but also the nearby healthy cells. However, radiation treatment is not always effective, as several forms of cancer, including gland and prostate cancer, have proven resistant to x ray therapy.

Radiation implant treatment involves placing a small container of radioactive material in the affected body cavity or directly into a cancer cell. By using radiation implants, doctors are able to give patients higher doses of radiation than are possible with external therapy, all the while sparing most of the healthy tissue around the tumor. Dr. Gerald DeNardo of the University of California, Davis, has treated 58 B-cell lymphoma patients with radiation implants. About two-thirds of the patients, according to an article by J. Bishop in the October 21, 1993 edition of *The Wall Street Journal*, responded to the treatments, and half of these are in complete remission.

Radiation therapy has strong side effects, including fatigue and skin reactions (such as rashes or red blotches) in the area being treated. It may also decrease the number of white blood cells, which help to protect the body against infection. The type and degree of side effects partially depend on the area of the body being treated.

Chemotherapy. Treatment with anticancer drugs, called chemotherapy, destroys cancer cells by disrupting their ability to multiply. Many different drugs are used to treat cancer and are given to patients either orally or by injection into a muscle, vein, or artery. Some drugs are given in cycles, followed by a rest period. Whether taken orally or by injection, chemotherapy drugs enter the bloodstream and are carried throughout the body; hence the name systemic. Depending on the drugs prescribed, most patients undergo chemotherapy as outpatients at a hospital. Sometimes it is necessary to stay in the hospital so that any side effects can be monitored.

While chemotherapy kills primarily cancerous cells, it also affects other rapidly growing cells, including hair cells and cells that line the digestive tract. As a result, patients often experience hair loss, nausea, and vomit-

Anticancer Chemicals in Foods

Chemical	Sources	Possible Protective Action
Carotene	Carrots, sweet potatoes, yams, pumpkins, squash, kale, broccoli, cantaloupe	Neutralizes free radicals and singlet oxygen radicals; enhances immune system; reverses pre-cancer conditions; high-intake associated with low cancer rate
Capsicum	Cayenne pepper	Antioxidant
Isoflavones	Legumes: beans, peas, peanuts	Inhibits estrogen receptor; destroys cancer gene enzymes; inhibits estrogen.
Terpene	Citrus fruit	Increases enzymes which break down carcinogens; decreases cholesterol
Lignans	Flaxseed, walnuts, fatty fish	Inhibits estrogen action; inhibits prostaglandins, hormones that cause cancer spread.
Polyacetylene	Parsley	Inhibits prostaglandins; destroys benzopyrene, a potent carcinogen.
Triterpenoids	Licorice	Inhibits estrogens, prostaglandins; slows down rapidly dividing cells, such as cancer cells.
Quinones	Rosemary	Inhibits carcinogens or co-carcinogens.
Various indoles	Cruciferous vegetables	Induces metabolism of estrogen to less carcinogenic forms.
Sulfides	Garlic, onions	Stimulates removal of carcinogens by liver.
Isothiocyanates	Mustard; radishes	Stimulates removal of carcinogens by liver.
Genistein	Soybeans, cruciferous vegetables	Antiangiogenesis.
Ellagic acids	Grapes, raspberries	May remove or block carcinogens.
Lycopene	Tomatoes	Antioxidant.
Monoterpenes	Carrots, cruciferous vegetables, squash, tomatoes	Antioxidant; removes carcinogens from liver.

Nutritional Guidelines for Common Cancer-Related Problems

Problems	Nutritional Intervention
Weight loss and muscle wasting	Consume high-calorie, protein-dense foods.
	Add powdered milk to foods and beverages to fortify protein.
	Use high-fat or high-calorie foods as tolerated (e.g,. ice cream or yogurt with higher milk fat, canned fruit packed in heavy syrup).
	Increase use of fats and gravies.
	Add glucose polymer supplements to beverages, juices, and gravies.
	Encourage between-meal snacks.
	Experiment with commercial supplements.
"Dumping syndrome"	Attempt small, frequent meals.
	Restrict simple carbohydrates, and increase protein and fat in diet.
	Restrict fluids to 30 minutes before a meal and 0-60 minutes after a meal.
Stomatitis and mucositis	Soft or liquid foods are usually better tolerated by the body.
	Avoid crisp or rough-textured foods.
	Salty, acidic, and spicy foods may be difficult to consume.
Diarrhea	Increase potassium-rich foods.
	Decrease lactose content of diet as needed.
	Adjust fat content of diet as needed.
	Increase fluid intake to replace losses.
	If diarrhea is not caused by infection, encourage high fiber intake with pectin. During acute state, fiber-restricted diet may be necessary.

ing. Most anticancer drugs also affect bone marrow, decreasing its ability to produce blood cells. As a result, some chemotherapy patients have weaker immune systems and are at a higher risk of infection. The side effects of chemotherapy vary depending on the drugs being given, the dosage, and the patient's age and general health. Patients should discuss fully all the advantages and disadvantages with their physician before undergoing treatment.

Alternative Cancer Treatments

Holistic physicians regard cancer as the manifestation of an unhealthy body whose defenses can no longer destroy or repair cells that turn cancerous. Holistic treatments therefore focus on strengthening the immune system of the cancer patient using physiological and psychological therapies. The therapies summarized in the following sections have either proven effective for some types of cancer or offer promise for further investigation. Patients with cancer should discuss all of the available proven treatments for specific cancers with their physician or health professional and together choose the most appropriate treatment (or combination of treatments).

Nutritional Therapies. There is mounting evidence that diet can play an important adjunctive role in treatment. Cancer specialist Dr. Keith Block believes that the foods people eat make a significant difference in the body's ability to resist disease and maintain health. His diet for cancer patients consists of whole grain cereals, vegetables, legumes, fruits, nuts and seeds, soy foods, fish, and free-range poultry. Restricted or eliminated food include most dairy products, eggs, red meat, refined sugar, caffeinated or alcoholic drinks, processed foods, some less healthy oils, and some vegetables in the nightshade family such as eggplant and green peppers. Block individualizes the diet based

on patients' physical condition, cultural background and tastes, climate and geographical condition, and activity level and physical needs, with extensive exchange lists making it easy for patients to "trade" different food or drinks from the same list. The Block diet provides 50-60% of nutrients in complex carbohydrates, and restricts fat intake to between 12 and 25% (primarily from vegetable sources), while the remainder of calories are derived from protein.

The Block diet is very similar to the diets the American Cancer Society, the National Cancer Institute, the American Academy of Sciences, and the American Heart Association have endorsed as having some preventive value in protecting against cancer and coronary disease.

Vitamin Therapies. Vitamin B_6 is one of the most promising B vitamins for cancer treatment. Hans Ladner and Richard Salkeld conducted a clinical trial treating cancer patients with vitamin B_6 in addition to radiotherapy. As cited in L. Poirier's *Essential Nutrients in Carcinogenesis*, B_6 was given to 105 endometrial cancer patients, aged 45 to 65, over a seven-week period. These patients had a 15% improvement in five-year survival rates compared to 105 patients who did not receive the B_6 supplements. No side effects from the B_6 supplementation were observed.

Ladner and Salkeld also confirmed the beneficial effects of B_6 on radiation-induced symptoms (nausea, vomiting, and diarrhea) in gynecological patients treated with high-energy radiation. They subsequently gave B_6 to 6,300 patients with cervical, uterine, endometrial, ovarian, and breast cancers, and concluded that both quality of life and survival rates significantly improved with B_6 supplementation.

Vitamin B_6 has also proved effective in inhibiting melanoma cancer cells. One

research team, as cited in *Esssential Nutrients in Carcinogenesis,* developed a topical B_6 pyridoxal that "produced a significant reduction in the size of subcutaneous cancer nodules and complete regression of cutaneous papules." While the results were considered preliminary, they may lead to a more successful topical B_6 treatment for several forms of skin cancer.

Folic Acid. Folic acid supplementation has been successfully used to regress precancerous cells in patients with cervical dysplasia. Cervical dysplasia is an abnormal condition of the cells of the cervix, which is usually regarded as a pre-cancerous lesion. When treated with folic acid, the regression-to-normal rate was observed to be 20% in one study and 100% in another, according to *Essential Nutrients in Carcinogenesis.*

Folic acid supplements may also decrease the risk of cardiovascular disease, colon cancer, and cervical cancer. The FDA currently restricts dosage of folic acid pills to 800 micrograms.

A high dietary folate intake also protects against colorectal adenoma, a pre-cancerous condition that can lead to colon cancer. Low folate intake also increases risk for cervical dysplasia. Although cervical cancer appears to be caused by a sexually transmitted virus, folate deficiency also appears to be a factor.

Unfortunately, few Americans consume enough fresh fruits and vegetables, the primary dietary source of folic acid. One study cited by Fugh-Berman found that 13-15% of American women 20-44 years of age showed biochemical evidence of folate deficiency.

Antioxidant Treatments. Combined antioxidant treatments may also extend survival times of cancer patients treated with chemotherapy or radiation. Twenty lung cancer patients in one study, reported in the May/June 1992 issue of *AntiCancer Research*, received antioxidant treatments of vitamins, trace elements, and fatty acids in combination with chemotherapy and/or irradiation at regular intervals. The average survival time for the entire group was 505 days. Fourteen (77%) survived for more than 12 months, and six patients (33%) for more than two years. One patient survived more than five years. Eight patients (44%) were still alive with a survival time of 32 months at the end of the study. Patients receiving antioxidants were also able to tolerate chemotherapy and radiation treatment well.

Vitamin E and Chemotherapy. Patients receiving chemotherapy often develop ulcers in the mouth or other parts of the digestive tract. In a controlled trial of 18 cancer patients, six out of nine receiving vitamin E oil experienced reversal of their ulcers within five days, compared to only one out of nine subjects receiving a placebo.

Botanical Therapies. As noted in Chapter 5, shiitake mushrooms (*Lentinus edodes*) have been successfully used by Japanese physicians to shrink several different types of tumors by as much as 80%. Nutritionist Dr. Donald Brown writes in the April 1994 *Townsend Letter for Doctors* that an extract of *Lentinus edodes* has been shown to suppress viral oncogenesis, and prevent cancer recurrence after surgery. Results of clinical trials indicate that shiitake mushrooms prolong the lifespan of patients with advanced and recurrent stomach, colorectal, and breast cancer with minimal side effects. The active ingredient, lentinan, appears to increase production of T-lymphocyte (natural killer) cells.

Maitake Mushrooms. Maitake mushrooms may also help treat cancer. Anthony Cichoke, writing in the May 1994 *Townsend Letter for Doctors*, claims that the compounds contained in maitake mushrooms stimulate immune function and inhibit tumor growth. Currently research is being conducted by Dr. Dennis Miller of the Cancer Treatment Centers of America on their effect in stabilizing tumors. Cichoke notes that Dr. Abram Ber, a homeopathic physician practicing in Phoenix, Arizona, has used maitake mushroom tablets to treat 12 patients with prostatic cancer. Not only were their symptoms ameliorated, but the patients reported improved urinary flow and a decreased need to urinate.

Shark Cartilage. Shark cartilage may also be an effective secondary cancer treatment. One reason tumors spread is because they develop their own blood supply–a process known as angiogenesis. Cartilage, a tough, elastic, connective tissue found in sharks and humans, does not develop a blood supply because it contains an "anti-angiogenic" substance that stops the blood supply from developing. Shark cartilage therapy is based on the premise that if the blood supply to tumors can be interrupted, they will stop growing and eventually die.

Dr. William Lane of New Jersey reports in *Sharks Don't Get Cancer* that the first study documenting the effectiveness of shark cartilage was conducted at the Hospital Ernesto Contreras in Tijuana, Mexico. The eight patients chosen for the study suffered from a variety of cancers, including cervical, colon, and breast, and all had life expectancies of three to six months. Shark cartilage, administered via retention enemas, was the only form of cancer treatment the patients received. After one month of therapy, seven of the eight patients experienced tumor reductions ranging from 30-100%. Symptomatic improvement was observed in all eight patients, including weight gain, improved energy, and pain control.

In a Cuban clinical trial reported by D. Williams in the February 1993 issue of *Alternatives Newsletter*, 19 terminal cancer patients experienced shrinking of their tumors after 16 weeks of shark cartilage therapy, with rates varying between 15 and 58%. No toxic side effects were reported.

Simone monitored 20 patients with advanced cancers using shark cartilage as a food supplement. He reported to the June 24, 1993 U.S. Senate Subcommittee on Appropriations Special Hearing on Alternative Medicine that after eight weeks, tumors were completely eliminated in four patients, and reduced in three others.

Shark Liver Oil. Shark liver oil is one of the best natural sources of alkoxyglycerols, natural alcohols that promote a generalized antibody response which may shrink cancer tumors. Judith Hooper, writing in the July 13, 1993 issue of *Your Health*, cites a study in Holland in which cervical cancer patients pretreated with shark liver oil before receiving radiation had far better survival rates than patients not receiving the treatment. In many cases, tumors shrank significantly before radiation began, thereby rendering the radiation more effective.

Hooper also claims that shark fin supplements inhibit angiogenesis, the development of tiny blood vessels, or capillaries, through which tumors spread. She cites studies conducted at several Boston hospitals associated with Harvard Medical School in which shark fin soup effectively inhibited the angiogenesis of several types of tumors.

Mistletoe. An extract of mistletoe (Iscador) has been used for 30 years in Europe as a potential anticancer agent. As reported by E. Kovacs in a 1991 issue of the *European Journal of Cancer*, Swiss scientists gave Iscador to 14 patients with advanced breast cancer. Twelve out of the 14 patients showed an improvement of DNA repair 2.7 times higher than before Iscador was administered.

Carnivora. According to Hooper's *Your Health* article, carnivora, an extract of the meat-eating Venus flytrap plant (*Dionaea muscipula*), has been used on more than 2,000 patients since 1981 to treat cancer, AIDS, and other immune-suppressed diseases. In an initial clinical study conducted by German physician Dr. Helmut Keller of 210 patients with a variety of cancers, all of whom had undergone unsuccessful chemotherapy or radiation, 40% were stabilized by carnivora treatment and 16% went into remission. According to Keller: "Carnivora proved to be extremely nontoxic and non-mutagenic," and its effects included cytostatis (destruction of cancer cells), immune enhancement, mitotic (cancer-cell division) inhibition, viricidal (virus-killing) effects, and pain relief.

Traditional Chinese Medicine (TCM).

Chinese physicians regard cancer as an imbalance of chi, and treat the whole person rather than just the specific disorder. They claim that treating the whole person avoids the phobia surrounding a diagnosis of cancer, and focuses on returning the patient to optimal health once the cancer has been stabilized or reversed. Chinese physicians report having successfully treated cancer with acupuncture, herbs, nutritional therapies, meditation, and exercise therapies such as qi gong.

However, it is difficult for Western scientists to evaluate the effectiveness of these therapies because clinical trials in China are not randomized or controlled. Given these reservations, J. Han, writing in a 1988 issue of the *Journal of Ethnopharmacology*, states that TCM has already yielded a significant number of anti-cancer botanical therapies, including indirubin (from dang gui lu hui wan), irisquinone (from iris *Lactea pallasii*), and zhuling polysaccharide (from polyporous umbellata). A study by Eric J. Lien at the University of Southern California School of Pharmacy, published in 1985, concluded that

Chinese herbs and plants from more than 120 species (belonging to 60 different families) have been used to successfully treat cancer.

Juzentaihoto (or JT-48, or JTT).

Juzentaihoto (or JT-48, or JTT) appears to be one of the most promising Chinese herbs for treating cancer. It has traditionally been used to relieve anemia, anorexia, extreme exhaustion, and fatigue. In November 1988, G. Wang reported to the First Shanghai Symposium on Gastrointestinal Cancer that patients given this herbal remedy had 3-10 year survival rates "significantly higher than commonly anticipated."

Herbal therapy using JTT in combination with chemotherapy and hormonal therapy has been shown to extend the life (and improve the quality of life) for metastatic breast cancer patients. A 1989 article by I. Adachi in the *Japanese Journal of Cancer and Chemotherapy* reported a controlled clinical trial at the National Cancer Center Hospital in Tokyo in which 119 advanced metastatic breast cancer patients were given either chemotherapy and endocrine therapy alone or in combination with JTT. After 38 months, the survival rate was significantly higher in the group receiving the herbal remedy. Quality of life was also better for those receiving JTT, including physical condition, appetite, and coldness of hands and feet. In addition, herbally treated patients were protected from the bone marrow suppression associated with chemotherapy.

The *Journal of the American Medical Association (JAMA)* reported at a Special Hearing on Alternative Medicine convened by the U.S. Senate Subcommittee on Appropriations on June 24, 1993 that a Chinese herbal therapy called Fu Zheng doubles the life expectancy of patients with rapidly advancing cancers when combined with Western treatment. The therapy, which consists of ginseng and astragalus, doubled the survival rate of patients with nasopharyngeal (nasal passage and pharynx) cancer from 24% to 53%.

Antineoplaston Therapy. Antineoplaston therapy was developed by Stanislaw Burzynski, a Polish physician who began practicing in the late 1960s in Houston, Texas, where he currently oversees the Burzynski Research Institute, a cancer treatment clinic. In an article entitled "Synthetic Antineoplastons and Analogs" appearing in a 1986 issue of *Drugs of the Future*, Burzynski explains that his cancer treatment is based on his theory that the body has a parallel biochemical defense system (BDS) independent of the immune system which helps reprogram defective cancer cells so that they begin to function normally. According to Burzynski, the BDS consists of short-chain amino acids, known as polypeptides, that are able to inhibit the growth of cancer cells.

Burzynski claims that the body of a cancer patient has only about two or three percent of the amount of antineoplastons contained in a healthy person. As a result, the BDS becomes deficient against chemical and physical carcinogens, viruses, and other cancer-causing agents. To rebuild the BDS, Burzynski has given synthetic antineoplastons to more than 2,000 patients (most of them diagnosed with advanced or terminal cancer). According to *Alternative Medicine: The Definitive Guide*, the majority of patients have benefited from antineoplaston therapy, experiencing complete or partial remission, or stabilization of their conditions. In addition, few side effects have been observed. The range of cancers he has treated include lymphoma, leukemia, and cancers of the breast, bone, prostate, lung, and bladder.

From 1988 to 1990, Burzynski conducted clinical trials investigating different forms of antineoplaston treatment, such as capsules or injections, in groups of 15-35 patients diagnosed with specific types of cancer. The first trial involved patients with astrocytoma, a highly malignant form of brain tumor. Most of the patients had already been unsuccessfully treated with surgery, radiation therapy, and/or chemotherapy. According to Burzynski, the majority of patients improved rapidly, and some of the adults were even able to resume working part-time after only six weeks of treatment. Eighty percent experienced "objective response," which Burzynski defines as complete or partial remission, or stabilization of their tumors. The National Cancer Institute subsequently issued its approval for Burzynski to undertake outside clinical trials involving various forms of brain tumors.

Livingston Therapy. In the 1940s, an American physician named Virginia Livingston discovered a bacterium, *Progenitor cryptocides*, which caused cancer in experimental animal studies. She contended it was present in virtually all human and animal cancers, and subsequently developed a vaccine derived from a culture of the patient's own bacteria–either from the tumor, urine, blood, or pleura (lung fluid). She also used the Bacillus Calmette-Guerin (BCG) vaccine, a mild tuburculin vaccine which stimulates white blood cells of the immune system to kill cancer cells. And, as Livingston believed that certain foods such as beef, chicken, eggs, and milk can be contaminated with *Progenitor cryptocides* (thereby providing a basis for the infectious transmission of cancer), her therapy to restore the immune system includes a primarily vegetarian whole-foods diet, along with nutritional supplements.

In her book, *Conquest of Cancer: Vaccines and Diet*, Livingston analyzed the effectiveness of her combined vaccine and nutritional therapies for 62 patients (17 of them diagnosed as terminal) with breast, lung, uterine, ovarian, colon, prostate, kidney, pancreatic, pelvic, esophageal, and larynx cancer.

Other patients were suffering from melanoma or skin basal cell cancer. According to Livingston, the success rate of therapy was 82%. However, as she did not conduct controlled clinical trails, her therapy has not been officially endorsed by the National Cancer Institute.

In another book, *Physician's Handbook: The Livingston-Wheeler Medical Clinic*, Livingston outlined her nutritional therapy which included individualized dosages of vitamins A, B_6, B_{12}, C, and E, liver supplements, organic iodine (which she felt was essential to the metabolism of thyroid, the oxidative hormone), additional thyroid supplements (whenever tolerated), and hydrochloric acid.

Livingston's diet emphasized raw or lightly cooked fresh vegetables, fresh vegetable juices, whole grain breads and cereals, fresh fruits, nuts, baked or boiled potatoes, salads, and homemade soups. No sugar, refined flours, processed or high-sodium foods were allowed, and few–if any–animal foods because of the likelihood of their being contaminated with *Progenitor cryptocides.* Smoking, alcohol, and coffee were also prohibited.

Livingston's patients were also given frequent baths in a hot tub with one cup of white vinegar to help eliminate toxins through the skin, along with purging and enemas. Her primary focus was instituting immunization, especially if patients were undergoing chemotherapy, because she believed patients could only survive cancer if they restrengthened their immune systems.

Hydrazine Sulfate. Dr. Joseph Gold, director of the Syracuse Cancer Research Institute in Syracuse, New York, began research in the late 1960s focusing on controlling the weight loss (cachexia) that often accompanies cancer. He discovered that the chemical hydrazine sulfate could reverse cachexia, providing the body with extra strength to fight cancer. In addition to weight gain, the benefit of this therapy according to *Alternative Medicine: The Definitive Guide* is the documented ability of hydrazine sulfate to shrink tumors, and even cause them to disappear completely. It has been particularly effective in treating cancers of the rectum, colon, ovaries, prostate, thyroid, breast, and lung, as well as for Hodgkin's disease, melanoma, and lymphoma.

Although Gold's experiments in the U.S. were controversial, Soviet scientists at the Petrov Research Institute of Oncology in Leningrad began testing the effectiveness of hydrazine sulfate therapy in 1976. Dr. V. Filov subsequently reported in a 1990 issue of *Voprosy Onkologii* that 740 terminal cancer patients with a broad range of tumors were treated with hydrazine sulfate over a 15-year period. According to Filov, approximately 50% of patients saw an improvement in their cachexia, 14% saw pronounced benefits, and all experienced a stabilization of the disease process.

Dr. Rowan T. Chlebowski of the University of California Los Angeles, writing in the January 1990 issue of the *Journal of Clinical Oncology*, reported hydrazine sulfate, used in conjunction with the best available conventional chemotherapeutic treatment, had significantly increased the survival rate in a controlled clinical trial of 65 patients with advanced inoperable, non-small-cell lung cancer (one of the most difficult of all cancers). Hydrazine therapy extended life to a median of 328 days, compared to a median of 209 days for patients who received chemotherapy alone.

Hydrogen Peroxide Therapy. Dr. Kurt W. Donsbach, in *Wholistic Cancer Therapy*, reports that food-grade hydrogen peroxide is also useful for reversing some cases of cancer. He believes that cancer cells are less virulent and may even be destroyed by the presence of a high oxygen environment. Hydrogen peroxide given orally and by transfusion has the ability to increase the oxygen content of the blood stream, which increases the oxygen environment of the cancer cell.

Donsbach states that he has helped hundreds of cancer patients using hydrogen peroxide therapy at his Hospital Santa Monica in Mexico. Approximately 70% of his patients, he adds, are alive three years after their first visit to his facility. In addition to hydrogen peroxide, Donsbach uses mineral therapies and hyperthermia and dimethly sulfoxide, DMSO, a solvent which facilitates the absorption of medicines through the skin.

Ozone Therapy. In a 1980 *Science* magazine article, Dr. Frederick Sweet of Washington University School of Medicine found that ozone therapy inhibited the growth of lung, breast, and uterine cancer cells when administered to patients over a period of eight days. Exposure to ozone at 0.8 parts per million inhibited cancer cell growth more than 90% and controlled cell growth to less than 50%. Sweet also observed that there was no growth inhibition of normal cells, which he states was due to the fact that "cancer cells are less able to compensate for the oxidative burden of ozone than normal cells."

Visualization. Dr. Carl Simonton and Stephanie Matthews-Simonton were the first to develop imagery therapy with the goal of physically reversing the development of cancer. In their best-selling book, *Getting Well Again*, they describe common mental images that can help cancer patients in their visualizations:

- The cancer treatment (either radiation or chemotherapy) is strong and powerful.
- The cancer cells are weak and confused.
- The healthy cells can repair any slight damage the treatment might do.

- The army of white blood cells is vast and destroys the cancer cells.
- The white blood cells are aggressive and quick to find the cancer cells and destroy them.
- The dead cancer cells are flushed from the body naturally.
- I am healthy and free of cancer.
- I still have many goals in life and reasons to live.

The Simontons varied their image visualizations to accommodate the belief systems of their cancer patients, and also encouraged the use of meditation, biofeedback, and hypnosis. The most important factor, the Simontons state, was whether patients visualized themselves returning to a healthy life. If they had positive reasons to live, patients usually were able to visualize themselves as being free of cancer.

The Simonton's imagery may not work for everyone and remains controversial. Many clinicians, including Bernie Siegel, suggest that symbolic imagery may be more powerful than the anatomically accurate visualizations used by the Simontons. Siegel states that the key factor in recovery is ending the imagery session by focusing clearly and powerfully on a healing image which is relevant, understandable, and powerful.

Hypnosis. Hypnosis has been found more effective than support groups for treating the pain that accompanies breast cancer. One study of 67 cancer patients undergoing bone marrow transplants compared hypnosis, cognitive behavioral skills, contact with a psychologist, and no treatment. Hypnosis proved to be effective in reducing oral pain associated with the cancer treatment, though nothing seemed to help nausea, vomiting, or the need to use painkillers.

In 49 children and adolescents with cancer, hypnosis with imagery proved more effective than nonhypnotic behavioral techniques (deep breathing, distraction, and practice sessions) in reducing pain and the anxiety connected with spinal taps and bone marrow biopsies.

Hypnosis and Chemotherapy. More than a quarter of patients undergoing chemotherapy develop such adverse reactions that they get nauseated or start vomiting even before the drugs are administered. There are many cases in which this problem–called anticipatory vomiting–has been relieved by hypnosis, as has been confirmed by two studies.

In one small study, three cancer patients were treated with hypnosis before some sessions of chemotherapy (but not before others), while three others were treated before all their sessions. Although none of the patients vomited after hypnosis, all vomited when they did not receive it. In another trial of 60 patients, hypnosis also significantly reduced anticipatory vomiting.

Positive Mental Attitudes and Social Support. A number of studies have now shown that positive mental states affect the outcome of cancer therapy, can assist the physician in making treatment more effective, minimize the negative side effects of medical treatments such as chemotherapy, and may even facilitate cures. As Siegel states in his best-selling book, *Love, Medicine & Miracles*, "We don't yet understand all the ways in which brain chemicals are related to emotions and thoughts, but the salient point is that our state of mind has an immediate and direct effect on our state of body. We can change the body by dealing with how we feel. If we ignore our despair, the body receives a 'die' message. If we deal with our pain and seek help, then the message is 'living is difficult but desirable,' and the immune system works to keep us alive."

The therapy group founded by Siegel, called Exceptional Cancer Patients (ECaP), is designed to help people mobilize their full resources–mental, emotional, physical, and spiritual–against their disease. Through regular group support meetings, nutritional counseling, exercise, meditation, visualization, and a trusting relationship with their physician (in which both take part in the decision-making process), patients "are accorded the conviction they can get well, no matter what the odds," Siegel explains. "If a person can turn from predicting illness to anticipating recovery," he continues, "the foundation for cure is laid."

Siegel, 1988 president of the American Holistic Medical Association, recommends that patients should not reject standard medical techniques such as radiation, chemotherapy, and surgery–at least as one option. "Drugs and surgery buy time, and may cure, while patients work to change their lives. The most important thing is to pick a therapy you believe in and proceed with a positive attitude," viewing therapy as energy that can heal.

Spiegel, a psychiatrist at the Stanford University Hospital, has also shown that psychosocial support can be of great benefit in coping with cancer. In a study of metastatic breast cancer patients cited in the October 14, 1989 issue of *Lancet*, women were randomly allocated into a control group that received standard medical therapy alone, or into one that attended weekly group therapy meetings and was taught self-hypnosis for pain. The patients who received therapy and learned hypnosis lived twice as long as the patients in the control group (36.6 months versus 18.9 months), and three of the women who received group therapy were still alive 10 years later.

Cancer patients are now offered a wide range of services to help them deal with the emotional and psychological aspects of the disease. Virtually every hospital serving cancer patients offers some form of psychosocial support, and many independent groups provide counseling, psychotherapy, and instruction in meditation, relaxation, and guided imagery or visualization. Biofeedback, hypnosis, and audio cassettes are other techniques. The common belief underlying these approaches is that patients' efforts to promote their emotional and spiritual well-being may also affect biological states and help restore them to wellness.

Expressing the negative emotions experienced by cancer patients is another important component in tipping the balance toward recovery. Psychologist Leonard Derogatis, in a study of 35 women with metastatic breast cancer, found that the long-term survivors had poor relationships with their physicians–as judged by the physicians. The survivors consistently questioned their doctors and expressed their emotions freely. Conversely, those dying within a year had relied heavily on repression, denial, and other psychological defenses.

National Cancer Institute psychologist Sandra Levy has further shown that seriously ill breast-cancer patients who expressed high levels of depression, anxiety, and hostility survived longer than those who showed little distress. As she reports in the September/October 1988 issue of *Psychosomatic Medicine*, Levy and other researchers have also found that aggressive "bad" patients tend to have more killer T cells–white cells that seek and destroy cancer cells–than docile "good" patients.

A group of London researchers under Keith Pettingale also reported a 10-year survival rate of 75% among cancer patients reacting to the diagnosis with a "fighting spirit," compared with a 22% survival rate among those who responded with "stoic acceptance" or feelings of helplessness or hopelessness.

Siegel agrees that "patients must be encouraged to express all their angers, resentments, hatreds, and fears. These emotions are signs that we care to the utmost when our lives are threatened. Time after time, research has shown that people who give vent to their negative emotions survive adversity better than those who are emotionally constricted. Unexpressed feelings depress your immune system," he claims.

The social support provided by family members helps cancer patients strengthen their immune system while undergoing treatment. In a study of cancer patients between the ages of 25 and 70, reported by Levy in the January/February 1985 issue of *Psychosomatic Medicine*, patients receiving high emotional support from a spouse or an intimate other had higher levels of natural killer (NK) cell activity. Perceived support from the patient's physician, and actively seeking social support as a major copying strategy, also increased NK activity.

Dr. Keith Block's Integrated Cancer Therapy. Dr. Keith Block of Evanston, Illinois, has developed a multifaceted cancer care program at Edgewater Medical Center in Chicago. The therapy, described in a November 1988 monograph prepared by Block for the Office of Technology Assessment (which was updated in 1990), is based on medical *caritas*, from the Latin meaning "compassionate caring for others." He says, "at the heart of the model is a carefully developed, very special doctor-patient relationship. The primary care physician seeks not only to understand and treat the patient's illness, but also to identify the patient's psychological, biomechanical, nutritional and physiological resources. In addition, the physician functions as a coordinator of medical care for patients."

Block's program is based on using the most effective, least invasive procedures first, before adopting more invasive prodcedures as, and if, they become necessary. He also uses innovative diagnostic and therapeutic tools which are noninvasive or low-invasive.

One of Block's fundamental premises is that his model of compassionate caring focuses not only on the diagnosis of a physical disease, such as cancer, but also "on a deep understanding of that patient's total psychosocial-cultural gestalt. Without a clear recognition of what is deeply important to the patient–e.g., prestige, libido, safety needs, control issues–the physician may propose a treatment that the patient cannot psychologically, culturally or socially accept. As many physicians have found to their dismay, treatment urged on a frightened or unwilling paient often compounds the problem rather than alleviating it."

Summary

Cancer is a group of diseases involving abnormal cell growth and proliferation. The holistic approach focuses on prevention, early detection, and treatment with a variety of therapies which restrengthen the immune system to stabilize malignant tumor cells and eliminate them from the body.

Human healing systems are both complex and varied, and the most effective treatments combine nutritional vitamin and mineral supplements, botanicals, and psychoimmunological therapies. The optimal therapeutic strategy will vary from patient to patient and from therapist to therapist.

Both holistic and conventional therapies, when given sufficient time to work, have helped people become healthier cancer patients–physically, emotionally, and mentally. Healthier cancer patients often do better with conventional therapies because their outlook makes them more resilient to both treatment and in some instances to the disease itself. Holistic approaches to cancer can make an enormous difference in life extension. The holistic psychoimmunological therapies developed by Siegel and others can help cancer patients achieve physical recovery. Conversely, long-term chronic depression, hopelessness, and cynicism tend to diminish resilience and increase physical vulnerability.

In summarizing the factors that lead to the onset of cancer and the most successful methods of treating it, Siegel concludes in *Peace, Love & Healing*: "Although there's no question that environment and genes play a significant role in our vulnerability to cancer and other diseases, the emotional environment that we create within our bodies can activate mechanisms of destruction or repair."

Resources

References

Adachi, I. "Role of Supporting Therapy of Juzenthaiho-to (JTT) in Advanced Breast Cancer Patients." *Gan To Kagaku Ryoho/Japanese Journal of Cancer and Chemotherapy* 16 (1989): 1538-43.

Altman, Nathaniel. *Oxygen Healing Therapies*. New York: Health Sciences Press, 1994.

Bishop, J. "Cancer Study Tries Lethal Warheads." *The Wall Street Journal* (October 21, 1993): B6.

Block, Keith I. "Part I: Block Nutrition Program." *New Clinical Care Model: Applications to Cancer-Patient Care*. Prepared for Office of Technology Assessment (November 1989): 1-2.

Brown, Donald. "Phytotherapy Review & Commentary." *Townsend Letter for Doctors* (April 1994): 406-07.

The Burton Goldberg Group. *Alternative Medicine: The Definitive Guide*. Payallup, WA: Future Medicine Publishing, Inc., 1993.

Burzynski, S. "Synthetic Antineoplastons and Analogs." *Drugs of the Future* 11, no. 8 (1986): 679.

Butler, Kurt, and Lynn Rayner. *The Best Medicine: The Complete Health and Preventive Medicine.* New York: Harper & Row Publishers, Inc., 1985.

Chlebowski, R.T., et al. "Influence of Hydrazine Sulfate on Nutritional Status and Survival in Non-Small Cell Lung Cancer." *Journal of Clinical Oncology* (January 1990): 9-15.

Cichoke, Anthony. "Maitake–The King of Mushrooms." *Townsend Letter for Doctors* (May 1994): 432-34.

"Diet and the Prostate." *Harvard Health Letter* (July 1994).

Donsbach, Kurt W. *Wholistic Cancer Therapy* Tulsa, OK: Rockland Corporation, 1992.

Filov, V., et al. "Results of Clinical Study of the Preparation Hydrazine Sulfate," *Voprosy Onkologii* 36, no. 2 (1990): 721-26.

Fugh-Berman, Adriane. *Alternative Medicine: What Works.* Tucson, AZ: Odonian Press, 1996.

Gold, Joseph. "Hydrazine Sulfate: A Current Perspective." *Nutrition and Cancer* 9 (1987): 59-66.

"Green Revolution." *Harvard Health Letter* (April 1995).

Han, J. "Traditional Chinese Medicine and the Search for New Antineoplastic Drugs." *Journal of Ethnopharmacology* 24 (1988): 1-17.

Hooper, Judith. "Unconventional Cancer Treatments." *Your Health* (July 13, 1993): 34-38.

Howe, G. "A Collaborative Case-Control Study of Nutrient Intake and Pancreatic Cancer." *International Journal of Cancer* (May 1992): 365-72.

Kovacs, E. "Improvement of DNA Repair in Lymphocytes of Breast Cancer Patients Treated with *Viscum Album* Extract (Iscador)." *European Journal of Cancer* 27 (1991): 1672-76.

Lane, William, and L. Cormac. *Sharks Don't Get Cancer.* Garden City Park, NY: Avery Publishing, 1992.

Levy, S.M. "Perceived Social Support and Tumor Estrogen/Progesterone Receptor Status." *Psychosomatic Medicine* (January/February 1985): 73-85.

Lien, Eric. *Structure Activity Relationship Analysis of Anti-Cancer Chinese Drugs and Related Plants* . Long Beach, CA: Oriental Healing Arts Institute, 1985.

Livingston-Wheeler, Virginia. *The Conquest of Cancer: Vaccines and Diet.* New York: Franklin Watts, 1984.

Marti, J. *Ultimate Consumer Guide to Diet and Nutrition.* Boston: Houghton Mifflin Inc., 1997.

Murray, Michael, and Joseph Pizzorno. *Encyclopedia of Natural Medicine.* Rocklin, CA: Prima Publishing, 1991.

Nixon, Daniel W. *The Cancer Recovery Eating Plan.* New York: Random House, Inc., 1994.

Poirier, L. *Essential Nutrients in Carcinogenesis.* New York: Plenum Press, 1986.

Pualesu, et al. "Studies on the ""Biological Effects Of Ozone: Induction of Tumor Necrosis Factor on Human Leukocytes." *Lymphokine and Cytokine Research* 10, no.5 (1991): 409-12.

Samid, Dvorit. "Trials Underway at Several Research Centers and Antineoplastons: New Antitumor Agents Stir High Expectations." *Oncology News* 16 (1990): 1, 6.

Shils, Maurice, James A. Olson, and Moshe Shike. *Modern Nutrition in Health and*

RESOURCES

Disease. Philadelphia, PA: Lea & Febiger, 1994.

Siegel, Bernie. *Love, Medicine & Miracles*. New York: Harper & Row, 1986.

Siegel, Bernie. *Peace, Love & Healing*. New York: Harper & Row, 1989.

Simone, Charles B. *Cancer & Nutrition*. Garden City Park, NY: Avery Publishing Group, 1992.

Simonton, Carl, and Stephanie Mathews. *Getting Well Again*. Los Angeles: Jeremy P. Tarcher, 1978.

"Special Hearing on Alternative Medicine." Subcommittee on Appropriations, United States Senate (June 24, 1993): 65, 69.

Spiegel, David. "Effect of Psychosocial Treatment on Survival in Patients with Metastatic Breast Cancer." *Lancet* (October 14, 1989): 888-91.

"Supplements Improve Response to Chemotherapy for Lung Cancer." *Anticancer Research* (May/June 1992): 599-606.

Sweet, F., et al. "Ozone Selectively Inhibits Growth of Cancer Cells." *Science* 209 (August 22, 1980): 931-32.

Tanouye, Elyse. "Folic Acid, An Ingredient In Vegetables, May Prevent Cancer, Say Researchers." *Wall Street Journal* (June 2, 1993): 7.

United States Congress Office of Technology Assessment. *Unconventional Cancer Treatments*. Washington, D.C.: Government Printing Office, September 1990.

Varro, J. "Ozone Applications in Cancer Cases." In *Medical Applications of Ozone*, Julius La Raus, ed. Norwalk, CT: International Ozone Association Pan American Committee (1983): 94-5.

Varro, J., et al. "Die Krebsbehandlung Mit Ozon." *Erfahrungsheilkunde* 23 (1974):178-81.

Wang, G.T. "Treatment of Operated Late Gastric Carcinoma with Prescriptions of 'Strengthen the Patient's Resistance and Dispel the Invading Evil,' in Combination with Chemotherapy: Follow-Up Study of 158 Patients and Experimental Study in Animals." *Meeting Abstract*. First Shanghai Symposium on Gastrointestinal Cancer (November 14-18, 1988): 244.

Williams, D.G. "The Final Results of the First Cuban Study." *Alternative Newsletter* 4 (February 1993): 20.

Wolf, Michele. "Can Exercise Ward Off Cancer?" *American Health* (October 1993): 77.

Pamplets

American Cancer Society. *Nutrition for Patients Receiving Chemotherapy and Radiation Therapy*. 1994. Booklets and further information available at 800/ACS0471.

Public Health Services, National Institutes of Health, National Cancer Institute. *Eating Hints: Tips and Recipes for Better Nutrition during Cancer Treatment*. NIH publication 91-2079. December 1990. Booklets and further information available from the Cancer Information Service, Office of Cancer Communications, National Cancer Institute, Building 31, Room 10a18, Bethesda, MD 20205. 800/CANCER.

Organizations

The Alliance for Alternative Medicine.
P.O. Box 59, Liberty Lake, WA 99019.

American Cancer Society.
1599 Clifton Road NE, Atlanta, GA 30329.

Burzynski Clinic.
6221 Corporate Drive, Houston, TX 77036.

Cancer Control Society.
2043 North Berendo Street, Los Angeles, CA 90027.

Foundation for Advancement in Cancer Therapy.
P.O. Box 1242, Old Chelsea Station, New York, NY 10113.

International Association for Cancer Victors and Friends.
7740 West Manchester Avenue, Suite 110, Playa del Rey, CA 90293.

Livingston Foundation Medical Center.
3232 Duke Street, San Diego, CA 92110.

National Cancer Institute.
Office of Cancer Communications, Building 31, 9000 Rockville Pike, Bethesda MD 20892.

Society of American Gastrointestinal Endoscopic Surgeons.
Thomas Jefferson University Hospital, 111 South 11th Street, Philadelphia, PA 19107.

Syracuse Cancer Research Institute.
Presidential Plaza, 600 East Genesee Street, Syracuse, NY 13202.

Additional Reading

Clark, Larry. *Selenium in Biology and Medicine*. New York: Van Nostrand Reinhold Co., 1991.

Gerson, Max. *A Cancer Therapy: Results of Fifty Cases*. 5th edition. Bonita, CA: Gerson Institute, 1990.

Lerner, Michael. *Choices in Healing: Integrating the Best of Conventional and Complementary Approaches to Cancer*. Cambridge, MA: MIT Press, 1994.

Revici, Emanuel. *Research in Physiopathology as a Basis of Guided Chemotherapy with Special Application to Cancer*. New York: American Foundation for Cancer Research, 1961.

Walters, Richard. *Options: The Alternative Cancer Therapy Book*. Long Island: Avery Publishing Group, 1993.

Chapter 18

HEART DISORDERS

More than 1.5 million people in the U.S. suffer from heart attacks every year, and 500,000 die as a result, nearly half of them women. In fact, more Americans die each year from cardiovascular disease–44%–than from all other causes of death combined, including cancer, AIDS, infectious diseases, accidents, and homicides. Cardiovascular disease is a general name for more than 20 different diseases of the heart and its blood vessels. Coronary artery disease (CAD), also referred to as coronary heart disease (CHD), is the most deadly of all heart disorders, accounting for approximately one out of every three heart disease deaths.

On a personal level, when people learn they have a heart disorder, some consult a conventional heart specialist who will provide the heart treatments recommended by the American Medical Association, including drugs and surgery. Others choose a holistic heart specialist who will suggest non-invasive, low-risk therapies based on lifestyle changes in such critical areas as nutrition, stress reduction, and exercise.

In 1989, 48 patients with severe coronary heart disease enrolled in a very unusual one-year experimental study conducted by heart specialist Dr. Dean Ornish. In Ornish's study, reported in *Dr. Dean Ornish's Program for Reversing Heart Disease,* participants were divided randomly into two groups. Patients in the usual care group were asked to follow their doctors' advice: to make moderate dietary changes (eat less red meat and more fish and chicken, use margarine instead of butter, and consume no more than three eggs per week), to exercise moderately, and to quit smoking. Patients in the other group were asked to follow Ornish's holistic heart reversal program, which included cessation of smoking, a vegetarian diet which allowed no more than

10% of calories to come from fat, stress management (including meditation, relaxation exercises performed one hour a day, and group support), and moderate exercise (30 minutes daily).

Both groups were given angiograms at the beginning of the study and one year later for comparison purposes. After only one year, 82% of the people who adopted Ornish's comprehensive lifestyle changes demonstrated "some measurable average reversal of their coronary artery blockages." Overall, the average blockage reversed from 61.1 to 55.8%; more severely blocked arteries showed even greater improvement. Four arteries that had been completely blocked began to open, even those that had been totally occluded for years. The group also experienced a 91% decrease in the frequency and severity of chest pain. According to Ornish, most coronary blockages take decades to build up, but even a small amount of reversal after one year in a severely blocked artery causes a great improvement in blood flow to the heart (as measured by a cardiac PET scan). As a result, these participants began to feel better very quickly. In contrast, the majority of heart patients in the comparison (usual care) group who were following their doctors' advice became measurably worse during the same one-year interval.

Ornish's breakthrough study provided the first solid evidence that major lifestyle changes can do what scientists thought impossible–reverse heart disease (unclog arteries) without the use of drugs or surgery. And the findings were so conclusive that one major insurance company, Mutual of Omaha, announced it would cover this diet and stress-reduction program, making it the first nonsurgical, nonpharmaceutical therapy for heart disease to qualify for insurance reimbursement. This chapter analyzes the holistic therapies developed by Ornish and others to pre-vent, treat, and even reverse major coronary heart disorders.

The Heart

The heart is one part of the cardiovascular system ("cardio" means heart and "vascular" refers to blood vessels). The heart's function is to pump blood (most adults have slightly more than a gallon of blood in their bodies) through more than 60,000 miles of blood vessels. Gordon Edlin and Eric Golanty estimate that the average adult's gallon of blood contains approximately 25 trillion red blood cells, which carry oxygen from the lungs to all of the body's tissues. More than 200 million new red blood cells are produced and released each day from bone marrow into circulation. Approximately the same number of old red blood cells are removed and recycled.

The heart, a strong and highly specialized muscle a little larger than a fist, pumps blood continuously through the circulatory system. It is divided into four chambers: the two upper chambers, called atria, receive blood returning from the body via the veins; the two lower chambers, called ventricles, pump blood out of the heart into the lungs and body through the heart's main artery, the aorta. The right atrium connects to the right ventricle and the left atrium connects to the left ventricle. A thin wall between the atria and ventricles divides the heart in half. Large blood vessels lead into the atria and leave the ventricles, passing through valves that separate the atria from the ventricles and allow blood to flow in only one direction when the heart expands and contracts (beats). Each day the heart beats approximately 100,000 times, depending on the body's activity, and pumps about 2,000 gallons of blood.

The heart does not use oxygen and nutrients from the blood which passes through its chambers. Instead, it depends on a series of arteries found on the outside surface of the heart. These are called the coronary arteries, so named for their crown-like appearance as they branch out from the aorta girdling the outer surface of the heart.

Angina. When the heart muscle does not get sufficient blood (and oxygen) for a given level of work, even for just a few minutes, chest discomfort called angina pectoris can develop. The pain, which radiates outward from the heart, usually subsides shortly if a person rests or uses nitroglycerine, a drug that dilates or opens blood vessels. Angina usually occurs when extra demands are placed on the heart–for instance, during periods of physical exertion or exposure to extreme cold or wind, or emotional stress or excitement. Some people also develop angina after eating a large meal, which requires increased blood flow to digest. Angina is not a heart attack, although it can be a warning sign that a person is at risk, and many people with angina never develop a heart attack.

Heart Attack

A heart attack, or myocardial infarction, occurs when the blood supply to part of the heart muscle itself (the myocardium) is severely reduced or stopped. This occurs when one of the coronary arteries (that supply blood and nutrients to the heart) is blocked by an obstruction. A heart attack can also be caused by a blood clot lodged in a coronary artery, which is called coronary thrombosis or coronary occlusion. The underlying cause of most heart attacks suffered by Americans is arterial disease–atherosclerosis–which also accounts for 85% of all cardiovascular (CVD) deaths in the U.S.

If blood supply to the myocardium is cut off drastically or for a long time, muscle cells suffer irreversible injury and die. Depending on where the blockage occurs and the amount of heart muscle that is damaged, a heart attack

Heart Attack Facts

- About 1.5 million Americans have heart attacks annually.
- About 500,000 of them will die as a result of a heart attack.
- Heart attacks are the leading killer of both American men and women.
- 85% of heart disorders are caused by atherosclerosis.
- 33% of all heart attacks in the U.S. are caused by atherosclerosis.
- 60% of heart attack deaths occur before the person reaches a hospital.
- 55% of people who have heart attacks are 65 years old or older.
- 80% of people who die of heart attacks are over age 65.

can be extremely serious or relatively minor. Even after a heart attack, the heart can recover so long as the damaged area is not too extensive. This is because small blood vessels within the heart may gradually reroute blood around the blocked or clogged arteries, in a process called collateral circulation.

Symptoms of a Heart Attack. According to the American Heart Association's *Fact Sheet on Heart Attack, Stroke and Risk Factors,* symptoms include uncomfortable pressure, fullness, squeezing, or pain in the center of the chest (which may spread to the shoulders, neck or arms) for more than a few minutes. Nausea, dizziness, sweating, fainting, a feeling of severe indigestion, and shortness of breath may also occur. Conversely, sharp, stabbing twinges generally are not signals of a heart attack. The importance of recognizing the symptoms of a

Coronary Artery Disease: Major Risk Factors that Can't be Changed

- **Heredity**: People with a parent or sibling who had a premature heart attack (before age 55 in a man or 65 in a woman) are at increased risk of CAD.
- **Sex**: Before age 55, men have a much higher rate of CAD than women, but by the time they reach 60, women develop CAD at the same rate as men at 50. Women who have a heart attack, especially at older ages, are more likely to die from it than are men.
- **Increasing age.** Approximately 55% of all heart attacks, and more than 80% of fatal ones, occur after age 65.
- **Race**. African-Americans have an elevated risk of CAD, primarily because they have a higher risk of hypertension and diabetes than whites.

heart attack and responding immediately cannot be overemphasized. More than 300,000 heart attack victims, the AHA warns, die before reaching the hospital each year, usually because they did not recognize the warning signals in time to receive emergency medical service.

Diagnosing Heart Disorders. Heart disorders are diagnosed on the basis of symptoms, medical history, and tests—for instance, a treadmill exercise test or coronary angiograph—which allow the physician to examine the coronary arteries themselves to determine the nature and extent of narrowing or blockage. Blood tests may also be used to detect abnormal levels of certain enzymes in the bloodstream, which are thought to be precursors of a heart attack. Additional tests may be needed in certain cases to rule out other conditions such as muscle disorders, infection, structural abnormalities, anxiety, or indigestion. A doctor may also test for signs of fluid accumulation in the lungs and tissues, or use an electrocardiogram (ECG or EKG) to discover any abnormalities of heart rhythm, insufficient blood flow to the heart muscle, or other problems. Ultrasound, another noninvasive procedure, defines heart size and pumping ability, and can also be used to check for problems with the functioning of the heart valves. The key is to identify the symptoms of heart disease in time to implement holistic strategies to counteract their effects.

The importance of early detection and diagnosis is underscored by the fact that as many as 25% of Americans who die of sudden cardiac death no previous symptoms of a heart problem, according to the March 1994 issue of *Graboys Heart Letter*. Sudden cardiac death (SCD) occurs when an already damaged heart muscle (caused by hardening of the arteries, viruses, drugs, or valve disorders) leaves a person susceptible to irregularities in the electrical signals that govern the heart's beating. When an incident occurs, the heart rhythm deteriorates into a fibrillation or twitching, and blood flow stops. If blood flow is not restored quickly, death will result. SCD kills 300,000 Americans each year–or one victim every 90 seconds. The average age of victims is between 55 and 60. As noted, the great majority of those who die suddenly have cardiovascular disease, in particular coronary artery disease (CAD), also sometimes called coronary heart disease (CHD).

Coronary Artery Disease Risk Factors. Unlike other organ systems of the body, most

Coronary Artery Disease: Major Risk Factors That Can Be Changed

- High blood cholesterol (≥ 240 mg/dl)
- Inactivity
- Obesity
- High blood pressure (≥ 140/90 mm Hg)
- Cigarette smoking
- Unmonitored diabetes
- Stress

heart diseases are not caused by infection (although cardiac infections can occur), but rather by atherosclerosis of the coronary arteries. According to the American Heart Association, the major risk factors for coronary artery disease include heredity, increasing age, high blood cholesterol levels, high blood pressure, and cigarette smoking. Coronary artery disease can also result from other contributing risk factors such as diabetes, obesity, physical inactivity, and emotional stress.

Conventional Treatments for Coronary Artery Disorders

Conventional heart specialists normally treat coronary artery disorders with drugs (which affect the supply of blood to the heart muscle or the heart's demand for oxygen) or surgery. Coronary vasodilators such as nitroglycerin, for example, cause blood vessels to relax, which, in turn, causes the opening inside the vessels to enlarge. Blood flow then improves, allowing more oxygen and nutrients to reach the heart. Coronary vasodilators also reduce the amount of blood returning to the heart, thus lessening the heart's need to

pump. Other drugs lower blood pressure and therefore reduce the heart's workload and need for oxygen. Drugs that slow the heart rate achieve a similar effect. All of these drugs have side effects, however, and have not proven effective in reversing coronary artery disease by removing the plaque that blocks coronary arteries.

Coronary bypass surgery, one of the most frequently recommended surgical procedures in the U.S., involves removing the diseased portions of the arteries and grafting a portion of a vein, usually taken from the patient's leg, onto the coronary arteries to replace the diseased segments, thus creating new pathways for blood flow to the heart. However, according to Ornish, heart attacks, strokes, infection, or death can occur as a result of bypass surgery, and up to one third of patients who undergo this operation suffer some form of transient or permanent neurological damage. Fifty percent of by-passed arteries clog up again within five years and 80% become blocked after seven years.

Reported in *Health and Wellness*, a study by the National Heart, Lung and Blood Institute showed that the five-year survival rate for patients with mild coronary artery blockage was the same whether they had coronary bypass surgery or used medication to treat symptoms. As a result of the study, the Institute concluded that as many as 25,000 bypass operations are performed unnecessarily every year.

Heart specialist Dr. Thomas Graboys reports in his *Graboys Heart Letter Special Report* that he and his colleagues at the Lown Cardiovascular Center in Boston conducted a study whereby they consulted with 168 patients seeking second opinions about undergoing coronary bypass surgery. They advised 83% of these patients not to have the operation. After four years, the death rate for those patients who declined the procedure was actually lower than the death rate for those who chose bypass surgery. In other words, 135 people in the study would have needlessly undergone an expensive and invasive procedure had they not sought a second opinion.

Balloon angioplasty, first employed by a Swiss cardiologist in 1977, is a relatively quick procedure that is less traumatic and expensive than bypass surgery, and is now used to treat hundreds of thousands of patients each year. In this procedure, a catheter with a deflated balloon on the end is threaded through an artery in the groin up into the patient's narrowed coronary artery. After the balloon is inflated to widen the artery, both the catheter and the balloon are removed. This compresses the plaque against the arterial walls (but does not remove it), and enlarges the inner diameter of the blood vessel so that blood can flow more easily to the heart. A newer form of angioplasty inserts a laser catheter and places it at the beginning of the blockage. The laser is activated and moved forward as it destroys fatty deposits and, after the artery is cleared, the laser catheter is removed. According to Ornish, one third of all patients that undergo balloon angioplasty find the same artery becoming narrowed or blocked within four to six months to the point

that another angioplasty is recommended. Despite this percentage, balloon angioplasty accounts for 90-95% of all angioplasty operations.

As serious as a heart attack can be, about 90% of patients who reach the hospital with a heart attack go home alive, and about 95% of those people live for at least a year. This survival rate is partly the result of new treatment strategies developed over the past three decades, including the use of aspirin and beta-blocking drugs (propranolol and atenolol, for example), to control the symptoms and reduce adverse outcomes of coronary artery disease. One of the most dramatic developments, according to the April 1994 issue of the *Harvard Heart Letter,* has been the use of thrombolytic agents or clot busting drugs that stop heart attacks in progress and thereby limit the amount of heart muscle damaged.

In a recent clinical trial called GUSTO (Global Utilization of Streptokinase and Tissue Plasminogen Activator [t-PA] for Occluded Coronary Arteries), reported in the April 1994 *Harvard Heart Letter*, more than 40,000 patients in 15 countries were treated with either streptokinase or t-PA, the two most popular clot busting drugs in the U.S. Both effectively dissolved the clots causing the heart attacks and kept the heart muscle alive. These medications are not always effective, however. In the GUSTO trial, 19% of patients receiving t-PA still had blocked arteries 90 minutes after treatment, as did 40% of patients receiving streptokinase. As with all medications, both drugs have been associated with some risks, particularly undesirable bleeding.

Holistic Treatments for Coronary Artery Disorders

Graboys asserts in the March 1994 *Graboys Heart Letter* that "everyone with a heart problem can benefit from an aggressive approach to the management of risk factors. Resetting life's priorities to include nutrition, exercise and stress management is necessary to continued heart health. I've worked with hundreds of patients who have recovered from a life-threatening heart problem using an 'holistic' approach to heart health."

Nutritional Therapies. Ornish claims that diet can almost immediately affect the heart. Even a single meal high in fat and cholesterol, he suggests, may cause the body to release a hormone, thromboxane, which causes the arteries to constrict and the blood to clot faster—one reason why heart patients often get chest pains after eating a fatty meal. According to Ornish, the diet he developed "allowed participants' arteries to dilate and blood to flow more freely because the fat and cholesterol content was so low."

Ornish's nutritional therapy focuses on lowering high blood cholesterol levels which form plaque and injure (tear) the linings of the coronary arteries. Ornish's vegetarian diet eliminates cholesterol, which is found in animal products (including meats), poultry, fish, and dairy products. Not only are vegetarian foods cholesterol-free but, with rare exception, they are low in saturated fat—a condition directly related to blood cholesterol levels. Ornish's diet excludes all oils and animal fats except nonfat milk and yogurt, as well as coffee, colas, MSG, tobacco, and other stimulants. All fried foods are strictly prohibited. Dairy foods high in vitamin D are also eliminated, including homogenized milk, because these products contain the enzyme xanthine oxidase which damages the arteries.

Ornish's diet allows only moderate use of salt and sugar. He also advises that eating increased amounts of dietary fiber, especially flax seed, oat bran and pectin, onions and garlic (both raw and cooked), vegetables, and fish can help reduce the consumption of saturated fats, cholesterol, sugar, and animal pro-

teins. The diet is not restricted in calories because the type of food eaten is more important than the amounts consumed. An important adjunct is reducing fat consumption to 10% of total caloric intake. However, Ornish suggests that omega-3 fatty acids (eicosopentanoic acid-EPA) may be beneficial for some patients, and these are provided by the fish included in his diet.

In their book *Prescription for Nutritional Healing,* James Balch and Phyllis Balch recommend a well-balanced diet that contains adequate amount of fiber. They suggest raw foods, broiled fish, turkey, chicken, garlic, onions, lecithin, almonds and nuts (no peanuts), olive oil, pink salmon, trout, tuna, Atlantic herring, and mackerel. All of these foods contain essential fatty acids, are low in fat, and provide nutrients needed for normal heart functioning. Balch and Balch also counsel that no salt should be included in the diet.

American Heart Association (AHA) Diet. The AHA's official diet for heart disease appears in *The American Heart Association Low-Fat, Low-Cholesterol Cookbook,* co-authored by Dr. Scott M. Grundy, one of the foremost lipid specialists in the U.S., and Mary Winston, senior science consultant for the AHA at its national headquarters in Dallas.

Grundy's book outlines the AHA's Step-One Diet and the Step-Two Diet, both of which are based on a nutritious eating plan calling for reductions in saturated fat and cholesterol. People concerned about preventing coronary artery disease by lowering their blood cholesterol levels are encouraged to first follow the Step-One Diet for three months. If they do not reach their target level by this point, they should adopt the Step-Two Diet.

Recommended Foods. The AHA diet recommends the following foods to prevent heart disorders:

AHA Step-One Diet Guideline

Nutrient	Recommended Intake
Total fat	30% or less of total calories eaten per day
Saturated fatty acids	Less than 10% of total calories
Polyunsaturated fatty acids	Up to 10% of total calories
Monounsaturated fatty acids	10% to 15% of total calories
Carbohydrates	50% to 60% of total calories
Protein	10% to 20% of total calories
Cholesterol	Less than 300 milligrams per day
Total calories	To achieve and maintain desirable weight

AHA Step-Two Diet Guideline

Nutrient	Recommended Intake
Total fat	30% or less of total calories eaten per day
Saturated fatty acids	Less than 7% of total calories
Polyunsaturated fatty acids	Up to 10% of total calories
Monounsaturated fatty acids	10% to 15% of total calories
Carbohydrates	50% to 60% of total calories
Protein	10% to 20% of total calories
Cholesterol	Less than 200 milligrams per day
Total calories	To achieve and maintain desirable weight

• *Fish*. Although fish is not entirely cholesterol-free, it generally contains less cholesterol than red meat. The AHA advises dieters to consume fish two to three times a week, especially fish high in omega-3 fatty acids (which may have cholesterol-lowering benefits), including: Atlantic and coho salmon, albacore tuna, club mackerel, carp, lake whitefish, sweet smelt, and lake and brook trout.

• *Meat Products*. Grundy's AHA diet permits a total of six ounces of poultry, fish, or lean meat per day (in one or two portions), provided that it is reasonably lean and contains between 500 and 600 calories. Red meat (including beef, lamb, pork, and veal) is permitted, so long as it contains a minimum of visible fat, and all outside fat is trimmed before cooking. Poultry is a good substitute for red meat only if it is a lean variety and if the skin is removed before cooking. Chicken and turkey are preferable to goose or duck.

- *Fruits, Vegetables, Grains, and Legumes.* These foods are low in cholesterol, tend to be low in fat, and, in many cases, are high in fiber and vitamins. A few exceptions include coconut meat (which is high in saturated fatty acids), olives, and avocados.

- *Nuts and Seeds.* Although both nuts and seeds tend to be high in fat and calories, Grundy states they do not contain cholesterol, and because most of their fat is unsaturated, they can replace high-protein, high-fat foods such as meat.

- *Dairy Products.* The AHA counsels dieters to virtually eliminate whole milk, and instead choose 1% or skim milk, both of which are rich in protein, calcium, and other nutrients without containing too much fat. Also recommended is consuming only low-fat or skim-milk cream, ice cream, and cheese, and substituting margarine for butter.

Restricted Foods. The following foods are restricted or eliminated in the AHA diet to reverse heart disorders:

- *Meat Products*. Processed meats that are high in fat and calories–including sausage, bologna, salami, and hot dogs–should be used only sparingly. Organ meats–including liver, sweetbreads, kidney, brain, and heart–are extremely high in cholesterol and should be restricted or eliminated.
- *Bakery Goods*. Bakery goods such as pies, cakes, cookies, candy, and doughnuts should be restricted on the AHA diet because they are typically high in calories and contain few beneficial nutrients. Homebaked goods prepared with unsaturated oils and egg whites instead of whole eggs are preferable.
- *Fats and Oils*. All fats and oils that tend to harden at room temperature are eliminated from the AHA diet, including butter, lard, and tallow from animal sources and palm, palm kernel, and coconut oils from plants. Margarines can be used that have hydrogenated oil listed as a second ingredient.
- *Beverages*. The AHA suggests avoiding very high consumption–10 or more cups a day–of coffee and possibly tea because they are suspected of raising cholesterol levels. However, one to two cups a day does not appear to pose a risk. In addition, alcohol in moderation (one ounce daily) does not appear to be harmful, although the AHA does not believe it helps prevent heart disease.

Phytoestrogens. As noted, Chinese and Japanese women who consume primarily vegetarian foods have lower heart disease rates than Western women. Adriane Fugh-Berman suggests that diets high in tofu, green soybeans, and other soy products that contain phytoestrogens (estrogen-like compounds found in plants) can decrease fat and calorie intake, and lower cholesterol levels. She cites a meta-analysis of 38 controlled trials that found that consumption of soy protein reduced total blood cholesterol levels by an average of 9%, LDL by 13%, and triglycerides by 10%.

Vitamin and Mineral Therapies. Atherosclerosis and heart disease take many years to develop, and a daily regimen of vitamin and mineral supplements may be helpful in preventing or treating both. The best procedure is to consult a heart specialist who may recommend vitamin and mineral supplements depending on a person's diet, body weight, medical status, and absorption levels.

Plaque formation in arteries usually follows prior damage to the inner lining of the arteries. A sudden increase in blood pressure due to chronic emotional stress, for example, can cause small tears in the arterial linings, as blood vessels do not always dilate rapidly enough to accommodate sudden increases in pressure. As noted in Chapter 3, deficiencies of vitamins B, C, and E and magnesium can make this inner lining more susceptible to damage and subsequent plaque formation.

Vitamin B_3 reduces cholesterol and tryglycerides in the blood and helps dilate the coronary arteries. Vitamin B_6 (pyridoxine) and B_{12} (necessary for the conversion of homocysteine to cystathionine) also help reduce cholesterol levels, especially oxidized cholesterols known as oxysterols. Homocysteine is derived from methionine (an amino acid found in red meat, milk, and milk products) and converted with the help of pyridoxine to a non-toxic derivative. A deficiency of pyridoxine leads to the accumulation of homocysteine, which is damaging to endothelial cells (which line the heart) and can contribute to atherosclerosis.

Vitamins C and E help prevent and dissolve coronary blood clots, prevent excessive scarring of the heart after a heart attack, and facilitate circulation by dilating capillaries and developing collateral blood vessels.

As cited in the May 20, 1993 editions of *The New York Times* and *The Wall Street Journal*, researchers at the Harvard School of Public Health and Brigham and Women's Hospital in Boston reported that people who take daily megadoses of vitamin E have a significantly reduced risk of heart disease, although they cautioned that it is still too soon to recommend widespread use. Separate studies of more than 120,000 men and women who took daily vitamin E supplements of at least 100 International Units–more than three times the current U.S. RDA–showed that they had a 40% lower risk of heart disease than those who did not.

The researchers found that the reduction in risk appeared after two years of taking the supplements, and that people who simply consumed a diet rich in vitamin E did not derive the same health benefits as those who took the supplements. They also found that the benefit was not enhanced when people took more than 100 units. The researchers concluded that vitamin E, as an antioxidant, might reduce heart disease by having an effect on low-density lipoprotein (LDL) cholesterol, the so-called "bad" cholesterol.

Magnesium. Ornish cites an impressive number of studies showing the benefits of taking magnesium for heart patients. Magnesium, according to Ornish, has been shown to reduce the risk of several different kinds of cardiac arrhythmias (abnormal heart rhythms). In two uncontrolled studies on a total of 18 patients suffering from a type of arrhythmia called *torsades de pointes*, magnesium reversed the arrhythmia in all cases. Another study of 18 patients with atrial fibrillation found that magnesium injections lowered their heart rates substantially. In 100 patients that had just received cardiac surgery, patients receiving intravenous magnesium suffered from only half the incidence of ventricle arrythmias that placebo subjects did. The hearts of the magnesium-treated subjects

also pumped more blood after the surgery.

A meta-analysis of magnesium treating acute heart attacks found eight randomized controlled trials involving 930 patients. The magnesium-treated group showed 49% fewer serious arrhythmias, 58% fewer cardiac arrests, and 54% fewer deaths than the control group. As this study suggests, magnesium given after a heart attack helps people live longer. In a later, larger study of 2,316 subjects four weeks after they suffered suspected heart attacks, there were 24% fewer deaths among those given magnesium. A long-term, follow-up of the same study found that the mortality rate of magnesium-treated subjects was reduced by 16%, and the reduction for ischemic (oxygen-deprived) heart disease was 21%.

Selenium. Selenium appears to have an effect on cardiovascular disease. One Danish study reviewed in *Alternative Medicine: What Works* found that men with the lowest selenium levels in their blood were 1.7 times as likely to suffer a cardiovascular event. Selenium is toxic in doses over 200 micrograms a day and an early sign of an overdose is a metallic taste in the mouth, dizziness, or nausea.

Pantethine. According to the *Encyclopedia of Natural Medicine*, carnitine, pantethine, and co-enzyme Q-10 help prevent the accumulation of fatty acids within the heart muscle by improving the breakdown of fatty acids and other compounds. Pantethine has been shown to reduce serum tryglyceride and cholesterol levels significantly while increasing HDL-cholesterol levels in clinical trials. It appears to accelerate fatty acid breakdown as well.

Co-enzyme Q-10. Co-enzyme Q-10, a vitamin that functions as a co-enzyme, protects against atherosclerosis by helping to prevent the formation of oxysterols. Co-enzyme Q-10 is an essential part of the mitochondria, the energy-producing part of a cell. Diseased hearts, according to studies reviewed by Fugh-Berman, tend to have less co-enzyme Q-10 in them, and supplementation with co-enzyme Q-10 appears to be treat various types of heart disease.

Karl Folders, a biomedical scientist at the University of Texas in Austin, suggests in the March/April 1994 issue of *Natural Health* that many heart patients suffer from a co-enzyme Q-10 deficiency. One study found co-enzyme Q-10 deficiencies in 75% of 132 patients undergoing heart surgery. Dr. Peter Langsjoen, a cardiologist in Tyler, Texas, states in the same article: "In 80 percent of my (heart) patients, I see a clinical improvement within four weeks of administering coenzyme Q10." According to Langsjoen, all forms of heart disease seem to respond to co-enzyme Q-10.

In a randomized, double-blind, controlled trial of 641 patients with congestive heart failure, patients receiving co-enzyme Q-10 required fewer hospitalizations and had fewer serious complications. And a small controlled study showed that exercise tolerance increased in 12 angina patients treated with co-enzyme Q-10.

In coronary artery bypass patients, co-enzyme Q-10 protected hearts from post-operative complications. In a controlled trial, 40 patients received co-enzyme Q-10 or a placebo for a week prior to their operation. The blood tests of treated subjects showed less evidence of heart injury than commonly occurs after this operation, and the treated group also had a lower incidence of arrhythmias during the recovery period.

Other minerals which have been linked with reducing cholesterol and platelet levels include calcium, chromium, and potassium. Dosages for these minerals should be prescribed by a heart specialist or physician.

Fish and Fish Oils. The arteries of patients who've undergone coronary angioplasty often close up again. Fugh-Berman reviews a meta-analysis of seven trials on these patients which found that fish oil reduces the rate at which the treated arteries clogged up again. In four studies in which pictures of the arteries were taken, the difference between the placebo and fish oil groups was 14%. The more fish oil consumed, the greater the effect.

Eating fish appears to thin the blood, which may partially explain how fish oil helps arterial problems. A large, population-based study found that people who ate fish once or more a day had the fewest clotting factors in their blood. Fish in the diet is also associated with less risk of chronic obstructive pulmonary disease (emphysema or chronic bronchitis) in smokers.

In a meta-analysis of 31 trials on 1,356 patients, fish oil reduced blood pressure in hypertensive people, but not in those whose blood pressure was normal.

Botanical Therapies. According to *Alternative Medicine: The Definitive Guide*, garlic, ginger, and hawthorn berry extract may be valuable in preventing and treating coronary heart disorders. Garlic contains sulfur compounds which work as antioxidants and help dissolve blood clots. Ginger has been shown to be effective in lowering cholesterol levels and making blood platelets less sticky.

A placebo-controlled, double-blind study reported by H. Kiesewetter in a 1993 issue of *Clinical Investigations* found that garlic-coated tablets reduced platelet aggregation. In this 12-week study, patients that took garlic significantly increased their walking distance by the fifth week of treatment. This increase was accompanied by a simultaneous decrease in platelet aggregation, blood pressure, plasma viscosity, and serum cholesterol levels.

Ginkgo biloba, according to nutritionist Donald J. Brown, writing in the May 1994 *Townsend Letter for Doctors*, is the premier botanical medicine used to treat intermittent claudication (clogging) caused by plaque or platelets. Brown suggests that using ginkgo biloba in conjunction with garlic should prove beneficial in treating coronary artery disease.

Michael Murray and Joseph Pizzorno report that hawthorn berry extracts are widely used in Europe to treat cardiovascular problems, and they cite nine studies demonstrating the effectiveness of the extracts in preventing angina attacks as well as lowering blood pressure and serum cholesterol levels.

Balch and Balch recommend barberry, black cohosh root, butcher's broom, cayenne pepper, dandelion, ginseng, hawthorn berries, red grape vine leaves, and valerian root. They suggest that some heart patients may benefit from suma herb tea, consumed three times a day with ginkgo biloba extract. These should all be prescribed by a physician, herbalist, or health practitioner.

Ayurvedic Medicine. Several Ayurvedic botanical supplements may be beneficial in lowering blood cholesterol levels, and thus indirectly lower the risk of coronary artery disease. MAK-5, a food supplement prepared with sweetened ghee (clarified butter), according to *Alternative Medicine: What Works* prevented human platelet aggregation in vitro in one small study, and may also have antioxidant properties. In another uncontrolled study of 35 men, some with high and some with normal cholesterol levels, 50 grams of ray amla, the ayurvedic herb *Emblica officinalis* (also called Indian gooseberry) lowered total blood cholesterol levels. After a month, however, there was no significant reduction in either total or LDL blood cholesterol levels.

Chelation Therapy. During chelation therapy a patient is given ehtylene-diaminertetraacetic acid (EDTA) to remove plaque and calcium deposits from the arterial walls. EDTA is usually administered intravenously several times a week over the course of two or three months in order to restore complete circulation. E. McDonagh reports in *A Textbook on EDTA Chelation Therapy* that 88% of patients receiving chelation therapy in one study exhibited improved blood flow to the brain. Dr. Charles Farr, co-founder of the American Board of Chelation Therapy, reports in *Alternative Medicine: The Definitive Guide* that he has given more than 500,000 chelation treatments to more than 20,000 patients in the last 20 years. Sixty to 70% of those with cardiovascular disease or circulatory problems improved. Many were originally scheduled to have bypass surgery or angioplasty. Farr claims that EDTA therapy is remarkably effective in removing arterial plaque, dissolving clots, dilating arterial blood vessels, and allowing essential nutrients to get to damaged tissues.

Homeopathic Medicine. In the January 1994 issue of the *Townsend Letter for Doctors*, nutritonist Luc Chaltin argues that atherosclerosis causes most cases of coronary artery disease, and can be effectively treated with combined homeopathic remedies such as Digitalis, Glonoinum and Crataegus, Lachesis Muta, Bathrops, and Crotalus Horridus. Cactus Grandiflorus is very effective for long-term chronic afflication of the arteries, especially the capillaries. Chaltin cautions, however, that these remedies must be combined with a diet low in protein, especially animal protein, to reduce the uric acid content of the blood which inflames the inner walls of the arteries.

Estrogen Replacement Therapy. Declining estrogen levels in women after menopause are believed to contribute to an increased risk of osteoporosis and heart attacks. Estrogen therapy, according to the May 1994 issue of the *UC Berkeley Wellness Letter*, raises HDL cholesterol. Hormone replacement therapy (HRT) usually includes progestin (a synthetic form of the hormone progesterone) along with estrogen. Recent studies cited by the *UC Berkeley Wellness Letter* suggest that the combined estrogen-progestin therapy also protects against heart disease. HRT is not appropriate for all women, however, and a physician should be consulted before starting treatment. The link between estrogen deficiency and an increased risk of heart disease varies with the age, health status, and nutritional and lifestyle habits of each individual.

There is preliminary evidence that low levels of sex hormones in men may play an indirect role in heart disease. A study reported in the June 1994 issue of the *Harvard Heart Letter* compared 49 heart attack victims, all of whom were under the age of 56, with an equal number of healthy volunteers. The two groups had similar levels of estrogen, the female hormone that is also present at low levels in normal men. Those suffering heart attacks, however, had levels approximately 20% lower of the male hormone dehydroepiandrosterone sulfate (DHEAS) than the healthy volunteers. How lower levels of male sex hormones might contribute to the development of heart disease is still not known.

Traditional Chinese Medicine. Traditional Chinese Medicine (TCM) views heart disease as a problem stemming from poor digestion, which causes the build-up of plaque in the arteries. Chung San Yuan reports in a 1973 issue of the *Chinese Medical Journal* that the Chinese herb Mao-tung-chinghas been successfully used to treat coronary heart disease. Mao-tung-ching was administered daily (both orally and intravenously) to 103 patients. In 101 out of 103 cases, significant improvement resulted. The herb is believed to dilate the blood vessels, although its

effectiveness in treating patients with coronary artery disease has not been confirmed in Western clinical trials. TCM practitioners often combine Chinese botanical therapies with acupuncture, believed to be an effective multiple treatment for chronic coronary heart disease cases. Further clinical trials are necessary, however, to evaluate the effectiveness of acupuncture in the treatment of cardiovascular disorders.

Exercise. Among healthy people, Ornish claims that exercise causes the arteries to secrete a substance called endothelium-derived relaxation factor (EDRF) that opens (dilates) the coronary arteries and allows more blood to flow to the heart. In people with coronary artery blockages, however, the coronary arteries constrict during exercise because less EDRF is produced in coronary arteries that are partially blocked. Smoking also decreases the production of EDRF. Therefore, people with a heart condition should consult with a physician before starting an exercise program. People over age 35 that have not exercised regularly for several years should also be examined by their physician before beginning regular exercise.

Vigorous exercise may actually increase the risk of heart attacks in people with coronary artery blockages, who eat a high-fat diet, smoke, manage stress poorly, and use stimulants. Moderate exercise, however, as long as it is combined with lifestyle changes–for example, a low-fat diet, stress reduction, and the elimination of stimulants and smoking–is beneficial in the treatment of coronary disorders.

Graboys recommends for his heart patients any form of exercise that "breaks a sweat" for at least 20-30 minutes, three to four times a week, including brisk walking, jogging, rowing, swimming, non-impact aerobics, and outdoor (or stationary) bicycling.

These aerobic exercises increase blood flow to the large muscle groups of the body, keeping the heart and circulatory system more healthy and functional. Regular exercise also contributes to weight loss or weight control, helps moderate the effects of stress, decreases the tendency of blood to form clots, helps the body use insulin, lowers blood pressure, and may boost HDL ("good") cholesterol.

D. Nieman reports that the U.S. Centers for Disease Control reviewed 43 studies of North American and European working-age men. Controlling for age, sex, blood pressure, smoking status, and total serum cholesterol levels, 68% of the studies reported a statistically significant relationship between physical activity and the risk of coronary heart disease (CHD). The studies confirmed that both physical fitness and physical activity (whether on the job or during leisure times) are associated with reduced risk of CHD, and that regular physical activity should be promoted in CHD prevention programs as vigorously as blood pressure control, dietary modification to lower serum cholesterol, and smoking cessation. Next to high blood cholesterol levels, Nieman notes, lack of physical activity is the second most important risk factor for heart disease in the U.S.

Aerobic Exercise. Any exercise program to reverse CAD must be moderate, progressive, and continuously monitored because overexercise can be dangerous. Regular aerobic exercise which is not extreme can be helpful because it helps dilate blood vessels, increase blood flow, and improve oxygenation of the blood.

Dr. Dean Ornish's Program for Reversing Heart Disease outlines a brief walking or jogging program three times a week for a minimum of 20 minutes, which, combined with a low-fat diet, reversed coronary artery disease in 41 patients. Ornish notes that the Cardiac Rehabilitation Program

Why Does Exercise Help Prevent Heart Disease?

1. Exercise works the heart, a muscle that must be stimulated to stay fit.

2. Exercise raises the maximal heart rate but lowers the resting heart rate once exercise is completed. Thus, it lowers the resting heart rate for 23 hours of the day, causing the heart to beat less but more efficiently.

3. Exercise helps in weight loss, a key factor in avoiding heart disease.

4. Exercise raises HDL cholesterol.

5. Exercise lowers LDL cholesterol and tryglycerides.

6. Exercise lowers blood pressure levels. Following aerobic exercise, blood pressure falls for at least 90 minutes. Studies have shown that both physical fitness and aerobic activity (at least three times a week for 20 minutes each session) are both associated with decreased risk of hypertension. Exercise training is also associated with lower blood pressure among hypertensive people.

at Providence Hospital (Rhode Island) also found that regular brisk walking lowers heart rates and increases the heart's pumping ability.

Lowering Blood Pressure. High blood pressure levels can permanently damage the heart, and many Americans take anti-hypertensive drugs to lower their blood pressure. However, Ornish states that these drugs often have severe side affects, including

Exercises That Help Prevent or Reverse Heart Disease

Stationary Bicycling. The Preventive and Cardiac Rehabilitation Program at Cedars-Sinai Medical Center (Los Angeles) has successfuly helped angina patients recover from surgery with 10-minute stationary bicycling sessions.

Treadmill. The Cedars-Sinai Program also incorporates treadmill walking in its treatment for angina patients, and has found that treadmill walking is equally as beneficial as stationary walking.

Running. A Swiss study of 39 sedentary men aged 30-50 found that jogging helped reduce blood pressure, cholesterol and triglyceride levels, and trimmed body fat–all of which are beneficial for preventing CAD.

Stairmaster. A University of Missouri study indicates that a 30-minute workout three times weekly burns 2,000 calories and lowers LDL, the "bad" cholesterol which can contribute to CAD.

Jumping Rope. Columbia Hospital Sports Medicine Center in Milwaukee found that a 30-minute workout (the equivalent to eight minutes of running) lowered LDL cholesterol levels.

Weight Training. A 10-week Canadian study of 18 men suffering from CAD found that those who weight-lifted in combination with aerobic exercise increased their muscle strength and cardiovascular fitness. CAD patients usually have weak upper body muscles. Low-weight, high-volume weight lifting done in 7-8 repetitions proved more helpful than doing aerobic exercise alone.

Bicycling. A University of Washington School of Medicine study found that walking, jogging, and bicycling increased blood levels of tissue plasminogen activator (TPA), which dissolves plaque in the blood.

---

impotence, fatigue, depression, and blood cell disorders. Most of the patients following Dr. Ornish's program, for example, were able to decrease or discontinue their blood pressure medications. Ornish feels that the safest and most effective way to lower blood pressure is to use natural stress reduction therapies such as yoga, meditation, and visualization.

As discussed in Chapter 9, studies by Dr. Herbert Benson at the Harvard Medical School clearly show that yoga, biofeedback, visualization, massage, and progressive relaxation help lower high blood pressure which

injures coronary artery linings and leads to the formation of coronary blockages. In Benson's studies, heart patients' blood pressure remained significantly reduced three to five years after making lifestyle changes that included meditation, group support, and exercise.

Ornish believes that deep breathing and imaging techniques aimed at reducing stress should be conducted frequently throughout the day to reduce the output of adrenal hormones and lower the level of platelet aggregation. He encourages patients to do these tech-

Deep Relaxation Technique

1. Lie on your back with your eyes closed.

2. Inhale deeply and progressively relax all your muscles.

3. Feel the gentle flow of air as it comes in and out of your nose.

4. Gradually allow the inhalations to become deeper with each breath.

5. Imagine that you are breathing in light and healing energy as well as oxygen that are revitalizing and recharging your body and mind.

Deep Breathing Exercise

1. Sit in a comfortable position and close your eyes.

2. Exhale fully.

3. Close off your right nostril with your thumb and inhale slowly through your left nostril.

4. Close off your left nostril and exhale through the right nostril.

5. Inhale through the right nostril.

6. Close off the right nostril and exhale through the left nostril.

7. Continue this pattern, changing the nostril after each inhalation.

8. Continue for 30 seconds to three minutes.

9. If you feel that you are not getting enough air at any time, simply resume breathing normally.

niques before meals and at bedtime, as they not only reduce stress but also improve digestion. Ornish's program is supported by Dr. William Lee Cowden, a cardiologist in Dallas, Texas, who notes in *Alternative Medicine: The Definitive Guide* that some nutrients which may help reverse coronary blockages (including magnesium and vitamins B, C, and E) must be absorbed out of the gastrointestinal tract. If the tract is in a stressed state, it cannot absorb these nutrients nearly as well as when it is relaxed.

Yoga. Both Ornish and Graboys recommend yoga as an adjunct to stress reduction therapies. The form of yoga used by Ornish's patients, hatha yoga, combines stretching and breathing techniques which produce a sense of equilibrium and rebalancing. It also includes visualization, progressive relaxation practices, self-analysis, and meditation.

Progressive Deep Relaxation and Alternate Nostril Breathing. In *Dr. Dean Ornish's Program for Reversing Heart Disease*, Ornish describes several progressive deep relaxation exercises which his patients have used to induce the relaxation response. Besides connecting the mind and body, breathing also decreases heart rate, blood pressure, muscular tension, and sympathetic nervous system stimulation.

Visualization. Visualization also directly produces the relaxation response, and lowers heart rate and blood pressure. According to Ornish, visualizing healing images can improve coronary blood flow by dilating the coronary arteries. Visualization also reduces the number and severity of irregular heartbeats. Ornish suggests that people with

Recovering from a Heart Disorder

Millions of people suffering from coronary artery disease have recovered fully and live long, happy, and productive lives. The following recommendations are an important part of this process.

- Keep your blood pressure low
- Maintain low blood cholesterol levels
- Exercise
- Return to work
- Lose Weight
- Reduce angry stress
- Join a heart rehabilitation support group
- Resume sexual relationships.

coronary blockages ask their cardiologist for a diagram showing the exact location of each blocked artery. Patients should choose a healing image that incorporates the following affirmations:

1. Your heart is beating regularly.

2. Your heart is pumping a healthy amount of blood with each beat.

3. The arteries in your heart are dilating and allowing more blood to flow.

4. New blood vessels are growing and supplying oxygen and other nutrients to your heart.

5. The blood is flowing smoothly and unobstructed.

Positive Thinking. Positive thinking and a healthy outlook help the heart to heal. One study conducted by Dr. Daniel Mark, a heart specialist at Duke University, and reported in April 15, 1994 edition of *The New York Times,* concluded that optimism was a powerful predictor of who will live and who will die after being diagnosed with heart disease. Mark conducted a follow-up study of 1,719 men and women that had undergone heart catheterization, a common procedure used to check the arteries for clogging. The patients typically underwent the test because of chest pain, and all were diagnosed with heart disease. When interviewed initially, 14% said they doubted that they would recover enough to resume their daily routines. After one year, 12% of these pessimists had died, compared with 5% of those optimistic about recovering. Even when the severity of people's conditions was taken into account, outlook was a crucial factor in survival. In fact, optimism often seemed to have little bearing on how sick people were. Some of those with very mild heart disease had the grimmest views of their prospects. Dr. Mark concluded: "The mind is a tremendous tool or weapon, depending on your point of view." In his study, pessimism appeared to be even more damaging to recovery than depression, which has also been shown to lower a person's chance of recovery from heart disease.

Hostility, anger, and anxiety may also play a key role in preventing heart disease. Psychologist Catherine Stoney of the American Psychosomatic suggests that hostile, anxious people metabolize fats more slowly than positive, relaxed persons, which may be a key reason hostility and heart attacks are linked. Those who seethe with anger–and usually try to suppress it–are slowest at ridding their bodies of dietary fat. Experts have known that hostile adults have higher cholesterol levels, and Stoney's finding–summarized in the April 15, 1994 edition of the *Marin Independent Journal*–may provide a partial answer.

Eliminating Smoking. According to Ornish, smoking causes "many more deaths" from heart disease than from lung cancer, in both men and women. The nicotine and other toxic substances in tobacco are absorbed into the blood and injure the lining of the coronary arteries. Nicotine also causes the coronary arteries to constrict, and can lead to the formation of blood clots.

Ornish cites recent studies demonstrating that quitting smoking reduces the risk of heart disease by 64% within the first three years after stopping. When people stop smoking, nicotine is eliminated from the body quickly, and the risk of blood clots or coronary artery spasms decreases rapidly.

Summary

Although heart disease causes half of all deaths in the U.S., it is one of the most preventable chronic degenerative disorders. Eighty-five percent of all heart attacks are caused by atherosclerosis–hardening of the coronary arteries which block blood flow to the heart. Overwhelming evidence suggests that the risk of coronary artery disease, including angina and myocardial infarction, can be prevented through dietary changes, vitamin and mineral therapies, botanical therapies, exercise, and stress reduction, all of which help prevent excessive oxidation of cholesterol in the bloodstream.

In the past three decades, significant progress has been made in the war against heart disease. Although the U.S. population has increased in size and become more elderly, the total annual number of heart attacks has remained relatively constant. Thus, the rate of heart attacks per 100,000 people of any given age has declined by approximately 40% since the early 1960s. According the April 1994 issue of the *Harvard Heart Letter*, prevention has played a major role in reducing the heart attack rate, and at least half of the credit for this improvement belongs to patients, who have modified their diets to reduce cholesterol levels, avoided cigarettes, controlled their blood pressure, and undertaken regular physical activity.

Resources

References

American Heart Association. *Fact Sheet on Heart Attacks, Stroke and Risk Factors.* 1987.

American Heart Association. *Heart and Stroke Facts.* 1992.

Balch, James F., and Phyllis Balch. *Prescription for Nutritional Healing.* Long Island, NY: Avery Publishing, 1993.

Benson, Herbert. *The Relaxation Response.* New York: William Morrow, 1975.

Brody, Jane. "Vitamin E Greatly Reduces Risk of Heart Disease, Studies Suggest." *The New York Times* (May 20, 1993): B7.

Brown, Donald J. "Garlic for Intermittent Claudication." *Townsend Letter for Doctors* (May 1994)): 546.

The Burton Goldberg Group. *Alternative Medicine: The Definitive Guide.* Payallup, WA: Future Medicine Publishing, Inc., 1993.

Chaltin, Luc. "Homeopathy & Electro-acupuncture." *Townsend Letter For Doctors* (January 1994): 39.

DeBakey, Michael E., Antonia M. Gotto, Lynee W. Scott, and John P. Foreyt. *The Living Heart Diet.* New York: Simon & Schuster, 1986.

Edlin, Gordon, and Eric Golanty. *Health and Wellness*. Boston: Jones and Bartlett Publishers, 1992.

Folders, Karl. "Heart Disease." *Natural Health* (March/April 1994): 3.

Fugh-Berman, Adriane. *Alternative Medicine: What Works*. Tucson, AZ: Odonian Press, 1996.

Graboys, Thomas B. "Avoiding Sudden Cardiac Death." *Graboys Heart Letter* (March 1994): 1-2.

——. "Choosing the Right Options for Heart Diagnosis and Treatment." *A Graboys Heart Letter Special Report* (1994): 1-4.

——. "Five Common Sense Ways to Stay Heart Healthy." *A Graboys Heart Letter Special Report* (1994): 1-4.

——. "Healing Your Own Heart: A Holistic Approach." *Graboys Heart Letter* (March 1994): 3.

——. "Nitroglycerine Can Eliminate Your Chest Pains." *Graboys Heart Letter* (May 1994): 3.

Grundy, Scott. *American Heart Association Low-Fat, Low-Cholesterol Cookbook*. New York: Random House, 1992.

"Hostility and Heart Attacks." *Marin Independent Journal* (April 15, 1994): A1.

"How Risky Is Physical Exercise?" *Harvard Health Letter* (May 1994): 13.

"Insurance to Cover Alternative Heart Treatment." *Natural Health* (November/December 1993): 18.

Kieswater, H. "Effects of Garlic Coated Tablets in Peripheral Arterial Occlusive Disease." *Clinical Investigations* 71 (1991): 383-86.

McDonagh, E. "An Oculocerebrovascullo-metric Analysis of the Improvement in Arterial Stenosis Following EDTA Chelation Therapy," in *A Textbook on EDTA Chelation Therapy* by E. M. Cranston. New York: Human Sciences Press, 1989, p.155.

"Men, Hormones, and Heart Disease." *Harvard Health Letter* (June 1994): 8.

"Mind/Body: Stress and Anger." *UC Berkeley Wellness Letter* (May 1994): 5.

Murray, Michael, and Joseph Pizzorno. *Encyclopedia of Natural Medicine*. Rocklin, CA: Prima Publishing, 1991.

Nieman, D. *Fitness & Your Health*. Palo Alto, CA: Bull Publishing Company, 1993.

"Optimism Can Mean Life for Heart Patients and Pessimism Death, Study Says." *The New York Times* (April 15, 1994): A11.

Ornish, Dean. *Dr. Dean Ornish's Program for Reversing Heart Disease*. New York: Ballantine Books, 1990.

"Progress in the War against Heart Attacks." *Harvard Health Letter* (April 1994): 1-5.

"Rating Your Risks for Heart Disease." *UC Berkeley Wellness Letter* (May 1994): 4-5.

Stipp, David. "Vitamin E Link Is Seen in Lowering Heart Disease Disease Risk." *The Wall Street Journal* (May 20, 1993): A10.

Yuan, Chung San. "Treatment of 103 cases of Coronary Diseases with *Ilex pubescens*." *Chinese Medical Journal* 1 (1973): 64.

Organizations

American Heart Association.
7320 Greenville Avenue, Dallas, TX 75231.

American Physical Therapy Association.
1156 15th St. N.W., Washington, DC 20005.

American Rehabilitation Foundation.
Kenny Rehabilitation Institute, 2727 Chicago Avenue, Minneapolis, MN 55407.

RESOURCES

Additional Reading

Butler, Kurt, and Lynn Rayner. *The Best Medicine: The Complete Health and Preventive Medicine Handbook*. San Francisco: Harper & Row Publishers, 1985.

Margolis, Simeon, and Hamilton Moses III. *The Johns Hopkins Medical Handbook*. New York: Medletter Associates, Inc., 1992.

Rees, Alan, and Charlene Willey. *Personal Health Reporter*. Detroit, MI: Gale Research, 1993.

RESOURCES

Chapter 19

AGING

Anna Mary Roberts ("Grandma") Moses took up painting at the age of 76. Norman Maclean published his first work of fiction, the award-winning *A River Runs Through It*, at the age of 75. Kurt Adler, the great conductor of the San Francisco Opera, was busy with music until he died in his mid-80s, and even fathered a child in his 70s.

Most of us know elderly persons who are quite remarkable in their own way—either staying fit by competing in athletics or keeping their minds agile through absorbing activities such as reading, writing, hobbies, or art. The last years of one's life, presumably, should be the most enjoyable, as they are usually years of leisure and reflection. No matter how healthy the lifestyle, however, as people become older certain basic biological changes occur. People lose their hair or their hair turns gray, their skin wrinkles, they lose muscle tone and physical stamina, their lungs decrease in size, and their heart and immune systems become less efficient.

While scientists have not yet been able to stop the normal processes of aging, it is possible for people to improve their strength, flexibility, and energy levels, and subsequently protect themselves against chronic illnesses associated with aging, including Alzheimer's disease, senile dementia and osteoporosis. This chapter describes the aging process and the holistic guidelines for retarding the aging process. Alternative treatments for common, age-related disorders, including Alzheimer's disease and osteoporosis, are discussed.

Causes of Aging

One genetic theory suggests that the human body has a biological aging clock in which each cell is genetically programmed to live a proscribed life span. The greater the maximum life span potential for a species, the greater the number of divisions a cell will undergo before its growth finally stops and the cell dies. Another theory, called the "error catastrophe" hypothesis, suggests that aging occurs as a result of accumulated genetic and cellular damage. The longer people live, for example, the more their bodies are exposed to radiation and cancer-causing chemicals. Eventually some essential cellular functions deteriorate due to mutations which inactivate the genes. Human cells possess a variety of enzymes that can repair damage to DNA and other vital cellular structures. If one or more of these enzymes becomes defective, however, it is possible that essential cellular functions will begin to fail.

A third theory proposes that decline in immune system functioning is key to the aging process. As discussed in Chapter 7, weakening of the immune system often results in increased susceptibility to many diseases, including cancer and atherosclerosis. As the body ages, the immune system at some point cannot recognize and eliminate damaged or foreign cells efficiently–and the elderly become particularly susceptible to infections and chronic diseases which can often be fatal.

Aging has also been attributed indirectly to the atrophy of the thymus gland. As people grow older, their thymus gland shrinks in size and produces less thymosin, an important hormone which may help regulate the biological aging clock. Another theory argues that aging is linked to cellular damage caused by free radicals–toxic molecules which can damage arterial walls and other healthy cells. Free radicals are normally neutralized or destroyed by protective enzymes in cells. However, cellular damage caused by free radicals may accumulate over time and contribute to the aging process.

A sixth theory suggests that aging may be related to dietary habits. Roy Walford, author of the book *Maximum Life Span*, has shown that the aging process in mammals is always in some degree related to caloric intake: the more calories they eat, the faster they age–and the fewer calories they consume, the slower they age. Walford has successively increased the lifespan of laboratory animals by reducing their caloric intake by 25%. Walford's anti-aging diet is summarized later in this chapter.

Finally, aging may be related to specific nutritional deficiencies, especially zinc. More than 100 enzymes in human cells require zinc to function properly. While a mild zinc deficiency may not produce any obvious clinical symptoms, a gradual depletion of zinc in the cells of older people could accelerate the aging process or increase their susceptibility to disease.

The most reasonable assumption about aging is that it is caused by both internal and external factors–including genetics–which interact in a complex way, and that those factors will affect each person differently. Because no scientific breakthroughs are anticipated which will prevent normal human aging or death, everyone should strive to maintain their mental and physical health throughout all stages of life.

Alternative Guidelines for Retarding the Aging Process

Nutrition. "There is no doubt that life can be shortened by a variety of forms of malnutrition," writes Alfred E. Harper of the departments of Nutritional Sciences and Biochemistry at the University of Wisconsin in *Forever Young*. He adds, "dietary modification can be used to reduce the

Physiological Changes of Aging

- **Loss of vision and hearing**: Visual function starts to decline at around age 45 and gradually worsens. By the age of 80, less than 15% of Americans have 20/20 vision. Gradual hearing loss generally begins at about age 20, and has been estimated to affect as many as 66% of people reaching the age of 80.

- **Loss of taste and smell**: The elderly often complain of a reduced ability to taste and enjoy food. Their taste buds diminish in number and size, and this affects sweet and salty tastes in particular. Approximately 40% of people over 80 years old appear to have difficulty identifying common substances by smell.

- **Dental bone loss**: The majority of the elderly suffer bone loss and disease in the tissues around the teeth. This makes it more difficult to chew, which leads to a reduced consumption of fresh fruit and vegetables high in dietary fiber.

- **Loss of lean body weight**: As people age their body fat tends to increase, while their muscle and bone (lean body weight) decrease. This leads to a reduction in energy expended during rest–which may explain why the elderly consume fewer calories than younger people.

- **Loss of bone mass**: Women lose significant amounts of their bone mass by the age of 65, which can lead to osteoporosis. The resulting fractures often mend slowly and result in long periods of reduced physical activity and social interaction.

- **Loss of mental clarity**: Nearly 60% of the elderly show some signs of senile dementia and problems associated with it, including impairment of memory, judgment, personality, and the ability to speak. Senile dementia of the Alzheimer's type accounts for at least half of all dementia experienced in old age.

- **Reduced ability to metabolize drugs**: The elderly less efficiently absorb, distribute, metabolize, and excrete nutrients as well as botanical and pharmaceutical drugs. The majority of the elderly regularly take more than one prescription drug, and these often interact with each other, causing severe side effects in some cases.

- **Urinary incontinence:** Up to 20% of the elderly living at home and 75% in long-term nursing facilities cannot control their urination. This often leads to social isolation and embarrassment.

- **Reduction in heart and lung fitness**: With aging, there is a reduction of 8-10% every decade in the ability of the heart and lungs to supply oxygen to the muscles. Most of this is due to the reduced physical activity of the elderly. The most important thing elderly people can do to extend their lifespan is to maintain the health of their hearts. If all forms of vascular heart disease were to disappear from our society, people could expect to live, on average, an additional 18 years.

Nutritional Recommendations to Increase Lifespan

1. **Eat fruits and vegetables.** The National Cancer Institute recommends five daily servings of fruits and vegetables, which is the key source of substances such as fiber, vitamins C and E, and betacarotene–all of which reduce the risk of cancer. They may also help prevent heart disease, cataracts, and other age-related illnesses.

2. **Eat less fat.** In a five-year Family Heart Study project conducted in Portland, Oregon, researchers found that people who adopted a low-fat diet suffered fewer day-to-day feelings of depression and anger. Reducing fat intake will also reduce the risk of heart disease and obesity.

3. **Reduce the consumption of alcohol.** Excess alcohol consumption puts a strain on the liver.

4. **Eat a hearty breakfast**. Research suggests that starting the day with a sensible meal is one of seven factors associated with longevity. A 10-year study of 7,000 men and women by UCLA's School of Public Health found that women who ate a healthy breakfast, along with never smoking, exercising regularly, drinking only moderate amounts of alcohol, sleeping seven to eight hours a night, maintaining proper weight, and not eating between meals, lived an average of eight years longer than women who followed only one to three practices.

5. **Eat dinner at lunchtime**. The French (who suffer fewer heart attacks than Americans even though they ingest the same amount of fat) consume 57% of their calories before 2 p.m., while Americans eat only 38% of their calories by that time. Researchers speculate that when people eat the bulk of their calories earlier in the day, their bodies are better able to metabolize fat. As a result, blood cells called platelets are less likely to aggregate–or stick together–which reduces the incidence of clotting that can lead to strokes and heart attacks.

6. **Eat foods rich in calcium**. The more calcium people store in their bones during their 20s and 30s, the less likely they are to suffer from osteoporosis in later years.

7. **Eat foods containing chromium.** Fresh fruits and vegetables, dairy products, whole wheat, and meat all contain small amounts of chromium, a trace mineral. Research conducted at the Human Nutrition Research Center in Beltsville, Maryland, suggests that people who do not get enough chromium cannot use their insulin as efficiently to get sugar out of the bloodstream and into the body tissues, which could be an early earning sign of diabetes.

severity of the signs and symptoms of a variety of genetic and pathological conditions that result in metabolic defects. Application of nutritional knowledge in these ways can prolong survival and increase longevity—within the biologically determined life span—just as can the application of other therapeutic measures or avoidance of environmental hazards."

To slow the general decline of bodily functions which occurs in aging, Dr. Sheldon Hendler, author of *The Complete Guide to Anti-Aging Nutrients*, suggests reducing fat intake to no more than 30% (preferably 20%) of total calories. He also recommends limiting red meat and animal protein intake because they are harder for the kidneys of elderly people to absorb, and increase the consumption of plant protein which enhances calcium consumption. According to Hendler, protein should comprise about 13% of total calorie intake, although some conditions such as surgery, chronic diseases, or skin ulcerations may increase this requirement.

James Balch and Phyllis Balch suggest that the elderly should restrict sugar and refined carbohydrates. Refined carbohydrates may also increase glucose intolerance, which occurs to an extent in normal aging. They recommend increasing the amount of fruits, vegetables, and fiber as substitutes for sugary foods. High-fiber foods are protein-rich and help ease constipation, another common complaint of older people.

According to the American Heart Association, eating less fat and salt, and more fresh fruits, vegetables, and whole grains, can reduce the risks of heart disease, cancer, and obesity. Ongoing research at the USDA Human Nutrition Research Center on Aging at Tufts University has found that cutting back on fat and stocking up on key nutrients can help increase life span.

In *The Anti-Aging Plan*, Dr. Walford describes his experience as a medical adviser to Biosphere 2, the one-year experiment in which he and seven other scientists lived in a massive closed ecological space on the Arizona desert near Tucson which housed

Ray Walford's Anti-Aging Diet

Required Foods. Only nutrient-dense, low-fat foods: vegetables, which are low in fat (especially saturated fats) and cholesterol, and high in fiber; and legumes (various types of beans), which are low in fat and high in complex carbohydrates.

Recommended Foods. Walford highly recommends vegetables and legumes; bran flakes, oat and wheat bran; kombu (a seaweed), nori (sea lettuce); nonfat dry milk; Brewer's yeast; shiitake mushrooms; soybeans; and wheat germ.

Eliminated Foods. Low-nutrient, high-calorie foods which are high in simple carbohydrates such as sugar. Processed and refined foods, such as ice cream, lemon meringue pie, pecan pie, hamburger, doughnuts, and whipped cream should be eliminated.

Restricted Foods: Alcohol. While Walford notes that dieters who consume only 1,800 calories daily may consume 100-200 calories of alcoholic beverages (one to two drinks daily) on his diet, he does not recommend this, although he notes that consuming alcohol is much healthier than consuming sugar. Some domestic beers and wines, he cautions, contain as many as 52 chemical additives and should be avoided. German beer and French wines are the best because they contain no additives.

more than 3,800 carefully selected species of plants and animals. Walford states that "we could only grow food enough to provide each

Antioxidant Recommendations of the Alliance for Aging Research

- **Vitamin C**: 250-1,000 milligrams, or four to 16 times the U.S. RDA of 60 milligrams.

- **Vitamin E**: 100-400 International Units (IUs), the equivalent of three to 13 times the U.S. RDA of 30 IUs.

- **Betacarotene** (a relative of vitamin A found only in plant foods): 17,000-50,000 IUs, or three to 10 times the recommended vitamin A allowance of 5,000 IUs.

member of the experiment with approximately 1,800-calories per day for the first six months." Nevertheless, he believes their 1,800-calorie diet of nutrient-dense vegetables, grains, complex carbohydrates, legumes, and fiber was ideal. Based on his Biosphere studies, Walford states that the Biospherians calorie-limited diet had important anti-aging effects. He relates that all of the volunteers who lived for a year inside Biosphere 2 decreased their average weight by 26 (men) and 15 pounds (women); cholesterol levels dropped by 68 points from average levels of 191 to 125; and blood pressure levels decreased from an average of 110/75 to 90/58 after only three months.

In *The Anti-Aging Plan*, Walford presents a gourmet version of the Biosphere diet which is: 1) generally moderate in protein, with emphasis on vegetable as opposed to animal protein sources; 2) low in fat with an emphasis of "quality" fats; 3) high in fiber; and 4) low in simple sugars but rich in complex car-

bohydrates. The diet provides approximately 75-80% of calories as complex carbohydrates, 10% as saturated fat, and 10-20% as protein.

Vitamin and Mineral Therapies. Although the role of vitamins and minerals in delaying the aging process is still debated by scientists, one public health organization, the Alliance for Aging Research, recommends vitamin supplements to reduce the risk of life-threatening medical disorders such as heart disease and cancer. According to an article in the May 1994 issue of the *Tufts University Diet & Nutrition Letter*, the Washington, D.C.-based health advocacy group now officially advises people to take large doses of vitamins C, E, and betacarotene–known as antioxidant nutrients–to supplement the amounts of these substances received from foods.

The Alliance's recommendations were developed after convening a panel of respected scientific experts from research and academic institutions around the country. The panel reviewed more than 200 studies of antioxidants conducted over the last 20 years, which together suggest that much larger amounts than the U.S. RDAs are necessary to combat free radicals–the highly toxic molecules which are produced as a natural byproduct during the chemical process of oxidation. Oxidation is triggered by environmental pollutants as well as by an individual's own metabolism. If free radicals are left unchecked, they can, according to the Alliance, damage the cells inside various tissues, potentially leading to the development of clogged arteries, various cancers, and other debilitating conditions.

Nutritionist Elizabeth Somer, author of *Nutrition for Women*, believes that the current RDAs for many vitamins and minerals are too low for people over 65. She argues that because it is often difficult for the elderly to purchase or prepare their own foods, they

RDAs and Elizabeth Somer's Optimal Dietary Allowances (ODAs) for the Elderly:

Nutrient	RDA	ODA
Protein	50 grams	62 grams
Vitamin A	4,000 IU	5,000 IU
Vitamin D	200 IU	400 IU
Vitamin E	12 IU	15 IU
Vitamin K	65 mcg	80 mcg
Vitamin C	60 mg	75 mg
Vitamin B_1	1 mg	1.25 mg
Vitamin B_2	1 mg	1.5 mg
Niacin	13 mg	16 mg
Vitamin B_6	1.6 mg	2 mg
Folic Acid	180 mcg	400 mcg
Vitamin B_{12}	2 mcg	2.5 mcg
Calcium	800 mg	1,000-1,500 mg
Phosphorous	800 mg	1,000 mg
Magnesium	280 mg	350 mg
Iron	10 mg	12.5 mg
Selenium	55 mcg	60 mcg
Copper	1.5-3 mg	3 mg
Manganese	2-5 mg	5 mg
Fluoride	1.5-4 mg	4 mg
Chromium	50-200 mcg	200 mcg
Molybdenum	75-250 mcg	250 mcg

should consider a supplement(s) that provides approximately 100-200% of the U.S. RDAs or 125% of the RDAs for vitamin D, the B vitamins, calcium, chromium, copper, iron, magnesium, manganese, selenium, and zinc. Betacarotene, vitamin C, and vitamin E can be consumed in slightly higher amounts, according to Somer, with no known harmful effects, and, in fact, large doses of these nutrients might be beneficial.

Human Growth Factor Supplements. In a landmark medical study published in July 1990 *Gerontologist*, Daniel Ruman and his colleagues at the Medical College of Wisconsin in Milwaukee gave injections of an anti-aging drug called human growth factor

(HGF) to 12 men aged 61-81 three times a week. Like most older adults, these men had been gaining fat. Yet, after six months of growth hormone injections, they had lost 14% of their body fat, gained nearly 9% in muscle mass, and their skin thickness and bone density had increased to levels typical of much younger adults. The men in the study looked noticeably more fit as well. Many of them told the researchers they had never felt better. The changes, according to the researchers, were equivalent in magnitude to a reversal of 10-20 years of aging.

Human growth factor is a potent, naturally occurring chemical produced by the pituitary gland. It is responsible for the beanstalk-like growth of childhood, spurring cell division and the maturation of various organs. Children who cannot produce the hormone grow barely beyond 4 1/2 feet tall. In adults, production of the growth hormone factor tapers off gradually after middle age–which has led some researchers to suggest that a shortage of the hormone late in life accounts for at least some of the physical deterioration that accompanies old age.

Preliminary research cited in *Alternative Medicine: The Definitive Guide* suggests that HGF causes dramatic shifts in the body's metabolic priorities, causing muscle-building proteins to be conserved efficiently while forcing the body to burn fat in order to meet its day-to-day energy needs. The resulting build-up of muscle and loss of fat gradually produce a fitter-looking body, although the benefits may well be more than cosmetic.

In addition, research suggests that growth hormone can reduce the risk of cardiovascular disease, not only because it reduces body fat, but because it also lowers total cholesterol levels and strengthens heart muscle. One study showed that older women who took growth hormone supplements increased their immune system stamina.

The National Institute of Health (NIH) has begun to conduct clinical trials of growth hormone in older adults. Many people who have taken the drug report improvement in their eyesight, noticeably more energy, and a more positive mental outlook. Some report that they sleep better. Others report that sun spots on their hands have disappeared.

Botanical Therapies. Dr. Ki C. Chen reports in the September 1993 issue of the *Journal of Traditional Chinese Medicine* that the Institute of Geriatrics at Xiyuan Hospital in Beijing is currently studying the anti-aging effects of 386 botanical medicines. Specifically, they are investigating the effects of each herb on cell generation, survival times, immunomudulation, improvement of visceral and metabolic functions, and inhibiting infections. Chen reports that preliminary results suggest that ginseng, *Radix astragali, Radix angelicae sinensis*, green tea, and ginkgo biloba compounds appear to delay some of the symptoms of aging and age-related diseases.

As noted in Chapter 5, green tea is now believed to help prevent some cancers because compound catechin and *Camellia sinensis* act as powerful antioxidants which help control the activity of free radicals, the unstable compounds that are implicated in premature aging and a host of diseases. In addition, ginkgo biloba extract has been remarkably effective in treating insufficient blood and oxygen supply in the brain, which is associated with common symptoms of aging such as short-term memory loss, dizziness, headaches, ringing in the ears, hearing and energy loss, and depression. Research in China, summarized by Dr. C. Liu in the February 1992 issue of the *Journal of Ethnopharmacology*, indicates that *Panax ginseng* "strengthens immune function and metabolism, possesses biomodulation action, and has effects on anti-aging and relieving stress."

Summary of Guidelines to Retard the Aging Process

1. **Maintain a Strong Immune System**: As the body ages, a decline in immune system or lymphatic functioning--or the ability to recognize and eliminate damaged or foreign cells--often results in increased susceptibility to many diseases, including infections, cancer, and atherosclerosis, which can be fatal. But even simple forms of exercise can strengthen the immune system and reduce susceptibility to disease.

2. **Maintain a Strong Thymus Gland**. As people grow older, their thymus gland shrinks in size and produces less thymosin, an important hormone which may help regulate the biological aging clock. Zinc, vitamin B_6, and vitamin C have been shown to increase thymic hormone function and cell-mediated immunity.

3. **Maintain Your Heart and Lung Fitness**. As noted, a key physiological change is the loss of heart and lung fitness which usually occurs with aging. By age 70, if a person does not exercise for 20 minutes three times a week, lung capacity can decrease by 40-50% and muscle strength by 20%.

4. **Maintain Low Blood Pressure.** Poor nutrition, a sedentary lifestyle, and an increasing intake of medications generally combine to increase blood pressure in the elderly. Stress reduction therapies such as yoga, meditation, hypnosis, biofeedback, and regular sustained exercise effectively lower blood pressure. The best exercises, according to clinical trials, are those that reduce the level of stress hormones in the bloodstream which constrict the arteries and veins.

5. **Maintain Your Muscle Mass**. As people age, they can lose as much as 10-12% of their muscle mass with no appreciable loss in overall body weight. Maintaining muscular strength is also important for the elderly because muscle weakness can make it difficult or impossible to carry out common daily activities.

6. **Maintain Your Ideal Body Weight**. Older people have a harder time losing weight because their metabolic rate is lower, and they have a higher proportion of body fat. Nevertheless, elderly people can have a level of body fat similar to that of younger people if they remain physically active and follow a nutrient-dense, low-fat diet.

7. **Maintain Normal Blood Glucose Levels**. Exercise and following a low-fat diet will not only help maintain ideal body weight, they also play an important role in improving glucose tolerance and reducing insulin resistance--both significant factors in the development of age-related disorders such as diabetes.

8. **Maintain Your Bone Mass**. Exercise and taking calcium supplements appear to stimulate bone mineralization and help both elderly men and women maintain, and in some cases, increase their bone mass.

9. **Preserve Your Joint Flexibility**. Joint flexibility is also a special concern of the elderly because the aging process gradually diminishes the amount of fluid in the joints. Exercises for rheumatoid arthritis sufferers help maintain cartilage, mineralize underlying bone (increase calcium absorption), strengthen shock-absorbing muscles and ligaments around joints, and increase joint flexibility.

The Chinese regard shiitake mushrooms as a plant which gives eternal youth and longevity. The Shiitake mushroom has been used in Traditional Chinese Medicine (TCM) to increase immune resistance to disease.

Exercise. Exercise, along with diet, also appears to increase longevity. Dr. Ralph Paffenbarger of Stanford University conducted a study of Harvard alumni which found that those whose weekly energy output in walking, stair climbing, and active sports totaled at least 2,000 calories had a 28% reduction in death rates from all causes. Paffenbarger suggests in a 1986 volume of the *New England Journal of Medicine* that this improvement in longevity–due to a reduced risk of major diseases–can be gained by walking or jogging 8-10 miles a week.

The benefits of exercise described in Chapter 6 are especially important for the elderly. Walking, running, swimming, and weight lifting (strength training), for example, make the heart more efficient at delivering blood to the muscles. Exercise relaxes the blood vessels so that blood flows through them more efficiently. It also helps increase cerebral blood flow, bone mass, and bone density, and improves mental functioning, including memory (see discussion of Alzheimer's disease and osteoporosis).

Meditation. In *Perfect Health: The Complete Mind/Body Guide*, Dr. Deepak Chopra cites several studies which suggest that relaxation exercises, especially meditation, help retard the aging process. A 1986 Blue Cross-Blue Shield insurance study, for example, based on 2,000 meditators in Iowa, showed that they were much healthier than the American population as a whole in 17 major areas of mental and physical disease. The meditation group was hospitalized 87% less often than nonmeditators for heart disease and 50% less often for all kinds of tumors. There were equally impressive reductions in disorders of the respiratory system, the digestive tract, and clinical depression.

Chopra also notes that research by Dr. Robert Keith Wallace has conclusively shown that meditation lowers blood pressure, and increases the acuteness of hearing and near-point vision (ability to see objects close-up) in elderly people. All three steadily deteriorate as the body ages, yet Wallace discovered that elderly people who meditated were significantly younger biologically than their chronological age would indicate. For instance, a typical 60-year-old meditating five years or more had the physiology of a 48-year-old.

According to Chopra, Dr. Charles Alexander, a Harvard psychologist, independently verified Wallace's research findings in 1980. Alexander compared three different types of relaxation techniques using 60 patients, all at least 80 years old in three separate retirement homes in the Boston area. He taught stress-management techniques to the first group, Transcendental Meditation (TM) to the second, and creative word games to the third. The meditation group scored highest in improved learning ability, low blood pressure, and mental health. They also reported that they felt happier and younger. When Alexander re-examined his elderly subjects in 1983, one third of the residents had died since he left, including 24% of the participants who had learned relaxation or words games. Among the meditative group, the death rate was zero.

Holistic Treatments for Age-Related Disorders

Alzheimer's and Senile Dementia

Alzheimer's disease–the most common form of dementia among the elderly–is a neurodegenerative disorder in which people progressively lose their ability to memorize, perceive, speak, solve problems, or make judgments. It was first described in 1906 by Alois Alzheimer, a German neurologist who discovered abnormal microscopic structures in the brain tissue of women who died of senile dementia. These structures were found primarily in the hippocampus, the part of the brain related to memory and intellectual function.

According to Alan Rees and Charlene Willey, an estimated 500,000 to 1.5 million older Americans are affected by Alzheimer's, although as many as 2.5 million may suffer from it. Alzheimer's is present in an estimated 25% of Americans who are 85 years or older, although it can occur in middle life as well. The Alzheimer's Association claims that the disease is the fourth leading cause of death in the U.S.

Alzheimer's disease—previously classified as senile dementia—is characterized by irreversible changes in nerve cells in certain vulnerable areas of the brain devoted to mental functions. This results in neurofibrillary tangles (tangles of threadlike nerve filaments in the outer layers), and many small plaques of a tough, fibrous protein called beta-amyloid–both of which indicate serious disruptions in the structural and functional connections between brain cells (neurons).

The disease usually has a gradual onset of symptoms, including difficulty with memory, especially in terms of recent events. Other symptoms include language problems, such as difficulty in finding the correct word when thinking abstractly. There can also be poor or decreased judgment, disorientation, inability to learn new material or concentrate, loss of initiative, changes in mood or behavior, changes in personality, paranoia, and motor activity problems. These symptoms typically cause difficulties in everyday activities. People may get lost in familiar surroundings,

for example, or lose their way to a familiar destination. They may also have difficulty handling money, getting dressed, reading, writing, or using keys or electrical appliances. The overall result is a noticeable decline in personal activity or work performance. How quickly these changes occur varies from person to person, but eventually the disease progresses to the stage where victims are unable to care for themselves.

Symptoms occurring before age 65 are designated presenile dementia of the Alzheimer's type (PDAT); after 65 they are called senile dementia of the Alzheimer's type (SDAT). Current diagnosis of Alzheimer's disease is extremely difficult as the only definitive diagnosis is a post-mortem biopsy of the brain.

No cause has been yet identified for Alzheimer's disease, although it might be infectious (viral), degenerative, or autoimmune. The disease is thought to be associated with a loss of acetycholine which functions as a transmitting agent in the brain, although there is a general reduction in the concentration of all neurotransmitting substances. It is likely that a combination of genetic and environmental factors contribute to its development. For example, Alzheimer's disease has been linked to a genetic abnormality on chromosome 19, one of the 23 pairs of human chromosomes, and the disease tends to run in families.

The fact that older people exhibit the symptoms of Alzheimer's does not necessarily mean they have the disease. For example, many elderly persons develop "benign forgetting" in which they have trouble remembering a word or thought and need a brief period of time to remember it. This and other conditions that produce symptoms similar to Alzheimer's are treatable if detected early enough. It is important for elderly people to get regular medical checkups which can help physicians isolate the common cause of the

Sources of Aluminum

- Foods additives
- Douches
- Antacids
- Buffered Aspirin
- Antidiarrheal Preparations
- Containers
- Shampoos
- Aluminum Cookware

symptoms, including a previous stroke, depression, drug intoxication, thyroid disease, nutritional deficiencies, brain tumors, head trauma, or conditions such as hydrocephalus which involves excessive amounts of water in the brain.

Dementia refers to a general mental deterioration, and in the elderly it is referred to as senile dementia. It can be marked by progressive mental deterioration, loss of recent memory, moodiness and irritability, self-centeredness, and childish behavior. This is often due to Alzheimer's disease, although there are many other causes of senile dementia.

Currently 1.3 million elderly people in the U.S. suffer severe dementia and approximately three million endure mild to moderate dementia–or a total of approximately 15% of all elderly Americans, reports Simeon Margolis. Dementia in the elderly is often a result of insufficient blood and oxygen flow to the brain. Also associated with these insufficiencies are short-term memory loss, vertigo, headaches, ringing in the ears, and depression. Much of this is due to the presence of atherosclerotic cardiovascular disease.

Many cases of dementia are entirely reversible. Michael Murray and Joseph Pizzorno claim that more than 80% of the eld-

erly are deficient in one or more vitamins or minerals which, if levels get too low, may induce dementia. In addition, more than 30% of the elderly use a number of prescription drugs daily. Drugs and drug interactions probably play a greater role in dementia and confused states than is currently realized.

Heavy Metal Poisoning. Research has revealed a strong correlation between Alzheimer's disease and excessive amounts of aluminum concentrated in the brain. Autopsies of victims of Alzheimer's disease reveal excessive amounts of aluminum and silicon in the brain. The hippocampus area and cerebral cortex of AD patients contained not only excess amounts of aluminum, but also of bromine, calcium, silicon, and sulfur. In addition, a deficiency of boron, potassium, selenium, vitamin B12, and zinc was found. These results may suggest that excessive amounts of aluminum in the diet, combined with a lack of several essential minerals, directly or indirectly predispose one to Alzheimer's disease. Although this information offers hope that Alzheimer's disease might some day be prevented, science does not yet know what can be done to allay the mental deterioration.

Nutritional Therapies. Although Alzheimer's disease is not yet curable or reversible, there are ways to alleviate symptoms and prevent or delay its onset. Diet is extremely important for Alzheimer's patients because many elderly tend to be undernourished, have food sensitivities, eat non-nutritious, easy-to-prepare foods–and have digestion and elimination problems due to these or other factors. Dr. William Crook of Jackson, Tennessee, as reported in *Alternative Medicine: The Definitive Guide*, has noted that many Alzheimer's patients have an overgrowth of the yeast *Candida albicans* in their gastrointestinal tract which often contributes to food allergies and poor

Drugs Associated with a Higher Incidence of Alzheimer's

According to the *Physician's Desk Reference,* the following drugs have been linked with side effects of mental confusion which are typical of AD. Statistics refer to the percentage of individuals affected.

Anestacon Solution (among most common)

Atrofen Tablets (1-11%)

Clozaril Tablets (3%)

Desyrel and Desyrel Dividose (5%)

Dilantin Infatabs, Kapseals, Parenteral (among most common)

Dilantin-30 Pediatric/Dilantin-125 Suspension, Dilantin with Phenobarbital Kapseals (among most common)

Duragesic Transdermal System (10% or more)

Eldepryl Tablets (3 of 49 patients)

Foscavir Injection (more than 5%)

Hylorel Tablets (14.8%)

IFEX (among most common)

Intron A (up to 12%)

Lioresal Tablets (1-11%)

Marplan Tablets (among most frequent)

Nipent for Injection (3-10%)

Permax Tablets (11.1%)

Roferon-A Injection (8%)

Sinemet CR Tablets (3.7%)

Stadol Injectable, NS Nasal Spray (3-9%)

Tonocard Tablets (2.1-11.2%)

Wellbutrin Tablets (8.4%)

Xanax Tablets (9.9-10.4%)

Xylocaine Injections, with Epinephrine Injections (among most common)

nutrient absorption. The inability to absorb nutrients needed for normal cardiovascular and brain functioning can result in depression, anemia and symptoms of dementia. Dr. Crook urges AD patients to follow a sugar-free diet, avoid antibiotic drugs, and consume adequate amounts of acidophilus (found in some yogurts) to restore their intestinal flora.

Balch and Balch also believe that nutritional factors can prevent or delay the onset of common symptoms such as memory loss associated with Alzheimer's disease and senile dementia. For example, patients with Alzheimer's disease tend to have lower body weight despite a high energy intake. They stress the importance of the B vitamins in maintaining memory, especially choline and B_6, and recommend frequent consumption of whole grains, tofu, farm eggs, legumes, wheat germ, soy beans, fish, brewer's yeast, nuts, millet, brown rice, and raw foods.

Vitamin and Mineral Therapies. Many nutritional deficiencies have been tentatively linked to Alzheimer's disease, including folic acid, niacin (vitamin B_3), thiamine (vitamin B_1), vitamins B_6 and B_{12}, vitamin C, vitamin D, vitamin E, magnesium, selenium, zinc, choline, L-glutamine, and lethicin.

Vitamins C and E, carotenes, flavonoids, zinc, and selenium are antioxidants which may neutralize the free radical-related processes thought by many to be involved in the development of Alzheimer's disease. Free radical damage is particularly detrimental to the immune system. Zinc supplements may help maintain the health of the immune system, and Murray and Pizzorno suggest that zinc picolinate is the best form of zinc supplementation for a majority of the elderly. Zinc may also play a role in normalizing cell replication, as zinc contains most of the enzymes involved in DNA replication and repair.

Dr. Abraham Hoffer, former president of the Canadian Schizophrenia Foundation, suggests in *Alternative Medicine: The Definitive Guide* that vitamin B_{12} deficiency is significantly common in Alzheimer's patients. There is often mistaken reliance on the presence of anemia to diagnose vitamin B_{12} or folic acid deficiency. However, deficiencies of either vitamin are associated with mental symptoms, including dementia, long before changes occur in the blood. In addition, changes in the blood may never take place, despite the fact that severe deficiencies are occurring in other tissues. Supplementation of B_{12} and/or folic acid may significantly improve symptoms in some patients, but there is usually little improvement for the majority.

Some patients with Alzheimer's have cardiovascular disorders which prevent enough blood and oxygen from reaching their brains. Vitamin and mineral therapies such as those used by Dr. Hoffer may improve mental alertness and memory. He combines niacin, which improves circulation and lowers cholesterol levels, with large doses of vitamins C and E. He also recommends folic acid because 40% of all senile patients are deficient in this B vitamin. Recently he has begun adding low daily doses of aspirin, which he regards as safe and helpful in preventing the platelets from sticking to each other—thus improving circulation in the brain.

As reported by M. Imagawa in the September 1992 issue of *Lancet,* studies in Japan have confirmed that daily supplements of vitamin B_6, co-enzyme Q-10, and iron returned some Alzheimer's-diagnosed patients to "normal mental capacity." In another study cited in *Alternative Medicine: The Definitive Guide,* Alzheimer's patients who took a daily regimen of evening primrose oil, zinc, and selenium showed significant improvements in alertness, mood, and mental ability.

Botanical Medicines. Ginkgo biloba has been shown to improve brain circulation and increase mental capacity in several clinical trials, according to M. Allard, writing in the September 1986 issue of *Presse Medicale.* In one clinical trial involving 112 geriatric patients diagnosed with cerebral vascular insufficiency, the administration of 120 milligrams per day of ginkgo biloba extract (GBE) resulted in a statistically significant regression of the major symptoms. As reported by Dr. G. Rai in a 1991 issue of *Current Medical Research & Opinion*, the regression of these symptoms suggests that a reduced blood and oxygen supply to the brain may be the major cause of the so-called age-related cerebral disorders (including senility), rather than a true degenerative process of nerve tissue. It appears that ginkgo biloba extract, by increasing blood flow to the brain, increases oxygen and glucose utilization, and offers relief from these presumed side effects of aging. "The results show," Rai concluded, "that GBE may be of great benefit in many cases of senility, including Alzheimer's disease." Balch and Balch suggest that the herbs blue cohosh and anise may also be effective, in combination with ginkgo biloba, in improving brain functioning by increasing the flow of oxygen to the brain.

Chelation Therapy. Dr. H. Casdorph, writing in *A Textbook on EDTA Chelation Therapy*, cites a number of studies which suggest that chelation therapy can improve the condition of some Alzheimer's patients. The therapy uses chelating agents such as EDTA (ethylenediaminetetraacetic acid), administered intravenously, to help restore normal circulation in the brain. EDTA therapy is believed to remove the calcium content of plaque which has formed in an Alzheimer patient's brain arterials. Chelation therapy, according to Casdorph, may also be beneficial for patients with senile dementia by removing aluminum, mercury, and other heavy metals from the body.

A new chelation therapy described by Dr. Charles Farr, co-founder of the American Board of Chelation Therapy, in *Alternative Medicine: The Definitive Guide* may be helpful for senile dementia. For patients whom he has diagnosed as having senile dementia due to atherosclerosis (hardening of the brain's arteries), he recommends 10-15 chelation treatments, alternating with intravenous hydrogen peroxide, in order to remove the plaque.

Estrogen Therapy. According to a University of Southern California study, reported in the March 8, 1994 edition of *The New York Times*, postmenopausal women who take estrogen replacement therapy (ERT) to prevent bone loss and heart disease are also less likely to develop Alzheimer's disease. And if they do develop the disease, their symptoms are less severe than those experienced by women who do not take ERT. Researchers examined 2,418 women over a period of 11 years, and found that those taking estrogen were 40% less likely to develop Alzheimer's.

The research suggests that estrogen plays an important role in maintaining connections between neurons (brain cells). When estrogen levels drop sharply upon menopause, the complexity of connections could slowly diminish, perhaps making neurons more likely to degenerate and die. In contrast, because males do not go through menopause and therefore retain higher levels of their sex hormone (testosterone), much of which is converted into estrogen in the brain, far fewer suffer from Alzheimer's.

Tips to Improve the Memory of Alzheimer's Patients

The most common causes of ordinary memory troubles include anxiety, fatigue, stress, grief, and mild depression. Using your memory–reading, playing chess, doing crossword puzzles, playing bridge–will help keep your memory fit. Here are specific tips:

- Make mental pictures of task, names, numbers, thoughts, words, or whatever it is that you want to remember.

- Talk about it; working over material in a conversation helps implant it in your memory.

- Eliminate distractions, background noise, and other things competing for your attention when trying to memorize something.

- Don't waste your attentiveness trying to remember things a mere piece of paper can retain. Keep lists and a daily calendar.

- Take occasional breaks to rest and refresh your mind, especially when trying to learn something new

Removing Mercury Dental Fillings. In *It's All in Your Head*, dentist Hal Huggins describes how he treated an elderly woman with advanced AD who hadn't spoken for 14 years. Huggins, director of the Huggins Diagnostic Center in Colorado Springs, Colorado, began removing all the woman's mercury dental fillings. On the twelfth day of the 14-day program, the woman completely recovered her memory and mental functioning.

Traditional Chinese Medicine. Dr. Maoshing Ni, vice president of Yo San University of Traditional Chinese Medicine in Santa Monica, California, reports in *Alternative Medicine: The Definitive Guide* that he has used a combination of acupuncture with Chinese herbs, nutrition, and exercise to halt the advance of Alzheimer's disease. He often urges patients to practice qi gong, a form of martial arts which restores deep breathing and improves cardiovascular functioning. Ni believes that because it combines concentration and visualization, gi qong balances the brain and body in very subtle ways which delay the development of hardening of the arteries in the brain.

Ayurvedic Medicine. Dr. Sodhi, director of the American School of Ayurvedic Sciences in Bellevue, Washington, as cited in *Alternative Medicine: The Definitive Guide*, has successfully treated Alzheimer's and senile dementia using a combination of homeopathic and Ayurvedic therapies. Although each patient's condition is caused by a unique combination of factors, he claims that more than 80% have environmental toxicities which must be eliminated first. He prescribes herbs which cleanse the liver, along with triphala, a combination of three herbs, and gotu kola, which increases brain cell functioning. For cerebral functioning, he prescribes ginkgo biloba or macunabrure along with vitamin B_1 and B_3 supplements, as long as patients do not have liver disorders.

Lifestyle Changes. Toxins such as food and tap water chemicals, carbon monoxide, diesel fumes, solvents, aerosol spray, and industrial chemicals can cause symptoms of brain dysfunctions which may lead to an inaccurate diagnosis of Alzheimer's or senile dementia. Avoiding external toxins and eliminating internal toxins by using the detoxification programs outlined in this book can be helpful in preventing the onset of these symptoms.

Tom Warren, in his book *Beating Alzheimer's*, describes his own poignant case in which he had his amalgam fillings removed, began an organic, whole foods diet (to eliminate allergic foods), took daily supplements of vitamin B_3, began a regular exercise regime, and practiced complete avoidance of household chemical pollutants. Four years after beginning this program, and 11 years after being diagnosed with Alzheimer's, Warren was able to return to work.

Osteoporosis

According to the June 1994 issue of the *Tufts University Diet & Nutrition Letter*, 24 million Americans, 80% of them women, suffer from osteoporosis, a progressive condition in which bones lose mass and become extremely brittleand prone to injury. Osteoporosis affects more women than heart disease, stroke, diabetes, breast cancer, or arthritis. It results in 1.5 million bone fractures annually, with yearly health care expenses exceeding $10 billion. And if steps are not taken to reduce the incidence of the disease, its prevalence is expected to double in the U.S. in just 25 years due to the aging of the population, with annual health care costs related to osteoporosis reaching $30 billion.

Osteoporosis begins when the body cannot make new bone fast enough to replace bone loss. Both men and women lose some bone mass as they age, but the rate of loss is much slower in men (who have denser bones to begin with) than in women, and osteoporosis is rarely a problem. Conversely, according to Kurt Butler and Lynn Rayner, women who live to the age of 80 usually lose a third to two-thirds of their entire skeletons and up to six inches of their height.

The process of bone loss typically begins in a woman's mid-30s, some 10-15 years before the onset of menopause, at a rate of

0.5-1% a year. This loss increases to 2-5% in the first 10 years following menopause, and then tapers off to about 1% per year. In the decade after menopause, women typically lose 5-10% of the bone-sustaining minerals in their spines alone. As a result, according to the National Osteoporosis Foundation, one-third of American women over 65 suffer spinal fractures and 15% break their hips because of osteoporosis.

Causes of Osteoporosis

Estrogen deficiency, according to Balch and Balch, is the leading cause of osteoporosis in menopausal females. Other causes include the decreasing ability to absorb sufficient amounts of calcium through the intestines, a calcium-phosphorous imbalance, lack of exercise, jaundice, gastrectomy, and lactose intolerance. Smoking, excessive use of alcohol, exposure to the toxic chemical cadmium, and taking certain prescription drugs have also been linked to osteoporosis, as has excessive consumption of sugar (which depletes the body of phosphorous), soft drinks (which upset the calcium/phosphorous balance required by the body), and caffeine (which reduces blood-calcium levels).

Nutritional Therapies. Many nutritionists and physicians believe that osteoporosis can be prevented by improved nutrition, calcium supplements, and implementation of lifestyles which include regular exercise and minimal use of alcohol and tobacco. Good sources of calcium include cheese, flounder, shrimp, clams, oysters, molasses, nuts and seeds, oats, seaweed, soybeans and soybean products such as tofu, wheat germ and whole wheat products, and yogurt. Kale, turnip, and dandelion greens, leafy green vegetables, and broccoli are excellent vegetable sources. Sardines and salmon contain high amounts of calcium as well. Balch and Balch recommend that cigarette smoking and alcohol be avoided

(as both interfere with estrogen's bone protecting effect), along with phosphate-containing drinks, high-protein animal foods (which deplete the body of calcium), and citrus fruits and tomatoes which may inhibit calcium absorption.

Butler and Rayner also counsel women to obtain adequate calcium and vitamin D well before their postmenopausal years, and to avoid too much phosphorous or protein. They recommend eating low-fat dairy products, soy products, sardines, salmon, beans, leafy greens, and a variety of vegetables.

Vitamin and Mineral Therapies. According to Balch and Balch, a diet that is adequate in protein, calcium, magnesium, phosphorus, and vitamins C and D can both prevent and treat osteoporosis. Since dietary calcium is so important, elderly people who have difficulty absorbing sufficient amounts of calcium may need to take calcium injections. Silica tablets contain high amounts of calcium in a form that is easily absorbed.

A July/August 1993 article in *Natural Health* entitled "Strong Bones" counsels women to consider supplemental calcium by their early 40s before the onset of menopause, particularly calcium citrate, calcium carbonate, or calcium lactate (forms that are easily absorbed by the body). Magnesium, another mineral essential for bone growth, can be found in nuts, seeds, fish, seafood, whole grains, legumes, and dark green leafy vegetables. In addition to calcium and magnesium, the body needs vitamin D to build bones. However, vitamin D is found in significant amounts in only a few foods–primarily egg yolks, fortified milk, butter, and fish liver oils. The article suggests that women consult a health practitioner to evaluate whether taking calcium, magnesium, or vitamin B supplements is advisable.

Sources of Dietary Calcium for Osteoporosis

Food	Serving	Calcium (Mg)
Nonfat plain yogurt	8 Ounces	452
Low-fat plain yogurt	8 Ounces	415
Sardines with bones	5 Ounces	372
Canned salmon with bones	3 1/2 Ounces	351
Part-skim ricotta cheese	1/2 Cup	336
Sesame seeds	1/2 Cup	331
Skim milk	8 Ounces	302
Romano cheese	1 Ounce	296
Whole milk	8 Ounces	291
Buttermilk	8 Ounces	285
Low-fat chocolate milk	8 Ounces	287
Swiss cheese	1 Ounce	272
Tofu set with calcium	1/2 Cup	258
Goat cheese (hard)	1 Ounce	254
Mackerel, canned	5 Ounces	250
Almonds	4 Ounces	250
Tahini (sesame butter)	1/4 Cup	250
Baked beans or pork and beans	2 Cups	250
Broccoli	1 1/2 Cups	250
Turnip greens	1 1/2 Cups	250
Bok choy	2 1/2 Cups	250
Dandelion greens	2 Cups	250
Kale	3 Cups	250
Mustard greens	3 Cups	250
Blackstrap molasses	2 Tablespoons	250
Orange juice (calcium-fortified)	8 Ounces	240
Cheddar cheese	1 Ounce	204
Cereal (calcium-fortified)	1 Cup	200
Mozzarella cheese (part-skim)	1 Ounce	183
Collards	1/2 Cup cooked	179
Okra (cooked)	1 Cup	176

Sources of Dietary Calcium for Osteoporosis (continued)

Food	Serving	Calcium (Mg)
American cheese	1 Ounce	174
Bread (calcium-fortified)	2 Slices	160
Feta cheese	1 Ounce	140
Parmesan cheese	2 Tablespoons	138
Spirulina	2 Tablespoons	131
Yams	2 Tablespoons	129
Vitamin D		**IU**
Sardines	3 1/2 Ounces	1,150
Mackerel, fresh	3 1/2 Ounces	1,100
Salmon, fresh	3 1/2 Ounces	550
Cod liver oil	1 Teaspoon	400
Herring, fresh	3 1/2 Ounces	315
Shrimp	3 1/2 Ounces	150
Milk, fortified	1 Cup	100
Vitamin K		**Mcg**
Turnip greens	2/3 Cup	650
Green peas	1/2 Cup	225
Broccoli	2/3 Cup	200
Lettuce	2 Cups	129
Cabbage	2/3 Cup	125

Skim Milk. Women of all ages, especially those at risk of osteoporosis, should consume high daily levels of vitamin D and calcium. The most beneficial source is fortified skim milk because it contains the most readily absorbable type of calcium along with all the essential amino acids and special protein substances that promote bone and muscle growth. Dr. George Blackburn advises everyone (except infants) to consume at least two 8-ounce servings of dairy products daily. Unfortunately, most Americans consume less than half this amount. Skim milk contains virtually no fat and a minimum of calories, and people who drink it tend to consume fewer caffeine-containing beverages such as coffee and tea, fewer sugary soft drinks, fewer sugary calorie-laden foods and juices, and less fat-heavy whole milk and other whole-milk dairy products. By switching to skim milk exclusively, Blackburn suggests that people can reduce their risk of osteoporosis and decrease their total fat intake to 25% of calories (most Americans currently consume

Dietary Guidelines to Prevent and Reverse Osteoporosis

1. Consume at least 1,500 milligrams of calcium daily, preferably in highly absorbable calcium-rich foods.

2. Carefully balance your family's daily calcium intake with phosphorus, manganese, magnesium, folic acid, zinc, silicon, and vitamin K.

3. Avoid consuming excessive amounts of daily fat, salt, and sugar which restrict calcium uptake.

4. Consume minimum amounts of coffee and tea, and be sure to add milk to your beverage.

5. Take vitamin and mineral supplements if you do not consume enough calcium or other nutrients each day to prevent osteoporosis.

6. Avoid taking more than 500 milligrams of calcium at one time. Calcium is best absorbed if taken in small amounts throughout the day. Avoid taking calcium with high-fiber meals or with bulk-forming laxatives as fiber can interfere with absorption.

7. Drink six to eight glasses of fluid a day.

8. Do not take an iron supplement at the same time as a calcium tablet because calcium can block iron absorption.

9. Excessive calcium intake can increase the likelihood of developing kidney stones. People with a history of kidney problems should consult their doctor before starting high-calcium supplementation. Most people can consume more than 2,000 milligrams daily without risking complications.

37% of daily calories from fat). Skim milk may also lower your cholesterol and blood pressure levels.

Soybean milk is also excellent for increasing bone mineral density (BMD) and mechanical bone strength. Several Japanese studies cited by Dr. N. Omihave shown that peptides in soybean milk accelerate intestinal calcium absorption.

Estrogen Replacement Therapy. Kurt Butler and Lynn Rayner describe taking daily estrogen and calcium supplements as an effective and safe treatment that, while it cannot rebuild bone already lost, can greatly decrease the incidence of fractures and slow further bone loss. They claim that small doses of estrogen substantially decrease the risk of breast cancer, and report that some studies suggest ERT also greatly decreases the incidence of heart attacks in postmenopausal women, perhaps by increasing HDL levels. A *New England Journal of Medicine* study reported in the November 30, 1993 issue of *Your Health* indicates women should take estrogen for up to seven years after menopause to derive long-term protection from brittle bones.

Botanical Therapies. One option for women who cannot take estrogen (those with congenital heart failure or migraines, for example) is to take plant estrogen (or "phytoestrogens"). Phytoestrogens such as soybeans, for example, may réduce osteoporosis without risking breast or uterine cancer. No clinical studies on the effectiveness of phytoestrogens have been reported, however.

Calcitonin. Calcitonin, a hormone isolated from salmon, has demonstrated remarkable effects in clinical studies and holds much promise in treating severe osteoporosis. Small amounts of calcitonin occur naturally in the body, as it is a hormone produced by the thyroid gland. It slows bone breakdown and is sold by prescription in synthetic form. According to Murray and Pizzorno, calcitonin acts to decrease serum calcium levels by increasing the activity of osteoblasts, cells that build bone. Low calcitonin levels are typically found in women with postmenopausal osteoporosis, and calcitonin replacement may prevent and reverse bone loss. Calcitonin was approved by the FDA for treating osteoporosis in 1984.

Calcitonin is currently the only pharmaceutical alternative to estrogen in the U.S. According to its manufacturers, Switzerland's Sandoz Ltd. and France's Poulenc S.A., calcitonin has not been associated with any cancer risks or heart benefits. It is, however, more expensive than estrogen, and must be taken every other day. Usually injected, patients normally take 1,500 milligrams of calcium and 400 I.U. per day of vitamin D during the treatment. The effectiveness of a nasal-spray form of calcitonin is currently being evaluated by the FDA.

Natural Progesterone (Wild Yams). According to Dr. John Lee, quoted in *Alternative Medicine: The Definitive Guide,* natural progesterone found in wild yams may be a safer and a more effective substitute for synthetic progesterone (progestin), which is currently used in combination with estrogen to treat osteoporosis. Progestin, he claims, does not keep sodium and water from moving into the cells as effectively, which

Daily Recommendations for Vitamin and Mineral Supplements

Vitamins:
- Vitamin B$_6$ — 5 to 50 mg
- Folic acid — 0.4 to 5 mg
- Vitamin C — 100 to 1,000 mg
- Vitamin D — 100 to 400 units
- Vitamin K — 100 to 500 micrograms

Minerals:
- Calcium — 400 to 1,200 mg
- Magnesium — 200 to 600 mg
- Zinc — 10 to 30 mg
- Copper — 1 to 2 mg
- Manganese — 5 to 20 mg
- Boron — 1 to 3 mg
- Silicon — 1 to 2 mg
- Strontium — 0.5 to 3 mg

can cause water retention and hypertension. Lee reports that a combined treatment program of diet, nutritional supplements and natural transdermal (absorbed through the skin), progesterone is virtually 100% successful in building bone mass.

According to Lee, the average increase in bone mass is 15% in women with postmenopausal osteoporosis. He suggests that both estrogen and natural progesterone supplements be taken together under the supervision of a physician or gynecologist. The Department of Obstetrics and Gynecology at Vanderbilt University now prescribes natural progesterone for both premenstrual syndrome and menopausal hormone replacement therapy.

Homeopathic Therapies. According to *Alternative Medicine: The Definitive Guide*, the following primary homeopathic constitutional remedies have been proven effective in reliving osteoporosis: Calcarea carbonica and Calcarea phosphorica, Calcarea fluorica, Carcinosin, Bufo, Silicea, and a complex formula called Vermiculate.

Traditional Chinese Medicine (TCM). Many people in China, once they turn 50, take low-dose herbal formulas that boost kidney energy. Two common formulas are "Two Immortals" (Er Sian Tang) and "Eight Flavor Rehmannia" (Shai Di Huang). American TCM practitioners have effectively treated osteoporosis with acupuncture and three botanicals: euconmia, dipsaci, and dong quai. According to *Alternative Medicine: The Definitive Guide*, this treatment can be very effective. After six weeks of treatment, bone mass is increased and estrogen and progesterone levels are stabilized.

Ayurvedic Medicine. A traditional Ayurvedic formula for osteoporosis detailed in *Alternative Medicine: The Definitive Guide* consists of one part sesame seeds, one-half part shatavari (Ayurvedic herb), and one-half part ginger with raw sugar added to taste. The Ayurvedic herb amla is also recommended for osteoporosis.

Exercise. There is strong evidence that exercise helps prevent osteoporosis. Bone is a fluid tissue that is constantly being broken and reformed throughout a person's lifetime. Until the age of 35, more bone is deposited than removed, leading to a net gain in bulk and strength. After 35, however, the balance gradually begins to reverse, and often leads to osteoporosis and subsequent fractures. This trend becomes particularly marked in postmenstrual women who lose the protective effect of estrogen against bone loss.

The best forms of exercise are those that increase calcium absorption and bone mass. Bones are living tissue that maintain their strength by having the muscles to which they are attached pull on them. As Jane Brody explains in the July 14, 1993 edition of *The New York Times*, this produces piezoelectricity, a force that results in bone deposition at the stress points. Exercise now appears to stimulate bone mineralization, particularly activities such as weight lifting that involve high loads and high stresses. Brody maintains that such activities (including strength training or working out on resistance machines) are more effective at building bone than activities which involve many repetitive cycles such as running, walking, or swimming.

Even though women who exercise regularly tend to have lower estrogen levels and be thinner (two states associated with higher risk for osteoporosis), the effect of exercise more than compensates for those factors, giving these women denser and stronger bones than women who do not exercise regularly. A 1987 study at the Queen Elizabeth Hospital in Toronto, Ontario, cited by Brody compared bone densities of sedentary women between the ages of 50 and 62 with those of women who engaged in aerobic exercise and others who did both aerobic and strengthening exercises. The active women of both groups experienced similar significant gains in bone mass, while the sedentary women showed a loss.

Brody goes on to state that after puberty, the only way women can maintain their bone mass is to continually exercise. Nancy Lane, a rheumatologist at the University of California in San Francisco, has extensively researched the bone density of older women runners. She suggests that exercise can slow the rate of bone loss during menopause and, by increasing a person's stability, strength, flexibility, and neuromuscular function, help decrease the likelihood of bone-breaking falls.

Brody cites several studies which confirm that exercise can help maintain and even increase bone density. For example, a large study by researchers in Durham, North Carolina, found that women aged 40-54 who were physically active had significantly higher bone mineral density in their spines and arms than a comparable group of nonexercisers. At the University of Missouri, a one-year study among previously sedentary women who had recently experienced menopause found that both low-impact and high-impact exercise three times a week for 20 minutes helped maintain their spinal bone. Another study of women in their 50s found that both brisk walking and aerobic dancing resulted in increased bone size and strength.

A study published in the *New England Journal of Medicine*, as reported in the June 23, 1994 edition of the *New York Times*, confirmed that even among the very old, it is never too late to exercise. The study involved 100 male and female nursing home residents with an average age of 87, although a third were in their 90s. Many suffered from a variety of medical disorders including dementia, arthritis, lung disease and high blood pressure. Participants were randomly assigned either to take part in ordinary nursing home activities, or to work out vigorously for 45 minutes three times a week. Those assigned to work out used exercise machines to strengthen their thighs and knees. The exercising residents increased their walking speed by 12% and their ability to climb stairs by 28%. Four who had needed walkers to get around became able to walk with just a cane. The people who worked out were also less depressed and more likely to take part in nursing home activities.

Together these studies indicate that elderly women can clearly maintain bone mass, and that by adopting other good health habits as well, they can forestall or prevent the damaging effects of osteoporosis.

Summary

As the ability to extend life through new technologies grows, so will the possibilities of improving the lifelong health of the elderly. New insights in molecular genetics and virology may allow most people to maintain full mental functions throughout their life span. Hormone replacement therapies may also prove effective in extending the life span and reducing the incidence of chronic generative diseases. Natural substances within the body may be discovered that will preserve the strength of the immune system and slow the aging process. Once the loss of bone mass and bone density can be delayed, frailty, imbalance, and walking disorders, now characteristic of many elderly persons, could be prevented. With more empirical studies of how nutritional, botanical, and psychoimmunological factors cause heart attacks and strokes, new gene-spliced drugs will help detect these disorders.

Resources

References

Adams, G. "Physiological Effects of Exercise Training Regimen upon Women Aged 51 to 79." *Journal of Gerontology* (1973): 50-55.

Allard, M. "Treatment of the Disorders of Aging with Ginkgo Biloba Extract: Pharmacology to Clinical Medicine." *Presse Medicale* (September 1986): 1540-45.

Allison, M. "Improving the Odds: Aging and Exercise." *Harvard Health Letter* (February 1991): 4.

Balch, James F., and Phyllis Balch. *Prescription for Nutritional Healing.* Long Island, NY: Avery Publishing, 1993.

"The Bare-Bones Facts for Avoiding Osteoporosis." *Tufts University Diet & Nutrition Letter* (June 1994): 3-6.

Blackburn, George. "Shake down Your Cholesterol and Blood Pressure (Skim Milk)." *Prevention* (August 1992): 101.

Brody, Jane. "Personal Health." *The New York Times* (July 14, 1993): B6.

The Burton Goldberg Group. *Alternative Medicine: The Definitive Guide.* Payallup, WA: Future Medicine Publishing, Inc., 1993.

Butler, Kurt, and Lynn Rayner. *The Best Medicine: The Complete Health and Preventive Medicine Handbook.* San Francisco: Harper & Row Publishers, 1985.

Casdorph, H. "EDTA Chelation Therapy: Efficacy in Brain Disorders," in E. Cranston's *A Textbook on EDTA Chelation Therapy.* New York: Human Sciences Press, 1989, pp. 131-53.

Chen, Li C. "Recent Advances in Studies on Traditional Chinese Anti-Aging Material Medica." *Journal of Traditional Chinese Medicine* (September 1993): 223-26.

Chopra, Deepak. *Perfect Health: The Complete Mind/Body Guide.* New York: Harmony Books, 1991

Doyne, E. "Running versus Weight Lifting in the Treatment of Depression." *Journal of Consultative Clinical Psychology* (1987): 748-55.

Edlin, Gordon, and Eric Golanty. *Health and Wellness.* Boston: Jones and Barlett Publishers, 1992.

"Estrogen Wards Off Alzheimer's." *Your Health* (January 11, 1994): 49.

"Exercise Found to Benefit Even the Very Old." *The New York Times* (June 23, 1994): A12.

Forever Young: New Medical Evidence of Age Reversal. Emmaus, PA: Rodale Press, Inc., 1988.

Gaby, Alan. *Preventing and Reversing Osteoporosis.* Rocklin, CA: Prima Publishing, 1994.

Gittleman, Ann Louise. "A Guide to Sturdy Bones." *Natural Health* (January/February 1994): 56-57.

Guiton, Arthur. *Textbook of Medical Physiology.* Philadelphia, PA: Harcourt Brace Jovanovich, 1991.

Hendler, Sheldon. *The Complete Guide to Anti-Aging Nutrients* . New York: Simon and Schuster, 1985.

Heyden, S. "Can Regular Exercise Prolong Life Expectancy?" *Sports Medicine* 6 (1988): 63-71.

Hoeger, W. "Effect of Low-Impact Aerobic Dance on the Functional Fitness of Elderly Women." *Gerontologist* 3 (1990): 189-92.

"How Risky Is Physical Exercise?" *Harvard Health Letter* (May 1994): 13.

Huggins, Hal. *It's All in Your Head.* New York: Basic Books, 1992.

Imagawa, M. "Coenzyme Q10, Iron and Vitamin B6 in Genetically Confirmed Alzheimer's Disease." *Lancet* (September 1992): 671.

Johnsgard, Keith. *The Exercise Prescription for Depression and Anxiety.* New York: Plenum Publishing, 1989.

Langreth, Robert. "Living to Be 150." *Your Health* (May 31, 1994): 33-38.

Lindner, Lawrence. "Smart Eaters Stay Healthier, Live Longer, Look Younger." *Fitness* (July/August 1993): 71.

Margolis, Simeon, and Hamilton Moses III. *The Johns Hopkins Medical Handbook.* New York: Medletter Associates, Inc., 1992.

Marti, James. *Consumer's Guide to Diets and Nutrition.* Boston: Houghton Mifflin Inc., 1997.

Morey, M.C. "Evaluation of a Supervised Exercise Program in a Geriatric Population." *Journal of the American Geriatric Society* 3 (1993): 348-54.

Murray, Michael, and Joseph Pizzorno. *Encyclopedia of Natural Medicine.* Rocklin, CA: Prima Publishing, 1991.

Nbiskane, L. "Resting Energy Expenditure in Relation to Energy Intake in Patients with Alzheimer's Disease." *Age & Aging* (March 1993):132-37.

Nehlsen-Cannarella, S. "The Effects of Moderate Exercise on Immune Response." *Medical Science Sports Exercise* (1991): 64-70.

Nieman, David. *Fitness and Sports Medicine: An Introduction.* Palo Alto, CA: Bull Publishing, 1990.

——. *Fitness & Your Health.* Palo Alto, CA: Bull Publishing Company, 1993.

Norris, R. "The Effects of Aerobic and Anaerobic Training on Fitness, Blood Pressure and Psychological Stress and Well-Being." *Journal of Psychosomatic Research* (1990): 367-75.

Omi, N. "Evaluation of the Effect of Soybean Milk and Soybean Milk Peptide on Bone Metabolism." *Journal of Nutritional Science & Vitaminology* (April 1994): 201-11.

Ornish, Dean. *Dr. Dean Ornish's Program for Reversing Heart Disease.* New York: Random House, 1990.

"Osteoporosis." *Your Health* (November 30, 1993): 45.

Paffenbarger, Ralph S. "Physical Activity, All-Cause Mortality and Longevity of College Alumni." *New England Journal of Medicine* 314 (1986): 605-13.

Peck, W.A. "Research Directions in Osteoporosis." *American Journal of Medicine* 84 (1988): 275-82.

"Progress in the War Against Heart Attacks." *Harvard Health Letter* (April 1994): 1-5.

Rai, G. "A Soluble-Blind, Placebo-Controlled Study of Ginkgo Biloba Extract ("Tanakan") in Elderly Outpatients with Mild to Moderate Memory Impairment." *Current Medical Research & Opinion* 6 (1991): 350-55.

Rees, Alan, and Charlene Willey. *Personal Health Reporter.* Detroit, MI: Gale Research Inc., 1993.

Schatz, Mary. *A Doctor's Gentle Yoga Program for Back and Neck Pain Relief.* Berkeley, CA: Rodmell Publishers, 1992.

Sheppard R.J. "The Scientific Basis of Exercise Prescribing for the Very Old." *JAMA* 314 (1990): 3862-70.

Somer, Elizabeth. *Nutrition for Women.* New York: Simon & Schuster. 1994.

Stamford B. "Exercise and the Elderly." *Sport Science Review* 16 (1988). 341-79.

Stevenson, J. "A Comparison of Land and Water Exercise Programs for Older Individuals." *Medical Science Sports Exercise* 6 (1988): 537.

"Strong Bones." *Natural Health* (July/August 1993): 31-32.

"To Take Antioxidant Pills or Not? The Debate Heats Up." *Tufts University Diet & Nutrition Letter* (May 1994): 3-5.

Walford, Roy. *Maximum Life Span.* New York: W.W. Norton & Company, Inc., 1983.

Warren, Tom. *Beating Alzheimer's.* Garden City Park, NY: Avery Publishing, 1991.

"You Can Prevent Many of the So-Called By-Products of Aging—Or Even Reverse Them—By Doing One Thing: Weight Lifting." *Healthy Woman* (Winter 1993): 42-43.

Organizations

Alzheimer's Association.
70 East Lake Street, Chicago, IL 60601.

Alzheimer's Disease Education and Referral Center.

P.O. Box 8250, Silver Spring, MD 20807-8250.

National Council on Aging, Family Caregivers Program.
600 Maryland Avenue S.W., Washington, DC 20024.

National Institute on Aging Information Center.
2209 Distribution Circle, Silver Springs, MD 20910.

National Osteoporosis Association.
1625 Eye Street N.W., Washington, D.C. 20006.

EPILOGUE: The Future of Alternative Medicine

Over the next 50 years, I believe that alternative medicine will change in astonishing ways. By 2050, for example, the most revolutionary technology in medicine will be the most familiar–the computer and the telephone–and will rank with antibiotics, x rays, and transplant surgery as milestones in the history of medicine. The life-saving potential of these new technologies will be most obvious in medical emergencies where patients–at the scene of an automobile accident, for example–will be aided by paramedics with video cameras and microphones that are patched directly to a hospital physician who can treat patients remotely.

Perhaps more importantly, advances in computer technology will give physicians a more precise method of predicting any person's genetic predisposition to disease. Collaborative Research, a Massachusetts company, and the Human Genome Project at Stanford University are currently developing maps of the 23 pairs of human chromosomes which they hope will help isolate the genes linked to more than 25 chronic illnesses, including heart disease and cancer. Genetic research may allow scientists in the relatively near future to diagnose and alter genetic abnormalities *in utero.*

Because alternative medicine is whole body medicine, precise genetic information about each individual will give physicians an unprecedented ability to tailor safe, holistic, noninvasive therapies. For example, people will be able to customize their personal intake of foods, vitamins, minerals, and botanical supplements to correct possible genetic defects. The current system of RDAs will probably be replaced by more sophisticated computer-based programs which allow individuals to design a specific diet given their genetic makeup, physical fitness, body weight, and body composition.

In the future, it is conceivable that people will be able to walk into any food store and purchase prepared "superfoods" based on recipes to reverse certain diseases. Stores may have sections devoted to specific health concerns such as "Heart Disease," "Cancer," "PMS," "Depression," and "Osteoporosis."

In the future, the vast majority of nonchronic conditions such as headaches and respiratory and digestive problems will be treated by people themselves with the help of software programs. An enormous amount of doctors' time is currently spent in administering routine tests. By 2050, parents will use CD-ROMs at home to diagnose and treat their children's common medical problems. In addition, scientists will more effectively treat many troubling mental health disorders such as schizophrenia, phobias, and depression using computer models of the human brain. These computer models may even help explain how natural therapies such as yoga and meditation prevent or reverse common emotional disorders.

The increasing reliance on genetic information and computer technology to predict, prevent, and reverse serious diseases may seem "anti-alternative." However, it is the human touch of alternative practitioners combined with cutting-edge technology that will distinguish "holistic telemedicine" in 2050. Technology will do us little good if it does not help all patients become better informed, more relaxed, and empowered to heal themselves. Holistic medicine in 2050 will not only heal you, it will *transform* you. Thus, when you walk into a holistic practitioner's office, you might first receive a head massage with sesame oil, listen to relaxing music, or take a mud bath to eliminate toxins. Your

physician may suggest that you meditate, or ask you to recite a mantra. If you should require surgery, your surgeon might ask you to watch a videotape beforehand so that you are fully informed about the procedure. Your preoperative education program might also include talking with former patients; preoperative care might involve acupressure, naturopathy, massage, and vitamin, mineral, amino acid, and botanical supplements.

During surgery, your surgeon will probably use a local anesthetic which will allow you to watch the procedure and talk with the surgical team throughout the operation. Your family might also watch the operation via video camera in an adjacent room. This holistic approach to surgery gives patients more confidence, comfort, and support, and increases their chances of recovery because patients tend to take better care of themselves when they feel they are controlling their own healing.

In the future, as it is now, this healing/ transformation approach will be at the center of holistic medicine, and, in fact, the leading proponents of today use words such as "transformation" or "transcendence" to describe their therapies. Dean Ornish states in his book, *Dr. Dean Ornish's Program for Reversing Heart Disease,* that while as a cardiologist he focuses on reversing coronary artery blockages, "I am even more interested in the power of my program to *transform* our lives in deeper ways." In *Peace, Love & Healing*, Dr. Bernie Siegel, a leading cancer surgeon, calls disease "an agent of *transformation*... We all have the ability to train our bodies to heal and eliminate illness," he states. "I think we can use meditative and lifestyle-altering techniques...to gain access to the superintelligence I'm convinced resides within each of us." Dr. Deepak Chopra, the leading proponent of Ayurvedic medicine, observes: "If you live in tune with your quantum mechanical body, all of your daily activities will proceed smoothly…breathing, eating, digestion, assimilation, and elimination. The most important routine to follow is *transcending*, the act of getting in touch with the quantum level of yourself."

James Marti
Holistic Medical Research Foundation
Clinica Holistica
Puerto Vallarta, Mexico
July 1997

EPILOGUE

GLOSSARY

absorption the process by which nutrients are taken up by the intestines and passed into the bloodstream.

acethylcholine one of the chemicals that transmits impulses between nerves.

acquired immune deficiency syndrome (AIDS) a disease involving a defect in cell-mediated immunity that has a long incubation period, follows a protracted and debilitating course, is manifested by various opportunistic infections, and has a poor prognosis.

acupressure a form of acupuncture where certain points of the body are pressed with the fingers and hands to release energy blocks.

acupuncture Chinese practice of inserting needles into specific body locations to relieve pain, to induce anesthesia, and for therapeutic purposes.

acute having a rapid onset, severe symptoms, and a short course; not chronic.

adenosine triphosphate (ATP) the energy source for muscular contraction.

adrenal gland the organ that sits on top of each kidney and makes epinephrine (adrenaline) and norepinephrine–which regulate blood pressure and heart rate.

adrenaline *See* epinephrine

aerobic exercise any exercise that requires additional effort by the heart and lungs to meet the increased demand by the skeletal muscles for oxygen.

AIDS *See* acquired immune deficiency syndrome (AIDS)

alkaloids a group of organic compounds produced by plants (including caffeine, morphine, and nicotine) which can also be made synthetically.

allergen a foreign substance (such as pollen, house dust, and various foods) that can produce a hyper-sensitive reaction in the body but is not necessarily intrinsically harmful.

allopathy the conventional method of medicine that combats disease by using active techniques specifically against the disease.

Alzheimer's disease   a form of senile dementia associated with atrophy of parts of the brain.

amenorrhea   the absence of menstruation.

amino acid   a group of nitrogen-containing chemical compounds that form the basic structural units of proteins.

aminocentesis   the obstetric procedure used to aid in diagnosing fetal abnormalities in which a small amount of amniotic fluid is removed for analysis.

anabolic steroids   a group of synthetic, testosterone-like hormones that promote muscle growth and masculinizing effects.

analgesic   a substance that reduces the sensation of pain.

androgen   a steroid that stimulates male characteristics.

anemia   a condition in which the oxygen-carrying pigment hemoglobin in the blood is below normal limits.

aneurysm   a localized abnormal dilation of a blood vessel due to weakness in the vessel wall.

angina   a choking or suffocating pain in the chest (angina pectoris) usually caused by insufficient flow of oxygen to the heart muscle during exercise or excitement.

anodyne   a pain reliever.

anorexia nervosa   a psychoneurotic disorder that involves a long-term refusal to eat, resulting in emaciation, lack of menstrual cycles, emotional disturbance regarding body image, and an abnormal fear of becoming fat.

anovulation   failure of the ovaries to produce, mature, or release ovum (eggs).

antibody   a molecule made by lymph tissue that defends the body against bacteria, viruses, and other foreign bodies (antigens).

antidote   a substance that neutralizes or counteracts the effects of a poison.

antigen   any substance or microorganism that, when it enters the body, causes the formation of antibodies against it.

antihypertensive   of or pertaining to a substance or procedure that has a blood-pressure lowering effect.

antioxidant   a substance capable of protecting other substances from oxidation; some are made by the body to inhibit the destructive actions of chemicals called free radicals; some, such as vitamins C and E, are nutrients.

antispasmodic   any agent that relieves spasms.

aorta   the major trunk of the system of arteries that carries blood away from the heart to the tissues.

apnea   a cessation of breathing, usually temporary.

arrhythmia   an irregular heartbeat.

arteries   vessels that carry blood away from the heart to the tissues of the body.

arteriosclerosis   a variety of conditions that cause the artery walls to thicken, lose elasticity, and calcify, resulting in a decreased blood supply, especially to the cerebrum and lower extremities.

asthma   a respiratory disease characterized by wheezing or coughing caused by a spasm of the bronchial tubes or by swelling of their mucous membranes.

astringent a substance that causes a contraction of the tissues upon application.

atheroma abnormal mass of fat, or lipids; as in deposits in an arterial wall.

atherosclerosis the most common form of arteriosclerosis in which the inner walls of the arteries are narrowed by deposits of cholesterol and other material.

atrophy the wasting or shrinking of muscles or glands due to disease, malnutrition, or lack of use.

Ayurvedic medicine in Sanskrit "Ayurveda" means "science of life and longevity"; based on the premise that health is a state of balance among physical, emotional, and spiritual systems.

basal metabolic rate the minimum energy required to maintain the body's life functions at rest.

benign not recurrent; favorable for recovery.

beta-carotene a previtamin A compound found in plants that the body converts to vitamin A.

binge eating the consumption of large quantities of foods within short periods of time.

biofeedback the use of electronic devices that amplify body electricity in order to help people monitor otherwise unconscious physiological processes such as heart rate and body temperature.

bioflavonoid a term for any of a group of substances found in many fruits and essential for the absorption and processing of vitamin C.

blood pressure the pressure exerted by the blood on the walls of the arteries. It is measured in millimeters of mercury (as in 120/80 mm Hg).

blood purifier a term used by herbalists to refer to an antibiotic action of certain botanical medicines.

body composition the proportion of fat, muscle, and bone making up the body. Body composition is usually expressed as percent of body fat and percent of lean body mass.

body mass index (BMI) body weight and height indices for determining a person's degree of obesity.

bone density the specific gravity of the body, which can be measured by underwater weighing.

botanical medicine therapies of or derived from plants.

bulimia an eating disorder characterized by episodes of binge eating, often followed by self-induced vomiting.

cachexia malnutrition and wasting usually linked with diseases such as tuberculosis and cancer.

calisthenics systematic, rhythmic body exercises performed usually without apparatus.

calorie a measure of the chemical energy provided by food. One calorie equals the amount of heat needed to raise the temperature of one gram of water one degree Celsius at one air pressure. One gram of carbohydrate or protein provides about four calories, while one gram of fat provides about nine calories.

canker an ulceration, usually of the mouth and lips.

capillaries tiny blood vessels that link the arteries and the veins.

carbohydrate a large group of sugars, starches, cellulose, and gums that all contain carbon, hydrogen, and oxygen in similar proportions.

carbon dioxide a colorless, odorless gas that is formed in the tissues by the oxidation of carbon, and is eliminated by the lungs.

carbon monoxide an odorless, colorless, poisonous gas, produced mainly during combustion of fossil fuels, such as coal and gasoline.

carcinogens substances that can cause cancer.

cardiac output the volume of blood pumped out by the heart in a given space of time. A normal heart in a resting adult ejects from 2.5 to 4 liters of blood per minute.

cardiovascular refers to the heart and blood vessel systems.

cataract a partial or complete opacity of one or both eyes, especially an opacity impairing vision or causing blindness.

cesarean section incision through the abdominal and uterine walls for the delivery of a baby.

chemotherapy the treatment of disease by chemical agents; as in radiation chemotherapy used to treat cancer patients.

chiropractic literally "done by hand," a science based on the theory that health and disease are life processes related to the function of the nervous system; a method of restoring wellness through adjustments of the spine.

cholesterol a fat-like substance found in all animal fats, bile, blood, and brain tissue.

chromosomes thread-like structures in the nucleus of a cell that carry genetic information.

chronic a disease or disorder that develops slowly and persists for a long period of time.

cocarcinogens substances that promote the action of a carcinogen.

coenzymes substances necessary for the action of any enzyme; many vitamins are coenzymes.

collagen a protein consisting of bundles of tiny fibers that forms connective tissue, including the white inelastic fibers of the tendons, ligaments, bones, and cartilage.

colon the part of the large intestine that extends to the rectum.

congenital an inherited physical characteristic that is present at birth, such as congenital heart disease.

conjunctiva the mucous membrane that lines eyeballs and inner eyelids.

constipation infrequent or difficult evacuation of the feces.

coronary arteries the arteries that feed oxygenated blood to the heart muscle.

corticosteroid any one of the hormones made in the outer layer of the adrenal gland that influence or control key functions of the body, such as making carbohydrates and proteins.

cortisone a steroid hormone made in the liver, or produced artificially, used to treat inflammation.

Crohn's disease a chronic inflammatory bowel disease of unknown origin affecting any part of the gastrointestinal tract from the mouth to the anus, but most commonly the ileum, the colon, or both structures.

cystitis inflammation of the urinary bladder and ureters that may be caused by a bacterial infection, stone, or tumor.

cytoplasm the protoplasm of a cell exclusive of that of the nucleus; the site of most of the chemical activities of the cell.

degenerative diseases diseases that cause permanent deterioration of the structure or function of tissues, such as osteoarthritis and arteriosclerosis.

dementia a disorder in which mental functions break down, characterized by personality change, confusion, and lack of energy.

demulcent oily substance used to soothe and reduce irritation of the skin.

detoxification the body's natural process of neutralizing or eliminating toxic substances, primarily through the skin, liver, kidneys, feces, and urine.

diaphoretic a substance that promotes perspiration and helps control body temperature.

diastolic the second number in a blood pressure reading that measures the pressure in the arteries during the relaxation phase of the heartbeat.

dilution making a solution less potent.

disaccharides sugars composed of two simple (monosaccharide) sugars, such as lactose and sucrose.

disc cartilage between the backbones.

diuretic a drug or other substance such as a botanical that promotes the formation and release of urine.

DNA (deoxyribonucleic acid) a large nucleic acid molecule found in the chromosomes of the nucleus of a cell; carries genetic information.

double-blind study a way of controlling against experimental bias by ensuring that neither the researchers nor the subjects know which treatment any subject is receiving.

douche a method in which a medicated solution or a cleansing agent in warm water is flushed into a body cavity under low pressure.

duodenum the upper part of the small intestine into which the stomach empties.

dysmenorrhea pain linked with menstruation that typically occurs in the lower stomach or back.

edema the abnormal pooling of fluid in tissues that can be caused by conditions such as congestive heart failure, cirrhosis, draining wounds, excessive bleeding, and malnutrition.

electrocardiography (ECG) a device that records the electric activity of the heart to detect abnormal electric impulses through the muscle.

electroconvulsive therapy (ECT) inducing convulsions by means of electric shock; also known as "electric shock therapy."

elimination diet a way to test for food allergies. Certain foods are eliminated from the diet one at a time until the allergy is identified.

embolism   the sudden obstruction of an artery, usually in the heart, lungs, or brain, by a clot or foreign substance.

emetic   substance that promote vomiting.

endocrine system   the network of ductless glands and other structures that secrete hormones into the bloodstream.

endometrium   the membrane lining the uterus.

endorphins   substances composed of amino acids and produced by the pituitary gland that act on the nervous system to reduce pain.

enzymes   substances, usually proteins formed in living cells, that cause or speed up chemical reactions such as the breakdown of protein to amino acids in the gastrointestinal tract.

epidemiology   the study of disease as it affects a particular part of the population.

epilepsy   any of various disorders marked by disturbed electrical rhythms of the central nervous system and usually demonstrated by convulsive attacks.

epinephrine   the hormone secreted by the adrenal gland that produces the "fight or flight" response.

epithelium   the cells that cover the entire surface of the body and line most of the internal organs.

essential amino acids   the nine amino acids that the body needs for protein synthesis and cannot produce itself.

essential fatty acids   fatty acids that the human body cannot manufacture, such as linoleic and linolenic acids.

estrogen   one of a group of hormonal steroid components that aid the development of female secondary sex traits such as breast development. Males also have estrogen in lesser amounts.

expectorants   substances that help to expel mucus or other fluids from the lungs.

fallopian tubes   the two tubes that carry the eggs from the ovaries to the uterus and through which sperm move toward the ovaries.

fibrin   a white, insoluble protein formed by blood clotting which serves as the starting point for wound repair and scar formation.

fibrocystic breast disease (FBD)   the presence of single or multiple cysts in the breasts, usually benign and fairly common.

flavonoids   plant pigments that contain several compounds which have beneficial physiological effects in the human body.

free radicals   highly reactive molecules that bind to and destroy cellular compounds.

fu zheng   Chinese herbal therapy, mostly ginseng and astragalus, that extends life expectancy of patients with rapidly advancing cancers.

gene   a segment of the DNA molecule that carries physical characteristics from parent to child.

gingivitis   inflammation of the gums.

glaucoma   a disease of the eye marked by increased pressure within the eyeball that can result in damage to the optic disk and vision loss.

glucose   a simple sugar found in foods, especially fruits, which is a major source of energy in body fluids.

glutamine   an amino acid found in many of

the body's proteins that helps remove ammonia.

glycogen   the major carbohydrate stored in animal cells, which is changed to glucose and released into circulation as needed for energy.

helper T-cells   white blood cells that help in immune system response.

hemorrhoid   a mass of dilated veins in swollen tissue near the anus or within the rectum.

homeopathy   system of therapeutics founded by Samuel Hahnemann in which diseases are treated by drugs which are capable of producing in healthy persons symptoms like those of the disease to be treated.

hormones   chemical substances produced in one part or organ of the body that trigger or regulate the activity of an organ or group of cells in another part of the body.

hydrotherapy   the application of water in any form, usually externally, in the treatment of disease.

hyperglycemia   a condition characterized by too much sugar (glucose) in the blood.

hypertension   a common disorder, often without symptoms, marked by high blood pressure persistently exceeding 140/90.

hypertrophy   the enlargement or overgrowth of an organ or part due to an increase in the size of its constituent cells; as in benign prostatic hypertrophy.

hypoglycemia   a less than normal level of sugar in the blood, usually caused by being given too much insulin, excessive release of insulin by the pancreas, or low food intake.

hypotension   an abnormal condition in which the blood pressure is too low for normal functioning.

hysterectomy   removal of the uterus by surgery.

immunoglobulins   any of five distinct antibodies in the serum and external secretions of the body.

immunotoxic   poisonous to the human immune system.

impotence   inability of the adult male to achieve penile erection, or less commonly, to ejaculate having achieved an erection; weakness.

in vitro   biological reactions produced in laboratory apparatus.

infarction   the development of an area of decay in a tissue, vessel, or organ resulting from an interruption of the blood supply to the area or, less often, by the blockage of a vein that carries blood away from the area.

inflammation   heat, redness, swelling, and pain caused by trauma, infection, allergic reactions, or other stress or injury to the tissue.

insomnia   the inability to sleep; abnormal wakefulness.

insulin   a hormone secreted by the pancreas that lowers blood sugar levels and promotes the entry of glucose into muscle, fat, and certain other cells.

interferon   a substance produced by living tissues following infection by a bacteria or virus.

international unit (IU)   a standard measurement of an antibiotic, vitamin, enzyme, or hormone, the amount of which produces a specific biological result.

intrauterine device (IUD) birth control device implanted within the uterus.

irritable bowel syndrome (IBS) chronic disorder of the small and large intestine causing abnormally increased motility of the bowels.

ischemia poor blood supply to an organ or part, often marked by pain and organ disorder.

jaundice a condition caused by elevation of bile pigment (bilirubin) in the body and characterized by yellow discoloring of the skin, mucous membranes, and eyes.

keratin a fibrous, sulfur-containing protein found in human skin, hair, nails, and tooth enamel.

ketones substances produced in the body through a normal change fats undergo in the liver.

lactase an enzyme that increases the rate of the change of milk sugar (lactose) to glucose and galactose.

lesions wounds, injuries, or other damage of body tissue.

lethargy abnormal tiredness, drowsiness, or lack of energy.

leukocytes white blood cells.

leukotrines a group of chemical compounds that occur naturally in white blood cells; they are able to produce allergic and inflammatory reactions, and may play a part in the development of asthma and rheumatoid arthritis.

libido the instinctual energy or drive associated with sexual desire.

ligaments white, shiny, flexible bands of fibrous tissue binding joints together and connecting various bones and cartilages.

lipid any of the various fats or fat-like substances in plant or animal tissues that serve as an energy reserve in the body.

lipoprotein a complex of protein and fat in one molecule.

lipotropic promoting the flow of lipids to and from the liver.

lymph a thin, clear, slightly yellow fluid originating in many organs and tissues of the body which circulates through the lymphatic vessels and is filtered by the lymph nodes.

lymphocytes white blood cells found primarily in lymph nodes.

macrophages large cells that can surround and digest foreign substances such as bacteria in the body. They are found in the liver, spleen, and loose connective tissue.

malabsorption a failure of the intestines to absorb nutrients, which may result from a birth defect, malnutrition, or an abnormal condition of the digestive system.

malignant a term used to describe a condition that tends to worsen and result in death.

malnutrition the condition of not receiving a proper balance of essential nutrients.

malocclusion abnormality in the coming together of teeth.

mandala a Hindu or Buddhist graphic symbol of the universe, specifically a circle enclosing a square with a deity on each side.

mastectomy surgical removal of one or both breasts.

materia medica the branch of medical study that deals with drugs, their sources, preparations, and uses; pharmacology.

megadose   a large dose, often 100 to 1,000 times as much as that recommended, to prevent or treat diseases believed to be caused by nutrient deficiencies.

megavitamins   massive quantities of a specific vitamin usually given for therapeutic purposes.

Meniere's disease   a chronic disease of the inner ear characterized by recurrent episodes of vertigo, progressive nerve deafness, and tinnitus.

menopause   cessation of menstruation in the human female, usually occurring around the age of 50.

menorrhagia   abnormally heavy or prolonged blood loss during menstruation.

menstruation   the monthly (approximately) discharge through the vagina of blood, secretions, and tissue debris from the shedding of the endometrium from the non-pregnant uterus.

metabolism   a collective term for all the chemical processes that take place in the body by which energy is produced and new material is assimilated for the repair and replacement of tissues.

metastasis   the spread of cancerous cells via the blood or lymph from one part of the body to another.

microbial   of or pertaining to or caused by microbes.

microflora   microorganisms present in or characteristic of a special location, e.g., the colon.

molecules   the smallest complete unit of a substance that can exist independently and still retain the properties of an element or compound.

monoclonal antibodies   genetically engineered antibodies specific for one particular antigen.

monosaccharide   a carbohydrate made up of one basic sugar unit such as fructose and glucose.

morning sickness   nausea and vomiting that occur especially during the early months of pregnancy.

mucous membrane   the soft, pink tissue that lines most of the cavities and tubes in the body, including the respiratory system, gastrointestinal and genitourinary tracts, and the eyelids.

mucus   the slimy substance that acts as a lubricant and mechanical protector of the mucous membranes. It is composed of mucin, white blood cells, water, and castoff tissue cells.

music therapy   a form of psychotherapy in which music is used as a means of recreation and communication and as a way to elevate the mood of depressed or psychotic patients.

myocardial infarction   death of an area of the heart muscle from the cessation of blood flow to the area due to arterial blockage.

myocardium   the middle and thickest layer of the heart wall.

naturopathy   a system of therapeutics based on natural foods, light, warmth, exercise, fresh air, massage, and the avoidance of medications. Advocates the belief that illness can be healed by the natural processes of the body.

neoplasm   a new and abnormal tissue growth which may be benign or malignant.

neurofibrillary tangles　a cluster of degenerated nerves.

neuron　the basic nerve cell of the nervous system.

neurotransmitters　chemicals such as norepinephrine, serotonin, and acetylcholine that travel across the synapse and communicate impulses.

norepinephrine　a neurotransmitter that functions mostly in the sympathetic nervous system and increases blood pressure by narrowing the blood vessels.

obesity　body weight beyond the limitation of skeletal and physical requirement, so much that the body cannot function normally.

occlusion　a blockage in a canal, artery or vein, or passage of the body. It can refer to any contact between the biting or chewing surfaces of the upper and lower teeth.

osteopathy　a system of medical practice based on the theory that diseases and illness are due to the loss of structural integrity, which can be restored by manipulating the joints and the spine supplemented by therapeutic measures.

osteoporosis　the common condition, found usually in aging women, of weak, demineralized bones.

otitis　inflammation or infection of the ear.

otosclerosis　growth of a spongy bone in the inner ear that results in gradual tinnitus, then deafness.

ovulation　the release of an egg from an ovary. This cycle usually occurs once a month in most women.

oxidize　to cause a substance to chemically combine with oxygen.

palpitation　a rapid or excessively forceful heartbeat.

panic disorder　a neurotic disorder characterized by persistent, uncontrollable anxiety.

Pap test (or Pap smear)　short for Papanicolaou's test, an examination of the cells of the cervix and vagina for precancerous or cancerous abnormalities.

parasympathetic nervous system　the branch of the autonomic nervous system that tends to slow the heart, constrict the pupils, and promote digestive and sexual functions.

Parkinson's disease　a chronic progressive nervous disorder marked by tremor and weakness of resting muscles and by a peculiar gait.

pathogens　microorganisms that are able to cause a disease.

phobia　an anxiety disorder characterized by an obsessive, irrational, and intense fear of a specific object, activity, or physical situation.

phytoestrogens　plant compounds that exert estrogen-like effects.

placebo　an inactive therapeutic substance, agent, or procedure that works (or appears to work) by suggestion, not by consistent physical effects on the body.

platelets　tiny disc-shaped cells in the blood that have no hemoglobin but are needed for blood clot formation.

polyp　a small tumor-like growth that projects from a mucous membrane surface.

polysaccharides carbohydrates such as starch that contain three or more simple carbohydrate molecules.

polyunsaturated fats fats, mostly from plants, with double bonds that can bind to hydrogen; these tend to be liquid at room temperature and are called oils.

premenstrual syndrome (PMS) syndrome of nervous tension, irritability, weight gain, headache, and edema occurring just before the onset of menstruation.

progesterone a natural hormone produced by the corpus luteum–the part of the ovary that the egg vacated–that prepares the uterus for the reception and development of the fertilized egg.

progestin any of a group of natural or synthetic hormones released by the corpus luteum, placenta, or adrenal cortex.

prostaglandins hormone-like compounds manufactured from essential fatty acids.

prostate the male gland that wraps around the neck of the bladder and produces a thin fluid that makes semen into a liquid.

prostatitis inflammation of the prostate gland.

pulmonary alveoli the tiny air sacs in the lungs from which oxygen enters the blood.

pyruvate an intermediate product in the breakdown of glucose to carbon dioxide and water.

qi gong a Chinese meditative exercise that relieves stress and improves cardiovascular functioning.

recommended daily (or dietary) allowance (RDA) the proper amount of nutrients needed for optimum health.

retinopathy a noninflammatory eye disorder resulting from changes in the retinal blood vessels.

rheumatoid arthritis a chronic disease characterized by pain, stiffness, inflammation, swelling, and destruction of joints.

RNA (ribonucleic acid) similar to DNA; there are several types that carry gene data from the nucleus to the cytoplasm.

saccharide any of a large group of carbohydrates, including all sugars and starches.

saturated fats fats that have no double bonds and cannot accept more hydrogen atoms; such fats tend to be solid at room temperature and are mostly from animal sources such as meat, whole milk, butter, and eggs.

SIDS *See* sudden infant death syndrome (SIDS)

sinusitis inflammation of the sinuses.

sorbitol a sugar-alcohol made from glucose, which, in diabetics, accumulates in peripheral nerves, the lens, and certain other tissues.

steroids a large number of chemicals including vitamin D, cortisone, testosterone, estrogen, and bile acids.

subluxation a partial dislocation.

sudden infant death syndrome (SIDS) the sudden, unexpected, and unexplained death of an apparently healthy infant, typically occurring between the ages of three weeks and five months.

suppressor T-cells lymphocytes that are controlled by the thymus gland and suppress the immune response.

sympathetic nervous system the branch of

the autonomic nervous system that tends to promote motor and mental excitation and is responsible for the "fight or flight" response, symptoms of which include a faster heartbeat, dilated pupils, and digestive and sexual inhibition.

synapse   the junction between two nerve cells.

syndrome   a group of signs and symptoms that occur together in a pattern characteristic of a particular disease or abnormal condition.

systolic   the pressure in the arteries during the contraction phase of the heartbeat. This is the first number in a blood pressure reading.

T-cells   lymphocytes that are under the control of the thymus gland.

tinnitis   tinkling or ringing in one or both ears.

toxicity   a poisonous effect produced when people ingest an amount of a substance that is above their level of tolerance.

triglyceride   a compound found in most animal and vegetable fats that is made up of a fatty acid and glycerol.

urinalysis   a physical, microscopic, or chemical examination of urine for color density, acidity, and other conditions.

vaginitis   inflammation of the vaginal tissues, as in a yeast infection.

varicose veins   unnaturally and permanently distended veins, usually in the legs.

vasoconstriction   the narrowing of any blood vessel, especially the arterioles and veins in the skin, stomach, and intestines.

vertigo   a disordered state in which the individual or his/her surroundings seem to whirl dizzily.

visulization   a variety of visual techniques used to treat disease based on inducing relaxation in the patient and having them actually will their disease away.

XJL   Chinese herb that interacts with neurotransmitters in the brain to curb the desire for alcohol.

GENERAL BIBLIOGRAPHY

A

Altman, Nathaniel. *Everybody's Guide to Chiropractic Health Care*. Los Angeles: Jeremy P. Tarcher, Inc., 1989.

Anderson, Robert A. *Wellness Medicine*. New Canaan, CT: Keats Publishing, Inc., 1990.

B

Balch, James F., and Phyllis Balch. *Prescription for Nutritional Healing*. Garden City Park, NY: Avery Publishing Group, 1993.

Benson, Herbert. *The Relaxation Response*. New York: William Morrow, 1975.

———, and William Proctor. *Beyond the Relaxation Response*. New York: Berkeley Publishing Group, 1987.

Beverly, Cal, ed. *Natural Health Secrets Encyclopedia*. Peachtree City, GA: FC&A Publishing, 1991.

Bricklin, Mark. *The Practical Encyclopedia of Natural Healing*. New York: Penguin Books, 1990.

Brody, Jane. *The Good Food Book*. New York: Bantam Books, 1990.

———. *Jane Brody's The New York Times Guide to Personal Health*. New York: Avon Books, 1982.

Bunyard, Peter. *Health Guide for the Nuclear Age*. London, England: Macmillan, 1988.

The Burton Goldberg Group. *Alternative Medicine: The Definitive Guide*. Puyallup, WA: Future Medicine Publishing, Inc., 1993.

Butler, Kurt, and Lynn Rayner. *The Best Medicine: The Complete Health and Preventive Medicine Handbook*. New York: Harper & Row Publishers, Inc., 1985.

C

Carper, Jean. *Creating Health: How to Make Up the Body's Intelligence*. Boston: Houghton Mifflin, 1987.

———. *The Food Pharmacy Guide to Good Eating*. New York: Bantam Books, 1988.

———. *Food–Your Miracle Medicine: How Food Can Prevent & Cure over 100 Symptoms & Problems*. San Francisco: HarperCollins, 1993.

Chaitow, Leon. *The Body/Mind Purification Program*. New York: Simon & Schuster, Inc., 1990.

————. *The Stress Protection Plan.* San Francisco: HarperCollins, 1992.

Chopra, Deepak. *Ageless Body, Timeless Mind.* New York: Harmony Books, 1993.

————. *Perfect Health: The Complete Mind/Body Guide.* New York: Harmony Books, 1991.

————. *Quantum Healing: Exploring the Frontiers of Body, Mind, Medicine.* New York: Bantam Books, 1993.

Culbreth, D. *A Manual of Materia Medica and Pharmacology.* Portland, OR: Eclectic Medical Publications, 1983.

Cummings, Stephen, and Dana Ullman. *Everybody's Guide to Homeopathic Medicine.* New York: St. Martin's Press, 1991.

D

Dharmananda, S. *Your Nature, Your Health–Chinese Herbs in Constitutional Therapy.* Portland, OR: Institute for Traditional Medicine and Preservation of Health Care, 1986.

Duke, J. *Handbook of Medicinal Herbs.* Boca Raton, FL: CRC Press, 1985.

E

Edlin, Gordon, and Eric Golanty. *Health and Wellness: A Holistic Approach.* Boston: Jones and Bartlett Publishers, Inc., 1992.

Eisenberg, D.M., et al. "Unconventional Medicine in the United States: Prevalence, Costs, and Patterns of Use." *New England Journal of Medicine* 328 (March 1993): 246-52.

Ellingwood, F. *American Materia Medica, Therapeutics and Pharmacognosy.* Portland, OR: Eclectic Medical Publications, 1983.

Epstein, Gerald. *Healing Visualizations.* New York: Bantam Books, 1989.

F

Felter, H. *The Eclectic Materia Medica.* Portland, OR: Eclectic Medical Publications, 1983.

G

Girdano, Daniel, and George Everly. *Controlling Stress and Tension: A Holistic Approach.* Englewood Cliffs, NJ: Prentice-Hall, 1986.

Goldstar, Rosemary. *Herbal Healing for Women.* New York: Simon & Schuster, Inc., 1993.

Goleman, Daniel. *The Meditative Mind.* Los Angeles: Jeremy P. Tarcher, Inc., 1988.

Goodhart, R., and V. Young. *Modern Nutrition in Health and Disease.* Philadelphia, PA: Lea & Febiger, 1988.

Griffith, H. Winter. *Vitamins.* Tucson, AZ: Fisher Books, 1988.

Guiton, Arthur. *Textbook of Medical Physiology.* Philadelphia, PA: Harcourt Brace Jovanovich, 1991.

H

Hahnemann, Samuel. *Organon of Medicine.* Translated by W. Boericke. New Delhi: B. Jain Publishers, 1992.

Hausman, Patricia, and Judith Been Hurley. *The Healing Foods.* Emmaus, PA: Rodale Press, Inc., 1989.

Hendler, Sheldon. *The Complete Guide to Anti-Aging Nutrients.* New York: Simon & Schuster, Inc., 1985.

Hoffer, A. *Orthomolecular Nutrition.* New Canaan, CT: Keats Publishing, Inc., 1978.

Hoffman, David. *The New Holistic Herbal.* Rockport, MA: Element Books, 1992.

K

Kabat-Sinn, J. *Full Catastrophic Living: Using the Wisdom of Your Body and Mind to Face Stress, Pain, and Illness.* New York: Delacorte Press, 1990.

Kahan, Barbara. *Healthier Children.* New Canaan, CT: Keats Publishing, Inc., 1990.

Kirchheimer, Sid. *The Doctor's Book of Home Remedies.* Emmaus, PA: Rodale Press, Inc., 1993.

Kutsky, Roman J. *Handbook of Vitamins, Minerals and Hormones.* New York: Van Nostrand Reinhold Co., 1973.

L

Lane, William, and L. Cormac. *Sharks Don't Get Cancer.* Garden City Park, NY: Avery Publishing Group, 1992.

Leung, A. *Encyclopedia of Common Natural Ingredients Used in Food, Drugs, and Cosmetics.* New York: John Wiley & Sons, 1980.

M

Margolis, Simeon, and Hamilton Moses III. *The Johns Hopkins Medical Handbook.* New York: Medletter Associates, Inc., 1992.

May, L. *Drug Information.* St. Louis, MO: Mosby Year Book, Inc., 1993.

Mills, Simon. *Out of the Earth: The Essential Book of Herbal Medicine.* New York: Penguin Books, 1991.

Monte, Tom, and the editors of *EastWest Natural Health. World Medicine: The EastWest Guide to Healing Your Body.* New York: Putnam Berkley Group, Inc., 1993.

Murphy, Michael. *The Future of the Body.* Los Angeles: Jeremy P. Tarcher, Inc., 1992.

Murray, Michael. *The Healing Powers of Herbs.* Rocklin, CA: Prima Publishing, 1992.

———, and Joseph Pizzorno. *Encyclopedia of Natural Medicine.* Rocklin, CA: Prima Publishing, 1991.

N

Newberry, Benjamin H., Janet Madden, and Thomas Gertsenberger. *A Holistic Conceptualization of Stress & Disease.* New York: AMS Press, Inc., 1991.

Nieman, D. *Fitness & Your Health.* Palo Alto, CA: Bull Publishing Company, 1993.

O

Ody, Penelope. *The Complete Medicinal Herbal.* London, England: Dorling Kindersley, 1993.

Ornish, Dean. *Dr. Dean Ornish's Program for Reversing Heart Disease.* New York: Ballantine Books, 1990.

———. *Eat More, Weigh Less.* San Francisco: HarperCollins, 1993.

Ornstein, R. *The Human Ecology Program.* San Francisco: San Francisco Medical Research Foundation, 1987.

P

Panos, Maesimund B., and Jane Heimlich. *Homeopathic Medicine at Home.* Los Angeles: Jeremy P. Tarcher, Inc., 1980.

Pauling, Linus. *How to Live Longer and Feel Better.* New York: W.H. Freeman and Co., 1986.

———. *Vitamin C and the Common Cold.* New York: W.H. Freeman and Co., 1971.

Porkett, Manfred. *Chinese Medicine.* New York: Henry Holt & Co., 1992.

R

Reid, Daniel. *Chinese Herbal Medicine.* Boston: Shambhala Publications Inc., 1993.

Riggs, Maribeth. *Natural Child Care: A Complete Guide to Safe & Effective Herbal Remedies & Holistic Health Strategies for Infants & Children.* New York: Crown Publishing Group, 1992.

S

Santillo, Humbart. *Natural Healing with Herbs.* Prescott, AZ: Hohm Press, 1991.

Schroeder, Steven. *Current Medical Diagnosis & Treatment.* Norwalk, CT: Appleton & Lange, 1992.

Selye, Hans. *Stress Without Distress.* New York: New American Library, 1975.

Shangold, Mona. *The Complete Sports Medicine Book for Women.* New York: Simon & Schuster, Inc., 1992.

Siegel, Bernie. *How to Live Between Office Visits.* New York: Harper & Row Publishers, Inc., 1993.

————. *Love, Medicine & Miracles.* New York: Harper & Row Publishers, Inc., 1986.

————. *Peace, Love & Healing.* New York: Harper & Row Publishers, Inc., 1989.

Simon, Harvey B., and Steven R. Levisohn. *The Athlete Within: A Personal Guide to Total Fitness.* Boston: Little, Brown, 1987.

Stanway, Andrew. *The Natural Family Doctor.* New York: Simon & Schuster, Inc., 1987.

Stein, Diane. *The Natural Remedy Book for Women.* Freedom, CA: The Crossing Press, 1992.

Stewart, Felicia. *Understanding Your Body: Every Woman's Guide to a Lifetime of Health.* New York: Bantam Books, 1987.

T

Tierra, Lesley. *The Herbs of Life.* Freedom, CA: Crossing Press, 1992.

U

Ullman, Dana. *Discovering Homeopathy.* Berkeley, CA: North Atlantic Books, 1989.

W

Walford, Roy. *Maximum Life Span.* New York: W.W. Norton and Co., Inc., 1983.

Walters, Richard. *Options: The Alternative Cancer Therapy Book.* Garden City Park, NY: Avery Publishing Group, 1993.

Weil, Andrew. *Health and Healing.* Boston: Houghton Mifflin Company, 1983.

————. *Natural Health, Natural Medicine.* Boston: Houghton Mifflin, 1990.

Weiner, Michael. *Weiner's Herbal.* Mill Valley, CA: Quantum Books, 1990.

Y

Yoder, Barbara. *The Recovery Resource Book.* New York: Simon & Schuster, Inc., 1990.

Z

Zimmerman, David. *Zimmerman's Complete Guide to Nonprescription Drugs.* Detroit: Gale Research, 1993.

INDEX

min B_1, 57; vitamin B_9 deficiency, 60

Aletris farinosa. See Unicorn root

Alexander, Charles, 400

Alexander Technique, 25, 175

Alfalfa, 148

Algae, 95, 236; blue green, 95; cancer, 96; hyperlipidemia, 96; hypertension, 96; immune system, 96; malnutrition, 96

Alkaloids, 103, 105

Alkoxyglycerols, 358

Allergies; ear infections, 328; otitis media, 328

Alliance for Aging Research, 396; dietary guidelines, 396

Alliance for Alternative Medicine, 367

Allium sativum. See Garlic

Aloe vera, 96, 148; abscesses, 306; antiviral properties, 96; kidney stones, 96; toothaches, 302

Alternative physicians, 13, 18, 369

Altman, Nathaniel, 25, 265; ozone therapy, 25, 245

Alum; canker sores, 337

Alzheimer, Alois, 401

Alzheimer's Association, 416

Alzheimer's disease, 400; Ayurvedic medicine, 406; botanical medicines, 404; chelation therapy, 404; dental fillings, 405; estrogen replacement therapy, 405; exercise, 406; heavy metal poisoning, 402; lifestyle, 406; memory improvement, 405; nutritional therapies, 402; Traditional Chinese Medicine, 406; vitamin and mineral therapies, 403; vitamin D, 68

Alzheimer's Disease Education and Referral Center, 416

Amalgam fillings, 294; American Dental Association (ADA), 294; mercury, 294

Amblyopia, 321

Amenorrhea; chaste tree, 95, 260

American Academy of Implant Dentistry, 313

American Academy of Periodontology, 313

American Academy of Sciences, 356

American Association of Acupuncture and Oriental Medicine, 118, 186, 335

American Association of Naturopathic Physicians, 118, 290

American Association of Orthodontics, 307

American Board of Chelation Therapy, 405

American Botanical Council, 118

American Cancer Society, 215, 356, 367; exercise, 10

American Chiropractic Association, 31

American College of Nurse-Midwives (ACNM), 282, 290

American College of Obstetricians and Gynecologists, 344

American College of Sports Medicine, 120, 129; aerobic exercise, 127, 134

American Council for Drug Education, 215

American Council on Alcoholism, 215

American Council on Science and Health, 41

American Dental Association (ADA), 292, 313

American Dietetic Association, 51

American Family Physician, 47, 49

American Health, 176, 255, 294, 301-302, 307, 323, 333, 351

American Heart Association (AHA), 137, 190, 356, 388; coronary artery disease, 373; dietary guidelines, 375, 377; symptoms of heart attacks, 371

American Herbalists Guild, 118

American Holistic Medical Association, 290, 363

American Institute of Homeopathic Education and Research, 31

American Institute of Homeopathy, 31

American Journal of Cardiology, 15

American Journal of Clinical Nutrition, 41, 47, 61, 64, 67, 72, 86

American Journal of Epidemiology, 168

American Journal of Hypertension, 180

American Lung Association, 215

American Materia Medica, Therapeutics and Pharmacognosy, 238

American Medical Association (AMA); homeopathic medicine, 11

American Nutritionists Association, 51

American Physical Therapy Association (APTA), 137, 388

American Psychiatric Association (APA), 221, 234

American Rehabilitation Foundation, 388

American School of Ayurvedic Sciences, 179, 242

American Sleep Disorders Association, 231

American Society for Clinical Nutrition, 51

American Society of Bariatric Physicians, 51

American Society of Clinical Hypnosis, 13, 31

American Speech and Hearing Association (ASHA), 325

American Tinnitus Association, 330, 340

Amino acid therapy; prostate enlargement, 242

Amino acids, 36; alcoholism, 199

Amino aspartate transferase, 299

Amla. *See* Indian gooseberry

Ammonia, 22, 145

Amphetamines, 202; dependence, 202

Anaprox, 186

Anatomy of an Illness, 166

Anderson, Robert, 90

Andropause, 235

sinusitis, 335; ulcers, 186-187; urinary tract infections, 245; vertigo, 332; vitamin and mineral therapies, 151, 407

Balloon angioplasty, 374

Balsalm pear. *See* Bitter melon

Baraiba, C, 107

Barbiturates, 22

Barnard, Julian, 175

Barrett, Richard, 335

Bartisch, Ernst, 255

Basal cell carcinoma. *See* Skin cancer

Basal ganglia, 72

Bassi, P, 108

Baylor College of Medicine, 16, 90

BDS. *See* Biochemical defense system (BDS)

Beating Alzheimer's, 406

Beckett, L, 19

Bedi, A, 113

Behavioral disorders; biofeedback, 6

Behavioral modification; bulimia, 48

Behavioral therapy; anxiety, 219; schizophrenia, 229

Bell peppers. *See* Capsicum

Belladonna, 176; ear infections, 329; earaches, 327; premenstrual syndrome (PMS), 260

Benign prostatic hypertrophy (BPH), 110; saw palmetto, 110

Bennings, M. A, 7

Benotti, Peter N, 46

Bensky, Dan, 110-111

Benson, Herbert, 158, 164-165; meditation, 13; yoga, 384

Bentonite, 148

Benzedrine, 202

Benzene, 22, 143

Benzocaine, 241

Benzodiazepine, 22

Ber, Abram, 358

Berberine, 105, 111

Bergner, Paul, 186

Beriberi, 57

Berkman, Lisa, 168

Berson, Eliot, 323

Best Medicine; The Complete Health and Preventive

Medicine Handbook, 171, 243, 330

Beta-blockers, 374

Betacarotene, 55; dietary sources, 150

Better Nutrition, 69-71, 296

Beyond Biofeedback, 11

Bicycling, 132

Bilberry extract, 97; capillaries, 97; eyesight, 320; glaucoma, 320

Bile; dandelion, 101

Binge eating, 49

Binge-purge cycle, 48

Binnie, N. R, 7

Biochemical defense system (BDS), 360

Biofeedback, 6, 163; alcoholism, 7, 200; cerebral palsy, 7; depression, 6; electromyographic (EMG) training, 177; eye disorders, 321; glaucoma, 320; headaches, 175, 177; heart disease, 7; hyperactivity, 7; hypertension, 179; incontinence, 7; macular degeneration, 322; panic disorders, 226; parasympathetic cardiac arrhymia, 7; pediatric sickle-cell anemia, 7; rectal ulcer syndrome, 7; sphincter incontinence, 7; tinnitus, 330; toothaches, 302; urinary incontinence, 7

Biological aging clock, 392

Birth control pills, 250

Bisabolol, 100

Bishop, J, 353

Bismuth, 187

Bitter melon, 98

Black cohosh, 255; menopause, 253

Black currant seeds, 97

Black ointment; abscesses, 306

Black snake root, 260

Black walnut, 260; cancer, 97

Blackburn, George, 46, 409

Bladder infections; cranberries, 100; natural treatment, 148

Blair, Steven; exercise, 352

Bleeding, excessive menstrual. *See* Menorrhagia

Bletilla rhizome. See Bai ji

Bletilla striata. See Bai ji

Block diet, 356

Block, Gladys, 64, 349

Block, Keith, 356

Bloksma, N, 106

Blood pressure; emotions, 386; exercise, 121; hawthorn berry, 105; mistletoe, 106; visualization, 385; yoga, 385

Bloom, Pamela, 25

Blue cohosh, 258; premenstrual syndrome (PMS), 260

Blumberg, Jeffrey, 71

Body/Mind Detoxification Program (Chaitow), 211

Body/Mind Purification Program (Chopra), 143

Bodywork therapies, 25; headaches, 175; hypertension, 179

Bone loss, 406

Bones; brittle. *See* Osteoporosis; softening. *See* Osteomalacia

Boomer Report, 8

Borage oil, 236

Botanical medicines, 7; abscesses, 305; aging, 398; Alzheimer's disease, 404; atherosclerosis, 172; cancer, 357, 359; canker sores, 337; cataracts, 318; dysmenorrhea, 257; ear infections, 329; earaches, 328; eyes, 324; glaucoma, 319; headaches, 175; heart disease, 380; hypertension, 180; irritable bowel syndrome (IBS), 183; male health problems, 237; menopause, 253; menorrhagia, 258; osteoporosis, 410; premenstrual syndrome (PMS), 259; schizophrenia, 228; sinusitis, 335; sore throats, 337, 339; stress reduction, 162; teeth, 295, 304; toothaches, 302, 304; ulcers, 186; uterine fibroids, 252; vertigo, 332; yeast infections, 265

Boyd, M, 96

Boyle, Wade, 22

BPH. *See* Prostate englargement

Braces, orthodontic, 293

Bradley method (childbirth classes), 281

Bradyarrhythmia, 105
Brain tumors; antineoplaston therapy, 360
Brandeis University, 213
Branewmark, Per-Ingvar, 308
Brazilian ginseng. *See* Suma
Breast cancer; juzentaihoto, 359; vitamin A, 55, 349; vitamin D, 67
Breast milk, 292
Breastfeeding, 288; benefits for babies, 285
Breasts; cysts, 249
Breathing exercises, 152
Bricklin, Mark, 78
Brigham and Women's Hospital, 379
British Journal of Cancer, 103
British Journal of Clinical Pharamacology, 110
British Journal of Psychiatry, 62, 228
British Medical Journal, 82, 85, 128, 181
Brody, Jane, 318; exercise, 238
Bromelain, 257; toothaches, 304
Bromocriptine, 250
Bronchitis, 22, 69, 106, 110, 112-113, 140-141, 209, 334
Brown, David, 108
Brown, Donald, 357, 381
Brown, Jonathan, 163
Brunner, E, 79
Brush massage; headaches, 176
Bruxism, 301
Bryonia, 176
Buckthorn; colon, 148
Bulimia, 48-49; behavioral modification, 48; treatment, 48-49
Buprenorphine, 203
Burns, P, 7
Burzynski Clinic, 367
Burzynski Research Institute, 360
Burzynski, Stanislaw, 360; antineoplaston therapy, 360; brain tumors, 360
Butler, Kurt; antacids, 186; atherosclerosis, 171; estrogen replacement therapy, 410; fiber, 173; hearing, 330; hydrochloric acid production, 185; hypertension, 178, 182; lecithin, 173; migraine headaches, 174; osteoporo-

sis, 406-407; prostate enlargement, 243; ulcers, 187-188
Butyl methacrylate, 145
Bypass surgery; vitamin E, 69. *See also* Coronary bypass surgery

C

CAD. *See* Coronary artery disease (CAD)
Cade, J, 57
Caffeine, 200; coffee substitutes, 201; dependence. *See also* Caffeinism
Caffeinism, 201; acupressure, 202; acupuncture, 202; botanical therapies, 201; exercise, 202; massage, 202; treatment, 201
Calan, 237
Calciportiol. *See* Vitamin D
Calcitonin; osteoporosis, 411
Calcitrol. *See* Vitamin D
Calcium; aging, 394; cholesterol, 77; deficiency, 76; food sources, 76; osteoporosis, 409; pregnancy, 291
Calcium channel blockers, 237
Calcium citrate, 77
Calcium deficiency; effects, 77; hypertension, 77, 181; hypoglycemia, 67
Calcium lactate, 185
Calcium sulphide, 329
Calisthenics, 135
Calories, 39, 42
Camellia sinensis. See Green tea
Camp, Joe, 304
Canadian Schizophrenia Foundation, 228, 404
Canadine, 105
Cancer; algae, 96; antineoplaston therapy, 360; antioxidants, 357; black walnut, 97; botanical medicines, 349, 357; carbohydrates, 346; carnivora, 359; children, 142; chromium, 81; diagnosing, 344; emotions, 363; estrogen, 351; exercise, 351-352; fiber, 345; food additives, 347; food carcinogens,

347; Fu Zheng, 359; garlic, 103; green tea, 398; hydrazine sulfate, 361; hydrogen peroxide, 361; hypnosis, 362; iodine deficiency, 84; juzentaihoto, 359; Livingston therapy, 360; lymphomas, 344; maitake mushrooms, 357; mistletoe, 107, 358; nutritional therapies, 345, 356; ozone therapy, 25, 362; radiation therapy, 353; shark cartilage, 358; shark liver oil, 358; shiitake mushrooms, 108; skin, 349; social support, 363; surgery, 353; Traditional Chinese Medicine, 359; types, 344; visualization, 18, 362; vitamin A, 55; vitamin and mineral therapies, 348, 356; vitamin B$_6$, 59, 356; vitamin C, 64; vitamin E, 69
Cancer and Nutrition, 149
Cancer Control Society, 368
Cancer Eating Recovering Plan, 345
Cancer, Immunology, Immunotherapy, 107
Cancer Treatment Centers of America, 358
Cancer Weekly, 64, 67, 69
Candida albicans. See Yeast infections
Canker sores; botanical medicines, 337; causes, 337; iron, 85; self-help treatments, 337; throat, 336; vitamin and mineral therapies, 336
Cannabis sativa. See Marijuana
Capillaries; bilberry extract, 97
Capoten, 237
Caprylic acid, 148
Capsaicin, 98
Capsella bursa-pastoris. See Shepherd's purse
Capsicum, 98
Captopril, 237
Carbohydrates, 37, 43; cancer, 346; complex, 37
Carbon dioxide, 2
Carbon monoxide, 140; toxic effects, 140
Carbon tetrachloride, 113, 143

Carcinogens; food, 347
Carcinomas. *See* Cancer
Cardene, 237
Cardizem, 237
Carduus mariana. See St. Mary's
thistle
Careiello, A, 79
Cargile, William, 186, 335
Carl Pfeiffer Treatment Center,
228
Carnitine, 173
Carnivora; cancer, 359
Carstens, Veronica, 105
Cascata, 241
Casdorph, H, 404
Cassia senna, 148
Cat's claw, 98; HIV/AIDS, 98
Cataracts, 316; botanical medi-
cines, 318; nutritional thera-
pies, 317; preventing, 316;
surgery, 318; Traditional
Chinese Medicine, 318; vita-
min A, 318; vitamin and
mineral therapies, 317; vita-
min B$_2$, 57; vitamin C, 63,
317; vitamin E, 318; zinc,
318
Cathcart, Robert, 151
Catuaba, 238
Caulophyllum thalictroides. See
Blue cohosh, 258
Cavities; infants, 292; prevention,
293
CCD. *See* Charged-couple device
(CCD)
CDA Journal, 294
CDC. *See* Centers for Disease
Control and Prevention
(CDC)
Cell therapy; impotence, 238
*Cellular & Molecular Biology
Research*, 100
Center for the Study of Anorexia
and Bulimia, 51
Centers for Disease Control and
Prevention (CDC), 120
Central nervous system (CNS)
depressants, 208
Cerebral palsy, 6-7
Certified nurse-midwives
(CNMs), 282
Cervical dysplasia; vitamin A, 55,
349; vitamin B$_9$, 61, 357
Cezheslovania Psychiatry, 20

Chaitow, Leon, 211, 222, 226;
pesticide poisoning, 143;
smoking, 211; soft water, 77
Chamaemelum nobile. See
Chamomile
Chamomile, 99; *Candida albi-
cans*, 100; digestion, 100;
ear infections, 329; earaches,
327; insomnia, 231; premen-
strual syndrome (PMS), 260;
sleep disorders, 231; stress
reduction, 163
Champault, G, 110
Change Your Smile, 309
Chapkin, R, 97
Charantin, 98
Charged-couple device (CCD),
311
Charles, V, 113
Chaste tree, 95; amenorrhea, 260;
premenstrual syndrome
(PMS), 259
CHD. *See* Coronary artery dis-
ease (CAD)
Chelation therapy, 151;
Alzheimer's disease, 404
Chelidanium majus (greater
celandine), 200
*Chemical & Pharmaceutical
Bulletin*, 100-101
Chemical Pharmacology Bulletin,
100
Chemotherapy; effects, 353; exer-
cise, 352; hypnosis, 363; vit-
amin E, 70, 357
Chen, Ki C, 398
Chi, 2; imbalance, 359; pregnan-
cy, 271
Chi-kuang. *See* Qi gong
Childbirth; certified nurse-mid-
wives (CNMs), 282; classes,
282; emotions, 283; free-
standing birth centers
(FSBCs), 284; holistic therapies, 280; home births, 284;
recovery. *See* Postpartum
recovery
Childbirth classes; Bradley
method, 281; Grantly Dick-
Read method, 281; Lamaze
method, 281; psychoprophylaxis method, 281
Children, 196; depression, 224-
225; earaches, 326; earwax,
326; electromagnetic fields,

142; exercise, 133; nutrition,
41; teeth, 297
Chili peppers. *See* Capsicum
Chimaphilia umbellata. See
Pipsissewa
*Chinese Herbal Medicine;
Materia Medica*, 110
*Chinese Journal of Integrated
Traditional & Western
Medicine*, 228
Chinese Medical Journal, 172
Chinese Medicine, 4
Chinese medicine. *See*
Traditional Chinese
Medicine
Chiropractic medicine, 8; dys-
menorrhea, 257; headaches,
176; lymphatic drainage
techniques, 153; pregnancy,
279
Chiropractors, 9; licensing, 9
Chlebowski, Rowan T, 361
Chlorhexidine, 300
Chloride, 77
Cholecalciferol. *See* Vitamin D
Cholesterol, 38, 375, 378; calci-
um, 77; copper deficiency,
82; gugulgum, 113;
hawthorn berry, 172; Indian
gooseberry, 113; levels, 38;
manganese, 86; vitamin B$_6$,
173; vitamin C, 63
Chopra, Deepak; Ayurvedic med-
icine, 6; meditation, 13, 400;
pranayama yoga, 275; tran-
scendental meditation (TM),
14-15
Chromium, 81; aging, 394; can-
cer, 81; dental cavities, 81;
dietary sources, 81
Chromium chloride, 81
Chronic fatigue; osteopathic med-
icine, 18; suma, 110
Chronic Fatigue and Immune
Dysfunction Syndrome
Association, 190
Chrysanthemum indicum. See Ye
ju hua
*Chung-Kuo Chung Hsi i Chieh
Ho Tsa Chih*, 106
Chuong, James C, 90
Cichoke, Anthony, 108, 357
Cimicifuga racemosa. See Black
cohosh
Cinnabar root. *See* Dan shen

Dental surgery, 310; laser surgery, 310

Dental x rays, 311

Dentists, holistic; choosing, 311

Dentures, 307; relieving discomfort, 308

Depression, 220; biofeedback, 6; botanical therapies, 223; children, 224-225; deep breathing exercises, 224; dysthmnia, 220; elderly, 221; exercise, 124; homeopathic medicine, 223; impotence, 239; major, 220; massage, 223; nutritional therapies, 222; schisandra, 109; St. John's wort, 109; symptoms, 221, 224; vitamin B_1, 57

Derogatis, Leonard, 364

Desipramine, 203

DET, 208

Detoxification programs, 153; side effects, 153

Dexedrine, 202

Deyo, Richard A, 125

Dharmananda, S, 240-241

DHEAS. *See* Dehydroepiandrosterone sulfate (DHEAS)

Diabetes; manganese, 86; retinopathy (RP), 323; zinc, 89

Diabetes Care, 79

Diagnostic and Statistical Manual of Mental Disorders, 259

Dickey, J. L, 18

Dietary guidelines, 40; aging, 395; antioxidants, 396; Food and Nutrition Board, NAS, 40; heart disease, 375, 377; men, 237; minerals, 151; osteoporosis, 410; pregnancy, 272; vitamin and mineral therapies, 151; World Health Organization (WHO), 40

Dietary sources; betacarotene, 150; folate, 150; iron, 150; molybdenum, 86; selenium, 86, 150; vitamin B_1, 56; vitamin A, 54, 150; vitamin B_{12}, 62; vitamin B_3, 58; vitamin B_5, 58; vitamin B_6, 59, 150; vitamin B_9, 60-61;

Vitamin C, 150; vitamin D, 66; vitamin E, 150; vitamins, 53

Diets and dieting; macrobiotic diet, 252. *See also* Weight loss

Digital radiography, 311

Digitalis, 8

Dihydrotachysterol. *See* Vitamin D

Dihydrotestosterone, 244

Diltiazem, 237; environmental, 237

Dioscorea villosa. See Yams, wild

Diosgenin, 110, 251; osteoporosis, 411

Dioxin, 143

Disabled; exercise, 134

Disabled American Veterans, 234

Discovering Homeopathy, 223, 260, 265

Diverticulosis, 98

DMT, 208

Doctor's Book of Home Remedies II, 323

DONA. *See* Doulas of North America (DONA)

Dong quai, 101, 238; menopause, 253, 255; premenstrual syndrome (PMS), 259

Donovan, Priscilla, 167

Donsbach, Kurt W, 361

Dopamine, 124

Dorant, E, 103

Doulas of North America (DONA), 290

Dr. Braly's Diet & Nutrition Revolution, 187

Dr. Dean Ornish's Program for Reversing Heart Disease, 1, 78, 172, 181

Dristan, 335

Drug abuse; adolescents, 194

Drug Information, 67

Drugs of the Future, 360

Dry mouth, 338

Dua, J. , 14

Duodenal ulcers, 185; fiber, 187

Dysentery, 111

Dysmenorrhea; acupuncture, 256; botanical medicines, 257; chaste tree, 95; chiropractic medicine, 257; osteopathic medicine, 18, 257;

Traditional Chinese Medicine, 257

Dysthmnia, 220

E

Ear disorders, 325; otosclerosis, 333

Ear Foundation, 331

Ear infections, 329; Ayurvedic medicine, 329; botanical medicines, 329; ferrum phas, 329; first aid, 327; heat therapy, 329; homeopathic medicine, 329; inner ear, 329; middle ear. *See* Otitis media, 328; neem, 329; relieving, 327; surgery, 329; vitamin and mineral therapies, 328

Earaches, 326; acupressure, 327; botanical medicines, 328; heat therapy, 334; nasal sprays, 333; relieving, 327; yoga, 327

Earches; botanical medicines, 328

Ears; acupuncture, 3; blockages, 326; cochlear implants, 333; components, 325; foreign bodies in, 326; high-impact aerobics, 330; nerve deafness, 326; nutritional therapies, 326

Ears, ringing in. *See* Tinnitus

Earthrise Company, 95

Earwax, 326; children, 326

Eating habits, 394

ECap. *See* Exceptional Cancer Patients (ECaP)

ECG. *See* Electrocardiogram (EKG)

Echinacea; abscesses, 306; colon, 148; eyes, 324; immune system, 102; lymphatic function, 148; otitis media, 329; prostatitis, 245; strep throat, 337; toothaches, 302

Echinacea angustifolia. See Echinacea

Echinacea purpurea. See Echinacea

Echinacea: The Immune Herb, 302

Eclectic Materia Medica, 238, 245

Eye drops, 325; glaucoma, 320; sties, 324

Eyebright; eyes, 324

Eyesight; bilberry extract, 320; smoking, 316; vision training, 322; vitamin B$_{12}$, 316

F

FA. *See* Ferulic acid (FA)

Fackelmann, Kathy A, 69, 90

Fahrion, Steve, 320

Fallopian tubes; surgery. *See also* Recanalization, 271

False unicorn root; menopause, 253

Farnesyl, 347

Farnsworth, N, 238

Farr, Charles, 381, 405

Farris, R. P, 41

Farsightedness. *See* Hyperopia

Fasting, 152

Fats, 38, 43; polyunsaturated, 68; saturated, 38

FDA Consumer Reports, 48, 308-309

FDA. *See* Food and Drug Administration (FDA)

FEBS Letter, 98

Federal Drug Administration (FDA); Bach flower therapy, 22; flower essences, 22; regulation of botanical medicines, 93

Feinstein, Alice, 331; earaches, 328

Feldene, 186

Feldenkrais method, 26, 175

Feldenkrais, Moshe, 26

Felter, H, 238, 245

Female health problems; exercise, 412; osteoporosis, 406; unicorn root, 255

Fennel; eyes, 324; menopause, 253

Ferrum phose. See Phosphate of iron

Ferulic acid (FA), 101

Fetal stimulation, 280

Fever; *Picorrhiza kurroa,* 113

Feverfew; headaches, 175

Fiber, 37, 43; cancer, 345; digestion, 37; hypertension, 181; ulcers, 187

Fibrocystic breast disease (FBD), 84, 249; Danazol, 250; hormone therapy, 250; iodine, 251; massage, 251; nutritional therapies, 251; vitamin and mineral therapies, 251

Fight or flight response, 158

Filov, V, 361

Finasterid, 242

First aid; ear infections, 327; teeth, 303-304

Fitness, 260

Fitness & Your Health, 148

Flap surgery, 300

Flavin adenine dinucleotide, 57

Flavin mononucleotide, 57

Flouidated water, 82

Flower essences, 21

Fluoride, 82, 295; benefits, 295; dietary sources, 82

Foeniculum vulgare, 255

Folate; dietary sources, 150

Folders, Karl, 380

Folic acid. *See* Vitamin B$_9$

Folic acid deficiency; Alzheimer's disease, 404

Folker, Keith, 99

Food additives; cancer, 347

Food and Drug Administration (FDA), 154; vitamin B$_9$, 60

Food and Life; A Nutrition Primer, 40

Food and Nutrition Information Center, 51

Food carcinogens, 347

Food Inisight, 126

Food intolerance; irritable bowel syndrome (IBS), 183

Food toxins, 143; combatting, 144

Forever Young, 392

Forse, Armour, 46

Foster, Steven, 103, 175

Foundation for Advancement in Cancer Therapy, 368

Foxglove; hepatitis, 111

Franger, Alfred, 262

Free radicals, 318; aging, 392; combatting, 396; vitamin E, 68-69, 71

Free-standing birth centers (FSBCs), 284

Freebase. *See* Cocaine

Frei, Jeffrey, 63

Frisch, Rose, 120, 351

Fructose, 37

Fu Fang Xi gua Shuang. *See* Watermelon frost

Fu Zheng; cancer, 359

Fu zi. *See* Aconite

Fugh-Berman, Adriane, 85; cervical dysplasia, 55; chiropractic medicine, 9; da qing ye, 111; headaches, 175; huang lian, 111; morning sickness, 60; phytoestrogens, 378; *Picorrhiza kurroa,* 113; vitamin A, 56; vitamin B$_9$, 61; yoga, 20

Full Catastrophic Living; Using the Wisdom of Your Body and Mind to Face Stress, Pain, and Illness, 165

Future of the Body, 163

G

Galactosemia, 316

Galen, 8

Gamble, Andrew, 110

Gamma-lineoleic acid, 95, 97

Gammainterferon, 83

Gan cao. *See* Licorice

Gard, Zane, 152

Garfinkel, P, 48

Gargling, 338-339

Garland, Frank, 67

Garlic, 103; abscesses, 306; cancer, 103; ear infections, 328; fibrin, 172

Gases; radioactive, 143

Gastric bypass surgery, 46

Gastric ulcers; symptoms, 185

Gastrointestinal Health, 183

Gatta, L, 97

Gelatin; sore throats, 339

Geleijnse, J. M, 181

Gelsenium, 176

General Adaptation Syndrome (GAS), 158

General Hospital Psychiatry, 13

Genital warts, 344

Geranium maculatum. See Spotted cranesbill

Gerhard, I, 271

Germanium, 82; dietary sources, 82; immune system, 83

Gerontologist, 397

Hearing; vitamin and mineral therapies, 330
Hearing loss, 326
Heart attacks; causes, 371; drug therapy, 374. *See also* Heart disease
Heart disease; biofeedback, 7; botanical medicines, 380; dan shen, 112; dietary guidelines, 375, 377; estrogen replacement therapy, 381; exercise, 382-383; hawthorn berry, 380; homeopathic medicine, 381; hormones, 382; ischemic, 70; magnesium, 379; nitroglycerin tablets, 373; phytoestrogens, 378; recovery, 386; selenium, 87, 379; surgery, 374; Traditional Chinese Medicine, 382; vitamin and mineral therapies, 378; vitamin E, 69-71, 379
Heart specialists; holistic. *See* Alternative physicians
Heat therapy; ear infections, 329; earaches, 334. *See also* Hyperthermia
Heavy metal poisoning, 141, 402; combatting, 141
Helium-neon laser treatment; vertigo, 333
Helixor, 107
Heller, Joseph, 26
Hellerwork, 26
Helonias opulus, 255
Hemochromatosis, 85
Hemorrhaging, postpartum, 287
Hemorrhoids, 25, 99
Hendler, Sheldon, 395
Henneberger, Melinda, 332
Henrikson, Robert, 95; algae, 95-96
Hepar sulph. See Calcium sulphide
Hepatitis; *Eclipta alba,* 113; foxglove, 111; licorice, 111
Herbal Healing for Women, 254
HerbalGram, 105, 109
Heroin, 206-207; acupuncture, 4
Heroin addiction; acupuncture, 207; treatment, 207
Herpes, 25, 344; aloe vera, 96; lithium, 85; shiitake mushrooms, 108

HGF. *See* Human growth factor
Hiatal hernias, 18
Hibbs, John, 329
High-density lipoproteins (HDL), 38
Hildreth, Suzanne, 165
Hilton, Eileen, 264
Hippocrates, 8
History of Nutritional Immunology, 89
Hitzenberger, G, 104
HIV/AIDS; acupuncture, 5; bitter melon, 98; cat's claw, 98; hyperthermia, 22; licorice, 106; maitake mushrooms, 108; ozone therapy, 25; skullcap, 100; vitamin A, 56; zinc, 89
Hoarseness, 336
Hobbs, Christopher, 105; echinacea, 302; St. John's wort, 109
Hodgkin's disease, 344
Hoffer, Abraham, 86, 228, 404
Hoffman, David, 183, 257
Holder, Jeffrey, 3, 204
Holistic dentists. *See* Alternative physicians
Holistic therapies; childbirth, 280; gingivitis, 300; teeth, 297
Holzman, David, 321
Home births, 284
Home Remedies Handbook, 308
Homeopathic doctors. *See* Alternative physicians
Homeopathic Education Services, 31
Homeopathic medicine, 10; abscesses, 306; alcoholism, 200; ear infections, 329; frequently used, 176; heart disease, 381; impotence, 238; osteoporosis, 412; pregnancy, 280; sinusitis, 335; sore throats, 338; teeth, 305; tinnitus, 330; toothaches, 302; vertigo, 332; yeast infections, 265
Homeopathic Remedies for Everyday Ailments and Minor Injuries, 176
Homeopathic therapies; headaches, 176; premenstrual syndrome (PMS), 260

Homeopaths. *See* Homeopathic physicans
Homes, Michelle, 47
Homocysteine, 378
Hooper, Judith, 358-359
Hops, 162; sleep disorders, 231
Hormone growth promoters, 36
Hormone therapy; fibrocystic breast disease (FBD), 250; sleep disorders, 231
Hormones; cancer, 352; heart disease, 382
Horsetail, 102; silica, 102; urinary tract infections, 245
Hospital Practice, 182
Hot baths. *See* Hydrotherapy
Hot flashes; vitamin E, 255
How Much Sleep Do You Need?, 231
How To Live Longer and Feel Better, 68
Hu, S, 19
Huang chi. *See* Astralagus
Huang lian, 111; dysentery, 111; fungi, 111; scarlet fever, 111
Huard, Pierre, 4
Hudson, Tori, 250, 259; fibrocystic breast disease (FBD), 251
Human Ecology Program, 83, 89
Human growth factor, 398
Human growth hormones; aging, 397; immune system, 398
Human immunodeficiency virus. *See* HIV/AIDS
Humor. *See* Emotions
Humulus lupulus. See Hops
Hunger, 44
Hydrastine, 105
Hydrastis canadensis. See Goldenseal
Hydrazine sulfate; cancer, 361
Hydrocarbons, 22
Hydrochloric acid, 77, 185
Hydrogen peroxide; cancer, 361
Hydrotherapy, 152; benefits, 22; irritable bowel syndrome (IBS), 183; pregnancy, 278; premenstrual syndrome (PMS), 260; prostate enlargement, 243; protatitis, 245; sinus congestion, 335; sore throats, 338
Hyperactivity; biofeedback, 6-7
Hypericum perforatum. See St. John's wort

Hyperlipidemia, 96

Hyperopia, 321

Hypertension, 15, 383; acupuncture, 179; algae, 96; alternative therapies, 179; Ayurvedic medicine, 179; biofeedback, 179; bodywork therapies, 179; botanical medicines, 180; calcium deficiency, 77, 181; essential, 178; exercise, 121, 124, 180; fiber, 181; hawthorn berry, 180; infants, 276; magnesium deficiency, 181; mineral salts, 181; mistletoe, 180; nutritional therapies, 181; oyster extract, 180; potassium, 80; stress reduction therapies, 181; sugar, 181; tai chi, 182; Traditional Chinese Medicine, 182; transcendental meditation (TM) , 15; types, 178; vitamin and mineral therapies, 182; vitamin C, 65; weight loss, 182; ye ju hua, 112

Hyperthermia, 22; contraindications, 23; hairy leukoplakia, 22; HIV/AIDS, 22; Kaposi's sarcoma, 22

Hypervitaminosis A, 55

Hypnosis, 11; asthma, 12; cancer, 362; chemotherapy, 363; irritable bowel syndrome (IBS), 184; smoking, 211; weight loss, 12

Hypnotherapists. *See* Alternative physicians

Hypoglycemia, 222; calcium deficiency, 67; vitamin D, 67

Hypothyroidism, 84; menorrhagia, 258

Hysterectomy Educational Resources and Services (HERS) Foundation, 253, 267

I

IBS. *See* Irritable bowel syndrome

I.B.S. Wellness Diet, 183

IHD. *See* Ischemic heart disease (IHD)

Ilex puibeceus. See Mao-tung-ching

Imagawa, M, 404

Immune system; aging, 392; algae, 96; detoxification, 147; detoxification programs, 153; echinacea, 102; elderly, 149; emotions, 149; exercise, 148-149; germanium, 83; human growth hormones, 398; macrophages, 351; natural killer (NK) cells, 351; nutritional therapies, 149-150; schisandra, 109; social support, 364; vitamin and mineral therapies, 151; zinc, 90

Immunobiology, 106

Immunoglobulins, 22

Immunostimulants, 83

Immunotoxins, 141

Implants, dental. *See* Dental implants

Impotence, 240; botanical medicines, 237-238; cell therapy, 238; exercise, 238; holistic therapies, 237; homeopathic medicine, 238; nutritional therapies, 239; papaverine injection therapy, 240; psychotherapy, 239; tai chi, 238; Traditional Chinese Medicine, 239; vitamin and mineral therapies, 240

In vitro fertilization (IVF), 271

Incontinence; biofeedback, 7

Indian gooseberry, 113; cholesterol, 113

Indian Journal of Medical Research, 19, 106

Indian Journal of Physiology and Pharmacology , 13, 19, 288

Indirubin, 359

Indoor air pollution, 145

INED, 18

Infants; breastfeeding, 285; cavities, 292; craniosacral therapy, 288; hypertension, 276; teeth, 292

Infertility, 271; vitamin B$_9$, 61

Insight, 321

Insomnia. *See* Sleep disorders

Institute for Aerobics Research, 351

Insulin; bitter melon, 98; zinc, 89

Interleukin, 108

Interleukin-2, 150

International Association for Cancer Victors and Friends, 368

International Chiropractors Association, 31

International Journal of Cancer, 345

International Journal of Obesity, 41

International Journal of Psychosomatics, 275

International Journal of Technology Assessment in Health Care, 303

Intrauterine devices; menorrhagia, 258

Inulin, 102

Involuntary nervous system; meditation, 13

Iodine, 83; deficiency, 83-84; dietary sources, 83; fibrocystic breast disease (FBD), 251; metabolism, 83

Iodized salt, 83

Iris versicolor, 176

Irisquinone, 359

Iron, 84; canker sores, 85; deficiency. *See* Anemia; detoxification, 85; dietary sources, 84, 150

Irradiation. *See* Radiation therapy

Irritable bowel syndrome (IBS), 182; botanical medicines, 183; colon therapy, 183; exercise, 183; food intolerance, 183; hydrotherapy, 183; hypnosis, 184; magnesium deficiency, 79; nutritional therapies, 184; stress reduction therapies, 184; vitamin and mineral therapies, 185; vitamin B$_9$, 61

Isatis tincotria. See Da qing ye

Iscador. *See* Mistletoe

Ischemic heart disease (IHD), 70

Isoleucine, 36

Isoptin, 237

It's All in Your Head, 405

Ito, N, 99

J

Jacob, A, 113
Jahnke, R, 164
JAMA. *See Journal of the American Medical Association* (JAMA)
Jane Brody's Guide to Personal Health, 292, 307
Janssen, O, 107
Japanese honeysuckle, 111
Japanese Journal of Cancer and Chemotherapy, 359
Japanese Journal of Clinical Oncology, 99
Jiang xiang, 112
Jin, P, 182
Jinyin hua. See Japanese honeysuckle
Jogging. *See* Running
Johns Hopkins Medical Handbook, 177, 180, 185, 240, 321-322, 333
Johns Hopkins Medical Letter, 178, 186, 318
Johns Hopkins Medical Letter: Health After 50, 221
Johnson Institute of Rehabilitation, 215
Johnson, Susan, 129
Johnstone, E, 228
Joint flexibility, 124
Jose Mercury News, 128
Journal of Asthma, 79
Journal of Biometerology, 20
Journal of Clinical Oncology, 361
Journal of Clinical Psychology, 7, 13, 200
Journal of Ethnopharmacology, 104, 110, 114, 359, 398
Journal of Holistic Nursing, 288
Journal of John Bastyr College of Natural Medicine, 96
Journal of Neuroscience, 19
Journal of Nursing, 101
Journal of Orthomolecular Medicine, 228
Journal of Pediatrics, 85
Journal of Physiology and Pharmacology, 13, 19
Journal of Psychosomatic Research, 182
Journal of School Health, 41

Journal of the American College of Nutrition, 78
Journal of the American Medical Association (JAMA) , 36, 61, 295, 359
Journal of the National Cancer Institute, 96
Journal of Traditional Chinese Medicine, 398
Journal of Traumatic Stress, 7
Journal of Tropical Medicine, 113
JT-48. *See* Juzentaihoto
JTT. *See* Juzentaihoto
Juglans nigra. See Black walnut
Juice fasts. *See* Fasting
Juice therapy; ulcers, 187
Juzentaihoto; cancer, 359

K

Kabat-Zinn, Jon, 165; meditation, 13
Kaiser, R, 6
Kali bichronicum, 176
Kaplan, H, 232
Kaposi's sarcoma; hyperthermia, 22
Kavner, Richard, 316, 322
Kegel exercises; pregnancy, 278; premature ejaculation, 241
Keim, Robert, 307
Keller, Helmut, 359
Kershan's disease, 87
Kidney stones; aloe vera, 96
Kidneys; toxins, 148
Kiecolt-Glaser, Janice, 149
Kiesewetter, H, 380
Kinesiology, 27
Kinetic cavity preparation (KCP), 294
Kirshna, Gopal, 80
Komori, A, 99
Kotsanis, Constantine A, 326; tinnitus, 330
Kovacs, E, 358
Kovacs, Maria, 224
Krotkiewski, M, 180
Kruzel, Tom; impotence, 239; prostate enlargement, 243; prostatitis, 246
Kuan Yin Clinic, 5
Kuba, M, 100
Kudzu, 199

Kulkalni, R, 113

L

L-Arginine, 185
Labor. *See* Childbirth
Lactea pallasii, 359
Lactobacillus acidophilus, 265
Lactose, 37
Ladner, Hans, 59
Lamarra, J. , 15
Lamaze method (childbirth classes), 281
Lambert, Craig, 6
Lancet, 18, 55-56, 68, 70, 81, 199, 329, 363
Lane, Nancy, 123, 412
Lane, William, 358
Langer, S, 71
Langsjoen, Peter, 380
Lark, Susan, 257, 263
Laryngoscope, 326
Lazy eye. *See* Amblyopia
LBG. *See* Light beam generators (LBG)
LDL. *See* Low-density lipoproteins (LDL)
Lead poisoning, 141; combatting, 142
Learning disabilities; anemia, 85
Lecithin, 173
Lectures in Naturopathic Hydrotherapy, 22
Lee, John, 250; diosgenin, 411
Lee-Huang, S, 98
Lehrer, Joel, 331
Lemon balm, 163
Lentinan, 108, 357
Lentinus edodes. See Shiitake mushroom
Leopard's bane. *See* Arnica
LeSassier, William, 252
Leucine, 36
Leukemias. *See* Cancer
Leukotrines, 87
Levodopa, 72
Levy, Sandra, 364
Li, B, 100
Licorice, 106, 238; hepatitis, 111; HIV/AIDS, 106; lymphatic function, 148; ma huang, 103; menopause, 253; premenstrual syndrome (PMS),

259; ulcers, 186; viruses, 106

Lidocaine, 241

Lien, Eric J, 359

Life expectancy, 124

Life Extension, 198

Light beam generators (LBG), 153

Ligusticum porteri. See Osha

Limberg, Pieter C, 72

Limbic system, 21

Lin, Yuan-Chi, 2; acupuncturists, 5

Lincoln Substance Abuse/Acupuncture Clinic, 204

Lipid, 260

Lipoproteins; high-density. *See* High-density lipoproteins (HDL), 38; low-density. *See* Low-density lipoproteins (LDL), 38

Lisinopril, 237

Lithium, 85; herpes, 85; manic-depressive disorder, 86

Liu, C, 104

Liver, 147; schisandra, 109

Liver cirrhosis, 22; *Eclipta alba,* 113

Living with Exercise, 352

Livingston Foundation Medical Center, 368

Livingston therapy, 360

Livingston, Virginia, 360

London, R. S, 78

London School of Hygiene and Tropical Medicine, 157

Lonicera japonica. See Japanese honeysuckle

Loomis, Evarts G, 152

Lotus seed, 241

Love, Medicine & Miracles, 13, 18, 343, 363

Love, Susan, 250

Low-density lipoproteins (LDL), 38

Lower Your Blood Pressure and Live Longer, 180

Lown Cardiovascular Center, 374

LSD. *See* Lysergic acid diethylamide (LSD)

Lu, W, 106

Ludvig Boltzmann-Institute, 107

Lukas Klinik, 107

Lust, Benedict, 15

Lyceum berries, 241

Lymphatic massage, 153

Lymphomas. *See* Cancer

Lysergic acid diethylamide (LSD), 208

Lysine, 36

M

Ma huang, 103

Ma, Q, 228

Maclean, C. , 14

Maclean, Norman, 391

Macrobiotic diet, 17, 252

Macrophages, 351

Macula, 322

Macular degeneration, 322; biofeedback, 322; nutritional therapies, 322; surgery, 322

Magnesium, 77; asthma, 79; food sources, 77; heart attacks, 78; heart disease, 379; premenstrual syndrome (PMS), 263

Magnesium chelate, 255

Magnesium citrate, 148

Magnesium deficiency, 77; angina, 78; hypertension, 181; irritable bowel syndrome (IBS), 79; premenstrual syndrome (PMS), 78

Magnets, dental, 307

Maitake mushrooms, 108; cancer, 357; HIV/AIDS, 108; hypertension, 180

Male erectile dysfunction. *See* Impotence

Male health problems; botanical medicines, 237; impotence, 237-239; premature ejaculation, 239-240; prostate, 238; prostate enlargement, 241; prostatitis, 244

Male Sexual Dysfunction Institute, 240

Malnutrition; algae, 96

Malocclusions, 306; braces, 306; dental magnets, 307; straightening, 307

Manganese, 86; cholesterol, 86; deficiency, 86; diabetes, 86; disease prevention, 86; epilepsy, 86; food sources, 86

Manic-depressive disorder; lithium, 86

Mantra, 13-14

Mao-tung-ching, 382; atherosclerosis, 172

Margolis, Simeon, 333; biofeedback, 177; glaucoma, 321; hypertension, 180; impotence, 240; macular degeneration, 322; peptic ulcers, 185

Marijuana, 206; effects, 205-206

Marin Independent Journal, 168

Marinelli, Rick, 242

Mark, Daniel, 386

Mark, H, 320, 325

Martin, M. F, 41

Massage, 23, 166; back pain, 23; caffeine withdrawal, 202; depression, 223; fibrocystic breast disease (FBD), 251; headaches, 176-177; lymphatic, 153; rolfing, 27; tonal, 167; uterine, 287

Matricaria chamomilla. See Chamomile

Maximum Life Span, 392

May, L, 67

Mayer, Roger, 288

Mayo Clinic Health Letter, 175, 210

McCabe, Edward, 246

McClanahan, T. , 15

McKinlay, John D, 237

M.D. Anderson Cancer Center, 55

Meadowlark, 152

Meat; growth hormones, 36

Medicine, Microbiology and Immunology, 85

Meditation, 13, 164; aging, 400; involuntary nervous system, 13; Personal Happiness Enhancement Program (PHEP), 14; pregnancy, 276

Meditative Mind, 164, 276

Meganutrients for Your Nerves, 59

Megavitamins, 228

Melanoma. *See* Cancer

Melatonin; sleep disorders, 231

Men; dietary guidelines, 237

Meniere's disease. *See* Vertigo

Menninger Clinic, 11

Menopausal Time of Life, 253

Menopause, 253, 255; botanical medicines, 253; deep breathing exercises, 254; diogenin, 254; estrogen replacment therapy (ERT), 254; exercise, 255; men. *See* Andropause, 235; nutritional therapies, 255; Vitamin K, 255

Menorrhagia, 258; blue cohosh, 258; botanical medicines, 258; gynecological exams, 258; nutritional therapies, 258; shepherd's purse, 258; spotted cranesbill, 258; thyroid hormones, 258; uterine fibroids, 258; witch hazel, 258

Menstrual cramps. *See* Dysmennorrhea

Menstruation, 256; excessive bleeding. *See* Menorrhagia, 258

Mental illness; acupuncture, 4; magnesium deficiency, 77

Mescaline, 208

Metabolism, 83

Methadone, 22

Methedrine, 202

Methionine, 378

Methionone, 36

Methotrexate, 61

Midwives. *See* Certified nurse-midwives (CNMs)

Migraine headaches, 174; feverfew, 176; food allergies, 177

Milk, 409; soybean, 410

Milk thistle, 106, 147

Miller, Dennis, 108, 358

Milne, Robert, 330, 332; ear infections, 329

Mindful exercise, 165

Mineral deficiencies; depression, 223

Mineral salts, 181

Minerals. *See* Vitamin and mineral therapies

Minerva Urologica, 108

Minimal brain dysfunction; skullcap, 100

Minton, John Peter, 251

Miracle Cure: Organic Germanium, 83

Misophobia, 226

Mistletoe, 106; blood pressure, 106; cancer, 107, 358; hypertension, 180

Mitchell, J, 87

Mitchell, W, 100

Modern Nutrition in Health and Disease, 49

Modern Synopsis of Comprehensive Textbook of Psychiatry, 232

Molhave, Lars, 145

Molybdenum, 86; dietary sources, 86

Momordica charantia. See Bitter melon

Monroe, Shafia, 252

Monte, Tom, 19

Mooradian, A, 86

Moorhead, Kelly J.; algae, 95

Morain, C. O, 82

Morgan, Helen C.; algae, 95

Morning sickness, 273; vitamin B$_6$, 60

Morphine, 206

Moses, Hamilton; biofeedback, 177; hypertension, 180; impotence, 240; peptic ulcers, 185

Mothad, Gowri, 281

Motherhood Report, 281

Motion sickness, 103

Mouth; abscesses, 305; ulcers. *See* Canker sores, 336

Mouth, dry. *See* Dry mouth

Mouthwash, 300

Movement therapy, 26-27

Mowrey, Daniel, 97; gotu kola, 102

Moyers, Bill, 3, 251

Mueller, E, 107

Murphy, Michael, 163

Murray, Frank, 55, 69; vitamin E, 71

Murray, Michael; aloe vera, 96; bitter melon, 98; botanical medicines, 162, 337; canker sores, 337; carnitine, 173; chamomile, 100; cholesterol, 172; cranberry juice, 101; dandelion, 101; dong quai, 101; ear infections, 329; fiber, 181, 187; food intolerance, 184; ginger, 104; ginseng, 104, 162; goldenseal, 105; gotu kola, 102;

headaches, 177; heart disease, 381; heavy metal poisoning, 141; hypertension, 180-181; intestinal toxins, 145; irritable bowel syndrome (IBS), 183; kidneys, 148; lymphatic function, 148; marapuama, 238; menopause, 255; milk thistle, 106; mistletoe, 106; obesity, 44; prostate enlargement, 244; sinusitis, 334-335; sore throats, 337; spleen, 147; stress, 187; stress reduction therapies, 184; ulcers, 186-187; vitamin and mineral therapies, 162, 335; vitamin B$_2$, 57; weight loss, 46

Music and the Brain, 167

Music therapy, 23-24, 166; childbirth, 280; grief, 25; stress, 25

Mutagens, 347

Myelomas. *See* Cancer

Myocardial infarction. *See* Heart attacks

Myocardium, 371

Myomectomy, 253

Myopia, 321-322

Myringotomy, 329

Myrrh; toothpastes, 296

N

NACA. *See* National Association of Childbirth Assistants (NACA)

Nacardipine, 237

Nadi Shodhana. *See* Pranayama yoga

Nagai, T, 100

Naprosyn, 186

Naproxen, 186

Nasal polyps, 336; vitamin A, 336; vitamin and mineral therapies, 336; vitamin C, 336

Nasal sprays; earaches, 333

National Academy of Sciences (NAS), 41

National Acupuncture Detoxification Association (NADA), 199

Nutrition Today, 46, 48
Nutritional deficiencies, 35, 149; aging, 392; Alzheimer's disease, 403
Nutritional therapies; abscesses, 305; Alzheimer's disease, 402; atherosclerosis, 172; cancer, 345, 356; cataracts, 317; ears, 326; fibrocystic breast disease (FBD), 251; headaches, 177; hypertension, 181; irritable bowel syndrome (IBS), 184; macular degeneration, 322; menopause, 255; menorrhagia, 258; osteoporosis, 407; otitis media, 328; postpartum recovery, 287; pregnancy, 272-273; premenstrual syndrome (PMS), 261; prostatitis, 245; sinusitis, 334; tinnitus, 330; ulcers, 187; uterine fibroids, 252; vertigo, 331; yeast infections, 265
Nux vomica, 176, 200; insomnia, 231, sinusitis, 335

O

O'Brien, Jim, 176
OAM. *See* Office of Alternative Medicine (OAM)
Oats, 211
Obeline (oats), 211
Oberg, O, 283
Obesity, 46; gastric bypass surgery, 46; holistic diet programs, 47; hypnotherapy, 12; weight loss, 46
Obsessive-compulsive disorders. *See* Compulsive disorders
Occupation Safety and Health Administration (OSHA), 155
Office of Alternative Medicine (OAM) , 9, 12, 20
Office on Smoking and Health, 215
Ohsawa, George, 17
Olive oil, 244
Olsten, Kristen, 238
Omi, N, 410

Ophediophobia; environmental, 226
Opium, 206
Optometric Extension Program Foundation, Inc, 341
Orchitis, 244
Orman, David, 105
Ornish, Dean, 369; atherosclerosis, 172; fiber, 181; holistic therapies, 17; hypertension, 181; magnesium, 78-79, 379; progressive relaxation, 385; smoking, 387; yoga, 385
Ornstein, R, 83
Orthomolecular Nutrition, 85
Orthomolecular therapy, 228
OSHA. *See* Occupation Safety and Health Administration (OSHA)
Osha; sore throats, 338; toothaches, 302
Osteoarthritis; acupuncture, 3; Articulin-F, 113; hypnotherapy, 12
Osteomalacia, 77
Osteopathic medicine, 17; dysmenorrhea, 18, 257; lympathic circulation, 153; physiologic motion disorders, 18
Osteopathic physicians. *See* Alternative physicians
Osteoporosis, 76, 78, 406; Ayurvedic medicine, 412; botanical medicines, 410; calcitonin, 411; calcium, 407; causes, 407; dietary guidelines, 410; diosgenin, 411; estrogen deficiency, 407; estrogen replacement therapy, 410; exercise, 412; homeopathic medicine, 412; nutritional therapies, 407; phytoestrogens, 410; Traditional Chinese Medicine, 412
Otitis media, 328; acute purient, 328; acute serious, 328; echinacea, 329; goldenseal, 329; nutritional therapies, 328; secretory, 328; symptoms, 328
Otosclerosis, 326, 333
Oxalic acid, 76

Oxygen Healing Therapies, 25, 245, 265
Oxysterols, 378
Oyster extract, 180
Ozaki, Y, 101
Ozone, 140
Ozone and Oxygen Therapy, 246
Ozone protection; vitamin E, 71
Ozone therapy, 25; cancer, 25, 362; HIV/AIDS, 25; types, 25; yeast infections, 265

P

PABA, 143
Paffenbarger, Ralph, 124-125, 135, 352
Pain in Infants, Children, and Adolescents, 2
Palmer, Daniel David, 8
Panax ginseng. See Ginseng
Panax quinquefolium. See Ginseng
Panic attacks. *See* Panic disorders
Panic disorders; biofeedback, 226; causes, 226; psychotherapy, 226
Panjwani, U. , 13, 19
Panos, Maesimund, 176
Pantethine, 379
Pantothenic acid. *See* Vitamin B$_3$
Pap smear, 344
Papaver somniferum, 206
Papaverine injection therapy, 240
Paranoid schizophrenia. *See* Schizophrenia
Parasympathetic cardiac arryhmia, 7
Parker, G, 176
Parkinson's disease; vitamin E, 72
Passiflora incarnata. See Passion flower
Passion flower, 163; hypertension, 180; insomnia, 231; menopause, 254; sleep disorders, 231
Patanjali, 19
Patient Care, 125, 128
Patient Education and Counseling, 13
Pauling, Linus, 53, 64, 68
PCBs. *See* Polychlorinated biphenyls (PCBs)

amin B$_9$ deficiency, 60; yoga, 274

Premature ejaculation, 239-240; botanical medicines, 241; Kegel exercises, 241; non-prescription medications, 240; nutritional therapies, 241; physical techniques, 241

Premenstrual syndrome (PMS); botanical medicines, 259; chaste tree, 95, 259; exercise, 260, 263; guidelines for relieving, 261; homeopathic therapies, 260; hydrotherapy, 260; magnesium deficiency, 78; nutritional therapies, 261; progesterone therapy, 262; qi gong, 262; sexual intercourse, 262; vitamin and mineral therapies, 263; vitamin B$_2$, 57; zinc, 90

Presbyopia, 321

Prescription for Nutritional Healing, 96, 108, 177, 183, 239, 241, 262, 319, 332

Presenile dementia of the Alzheimer's type (PDAT), 401

Presse Medicale, 404

Prevention Magazine, 45, 63, 77, 80, 89, 254

Preventive Medicine, 103

Priessnitz, Vinzenz, 22

Priestley, Joan, 108

Primary Cardiology, 181

Primavera, Joseph, 176

Prinivil, 237

Pritchard, Jack, 283

Procardia, 237

Proceedings of the National Academy of Sciences, 99

Progenitor cryptocides, 360-361

Progesterone; cream, 250

Progesterone therapy; premenstrual syndrome (PMS), 262

Progressive relaxation, 161, 384; blood pressure, 385; pregnancy, 276

Propolis; abscesses, 306

Propranolol, 374

Proscar. *See* Finasterid

Prostaglandins, 87, 236

Prostate cancer; zinc, 88

Prostate enlargement, 241; acupuncture, 242; amino acid therapy, 242; Ayurvedic medicine, 242; botanical medicines, 242-243; drug therapies, 242; nutritional therapies, 243; vitamin and mineral therapies, 243; zinc, 88

Prostatic hypertrophy, benign, 110

Prostatitis, 244; Ayurvedic medicine, 244; botanical medicines, 245; homeopathic medicine, 245; hydrotherapy, 245; nutritional therapies, 245; ozone therapy, 245; Traditional Chinese Medicine, 246; vitamin and mineral therapies, 246

Proteins, 36, 43

Pseudoephedrine, 103

Psoriasis; vitamin D, 67

Psychedelic drugs, 207-208

Psychoactive drugs, 193

Psychological disorders; aromatherapy, 21; vitamin B$_9$, 61

Psychological Report, 15

Psychopharmacology, 231

Psychoprophylaxis method (childbirth classes), 281

Psychosomatic Medicine, 364

Psychotherapy, 169; compulsive disorders, 230; impotence, 239; panic disorders, 226; schizophrenia, 229

Pulsatilla, 260; ear infections, 329; earaches, 327

Pumpkin seeds, 89

Pygeum, 108, 110, 243; urinary disorders, 242

Pygeum africanum. See Pygeum

Pyridoxine. *See* Vitamin B$_6$

Q

Qi gong, 164; Alzheimer's disease, 406; pregnancy, 279; premenstrual syndrome (PMS), 262

Quantum Healing, 275

R

Radial keratotomy, 321

Radiation therapy; cancer, 353; implant therapy, 353

Radioactive gases, 143

Radiotherapy. *See* Radiation therapy

Radon. *See* Radioactive gases

Rai, G, 104, 404

Raju, P, 19

Rama, Swami, 19

Rauch, Erich, 152

Rawal, S, 20

Rayner, Lynn; antacids, 186; atherosclerosis, 171; fiber, 173; hearing, 330; hydrochloric acid production, 185; hypertension, 178, 182; lecithin, 173; migraine headaches, 174; osteoporosis, 406-407, 410; prostate enlargement, 243; ulcers, 187-188

Recanalization, 271

Recommended Dietary Allowances (RDA). *See* Dietary guidelines

Rectal ulcer syndrome, 7

Redbook, 335

Rees, Alan, 203; dentures, 307; exercise, 119; macular degeneration, 322; menstruation, 256; obesity, 46; sinusitis, 335; stress, 157

Reflex sympathetic dystrophy (RSD) , 7

Rehmannia glutinosa. See Chinese foxglove root

Reid, Bill, 331

Relaxation, 158; progressive, 161, 276; spiral, 161; tinnitus, 331

Relaxation response, 14, 158

Resistance phase (stress), 158

Respiratory infections; pokeweed, 107

Retalin, 100

Retinoic acid, 329, 333

Retinol, 54-55

Retinopathy (RP), 323

Reynold, E, 62

Reynold, Robert D, 59-60

Rheumatoid arthritis; vitamin E, 72; zinc, 90

Ribes nigrum. See Black currant seed
Riboflavin. *See* Vitamin B$_2$
Riemersma, R. A, 68
Riley, K, 96
Ringing in the ears. *See* Tinnitus
Riodan, Hugh, 223-224
Risperdal. *See* Risperidone
Risperidone, 229
Roberts, Joyce, 282
Roberts, S. B, 41
Rolf, Ida, 27
Rolfing, 27
Rosacea, 57
Rosen, Marion, 27
Rosen method, 27
Ross, Harvey, 222
Rowing, 131
RP. *See* Retinopathy (RP)
RSD. *See* Reflex sympathetic dystrophy (RSD)
Rubia, 148
Ruch, Meredith, 23, 223
Running; benefits, 130; safety tips, 130

S

Sahaja yoga. *See* Yoga
Saine, Andre, 22
Salkeld, Richard, 59, 356
Salt, iodized, 83
Salt substitutes, 77, 181
Salvia. *See* Dan shen
Salvia miltiorrhiza. See Dan shen
San Francisco Chronicle, 37, 229, 300, 333
San Jose Mercury News, 163, 297, 329, 331-332
Sanguinaria; toothpastes, 296
Sanguinaria canadensis. See Sanguinaria
Santhi kriya yoga. *See* Yoga
Saponins. *See* Pfaffosides
Sarcomas. *See* Cancer
Sarkar, S, 108
Saturated fats, 38
Satyanarayana, M, 19
Saw palmetto, 110; benign prostatic hypertrophy (BPH), 110; impotence, 238; prostate enlargement, 242
Saxb, E. , 7, 200

Scandinavian Journal of Psychology, 14
Scandinavian Journal of Rheumatology, 87
Scanlon, Deralee, 183; irritable bowel syndrome (IBS), 185
Scarlet fever; huang lian, 111
SCD. *See* Sudden cardiac death (SCD)
Schatz, Mary, 275
Schecter, Steven, 142
Scheel, John, 15
Schisandra chinensis. See Schisandra
Schisandra, 109; depression, 109; immune system, 109; liver, 109
Schizophrenia, 227; botanical medicines, 228; causes, 227; drug therapies, 229; orthomolecular therapy, 228; psychotherapy, 229; vitamin and mineral therapies, 228; vitamin B$_{12}$, 62
Schizophrenia: Questions and Answers, 226
Schnaubelt, Kurt, 21
Schroeder, Steven, 197
Science, 78, 333, 362
Science News, 69, 90
Scientific Validation of Herbal Medicine, 97
Sclera, 318
Scutellaria baicalensis. See Skullcap
Scutellaria latriflora. See Skullcap
SDAT. *See* Senile dementia of the Alzheimer's type (SDAT)
Seaweed; hypertension, 180
Secondhand tobacco smoke; effects, 209
Secrets of Serotonin, 260
Selenium, 86-87, 199; dietary sources, 86, 150; gout, 87; heart disease, 87, 379; yeast infection, 87
Selenium in Biology and Medicine, 87
Self, 302
Seligman, Martin, 224
Sellach, I, 296

Senile dementia of the Alzheimer's type (SDAT), 401
Sepia. See Cuttlefish
Serenoa repens. See Saw palmetto
Serotonin, 49, 98, 124, 221; antidepressants, 98; black walnut, 98, 260; feverfew, 175
Sexual intercourse; headaches, 176; premenstrual syndrome (PMS), 262
Sexuality; vitamin B$_5$, 240
Seyle, Hans, 158
Shangold, Mona, 263
Shared Guide, 294
Shark cartilage; cancer, 358
Shark liver oil; cancer, 358
Sharks Don't Get Cancer, 358
Shaw, Sandy, 198
Sheng di huang, 111
Shepherd's purse, 258
Sherman, A, 89
Shiatsu. *See* Acupressure
Shields, Jack, 152
Shiitake mushrooms; aging, 400; cancer, 108; herpes, 108; tumors, 108, 357
Shils, Maurice, 49
Shriner's Burn Institute, 149
Siegel, Bernie, 13, 18; emotions, 363; meditation, 13; visualization, 18, 362
Silica, 88; horsetail, 102
Silicon, 88
Silybum marianum. See Milk thistle
Simkin, Penny, 282
Simone, Charles, 347, 351; elderly, 149; exercise, 352; food additives, 347; juice therapy, 149; nutritional deficiencies, 149; shark cartilage, 358
Sin Shen Ling (XSL); schizophrenia, 228
Sinus congestion; hydrotherapy, 335
Sinusitis, 334; acupuncture, 335; antibiotics, 335; botanical medicines, 335; chronic, 334; homeopathic medicine, 335; nutritional therapies, 334; symptoms, 334; vitamin and mineral therapies, 334; zinc, 334

Sitz baths; benign prostatic hypertrophy (BPH), 243; childbirth, 287; irritable bowel syndrome (IBS), 183; neutral, 243. *See also* Hydrotherapy

Skiing, cross-country, 131

Skin cancer, 142; vitamin A, 349

Skullcap, 100, 163; HIV/AIDS, 100; minimal brain dysfunction, 100; sleep disorders, 231

Sleep; guidelines, 231

Sleep disorders, 230; biofeedback, 6; exercise, 232; hormone therapy, 231

Sleep therapy, 232

Smith, Michael, 207

Smith, W. , 13

Smog, 72, 140

Smoking, 209, 387; acupressure, 211; acupuncture, 211; aids for stopping, 212-213; eyesight, 316; hypnosis, 211; quitting, 210-211

Social Readjustment Rating Scale, 158-159

Social support; cancer, 363; immune system, 364

Society of American Gastrointestinal Endoscopic Surgeons, 368

Sodhi; Alzheimer's disease, 406

Sodhi, Virender; atherosclerosis, 172; ear infections, 326, 329; hypertension, 179; prostate enlargement, 242; ulcers, 186; vertigo, 332

Sodium, 80; deficiency, 80; dietary sources, 80; excessive intake, 80

Somer, Elizabeth, 396

Soot, 141

Sorbitol gum, 298

Sore throats; antibiotics, 338; botanical medicines, 337, 339; cleaning, 338; gargling, 338; gelatin, 339; glycerin, 339; homeopathic medicine, 338; hydrotherapy, 338; osha, 338; pectin, 339; vitamin and mineral therapies, 337

Sound, Listening and Learning Center, 341

Southern Medical Journal, 326

Southwest College, 16

Sphincter incontinence, 7

Spiegel, David, 363

Spinal misalignment, 8

Spiral relaxation, 161; pregnancy, 276

Spirulina. *See* Algae

Spirulina: Nature's Superfood, 95

Spleen, 147

Sports, 133

Squamous-cell carcinoma, 142

St. John's wort, 109; depression, 109, 223

St. Mary's thistle, 200

Staying Healthy with Nutrition, 201

Steinberg, Phillip, 98

Steinman, David, 99

Stephan Clinic, 238

Stephens, Paul, 295

Sties, 323; eye drops, 324; treatment, 324

Still, Andrew Taylor, 17

Stomach acid. *See* Hydrochloric acid

Stoney, Catherine, 386

STP, 208

Strabismus, 321

Stramonium. *See* Thorn-apple

Strep throat, 337

Stress, 157-158; alarm reaction, 158; coping with, 158; dance therapy, 164; exhaustion phase, 158; measurement, 158; music therapy, 25; nutritional therapies, 162; potassium, 80; resistance phase, 158; Social Readjustment Rating Scale, 158; vitamin and mineral therapies, 162; yoga, 164

Stress Protection Plan, 222, 226

Stress reduction; acupuncture, 166; aromatherapy, 163; biofeedback, 163; botannical medicines, 162-163; exercise, 163-164; humor. *See* Emotions, 166; massage, 166; meditation, 164-165; music, 166; pregnancy, 273; psychotherapy, 169; relaxation exercises, 167; social support, 168; tonal massage,

167; visualization, 166; Zen breathing, 165

Stress Reduction Clinic, University of Massachusetts, 165

Stress reduction therapies for; headaches, 177; hypertension, 181; irritable bowel syndrome (IBS), 184; ulcers, 187

Stress Without Distress, 158

Strome, M, 326

Styrenes, 22

Subluxations, 8

Sucrose, 37

Sudden cardiac death (SCD), 372

Sugar, 43; excessive intake, 37; hypertension, 181; simple, 37

Suharno, D, 56

Sulfur, 81

Suma, 110, 238; chronic fatigue, 110; heart disease, 381

Sunlight; cataracts, 318; radiation, 142; toxic effects, 142

Super Nutrition for Men, 235

Surgeon General's Report on Nutrition and Health, 33, 41, 43

Surgery; balloon angioplasty, 374; cancer, 353; coronary bypass, 373; ear infections, 329; eye disorders, 321; glaucoma, 320-321; macular degeneration, 322; radial keratotomy, 321; uterine fibroids, 253; vertigo, 332

Sushruta Samhita, 112

Swartwout, Glen, 316

Sweet, Frederick, 362

Swimming, 132

Symptoms: Their Causes & Cures, 328, 331

Syracuse Cancer Research Institute, 361, 368

T

T-cells, 90

Tai chi, 10, 135, 164; hypertension, 182; impotence, 238

Tamoxifen, 250

Taraxacum officinale. See Dandelion

tion, 76; deficiency symptoms, 66; dietary sources, 66; elderly, 67; excessive intake, 66; hypoglycemia, 67; magnesium deficiency, 78; osteoporosis, 409; pregnancy, 292; psoriasis, 67

Vitamin E, 72; Alzheimer's disease, 68; angina, 68; anticoagultion, 69; arthritis, 72; atherosclerosis, 173; benefits, 67, 71; bypass surgery, 69; cancer, 69; canker sores, 336; cataracts, 318; chemotherapy, 70, 357; deficiency, 68; dietary sources, 68, 150; epilepsy, 70; fibrocystic breast disease (FBD), 251; free radicals, 68-69, 71; heart disease, 69-71, 379; hot flashes, 255; longevity, 71; ozone protection, 71; Parkinson's disease, 72; rheumatoid arthritis, 72; selenium, 86; smoking, 211; ulcers, 188

Vitamin K; menopause, 255

Vitamins, 53, 82; dietary sources, 53; supplements, 54. *See also* Vitamin and mineral therapies

Vitex agnus-castus. See Chaste tree

Voison, Andre, 88

Von Kreisler, Kirstin, 176

Voprosy Onkologii, 361

Vulvovaginitis, 25

W

Wagner, D, 113

Walford, Ray; diet, 392, 395

Walker, Morton, 242, 262

Walking, 128; benefits, 128; bones, 413; brisk, 130

Walking Handbook, 129

Wall Street Journal, 199, 349, 353

Wallenweber, E, 95

Walsh, B, 101

Wang, G, 359

Wang, Ping, 323

Warren, Tom, 406

Water; healing properties of, 22; soft, 77; toxins, 143

Water fluoridation, 82

Watermelon frost, 306

Wax, ear. *See* Earwax

Wedelia calendulacea, 113

Weight loss, 45; emotions, 44; hypertension, 182; hypnosis, 12

Weil, Andrew, 8; homeopathic medicine, 10, 17

Weiner, M, 109

Weiner's Herbal, 109-110

Weintraub, Michael, 330

Weisman, Thomas, 8-9; chiropractic medicine, 9

Weizman, Jody, 260

Well Baby Book, 280

Well Being Journal, 182

Wellness Medicine, 90

WHO. *See* World Health Organization (WHO)

Whole body medicine, 1

Whole-Brain Thinking, 167

Wholistic Cancer Therapy, 361

Wiener Medizinische Wochenschrift, 104

Wikstrom, J, 87

Wilbur, JoEllen, 255

Wild chrysanthemum flower. *See* Ye ju hua

Willey, Charlene, 203; dentures, 307; exercise, 119; macular degeneration, 322; obesity, 46; sinusitis, 335; stress, 157

Williams, D, 358

William's Obstetrics, 283

Winston, Mary, 375

Wisdom teeth, 303

Withania somnifera, 113

Woad. *See* Da qing ye

Wolf, Michele, 120; cancer, 351

Wolfe, Honora Lee, 257

Wonder, Jacquelyn, 167

Wong, Ming, 4

Wood leaf. *See* Da qing ye

Woodside, D. B, 48

World Health Organization (WHO), 3; dietary guidelines, 40; traditional medicines, 8; vitamin E, 70

World Journal of Surgery, 7

World Medicine: The EastWest Guide to Healing Your Body, 19

Wray, D, 85

X

X rays, dental, 311

X-ray therapy. *See* Radiation therapy

Xerophthalmia, 55

Xerostomia. *See* Dry mouth

Xi gua Shuang. *See* Watermelon frost

XJL, 198

XSL. *See* Sin Shen Ling (XSL)

Xylitol gum, 298

Y

Yams, wild, 110, 259, 411; menopause, 254

Yang, 2

Yarrow; toothaches, 302

Ye ju hua; hypertension, 111-112; viruses, 112

Yeast infections, 264; acidophilus, 264; berberine, 105; botanical medicines, 265; chamomile, 100; homeopathic medicine, 265; nutritional therapies, 265; ozone therapy, 265; selenium, 87; symptoms, 264; vitamin and mineral therapies, 265

Yeat, John, 278

Yee, John D, 2

Yin, 2

Yo San University of Traditional Chinese Medicine, 406

Yoder, Barbara, 211

Yoga, 19, 164, 182; asanas, 20, 275; blood pressure, 385; compulsive disorders, 19; earaches, 327; hatha, 275; postpartum recovery, 287; pranayama, 275; pregnancy, 274; stress-reduction therapies, 20

Yogi, Maharishi Mahesh, 14

Your Health, 176-177, 198, 232, 262, 307, 317-318, 328, 358-359, 410

Your Nature, Your Health-Chinese Herbs in